LIST OF OFFICERS AND MEN

Serving in the

FIRST

Canadian Contingent

of the

British Expeditionary Force,

1914.

COMPILED BY PAY AND RECORD OFFICE,
Canadian Contingent,
36, VICTORIA STREET, LONDON, S.W.

INTRODUCTION

When Britain declared war on Germany in August 1914 Canada was automatically at war as well. Her constitutional position as a Dominion gave her no say in declaring war or making peace, but she had the right to decide what form any contribution to the war effort would take. Loyalty to the Empire, ties with the Motherland and the sense of patriotism were very strong then, and there was never any doubt that Canada's response would be anything other than wholehearted. Sir Robert Borden, the Prime Minister, expressed the feeling of the nation at the opening of a special war session of Parliament on 18 August: "As to our duty", he said, "we are all agreed; we stand shoulder to shoulder with Britain and the other Dominions in this quarrel. And that duty we shall not fail to fulfil as the honour of Canada demands."

At the outbreak of war the Canadian regular army, or, to give it its proper title, the Permanent Active Militia, numbered just over 3,000. It consisted of two cavalry regiments, The Royal Canadian Dragoons and Lord Strathcona's Horse; one infantry battalion of the Royal Canadian Regiment (RCR); and some artillery, engineer and service support units. This small force was strengthened a few days after the declaration of war by the creation of a new infantry regiment, Princess Patricia's Canadian Light Infantry (PPCLI), named after the daughter of the Governor-General, HRH Prince Arthur, Duke of Connaught. Raised by Captain Hamilton Gault, who put up one hundred thousand dollars towards the cost, and planned to make use of the many men who had already seen service, it was rapidly brought up to strength with veterans volunteering from all over Canada. In less than three weeks from the time Gault put forward his proposal the new regiment was at full strength, 1098 chosen from nearly 3,000 applicants; 1,049 of them had previous service with the Colours and about 90% had been born in the UK. According to the regimental history every regiment of the regular British Army bar one was represented on battalion parade.

The PPCLI was the first Canadian battalion into the front line, crossing to France in the last days of 1914 as part of 80th Brigade, 27th Division, a newly formed British division made up of regular battalions returning from India, Hong Kong and Tientsin. Again, statistics

i

published in the regimental history show that by the end of the war 5,086 officers and men had served in the battalion, casualties totalled 4076 of whom 1,300 were dead. Today the PPCLI is one of the three infantry regiments of Canada's regular army. Ironically, the only pre-war regular infantry unit, the RCR, was sent to Bermuda to relieve the 2nd Lincolns and although this gave them the distinction of being the first Canadian unit to serve outside Canada in the Great War, it also meant they did not get to France till November 1915, almost a year after the PPCLI.

Behind the small regular force stood the Non-Permanent Active Militia (NPAM), equivalent to the Territorials in the UK. Numbering some 60,000 it included 36 cavalry and 106 infantry regiments distributed among six Divisional Areas and three Military Districts. The Divisional Areas, numbered 1 to 6, were located as follows: 1st, Western Ontario (HQ London); 2nd, Central Ontario (Toronto); 3rd, Eastern Ontario (Kingston); 4th, Western Quebec (Montreal); 5th, Eastern Quebec (Quebec); and 6th, Maritime Provinces (Halifax). The three Districts were numbered 10th, 11th and 13th and were located at Manitoba and Saskatchewan (HQ Winnipeg); British Columbia and Yukon (Victoria); and Alberta (Calgary). In April 1916 the Divisional areas were renamed Military Districts to avoid any confusion with the divisions on active service on the Western Front.

Plans had been drawn up just before the war for the general mobilization of the Militia and for the provision of a contingent for overseas service amounting to an infantry division and a cavalry brigade. The scheme involved each divisional area and district providing their quota of troops, all of whom would be volunteers with preference given to those with previous or military training. As soon as war broke out the Canadian government offered to send a contingent, an offer gratefully and promptly accepted by Britain. The War Office advised that an infantry division, organized on British lines, would be the most suitable composition of such a force and the strength was set at 25,000 which would provide adequate reserves. This was very much what the existing mobilization plan envisaged. But things did not go according to plan.

The Minister of Militia was Colonel Sam Hughes, an arrogant and overbearing though very energetic individual, full of zeal for the cause of the Empire; at times he was something of a loose cannon. He had his own ideas about mobilization which ignored any existing plans. He addressed his own, personal "call to arms" to all non-permanent militia unit commanders over the heads of Divisional and District staffs, requiring volunteers to be sent to a concentration area at Valcartier, a few miles north-west of Quebec, where no facilities of any sort then existed. With commendable speed, in fact within a month, a camp had been erected with sufficient tented accomodation for 35,000 men with electric light, drains, water mains, a spur line and sidings, over three miles of rifle ranges with 1,500 targets and all the necessary services and administration. In the event 32,665 volunteers were brought in by one hundred trains from all over Canada between mid-August and mid-September. They represented virtually every militia regiment and the first problem was to organize them in some shape of military formation. It was quite clear that it was impossible for each militia regiment to go overseas as an individual unit, many of them had provided not even enough men to form a company let alone a battalion. Valcartier Camp Order No 241 of 2 Sep 1914 published a strength return by regiments which showed, at one end of the scale, the 101st (Edmonton Fusiliers) and the 5th (Royal Highlanders of Canada) had fielded 1,247 and 996 respectively, while at the other end the 92nd (Dorchester) and 66th (Princess Louise Fusiliers) provided 9 (5 officers and four men) and 32. Sam Hughes decided to ignore regimental titles but incorporate them into provisional battalions based on the regions from which the component regiments had come. The only exception to this was the newly raised PPCLI which remained separate and retained its identity. The 1st Provisional Battalion, for example, was based on Western Ontario and no less than 16 Militia regiments contributed to its composition. The loss of regimental titles caused some mutterings in the ranks but this seemed to be the only practical solution.

Sixteen Provisional Battalions were formed, numbered from 1st through to 16th, and allotted to four Provisional Brigades (1st to 4th), four battalions to each. When numbers of infantry exceeded the required establishment figures a 17th Battalion was formed to take the surplus; an 18th Battalion but was likewise authorised but was disbanded before the contingent sailed. Of the four brigade commanders - Mercer, Currie, Turner VC and Cohoe - the first three would go to France as brigade commanders with the Canadian Division; one of them, Arthur Currie, would rise to command the Canadian Corps and become Canada's greatest soldier.

Embarkation began on 25th September at Quebec amid scenes of some chaos, but eventually, at 1500 hours on 3rd October, 30 ships set sail carrying 30,605 officers and men, 6,816 horses, 127 guns, 595 motor and horse-drawn vehicles and 82 bicycles. It is of interest to note that figures compiled in 1936 show that of this first contingent 9,159 were born in Canada and 18,495 in the British Isles. The ships were joined at the mouth of the St Lawrence by SS Canada which had brought 2nd Lincolns from Bermuda, where they had been relieved by the Royal Canadian Regiment, and two days later by SS Florizel off Cape Race, carrying 539 officers and men of the Newfoundland contingent. One ship, SS Manhattan, sailed independently on 5th October with 863 horses, 90 motor vehicles, 130 horse-drawn carts and a great quantity of miscellaneous stores and equipment left behind by the other ships.

Originally destined for Southampton, the convoy was diverted to Plymouth just two days before it was due to arrive because of reported U-boat activity in the Channel. Disembarkation was, if anything, a scene of even greater confusion than embarkation; it took nine days before the last of the troops came ashore and finally the first Canadian contingent arrived at its home for the next few months - Salisbury Plain.

So the first Canadian volunteers arrived in the UK, and in this book their names are listed, by company, battalion and brigade and by units of all arms of the service - cavalry, artillery, engineers, medical, transport and so on - a truly remarkable record, compiled by the Pay and Records Office of the Canadian Contingent, then located at 36, Victoria Street, London SW1, published by Canadian Pacific (The Empire's Greatest Railway), and sold for the benefit of the Queen's Canadian Military Hospital, Beachborough Park, Shorncliffe. They were the first of what was to be a tremendous response. By the end of August 1916 there were four Canadian divisions in France, forming the Canadian Corps, which was to become one of the most formidable fighting formations on the Western Front.

The Canadian Official History shows 619,636 men and women served in the Canadian army and of these 51,748 were killed in action or died of wounds; a further 7,796 died of disease, illness or injury bringing the total number of army fatalities to 59,544. The total figure of Canadian army casualties of all natures in all theatres amounted to 232,494. Sixty-four Canadians won the VC, fifty-eight of them while serving with the Canadian Corps (the other six were shared equally by the Canadian Cavalry Brigade and Canadians serving with the RFC/RAF); a further 21,763 British honours and decorations were awarded, 13,190 of these being Military Medals.

The 1st Canadian Division, made up from the units and personnel listed in this book, was the first non-regular division to join the BEF, and as the force grew in numbers so did the men's confidence in themselves and in their officers. The high point was, undoubtedly, the capture of Vimy Ridge in April 1917 when, for the first time, all four divisions went into action side by side. It can be argued that this was a watershed in Canada's history. From Vimy on, the Corps' record of successes was unbroken and its contribution to final victory immeasurable. Canada took great pride in her soldiers' achievements, and her new found status and prestige, won for her by her fighting men, was duly acknowledged; her separate signature was on the Peace Treaties and she had a separate seat at the League of Nations. She had achieved full nationhood.

Terry Cave
Worthing 1998

NON-PERMANENT ACTIVE MILITIA REGIMENTS, AUGUST 1914

CAVALRY

	The Governor General's Body Guard
1st	Hussars
2nd	Dragoons
3rd	The Prince of Wales's Canadian Dragoons
4th	Hussars
5th	Princess Louise Dragoon Guards
6th	Duke of Connaught's Royal Canadian Hussars
7th	Hussars
8th	Princess Louise's New Brunswick Hussars
9th	Mississauga Horse
10th	No regiment with this number
11th	Hussars
12th	Manitoba Dragoons
13th	Scottish Light Dragoons
14th	King's Canadian Hussars
15th	Light Horse
16th	Light Horse
17th	Duke of York's Royal Canadian Hussars
18th	Mounted Rifles
19th	Alberta Dragoons
20th	Border Horse
21st	Alberta Horse
22nd	Saskatchewan Light Horse
23rd	Alberta Rangers
24th	Grey's Horse
25th	Brant Dragoons
26th	Stanstead Dragoons
27th	Light Horse
28th	New Brunswick Dragoons
29th	Light Horse

30th	British Columbia Horse
31st	British Columbia Horse
32nd	Manitoba Horse
33rd	Vaudreuil and Soulanges Hussars - Note 1
34th	Fort Garry Horse
35th	Central Alberta Horse
36th	Prince Edward Island Light Horse

Note 1. Disbanded, 1 October 1914.

INFANTRY

	The Governor General's Foot Guards
1st	Canadian Grenadier Guards
2nd	Queen's Own Rifles of Canada
3rd	Victoria Rifles of Canada
4th	Chasseurs Canadiens
5th	Royal Highlanders of Canada
6th	Duke of Connaught's Own Rifles
7th	Fusiliers
8th	Royal Rifles
9th	Voltigeurs de Quebec
10th	Royal Grenadiers
11th	Irish Fusiliers of Canada
12th	York Rangers
13th	Royal Regiment
14th	Princess of Wales's Own Rifles
15th	Argyll Light Infantry
16th	Prince Edward
17th	Regiment of Infantry
18th	Francs-Tireurs de Saguenay
19th	Lincoln
20th	Halton Rifles
21st	Essex Fusiliers
22nd	Oxford Rifles
23rd	Northern Pioneers

24th		Kent
25th		Regiment
26th		Middlesex Light Infantry
27th		Lambton (St Clair Borderers)
28th		Perth
29th		Waterloo (note 1)
30th		Wellington Rifles
31st		Grey
32nd		Bruce
33rd		Huron
34th		Ontario
35th		Simcoe Foresters
36th		Peel
37th		Haldimand Rifles
38th		Dufferin Rifles of Canada
39th		Norfolk Rifles
40th		Northumberland
41st		Brockville Rifles
42nd		Lanark and Renfrew
43rd		Duke of Cornwall's Own Rifles
44th		Lincoln and Welland
45th		Victoria and Haliburton
46th		Durham
47th		Frontenac
48th		Highlanders
49th		Hastings Rifles
50th		Victoria
51st		Soo Rifles
52nd		Prince Albert Volunteers
53rd		Sherbrooke
54th		Carabineers de Sherbrooke
55th		Note 2
56th		Grenville
57th		Peterborough Rangers
58th		Note 3
59th		Stormont and Glengarry
60th		60th Rifles of Canada

61st	Montmagny and L'Islet
62nd	Saint John Fusiliers
63rd	Halifax Rifles
64th	Chateauguay and Beauharnois
65th	Carabiniers Mont Royal
66th	Princess Louise Fusiliers
67th	Carleton Light Infantry
68th	Earl Grey's Own Rifles
69th	Annapolis
70th	Note 4
71st	York
72nd	Seaforth Highlanders of Canada
73rd	Northumberland
74th	New Brunswick Rangers
75th	Lunenburg
76th	Colchester and Hants Rifles
77th	Wentworth
78th	Pictou (Highlanders)
79th	Cameron Highlanders of Canada
80th	Nicolet
81st	Hants
82nd	Abgeweit Light Infantry
83rd	Joliet
84th	St Hyacinthe
85th	Regiment
86th	Note 5
87th	Quebec
88th	Victoria Fusiliers
89th	Temiscouata and Rimouski
90th	Winnipeg Rifles
91st	Canadian Highlanders
92nd	Dorchester
93rd	Cumberland
94th	Victoria (Argyll Highlanders)
95th	Saskatchewan Rifles
96th	Lake Superior
97th	Algonquin Rifles

98th	Infantry
99th	Manitoba Rangers
100th	Winnipeg Grenadiers
101st	Edmonton Fusiliers
102nd	Rocky Mountain Rangers
103rd	Calgary Rifles
104th	Westminster Fusiliers of Canada
105th	Saskatoon Fusiliers
106th	Winnipeg
107th	East Kootenay

The 108th Regiment was raised on 21 Sep 1914 and the 109th on 15 Dec 1914.

Notes
1. Redesignated Highland Light Infantry of Canada 15 Apr 1915.
2. 55th Megantic Light Infantry disbanded 3 Sep 1912, re-formed as 55th Infantry 29 Aug 1914.
3. 58th Westmount Rifles formed 2 Nov 1914. Previously 58th Compton Regiment, converted to cavalry as 7th Hussars 1 May 1903.
4. 70th Colchester and Hants renumbered 76th 2 May 1910; 70th Regiment formed 7 Aug 1914.
5. 86th Three Rivers Regiment disbanded 1 Apr 1914, re-formed 1 Oct 1915

INDEX.

	PAGES.
HEADQUARTERS, FIRST CANADIAN CONTINGENT	5, 6
DIVISIONAL HEADQUARTERS SUBORDINATE STAFF	6–8
FIRST INFANTRY BRIGADE—	
HEADQUARTERS	8
1ST BATTALION	9–21
2ND BATTALION	21–34
3RD BATTALION	34–47
4TH BATTALION	47–60
SECOND INFANTRY BRIGADE—	
HEADQUARTERS	60, 61
5TH BATTALION	61–74
6TH BATTALION	75–87
7TH BATTALION	88–101
8TH BATTALION	101–114
THIRD INFANTRY BRIGADE—	
HEADQUARTERS	114
13TH BATTALION	115–128
14TH BATTALION	128–141
15TH BATTALION	141–153
16TH BATTALION	154–167
FOURTH INFANTRY BRIGADE—	
STAFF, &C.	167
9TH BATTALION	168–180
10TH BATTALION	181–192
11TH BATTALION	192–206
12TH BATTALION	206–217
17TH BATTALION (NOT BRIGADED)	217–227
PRINCESS PATRICIA'S CANADIAN LIGHT INFANTRY	227–238
DIVISIONAL SIGNAL COMPANY	238–240
DIVISIONAL CAVALRY	241, 242
DIVISIONAL CYCLIST COMPANY	243
ROYAL CANADIAN DRAGOONS	244–250
LORD STRATHCONA'S HORSE (R.C.)	251–257
DIVISIONAL ARTILLERY HEADQUARTERS	258
FIRST ARTILLERY BRIGADE AND AMMUNITION COLUMN	258–267

INDEX—*continued.*

	PAGES.
SECOND CANADIAN FIELD ARTILLERY BRIGADE—	
BRIGADE STAFF	267, 268
4TH BATTERY	268–270
5TH BATTERY	270–272
6TH BATTERY	272–274
AMMUNITION COLUMN	274–276
THIRD CANADIAN FIELD ARTILLERY BRIGADE—	
BRIGADE STAFF	277
7TH BATTERY	277–279
8TH BATTERY	280, 281
9TH BATTERY	282–284
AMMUNITION COLUMN	285, 286
NO. 1 HEAVY BATTERY	286–288
ROYAL CANADIAN HORSE ARTILLERY	289–294
DIVISIONAL ENGINEERS	294–302
DIVISIONAL TRAIN	303–308
DIVISIONAL SUPPLY COLUMN, M.T.	308–311
DIVISIONAL AMMUNITION COLUMN	311–318
DIVISIONAL AMMUNITION PARK, WITH C.F.A. (ATTACHED)	318–323
NO. 1 RESERVE PARK	323–326
DEPÔT UNITS OF SUPPLY, C.A.S.C.	326, 327
RAILWAY SUPPLY DETACHMENT	327, 328
NO. 1 FIELD AMBULANCE	328–331
NO. 2 FIELD AMBULANCE	332, 333
NO. 3 FIELD AMBULANCE	333–336
CLEARING HOSPITAL	336, 337
NO. 1 GENERAL HOSPITAL	337–339
NO 2 GENERAL HOSPITAL	340, 341
NO. 1 STATIONARY HOSPITAL, A.M.C.	342
NO. 2 STATIONARY HOSPITAL, A.M.C.	343, 344
ADVANCED MEDICAL DEPÔT STORES	344
CANADIAN ARMY VETERINARY CORPS	345–347
CANADIAN MOBILE VETERINARY SECTION	347
CANADIAN VETERINARY BASE SUPPLY DEPÔT	348
REMOUNT DEPÔT	348, 349
AUTO MACHINE GUN BRIGADE, NO. 1	349, 350
BASE PAY DEPÔT UNIT	351
PAY AND RECORD OFFICE, LONDON	351
CANADIAN ORDNANCE CORPS	351
POSTAL DETACHMENT	352
NURSING MATRONS AND NURSING SISTERS	352, 353

HEADQUARTERS, FIRST CANADIAN CONTINGENT.

General Officer Commanding ...	Lt.-General E. A. H. Alderson, C.B.
Military Secretary	Colonel J. C. MacDougall
Aide-de-camp	Major C. H. L. Beatty, D.S.O.
,, ...	Captain A. C. F. Butler
,, ...	,, G. K. Killam
,, ...	Lieutenant W. B. Sifton
,, ...	,, T. Williams-Taylor.

General Staff.

General Staff Officer, 1st Grade ...	Colonel E. S. Heard
,, ,, 2nd ,, ...	Lieut.-Col. A. H. Macdonnell, D.S.O.
,, ,, 2nd ,, ...	,, G. C. W. Gordon-Hall
,, ,, 3rd ,, ...	,, C. H. Mitchell
,, ,, 3rd ,, ...	,, H. T. Lamb

Administrative and Departmental Staff.

Asst. Adjt. and Qr.-Mr.-General ...	Colonel T. Birchall Wood
Dep. Asst. Adjt. and Qr.-Mr.-General	Major J. H. McBrien
Dep. Asst. Adjt.-General	,, G. T. Hamilton
Dept. Asst. Qr.-Mr.-General ...	,, J. S. Brown
Director of Medical Services ...	Colonel G. Carleton Jones
Asst. Director of Med. Services ...	Lieut.-Colonel G. la F. Foster
Dep. Asst. Director of Med. Services	Captain H. A. Chisholm
Asst. Director of Veterinary Services	Lieut.-Colonel W. J. Neill
Dep. Asst. Director Ord. Services ...	,, F. Strange (acting)
Field Cashier	Major J. T. E. Gagnon
Asst. ,, ...	Lieutenant O. R. Lobley
Senior Chaplain	Hon. Major Rev. R. H. Steacy
Postmaster	Lieutenant K. A. Murray
Asst. Provost Marshal	Captain E. S. Clifford, D.S.O.

Attached.

General Camp Commandant ...	Colonel V. A. S. Williams
Water Expert	Lieut.-Colonel G. G. Nasmyth
Sanitary Adviser	Major R. E. Wodehouse
Chaplain (Roman Catholic) ...	Hon. Major Rev. Father S. Jolicœur
Interpreter	Captain J. E. Hahn
,, ...	Lieutenant P. Newhouse
Staff Officer for Musketry	Captain H. R. Sandilands
Supernumerary	Major E. de B. Panet
,, ,, ...	Lieut.-Colonel E. B. Worthington
,, ,, ...	,, E. E. W. Moore
,, ,, ...	,, F. A. Reid
,, ,, ...	,, J. G. Rattray
,, ,, ...	,, E. B. Clegg

Canadian Pacific—The Empire's Greatest Railway.

HEADQUARTERS—*cont.*

Staff Specially Employed.

Chief Paymaster and officer in charge of Records } Colonel W. R. Ward
D.A.A.G. for Records ... ... Major F. Logie Armstrong

DIVISIONAL HEADQUARTERS SUBORDINATE STAFF.

Acting Quartermaster-Sergeant.

1807 Sergt.-Major B. E. Purdy (W.O.), (R.C.D.)

Clerks.

General Staff Branch—
    1801 Sergt.-Major J. S. Chenay (W.O.), C.M.S.C. (Supt. Clerk.)
    1803 Q.M.-Sergt. G. T. E. Martin, C.M.S.C.
    1804   ,,   H. F. Moody, C.M.S.C.
    1805   ,,   P. M. Orbinski, C.M.S.C.

Administrative Branch—
    1802 Sergt.-Major A. W. Kelly (W.O.), C.M.S.C.
    1806 Q.M.-Sergt. G. W. Cragg, C.M.S.C.
    1809 Staff Sergt. E. W. Johnston, C.M.S.C.
    1808   ,,   J. F. Cummins, C.M.S.C.
    1811 Sergeant Stanley Smith

Central Registry—
    1810 Sergeant G. E. Berry, C.M.S.C.

A.D.M.S. Branch—
    1821 Sergt.-Major J. E. Lawrence, A.M.C.
    48009   ,,   A. E. Clifton
    1822 Staff Sergt. G. S. Cooke, A.M.C.
    1825 Sergeant H. G. B. Butt, A.M.C.
    1824   ,,   W. J. Phillips
    1823   ,,   Tythridge, A.B.
    1899 Private H. Whitney

A.D.V.S. Branch—
    1826 Quartermaster-Sergeant A. Newell, C.P.A.V.C.
    1812 Sgt. Farrier H. E. Dyball
    1818 Shoesmith R. Teasdale

D. Asst. Director O.S. Branch—
    48014 Sub-Conductor J. D. Pitman, C.O.C

To Field Cashier—
    35005 Sergeant Taschereau, E. de G.
    10531   ,,   J. J. Scanlan

Canadian Pacific—The Empire's Greatest Railway.

DIVISIONAL HEADQUARTERS—cont.

Postal Corps.

Regl. No.	Rank.	Name.	Regl. No.	Rank.	Name.
1827	Sergt.	G. W. Ross	1829	Private	G. H. Baldock
1820	Private	B. J. Terry	1830	,,	C. Smith

Military Police.

1842	Sgt.Maj.	J. L. Smuck (W.O.), R.C.D.	1847	Private	H. Stanley
			1848	,,	G. Stevenson
1843	Private	A. E. Booth	1849	,,	F. Waters
48010	,,	J. Bowen	1850	,,	T. F. Williams
1844	,,	T. Carbin	1851	,,	S. Williams
1845	,,	W. G. Knyvett			

Transport Drivers, A.S.C.

1816	Private	W. B. Carley	1817	Private	E. J. Vickery

Water Detail, A.M.C.

1882	Corpl.	G. Martin	48013	Private	E. B. Beecroft

Drivers—Mechanical Transport

1831	Sgt.-Maj.	Roberts, H. D.	1835	Sergt.	Smillie, H. M.
1832	Sergt.	Ramus, H. R.	1838	,,	Mothersill, F.
1833	,,	Dyball, R. S.	48012	,,	Arnold, L. A.
1834	,,	McIver, Eric			

Attached.

1836	Sergeant	Reece, L. R. (chauff.)	48001	Sergt.	Chisholm, G. H.(chauff.)
1839	,,	Packen, A.	1837	,,	Radermacher, H. M.
1840	,,	Farr, Harry A.			

Batmen.

1853	Private	Butcher, A. R.	1869	Private	Green, John Thomas
1854	,,	Badger, Robert	1815	,,	Hewson, John Henry
1855	,,	Baxter, John Mills	1870	,,	Highfield, Eyre
1856	,,	Bradley, W. M.	1871	,,	Howe, Thomas
1857	,,	Barker, George A.	1872	,,	Hill, Elliot
48011	,,	Beeston, Thomas B.	1873	,,	Howe, Gordon
1860	,,	Cavanagh, G. B.	48000	,,	Hockney, John W.
1858	,,	Corner, Frederick	1875	,,	Johnstone, W. J.
1859	,,	Clinton, Thomas P.	1874	,,	Johnston, John
1861	,,	Curle, Horace B.	1876	,,	Karner, F. le Roy
1862	,,	Clair, Charles	1877	,,	McCallum, Robert
1863	,,	Cooke, F. W.	1878	,,	McLean, Joseph
1864	,,	Chalcraft, George	1879	,,	Malcolm, Ivan W.
48002	,,	Fortune, William	1880	,,	McDonnel, James
1866	,,	Garvin, M. J.	1881	,,	McBeath, Donald
1867	,,	Goodband, George	48616	,,	Melvin, Joseph
1865	,,	Grant, Charles S.	48008	,,	Neal, William
1868	,,	Grainger, James	1852	Corpl.	Oborn, Stanley M.

Canadian Pacific—The Empire's Greatest Railway.

DIVISIONAL HEADQUARTERS—cont.

Batmen—cont.

Regl. No.	Rank.	Name.	Regl. No.	Rank.	Name.
48005	Private	Redmond, Albert E.	1892	Private	Thomas, Kemster
1886	,,	Robertson, A.	1893	,,	Trounce, Louis J.
1884	,,	Rees, Albert	1894	,,	Taylor, William H.
1885	,,	Roche, William H.	1890	,,	Thornbeck, W. H.
1883	,,	Ryan, William E.	1898	,,	Warwick, C.
1814	,,	Robeson, Alfred A.	48004	,,	Walters, Sydney S.
1887	,,	Sherlock, Henry	1896	,,	Wamsley, C. H.
1888	,,	Smith, George	1895	,,	Wilcocks, John B.
1889	,,	Skinner,	1897	,,	Winning, William
1900	,,	Stanbrook, Henry	48007	,,	Wood, Thomas
1891	,,	Trudel, Ernest	48006	,,	Woolison, R. F.

Cooks.

1813	Private	Bradley, Ernest H.	1819	Private	Watson, Henry
1820	,,	Metcalf, John M.			

1st INFANTRY BRIGADE.
HEADQUARTERS.

Lieut.-Colonel ... ... Mercer, Malcolm Smith
Major ... ... Hayter, Ross John Finnis
Captain ... ... Ware, Francis Bethel
Lieutenant ... ... Wedd, William Basil
,, ... Teed, Hugh Mariner
,, ... Walsh, Frederick

Regl. No.	Rank.	Name.	Regl. No.	Rank.	Name.
6001	Q.M.S.	Barker, Charles	6013	Private	McEntire, H. S.
6024	Sergt.	Gill, Wm. J. N.			McCready
6002	,,	Milvain, Charles E. F.	35209	,,	Murray, Thos. H.
35208	Corpl.	McPherson, Dan. V.	6004	,,	Parlow, Allan Edward
6011	Private	Ashley, Howard John	6015	,,	Roebroek, Harry
6006	,,	Bowhay, Lance Gil.	6014	,,	Rogers, Frederick
35210	,,	Edwards, Ledman	6009	,,	Tournigny, Wilfred
6008	,,	Deremo, James Carlos	6012	,,	Waller, George
6005	,,	Gilbert, Charles	6019	,,	Williams, Thomas B.
6010	,,	Harris, Thomas	6007	,,	Wragge, Lemuel
6008	,,	MacDonald, Ron. J.			

Military Mounted Police.

6016	Sergt.	O'Neill, Patrick	6017	Private	Mitchell, William
6023	Private	Carroll, William	6018	,,	Perry, John

Army Service Corps Drivers.

30217	Private	Haines, Oscar	30226	Private	Mainwaring, George
30218	,,	Hill, Albert William	30228	,,	McCubbin, Thomas
30219	,,	Johnstone, Robert			

Canadian Pacific—The Empire's Greatest Railway.

1st BATTALION (ONTARIO REGIMENT), 1st INFANTRY BRIGADE.

HEADQUARTERS.

Officer Commanding	Lieut.-Colonel Hill, Frederic W.
—	Major Becher, Henry C. KIA 15/6/15
—	,, Welch, Thomas B.
Adjutant	Captain Brook, Reginald, J.
Asst. Adjutant	Captain Coghill, Harry J.
Quartermaster	Captain Pembroke, Harry E.
Signalling Officer	Lieutenant Butler, Walter Chester
Transport Officer	Major Ross, Robt. B.
Machine Gun Officer	Lieutenant Campbell, Fred DOW 18/6/15

Attached.

Medical Officer	Captain Robertson, David E.
Paymaster	Hon. Capt. Bottomley, Jn. W.
Chaplain	,, Rev. Warner, D. V.
,,	,, ,, Arts, J.

Subordinate Staff.

Regl. No.	Rank.	Name.	Regl. No.	Rank.	Name.
6101	W.O.	McKinney, Danl. J.	6995	Cook Sgt.	Charman Stanley, J.
6102	Q.M.S.	McClymont, Andrew C.	7214	Trans. Sgt.	Burns, Leslie J.
			7213	Signl. Sgt.	Farrell, Edgar
6105	Drum. Sgt.	Andrews, Wm. C.	7233	Sergt.	Bennett, Joseph
6106	Pion'r Sgt.	Barrett, Wm. Jas.	6126	,,	Johnson, Ralph J.
6529	O.R.Sgt.	Thwaites, W. F.	6108	Shoe. Pte.	Dilkes, Wm. P.

Signallers.

7205	Private	Buck, Chas. S.	7209	Private	Hughes, Edward
6308	,,	Capswell, W. E.	7210	,,	Hull, Frederick W.
7206	,,	Carey, Philip	7211	,,	Sheard, Fred
7207	,,	Collyer, Ralph P.	7212	,,	Sullivan, Leo. I.
7208	,,	Gould, Herbert L.			

Medical Orderlies.

6110	Private	Atkinson, Charles H.	6109	Private	Jones, W. E.

Transport.

7225	Corpl.	Mullin, Milton	7228	Private	Muir, Robt. A.
7216	Private	Campbell, John	7220	,,	McCrossin, Jas.
7224	,,	Campbell, Mathew	7229	,,	Patton, Wm.
7217	,,	Fox, Stanley R.	7221	,,	Rudall, Adolphis
7218	,,	Fraser, John	7230	,,	Smith, W.
7226	,,	Falconham, W. R.	7222	,,	Walsh, Oscar
7219	,,	Lawson, James	7223	,,	White, James G.
7227	,,	Morrison, H.			

Canadian Pacific—The Empire's Greatest Railway.

1ST BATTALION, 1ST INFANTRY BRIGADE—cont.

Batmen.

Regl. No.	Rank.	Name.	Regl. No.	Rank.	Name.
6119	Post Sgt.	Smith, Douglas M. L.	6111	Private	Knight, Wm. H.
7231	Private	Bonser, Walter	6112	,,	Newport, Isaac
6116	,,	Clements, David	7072	,,	Pendergast, A.
6120	,,	Gardner, Harry W.	6119	,,	Smith, Douglas M. L.
7174	,,	Garton,	6118	,,	Weston, Wm.
6330	,,	Glenday, D.	6114	,,	Whitworth,
6113	,,	Kellman, A.			

Machine Gun Section.

Regl. No.	Rank.	Name.	Regl. No.	Rank.	Name.
6148	Sergt.	Jones, McCulloch Hill	6156	Private	Jewel, Arthur Ed.
6149	Corpl.	Scott, William	6157	,,	Jones, Herbert Ed.
6661	Private	Ballantyne, John	6158	,,	Knight, George
6150	,,	Bickerson, Lester E.	6159	,,	Logan, Arnold
6151	,,	Biggs, Ernest Wm.	6160	,,	Murphy, Tim.
6152	,,	Cameron, Donald S.	6161	,,	Phillips, Harold
6153	,,	Campbell, Duncan T.	6162	,,	Plaskett, Ivor C.
6154	,,	Caudle, Frank	6163	,,	Ritchie, Alexander
6155	,,	Hobson, Wm. John	6164	,,	Reaume, Ralph A.

Attached—O.R. (Water Detail).

Regl. No.	Rank.	Name.	Regl. No.	Rank.	Name.
33601	Corpl.	La Marsh, Wilfred	33605	Private	Stanley, Charles
33604	Private	Bartlet, Frank Alex.	33603	,,	Wigle, Arthur M.
33602	,,	Rayner, George			

Company Officers.

Captain	Delamere, Thos Gillmore
,,	Grover, Lucius Halen
,,	Kimmins, Albert Edw.
,,	Osborne, Baron
,,	Smith, Geo. John Lorne
,,	Sutherland, Donald Matheson
,,	Watson, G. B.
,,	Wilkinson, Geo. Henry
Lieutenant	Brown, Robt. Renwick
,,	Creighton, Frank
,,	Clifford, E. W.
,,	Chesham, E. N.
,,	Douglas, Donald Eric
,,	Greenwood, Ernest Herbert
,,	Gordon, Glen Napier
,,	Galaugher, Wm. Nelson
,,	Helliwell, Jos. Grant
,,	Hinderson, Ernest Boran
,,	Hunt, G. C.
,,	Hodson, C. W.
,,	James, Cecil Arthur
,,	Lockhart, Thos. Downie
,,	Lalor, W. J.

Canadian Pacific—The Empire's Greatest Railway.

1st BATTALION, 1st INFANTRY BRIGADE—cont. 11

Company Officers—cont.

Lieutenant	...	...	...	Lodge, Fred Laing
,,	...	...	...	Metcalfe, Geo. Andrew
,,	...	...	...	Mahaffy, K. A.
,,	...	...	...	Pick, P. W.
,,	...	...	...	Robinson, Fred. Wm.
,,	...	...	...	Swift, Thos, C. L. (Lemon)
,,	...	...	...	Stapleford, R. H.
,,	...	...	...	Tranter, J. L.
,,	...	...	...	Thomas, Llywellyn Murray
,,	...	...	...	Youngs, John Laut

Non-commissioned Officers and Men.

Regl. No.	Rank.	Name.	Regl. No.	Rank.	Name.
6755	Col.-Sgt.	Barry, Robt.	6523	Sergt.	McMurphy, Archibald
6401	,,	Garswood, FrankAlbro	6876	,,	Newell, L. G.
6637	,,	Hall, Frederick W.	6403	,,	Purchase, John
6519	,,	McDonald, John W.	7111	Sgt.M.-T.	Whyte, Alexander
6873	,,	Owens, A. E.	6405	Private	Fisher, Edward G.
6283	,,	Stevenson, William R.	6284	,,	Humphries, John J.
6165	,,	Warwick, William T.	6520	,,	Hill, Matthew
6874	Sergt.	Ashton, G. H.	6993	,,	Husband, FrederickW.
6875	,,	Barron, R. E.	6757	,,	Leggitt, William
7110	Band-Sgt.	Burdett, Henry H.	6287	,,	McBeth, James
6166	Sergt.	Bushby, George W.	6402	,,	McMaster, Dalton C.
6167	,,	Bowers, Wm.	6992	,,	Mills, Chas. Frederick
6638	,,	Burgin, James	7113	,,	Nash, Henry J.
6639	,,	Buchanan, John R.	6286	,,	Oliver, Thos. Henry
6758	,,	Blake, Wm.	6991	,,	Pratt, Wm. John
6168	,,	Chivers, William	6877	,,	Randal, R. G.
6545	O.R.Sgt.	Coghill, F.	6994	,,	Rowley, John Henry
6285	Sergt.	Colson, William John	6996	,,	Skidmore, James W. P.
6522	,,	Collins, John	6521	,,	Wilson, John George
7112	,,	Cuddy, W. M.	6640	,,	Ward, Henry George
6169	,,	Davis, Arthur D.	6641	,,	Whitfield, Robert
6756	,,	Hoey, Norman	6404	,,	Young, Thomas
6759	,,	Kilt, Davis			

Regl. No.	Rank.	Name.	Regl. No.	Rank.	Name.
7115	Private	Adams, W. F.	6171	Private	Anderson, Jos.
6770	,,	Agombar, Bertie	6766	,,	Anderson, Lorne
6771	,,	Aiken, Milton J.	6421	,,	Anderson, Robt.
7109	,,	Aikman, H.	6769	,,	Anderson, Thos. John
6883	,,	Aitchson, L. C.	6412	,,	Andrews, Robt.
6767	,,	Alexander, Hector	6646	Corpl.	Ansell, Ernest
7114	,,	Allan, G. D.	6172	Private	Apps, Geo.
6170	,,	Allan, Wm.	7012	,,	Arbor, Arthur
6884	,,	Allen, Robt.	6768	,,	Armstrong, Percy
7116	,,	Alvey, William	6532	,,	Arnold, Andrew S.
6293	,,	Anderson, David	6422	,,	Arnold, Elijah

Canadian Pacific—The Empire's Greatest Railway.

1st BATTALION, 1st INFANTRY BRIGADE—*cont.*

Regl. No.	Rank	Name	Regl. No.	Rank	Name
6685	Private	Arnold, G. E.	6428	Private	Binny, James Bruce
6651	,,	Ash, John	6544	,,	Bint, Arthur Stanley
6292	,,	Atkinson, Harold	6764	Sergt.	Birch, Saml.
6173	,,	Atkinson, Harold L.	7019	Private	Bird, Edward
6765	,,	Atkins, Robt.	6895	,,	Burkinham, William
7234	,,	Babbs, Geo.	6178	,,	Biswarwick, Thos.
6535	,,	Bailey, Victor	7123	,,	Blair, James
6893	,,	Baillie, Robt. Winter	6666	,,	Blair, Robert
7127	,,	Baines, Bert Chas.	6180	,,	Blakely, William
6423	,,	Bain, E. M.	6889	,,	Blanchard, George
7015	,,	Baker, E. Chas.	6776	,,	Bleich, John
6174	,,	Baker, Ernest H.	6894	,,	Blondell, Martin
6181	,,	Balderick, Wm. T.	6892	,,	Blunt, William
6528	,,	Banks, Edwin	6654	,,	Blunt, William
6424	,,	Barden, Jn.	6660	,,	Boland, Joseph
7120	,,	Barker, Geo. C.	6182	,,	Bolton, Frederick E.
6538	,,	Barker, Nathan	6183	,,	Bond, John Henry
7121	,,	Barker, William	6533	,,	Bonnett, Herbert
6652	,,	Barlow, Frank	6541	,,	Bowerman, Alfred J.
6175	,,	Barney, Edward S.	6539	,,	Bowers, Maurice D.
7117	,,	Barrass, Wm. E.	7125	,,	Bowie, Wm.
7020	,,	Barrett, Jas. Jo.	6185	,,	Bowles, Sydney J.
6425	,,	Barrie, Joseph C.	6430	,,	Bowman, Samuel
6896	,,	Barry, Joseph	6186	,,	Boyce, Thos.
6540	,,	Bartholomew, Frederick J.	6997	Corpl.	Brade, Henry Chas.
			6296	Private	Bradford, Noel Geo.
6773	,,	Bartholomew, Jonah	6642	Lce.-Sgt.	Bradley, William F.
6294	,,	Bartram, Augustus E.	6534	Private	Brandnum, Percy
7009	,,	Basley, John James	6187	Sergt.	Brady, Wm. Bedfort
6659	,,	Batis, Albert	6664	Private	Brebner, Harry
6887	,,	Baxter, Duncan	6663	,,	Brebner, James
6998	Sergt.	Bay, William	6774	,,	Brennen, Thomas
6653	Private	Beals, George	6431	,,	Brereton, Laurence
6426	,,	Beardmore, Harold	7007	,,	Bricker, Roger
6542	,,	Beattie, W. H.	6295	,,	Bridge, Henry
6667	,,	Bell, George	6777	,,	Bridge, Percy
6305	,,	Bell, George Victor	6655	,,	Britton, William
6176	,,	Bendall, Ernest C.	6665	,,	Brock, Harry
7125	,,	Benn, Louis K.	6432	,,	Brompton, James
7122	,,	Bennett, George	6433	,,	Brompton, Witty
6886	,,	Benware, Neil	6434	,,	Brookfield, Andrew
6427	,,	Bemey, Edgar	6537	,,	Brown, Albert
7118	,,	Berber, Richard	6188	,,	Brown, Arthur K.
7017	,,	Bertram, Leonard	6890	,,	Brown, John
7014	,,	Bevan, Henry Arthur	6435	,,	Brown, John George
7119	,,	Bezzo, William C.	6189	,,	Brown, Maurice H.
7235	,,	Bigby, William	6772	,.	Brown, Robt.
6179	,,	Biggar, John	6662	,,	Brunning, William
7016	Arm. Cpl.	Biggs, Daniel	6190	,,	Bryant, Robt. I.
6543	Private	Biggs, Stanley Geo.	6436	,,	Buchanan, Arthur G.
6177	,,	Bigiron, Franklin B.	6775	,,	Buchanan, Thomas
7245	,,	Binette, Marcisse	6878	,,	Budge, John

Canadian Pacific—The Empire's Greatest Railway.

1ST BATTALION, 1ST INFANTRY BRIGADE—cont.

Regl. No.	Rank	Name	Regl. No.	Rank	Name
6191	Private	Bullen, Geo.	6410	Private	Clayton, James H.
6192	Corpl.	Burchett, Henry F.	6200	,,	Cleaves, Jas. G.
7013	Private	Burgess, Albert Thos.	7022	,,	Cochrane, Frank
6297	,,	Burns, John	6201	,,	Cocoran, Jas. T.
7124	,,	Burratt, Frank T.	6413	,,	Codogan, Alexander
6429	,,	Burtch, Homer P.	6316	,,	Coghan, Leo. B.
7018	,,	Butcher, Albert Edw.	6439	,,	Coldwell, Edwin
6657	,,	Butler, Harry	6781	,,	Cole, Frederick
6536	,,	Butler, James	6782	,,	Cole, George
6658	,,	Butler, William	6778	,,	Cole, Thomas
6891	,,	Buttery, Albert	7106	,,	Cole, Wm. Fredk.
6437	,,	Bye, Edwin	7129	,,	Collins, Edward
6656	,,	Byfield, Kenneth	6546	,,	Conyard, Henry
6438	,,	Byng, Joseph	6780	,,	Cook, Edgar
7136	,,	Cameron, Allan	6779	,,	Cook, Guy
7135	,,	Campbell, Archibald	6443	,,	Cook, Harry
6999	Corpl.	Campbell, Donald H. B.	6198	,,	Cook, John D.
6313	Private	Campbell, Matthew	6301	,,	Cookson Bertram
6547	,,	Campbell, Robt. H.	6317	,,	Cope, William
6304	,,	Campbell, William	6898	,,	Copeland, E. S.
6548	,,	Capley, H.	6882	Bugler	Cordray, William
6298	,,	Cairns, George	7134	Private	Corrigan, Thos. L.
6648	,,	Callery, William	7021	,,	Cosgrave, David
6897	,,	Carloan, John	6901	,,	Cottell, Harry
6899	,,	Carruthers, D.	7130	,,	Coulay, William
6193	,,	Carruthers, William	6444	,,	Courtney, John Henry
6300	,,	Carter, Arthur Geo.	7024	,,	Cowper, John W.
6299	,,	Carter, Thomas	6549	,,	Cracknell, George
7025	,,	Casey, Michael J.	7128	,,	Craddock, Frank
6194	,,	Catchpole, Alfred Jas.	6445	,,	Craig, George F.
6670	,,	Chamberlain Sydney	6903	,,	Creighton, Chas.
6303	,,	Chance, Edwin	6902	,,	Creighton, F. A.
6440	,,	Chance, Edward	6319	,,	Crimson, John Francis
6184	,,	Chantler, L.	6552	,,	Crockett, Samuel A.
6551	,,	Chapman, Edwin	6315	,,	Crooks, James T.
6195	,,	Chappel, Albert E.	6668	,,	Crosier, Charles
6318	,,	Charlwood, Sam. G.	6446	,,	Cross, Joseph
7131	,,	Cheesman, Cedric	6671	,,	Croucher, Hone
6441	,,	Chew, George A.	6669	,,	Crowther, Fredk.
6442	,,	Chiffins, William J.	7026	,,	Cullen, David
6196	,,	Chisholm, W. C. H.	6447	,,	Cunningham, A. S.
6527	Corpl.	Christie, George	6900	,,	Cunningham, M.
6197	Private	Christison, David John	6202	,,	Curtis, Roy Barnet
6109	,,	Clare, Jean	6526	,,	Cuthill, Thos.
7133	,,	Clark, Chas. V.	6483	Arm. Cpl.	Dagg, Hueston Roy
6302	,,	Clark, James P.	6676	Private	Dalziel, Peter
6550	,,	Clark, James Thomas	6910	,,	Darniell, A. Thomas
7023	,,	Clarke, Ernest V.	6323	,,	Daw, Ernest
6199	,,	Clark, Robt. Wm.	6911	,,	Dawson, G. D.
6419	Bugler	Classon, Wilfred A.	6203	,,	Davey, George J.
6672	Private	Claus, Abner	6906	,,	Davidson, Thomas
7132	,,	Claxton, George	6320	,,	Davis, Edwin John

Canadian Pacific—The Empire's Greatest Railway.

14   1st BATTALION, 1st INFANTRY BRIGADE—cont.

Regl. No.	Rank.	Name.	Regl. No.	Rank.	Name.
6321	Private	Davis, Frederick	6453	Private	Feulger, William H.
6204	,,	Davis, William M.	7031	,,	Fields, William L.
7027	,,	Davis, William	7032	,,	Finlay, William
6324	,,	Deakin, Thomas	7141	,,	Finley, Frank
6205	,,	Deane, Arthur L. S.	6210	Corpl.	Fisher, Ellis W.
6783	,,	Delisle, Edgar	6683	Private	Fisher, Horace
6674	,,	Dennington, Alfred	6211	,,	Fisher, James Clair
6675	,,	Dennis, Richard	6793	,,	Fisher, John
7137	,,	Dent, Harold	6309	,,	Fitzsimons, Henry
6448	,,	Denvir, Patrick	6913	,,	Fleming, Hugh
6761	Sergt.	Denvil, Thomas	6212	,,	Fletcher, Joseph F.
6784	Private	Depencier, John	6553	,,	Flynn, James
6326	,,	Devitt, James	6454	,,	Foracre, Harry
6206	,,	Dickinson, Frank	6915	Corpl.	Ford, Peter
6449	,,	Dirsch, Horace	7143	Private	Ford, Thomas
7025	,,	Dixon, William	7144	,,	Ford, William
6907	,,	Dodds, Thomas	6794	,,	Forrester, William
7107	,,	Dolson, Charles	6916	,,	Forsyth, R. M.
6673	,,	Done, Alfred	6679	,,	Fox, Albert
6908	,,	Doran, Daniel	6213	,,	Fox, William, H.
6905	,,	Dorrance, H. J.	7142	,,	Foster, John F.
6755	,,	Doughty, Alfred	6789	,,	Francis, Claude
6904	,,	Downey, William	6791	,,	Fraser, Donald
6290	,,	Dudgeon, John	6329	,,	Fraser, George
6909	,,	Dudley, Harold	6681	,,	Freeman, George
6322	,,	Duffy, Oliver	6684	,,	French, Herbert
6325	,,	Dunbar, James	7145	,,	French, Hubert
7029	,,	Duncan, John	6455	,,	Fridd, John
6420	,,	Durrant, Wm. T.	7030	,,	Frostick, William.
6677	,,	Dye, Arthur	6792	,,	Fryer, Edward B.
6450	,,	Edmond, John	6795	,,	Fry, Lester
6786	,,	Edwards, Charles	6682	,,	Fry, Lewis
6678	,,	Edwards, Edward	7000	,,	Gaines, Wm. H.
6635	,,	Edwards, Wm. H.	6337	,,	Galbraith, Andrew
6780	,,	Edy, Harry	6686	,,	Gale, William
6787	,,	Eldridge, John	6456	,,	Garrett, Cecil S.
6328	,,	Elerton, Frank	7147	,,	Garton, Chas. Herb.
6327	,,	Elliott, Alex. McL.	6556	,,	German, Laurel
7139	,,	Ellis, Clarence A.	7002	Bugler	Gibb, William K.
6207	Arm. Cpl.	Ellwood, Wm. O.	6331	Private	Gibb, Andrew
6457	Private	Elstone, Stanley W.	7108	,,	Gibbard, Arthur John
7138	,,	English, Charles	6457	,,	Gibbard, Stanley A.
7006	,,	Essery, Alfred E.	6796	,,	Gibbs, Arthur
6912	,,	Evans, Thos.	6555	,,	Gibson, Wilfred E.
6452	,,	Eversfield, Leslie	6339	,,	Gilbert, Edgar
6790	,,	Failis, Vernon	6685	,,	Gilbert, Sydney
6914	,,	Fair, Roy	6214	,,	Gillespie, Robert M.
7146	,,	Falstaid, Charles J.	7150	,,	Gilliman, Albt. Ed.
6209	,,	Feilder, Frank K.	6650	,,	Gillingham, Charles
6282	,,	Fenn, John A.	6215	,,	Gillroy, Harold Evans
6554	,,	Fennie, Frank Wm.	6629	,,	Gimfoyle, James E.
7140	,,	Ferguson, Joseph	7149	,,	Ginney, William

Canadian Pacific—The Empire's Greatest Railway.

1ST BATTALION, 1ST INFANTRY BRIGADE—cont. 15

Regl. No.	Rank.	Name.	Regl. No.	Rank.	Name.
6797	Private	Girouard, George	6349	Arm. Cpl.	Harris, Thos.
7151	,,	Girsch, Harold	6345	Private	Harris, Walter
6340	,,	Glasser, Henry R.	7037	,,	Harrison, Thomas W.
6216	,,	Gleason, Francis	6557	,,	Harrison, Henry
7034	,,	Gleave, Hugh	6224	,,	Harte, George Harry
6920	,,	Gledhill, Verne	7044	,,	Haskell, Charles
6458	,,	Glidden, Jos. Chas.	6462	,,	Haskins, Harry C.
6633	,,	Goble, George	6565	,,	Hastings, James
6799	,,	Godfrey, Arthur	7043	,,	Haughton, Peter
6801	,,	Gooch, Albert	6563	,,	Hawes, Frank
6333	,,	Goodall, Patrick	7155	,,	Hawkins, Alfred
6217	,,	Goodall, Wesley M.	6689	,,	Hawkins, Steven
6338	,,	Gordon, Christopher	7156	,,	Hawthorne, Alex.
6986	,,	Gordon, James	6687	,,	Hayes, John
6218	,,	Gordon, Robert	6921	Corpl.	Hayles, Wm.
6335	,,	Gordon, Thomas H.	6341	Private	Havard, Jack
7152	,,	Gowie, Hugh	6351	,,	Hazel, Alfred C.
6220	,,	Graham, Charles A.	6463	,,	Headon, Frederick
7036	Corpl.	Graham, Geo. Wm.	6688	,,	Heather, James
6336	Private	Graham, H. W.	7039	,,	Heavens, Jos. J.
6800	,,	Gransden, Austin	6564	,,	Hemming, John
7033	,,	Grant, Alex Walker	6566	,,	Henley, John
7237	,,	Grant, James	6346	,,	Herage, Leonard
6763	,,	Grant, John	6226	,,	Higgins, John K.
6524	Corpl.	Grant, Samuel	6813	,,	Hill, Albert
7148	Private	Graves, Frederick	6464	,,	Hill, Ernest S.!
6918	,,	Green, David	6227	,,	Hill, John William
6798	,,	Green, George	7041	,,	Hill, William
6222	,,	Greenwood, Robert	6225	,,	Hiller, Adam A.
6221	,,	Gregson, David A.	6809	,,	Hilmkay, Arch.
6917	,,	Griffin, Harry	6350	,,	Hilton, John
6334	,,	Griffiths, Steven	7046	,,	Hislop, Chas. A.
6219	,,	Grosse, Alfred S.	6803	,,	Hobson, Harry
6460	,,	Grouden, Walter	6636	,,	Hodsol, Frank H.
6919	,,	Groves, Frederick	6561	,,	Hogan, Frank H.
7236	,,	Gruchey, Charles	6560	,,	Hogan, Valentine
6332	,,	Gurney, Guy V.	6568	,,	Holdernesse, Arthur
7035	,,	Gwyn, Charles C.	7045	,,	Holland, Richard
6461	,,	Habel, Harry Duncan	6806	,,	Hollingworth, John
7157	,,	Hachett, Joseph	6228	,,	Holmes, Alfred
6805	,,	Hadley, Arthur	6342	,,	Holmes, Charles
6223	,,	Hamilton, James	7153	,,	Holmes, Cecil
6559	,,	Hamilton, John	7038	,,	Holmes, Harry
6107	,,	Hancock, George	6810	,,	Holt, Harry
6922	,,	Handsley, Thos.	6343	,,	Holtnur, George
6567	,,	Hannaberry, William	6229	,,	Hopwood, Laurence
6802	,,	Hannah, Robert	6465	,,	Horne, Geo. Wm.
6924	,,	Hardy, Herbert	6811	,,	Horne, Thos.
6562	,,	Harefield, Claude G.	6348	,,	Hoskin, Henry
6925	,,	Harkness, James	7042	,,	Housler, A. Patterson
6804	,,	Harreman, John	6923	,,	Howard, Henry
6926	,,	Harrington, G. E.	7040	,,	Howe, V. C.

Canadian Pacific—The Empire's Greatest Railway.

1st BATTALION, 1st INFANTRY BRIGADE—cont.

Regl. No.	Rank.	Name.	Regl. No.	Rank.	Name.
6808	Private	Howell, Ernest	7163	Private	Kirk, Andrew
6558	,,	Hoyle, Arthur	6236	,,	Kirk, Robert John
6812	,,	Hudson, Robt.	6469	,,	Knight, Frederick
6347	,,	Humphry, Francis	6818	,,	Knight, G.
6344	,,	Hughes, Carl Ellis	7050	,,	Knill, John H.
6807	,,	Hughes, David	6819	,,	Knowles, William
6987	,,	Hurlbert, George	6820	,,	Kretchel, Clayton
7154	,,	Hutchison, Ernest	6827	,,	La Force, Angus
6466	,,	Hyatt, Arthur	6826	,,	Lalonde, Jos.
6927	,,	Iliffe, Roy	6698	,,	Lamk, Joseph
6814	,,	Ilott, Joseph	6459	,,	Lamky, Milton J.
6816	,,	Ince, Wm.	6470	,,	Lancaster, Charles
7158	,,	Irons, Edward	6471	,,	Langford, John B.
6691	,,	Irvine, E.	7008	,,	Langridge, Edward
6815	,,	Isaac, Samuel	7053	,,	Lanning, Henry
6690	,,	Ivison, Joseph	6472	,,	Large, William Chas.
7159	,,	Jackman, Geo.	6237	,,	Laufers, B. Frank
6570	,,	Jackson, John Murry	6823	Private	Laughrin, Conrad
6354	,,	Jamieson, Arthur E.	6238	,,	Laurie, John Alfred
6230	,,	Jennings, Edward	7168	,,	Lavender, John
6352	,,	Johns, Frank	7055	,,	Lavender, Thos. John
6817	,,	Johnson, Hilton	6239	,,	Lawrence, William C.
6928	,,	Johnson, L. F.	6574	,,	Lea, Harry
6929	,,	Johnson, Roy Alex.	7170	,,	Lee, Ernest E,
6984	,,	Johnson, Wentworth	7054	,,	Leith, James
7047	,,	Johnson, William	6880	Sergt.	Leithbridge, John
6692	,,	Joiner, Joseph	6932	Private	Leithbridge, William
6353	,,	Jones, Benj.	7003	Bugler	Lewis, Albert C.
7160	,,	Jones, Charles	6355	Private	Lewis, Joseph H.
6930	,,	Jones, Frederick A.	6240	,,	Lillie, Mark
7048	,,	Jones, George A.	6408	,,	Lirdwall, Gunnis A.
6693	,,	Jones, Richard	6699	,,	Ling, Percy
6569	,,	Jones, Wilfrid	6697	,,	Littlejohn, Wilfred
6571	,,	Kane, Alex. H.	6358	,,	Lloyd, Sydney S.
6573	,,	Kane, James	6473	,,	Lloyd, William
6933	,,	Kavanagh, Gerald T.	6649	,,	Look, Henry
6695	,,	Kay, Robert	6700	,,	Locke, Ernest
7164	,,	Kearney, William	6821	,,	Lockwood, John
6988	,,	Keemles, C. E.	7167	,,	Long, Elwyn Arthur
7162	,,	Keir, Ed. Alex.	7165	,,	Long, Gilbert
7161	,,	Kelly, James	6825	,,	Longman, George
6931	,,	Kendall, John	6824	,,	Longmire, Harold
6467	,,	Kendall, Jos.	6357	,,	Lonie, James
6468	,,	Kendrick, B. H.	6474	,,	Loveland, Harvy H.
7049	,,	Kennedy, Samuel W.	6701	,,	Lovell, Stephen
6232	,,	Kett, George E.	6356	,,	Lowe, Geo. Henry
6231	,,	Kett, Irwin A.	6996	,,	Lowe, Robert
6572	,,	Kilgour, Frank B.	6575	,,	Luce, John R.
6235	,,	Kinsella, James	7051	,,	Lumber, Walter Chas.
6233	,,	King, Frederick G.	6822	,,	Lund, Oscar
6234	,,	King, Herbert	7169	,,	Lunham, Ross
6694	,,	Kingston, Richard	7166	,,	Lunn, Arthur H.

Canadian Pacific—The Empire's Greatest Railway.

1st BATTALION, 1st INFANTRY BRIGADE—cont. 17

Regl. No.	Rank.	Name.	Regl. No.	Rank.	Name.
6362	Private	McAllister, Harvey	6476	Private	Martle, Wm. Geo.
6583	,,	McAuley, William	6576	,,	Maslem, John
6582	,,	McCarthy, Frank	7174	,,	Mason, George
6990	,,	McCarthy, Jos.	7177	,,	Mason, Harold Edwin
6360	,,	McComb, Alexander	6715	,,	Massacar, Edwin
6241	,,	McConnell, Charles	6832	,,	Matheson, Alex.
6242	,,	McCoy, Charles	6706	,,	Matheson, William
6244	,,	McCreedy, Bernard H.	6363	,,	Matthews, Alfred J.
6245	,,	McCrinnon, Hugh W.	7173	,,	Matthews, Geo. G.
6941	,,	McDonald, Donald	6940	,,	May, James
6630	,,	McDonald, George	6830	,,	May, William
6581	,,	McDonald, George	6710	,,	Mayberry, Edward
6477	,,	McDonald, George	7181	,,	Mays, Ulysses
6246	,,	McDonald, John Chas.	6718	,,	Medows, Frederick
6836	,,	McDonald, Nicholas	6711	,,	Meehan, Mathew
6828	,,	McDonald, William	7176	,,	Meley, John
7058	,,	McDougal, David	6365	,,	Melhurst, Arthur J.
6833	,,	McFarland, Claude	6367	,,	Metcalf, Arthur
6704	,,	McGee, Patrick	6479	,,	Metcalf, Oswald
6243	,,	McGowan, Mathew C.	7179	,,	Meyer, Albert H.
7056	,,	McGuinness, James	6716	,,	Middleton, William
6702	,,	McIntosh, Donald	6935	,,	Miller, Alexander
6713	,,	McIntosh, James	7059	,,	Milligan, Wm. Alex.
6478	,,	McKinley, Thos.	6720	,,	Mills, Robert
7175	,,	McKinstray, Thomas	6311	,,	Milmine, Harry
6359	,,	McLaren, Charles	6482	,,	Milner, Archie E.
6871	,,	McLaren, Harold	6250	,,	Minchen, Milton O.
7178	,,	McLellan, Arch.	7239	,,	Minorgan, Jas.
7180	,,	McLeod, Alex.	6251	,,	Mitchell, Robert
6361	,,	McLeod, Ross John	6411	,,	Mitchell, Wilfred E.
7057	Lce.-Cpl.	McMaster, John T.	6480	,,	Mitchell, William O.
6580	Private	McMeekin, William	7171	,,	Mitchison, Thos. W.
6839	,,	McMillan, Joseph	6579	,,	Montier, Albert V.
6584	,,	McMillan, Thos. H.	6254	,,	Monynihan, James
6934	,,	McPherson, Alexander	6834	,,	Moore, Arthur
6835	,,	Macfie, Robert	6719	,,	Moore, John
6578	,,	Maddox, George	6712	,,	Moore, George
6364	,,	Mageehan, James	6252	,,	Moore, George
6247	,,	Magnus, George H.	6253	Lce.-Cpl.	Morey, Albert
6942	,,	Maher, Richard	6709	Private	Morrice, C.
6255	,,	Malarkey, James	6703	,,	Morris, Stanley
6714	,,	Malding, Frederick	6717	,,	Morse, Charles
6938	,,	Manning, C. F.	6484	,,	Motby, John
6475	,,	Marks, Harry	6829	,,	Moulder, Herbert
6841	,,	Marmelstein, Peter	6939	,,	Mouldring, C.
6248	Corpl.	Marsden, George	6840	,,	Moulke, William
6249	,,	Marsh, Herbert W.	6366	,,	Moy, Walter
6936	Private	Marshall, Chas. J.	6485	,,	Munn, Harry
7172	,,	Marshall, Geo.	6842	,,	Munro, John
6312	,,	Marr, John	6488	,,	Munro, William D.
6837	,,	Martin, Alexander	6708	,,	Murdoch, James
6831	,,	Martin, James	6707	,,	Murdoch, William

Canadian Pacific—The Empire's Greatest Railway.

B

1st BATTALION, 1st INFANTRY BRIGADE—cont.

Regl. No.	Rank.	Name.
6937	Private	Murich, E. J.
6208	,,	Murphy, F. N.
6486	,,	Murphy, John
6160	,,	Murphy, Tim
6256	,,	Murray, James F.
6838	,,	Murray, John
6705	,,	Murray, Thos.
7238	,,	Murray, Thomas
6577	,,	Murray, Wilson
6487	,,	Musser, Samuel
6291	,,	Mutton, Charles
6368	,,	Nash, Alfred A.
6586	,,	Neil, George
7062	,,	Nellthrop, Herbert H.
6843	,,	Nelson, Charles
7060	,,	Nelson, Peter
6943	,,	Nesbit, Robert
6879	,,	Newell, F. C.
6369	,,	Newman, Nathaniel
6722	,,	Nicol, James
6944	,,	Nicol, Wm. Glen
7061	Corpl.	Nightingale, Geo. E.
6307	Private	Nixon, David
6370	,,	Nixon, Robert
6585	,,	Norris, C.
6587	,,	Nunn, John James
6989	,,	O'Brien, Henry
7241	,,	O'Brien, James
7185	,,	O'Connor, Pat.
6531	Corpl.	Odell, Oscar W.
6945	Private	O'Farrell, Arthur
6489	,,	Offer, Sidney T.
7183	,,	O'Hare, James
6588	,,	Oliver, David L.
7063	,,	O'Neill, James
7184	,,	Osmond, Stanley
7182	,,	Otto, Eric Arnold
7064	,,	Oughton, Chas. J.
6049	,,	Owen, Charles
7074	,,	Pacey, John W.
6490	,,	Page, Fredk. C. B.
6374	,,	Paget, Louis
6728	,,	Palmer, Ernest
6950	,,	Palmer, Wm.
6845	,,	Park, Joseph
7070	,,	Parke, Robert
7189	,,	Parker, Harry
6847	,,	Parsons, Ernest
6491	,,	Pascoe, Franklin
6257	Corpl.	Patterson, Andrew
7240	Private	Patterson, James
6258	,,	Patmore, Cecil M.
7069	Private	Pattinson, John
7246	,,	Payne, H.
7066	,,	Payne, Walter C.
7065	,,	Payne, Walter H.
7073	,,	Peacock, Robert
6594	,,	Peak, William
6492	,,	Pearce, Albert E.
6595	,,	Pedden, John A.
6259	,,	Peer, Leonard L.
6846	,,	Pegahmegabow, Francis
6596	,,	Pembleton, Laurence
7075	,,	Pennigar, Charles
6493	,,	Perry, Leonard
7071	,,	Peterson, Leonard
6631	,,	Pethick, Manford
6590	,,	Pouprase, Harry
6844	,,	Peur, Percy
6946	,,	Phelps, Jacob F.
6949	,,	Philcox, H. Milton
6726	,,	Philips, John
6260	,,	Phillips, Chas. Wm.
6725	,,	Phillips, Ernest
7186	,,	Phyllis, Robt.
6373	,,	Pile, Sidney P.
6371	,,	Pike, Geo. R. C.
6589	,,	Pinner, Bertie Geo.
7076	,,	Pirie, Geo. McC.
6375	,,	Pitman, Francis E.
6724	,,	Pitt, Frederick
6593	,,	Plante, Chester C.
6985	,,	Playne, Leslie
6947	,,	Plumridge, Thos.
6592	,,	Polly, Charles
6494	,,	Poole, George
6591	,,	Pope, Robt. H.
6723	,,	Popham, William
6261	,,	Porte, Nelson
7187	,,	Postill, Frank
7067	,,	Potts, Geo. C.
6948	,,	Powell, Thos. E.
6263	,,	Pratley, Robert
6643	Corpl.	Pratt, Ernest
7068	Private	Pratt, Frank
7188	,,	Preston, Sidney
6372	,,	Price, Herbert J.
7190	,,	Prince, James
6727	,,	Pyne, Victor
6262	Lce.-Sgt.	Pyper, Frederick A.
6734	Private	Rabbitt, James
6731	,,	Rae, Allen
6850	Corpl.	Ramsden, H.

Canadian Pacific—The Empire's Greatest Railway.

1ST BATTALION, 1ST INFANTRY BRIGADE—cont. 19

Regl. No.	Rank	Name	Regl. No.	Rank	Name
6730	Private	Randall, John	6500	Private	Seibert, Robt. A.
6495	,,	Ransom, John J.	7083	,,	Selves, Alfred
6377	,,	Rawlins, Geo. A.	7087	,,	Senior, A.
6602	,,	Ray, Charles	6855	Arm.-Cpl.	Serle, G. H.
6416	,,	Raymond, Alfred W.	6608	Private	Sewell, Fredk.
6848	,,	Raymond, Bert	6607	,,	Sewell, Thomas
7193	,,	Raymond, Charles	6737	,,	Sexton, Thomas
7005	,,	Raynor, Burns	6851	,,	Shaw, John
6599	,,	Read, Alexander	6380	,,	Shaw, Thos.
6496	,,	Read, Ernest	7211	Corpl.	Sheard, —
6952	,,	Redburn, C. H.	7010	Private	Shepherd, George
6634	,,	Reed, Robert	6960	,,	Shepley, Adam E.
6598	,,	Reed, William	7195	,,	Sheppard, Arthur
6632	,,	Rees, Henry A.	6530	Lce.-Cpl.	Shillings, John
6604	,,	Regan, Jerimiah	7194	Private	Shuel, Robt.
7192	,,	Reid, Jas. Henry	7084	,,	Simmers, Geo. A. E.
6733	,,	Renshaw, Laurence	6382	,,	Simmons, Reginald T.
6497	,,	Revell, Francis C.	6742	,,	Skiggs, William
7077	,,	Richardson, Wm. W.	6407	,,	Skinner, Alex.
6376	,,	Riddaway, Arthur J.	7007	,,	Skinner, Harry
6597	,,	Rigg, Thomas	6379	,,	Skrimshire, Howard
6163	,,	Ritchie, A.	6988	,,	Slade, W.
6953	,,	Rivers, A.	6888	,,	Slade, William
6289	,,	Robertson, David	6609	,,	Slater, Jos.
6954	,,	Robertson, G. E.	6741	,,	Slipper, Nathaniel
6732	,,	Robinson, John	6266	Lce.-Cpl.	Smale, Geo. S.
7242	,,	Rolfe, Frederick	6959	Private	Smith, Albert
7078	,,	Rolfe, James E.	6501	,,	Smith, Allan
6955	,,	Rose, H. E.	6856	,,	Smith, Charles
6849	,,	Roseby, Harold	6267	,,	Smith, Chas. Wm.
7191	,,	Rosmond, Robert	6383	,,	Smith, Clarence
6264	,,	Rouse, Charles	6956	,,	Smith, E. W.
7001	Sergt.	Rowe, E.	6644	Corpl.	Smith, George
6603	Private	Rudkin, Robert S.	6502	Private	Smith, Harry J.
7079	,,	Rushmere, Sidney R.	6957	,,	Smith, James
6951	,,	Russell, F. J.	6958	,,	Smith, Jas. Chas.
6399	,,	Russell, James	6306	,,	Smith, John
6762	Corpl.	Russell, John	6739	,,	Smith, McLean
6601	Private	Ruwald, Horace	6268	,,	Smith, Stephen
6378	,,	Ryan, Frank	6612	,,	Smith, Thos. S.
6729	,,	Ryan, James	6384	,,	Smith, William H.
6498	,,	Ryder, Harry	6738	,,	Snelgrove, Oliver
6600	,,	Ryder, Harry	6381	,,	Snook, Morris
6265	,,	Sanders, Henry	6613	Lce.-Cpl.	Sommerville, Hugh
6852	,,	Sargent, Thos.	6503	Private	Souvay, William F.
7082	,,	Saunders, David	6504	,,	Spray, Cyril H.
6647	Lce.-Cpl.	Scheff, John	6743	,,	Spurgeon, Frederick
6499	Private	Schultz, Frederick	6610	,,	Spyer, Thos. J.
6605	,,	Scott, David	6269	,,	Stacke, Thos. G.
6314	,,	Scott, William	6505	,,	Stanton, Archie A.
6606	,,	Scott, William A.	6735	,,	Stanton, Thomas
6853	,,	Scriver, Saml.	6611	,,	Stayte, Danl.

Canadian Pacific—The Empire's Greatest Railway.

1st BATTALION, 1st INFANTRY BRIGADE—cont.

Regl. No.	Rank.	Name.	Regl. No.	Rank.	Name.
6385	Private	Steele, John A.	6858	Private	Tuomi, John
6270	,,	Steele, Louis A.	7088	,,	Turner, Arthur E. R.
6507	,,	Stephens, Joseph	6617	,,	Turner, Harry E.
7081	,,	Stevenson, Norman	7090	,,	Turner, Lewis
6854	,,	Stewart, Jos.	6389	,,	Turpin, Walks
6963	,,	Stewart, Sydney	6526	Corpl.	Tuthill, L.
6271	,,	Stinchombe, Andrew	6749	Private	Tweede, Charles
6525	Corpl.	Stockwell, Alfred	6618	,,	Tye, Harry
6961	Private	Stone, Alfred W.	6616	,,	Tyrie, Kenneth
6740	,,	Stonefish, George	7092	,,	Upton, Philip E.
6736	,,	Stringer, Cecil	6273	,,	Urquhart, Alex.
6506	,,	Style, Henry D.	6864	,,	Van der Toon, Frips
7080	,,	Summerfield, Roland	6862	,,	Van Hess, Jas.
6272	Lce.-Cpl.	Summers, Edw. T.	6510	,,	Vannon, Donald
7085	Private	Sutton, Edw. Jos.	6872	,,	Van Oss, Joseph
7086	,,	Sutton, James	6863	,,	Valkers, Gerrett
6406	Sergt.	Swanson, Harry	6391	,,	Vaughan, Griffith
6962	Private	Syder, Percy Geo.	6750	,,	Verrell, Percy
6744	,,	Tack, Henry	6861	,,	Vincent, Howard
6280	,,	Talbot, Frank	6518	,,	Wackett, Edgar
6619	,,	Tanner, Albert	6982	,,	Waddell, Archibald
7197	,,	Taylor, Arthur	7011	,,	Waddell, J.
6747	,,	Taylor, Arthur	6983	,,	Waddell, William
6622	,,	Taylor, Frank	7100	,,	Wade, William
6508	,,	Taylor, James A.	7099	,,	Wainwright, Robt. J.
6748	,,	Taylor, Walter	6625	,,	Wakefield, Fred. K.
6967	,,	Templeman, Fredk.	6972	,,	Wakelin, Fred B.
6965	,,	Terry, George E.	6973	,,	Wakelin, Thomas
6388	,,	Tessier, Arthur E.	6288	,,	Walker, Alfred
6415	,,	Thomas, Albert E.	7199	,,	Walker, George
6614	,,	Thomas, Geo.	6971	,,	Walker, Gordon
7091	,,	Thomas, Ivan H.	6512	,,	Walker, Herbert
6387	,,	Thomas, Jacob	6396	,,	Walkerdine, William
6966	,,	Thomas, Rex	6751	,,	Wall, William
6281	,,	Thompson, Wm. Day	7093	,,	Waller, Charles A.
6968	,,	Thompson, Geo. H.	6513	,,	Walmsley, William
6746	,,	Thompson, Oliver	6395	,,	Walsh, Cecil
6615	,,	Thompson, Thomas	6866	,,	Walsh, Fredk.
6857	,,	Thoms, John	6975	,,	Ward, Charles
6390	,,	Thorne, Ralph E.	6626	,,	Ward, John
7196	,,	Thornton, John	6974	,,	Ward, John
6620	,,	Tidy, Harry	6981	,,	Ward, Samuel F
6964	,,	Tobias, Stirling S.	6881	,,	Ward, Thos. C.
6509	,,	Todd, Henry	7098	,,	Ward William L.
6859	,,	Tomkins, Cecil	7244	,,	Wardell, Sydney
6621	,,	Tonge, Joseph F.	6645	Corpl.	Ware, Charles
7243	,,	Tooney, Fredk.	6400	Private	Warren, Reginald
6969	,,	Toope, Cyril L.	6274	,,	Warrington, Leonard
7089	,,	Tracey, Walter F.	6275	,,	Warwick, Samuel T.
6860	Corpl.	Tranter, William	6752	,,	Watkins, Frank
6745	Private	Trudell, Thos.	6397	,,	Watson, James
6386	,,	Tunnicliff, Edw. P.	6515	,,	Watson, John

Canadian Pacific—The Empire's Greatest Railway.

1st BATTALION, 1st INFANTRY BRIGADE—cont.

Regl. No.	Rank.	Name.
6514	Private	Watson, Thos. T.
6623	,,	Watson, William
6276	,,	Watt, Wm. G.
6516	,,	Watts, Richard
6865	,,	Weaver, Patrick
7198	,,	Weaving, Victor
6868	,,	Webster, Fredk.
6978	Corpl.	Welch, Sydney
7104	Private	Wells, Wm. F.
6277	,,	Welsh, William
6818	,,	Weston, Philip H.
6628	,,	Whittaker, Edwin
6398	,,	White, James Geo.
6511	,,	White, Thos.
7097	,,	Whitla, William
6977	,,	Whitsett, Henry
6978	,,	Whitworth, John H.
6980	,,	Wiley, Edw. Frank
7094	,,	Wilkins, Albert E.
6517	,,	Williams, Bert
6970	,,	Williams, John M.
7203	,,	Williams, Thos.
7105	,,	Williams, Thomas M.
6393	,,	Wilmot, Joseph
7201	,,	Wilson, Edw. G.
7202	,,	Wilson, Frank

Regl. No.	Rank.	Name.
6392	Private	Wilson, Richard
6310	,,	Windsor, Frederick C.
6394	,,	Winegarden, Harold L.
6627	,,	Winterbottom, Jas.
7200	,,	Wood, Charles
6278	,,	Woodgate, Harold
6279	,,	Woods, James
6976	,,	Woodward, Alfred
7103	,,	Woodward, J.
7102	,,	Woodward, Wm. R.
6417	,,	Wormould, Wm. H.
6418	,,	Worrell, Albert
6624	,,	Wraith, Allan
6760	Sergt.	Wrigglesworth, John
6867	Corpl.	Wright, Fredk.
7101	Private	Wright, William
6414	,,	Wygall, Alfred W.
7095	,,	Wylie, Thomas
7096	,,	Wylies, Samuel
7204	,,	Yabsby, Albert
6754	,,	Yates, William
6753	,,	Young, Edgar
6869	,,	Young, John
6870	,,	Young, Joseph
6481	,,	Zapski, Walter S.

2nd BATTALION, 1st INFANTRY BRIGADE.

HEADQUARTERS.

Lieut.-Colonel *illegible* ... Watson, David
Major ... ... Rogers, Chas. Herman (Lt.-Col. C.M.)
,, ... Howard, Frank A. (Lt.-Col. C.M.)
Quartermaster ... ... Major Mills, Joseph
Chaplain ... ... ,, Beattie, William
Adjutant ... ... Captain Willis-O'Connor, Henry
Medical Officer ... ... ,, Greer, George Garnet
Transport Officer *illegible* Lieut. Jones, Richard William Fisher *124*
Machine Gun Officer ... ... ,, Hodge, Henry Edmund
Paymaster ... ... Hon. Capt. Houghton, Thos. Middleton
Asst. Adjutant ... ... Lieut. Turner, Alfred George
Signalling Officer ... ... ,, Curry, Frederick Crawford

Regl. No.	Rank.	Name
8592	S.M. (W.O.)	White, Wilfrid O.
8593	,, ,,	O'Brien, John E.
8594	Q.M.S.	Taylor, Harry
8595	Sgt.-Bugler	Day, Charles A.

Regl. No.	Rank.	Name.
8596	Pnr-Sgt.	Smith, William A. F.
8597	Cook-Sgt.	Murphy, John Francis
8598	Trspt.-St.	Graham, James Henry
8599	Sgl.-Sgt.	Unwin, Valentine W.

Canadian Pacific—The Empire's Greatest Railway.

2ND BATTALION, 1ST INFANTRY BRIGADE—cont.

Regl. No.	Rank.	Name.	Regl. No.	Rank.	Name.
8600	S.-Shmkr.	Futter, Albert	8631	Corpl.	Gardiner, Edward
8601	Arm-Sgt.	Antell, George Francis	8632	Private	Adam, Fredk. Martin
8602	Pay-Sgt.	Laing, George Norman	8633	,,	Blood, Daniel Charles
8603	Sergt.	Bussell, Ebinezer W.	8634	,,	Caldwell, Robert Allan
8604	Private	Warner, Roy Lindsay	8635	,,	Giles, Frank Egerton
8605	,,	Parker, Percy George	8636	,,	Honeyman, Edward F.
8606	,,	Wilson, Charles	8637	,,	Folkard, Arthur
8607	,,	Kyle, John	8638	,,	Jones, John David
8608	,,	Wren, Alexander	8639	,,	Malone, Edward Geo.
8609	,,	Rowles, Wm. Henry	8640	,,	Rolfe, Reginald Dennis
8610	,,	Trudell, Regis Adalard	8641	,,	Burns, George
8611	,,	Leonard, Charles	8642	,,	Bostridge, Charles
8612	,,	Carse, Thomas	8643	,,	Anderson, James
8613	,,	Underwood, Harold E.	8644	,,	Callahan, Fred
8614	,,	Besant, Thomas Wm.	8645	,,	Broadbent, Thomas
8615	,,	Gordon, George	8646	,,	Cardew, Richard Thos.
8616	,,	McMillan, John	8647	,,	McLachlin, Andrew
8617	,,	Smith, Thos. Aldershaw	8648	,,	Salway, Edward Wm.
8618	,,	Staback, James Elliot	8649	,,	Pitreson, George
8619	,,	Stuart, Henry Cuthbert	8650	,,	Pulley, Albert
8620	,,	Wilder, Sherbourne	8651	,,	Pengelly, Thos. Henry
8621	,,	Lewis, Fred	8652	,,	Nicholson, Alfred
8622	,,	Bristow, Jesse John	8653	,,	Patterson, Walter Steel
8623	,,	Bisnaw, Wm. Arthur	8654	,,	Brown, Charles Henry
8624	,,	Clarke, Fredk. Archer	8655	,,	Bovey, Frederick
8625	,,	Day, Charles Fowler	8656	,,	Shotter, William
8626	,,	Frego, John Joseph	8657	Corpl.	Knapp, William James
8627	,,	Mitchell, Douglas G.	8658	Private	Gould, William
8628	,,	Sandford, Walter Thos.	8569	,,	Gracey, William
8629	,,	Le Bar, Lyle	8660	,,	Cline, Percy
8630	M.G.-Pte.	Young, James Kenneth	8661	,,	Hunter, Robert Edgar

"A" COMPANY.

Captain ... Maj. (K'M) 23/4/15... Bennett, George W.
Lieutenant ... ... McLennan, Andrew Gordon
,, ... Ackerman, Charles Hadyn
,, ... Whelen, Otis Goodwin

Regl. No.	Rank.	Name.	Regl. No.	Rank.	Name.
7576	Col.-Sgt.	Howarth, Fred	7586	Lce.-Cpl.	Ackerman, Arthur R.
7577	Sergt.	Allen, John Matthew	7587	,,	Ellis, Gerald William
7578	,,	Griffin, Thomas	7588	,,	Cumberland, Keith O.
7579	,,	Nicholls, Ernest	7589	,,	Collins, Thomas
7580	,,	King, George William	7590	,,	Yates, Harry Richard
7581	Lce.-Sgt.	Victor, Peter	7591	,,	Stevens, Fred
7582	Corpl.	Savage, Wm. Alexander	7592	Private	Collins, Thomas Ernest
7583	,,	Field, Fredk. Arthur	7593	,,	Banks, Charles Henry
7584	,,	Hale, Eric George	7594	,,	Smith, John Arthur
7585	,,	Carpenter, Herbert E.	7595	,,	Wood, William Arthur

Canadian Pacific—The Empire's Greatest Railway.

2ND BATTALION, 1st INFANTRY BRIGADE—cont. 23

Regl. No.	Rank	Name	Regl. No.	Rank	Name
7596	Private	Brown, Edgar	7645	Private	Kendall, Albert
7597	,,	Kelsey, Harry George	7646	,,	Kendry, David Roscoe
7598	,,	Griffiths, Thos. Henry	7647	,,	Kingston, James Elmer
7599	,,	Jeffries, Charles Walter	7648	,,	Leal, Douglas
7600	,,	James, Richard Fred	7649	,,	Levoir, Robert
7601	,,	Affleck, William	7650	,,	Levoir, Thomas
7602	,,	Aspey, John	7651	,,	Levoir, William
7603	,,	Bills, James	7652	,,	Long, William James
7604	,,	Brisco, Fred	7653	,,	Levere, Arthur Stanley
7605	,,	Bartle, Eric Lenoard	7654	,,	Legg, John
7606	,,	Brunton, George Wm.	7655	,,	Middleton, George
7607	,,	Butler, Peter John	7656	,,	McKinley, Samuel
7608	,,	Boswell, Ernest B.	7657	,,	Mills, Samuel Albert
7609	,,	Boyce, George Arthur	7658	,,	Mongour, Charles A.
7610	,,	Brooks, Oswald R.	7659	,,	Minorgan, Geo. Elliot
7611	,,	Bucknell, Stanley H.	7660	,,	Mills, Bruce Albert
7612	,,	Bailey, William Arthur	7661	,,	Morgan, Wm. Edgar
7613	,,	Cook, Joseph	7662	,,	Mockett, Fredk. Wm.
7614	,,	Cummings, David	7663	,,	Mesley, Ernest
7615	,,	Cockerill, Allan	7664	,,	Nicholls, Thomas
7616	,,	Cole, William	7665	,,	Northcote, Victor Jas.
7617	,,	Curtis, George Norman	7666	,,	Newell, James Gordon
7618	,,	Caillard, Henry	7667	,,	Packwood, Walter D.
7619	,,	Clarke, Fred	7668	,,	Parrington, Thomas A.
7620	,,	Cursen, George	7669	,,	Prosser, Edward
7621	,,	Clarke, Noel Hughes	7670	,,	Pimblott, Fred
7622	,,	Cook, Hiram Delbert	7671	,,	Pellow, Sydney
7623	,,	Christie, G. McPherson	7672	,,	Powell, Charles
7624	,,	Connelly, Daniel	7673	,,	Phipps, Arthur Wm.
7625	,,	Dudley, Frank	7674	,,	Quinn, Theodore
7626	,,	Dummitt, Ernest Isaac	7675	,,	Richardson, Frank
7627	,,	Davis, George	7676	,,	Rogers, Heber S.
7628	,,	English, James Herbert	7677	,,	Robertson, James
7629	,,	Ellis, Henry	7678	,,	Scollie, Harold
7630	,,	Fitz-Clarence, Henry	7679	,,	Sheperdson, William
7631	,,	Ford, John	7680	,,	Sherwood, Herbert S.
7632	,,	Gifford, Victor	7681	,,	Saunders, Harold Wm.
7633	,,	Gibson, Wm. Fordyce	7682	,,	Simmons, Wm. Wilson
7634	,,	Garrett, Stanley	7683	,,	Sheehan, William
7635	,,	Gladdon, George	7684	,,	Stenson, Charles
7636	,,	Gray, George Ernest	7685	,,	Taylor, Odley David
7637	,,	Hayden, Ernest Edwin	7686	,,	Vincent, John
7638	,,	Hayes, Stuart Fin-Bar	7687	,,	White, Arthur Wm.
7639	,,	Hartley, Leonard R.	7688	,,	White, Albert Edward
7640	,,	Hele, William Copley	7689	,,	Wood, Harry
7641	,,	Hawkins, Albert K.	7690	,,	Wilson, John
7642	,,	Hunt, John William	7691	,,	Wardlow, Walter
7643	,,	Jolly, Thomas William	7692	,,	Worles, Albert Edward
7644	,,	Johnson, John			

Canadian Pacific—The Empire's Greatest Railway.

24   2ND BATTALION, 1ST INFANTRY BRIGADE—cont.

"B" COMPANY.

Major	Thorne, Sydney Lodge
Lieutenant	Gordon, Walter Leslie Lockhart
,, ...	Strathy, John Henry Grasset
,, ...	Klotz, Herbert Norman

Regl. No.	Rank.	Name.	Regl. No.	Rank.	Name.
7693	Col.-Sgt.	Paton, David	7737	Private	Devonshire, Jas. Elliot
7694	Sergt.	Seddon, Arthur Wm.	7738	,,	Edwards, Fred John
7695	,,	Kirk, Robert John	7739	,,	Ferris, Frederick
7696	,,	Howard, Harry	7740	,,	Glover, Frank
7697	,,	Parker, Bertram John	7741	,,	Gohn, Wm.
7698	Lce.-Sgt.	Bayliss, Joseph John	7742	,,	Graham, Wm.
7699	Corpl.	Huggett, Ed. Walter	7743	,,	Graves, Sydney Charles
7700	,,	Bettens, John Francis	7744	,,	Gray, Chas.
7701	,,	Bailey, Wm. Frederick	7745	,,	Gray, George Henry
7702	,,	Starr, Clarence Leslie	7746	,,	Green, John Francis
7703	Lce.-Cpl.	Faulkner, Freeman	7747	,,	Harris, Robert Hewson
7704	,,	Sawyer, Frank	7748	,,	Henfrey, George
7705	,,	Douse, Edwin Thomas	7749	,,	Hicks, Gerald William
7706	,,	Green, Thomas	7750	,,	Hicks, Burwill
7707	,,	Morgan, James Chas.	7751	,,	Hood, Frank
7708	,,	Owen, Ernest Joseph	7752	,,	Ingham, Robert
7709	Private	Allen, Ernest	7753	,,	Jones, Claude Sam.
7710	,,	Arthur, William	7754	,,	Jones, Percy Robert
7711	,,	Barnhart, Con.	7755	,,	Jones, Douglas Crosbie
7712	,,	Beck, Wm. John	7756	,,	Kemsley, Ernest Wm.
7713	,,	Bennett, Henry Leigh	7757	,,	Kennedy, W. J. McK.
7714	,,	Bennett, Russell	7758	,,	Kennett, John
7715	,,	Blair, Robert	7760	,,	Lavin, John
7716	,,	Booker, John	7761	,,	Lightwood, Alfred
7717	,,	Bolan, Wm. Thomas	7762	,,	Miller, Chas. Albert
7718	,,	Bolus, Chas. Harold	7763	,,	Mangan, Robert
7719	,,	Brassey, Wm. Leslie	7764	,,	Markey, Arthur Wm.
7720	,,	Briggs, Albert	7765	,,	Martin, Nilson
7721	,,	Bromley, Jas. Wm. B.	7766	,,	Massey, Alfred
7722	,,	Brown, George Herbert	7767	,,	Maynes, Ricd. Norman
7723	,,	Cameron, Wm. Hugh	7768	,,	McCarthy, Bryan D.
7724	,,	Carey, James	7769	,,	McCaul, Gordon.
7725	,,	Carson, Fred David	7770	,,	McDowell, Wm. Robert
7726	,,	Cashman, Fredk. Geo.	7771	,,	Meff, Jas. Henderson
7727	,,	Cathcart, Wm.	7772	,,	Medowcraft, John
7728	,,	Catto, Dashwood	7773	,,	Massett, Ralph
7729	,,	Chantry, Alfred	7774	,,	Miller, Harold Joseph
7730	,,	Chantry, Wm. Henry	7775	,,	Million, George
7731	,,	Chittenden, Wm.	7776	,,	Moore, Horace
7732	,,	Cleveland, Bertram S.	7777	,,	Niddery, Edward John
7733	,,	Cole, Bruce	7778	,,	O'Connor, Wm.
7734	,,	Cottrill, Walter	7779	,,	Page, Fred
7735	,,	Davis, George	7780	,,	Parker, George Charles
7736	,,	Derbyshire, Oswin	7781	,,	Pearce, Fred

Canadian Pacific—The Empire's Greatest Railway.

2ND BATTALION, 1ST INFANTRY BRIGADE—cont.

Regl. No.	Rank	Name	Regl. No.	Rank	Name
7782	Private	Perks, Clarence Henry	7796	Private	Stephens, Leonard V.
7783	,,	Perry, Ernest Berry	7797	,,	Stevenson, Geo. Albert
7784	,,	Powles, David Austin	7798	,,	Styles, George
7785	,,	Reid, Joseph	7799	,,	Stubington, Frank
7786	,,	Reid, Everitt	7800	,,	Thomson, Eric B.
7787	,,	Reynolds, Wm.	7801	,,	Tuttle, Ernest Garfield
7788	,,	Rigby, Joseph	7802	,,	Ventris, Frank Eden
7789	,,	Rowe, Archie.	7803	,,	Walker, Leslie George
7790	,,	Rutherford, Wm.	7804	,,	Ward, Harold Edward
7791	,,	Sadler, Eric	7805	,,	Ware, Ernest Leigh S.
7792	,,	Saunders, Herbert	7806	,	Watson, Robert
7793	,,	Seddon, Saml. Henry	7807	,,	Winslow, Alfred
7794	,,	Skewis, Wm. James	7808	,,	Young, Russell
7795	,,	Snider, Sherman Jay	7809	,,	Young, Sherman

"C" COMPANY.

Captain ... ... Chrysler, Geoffrey G.
Lieutenant ... ... Culling, Evelyn Claude
,, ... Hugill, Archibald Henry
,, ... Earl, Rollo Othwell

Regl. No.	Rank	Name	Regl. No.	Rank	Name
7810	Col.-Sgt.	Landriau, Francis A.	7837	Private	Brown, Reg. Geo.
7811	,,	Neilson, Malcolm A.	7838	,,	Chenevert, Roscoe
7812	Private	Riddle, Wm. van Buren	7839	,,	Cobourn, Allen L.
7813	Sergt.	Ablard, Harry Chas.	7840	,,	Coleman, Ernest
7814	,,	Neal, Cyril Wilfrid	7841	,,	Comiskey, Thomas
7815	Corpl.	Guigues, Frdk. Stanley	7842	,,	Cooper, Thomas
7816	,,	Simons, Daniel Alex.	7843	,,	Crawley, Percy Wm.
7817	,,	Stoddart, Daniel	7844	,,	Crean, Chas.
7818	,,	Mates, John	7845	,,	Curtis, Walter Henry
7819	Lce.-Cpl.	Howden, Hay	7846	,,	Dean, Thomas
7820	Private	Fennell, George	7847	,,	Dobbin, Edward
7821	Lce.-Cpl.	Tressider, George	7848	,,	Dowse, Saml. Jas.
7822	,,	McMahn, Michael	7849	,,	Down, James
7823	,,	Hawken, Frank Jos.	7850	,,	Dunne, Patrick Leonrd.
7824	,,	Anderson, Alex.	7851	,,	Etherington, Joseph
7825	Private	Abrahamson, John	7852	,,	Fillion, Hector Ovide
7826	,,	Acton, George Dunbar	7853	,,	Fisher, Thomas Wm.
7827	,,	Alexander, Walter C.	7854	,,	Foley, Raymond
7828	,,	Andrews, Wm.	7855	,,	Gardner, Richard
7829	,,	Arbuckle, Percy Robt.	7856	,,	Glover, George
7830	,,	Armstrong, Wm.	7857	,,	Graham, Kenneth
7831	Bugler	Hunt, Horace	7858	,,	Grant, Harry
7832	Private	Pearce, Philip	7859	,,	Grant, Wm. Jas.
7833	,,	Bliss, Alder Eardley	7860	,,	Graystone, Herbert
7834	,,	Bolter, Frederick Jas.	7861	,,	Gregory, Chas.
7835	,,	Bradley, Edward	7862	,,	Hall, Wm.
7836	,,	Bramley, Percy Allen	7863	,,	Hilliar, Wm. John

Canadian Pacific—The Empire's Greatest Railway.

2ND BATTALION, 1ST INFANTRY BRIGADE—cont.

Regl. No.	Rank.	Name.	Regl. No	Rank.	Name.
7864	Private	Hoffman, Wm.	7896	Private	Reid, Benj.
7865	,,	Hope, Henry Thomas	7897	,,	Reid, Marshall
7866	,,	Hughes, Frank	7898	,,	Rew, Frederic Herbert
7867	,,	Jenkins, Michael John	7899	,,	Rochon, Joseph
7868	,,	Johnston, James Chas.	7900	,,	Rooney, Arthur
7869	,,	Knox, Lawrence B.	7901	,,	Salt, John
7870	,,	Lane, George	7902	,,	Sheridan, Lawrence
7871	,,	Lauder, Joseph	7903	,,	Shearman, Frederick J.
7872	,,	Lloyd, Henry	7904	,,	Simkins, Edwd. Walter
7873	,,	Longprey, Eddy S. M.	7905	,,	Simpson, Peter Orton
7874	,,	Lord, James	7906	,,	Summerfield, Wm.
7875	,,	Major, John	7907	,,	Smith, George Jas.
7876	,,	Mallard, James Patrick	7908	,,	Smith, Wm.
7877	,,	Mason, Frank Hubert	7909	,,	St. Germain, Benj. C.
7878	,,	May, Oscar Victor Alf.	7910	,,	Tasse, Rodolfe
7879	,,	Miller, George	7911	,,	Tenne, Chas. Edward
7880	,,	Mills, Arthur	7912	,,	Thomas, Fredk. Geo.
7881	,,	Mison, Chas. Wm.	7913	,,	Tubman, Leslie Walter
7882	,,	Moore, Wm.	7914	,,	Waddy, Harry Clifford
7883	,,	Moyes, Wm.	7915	,,	Walters, Richard
7884	,,	McDonald, Daniel E.	7916	,,	Whyte, Wm. Steven
7885	,,	McDougall, Lorne H.	7917	,,	Williams, Joseph
7886	,,	McGillicuddy, Arthr. J.	7918	,,	Wilson, Byron
7887	,,	McGurk, Peter	7919	,,	Wilson, Moore
7888	,,	McKay, George	7920	,,	Winton, Thomas
7889	,,	McLaughlin, Alfred J.	7921	,,	Wood, John Howard
7890	,,	Nichol, Herbert Lucien	7922	,,	Wooding, Alfred
7891	,,	O'Higgins, Dennis	7923	,,	Woodruff, Bernard Jn.
7892	,,	Parsons, Bernard W.	7924	,,	Yarrow, Charles
7893	,,	Porter, Robert Jordan	7925	,,	Yarrow, Frederick
7894	,,	Racette, Joseph	7926	,,	Young, Walter Jas.
7895	,,	Rainey, Wm. Hill			

"D" COMPANY.

Captain	...	...	...	Verret, Hector Bacon
Lieutenant	...	...	...	De Salaberry, Rene
,,	...	...	...	Kidd, Thomas Ashmore
,,	...	...	...	McLurg, John Ernest

Regl. No.	Rank.	Name.	Regl. No.	Rank.	Name.
7927	Col.-Sgt.	Gibson, Frederick	7936	Corpl.	Vaughan, Leonard
7928	Sergt.	Stone, Joseph Scott	7937	Lce.-Cpl.	Lawlor, Leonard
7929	,,	Smith, Geoffry Leigh	7938	,,	Millward, Ernest
7930	,,	Hamilton, Henry Sid.	7939	,,	Ford, F. MacDonald
7931	,,	Foote, Walter Percival	7940	,,	Ryan, James
7932	Lce.-Sgt.	Brettle, James	7941	,,	Fouchette, Williard
7933	Corpl.	Baggs, Alfred	7942	,,	Cotgrave, M. Larmer
7934	,,	Sutton, Ernest Nathl.	7943	Private	Anderson, Thomas
7935	,,	Lewis, Wm. James	7944	,,	Albrough, John Albion

Canadian Pacific—The Empire's Greatest Railway.

2ND BATTALION, 1ST INFANTRY BRIGADE—cont.

Regl. No.	Rank.	Name.	Regl. No.	Rank.	Name.
7945	Private	Bailey, John Kennedy	7994	Private	Lightfoot, James
7946	,,	Bowker, Frank Stan.	7995	,,	Lucas, Wm.
7947	,,	Coe, Thomas	7996	,,	Miron, Charles
7948	,,	Cameron, Donald Alex.	7997	,,	Monk, George Henry
7949	,,	Conner, Harry S.	7998	,,	Murray, Thomas
7950	,,	Cooper, David George	7999	,,	Major, Frank
7951	,,	Collins, Eden Ambrose	8041	,,	Malone, Edward
7952	,,	Carruth, James J.	8000	,,	Merrifield, William
7953	,,	Denman, Oliver	8001	,,	Martin, Chas.
7954	,,	Durham, E. Thompson	8002	,,	MacMillan, Donald
7955	,,	Durham, Elliot Manery	8003	,,	MacNab, John Ide
7956	,,	Davis, Leonard	8004	,,	McDonald, Charles
7957	,,	Dunn, Joseph	8005	,,	MacAllister, David
7958	,,	Donnan, B. C.	8006	,,	McLeod, J. McDonald
7959	,,	Dederer, Matt. L.	8007	,,	McCarthy, John Carl
7960	,,	Day, Alex.	8008	,,	McKay, Andrew
7961	,,	Dunsmore, Wm. John	8009	,,	Munroe, James
7962	,,	Furlong, Wm. A.	8010	,,	Mahulak, Peter
7963	,,	Furber, Allan	8011	,,	Nicholls, F. Randolph
7964	,,	Finch, Llewellen	8012	,,	Nicholson, Andrew
7965	,,	Firth, Wm.	8013	,,	O'Rourke, Wm.
7966	,,	Fox, Michael	8014	,,	Pringle, Geo. Wm.
7967	,,	Franks, Archi.	8015	,,	Pim, Michael
7968	,,	Grant, John	8016	,,	Partington, Charles
7969	,,	Grey, Wm.	8017	,,	Pomeroy, Harved
7970	,,	Grant, Peter	8018	,,	Paice, Ernest Wm.
7971	,,	Goodman, Thos.	8019	,,	Reed, Brian Lee
7972	,,	Gourley, John	8042	,,	Reid, Lawrence Wm.
7973	,,	Green, Herbert	8020	,,	Rout, Frederick Walter
7974	,,	Hardiman, F. Napier	8021	,,	Ribout, Fred Honore
7975	,,	Humphries, Harry	8022	,,	Roddy, Wm.
7976	,,	Huyson, Herbert	8023	,,	Rowlands, Benj.
7977	,,	Hand, Percy	8024	,,	Sherwood, Clifford
7978	,,	Hallimond, Wm.	8025	,,	Stephens, J. Martin
7979	,,	Hindmarsh, John	8026	,,	Sayers, Edward
7980	,,	Highstone, Albert S.	8027	,,	Smiganoski, W. M.
7981	,,	Hughes, Ellis Duncan	8028	,,	Strudwick, Walter G.
7982	,,	Heard, Chas.	8029	,,	Sorley, Charles H.
7983	,,	Holgate, Bert.	8030	,,	Saunders, Wm.
7984	,,	Herr, Philip L.	8031	,,	Thompson, T. C.
7985	,,	Hounsell, James	8032	,,	Taylor, Thomas
7986	,,	Hounsell, Wilbert	8033	,,	Taylor, Edward
7987	,,	Ironsides, Will	8043	,,	Thomas, Harry
7988	,,	Jackson, Wilfred	8034	,,	Turner, John William
7989	,,	Jarrett, George	8035	,,	Venn, Archie
7990	,,	Jarbeau, Eddy	8036	,,	Wilson, Geo. Neilson
8040	Bugler	Johnston, Thomas	8037	,,	Wheeler, Richard
7991	Private	Kennedy, Stuart	8038	,,	Wilks, Albert
7992	,,	Kennedy, Thomas	8039	,,	Wines, Percy
7993	,,	Leffler, Raymond			

Canadian Pacific — The Empire's Greatest Railway.

2ND BATTALION, 1st INFANTRY BRIGADE—cont.

"E" COMPANY.

Captain	... ...	Guttman, Leo Frank
Lieutenant	... ...	Richardson, George Taylor
,,	... ...	Stewart, John.Herchner
,,	... ...	Day, Calvin Wellington

Regl. No.	Rank.	Name.	Regl. No.	Rank.	Name.
8044	Col.-Sgt.	Tierney, Michael	8089	Private	Darling, C. Douglas
8045	Sergt.	Cross, Albert Edward	8090	,,	Davy, Mark
8046	,,	Lyons, George Wm.	8091	,,	Ewart, Joshia Charles
8047	,,	Bentley, John	8092	,,	Foster, Frank William
8048	,,	Mahoney, Thomas	8093	,,	Flannagan, Daniel
8049	Lce.-Sgt.	King, Alfred	8094	,,	Fillion, Oscar Gardier
8050	Corpl.	Singleton, Harry	8095	,,	Fleet, William
8051	,,	Edwards, Fredk. John	8096	,,	Filtz, John
8052	,,	Langton, Harry Wm.	8097	,,	Haynes, L. Harrison
8053	,,	Murray, Samuel John	8098	,,	Havery, Wm. Thomas
8054	Lce.-Cpl.	Hicks, Charles	8099	,,	Hagon, Geo. Thomas
8055	,,	Rogers, John Francis	8100	,,	Handcock, Thomas
8056	,,	Burton, William	8101	,,	Herman, Robert Rose
8057	,,	Hannaford, J. Haines	8102	,,	Heagle, Marquis
8058	,,	Smith, Frank Francis	8103	,,	Hill William
8059	,,	Wright, Thomas	8104	,,	Howard, John Henry
8060	Private	Adams, Fredk. Samuel	8105	,,	Holtham, W. Clement
8061	,,	Atkins, James Alex.	8106	,,	Holden, George
8062	,,	Ayres, Walter John	8107	,,	Hutton, George
8063	,,	Barry, John Edward	8108	,,	Hughes, Robert
8064	,,	Barry, George	8109	,,	Hutchings, Cyril
8065	,,	Banbrook, Fredk.Wm.	8110	,,	Judge, Richard
8066	,,	Bean, Edward Roy	8111	,,	Johnson, William
8067	,,	Bingham, Albert Jas.	8112	,,	Kelly, Aringo Thos.
8068	,,	Bury, Harry Garfield	8113	,,	Kelly, Alfred Edward
8069	,,	Broad, Robert Newell	8114	,,	Kelly, Chas. Frederick
8070	,,	Brown,GeorgeEdward	8115	,,	Kelso, Wm. Alexander
8071	,,	Brown, Mark Bignell	8116	,,	Litchfield, Thomas
8072	,,	Bush, William Forest	8117	,,	Lott, Henry
8073	,,	Buse, Edwin William	8118	,,	Lucas, Percy Borden
8074	,,	Billings, James Geo.	8119	,,	Letts, Thomas Hugh
8075	,,	Bryant, Clive	8120	,,	McDonald, Geo.Alfred
8076	,,	Byron, Gordon	8121	,,	McDonald, Alfd. John
8077	,,	Burrows, Wm. Provis	8122	,,	McDonald, D. Edward
8078	,,	Butcher, Robt. Leslie	8123	,,	McClelland, John
8079	,,	Clarke, E. Gladstone	8124	,,	Marguery, F. Gaston
8080	,,	Connolly,Thos.Patrick	8125	,,	Matthews, Wm. John
8081	,,	Charlton, Burt	8126	,,	McGall, Hugh John
8082	,,	Chambers, C. A. Wm.	8127	,,	Montgomery, Edmund
8083	,,	Cowie, John	8128	,,	Murphy, William
8084	,,	Christie, John	8129	,,	Mack,JamesFrederick
8085	,,	Crickenton, Frederick	8130	,,	Murray, Saml. Brown
8086	,,	Cox, Lewis	8131	,,	Murray,Wm. Hanning
8087	,,	Davidson,JohnWalker	8132	,,	Newman, John Wm.
8088	,,	Davidson, Allan Wm.	8133	,,	Neilson,RaymondEarl

Canadian Pacific—The Empire's Greatest Railway.

2ND BATTALION, 1ST INFANTRY BRIGADE—cont.

Regl. No.	Rank.	Name.	Regl. No.	Rank.	Name.
8134	Private	Nicholls, Thomas	8148	Private	Stanley, William
8135	,,	Nolan, William Henry	8149	,,	Schemerhorn, Ross
8136	,,	Oldfield, Alford	8150	,,	Sullivan, Thomas
8137	,,	Pirie, William	8151	,,	Sidore, W. Franklin
8138	,,	Pace, George	8152	,,	Shangrow, John L.
8139	,,	Pollard, James Gerald	8153	,,	Treneer, William C.
8140	,,	Ramsey, William	8154	,,	Unwin, William David
8141	,,	Stacey, George	8155	,,	Wilson, John
8142	,,	Smallridge, W. Stanley	8156	,,	Wheatley, Lewis A.
8143	,,	Smith, Ernest	8157	,,	Warren, Eden Wright
8144	,,	Smith, Alfred James	8158	,,	Warmington, Joseph
8145	,,	Smith, Thomas Joseph	8159	,,	Wiles, Charles
8146	,,	Stephenson, Thomas	8160	,,	Wickham, George H.
8147	,,	Stanfield, David Henry			

"F" COMPANY.

Captain	... ...	Abell, T. S. Hall
Lieutenant	... ...	Ponton, Richard Douglas
,,	... ...	Ferguson, Kenneth Douglas
,,	... ...	Fraser, Hugh Neil

Regl. No.	Rank.	Name.	Regl. No.	Rank.	Name.
8161	Col.-Sgt.	Howard, Lawrence F.	8191	Private	Clarke, Edward M.
8162	Sergt.	Latimer, D'Arcy A.	8192	,,	Casselman, Homer W.
8163	,,	Conroy, Philip S.	8193	,,	Clarke, Clemen Carl
8164	,,	Woollcombe, P. H. P.	8194	,,	Craig, Walter Stethem
8165	,,	Hutchinson, Walter A.	8195	,,	Couch, Stanley M.
8166	Lce.-Sgt.	Webster, Fred T.	8196	,,	Coburn, Frederick G.
8167	Corpl.	Scott, James Goodie	8197	,,	Dussault, Olliver
8168	,,	Gibson, Charles A.	8198	,,	David, Joseph
8169	,,	Beddoe, Alan B.	8199	,,	Degagne, Raoul
8170	,,	Lancaster, George B.	8200	,,	Dingman, William A.
8171	Lce.-Cpl.	Gunn, William	8201	,,	Dalglish, William A.
8172	,,	Cooke, Archibald	8202	,,	Deslaurier, Harry Jos.
8173	,,	Donaldson, Dwight L.	8203	,,	Dobson, Charles Joseph
8174	,,	Lindesay, Hugh H.	8669	,,	Duffy, Edward
8175	,,	Pelletier, Donat	8204	,,	Eaton, Henry Thos.
8176	,,	Richards, William A.	8205	,,	Earle, Colin Victor
8177	Private	Ainsborough, Wm. P.	8206	,,	Fulton, David James
8178	,,	Anderson, James	8207	,,	Grant, Richard
8180	,,	Bacon, Fredk. George	8208	,,	Gorman, Jas, Herbert
8181	,,	Benoit, Albert Joseph	8209	,,	Gilbey, John
8182	,,	Blewden, Frederick J.	8210	,,	Graham, David G.
8183	,,	Bonnar, Robert	8211	,,	Grant, Mac
8184	,,	Bradley, John Herbert	8212	,,	Hood, William
8185	,,	Brennan, Peter Donald	8213	,,	Harrison, John B.
8186	,,	Brooke, William	8188	,,	Barnum, Frank
8187	,,	Brown, Albert Ernest	8214	,,	Houghton, Harvey W.
8189	,,	Caty, Paul	8215	,,	Humphries, George C.
8190	,,	Calderon, Frederick E.	8216	,,	Hollister, John Milton

Canadian Pacific—The Empire's Greatest Railway.

2ND BATTALION, 1ST INFANTRY BRIGADE—cont.

Regl. No.	Rank.	Name.	Regl. No.	Rank.	Name.
8217	Private	Hetherington, Thos. J.	8248	Private	Pearson, Atkinson
8218	,,	Hartley, Thomas James	8250	,,	Potter, Thomas
8219	,,	Hobin, Archibald	8251	,,	Pearson, Alfred
8220	,,	Hamlin, Harry	8668	,,	Price, Hilburn M.
8221	,,	Hope, William	8249	,,	Rawlingson, William
8222	,,	Jarvie, Alexander W.	8252	,,	Royall, Albert
8223	,,	Lloyd, Alexander	8253	,,	Reynolds, Richard H.
8224	,,	Lavender, Bert	8254	,,	Roberts, George May
8225	,,	Leblanc, Stephen	8255	,,	Sheridan, Thomas A.
8226	,,	Lubin, Alfred	8256	,,	Sutherland, Harry W.
8227	,,	Lacelle, Eugene	8257	,,	Smellie, Edward Geo.
8228	,,	Mann, Duncan	8258	,,	Smith, James J.
8229	,,	Malloy, John	8259	,,	Smith, Wilfred J.
8230	,,	Marr, William	8260	,,	Smith, Edward George
8231	,,	McNally, Thomas	8261	,,	Styles, William
8232	,,	McNaughton, Dnld. J.	8262	,,	Sheard, Harold
8233	,,	McDonald, William	8263	,,	Sparks, Wilfrid Eska
8234	,,	Matthews, Albert E,	8264	,,	Tunnicliffe, Charles
8235	,,	McConnell, Walter C.	8277	,,	Tyo, Frederick
8236	,,	Morgan, Owen L.	8265	,,	Urquhart, Arpad Grant
8237	,,	Norton, Thomas	8266	,,	Vance, Thomas
8238	,,	Nairn, William	8267	,,	Vandervoort, Milton
8239	,,	O'Hara, Thomas G.	8268	,,	Venasse, Oscar A.
8240	,,	O'Neill, William	8269	,,	Webster, Henry E.
8241	,,	Owens, Cecil C.	8270	,,	Wylie, William Ralph
8242	,,	Pace, Arthur Howard	8271	,,	Warner, Albert
8243	,,	Potter, Frank	8272	,,	Webb, Brook
8244	,,	Palmer, Arthur C.	8273	,,	Wilkinson, Arthur B.
8245	,,	Patrick, George	8274	,,	Wiggins, Roy Harold
8246	,,	Plet, Arthur Carl	8275	,,	Wiseman, Hugh
8247	,,	Prince, John Charles	8276	,,	Wanless, H. McDonnell

"G" COMPANY.

Major	...	...	...	...	Bolster, Herbert George
Captain	...	...	...	...	Birdsall, Francis Everett
Lieutenant		...	...	...	Doxsee, William John
,,		...	...	...	Wallace, Ernest Donald *Accident?*

Regl. No.	Rank.	Name.	Regl. No.	Rank.	Name.
8278	Col.-Sgt.	Cooper, William	8287	Corpl.	Ledger, Harry
8279	Sergt.	Davis, George Edward Holborck	8288	Lce.-Cpl.	Rowntree, Thomas
			8289	,,	Johns, Frank
8280	,,	Richardson, Joseph	8290	,,	Martin, Richard
8281	,,	Winterbottom, G.	8291	,,	Newman, Thomas
8282	Lce.-Sgt.	Lacey, William	8292	,,	Ryan, Stephen
8283	Sergt.	Leyland, John	8293	,,	Brooks, Bruce Howard
8284	Corpl.	Aitchison, Thomas J.	8294	Bugler	Jenkinson, Arthur
8285	,,	Graham, Marshall	8295	,,	Townsend, George
8286	,,	Shirra, William	8296	Signaller	Ling, Fred Edward

Canadian Pacific—The Empire's Greatest Railway.

2ND BATTALION, 1ST INFANTRY BRIGADE—cont. 31

Regl. No.	Rank.	Name.	Regl. No.	Rank.	Name.
8297	Signaller	Stuart, Robert William	8345	Private	Little, William
8298	Private	Abbot, John Francis	8346	,,	Lewis, John
8299	,,	Butterfield, William	8347	,,	Merrill, Frederick C.
8300	,,	Bastin, George	8348	,,	Moore, Harry
8301	,,	Briggs, William James	8349	,,	Mitchell, Geo. L. G.
8302	,,	Brown, Walter George	8350	,,	McCrossen, Michael
8303	Corpl.	Beavis, James	8351	,,	Munroe, George
8304	Private	Brown, David	8352	,,	McFarlane, Parlane
8305	,,	Barrell, Thomas	8353	,,	Mitchell, William
8306	,,	Bloom, Leslie	8354	,,	Noble, Charles Roy
8307	,,	Bishop, William	8355	,,	Nash, Joseph
8308	,,	Beatty, James Marcus	8356	,,	Payne, Fred
8309	,,	Bartleman, Henry	8357	,,	Peters, Arthur Everett
8310	,,	Cowan, Charles	8358	,,	Parks, Glen
8311	,,	Crump, Joseph	8359	,,	Peggs, Herbert
8312	,,	Chapman, Charles	8360	,,	Pick, William
8313	,,	Craig, George	8361	,,	Richardson, Frank
8314	,,	Charleton, Fred	8362	,,	Robertson, Alexander
8315	,,	Cooper, Willfred	8363	,,	Rutherford, James W.
8316	,,	Carpenter, John	8364	,,	Reeves, George Henry
8317	,,	Davies, Mark	8365	,,	Reeves, Charles
8318	,,	Dennis, Harry	8366	,,	Raby, Noel Frederick
8319	,,	Davies, John Robby	8367	,,	Robus, Thomas Walter
8320	,,	Emes, Preston	8368	,,	Robinson, Percy
8321	,,	Fowler, Francis	8369	,,	Richmond, Frank
8322	,,	Foskett, John	8370	,,	Stacey-Bush, Geo. Wm.
8323	,,	Fudge, Robert	8371	,,	Simpson, Alex
8324	,,	Garratt, Ronald Vivian	8372	,,	Swift, John
8325	,,	Gibson, John	8373	,,	Sudell, Robert
8326	,,	Gold, Fred William	8374	,,	Sweet, Everet John
8327	,,	Griffiths, John Francis	8375	,,	Siburn, Wm. George
8328	,,	Gotts, George	8376	,,	Smith, Harry Nathan
8394	,,	Gordon, Henry	8377	,,	Saunders, James W.
8329	,,	Gardiner, William W.	8378	,,	Smith, Reuben
8330	,,	Graham, Robert	8379	,,	Taylor, Walter
8331	,,	Graham, Thomas	8380	,,	Tomson, George
8332	,,	Hare, Stanley	8381	,,	Tough, John
8333	,,	Houston, David	8382	,,	Windover, Harry
8334	,,	Hannaburg, George C.	8383	,,	Watering, Walter C.
8335	,,	Huggins, Roy	8384	,,	Withers, George
8336	,,	Harding, James	8385	,,	Weeks, Ernest
8337	,,	Hother, Edward James	8386	,,	Wilson, John
8338	,,	Hubble, Charles	8387	,,	Wood, Leon
8339	,,	Herrington, Kelvin	8388	,,	Waring, Elvin
8340	,,	Jones, Lancelot H.	8389	,,	White, Howard
8341	,,	Kirk, Thomas George	8390	,,	Wilcox, George
8342	,,	Kilburn, Percy John	8391	,,	Waite, George
8343	,,	Lovell, James	8392	,,	Wilson, Robert Henry
8344	,,	Lewis, Ernest	8393	,,	Waller, Henry George

Canadian Pacific—The Empire's Greatest Railway.

32 2ND BATTALION, 1ST INFANTRY BRIGADE—cont.

"H" COMPANY.

Captain ... ... Hooper, William Henry Vickers
Lieutenant ... ... O'Flynn, Edmund Duckett
„ ... ... Scott, Clyde Rutherford
„ ... ... Garrison, Floyd McKim

Regl. No.	Rank.	Name.	Regl. No.	Rank.	Name.
8395	Col.-Sgt.	Wright, William	8440	Private	Fraser, Edwin
8396	Sergt.	Larkin, James	8441	„	French, John Ben.
8397	„	Flinter, Percy Stuart	8442	„	Frood, Lorne
8398	„	Elliott, Hubert Thos.	8443	„	Garvie, John
8399	„	Pearce, Victor George	8444	„	Graham, Gordon H.
8400	Lce.-Sgt.	Reilly, William	8445	„	Graham, William
8401	Corpl.	Elliott, William Robt.	8446	„	Hall, Clarence James
8402	„	Romans, Charles	8447	„	Halsey, Leonard
8403	„	Lucas David Henry	8448	„	Hamilton, John
8404	„	Brown, Horace	8449	„	Harty, James
8405	Lce.-Cpl.	New, George	8450	„	Hastings, John
8406	„	Goodman, Charles	8451	„	Honour, Ernest
8407	„	Ormsby, William Geo.	8452	„	Hughes, William S.
8408	„	Gallagher, George B.	8453	„	Ireland, Harry
8409	„	Martin, Kenneth C.	8454	„	Jamieson, Fred
8410	„	McHurd, Ross	8455	„	Joynt, William
8411	Private	Armstrong Noble	8456	„	Jones, Owen
8412	„	Ashman, John Charles	8457	„	Kelman, Walter Jas.
8413	„	Barrett, Charles	8458	„	Kershaw, Fredk. Nat.
8414	„	Beeman, Harry	8459	„	Kershaw, Alfred Wm.
8415	„	Bennett, Donald	8460	„	Kittner, Bert
8416	Signaller	Butler, Thomas Abbott	8461	„	Kurkravitch, Isaac
8417	Private	Bigham, George	8462	„	Knight, Archibald
8418	„	Bremner, Ferguson	8463	„	Lambon, Peter
8419	„	Brown, Arthur Ernest	8464	„	Lawson, James
8420	„	Borland, Robert John	8465	„	Lindsay, George
8421	„	Calvin, Thomas Geo.	8466	„	Love, Edward Edmond
8422	„	Cameron, George H.	8467	„	Lucas, Albert Edward
8423	„	Campbell, Lockhart	8468	„	Lynch, Robert J.
8424	„	Carey, Harold	8469	„	MacCallum, John A.
8425	„	Carr, Fred	8470	„	Maclaren, Alexander
8426	(Bugler)	Cassidy, Charles Hen.	8471	„	McClement, Thomas
8427	Private	Crockford, Albert	8472	„	McDonald, Alex. D.
8428	„	Davis, Jack	8473	„	McDonald, David S.
8429	„	Dempsey, Nelson	8474	„	McDonald, Roy
8430	„	Dewell, Matthew	8475	„	McDougall, James G.
8431	„	Dewell, Wilfred	8476	„	McGill, James Wilfred
8432	„	Doughton, Thomas R.	8477	„	McIntyre, Roy
8433	„	Douglas, Daniel M.	8478	„	Maclaren, Henry H.
8434	„	Duncan, William	8479	„	McPhee, John Neil
8435	„	Edgerton, John Herbt.	8480	„	Mackay, Cameron
8436	„	Fairbairn, George W.	8481	Bugler	Mantell, Arthur John
8437	„	Fairbairn, William	8482	Private	Monteville, George
8438	„	Ferguson, Thomas C.	8483	„	Moody, Edward
8439	„	Field, Alfred	8484	„	Morgan, William

Canadian Pacific—The Empire's Greatest Railway.

2ND BATTALION, 1ST INFANTRY BRIGADE—cont.

Regl. No.	Rank.	Name.	Regl. No.	Rank.	Name.
8485	Private	Munro, Wilmer	8499	Private	Sinclair, Archibald
8486	Signaller	Murphy, Robert Alex.	8500	,,	Slater, Bernard Geo.
8487	Private	Norlock, Michael	8501	,,	Smith, Harold
8488	,,	Oxley, Alfred John	8502	,,	Somers, Charles
8489	,,	Pierron, Leo	8503	,,	Spalding, Eric
8490	,,	Powell, Garth Hen. M.	8504	,,	Wallace, Andrew
8491	,,	Reynolds, Ernest C.	8505	,,	Watson, Andrew
8492	,,	Richardson, John	8506	,,	Watts, Alfred
8493	,,	Ring, Alexander	8507	,,	White, Arthur
8494	,,	Sample, Thomas	8508	,,	Wicks, Robert
8495	,,	Scott, Ira Calvin	8509	,,	Wilson, Alexander
8496	,,	Scrimminger, Arch.	8510	,,	Winmill, Charles Cyril
8497	,,	Simmons, Sydney	8511	,,	Wright, William
8498	,,	Simons, Arthur John			

BASE OR "I" COMPANY.

Captain (K/A) 11/12/15 ... Mercer, Arthur Edward

Regl. No.	Rank.	Name.	Regl. No.	Rank.	Name.
8512	Col.-Sgt.	Brister, Albert John	8538	Private	Davidson, Brice D.
8513	Sergt.	Mansell, Albert James	8539	,,	Denike, Anselm
8514	,,	McHugh, Francis G. J.	8540	,,	De Paiva, Alfred Joh.
8515	Lce.-Cpl.	Brindley, William E.	8541	,,	Davis, Charles Erastus
8516	,,	Meister, Alfred Edwd.	8542	,,	Earls, George Edward
8517	,,	McCaw, Gilbert G.	8543	,,	Green, William Edwd.
8518	,,	Piper, William	8544	,,	Gray, Edward
8519	,,	Reuben, Aaron	8545	,,	Gardiner, Bruce Edgar
8520	,,	Topham, James	8546	,,	Graham, William F.
8521	Private	Armstrong, Sydney	8547	,,	Harribin, Arthur
8675	,,	Barker, John Reid	8548	,,	Head, William Earle
8522	,,	Bigras, Walter	8549	,,	Heineman, Clayton C.
8523	,,	Blake, John	8550	,,	Haight, Grant A.
8524	,,	Bond, James	8551	,,	Holland, John Arthur
8525	,,	Bullied, George	8552	,,	Hicken, Charles
8663	,,	Brishois, John	8674	,,	Hill, Rowland
8526	,,	Brule, Hector Joseph	8553	,,	Henderson, Wesley
8527	,,	Beavan, Wilfred	8554	,,	Jenkinson, Charles T.
8528	,,	Buchanan, George	8664	,,	Jollineau, Frank F.
8662	,,	Case, Charles Frederick	8555	,,	Jones, William Edwd.
8529	,,	Clarke, John Harry	8672	,,	King, Fred
8530	,,	Conlon, Matthew	8556	,,	King, William Stanley
8531	,,	Cumming, Wm. Turpie	8557	,,	Lewis, Charles Fredk.
8532	,,	Coleman, Richard H.	8558	,,	Love, Clifford W. A.
8533	,,	Clark, Bert William	8559	,,	Lince, Alfred Victor
8534	,,	Cook, Frederick	8560	,,	Lacelle, Fred Joseph
8535	,,	Campbell, David	8667	,,	Le Clerc, Rudolph
8536	,,	Chard, Ezra	8561	,,	Lindop, James Henry
8671	,,	Cox, William Henry	8562	,,	La France, Joseph
8537	,,	Cheesewright, Alfred	8563	,,	Mason, Kenneth C.

Canadian Pacific—The Empire's Greatest Railway.

34 2ND BATTALION, 1ST INFANTRY BRIGADE—cont.

Regl. No.	Rank.	Name.	Regl. No.	Rank.	Name.
8564	Private	Meister, William Jos.	8578	Private	Roberts, James
8565	,,	Mercer, William R.	8579	,,	Redden, James Jacob
8566	,,	Massey, Frederick	8580	,,	Sherwood, Frank
8567	,,	Macfarlane, Michael	8673	,,	Stafford, George Edw.
8568	,,	Matthews, James	8581	,,	Steele, George
8569	,,	McGuire, Terrance	8582	,,	Sisson, Howard
8570	,,	Maughton, Arthur	8583	,,	Sinclair, Archibald M.
8571	,,	Montgomery, O. H.	8665	,,	Sullivan, Michael J.
8676	,,	Marskell, William J.	8584	,,	Thompson, Gilbert
8572	,,	McLeod, Ralph G.	8585	,,	Troy, Jock
8573	,,	Mercer, George	8586	,,	Van Dusen, Arthur
8666	,,	Miller, Robert F.	8587	,,	Weeks, William
8670	,,	O'Brien, Maurice M.	8588	,,	White, Harry
8574	,,	Perrault, George	8589	,,	Watts, William
8575	,,	Powell, Albert	8590	,,	Williams, Harry Jas.
8576	,,	Pargetter, Gordon	8591	,,	York, Samuel Herbert
8577	,,	Rogers, John Arthur			

3rd BATTALION (TORONTO REGIMENT), 1st INFANTRY BRIGADE.

HEADQUARTERS STAFF.

Officer Commanding ... ... Lieut.-Colonel R. Rennie, M.V.O.
Senior Major (K/A) ... ... Major G. M. Higinbotham, M.V.O.
Junior Major ... ... ,, A. J. E. Kirkpatrick
Adjutant ... ... Lieutenant M. B. Duncan
Asst. Adjutant ... ... ,, M. S. Gooderham
Quartermaster ... ... Captain John Hutcheson
Transport Officer ... ... Lieutenant J. Cameron
Signalling Officer ... ... Captain D. H. C. Mason
Machine Gun Officer ... ... Lieutenant M. D. MacDonald

Attached.

Medical Officer ... ... Lieutenant A. K. Haywood.
Paymaster ... ... Hon. Captain H. G. Wickens.

Subordinate Staff.

Regl. No.	Rank.	Name.	Regl. No.	Rank.	Name.
	Sgt.-Maj. (W.O.)	Blake-Forster, A.B.	9056	Trans.Sgt.	Whitney, W. C.
			9057	Sign. Sgt.	Clifton, H. K.
9051	Q.M.S.	Mathews, J. I.	9058	Shoe Sgt.	Osborne, F.
9052	O.R.S.	Houston, A. S.	9059	Sign. Cpl.	Easterbrook, E.G.B.
9053	Sgt. Drum.	Evans, G. E.	9060	Private	Flint, I.
9054	Pion'r Sgt.	Fox, C. J.	9061	,,	Glover, T. S.
9055	Cook Sgt.	Salvaneschi, J. C.	9062	,,	Graveley, W. K.

Canadian Pacific—The Empire's Greatest Railway.

3RD BATTALION, 1ST INFANTRY BRIGADE—cont. 35

Subordinate Staff—cont.

Regl. No.	Rank.	Name.	Regl. No.	Rank.	Name.
9063	Private	Jones, E. H.	9082	Private	Delaney, L. E.
9064	,,	Jones, R. G.	9083	,,	Risk, James
9105	,,	Ottey, R. G.	9084	,,	Montgomery, S. B.
9065	Arm. Sgt.	Jeffries, W. G.	9085	,,	Andrews, J. B.
9102	Sergt.	Dube, H. G.	9086	,,	Honeycombe, H. R.
9066	Private	Williams, F.	9087	,,	Anderson, A. S.
9067	,,	Adamson, S.	9088	,,	Green, G.
9068	Lce.-Cpl.	Spence, H. V.	9089	,,	Zussman, H.
9069	,,	Dean, Thos.	9090	,,	Shanahan, J. J.
9070	Private	Thorne, N.	9091	,,	Wilkinson, T.
9071	,,	Legate, T. G.	9092	,,	Spain, Fred
9072	,,	Wallen, A. J.	9093	,,	Burningham, G.
9073	,,	Maitland, Wm.	9094	,,	Brown, A. G.
9074	,,	Mullen, Jas.	9096	,,	Keown, F. J.
9075	,,	Norris, T.	9103	Pay Sergt.	Grant, Wm. J.
9076	,,	Mussen, Wm.	9097	Corporal	Shaw, D. D.
9077	,,	Westover, W. J. L.	9098	Private	Melmer, C.
9078	,,	Spinks, J.	9099	,,	Corcoran, W. W.
9079	,,	Cobbold, H. F.	9100	,,	Eccles, T.
9080	,,	Peters, H. L.	9101	,,	Percy, A.
9081	,,	Steward, S.	9104	,,	Thompson, Wm.

Machine Gun Section.

Regl. No.	Rank.	Name.	Regl. No.	Rank.	Name.
10201	Sergt.	Lyall, C. R.	10210	Private	Grasett, H. M.
10202	Corpl.	Townsend, A. J. H.	10211	,,	Griffin, S. H.
10203	Private	Bayly, G. W.	10212	,,	Jackson, C. H.
10204	,,	Bell, Joseph	10213	,,	Levy, N. M.
10205	,,	Binkley, J. R.	10214	,,	Lyall, R. L.
10206	,,	Cameron, E. R. C.	10215	,,	Smith, W. S. E.
10207	,,	Cameron, H. C.	10216	,,	Stevenson, C. E.
10208	,,	Cartwright, J. R.	10217	,,	Williams, L. G.
10209	,,	Cotton, J. D.			

"A" COMPANY.

Captain ... ... Allan, W. D.
Lieutenant ... ... George, R.
,, ... Medland, F. R.
,, ... Alley, H. R.

Regl. No.	Rank.	Name.	Regl. No.	Rank.	Name.
9151	Col.-Sgt.	Thomson, A. E.	9158	Corpl.	Johnson, L.
9152	Sergt.	Kerr, H. G.	9159	,,	Baker, J. G.
9153	,,	Pratt, W.	9160	,,	Lorsch, F. D.
9154	,,	Eddis, A. G.	9161	Bugler	Dudley, P.
9155	,,	Seeley, R. L.	9162	,,	Bedford, C.
9156	Lce.-Sgt.	Roberts, G. B.	9163	Pioneer	Merson, E.
9157	Corpl.	Slatter, A. J.	9164	Signaller	Fielding, L. M.

Canadian Pacific—The Empire's Greatest Railway.

c 2

3RD BATTALION, 1ST INFANTRY BRIGADE—cont.

Regl. No.	Rank	Name	Regl. No.	Rank	Name
9165	Signaller	Flint, H. R.	9216	Private	Jones, R. A.
9166	Str. B'rer	Brailsford, W. C.	9217	,,	Kelleher, H.
9167	,,	Bennyworth, G. F.	9218	,,	Kenyon, F. W.
9168	Private	Anglin, J. T.	9219	,,	King, R. J.
9169	,,	Alexander, P. N.	9220	,,	Langford, W.
9170	,,	Ashbourne, F. V.	9221	,,	Lewis, E. H.
9171	,,	Ashbourne, B. N.	9222	,,	Littlewood, B.
9172	,,	Balchin, W. H.	9223	,,	Marriott, J. A.
9173	,,	Baird, F.	9224	,,	Mertens, A. B.
9174	,,	Bond, F.	9225	,,	Munn, H. E.
9175	,,	Broughall, D.	9226	,,	Murdock, R.
9176	,,	Bushey, G. E.	9227	,,	McManus, S.
9177	,,	Clark, F.	9228	,,	Musgrove, C. H.
9178	,,	Caldwell, R.	9229	,,	Norris, T. A.
9179	,,	Cowling, C. E.	9230	,,	Ogden, C. E.
9180	,,	Cranston, G. H.	9231	,,	Owen, E. L.
9181	,,	Creighton, W. A.	9232	,,	Pennington, T.
9182	,,	Culbert, W.	9233	,,	Platt, W. J.
9183	,,	Curry, F. T.	9234	,,	Palmer, A.
9184	,,	Curry, C. T.	9235	,,	Painter, H.
9185	,,	Cross, H. C.	9236	,,	Prestidge, W.
9186	,,	Davis, W.	9237	,,	Rice, G. D. L.
9187	,,	Davis, W. S.	9238	,,	Ransom, A. F.
9188	,,	Davison, E.	9239	,,	Robinson, H.
9189	,,	Donnelly, T. J.	9240	,,	Rogers, E. A.
9190	,,	Drew, L.	9241	,,	Reid, E. A.
9191	,,	Durham, P.	9242	,,	Secord, E. L.
9192	,,	Elliott, W. N. J.	9243	,,	Sewell, A. V.
9193	,,	Farnell, J. B.	9244	,,	Sibbald, W. M.
9194	,,	Fisher, W. S.	9245	,,	Simpson, R. L.
9195	,,	Fitzsimmons, C.	9246	,,	Shields, L. S.
9196	,,	Fitzpatrick, J. F.	9247	,,	Smallman, F.
9197	,,	French, R.	9248	,,	Stevens, E. P.
9198	,,	Giddens, E.	9249	,,	Stuart, P. C.
9199	,,	Gillard, W.	9250	,,	Spalding, R. C.
9200	,,	Gordon, H. R.	9251	,,	Sanderson, H.
9201	,,	Grossi, S.	9252	,,	Taylor, S. H.
9202	,,	Hamilton, J. S.	9253	,,	Tellett, C.
10196	,,	Harris, A.	9254	,,	Thomas, C. A.
9203	,,	Hazlett, T. A.	9255	,,	Thomas, W. S.
9204	,,	Heintzman, F. C.	9256	,,	Tilley, F. W.
9205	,,	Hertzberg, O. P.	9257	,,	Van Ryn, A. H.
9206	,,	Hewitt, J.	9258	,,	Vigus, T.
9207	,,	Hogan, J. C.	9259	,,	Warden, W. G.
9208	,,	Howard, E. F.	9260	,,	Wedd, L. M.
9209	,,	Howard, S, T.	9261	,,	White, N. D.
9210	,,	Hughes, G. R.	9262	,,	Wilcocks, J. H.
9211	,,	Hunt, H.	9263	,,	Watson, J.
9212	,,	Hills, E. A.	9264	,,	Wolstenholme, C.
9213	,,	Hutchcroft, W. B.	9265	,,	Williams, R. H.
9214	,,	Harper, H. E.	9266	,,	Wallwork, S.
9215	,,	Jackson, R.	9267	,,	Zufelt, N.

Canadian Pacific—The Empire's Greatest Railway.

3RD BATTALION, 1ST INFANTRY BRIGADE—cont. 37

"B" COMPANY.

Captain	... ...	Morrison, L. S.
Lieutenant	... ...	Cronyn, J. K.
,,	... ...	Vander Smissen, W. H.
,,	... ...	Clark, C. L.

Regl. No.	Rank.	Name.	Regl. No.	Rank.	Name.
9268	Col.-Sgt.	Addy, W. J.	9313	Private	Davis, S. G.
9269	Sergt.	Pittam, F. H.	9314	,,	Fluck, T. A.
9270	,,	Blackey, P.	9315	,,	Frisby, T. W.
9271	,,	Williams, D. F.	9316	,,	Fogden, H. V.
9272	,,	Bushell, A. J.	9383	,,	Forster, A. V.
9273	Lce.-Sgt.	Good, H. C.	9317	,,	Giles, D. E.
9274	Corpl.	Scott, E. J.	9318	,,	Gearin, W. J.
9275	,,	Poulton, M. J.	9319	,,	Gifford, E.
9276	,,	Tarbet, D. H.	9320	,,	Gates, W. G.
9277	,,	Blackhall, J. P.	9321	,,	Goddard, A. P.
9278	Bugler	Baxter, R. D.	9384	,,	Hall, J. H.
9279	,,	Cargill, G. D. D.	9322	,,	Holland, R. J.
9280	Pioneer	Philip, F. F.	9323	,,	Hewitt, Robert
9281	,,	Townsend, W. B.	9324	,,	Hider, J. R. S.
9282	Signaller	Calverley, H. S.	9325	,,	Hemming, T. J.
9283	,,	Coulthard, A. K.	9326	,,	Haight, C. E.
9284	Str. B'rer.	Boyd, H. H.	9327	,,	Howarth, J. W.
9285	,,	Trull, T. E.	9328	,,	Jefferies, V. A.
9286	Driver	Britton, J. A.	9329	,,	Kirkaldy, Robert
9287	,,	Price, William	9330	,,	Kidd, C. E.
9288	Cook	Upton, F. M.	9331	,,	Lock, Ed. J.
9289	,,	Hopkins, A. T.	9332	,,	Lukeman, A. S.
9290	Private	Adcock, F.	9333	,,	Long, Henry
9291	,,	Austin, J. L.	9334	,,	Lowrie, P.
9292	,,	Brookes, Z.	9335	,,	Lussier, R.
9293	,,	Noverre, P. W.	9336	,,	Lindsell, C. C.
9294	,,	Burger, F. M.	9337	,,	MacLennan, John
9295	,,	Bright, E.	9338	,,	Murray, K.
9296	,,	Burns, W. G.	9339	,,	McDonald, K.
9297	,,	Bell, J. H.	9340	,,	Milne, J.
9298	,,	Bassett, H.	9341	,,	Minns, A. G.
9299	,,	Baird, A.	9342	,,	Minns, E. H.
9300	,,	Bloxham, H. C.	9343	,,	Moore, N. C.
9301	,,	Braddick, A.	9344	,,	Mundy, H. A.
9302	,,	Copping, A.	9345	,,	Metcalfe, J. A.
9303	,,	Calhoun, C. S.	9346	,,	Mansbridge, H.
9304	,,	Cuss, A. G.	9347	,,	Mullins, S.
9305	,,	Caldow, F. J.	9348	,,	Johnston, E.
9306	,,	Clapton, R. J.	9349	,,	Nixon, J. F. J. M.
9307	,,	Carless, H.	9350	,,	Nolan, H. M.
9308	,,	Crossley, H.	9351	,,	Patterson, A. H.
9309	,,	Dunstall, S. G.	9352	,,	Ogle, A. A.
9310	,,	Deas, A. M.	9353	,,	Oliver, E. J.
9311	,,	Davis, F. J.	9354	,,	Pack, W. H.
9312	,,	Davis, T. E.	9355	,,	Poulton, R. R.

Canadian Pacific—The Empire's Greatest Railway.

3RD BATTALION, 1st INFANTRY BRIGADE—cont.

Regl. No.	Rank.	Name.	Regl. No.	Rank.	Name.
9356	Private	Pollock, G. R.	9370	Private	Slater, F. E.
9357	,,	Perry, Wm. J.	9371	,,	Sproul, Jas.
9358	,,	Parriss, Walter	9372	,,	Sawyer, C. C.
9359	,,	Pannell, W. H.	9373	,,	Smith, H. F.
9360	,,	Rosebatch, A. N.	9374	,,	Sharpe, L. W.
9361	,,	Randall, S.	9375	,,	Shaw, J. T.
9362	,,	Rattray, Wm. J.	9376	,,	Shipman, J. W.
9363	,,	Sawyer, Ernest	9377	,,	Thompson, C. M.
9364	,,	Short, G. E.	9378	,,	Waters, F. J.
9365	,,	Shearer, Jas.	9379	,,	Whiteacre, A. S.
9366	,,	Sloan, J. G.	9380	,,	Walsh, W. J.
9367	,,	Symons, W. R.	9381	,,	Wilson, D. D.
9368	,,	Stewart, N.	9382	,,	Wilson, Jas.
9369	,,	Smith, C. F.			

"C" COMPANY.

Captain	...	...	...	Muntz, H. G.
Lieutenant	...	...	...	Rogers, J. B.
,,	...	...	...	Nicholls, Walter
,,	...	...	...	Hagarty, D. G.

Regl. No.	Rank.	Name.	Regl. No.	Rank.	Name.
9386	Col.-Sgt.	Ricketts, N. H.	9414	Private	Bridges, H. R.
9387	Sergt.	Esten, G. P.	9415	,,	Bartholomew, J. C.
9388	Private	Braden, C. E.	9416	,,	Bradt, J.
9389	Sergt.	Mote, G. A.	9417	,,	Brickles, I.
9390	,,	Marani, F. H.	9418	,,	Blackhall, J.
9391	Lce.-Sgt.	Crang, F. L.	9419	,,	Brown, H.
9392	Corpl.	O'Connor C. L. B.	9420	,,	Buse, H.
9393	,,	Bennie, W.	9421	,,	Burrows, A. R.
9394	,,	Parker, J.	9422	,,	Caswall, F.
9395	,,	Salvaneschi, V.	9423	Corpl.	Cliff, N. V.
9396	Bugler	Morris, H.	9424	Private	Clough, E. M.
9397	,,	Cunnington, G.	9425	,,	Crighton, M.
9398	Pioneer	Temple, G. S.	9426	,,	Croft, J. W.
9399	Signaller	Tyler, E. C.	9427	,,	Crossland, J.
9400	,,	Rush, C. W.	9428	,,	Crossland, E. F.
9401	Str. B'rer	McIntosh, R. K.	9429	,,	Cook, A. F.
9402	,,	Hardy, W. J.	9430	,,	Cook, J. W.
9403	Driver	Scott, T.	9431	,,	Carradus, M. C.
9404	,,	Higginson, John W.	9432	,,	Dawson, S.
9405	Batman	Rogers, T. B.	9433	,,	Davey, J. M.
9406	,,	Varney, C. T.	9434	,,	Dent, G. W.
9407	Private	Littlehales, H.	9435	,,	Dillon, Thos. E.
9408	Cook	Carrington, C. G.	9436	,,	Dobson, W. J.
9409	,,	Everest, E.	9437	,,	Duff, E. A.
9410	Private	Armstrong, F. C.	9438	,,	Duncanson, T. S.
9411	,,	Bain, H.	9439	,,	Dolan, H. E.
9412	,,	Ball, D.	9440	,,	Davies, M. C.
9413	,,	Bennett, W. H.	9441	,,	Featherstonhaugh, E.H.

Canadian Pacific—The Empire's Greatest Railway.

3RD BATTALION, 1ST INFANTRY BRIGADE—cont.

Regl. No.	Rank	Name	Regl. No.	Rank	Name
9442	Private	Fitzgerald, T.	9472	Private	McGivern, J.
9443	,,	Fitzpatrick, H.	9473	,,	MacMurchy, W. C.
9444	,,	Fowler, G. H.	9474	,,	Metcalf, R.
9445	,,	Freebairn, T. S.	9475	,,	Newton, D.
9446	,,	Gardner, W.	9476	,,	Oliver, A. W.
9447	,,	Gill, J.	9477	,,	Oliver, J.
9448	,,	Grant, R. M.	9478	,,	Potter, F. W.
9449	,,	Haggart, G. B.	9479	,,	Palmer, O. B.
9450	,,	Harris, H. S.	9480	,,	Poste, H. S.
9451	,,	Howison, H.	9481	,,	Parsons, W. G.
9452	,,	Harrison, F.	9482	,,	Quin, W. H.
10218	,,	Hollis, C. H.	9483	,,	Reith, G. T.
9453	,,	Hughes, T. W. R.	9484	,,	Roper, F. S.
9454	,,	Hall, W. T.	9485	,,	Reeve, A.
9455	,,	Hunter, S. H.	9486	,,	Reid, A. D.
9456	,,	Harvey, E. C.	9487	,,	Richardson, J. C.
9457	,,	Hally, R. A.	9488	,,	Richmond, S. B.
9458	,,	Kinghan, A. E.	9489	,,	Roberts, J.
9459	,,	Knight, F. W.	9490	,,	Sproule, N.
9460	,,	Irving, W. P.	9491	,,	Steele, E.
9461	,,	Jackson, W.	9492	,,	Sears, R. R.
9462	,,	Jones, W. H.	9493	,,	Stevens, J.
9463	,,	Legier, W.	9494	,,	Theberge, P. H.
9464	,,	Le Thicke, G. M.	9495	,,	Thompson, A. B.
9465	,,	Leader, K. M.	9496	,,	Thompson, R. V.
9466	,,	Little, C.	9497	,,	Thorne, E. W.
9467	,,	Lobb, M. E.	9498	,,	Temple, H.
9468	,,	Manning, L.	9499	,,	Walker, H. W.
9469	,,	Martin, E. A.	9500	,,	Whitter, Ed. L.
9470	,,	Murphy, F.	9501	,,	Whittaker, R. H.
9471	,,	Matthews, A. D.	9385	,,	Webster, H.

"D" COMPANY.

Captain ... ... Tidy, F. O.
Lieutenant ... ... Crowther, W. B.
,, ... McCormack, C. A. V.
,, ... Anderson, T. W.

Regl. No.	Rank	Name	Regl No.	Rank	Name
9502	Col.-Sgt.	Coulter, A. W.	9511	Corpl.	Coulter, A. K.
9503	Sergt.	Reddock, S. A.	9512	Bugler	Hanbridge, F. E.
9504	,,	Galloway, A.	9513	,,	Kinsley, H.
9505	,,	McLean, J. H.	9514	Pioneer	Bicknell, A. J.
9506	,,	Boyd, D. G.	9515	Signaller	Kippen, W.
9507	Lce.-Sgt.	Dingle, G. R.	9516	,,	Presant, C. H.
9508	Corpl.	Hannan, S. F.	9517	Str. B'rer	Jones, W. E.
9509	,,	Dymond, J. M.	9518	,,	Grundy, A. J.
9510	,,	Wiles, H. A.	9519	Driver	Pollard, G. A.

Canadian Pacific—The Empire's Greatest Railway.

3RD BATTALION, 1ST INFANTRY BRIGADE—cont.

Regl. No.	Rank.	Name.	Regl. No.	Rank.	Name.
9520	Driver	Burleigh, W.	9570	Private	Kerr, T. F.
9521	Batman	Hudson, J. G.	9571	,,	King, H. R.
9522	,,	Lee, R.	9572	,,	Kemble, A. F.
9523	,,	Wheaton, E.	9573	,,	Kellman, E. D.
9524	,,	McMillan, H. R.	9574	,,	Kaye, J. F. B.
9525	Cook	Fossett, J.	9575	,,	Lancey, A. W.
9526	,,	Kidman, E.	9576	,,	Luck, E. T.
9527	Private	Austerbury, J. H.	9577	,,	Millet, G.
9528	,,	Allen, E. W.	9578	,,	Mason, Thos.
9529	,,	Brown, G.	9579	,,	Martin, A. T.
9530	,,	Barker, T. E.	9580	,,	Murray, A. A.
9531	,,	Bunner, A.	9581	,,	Marriott, W.
9532	,,	Bowers, C. D.	9582	,,	Martin, T. J.
9533	,,	Best, A. L.	9583	,,	Morris, B. L.
9534	,,	Byrne, T. W. D.	9584	,,	Macdonald, A. R.
9535	,,	Beaumont, G. J.	9585	,,	Macdonald, D.
9536	,,	Berrall, E. C.	9586	,,	McIlhagga, S.
9537	,,	Bent, J.	9587	,,	McCreery, J. B.
9538	,,	Bye, G. F.	9588	,,	McGowan, W.
9539	,,	Cole, J. J.	9589	,,	McJannett, J. H.
9540	,,	Card, R. W. G.	9590	,,	McLeod, P.
9541	,,	Cridland, R. C.	9591	,,	Markham, G.
9542	,,	Cowell, J. E.	9592	,,	Mills, J. W.
9543	,,	Cox, E. B.	9593	,,	Nevitt, B.
9544	,,	Carter, L.	9594	,,	Nye, C.
9545	,,	Conley, G. H.	9595	,,	Potter, G. W.
9546	,,	Cockburn, G. A.	9596	,,	Pope, C. S.
9547	,,	Coffey, J. J.	9597	,,	Phillips, F. E.
9548	,,	Cohen, I.	9598	,,	Pearson, C. W.
9549	,,	Curtis, H.	9599	,,	Rogers, J. L.
9550	,,	Dashwood, F. A.	9600	,,	Roe, R. K.
9551	,,	Darrington, J. W.	9601	,,	Ruse, J. C.
9552	,,	Durward, Q.	9602	,,	Rennie, S. G.
9553	,,	Dilnot, K.	9603	,,	Smith, R. F.
9554	,,	Eastwood, J. F.	9604	,,	Stevenson, A. G.
9555	,,	Fisher, G. C.	9605	,,	Smith, A. J.
9556	,,	Fox, J. B.	9606	,,	Slack, G. J.
9557	,,	Finlay, W.	9607	,,	Sargent, J. M.
9558	,,	Gray, J. H.	9608	,,	Spraggett, G.
9559	,,	Graham, R. N.	9609	,,	Tait, J.
9560	,,	Gardner, C. E.	9610	,,	Varney, S.
9561	,,	Graves, R. A.	9611	,,	Wilkinson, R. F.
9562	,,	Griffin, J. W.	9612	,,	Wilkinson, O. G.
9563	,,	Hall, H. W.	9613	,,	West, E. C.
9564	,,	Hearn, W. C.	9614	,,	White, W. S.
9565	,,	Heighway, F.	9615	,,	Wood, T.
9566	,,	Holmes, O. R.	9616	,,	Walsh, J. I.
9567	,,	Jowsey, F. W.	9617	,,	Wisbey, P. T.
9568	,,	Jewell, H.	9618	,,	White, J. R.
9569	,,	Jack, W.			

Canadian Pacific—The Empire's Greatest Railway.

3RD BATTALION, 1ST INFANTRY BRIGADE—cont. 41

"E" COMPANY.

Captain ... ... Hovelt, A. E. B.
Lieutenant ... ... Curry, W. E.
„ ... ... Chitty, R. M. W.
„ ... ... Davis, R. N. C.

Regl. No.	Rank.	Name.	Regl. No.	Rank.	Name.
9619	Col.-Sgt.	Pritchard, C. G.	9664	Private	Dwyer, S.
9620	Sergt.	Vickers, W.	9665	„	Darcy, F. J.
9621	Private	Ingram, P. J.	9666	„	Davey, C.
9622	Sergt.	Smith, B. M.	9667	„	Egan, H.
9623	„	Cronin, M.	9668	„	Farrer, D.
9624	„	Holt, J.	9669	„	Foote, H. H.
9625	Corpl.	Buckman, W. C.	9670	„	Fitzwalters, W. J.
9626	Lce.-Sgt.	Harkens, F. G.	9671	„	Francis, C.
9627	Corpl.	Rainbow, H.	9672	„	Foy, H.
9628	„	Holland, V.	9673	„	Fisher, A.
9629	Bugler	Hoaken, F. A.	9674	„	Franks, H.
9630	„	Sanders, W. H.	9675	„	Freeman, H. G.
9631	Pioneer	Trowbridge, T.	9676	„	Forster, G.
9632	„	Hanna, N. W.	9735	„	Fraser, Wm.
9633	Signaller	Hunter, J. S. M.	9677	„	Goodall, E.
9634	„	Gurnett, N. A.	9678	„	Green, M. E.
9635	Str. B'rer	McIntyre, L.	9679	„	Germon, J. J.
9636	„	Gibson, D.	9680	„	Grady, J.
9637	Driver	Chenery, F. L.	9681	„	Harland, A.
9638	„	Corbett, J.	9682	„	Hamilton, J. J.
9639	Batman	Evans, T.	9683	„	Kennedy, J.
9640	„	Yule, S. R.	9684	„	Kaelin, C. D.
9641	Cook	Beckett, P.	9685	„	Kirkpatrick, J.
9642	„	Geddes, P. M.	9686	„	Latimer, G.
9643	Private	Aylott, T. H.	9687	„	Leviseur, H. J.
9644	„	Barrett, L.	9688	„	Love, T. H.
9645	„	Basher, G. H.	9689	„	Lynn, E.
9646	„	Beckett, A. W.	9690	„	Loty, F.
9647	„	Boulton, H.	9691	„	Lovell, E. S.
9648	„	Bruno, J.	9692	„	Mills, A. M.
9649	„	Blake, A. G.	9693	„	McCallister, W. H.
9650	„	Bamford, W.	9694	„	Mackay, F.
9651	„	Brown, H. B.	9695	„	Meares, J.
9652	„	Carr, C. C.	9696	„	Martin, J. L.
9653	„	Cooper, E.	9697	„	Martin, B. H.
9654	„	Crummey, E. W.	9698	„	Marley, W. E.
9655	„	Caulfield, J.	9699	„	Morris, H.
9656	„	Clark, G. B.	9700	„	Moulton, R.
9657	„	Callingham, A. E.	9701	„	Neilson, J. H.
9658	„	Clarke, R. J.	9702	„	Newdick, S. G.
9659	„	Collier, A.	9703	„	Newdick, T. W.
9660	„	Dowall, C.	9704	„	Olmstead, C. H.
9661	„	Davis, T. M.	9705	„	Pegler, T. H.
9662	„	Dent, R. E.	9706	„	Pound, G.
9663	„	Dearman, H.	9707	„	Penno, L. L.

Canadian Pacific—The Empire's Greatest Railway.

3RD BATTALION, 1ST INFANTRY BRIGADE—cont.

Regl. No.	Rank.	Name.	Regl. No.	Rank.	Name.
9708	Private	Parliament, G. H.	9722	Private	Smith, B.
9709	,,	Polson, G.	9723	,,	Scott, J. D.
9710	,,	Pillar, F. H.	9724	,,	Stanton, G. J.
9711	,,	Penfold, E.	9725	,,	Taylor, C.
9712	,,	Peace, E.	9726	,,	Thomson, J.
9713	,,	Roberts, J. B.	9727	,,	Thomas, C. E.
9714	,,	Renfrey, W.	9728	,,	Tynan, S. P.
9715	,,	Ross, C.	9729	,,	Taylor, H. V.
9716	,,	Rose, H.	9730	,,	Taylor, T.
9717	,,	Spademan, G.	9731	,,	Upton, T. F.
9718	,,	Shanks, D.	9732	,,	Webster, J.
9719	,,	Sinclair, J. W.	9733	,,	White, R. H.
9720	,,	Smith, H.	9734	,,	Wood, J. H.
9721	,,	Saunders, G.			

"F" COMPANY.

Captain ... ... Streight, J. E. L.
Lieutenant ... ... Jarvis, W. D. P.
,, ... Smith, Geo.
,, ... Kirkpatrick, A. D.

Regl. No.	Rank.	Name.	Regl. No.	Rank.	Name.
9736	Col.-Sgt.	McKinley, F.	9765	Private	Bowyer, C. P.
9737	Sergt.	Bacon, J. C.	9766	,,	Burton, T. W.
9738	,,	Cameron, J.	9767	,,	Barker, W.
9739	,,	Palmer, T. W.	9768	,,	Bushell, Wm.
9740	,,	Newman, V.	9769	,,	Beattie, J.
9742	Corpl.	Allingham, F.	9770	,,	Blacklock, F. A.
9743	,,	Shea, G. W.	9771	,,	Best, D. T. W.
9744	,,	Aldridge, R.	9772	,,	Bennett, F.
9745	,,	Chambers, A.	9773	,,	Barfield, H. R.
9746	Bugler	Adams, F. G. A.	9774	,,	Berry, H. L.
9747	,,	Spring, G. J.	9775	,,	Bittle, R. N.
9748	Pioneer	Pilling, S. H.	9776	,,	Clancy, Jos. J.
9749	Signaller	Beahan, F. P.	9777	,,	Cowan, T. E.
9750	,,	Harvey, J. W.	9850	,,	Connor, J. E.
9751	Str. B'rer	Price, A.	9778	,,	Dalliday, J. W. H.
9752	,,	McLeod, J.	9779	,,	Edge, H.
9753	Driver	McBride, A. D.	9780	,,	Edmondson, M. P.
9754	,,	Gray, J.	9781	,,	Finnimore, F. A.
9755	Batman	Kensitt, J. G.	9785	,,	Finnimore, J. W.
9756	,,	Roberts, E. C.	9782	,,	Foster, A.
9757	,,	Robertson, J.	9783	,,	Fellowes, J. J.
9758	Private	Arnold, Thos.	9784	,,	Fenton, F.
9759	Cook	Bacon, Ed.	9741	,,	Foster, M.
9760	Private	Bacon, R. C.	9786	,,	Gallagher, G. M.
9761	,,	Barham, R. S.	9787	,,	Gamey, O. A.
9762	,,	Beatty, J. J.	9788	,,	Gardner, H.
9763	,,	Browne, H. W.	9789	,,	George, A. J.
9764	,,	Bowman, L. W.	9790	,,	Guild, W. S.

Canadian Pacific—The Empire's Greatest Railway.

3RD BATTALION, 1ST INFANTRY BRIGADE—cont.

Regl. No.	Rank.	Name.	Regl. No.	Rank.	Name.
9851	Private	Glover, H.	9820	Private	Pearce, F.
9791	,,	Gibb, A.	9821	,,	Pears, Joseph
9792	,,	Hammond, D. V.	9822	,,	Rankin, K. S.
9793	,,	Horn, H. G.	9823	,,	Rush, G. W.
9794	,,	Hossack, Robt. A.	9824	,,	Russell, S. L.
9795	,,	Holyoak, Chas.	9825	,,	Seaman, E. R.
9796	,,	Hyde, Ed.	9826	,,	Silvester, Chas. H.
9852	,,	Hurd, G. K.	9827	,,	Sheahan, T.
9797	,,	Jeffrey, E. H.	9828	,,	Smith, W.
9798	,,	Kerr, A.	9829	,,	Stewart, C.
9799	,,	Kidd, D.	9830	,,	Swinford, Chas.
9800	,,	Lasoff, S.	9831	,,	Stevens, H.
9801	,,	Leathem, W. J.	9832	,,	Sloane, A. J.
9802	,,	Loveday, O. H.	9833	,,	Taverner, G. R.
9803	,,	Lucas, Joe	9834	,,	Theobald, Joseph
9804	,,	Livingston, W.	9835	,,	Thomas, F. W.
9807	,,	McDonald, T. C.	9836	,,	Tyler, A.
9806	,,	McConnell, B.	9839	,,	Taylor, P.
9805	,,	McDowell, O. F.	9838	,,	Taylor, B. M.
9808	,,	Matthews, H.	9837	,,	Taylor, A. C.
9809	,,	Mesley, W. F.	9840	,,	Tindale, W. O.
9810	,,	Moulds, W.	9841	,,	Vear, A.
9811	,,	Morton, N.	9842	,,	Worsell, H. D.
9812	,,	Moffit, C. E.	9843	,,	Welch, R. B.
9813	Lce.-Sgt.	Murdock, Chas.	9844	,,	Welton, R. D.
9814	Private	Murray, James	9845	,,	Wilson, W. W.
9815	,,	Marchington, A.	9846	,,	Wix, J. R.
9816	,,	Newport, R. W.	9847	,,	Ward, Geo.
9817	,,	Nott, Jas. J.	9848	,,	Yates, J. F.
9818	,,	Owens, J.	9849	,,	Yates, W. F.
9819	,,	Pipher, R.			

"G" COMPANY.

Captain	Ryerson, G. C.
Lieutenant	Sanderson, A. M.
,, ...	Allan, D. G.
,, ...	Kelley N. P.

Regl. No.	Rank.	Name.	Regl. No.	Rank.	Name.
9853	Col.-Sgt.	Freemantle, A. H. O.	9863	Bugler	Green, R. H.
9854	Sergt.	Craddock, Jas.	9864	,,	Morgan, W. R.
9855	,,	Wilkie, J. L.	9865	Pioneer	Myers, T. F.
9856	Private	McCleary, R.	9866	Signaller	Martin, J. S.
9857	Sergt.	Murphy, A. J.	9867	,,	Page, J. A.
9858	Lce.-Sgt.	Nicholson, E. C.	9868	Str. B'rer.	Boyce, W. H.
9859	Corpl.	Pickering, H.	9869	,,	Edwards, H.
9860	,,	Birks, C. D.	9870	Driver	Pantling, F.
9861	,,	Hill, R. C.	9871	,,	Woods, W. J.
9862	,,	Ives, P.	9872	Batman	Barton, G.

Canadian Pacific—The Empire's Greatest Railway.

3RD BATTALION, 1st INFANTRY BRIGADE—cont.

Regl. No.	Rank.	Name.
9873	Batman	Edwards B.
9874	,,	Carroll, J.
9875	Cook	Watson, H.
9876	,,	Cross, C.
9877	Lce.-Cpl.	Ferguson, W.
9878	Private	Austin, F.
9879	,,	Abbey, G.
9880	,,	Alderton, W.
9881	,,	Baxter, J. W.
9882	,,	Bertram, W.
9883	,,	Bethune, D.
9884	,,	Barnes, R. H.
9885	,,	Black, H.
9886	,,	Boulton, A.
9887	,,	Bell, R. W.
9888	,,	Birch, E.
9889	,,	Bennett, W.
9890	,,	Brown, R. E.
9891	,,	Brandreth, E.
9892	,,	Barlow, H. E.
9893	,,	Boal, H. R.
9894	,,	Barclay, R.
9895	,,	Castas, T.
9896	,,	Cornish, C. F.
9897	,,	Crowley, J.
9898	,,	Cannon, A. E.
9899	,,	Chisman, R.
9900	,,	Clarke, T.
9901	,,	Denoon, J.
9902	,,	Eastman, G. L.
9903	,,	Fletcher, H.
9904	,,	Francis, W. E.
9905	,,	Feller, A.
9906	,,	Graham, R.
9907	,,	Gardiner, F.
9908	,,	Green, H. J.
9909	,,	Green, E.
9910	,,	Green, N. I.
9911	,,	Green, J. F.
9912	,,	Green, J. G.
9913	,,	Gregg, D.
9914	,,	Greig, N.
9915	,,	Guest, W.
9916	,,	Gilfillan, J.
9917	,,	Goddard, G. W.
9918	,,	Gibson, W. H.
9919	,,	Guinyon, J.
9920	,,	Green, H.
9921	,,	Howe, William J.
9922	Private	Hedderson, G. A.
9923	,,	Hazlett, J.
9924	,,	Hatton, W.
9925	,,	Holmes, S.
9926	,,	Hicks, E. J.
9927	,,	Jacobs, W.
9928	,,	Johnston, S.
9929	,,	Jones, F.
9930	,,	Irvine, J. E.
9931	,,	Kirk, T.
9932	,,	Kelly, S.
9933	,,	Keenan, J.
9934	,,	McKelvie, J.
9935	,,	McIntyre, W.
9936	,,	MacNaughton, A. S.
9937	,,	McHugh, E. M.
9938	,,	McBratney, H.
9939	,,	McKeown, W. G.
9940	,,	May, W. H.
9941	,,	Miller, C. D.
9942	,,	Moulds, T. J.
9943	,,	Nugent, A. G.
9944	,,	O'Donohoe, F.
9945	,,	Page, R.
9946	,,	Payne, C. F.
9947	,,	Phillips, J. D.
9948	,,	Phillips, H. H.
9949	,,	Peters, S. J.
9950	,,	Randle, G.
9951	,,	Robinson, H.
9952	,,	Richardson, A. V.
9953	,,	Rose, J. C.
9954	,,	Rainey, A.
9955	,,	Summers, A.
9956	,,	Shepherd, E. G.
9957	,,	Stephenson, P. C.
9958	,,	Smith, W.
9959	,,	Smith, S.
9960	,,	Stanford, E.
9961	,,	Stanford, J. J.
9962	,,	Sullivan, J.
9963	,,	Thompson, H. E.
9964	,,	Vincent, R.
9965	,,	Wardlaw, P.
9966	,,	Wilkie, R. D.
9967	,,	Warburton, J.
9968	,,	Willis, F.
9969	,,	Woods, J.

Canadian Pacific—The Empire's Greatest Railway.

3RD BATTALION, 1ST INFANTRY BRIGADE—cont.

"H" COMPANY.

Captain ... ... Morton, C. E. H.
Lieutenant ... ... Neale, J. B.
„ ... ... Greene, G. E. D.
„ ... ... Davison, H. J.

Regl. No.	Rank.	Name.	Regl. No.	Rank.	Name.
9971	Col.-Sgt.	Cooper, C. E.	10017	Private	Cleverley, A. C.
9973	Sergt.	Curlew, F.	10018	„	Corby, H. G.
9974	„	Saunders, A. G.	10019	„	Conyers, G. S.
9975	Lce.-Sgt.	Roberts, H. W.	10086	„	Cole, F.
9976	Corpl.	Webber, A. J.	10020	„	Daly, A. P. V.
9977	„	Harrison, F.	10021	„	Dickens, J. J.
9978	„	Haines, F. J.	10022	„	Douglas, W.
9979	„	Bailey, D.	10023	„	Dickson, A.
9980	Bugler	Swan, J.	10024	„	Earls, J. G.
9981	„	Doyle, E.	10025	„	Edie, G. B.
9982	Pioneer	Bevington, A.	10026	„	Franklin, T.
9983	Signaller	Field, A.	10027	„	Fielder, J.
9984	„	Maclean, R.	10028	„	Fitzpatrick, K. J.
9985	Str.-B'rer	Burke, C. A.	10029	„	Fulton, R.
9986	„	Speight, F.	10030	„	Forgie, D.
9987	Driver	Rainor, W.	10031	„	Greetham, F.
9988	„	Sibley, A. G. H.	10032	„	Graham, T. M.
9989	Batman	McVicar, W.	9972	„	Greenhow, G. O. R.
9990	„	Carter, L. H.	10033	„	Gamey, T. A.
9991	„	Kent, F.	10034	„	Gunning, A.
9992	„	Corfield, C. H.	10035	„	Harley, S. J.
9993	Cook	Courts, F.	10036	„	Henderson, S. L.
9994	„	Beaton, T. J.	10037	„	Hilliar, F.
9995	Private	Armitage, D. R.	10038	„	Harries, J. S.
9996	„	Attree, A.	10039	„	Harrison, A. E.
9997	„	Adams, R.	10040	„	Harrell, P.
9998	„	Armstrong, F.	10041	„	Howard, T.
9999	„	Biggs, W. J.	10042	„	Ivy, W. R.
10000	„	Brown, O. Y.	10043	„	Jackson, F. A.
10001	„	Beard, W. B.	10044	„	Johnson, G. H.
10002	„	Byrne, J.	10045	„	Kidney, T. J.
10003	„	Brown, C. M.	10046	„	Keele, T.
10004	„	Bradshaw, F. W.	10047	„	Lewis, A. T.
10005	„	Bradbrook, W.	10048	„	Lennox, J. H.
10006	„	Brown, W. A.	10049	„	Lendon, A. F.
10007	„	Blayney, R. H.	10050	„	MacPherson, R.
10008	„	Bullick, A. H.	10051	„	Metcalfe, J. M.
10009	„	Bickerstaff, E. M.	10052	„	Madill, R. M.
10010	„	Bromley, T.	10053	„	Moore, J. G.
10011	„	Batley, F. E.	10054	„	Martin, W. C.
10012	„	Cusin, E.	10055	„	O'Brien, D.
10013	„	Comins, E.	10056	„	Pritchard, C. R.
10014	„	Cully, T.	10057	„	Pascoe, T.
10015	„	Coles, E. C.	10058	„	Pattison, W.
10016	„	Cox, A.	10059	„	Porter, T. H.

Canadian Pacific—The Empire's Greatest Railway.

3RD BATTALION, 1ST INFANTRY BRIGADE—cont.

Regl. No.	Rank	Name
10060	Private	Palmer, W. H.
10061	,,	Platten, T.
10062	,,	Pickup, G.
10063	,,	Perry, H.
10064	,,	Pope, H. A.
10065	,,	Porter, S.
10066	,,	Peters, W. K.
10087	,,	Peters, A.
10067	,,	Ryder, L.
10068	,,	Rushton, E.
10069	,,	Reeves, O.
10070	,,	Shields, H.
10071	,,	Savory, F. E.
10072	,,	Smith, G.
10073	Private	Stringer, C. R.
10074	,,	Thomas, J. H.
10075	,,	Thomson, H. C.
10076	,,	Templeton, C. B.
10084	,,	Venables, W. H.
10077	,,	Watts, S. J.
10078	,,	Westmorland, A. W. G.
10079	,,	White, G.
10080	,,	Wilson, T. A.
10081	,,	Weller, G.
10082	,,	Whitworth, G.
10083	,,	Wright, D. T.
10085	,,	Young, G.

BASE DETAIL.

Lieutenant ... ... Johnston, B. L.

Regl. No.	Rank	Name
10089	Mstr.Tlr.	Rodgman, F. C.
10191	O.R.S.	Mulloy, E. H.
10144	Band Sgt.	MacAgy, G. P.
10090	Sergt.	Evason, U.
10091	,,	Scovell, A. G.
10092	Storeman	Smyth, R. F.
10093	,,	Lennox, O. E.
10094	Private	Adams, J. R.
10095	,,	Addison, R.
10096	,,	Andrews, H. W.
10097	,,	Arnoldi, A. C.
10098	,,	Ashford, W. H.
10099	,,	Ashleigh, A. A.
10100	,,	Ashby, A.
10101	,,	Atkinson, R.
10102	,,	Attfield, N. C.
10103	,,	Blower, J. W. H.
10104	,,	Beattie, E.
10105	,,	Bourlet, W. J.
10106	,,	Bradshaw, H.
10107	,,	Campbell, A.
10187	,,	Campbell, R. G.
10108	,,	Cartwright, T.
10109	,,	Chambers, F.
10110	,,	Chaney, J.
10111	,,	Clark, G. H.
10112	,,	Conroy, A. V.
10192	,,	Cramp, H. M.
10113	,,	Cuthbert, S.
10114	,,	Dean, K. L.
10115	,,	Dickson, S.
10188	Private	Dickson, W. M.
10116	,,	Deeks, W. H.
10117	,,	Eakins, F. C.
10118	,,	Elliott, F.
10119	,,	Elliott, G. W.
10120	,,	Francis, G.
10121	,,	Fletcher, W. G.
10189	,,	Forrest, P. A.
10088	,,	Gamble, F. J.
10122	,,	Gibbons, A.
10123	,,	Gilmore, R.
10124	,,	Glockling, P. J.
10125	,,	Graham, W. J.
10126	,,	Gray, J. R.
10127	,,	Gonneau, O. E.
10128	,,	Hamilton, W. H.
10129	,,	Harrington, S. R.
10130	,,	Hawken, R. H.
10131	,,	Hoban, R. E.
10132	,,	Hobbis, G. J.
10133	,,	Hobson, J.
10134	,,	Howard, L.
10135	,,	Irons, B.
10136	,,	Jackman, N. J.
10137	,,	Kirwin, W. H.
10138	,,	Lindner, W. M.
10139	,,	Lookton, A.
10140	,,	Lowther, G. C.
10141	,,	Lyon, L. D.
10142	,,	Lyon, L. M.
10143	,,	Lyon, I. C.

Canadian Pacific—The Empire's Greatest Railway.

3RD BATTALION, 1ST INFANTRY BRIGADE—cont.

Regl. No.	Rank.	Name.	Regl. No.	Rank.	Name.
10145	Private	Mahon, J. L.	10166	Private	Sloan, D.
10146	,,	Marr, A.	10167	,,	Smith, Oscar
10147	,,	Marriner, N.	10168	,,	Smythe, W. P.
10148	,,	Martin, S. J.	10169	,,	Sproule, H. C.
10150	,,	Matthews, W. J.	10190	,,	Steane, B. C.
10151	,,	McDonald, A.	10170	,,	Stickley, F. W.
10195	,,	McGee, Patrick	10171	,,	Stretton, G.
10152	,,	Mead, F. W.	10172	,,	Sutherland, W. A.
10153	,,	Minett, W. H.	10173	,,	Thornton, T.
10154	,,	Montgomery, R.	10174	,,	Tunstead, R. F.
10155	,,	Moss, P. R.	10175	,,	Walton, R.
10156	,,	Mulcahy, R.	10176	,,	Waters, A.
10157	,,	Munn, W. P.	10177	,,	Watson, C.
10158	,,	O'Brien, D.	10178	,,	Webb, E.
10159	,,	Oliver, A. W.	10179	,,	Webster, C. F.
10160	,,	Parsons, A. H.	10180	,,	Whittle, H. C.
10161	,,	Perry, C. H.	10181	,,	Williams, C. H.
10162	,,	Ridout, T. R.	10182	,,	Williams, H. J.
10163	,,	Robertson, A. C.	10183	,,	Wills, P.
10193	,,	Scott, H.	10184	,,	Wurtele, E. G. M.
10194	,,	Scarboro, R.	10185	,,	Young, A. A.
10164	,,	Seabrook, H. G.	10186	,,	Young, W. J.
10165	,,	Smales, P.			

4th BATTALION, 1st INFANTRY BRIGADE.

HEADQUARTERS.

Officer Commanding ...	Lieut.-Colonel R. H. Labatt
Major	,, W. S. Buell
Adjutant	Captain J. D. Glover
Asst. Adjutant	Lieutenant D. W. Megaffin
Transport Officer	,, H. A. Cozzens
Signalling Officer	,, V. Dyas
Machine Gun Officer	,, H. H. Washington
Medical Officer	Major R. Raikes
Paymaster	Hon. Captain H. P. Johnson
Chaplain	Hon. Major F. C. Piper
Quartermaster	Major A. Gillies

Regl. No.	Rank.	Name.	Regl. No.	Rank.	Name.
10526	Sgt.-Maj.	Galloway, G. W.	10547	Trans.Sgt.	Mounce, J.
10527	Q.M.Sgt.	Kerry, W.	10532	Sgl. Sgt.	Basnett, H.
10528	Sgt. Dmr.	Summerville, H.	10578	Shoe Sgt.	Robb, W.
11264	O.R. Sgt.	McGregor, J.	10862	Pnr. Sgt.	Smith, G.
10576	Paymr.Sgt.	Hollister, E. A.	10577	Arm. Sgt.	Grassby, G.
11538	Cook Sgt.	Carey, H.			

Canadian Pacific—The Empire's Greatest Railway.

4TH BATTALION, 1st INFANTRY BRIGADE—cont.

Signallers.

Regl. No.	Rank.	Name.	Regl. No.	Rank.	Name.
10533	Lce.-Cpl.	Robins, H.	10537	Private	Martin, G.
10540	,,	Emmett, J.	10729	,,	Murray, J.
10535	Private	Donoghue, J.	11433	,,	Payne, A.
10538	,,	Hart, W.	10534	,,	Payne, H.

Orderlies for Medical Officers.

11317	Lce.-Cpl.	Elliott, T.	10542	Private	Richardson, D.

Drivers.

10556	Private	Baird, H.	10563	Private	Macwhenney, G.
10555	,,	Bell, R.	10551	,,	McDonald, E.
10558	,,	Bowman, J. S.	11078	,,	O'Higgin, F. M.
10550	,,	Cara, S.	10553	,,	Painter, A.
10548	,,	Gardner, G.	11514	,,	Smith, W. R.
10552	,,	Garrow, H. A.	10543	,,	Solomon, J. J.
10549	,,	Hulme, W.	10554	,,	Whelan, P. T.
10544	,,	Johnston, R.			

Batmen.

10766	Private	Dawson, W.	11666	Private	Swan, G.
10713	{Chapl's. Batman}	Higham, H. C.	10559	,,	Tearney, J. J.
10568	Private	Murray, H.	10698	{S.M.'s Batman}	Verrell, H.
10560	,,	Rhodes, W.	10561	Private	Wakeling, R.
10564	,,	Roberts, A.			

Water Detail.

33616	Corpl.	Rodgers, G.	33619	Private	Moffat, W. B.
33618	Private	Heppell, G.	33617	,,	O'Day, D. M.
33620	,,	Lennox, H.			

Machine Gun Section.

10579	Sergt.	Crook, J. T.	10591	Private	Kift, A. J.
10588	Corpl.	Walker, A. E.	10586	,,	Kirby, T.
10595	Batman	Brooks, J.	10582	,,	Murray, J.
10585	Private	Charlton, C. F.	10581	,,	Nesbitt, J.
10592	,,	Cross, J. B.	10583	,,	Nolan, W.
19587	,,	Doy, J.	10590	,,	Phillips, W.
10594	Driver	Hunter, J.	10589	,,	Russell, J.
10584	Private	Kemp, W.	10580	,,	Sage, S. C.

Canadian Pacific—The Empire's Greatest Railway.

4TH BATTALION, 1ST INFANTRY BRIGADE—cont.

"A" COMPANY.

Captain	... ...	Major J. Ballantine
Lieutenant	... ...	McKinley, J. M.
,,	... ...	Conover, R.
,,	... ...	Brown, G. O.

Regl. No.	Rank.	Name.	Regl. No.	Rank.	Name.
11079	Col.-Sgt.	Jamieson, S. J.	11155	Private	Green, G.
11080	Sergt.	Hucklebridge, G.	11163	,,	Gibb, J.
11081	,,	Duffy, T. P.	11177	,,	Grainge, H.
11082	,,	Outhwaite, W. F.	11184	,,	Grieve, C.
11083	,,	Bradley, L. W.	11092	,,	Harrison, S.
11084	Corpl.	Burrows, W.	11093	,,	Hall, T.
11086	,,	Harwood, H.	11137	,,	Herbert, A.
11087	,,	Wray, J.	11138	,,	Hart, A.
11088	,,	McMaster, M.	11140	,,	Harper, H.
11105	,,	Andrew G. (Armrer.)	11142	,,	Holahan, D.
11085	,,	Cummings, A. C.	11144	,,	Henderson, H. D.
11101	Private	Alder, A.	11147	,,	Healey, M.
11102	,,	Algeo, A.	11643	,,	Johnson, F.
11103	,,	Anderson, W.	11642	,,	Kelby, G.
11104	,,	Armstrong, T.	11090	,,	Lee, W.
11106	,,	Best, W.	11145	,,	Lamb, R.
11107	,,	Burkenshaw, F. G.	11160	,,	Lees, W.
11108	,,	Bayliss, G. W.	11135	,,	Mills, W.
11109	,,	Bradley, L.	11136	,,	Matheson, W.
11110	,,	Barnes, J.	11143	,,	Madden, J.
11111	,,	Busby, G.	11164	,,	Mander, V.
11112	,,	Butler, J.	11175	,,	Marsden, W.
11113	,,	Bird, G. D.	11182	,,	Main, A.
11114	,,	Bunker, A.	11416	,,	McCartney, R.
11091	,,	Clarke, H.	11185	,,	McCauley, J.
11115	,,	Carr, W.	11191	,,	McLeod, A.
11116	,,	Cole, J. H.	11132	,,	Nelle, T.
11117	,,	Cannon, H.	11154	,,	Norman, D.
11118	,,	Cockington, J.	11150	,,	Oakes, A.
11119	,,	Church, J. L.	11099	,,	Oliver, G.
11120	,,	Cormack, D.	11139	,,	Peace, J.
11121	,,	Cooper, G.	11141	,,	Platt, E.
11122	,,	Cook, J.	11148	,,	Peaks, W. H.
11190	,,	Dickson, J.	11157	,,	Patterson, D.
11094	,,	Doudney, J.	11171	,,	Plant, G.
11123	,,	Debenham, F. R.	11174	,,	Pratt, G.
11124	,,	Dunbar, A. R.	11179	,,	Rodger, A.
11125	,,	Dymott, W.	11181	,,	Pickup, R.
11126	,,	Davis, A. E.	11100	,,	Roult, F.
11127	,,	Douglas, D.	11149	,,	Reid, C.
11095	,,	Eden, A.	11162	,,	Robertson, J.
11128	,,	Edwards, A.	11189	,,	Riding, H.
11089	,,	Fincher, F.	11622	,,	Scott, R.
11133	,,	Francis, H. W.	11192	,,	Stanley, J. T.
11146	,,	Farries, T.	11097	,,	Stewart, J.

Canadian Pacific—The Empire's Greatest Railway.

D

4TH BATTALION, 1st INFANTRY BRIGADE—cont.

Regl. No.	Rank.	Name.	Regl. No.	Rank.	Name.
11130	Private	Sloane, J.	11156	Private	Watmough, J.
11134	,,	Sanderson, A.	11158	,,	Ward, D. H.
11153	,,	Saunders, R.	11165	,,	Williams, H.
11161	,,	Singleton, R.	11166	,,	Wade, D.
11159	,,	Sahli, J.	11167	,,	Wilson, R.
11172	,,	Swindale, J.	11168	,,	Winterburn, A.
11098	,,	Toon, A.	11169	,,	Wisson, G.
11151	,,	Tarry, W.	11170	,,	Wales, A.
11173	,,	Towland, R.	11176	,,	Wilson, A.
11152	,,	Tuxford, V.	11178	,,	White, J.
11180	,,	Vernon, W.	11186	,,	Wills, F.
11633	,,	Walton, T.	11187	,,	Wright, F.
11129	,,	Wildispin, J.	11188	,,	Williams, S.
11131	,,	Winter, G.			

"B" COMPANY.

Captain ... ... Huggins, S. J.
Lieutenant ... ... Megaffin, W. W.
    ,, ... Sprinks, W.
    ,, ... Bennett, J. H.

Regl. No.	Rank.	Name.	Regl. No.	Rank.	Name.
10854	Col.-Sgt.	Easterbey, T. A.	10708	Private	Clarke, T. W.
10597	Sergt.	Mitchell, C.	10733	,,	Cronie, A.
10598	,,	Moore, A. E.	10710	,,	Driver, F.
10599	,,	Hay, R.	10636	,,	Done, C.
10600	,,	Coulter, J.	10637	,,	Delaney, T.
10602	Corpl.	Thompson, G.	10638	,,	Drabble, F.
10603	,,	Kennedy, A.	10639	,,	Davidson, W.
10605	,,	Clarke, G. W. (Armourer)	10640	,,	Dutton, T.
			10641	,,	Dew, W.
10619	Private	Atwell, F.	10642	,,	Dunlop, W.
10620	,,	Arms, F.	10643	,,	Dolan, F.
10621	,,	Adams, A.	10644	,,	Don, S.
10622	,,	Amory, E.	10645	,,	Dalrymple, F.
10712	,,	Benson, A.	10646	,,	Earle, J. W.
10607	,,	Beatty, E.	10647	,,	Farrell, J.
10608	,,	Bohme, H. D.	10562	,,	Ferguson, T. A.
10618	,,	Bennett, C. F.	10604	,,	Flynn, G.
10623	,,	Berridge, E.	10648	,,	Foley, R.
10624	,,	Biggs, E.	10649	,,	Freeman, H.
10625	,,	Bryant, H.	10650	,,	Goldstien, H.
10626	,,	Baker, A.	10651	,,	Gologly, J.
10628	,,	Collins, C.	10652	,,	Granger, C.
10629	,,	Case, N.	10709	,,	Hunt, E. C.
10630	,,	Copley, J.	10613	,,	Huff, G. E.
10631	,,	Conden, J.	10653	,,	Hall, W.
10632	,,	Calvert, W.	10654	,,	Haslam, J.
10634	,,	Cooper, C.	10655	,,	Hogan, F.
10635	,,	Cairns, C.	11660	,,	Hougton, J.

Canadian Pacific—The Empire's Greatest Railway.

4TH BATTALION, 1ST INFANTRY BRIGADE—cont.

Regl. No.	Rank.	Name.
10656	Private	Hollands, W. S.
10657	,,	Humbert, R.
10658	,,	Harrison, W.
10659	,,	Hart, G.
10660	,,	Hogan, C.
10661	,,	Harrison, C. A.
10662	,,	Hubbling, C.
10612	,,	Jackson, A.
10663	,,	Johnston, W.
10711	,,	Kent, E.
10664	,,	Kerr, G.
10665	,,	Kelly, T. E.
10666	,,	Knight, J.
10570	,,	Kirkpatrick, A.
10590	,,	Kinghorn, J.
10610	,,	Lockyer, W.
10667	Asst. Cook	Linfoot J.
10668	Private	Lynch, J.
10669	,,	Lawrence, C. M.
10606	,,	McDaniel, E.
10611	,,	Mercer, J.
10616	,,	Mountain, W. J.
10670	,,	Maffey, H.
10671	,,	Meyer, H.
10672	,,	Mills, F.
10673	,,	Muten, W. F.
10674	,,	Morris, W.
10675	,,	Martin, S. G.
10676	,,	Muir, J.
10677	,,	Miles, J.
10678	,,	Morris, F.
10679	,,	McDonald, J.

Regl. No.	Rank.	Name.
10680	Private	Moody, W.
10681	,,	Matthewson, J.
10682	,,	Morris, E.
10683	,,	McQuay, R. (Cook).
10684	,,	Nutt, C.
10685	,,	Pope, W.
10686	,,	Parker, A.
10609	,,	Pepperill, W.
10615	,,	Peacey, C. H.
11612	,,	Reeves, F. W.
10617	,,	Rouse, T.
10687	,,	Rider, J.
10688	,,	Rooney, G.
10689	,,	Reynolds, H.
10690	,,	Raynor, G.
10691	Corpl.	Salmond, H. J.
10692	Private	Smith, J. A.
10693	,,	Shaw, W. F.
10694	,,	Sinan, E.
10695	,,	Stovall, C.
10696	,,	Skiffington, P.
10697	,,	Terrell, C.
10707	,,	Verrall, E.
10614	,,	Williams, A.
10699	,,	Wood, W. (Cook)
10700	,,	Walton, L.
10701	,,	Wilson, G. H.
10702	,,	Whitley, T.
10703	,,	Wilkinson, W.
10704	,,	Williamson, A.
10705	Corpl.	Wilson, W. A.

"C" COMPANY.

Captain ... ... Major B. H. Belson
Lieutenant ... ... McLaren, F. G.
,, ... Wright, G. C.
,, ... Ballard, G. W. M.

Regl. No.	Rank.	Name.
10852	Col.-Sgt.	Hunt, R. W.
10853	Sergt.	Letten, J.
10855	,,	Ross, D.
10856	,,	Towlson, T. W.
10596	,,	Howard, C.
10857	Corpl.	Kaye, A.
10893	,,	Dukeman, H.
10910	,,	Hanford, B.
10954	,,	Wood, E.
10860	,,	Rabbit A.

Regl. No.	Rank.	Name.
10861	Corpl.	Trenwith, F. D. (Armourer)
10874	Private	Anderson, J.
10875	,,	Arnold, T.
10864	,,	Barrett, E.
10868	,,	Brown, W.
10870	,,	Batson, G.
10876	,,	Bennie, A.
10877	,,	Blunt, A.
10878	,,	Blunt, H.

Canadian Pacific—The Empire's Greatest Railway.

4TH BATTALION, 1ST INFANTRY BRIGADE—cont.

Regl. No.	Rank.	Name.	Regl. No.	Rank.	Name.
10879	Private	Bland, F.	10920	Private	Jarvie, A.
10880	,,	Brown, W. C.	10921	,,	Jones, W. C.
10881	,,	Baillie, N.	10922	,,	Jones, J. H.
10882	,,	Brogan, T.	10923	,,	Jennings, S.
10883	,,	Browett, W.	10873	,,	Kelly, Jno. W.
10884	,,	Bolton, J.	10924	,,	Kelly, Jas. W.
11669	,,	Booker, J.	10925	,,	Leslie, J. J.
10885	,,	Butler, T. A.	10926	,,	Lewes, R.
10886	,,	Clay, D.	10960	,,	Lawrence, R.
10887	,,	Crossan, R.	10927	,,	Mercer, J. E.
10888	,,	Capell, F.	10928	,,	Marrell, J.
10889	,,	Comeau, L.	10929	,,	Mountain, S.
10890	,,	Clarkson, W. J.	10930	,,	Marshall, F.
10891	,,	Curtis, F.	10931	,,	Marr, A.
10892	,,	Davis, W.	10932	,,	McGregor, H.
10894	,,	Dodd, N.	10933	,,	McGinn, J.
10895	,,	De Bues, P.	10934	,,	McHarg, D.
10896	,,	Edwards, J.	10871	,,	Miller, H.
10897	,,	Espley, E.	11670	,,	McEwen, R.
10869	,,	Etty, A.	10863	,,	Nixon, J.
10898	,,	Edgerley, G.	10935	,,	Pickup, R.
10899	,,	Fairclough, W.	10936	,,	Priest, C.
10900	,,	Flynn, J.	10937	,,	Robinson, A.
10859	,,	Fraser, J.	10865	,,	Sheppard, A.
10901	,,	Galpin, R.	10867	,,	South, J.
10902	,,	Ginn, A.	10938	,,	Stinson, J.
10903	,,	Glazier, L.	10939	,,	Swan, G. L.
10904	,,	Graves, T.	10940	,,	Shipman, E.
10905	,,	Griffiths, H.	10941	,,	Sloan, F.
10906	,,	Gratton, J. W.	10942	,,	Sinclair, W. J.
10907	,,	Goodyear, W.	10943	,,	Sprowson, A.
10908	,,	Gilks, J.	10944	,,	Saddler, G.
10909	,,	Gale, G.	10961	,,	Stone, A. W.
10959	,,	Glass, W.	11664	,,	Stone, H.
11662	,,	Gregson, G.	11665	,,	Saywell, S.
11663	,,	Griffin, T.	10945	,,	Taylor, J.
10872	,,	Graham, T.	10946	,,	Todd, J. D.
10866	,,	Holland, A. G.	10947	,,	Telford, A.
10911	,,	Huckstep, R.	10948	,,	Thomas, W. E.
10912	,,	Hendrie, J.	10949	,,	Todd, J. J.
10913	,,	Haygarth, S.	10950	,,	Thompson, J.
10914	,,	Humphreys, W.	10951	,,	Vincent, E.
10915	,,	Hall, W.	10952	,,	Venn, E.
10916	,,	Hearle, E.	10953	,,	Wilkinson, C. E.
10917	,,	Hilton, F. C.	10955	,,	Wilson, J. A.
10918	,,	Hollinsed, R.	10858	,,	Withun, H.
10962	,,	Hollands, A. V.	10956	,,	Wyndham, S.
10963	,,	Holt, F.	10957	,,	Wright, P. C.
10919	,,	Ireland, A.	10958	,,	Wilson, W.

Canadian Pacific—The Empire's Greatest Railway.

4TH BATTALION, 1ST INFANTRY BRIGADE—cont. 53

"D" COMPANY.

Captain	... ...	Beggy, G. B.
Lieutenant	... ...	Bastedo, A. C.
,,	... ...	Brant, C. D.
,,	... ...	Hoshal, A. J.

Regl. No.	Rank	Name	Regl. No.	Rank	Name
10964	Col.-Sgt.	White, A. A.	10985	Private	Hargraives, J.
10965	Sergt.	Michelin, H. A.	10990	,,	Huggins, J.
10966	,,	Williams, J.	11004	,,	Hatton, W. J.
10967	,,	Dealtry, P.	11006	,,	Heally, J.
10968	,,	Gillingwater, P. H.	11007	,,	Hill, J.
10971	,,	Stacey, J.	11033	,,	Hannigan, N.
10969	Corpl.	Sloan, W.	11052	,,	Heasley, G.
10970	,,	Crain, A.	11069	,,	Hawkins, R. R.
10972	,,	Styres, A.	11070	,,	Hoskins, A.
10973	,,	Clark, J. (Armourer)	11078	,,	O'Higgins, F. M.
10991	Private	Adams, J.	11585	,,	Inglis, J.
10992	,,	Allison, J.	11068	,,	Innes, W.
11066	,,	Atkin, H.	11008	,,	Kempling, H. H.
11076	,,	Anchor, F.	11046	,,	King, G.
10993	,,	Berry, F. A	11072	,,	Keates, A.
10994	,,	Bowley, G.	11009	,,	Large, A.
10995	,,	Barton, T.	11048	,,	Lambourne, F.
10996	,,	Bayless, F.	11658	,,	Lay, J.
10997	,,	Bradshaw, P. A.	11594	,,	Lewis, V.
11039	,,	Bennett, W.	11592	,,	Lowe, S.
11040	,,	Baker, C.	10982	,,	McQuinn, F.
11041	,,	Brooker, P.	11010	,,	McDonald, F.
11042	,,	Brown, G.	11011	,,	McKnight, E.
11067	,,	Binch, A.	11034	,,	Montour, F.
11060	,,	Birch, F.	11035	,,	Montour, N.
10998	,,	Challis, G.	11036	,,	Montour, W.
10999	,,	Coulthart, J.	11063	,,	MacKenzie, A.
11000	,,	Crawford, W.	11012	,,	Nortcliffe, E.
11065	,,	Cullum, A. E.	11053	,,	Osborn, A.
11001	,,	Donaldson, A.	10987	,,	Palmer, J.
11043	,,	Doan, P.	11056	,,	Pannell, H.
11002	,,	Edge, S.	11013	,,	Patterson, E.
11003	,,	Edge, W.	11014	,,	Patterson, G. S.
11567	,,	Elmsley, A. H.	11077	,,	Perrett, M.
11005	,,	Farebrother, S.	10978	,,	Rowling, R.
11044	,,	Fralick, W.	11015	,,	Rance, F.
11045	,,	Fralick, G.	11016	,,	Rendall, F.
11571	,,	Freemantle, H.	11017	,,	Reynolds, W.
11062	,,	Fisher, C.	11038	,,	Rodger, M.
11064	,,	Fox, D.	11031	,,	Mike, J.
10989	,,	Goldsmith, F.	10986	,,	Sheridan, H.
11073	,,	Gillies, W.	10988	,,	Slack, W.
11059	,,	Hall, P.	10976	,,	Smith, J.
10977	,,	Howard, T.	11018	,,	Scott, W. D.
10984	,,	Harvey, C.	11619	,,	Shanley, A.

Canadian Pacific—The Empire's Greatest Railway.

54 4TH BATTALION, 1ST INFANTRY BRIGADE—cont.

Regl. No.	Rank.	Name.	Regl. No.	Rank.	Name.
11019	Private	Shephard, H. T.	11025	Private	Turnbull, A.
11020	,,	Sloan, G.	11037	,,	Turnbull, W.
11021	,,	Sommerville, W.	11075	,,	Trowles, V.
11022	,,	Spence, R.	10980	,,	Wells, D. H.
11030	,,	Stewart, E. W.	11026	,,	Watson, J.
11049	,,	Sims, R.	11629	,,	Watson, J.
11050	,,	Smith, J.	11027	,,	White, B. C.
11051	,,	Smith, B.	11029	,,	Wolhampster, H.
11054	,,	Secord, T.	11028	,,	Worrall, W.
11061	,,	Stephenson, R.	11055	,,	Wheeler, C.
11074	,,	Simpson, G.	11059	,,	Ward, E.
11659	,,	Sartain, J.	11071	,,	Woods, T. L.
11023	,,	Taylor, J.	11057	,,	York, W.
11024	,,	Tobin, K. E.			

"E" COMPANY

Captain ... ... Rodgers, G. R.
Lieutenant ... ... Allen, J.
      ,, ... Young, N. F.
      ,, ... Wallace, J. C.

Regl. No.	Rank.	Name.	Regl. No.	Rank.	Name.
10714	Col.-Sgt.	Groom, C.	10751	Private	Case, T.
10718	Sergt.	Benton, B.	10752	,,	Dorricott, E. A.
10716	,,	Smith, R.	10753	,,	Drinkwater, W.
10717	,,	Weeks, H.	10833	,,	Evans, E. R.
10719	Corpl.	Lake, W.	10754	,,	Falconer, R.
10721	,,	MacGuire, R.	10755	,,	Ferrier, H.
10720	,,	Pearce, S.	11569	,,	Foster, C. N.
10722	,,	Westlake, E.	10847	,,	Fraser, J.
10736	Private	Abell, C.	10849	,,	Fraser, J. A. S.
10728	,,	Alger, T.	10756	,,	Griffiths, H.
10851	,,	Bennett, R. (Act. Provost Sergeant.)	10727	,,	Gillen, T.
			10757	,,	Garland, A.
10737	,,	Betts, R.	10758	,,	Goddard, F.
10738	,,	Baxter, W.	10759	,,	Gazley, R.
10739	,,	Bonton, A.	10760	,,	Glidden, A. C.
10740	,,	Bradbury, G.	10725	,,	Herrill, C.
10741	,,	Blake, J. E.	10761	,,	Hartell, E.
10742	,,	Bayley, J.	10762	,,	Henry, W.
10726	,,	Curtiss, L. G.	10763	,,	Hall, B.
10733	,,	Cronie, A.	10764	,,	Hanna, W.
10743	,,	Craven, E. H.	10785	,,	Hermiston, F.
10744	,,	Carbury, A.	10786	,,	Hunter, W.
10745	,,	Cook, J.	10787	,,	Henderson, R.
10746	,,	Crouch, J.	10788	,,	Harrison, G.
10747	,,	Cohen, A.	10789	,,	Holmes, J. W.
10748	,,	Cummings, P.	10790	,,	Hearn, W.
10749	,,	Carmichael, L.	10791	,,	Henderson, J.
10750	,,	Clarke, C.	11426	Arm'rer	Hurst

Canadian Pacific—The Empire's Greatest Railway.

4TH BATTALION, 1ST INFANTRY BRIGADE—cont. 55

Regl. No.	Rank.	Name.	Regl. No.	Rank.	Name.
10838	Private	Iddendon, A.	10840	Private	Reason, F. G.
10792	,,	Johnston, J.	10715	,,	Saunders, E. C.
11442	,,	Jacobs, H.	10723	Corpl.	Smith, J. W.
10793	,,	Jones, A. L.	10730	Private	Strathern, W.
10794	,,	Kelly, T.	10735	,,	Smith, E. H.
10795	,,	Klipper, J.	10813	,,	Sharpe, T.
10835	,,	Leigh, H.	10814	,,	Smith, M.
10796	,,	Lawton, C.	10815	,,	Smith, E. J.
10797	,,	Leslie, J. A.	10816	,,	Smith, A.
10798	,,	Lynch, E.	10817	,,	Sheddon, W.
10799	,,	Mackness, F.	10818	,,	Small, H.
10800	,,	Maines, J.	10819	,,	Stephens, A.
10801	,,	Melody, G.	10820	,,	Smith, T. D.
10802	,,	Millis, A.	10821	,,	Seward, J.
10803	,,	MacReady, D.	10837	,,	Shepherd, T.
10834	,,	Muir, W.	10836	,,	Stork, L.
10843	,,	Murphy, J.	10822	,,	Tooke, A.
10844	,,	Milton, G.	10845	,,	Tollemache, H.
11667	,,	Montgomery, F. J.	10823	,,	Vickers, J.
10804	,,	Newbury, W. C.	10824	,,	Wiles, L.
10805	,,	Norton, A.	10825	,,	Whiting, G.
10806	,,	Othen, H.	10826	,,	Wallace, J.
11609	,,	Patterson, A.	10828	,,	Watson, W.
10807	,,	Price, A. S.	10829	,,	Wynne, A.
10808	,,	Paprosky, G.	10830	,,	Wheeler, W.
10732	,,	Rowe, H.	10831	,,	Walmsley, M.
10734	,,	Roberts, H.	10841	,,	Wallace, C. B.
10809	,,	Robinson, C.	10846	,,	Wood, J.
10810	,,	Reynolds, F.	10850	,,	Westley, J.
10811	,,	Ralston, E.	10842	,,	Wiseman, A.
10812	,,	Roberts, F.	10832	,,	Zittermann, J. S.
10839	,,	Richardson, G.			

"F" COMPANY.

Captain ... ... Collins, G. R. N.
Lieutenant ... ... McGuire, H. B.
,, ... Bleakley, H. T.

Regl. No.	Rank.	Name.	Regl. No.	Rank.	Name.
11194	Col.-Sgt.	McInerney, T. J.	11220	Corpl.	Davis, E. R. N.
11196	Sergt.	Mills, J.	11204	Private	Anderson, H. J.
11197	,,	Lilley, A.	11205	,,	Bent, S.
11195	,,	Marsh, W.	11206	,,	Bailey, J.
11198	,,	Twigg, G. W.	11207	,,	Bracey, E. G.
11199	Lce.-Sergt.	Austin, A. D.	11208	,,	Barr, S.
11200	Corpl.	Ryan, T. (Armr.)	11209	,,	Britcher, W.
11202	,,	Hickey, H.	11646	,,	Bridgeman, E.
11203	,,	Andrews, P.	11649	,,	Bevan, C. J.
11201	,,	Scott, A. J.	11554	,,	Blake, H. W.

Canadian Pacific—The Empire's Greatest Railway.

4TH BATTALION, 1ST INFANTRY BRIGADE—cont.

Regl. No.	Rank.	Name.	Regl. No.	Rank.	Name.
11551	Private	Brooks, R. W.	11255	Private	Lendridge, G.
11210	,,	Ceeley, E. H.	11256	,,	Latimer, W.
11211	,,	Cavers, L.	11257	,,	Mallen, H.
11212	,,	Carlton, J.	11258	,,	Maslin, W.
11213	,,	Campbell, T.	11259	,,	Milligan, J.
11214	,,	Chambers, P.	11260	,,	Makepeace, A.
11215	,,	Chappell, C.	11261	,,	Mason, W. N.
11216	,,	Cordoza, G.	11262	,,	McCauley, H.
11217	,,	Cane, W. C.	11263	,,	McLennan, A. R.
11652	,,	Coleman, R.	11266	,,	Millan, H.
11218	,,	Downs, W.	11267	,,	Mills, G. E.
11219	,,	Doyley, J.	11605	,,	Milford, J.
11221	,,	Everett, W.	11268	,,	Morris, R. A.
11222	,,	Edwards, C.	11269	,,	Morrison, V.
11233	,,	Foy, A.	11270	,,	Middleton, H. H.
11224	,,	Frost, H.	11271	,,	Murray, M.
11225	,,	Frazer, G.	11272	,,	Nichol, C. C.
11226	,,	Farr, W.	11273	,,	Norris, F. E.
11227	,,	Giffen, W. H.	11275	,,	Pearson, G. A.
11228	,,	Green, W.	11276	,,	Pagan, J. L.
11229	,,	Grieve, T.	11277	,,	Patterson, G.
11230	,,	Gunn, L.	11278	,,	Parbury, S. J.
11231	,,	Glenn, W. G.	11279	,,	Perdue, J.
11232	,,	Gordon, C.	11645	,,	Palmer, W.
11233	,,	Grice, J.	11280	,,	Robinson, F.
11234	,,	Gandy, G. T.	11281	,,	Robotham, E.
11235	,,	Golding, A.	11282	,,	Roe, B.
11236	,,	Gardner, W.	11283	,,	Richards, A.
11648	,,	Gaiger, E.	11284	,,	Reid, W. T.
11653	,,	Hare, F.	11651	,,	Robinson, R.
11237	,,	Hailey, C.	11285	,,	Sheffield, W.
11238	,,	Harvey, B.	11286	,,	Swain, G.
11239	,,	Healey, A. E.	11287	,,	Strickland, S.
11240	,,	Hibbert, T.	11288	,,	Smith, F.
11241	,,	Hutchison, N. E.	11289	,,	Short, J.
11242	,,	Hart, W. C.	11290	,,	Schier, D. J.
11243	,,	Holmes, R.	11644	,,	Seddon, W.
11244	,,	Howell, G.	11647	,,	Spademan, E.
11245	,,	Hanna, M.	10569	,,	Smith, W. G.
11246	,,	Hamilton, R.	11291	,,	Tweedle, J. A.
11247	,,	Harbord, J.	11292	,,	Tapp, C. A.
11248	,,	Harbord, L.	11293	,,	Vintiner, A.
11249	,,	Ironsides, J.	11294	,,	Waters, B.
11250	,,	Jackson, F. S.	11295	,,	Woodhouse, J.
11251	,,	Jensen, H.	11296	,,	Weeks, E. J.
11650	,,	Jackson, L.	11297	,,	Walker, W. E.
11252	,,	Kearney, M.	11298	,,	Woods, J.
11253	,,	Leviston, W.	11299	,,	Watson, A.
11254	,,	Lockear, F.	11654	,,	Watson, J.

Canadian Pacific—The Empire's Greatest Railway.

4TH BATTALION, 1ST INFANTRY BRIGADE—cont. 57

" G " COMPANY.

Captain ... ... Colquhoun, M. A.
Lieutenant ... ... Jones, T. P.
,, ... Miller, F. W.
,, ... Towers, W. C.

Regl. No.	Rank.	Name.	Regl. No.	Rank.	Name.
11300	Col.-Sgt.	Mott, A. J.	11352	Private	Gage, R. B.
11301	Sergt.	Prior, E. H.	11353	,,	Greenwood, F.
11302	,,	Dockray, J.	11354	,,	Godfrey, S.
11303	,,	Crouch, G.	11355	,,	Gaydon, J. H.
11304	,,	Davis, A. H.	11356	,,	Grant, W. J.
11305	Corpl.	Pilley, G.	11357	,,	Graham, H.
11306	,,	Simpson, T.	11358	,,	Gallagher, J.
11307	,,	Lofty, W.	11359	,,	Guy, P.
11308	,,	Orr, H.	11313	,,	Hayward, L.
11309	,,	McKay, D. (Armourer)	11360	,,	Hollway, A. G.
			11361	,,	Harrington, E. J
11322	Private	Atkinson, W.	11362	,,	Hilborn, E.
11323	,,	Adams, A.	11363	,,	Houliston, W. J.
11324	,,	Atkins, R. A.	11364	,,	Hall, W.
11325	,,	Anthoney, R.	11414	,,	Harris, H.
11326	,,	Anderson, T.	11365	,,	Hamilton, R.
11327	,,	Baker, P.	11366	,,	Hamilton, A.
11328	,,	Braund, G. E.	11367	,,	Hawke, J.
11329	,,	Bull, J.	11368	,,	Hooper, E.
11330	,,	Bell, J.	11369	,,	Huggings, G.
11331	,,	Brimmer, C.	11370	,,	Houlding, H.
11332	,,	Burnham, G.	11316	,,	Jarvis, W. R.
11333	,,	Babcock, W.	11371	,,	Johnson, F. L.
11553	,,	Bancroft, M.	11372	,,	Jubber, G.
11334	,,	Blacker, W.	11373	,,	Johnson, A. J.
11335	,,	Barnes, A. J.	11374	,,	Keighley, W.
11336	,,	Bingham, W.	11375	,,	Keighley, J.
11337	,,	Bater, A.	11376	,,	Kinsella, C.
11338	,,	Burkhard, F.	11377	,,	Kenyon, C.
11315	,,	Baulcomb, E.	11378	,,	Kneill, S.
11339	,,	Cross, R.	11379	,,	Kerr, W.
11340	,,	Coppin, H.	11380	,,	Lahque, W. J.
11341	,,	Daddswell, C. H.	11381	,,	Lockyer, T.
11342	,,	Davis, H.	11382	,,	Lee, J.
11343	,,	Dumble, G.	11661	,,	Lee, T.
11344	,,	Dockray, J.	11383	,,	Lacey, E. H.
11345	,,	Duff, A.	11384	,,	Larin, N.
11314	,,	Dudden, C. G.	11385	,,	Mockford, G.
11346	,,	Ellis, F.	11386	,,	Massengale, F.
11347	,,	Edwards, E.	11387	,,	McLaren, J.
11348	,,	Forsyth, C.	11388	,,	Nuttycombe, A.
11349	,,	Fitzpatrick, A.	11389	,,	Pratt, J.
11350	,,	Freeman, H. E.	11390	,,	Prosser, W. H.
11351	,,	Fraser, A. D.	11391	,,	Phillips, L. W.
11318	,,	Grand, A.	11392	,,	Phipps, E.

Canadian Pacific—The Empire's Greatest Railway.

4TH BATTALION, 1ST INFANTRY BRIGADE—cont.

Regl. No.	Rank.	Name.	Regl. No.	Rank.	Name.
11393	Private	Powell, J.	11404	Private	Taylor, W.
11394	,,	Patterson, T.	11405	,,	Taylor, S.
11395	,,	Price, J.	11406	,,	Thompson, J.
11396	,,	Podd, T. H.	11310	,,	West, B.
11397	,,	Rose, T.	11319	,,	Westlake, H.
11398	,,	Ross, D.	11321	,,	Wakeling, A.
11311	,,	Smith, H.	11407	,,	Webb, T. D.
11312	,,	Stanley, J.	11408	,,	Westacott, F.
11320	,,	Stodden, C.	11409	,,	Williams, C. T.
11399	,,	Scanlon, J.	11410	,,	Walters, C. A.
11400	,,	Scott, J. F.	11411	,,	Wood, W. J.
11401	,,	Shaw, H.	11412	,,	Watson, H.
11402	,,	Small, P.	11413	,,	Wright, B.
11403	,,	Symington, W.	11415	,,	Wood, M. M.

"H" COMPANY.

Captain	...	...	...	Kelley, E. T.
Lieutenant	...	...	...	Reilly, J. R.
,,	...	...	...	Dent, F. S.
,,	...	...	...	Stirling, W. S.

Regl. No.	Rank.	Name.	Regl. No.	Rank.	Name.
11418	Sergt.	Watkins, G.	11459	Private	Bull, G.
11419	,,	McDonald, J.	11460	,,	Brooks, W.
11421	,,	Neville, T.	11461	,,	Clark, G.
11429	,,	Meek, R.	11438	,,	Chambers, J.
11428	,,	Rothery, F.	11462	,,	Connors, C.
11422	Corpl.	Young, C. G.	11463	,,	Coryn, H.
10849	Arm. Cpl.	Cunningham, J.	11464	,,	Carter, C.
11316	Corpl.	Garraty, H.	11465	,,	Crew, J.
10541	,,	Dibbin, W. E.	11466	,,	Curry, F.
11432	,,	Johnson, E.	11467	,,	Costello, P.
11443	Private	Aslin, T.	11468	,,	Christie, C.
11444	,,	Alexander, T.	11430	,,	Deveaux, H.
11445	,,	Arber, H.	11431	,,	Daley, J.
11446	,,	Anderson, F.	11440	,,	Dodd, C. F.
11447	,,	Armstrong, C.	11469	,,	Deans, D.
11424	,,	Bruce, Alex.	11470	,,	Davidson, R.
11448	,,	Burt, G.	11471	,,	Drew, C.
11449	,,	Bergstron, G.	11472	,,	Diver, A. E.
11434	,,	Brock, H. W.	11473	,,	Dunbar, J.
11450	,,	Barclay, C.	11474	,,	Denvir, J.
11451	,,	Boles, J. E.	11475	,,	Dobie, J.
11452	,,	Bromley, H.	11476	,,	Eagen, L.
11453	,,	Barker, W.	11531	,,	Fallowes, J. T. C.
11454	,,	Baker, F.	11477	,,	Fulcher, J.
11455	,,	Blake, J.	11478	,,	Flaherty, J.
11456	,,	Bentley, W.	11479	,,	French, F.
11457	,,	Bryan, J.	11480	,,	Falen, J. E.
11458	,,	Broome, A.	11441	,,	Godfrey, S.

Canadian Pacific—The Empire's Greatest Railway.

4TH BATTALION, 1ST INFANTRY BRIGADE—cont. 59

Regl. No.	Rank.	Name.	Regl. No.	Rank.	Name.
11481	Private	Gregorieff, J.	11503	Private	Middlemore, P.
11482	,,	Gregory, G.	11504	,,	Morrison, G.
11483	,,	Greene, W.	11506	,,	Miller, J.
11484	,,	Grant, E.	11529	,,	Milner, A.
11485	,,	Henry, F.	11534	,,	Morgan, T.
11486	,,	Hanlin, E.	11533	,,	McGinnes, W.
11487	,,	Hatt, J.	11508	,,	Nelson, T.
11488	,,	Harding, V.	11509	,,	Newman, T.
11489	,,	Hartnett, W.	11507	,,	Norman, T.
11490	,,	Harshaw, E.	11439	,,	O'Brien, J.
10768	,,	Howe, E.	11425	,,	Offord, S.
11491	,,	Hester, J.	11511	,,	Perry, A.
11492	,,	Hubbard, W.	11530	,,	Perry, C.
11527	,,	Hall, F. C.	11518	,,	Russell, J.
11535	,,	Headon, R. B.	11519	,,	Ryan, W.
11437	,,	Jones, H. J.	11520	,,	Reeves, A.
11493	,,	Kelly, P. J.	11528	,,	Russell, W.
11047	,,	Kelly, T.	11512	,,	Sterling, A.
11494	,,	Kerr, J.	11617	,,	Sullivan, J. F.
11495	,,	Kinsley, M.	11532	,,	Saunders, W.
11496	,,	Leahey, P. A.	11427	,,	Taylor, A.
11497	,,	Longstaff, T.	11513	,,	Trigg, C.
11435	,,	McDonald, T.	11515	,,	Thompson, J.
11603	,,	McFarlane, J. J.	11516	,,	Thompson, A.
11506	,,	McIntyre, E.	11517	,,	Vass, D.
11436	,,	Mack, J.	11521	,,	Wyss, A.
11423	,,	Moir, R.	11522	,,	Whybra, H.
11498	,,	Morgan, C.	11523	,,	Wilson, S.
11499	,,	Marchant, A.	11524	,,	Weaver, C.
11500	,,	Mallen, W. C.	11525	,,	Wilson, A.
11501	,,	Matheson, C.	11526	,,	White, A.
11502	,,	Minor, G.			

"BASE" COMPANY.

Captain ... ... Major H. Graham
Supernumerary ... ... ,, A. T. Hunter

Regl. No.	Rank.	Name.	Regl. No.	Rank.	Name.
11536	Col.-Sgt.	Wade, H.	11550	Private	Baskin, F.
11537	O.-R.Sgt.	Murrow, L. H.	11552	,,	Beals, W. T.
11540	Sergt.	Denton, H.	11555	,,	Bradford, S.
11541	Lce.-Sgt.	Woods, J. R.	11556	,,	Betts, W.
11542	Mr.Tailor	McGarvey, P.	11557	,,	Butts, W. A.
11543	Corpl.	Baker, W.	11558	,,	Barnard, C.
11544	,,	Evans, J.	11559	,,	Bayless, F.
11545	,,	Gibbard, C.	11560	,,	Brinkworth, F.
11546	,,	Jones, C.	10546	,,	Bain, W. E.
11539	,,	Dean, G.	11655	,,	Betts, F.
11547	Private	Amos, J.	11656	,,	Brough, W.
11549	,,	Anderson, G.	11657	,,	Blanchard, H.

Canadian Pacific—The Empire's Greatest Railway.

4TH BATTALION, 1ST INFANTRY BRIGADE—cont.

Regl. No.	Rank.	Name.	Regl. No.	Rank.	Name.
10627	Private	Barker, H.	11599	Private	McDonald, J. B.
11561	,,	Cuthbertson, W.	11600	,,	McAsklin, A.
11563	,,	Conlin, H. J.	11601	,,	McFarlane, W. W.
10566	,,	Dawson, W.	11602	,,	McFarlane, E. J.
11564	,,	Dewar, B.	11604	,,	Murphy, T. V.
11565	,,	Dickson, H.	11666	,,	Murphy, P.
11566	,,	Elliott, J.	10633	,,	Morgan, W.
11568	,,	Farndon, H.	10765	,,	Marment, W. H.
11569	,,	Foster, C. N.	11667	,,	Montgomery, F.
11570	,,	Free, J. F.	11606	,,	Norman, H.
11572	,,	Fecteau, A.	11607	,,	Pidd, J. H.
11573	,,	Fisher, H.	11608	,,	Phillips, T.
11574	,,	Ferguson, J. W.	11609	,,	Patterson, A.
10601	,,	Foord, R. J.	11610	,,	Revell, W. J.
11575	,,	Gibson, W.	11611	,,	Read, D.
10552	,,	Garrow, H. A.	11613	,,	Richardson, W.
11576	,,	Goodwin, L.	10769	,,	Richardson, W.
11577	,,	Gauntlett, H.	11614	,,	Roncliffe, C. H.
11578	,,	Garretty, H.	11615	,,	Robinson, J.
11579	,,	Gray, P.	11616	,,	Reid, J.
11580	,,	Hall, J. R.	11618	,,	Seymour, W. J.
11581	,,	Hare, W. J.	11620	,,	Sinclair, J.
11582	,,	Houston, G.	11621	,,	Sloat, N.
11583	,,	Humphries, C.	11623	,,	Skelton, E.
11584	,,	Hatch, A.	11624	,,	Stanley, G.
10549	,,	Hulme, W.	11625	,,	Teague, A. E.
11586	,,	Jones, T. J.	11626	,,	Thompson, G.
11587	,,	Jeffries, F. N.	11627	,,	Van Flett, H.
11588	,,	Knowles, T.	11628	,,	Weston, H.
11589	,,	Knowles, G.	11630	,,	Webb, G.
11591	,,	Lofting, E.	11632	,,	Wallison, E. H.
11592	,,	Lawton, W.	11634	,,	Wilson, W. H.
11595	,,	Lane, F.	11635	,,	Walker, A.
11596	,,	Lankey, C.	11636	,,	Wallace, E. P.
11597	,,	Linwood, J.	11637	,,	White, J.
11416	,,	McCartney, R.	11638	,,	Wright, A. B.
11506	,,	McIntyre, E. H.	11639	,,	Watham, T.
11598	,,	McCoy, G.	11640	,,	Yallop, H.

2nd INFANTRY BRIGADE (WESTERN CANADA).
HEADQUARTERS.

Lieut.-Colonel ... ... Currie, Arthur William
Major ... ... Kemmis Betty, Hubert
Captain ... ... Clark, Robert Percy
,, ... Foulkes, John Fortescue
,, ... Napier, Rob Ross
,, ... Greene, Murray Kirk
Lieutenant ... ... Colebourn, Harry

Canadian Pacific—The Empire's Greatest Railway.

HEADQUARTERS, 2ND INFANTRY BRIGADE—cont.

Regl. No.	Rank.	Name.	Regl. No.	Rank.	Name.
12001	Sgl.-Sgt.	Sprange, Arthur P.	12012	Private	Evans, Thomas
13153	Sergt.	Smith, Thomas Wm.	12013	,,	Barlow, Jn.Ronald T.
12002	,,	Pigou, Hen. La Trobe	12014	,,	Jackson, Daniel
12007	,,	Graham, Stuart M.	12015	,,	Auvache,Alfred Chas.
12004	,,	Gow, Walter John	12016	,,	Bryce, David Stewart
12023	Private	Belanger, J. H.	12022	,,	Stroud, Thomas
653	,,	Couture, G.	30289	Driver	Openshaw, William
12009	,,	Wilkes, John W. Hy.	30285	,,	McLaughlin,William
12008	,,	Waddy, Baruck A.	12019	Private	Hazel, John Thomas
12010	,,	Champion, Albert	12021	,,	Gosnell, Albert M.
12017	,,	Scobie, Stewart H.	30288	Driver	Oddie, William
12018	,,	Rhodes, Murray	30299	,,	Ring, E. E.
12011	,,	Wadman, Edwin T.	12020	Private	Martin, Albert

5th BATTALION, 2nd INFANTRY BRIGADE.

HEADQUARTERS.

Lieut.-Colonel	Tuxford, George Stuart
Major	Dyer, Hugh Marshall
,, ...	Morriss, George Gordon
Adjutant	Captain Edward Hilliam
Asst. Adjutant	Lieutenant William Tulloch Daniel
Machine Gun Officer ...	,, Guy Cyril de Dombasle
Signalling Officer ...	,, John Foster Paton Nash D S O
Quartermaster	,, William Cooley Ellis
Medical Officer	Major Ashron Sill Langrill
Paymaster	Hon. Captain Frederick Davy
Chaplain	,, ,, Bertram Loftus Whittaker
Transport Officer ...	Major Ernest Thornton

Regl. No.	Rank.	Name.	Regl. No.	Rank.	Name.
12601	B.S.-M.	Mackie, Alexander G.	12954	Q.M.Sgt.	Scott, John McIntyre
12807	O.-R.Sgt.	Bagshaw, Fredk. B.	12607	Sgt. Cook	Howlett, Arthur G.
12608	Sgt. Dmr.	Butterfield, Thomas	12610	Shoe Sgt.	Hall, Mark
12603	Arm. Sgt.	Bernard,AugusteC.J.	12635	Trans. Sgt.	Miller, Henry
12606	Pay Sgt.	Bolster,Hrbt.D'Alton	12609	Sgl. Sgt.	McNeil, William B.
12602	Q.M.Sgt.	Chatterton, George			

M.O. Orderlies.

12612	Lce.-Cpl.	Colwell, George Herbert
12613	Private	McLean, Donald Gladstone

Canadian Pacific—The Empire's Greatest Railway.

5TH BATTALION, 2ND INFANTRY BRIGADE—cont.

Transport Drivers.

Regl. No.	Rank.	Name.	Regl. No.	Rank.	Name.
12628	Private	Bonnell, Wm. Norman	12632	Private	Harrison, James Wm.
12631	,,	Barber, Frank	12639	,,	Hughes, Neville
12629	,,	Cobham, Hubert	12636	,,	Lynch, Geo. Stailing
12627	,,	Dennis, John Herbert	12637	,,	Parkin, Ben
12636	,,	Dean, John Frederick	12638	,,	Patterson, A.
12640	,,	Fisher, Osmond Edw.	12630	,,	Sullivan, Philip James
12633	,,	Glendinning, Thomas	12634	,,	Sparling, Edward

Batmen.

12620	Private	Boam, Frederick C.	12616	Private	Robertson, Frank Henry May
12621	,,	Davies, Francis H.			
12622	,,	Gill, Herbert	12618	,,	Saunders, Samuel
12617	,,	Grimes, Ernest	12615	,,	Thompson, Frederick
12992	,,	Honey, Frank Horace	12619	,,	Williams, Frank E.
12624	,,	Kearns, David Wright	12614	,,	Whitehorn, Mark

Machine Gun Section.

12665	Sergt.	Carter, Harry	12663	Private	Edgar, Stanley H.
12657	Corpl.	Stewart, Robt. McP.	12651	,,	Ford, Fredk Wm.
12662	Private	Bradley, John Francis	12652	,,	Harris, Fredk. Wm.
12655	,,	Bradley, Geo. Francis	12660	,,	Hart, Wm. Malloch
12659	,,	Currie, Alfred Cecil	12654	,,	Jenkins, Robt. H. C.
12661	,,	Cove, Thomas	12664	,,	Martin, Wm. Pryde
12656	,,	Cockerill, Ashton D.	12653	,,	Parker, John Thomas
12666	,,	Deane, Clifford	12667	,,	Rowan, William
12658	,,	De Laney, Ernest			

Signalling Staff.

12642	Private	Durkin, Hugh John	12645	Private	Pedley, James
12644	,,	Holmes, William M.	12646	,,	Sopp, Ernest John
12641	,,	Lingford, Reginald	12647	,,	Tosh, George Smith
12643	,,	Leonard, Percy O.	12648	,,	Wickham, N. Wyke

(Attached) Army Medical Corps.

33621	Corpl.	Lowery, Albert E.	33625	Private	Bulmer, Leonard C.
33624	Private	Atkinson, John Samuel	33622	,,	McIntyre, Donald
			33623	,,	Watson, C. V.

Canadian Pacific—The Empire's Greatest Railway.

5TH BATTALION, 2ND INFANTRY BRIGADE—*cont.* 63

"A" COMPANY.

Major	Tenaille, Daniel Jean
Captain	Candlish, John William
Lieutenant	Ravenhill, Edmund Lawrence Bartelot
„	Crossman, Alan Fairfax

Regl. No.	Rank.	Name.	Regl. No.	Rank.	Name.
12720	Col.-Sgt.	Hobday, Leonard S.	12707	Private	Forgie, John Robert
12697	Sergt.	Church, John William	12708	„	Fisher, Thomas
12731	„	McCuaig, Archibald	12709	„	Gilliard, John
12673	„	Bissett, Daniel A.	12710	„	Gerrand, Thomas
12706	Lce.-Sgt.	Dunbar, Henry	12711	„	Green, John
12712	Corpl.	Grant, John Nicholas	12713	„	Harrington, John
12686	„	Barfield, Henry	12715	„	Hesketh, John
12762	„	Sims, Frederick Geo.	12716	„	Hubert, Ronald
12714	„	Hunsley, Cyril	12717	„	Hulbert, Cyril K.
12698	„	Dyer, Wilfred Harry	12718	„	Hart, Percy
12785	Lce.-Cpl.	Woolven, George	12719	„	Harvey, Harold
12743	„	Prescott, William	12721	„	Hodgson, Edward
12751	„	Ross, James	12722	„	Kerr, Charles
12732	„	McAllister, George	12723	„	Knighton, Leo S.
12678	„	Brown, Charles R.	12724	„	Kirk, Thomas Peter
12747	„	Pearson, Wm. Ross	12725	„	Jones, Wm. Erskine
12671	Private	Adair, David	12726	„	Linaker, William
12672	„	Attenborough, John	12727	„	Logan, Walter James
12674	„	Burgess, William	12728	„	Mills, Albert William
12676	„	Berry, Walter	12729	„	Marshall, Jas. Henry
12677	„	Black, George Wm.	12730	„	Michaud, Alexander
12679	„	Brown, William	12733	„	McGregor, M. McA.
12680	„	Bateman, William A.	12734	„	McGregor, James
12681	„	Broad, Thomas	12735	„	McGlashan, Robert S.
12682	„	Brown, David Hugh	12736	„	McFeat, Edward G.
12683	„	Bierd, Victoria L.	12737	„	McQuarrie, Donald A.
12684	„	Belcher, Arthur	12738	„	McEwen, James
12685	„	Barclay, Harry M.	12739	„	Newton, Thomas
12687	„	Belanger, Fred.	12740	„	Ogilvie, Lancelot B.
12688	„	Bell, Andrew Robert	12741	„	Oliver, Geo. Johnston
12689	„	Bingham, Frank N.	12742	„	Pigg, William Lisle
12691	„	Constable, Ernest	12744	„	Payne, Ernest A. D.
12692	„	Coomb, Roy	12745	„	Pikes, William James
12693	„	Cameron, Archibald	12746	„	Pedersen, William
12694	„	Cameron, Walter	12748	„	Porteous, Robt. McL.
12695	„	Cumming, Wallace	12749	„	Pettifer, Charles
12696	„	Crockart, Jesse E.	12750	„	Ross, Alexander
12699	„	Duffin, Joseph Wm.	12752	„	Rosenberg, Harry W.
12700	„	Daynes, William	12753	„	Russell, Robert Evans
12701	„	Dingwall, Roderick	12754	„	Rea, Harvey
12702	„	Durham, James F.	12755	„	Rogan, John Felix
12703	„	Depever, Joseph	12756	„	Ramsay, Thomas
12704	„	Devaney, John	12757	„	Ramsay, William
12705	„	Dixon, Rydan	12758	„	Robins, Stephen Thos.

Canadian Pacific—The Empire's Greatest Railway.

64 5TH BATTALION, 2ND INFANTRY BRIGADE—cont.

Regl. No.	Rank.	Name.	Regl. No.	Rank.	Name.
12759	Private	Robinson, Robert	12774	Private	Thompson, Albert E.
12760	,,	Rutherford, John G.	12775	,,	Urquhart, Aldo
12763	,,	Sewell, Frank F.	12776	,,	Wall-Row, Rich. G.
12764	,,	Saunders, Stanley	12777	,,	Withers, PercyHenry
12765	,,	Smith, Andrew G.	12778	,,	Wilson, Robert F. S.
12766	,,	Stout, Chas. Elsworth	12779	,,	Walton, John William
12761	,,	Stuart, George	12780	,,	Waller, Richard R.
12767	,,	Sutherland, A. G.	12781	,,	Warren, Frederick
12768	,,	Sparling, Geo. Boyd	12782	,,	Wake, Henry James
12769	,,	Tierney, Jack	12783	,,	White, John Crooket
12770	,,	Taylor, Frank	12784	,,	Walwyn, Henry A.
12771	,,	Taylor, Berton	12786	,,	Watt, Alexander P.
12772	,,	Thorvaldson, Walter	12787	,,	Youngs, Herbert C.
12773	,,	Tuttle, Frank Lipsett			

"B" COMPANY.

Major	... ...	Edgar, Norman Samuel
Captain	... ...	Currie, James Maxwell
Lieutenant	... ...	Nicholl, Christopher Benoni
,,	... ...	Mundell, David

Regl. No.	Rank.	Name.	Regl. No.	Rank.	Name.
12802	Col.-Sgt.	Domaille, Thomas	12830	Private	Berry, George Henry
12804	Sergt.	Sculthorpe, George	12831	,,	Chalmers, Warner
12805	,,	Wright, Robert Wm.	12832	,,	Cowan, Hugh Stewart
12809	,,	Butler, John	12833	,,	Calder, John Robert
12810	,,	Adamson, Alfred	12834	,,	Connell, Richard F.
12806	Lce.-Sgt.	Cox, Sidney Henry	12835	,,	Craig, Daniel
12808	Corpl.	Campbell, William	12836	,,	Cullen, Edward
12813	,,	Bright, Oliver	12837	,,	Campbell, Roy
12849	,,	Hosie, Andrew John	12838	,,	Cameron, Charles
12900	,,	Smith, David Alpine	12839	,,	Chandler, Hardy
12811	Private	Abel, George	12840	,,	Chilton, Henry
12812	,,	Armstrong, Wm. John	12841	,,	Davis, Thos. Arthur
12814	,,	Barnes, John Ernest	12843	,,	Dedman, John
12815	,,	Bremner, James G.	12803	,,	Donnelly, Geo. Henry
12816	,,	Bell, William	12844	,,	Edwards, Wm. Jos.
12817	,,	Beale, Arthur Thos.	12845	,,	Edwards, Albert E.
12818	,,	Brooks, Wm. Henry	12846	,,	Earnshaw, Edward
12819	,,	Brown, Thomas	12847	,,	Forder, Ernest Geo.
12820	,,	Brasnett, John	12848	,,	Forstan, Andrew
12821	,,	Birrell, Morrison	12850	,,	Hamer, Roy
12822	,,	Bramley, Wm. Henry	12918	,,	Harding, Hy. Arthur
12823	,,	Bamfield, Percy	12851	,,	Holmden, George L.
12824	,,	Bell, Oliver Ewart	12852	,,	Hunter, Percy
12825	,,	Ballard, Arthur Hy.	12853	,,	Herrington, George
12826	,,	Brydges, Godfrey Ed.	12854	,,	Hailstone, Robert
12827	,,	Burns, Henry Robt.	12855	,,	Hawkes, Philip
12828	,,	Bannister, George S.	12856	,,	Hazeldine, Frederick
12829	,,	Boffin, Alfred Sidney	12857	,,	Hennessey, John H.

Canadian Pacific—The Empire's Greatest Railway.

5TH BATTALION, 2ND INFANTRY BRIGADE—cont. 65

Regl. No.	Rank.	Name.	Regl. No.	Rank.	Name.
12858	Private	Inall, Edward	12889	Private	Russell, John Findlay
12859	,,	Irvine, Nelson James	12890	,,	Rooke, Francis Hy.
12860	,,	Ireland, James Jos.	12891	,,	Reid, Alex.
12861	,,	Johnson, Chas. Hedley	12892	,,	Richard, Arthur W.
12862	,,	Johnson, Fredk. Wm.	12893	,,	Sasseville, Theodore
12863	,,	Jenkins, D. J. C.	12894	,,	Spicer, Angel C.
12864	,,	Jones, Wm. Edward	12895	,,	Swanston, Victor N.
12865	,,	Koss, Michael	12919	,,	Swanston, Ernest
12866	,,	Knop, Daniel	12896	,,	Smith, Albert
12867	,,	Lamb, Godfrey	12897	,,	Sampson, Frank C.
12868	,,	Lindsay, Arthur P.	12898	,,	Smallwood, Albert E.
12869	,,	Marshall, Frank Hy.	12899	,,	Smith, George Lacey
12870	,,	Miles, Richard	12901	,,	Smith, Rich. Chas.
12871	,,	Moore, Wm. John	12902	,,	Spencer, Frdk. Albert
12872	,,	McDougall, Jas. Wm.	12903	,,	Stroud, Rich. Sidney
12873	,,	McClinton, George	12904	,,	Shore, Richard
12874	,,	McCaig, John D.	12905	,,	Smart, Gerald Claud
12875	,,	McCormick, Alex.	12906	,,	Stutters, James
12876	,,	McPherson, George	12907	,,	Shane, John Harold
12877	,,	McKie, Jos. Mason	12908	,,	Stewart, Allan Carl
12878	,,	Osborne, Thos. Wm.	12909	,,	Tarzwell, Laurence
12880	,,	Ormiston, Douglas C.	12910	,,	Wicking, John
12881	,,	Price, Ernest	12911	,,	Woods, Samuel Geo.
12882	,,	Ptolemy, Archibald	12912	,,	Westerman, Walter
12883	,,	Patterson, Cyril	12913	,,	Williams, Richard
12884	,,	Pollard, Mark Smith	12914	,,	Watson, Alfred
12885	,,	Ramsay, Thomas	12915	,,	Willis, Roland Arthur
12886	,,	Robinson, Henry P.	12916	,,	Woods, Philip
12887	,,	Roberts, Geo. Ernest	12917	,,	West, Edward Albert
12888	,,	Reed, Ray Ralph	12801	,,	Wright, George

"C" COMPANY.

Major	... ...	Robson, Norman Lionel
Lieutenant	... ...	Graham, M. John
,,	... ...	Meikle, David
,,	... ...	Bellamy, George

Regl. No.	Rank.	Name.	Regl. No.	Rank.	Name.
12931	Col.-Sgt.	Adams, Walter	12942	Lce.-Cpl.	Campbell, William
12933	Sergt.	Savage, Chas. Edwd.	12944	,,	Russell, Hy. Norton
12934	,,	Strachan, Ernest F.	12945	,,	Dunlop, Albert
12935	,,	Brierley, William	12946	,,	Rowe, James
12936	,,	Hayden, Ernest	12947	,,	Price, Hendry James
12939	Corpl.	Berwick, Cyril	12960	Private	Aston, George
12940	,,	Cobham, Arthur	12961	,,	Allan, Albert
12941	,,	Wade, Herbert	12962	,,	Allan, Ernest Walter
13037	,,	Stockdale, Percy	12963	,,	Balmer, William

Canadian Pacific—The Empire's Greatest Railway.

5TH BATTALION, 2ND INFANTRY BRIGADE—cont.

Regl. No.	Rank.	Name.	Regl. No.	Rank.	Name.
12964	Private	Bradley, John	13003	Private	Lee, Norman R.
12965	,,	Bertram, George	12950	,,	Leckie, William
12966	,,	Blatchford, John	13004	,,	Lawrence, John
12967	,,	Bye, George	13005	,,	McDonald, Thos.Geo.
12623	,,	Berry, Walter	13006	,,	McCormack, Hugh
12952	,,	Bailey, Louis Monelle	13007	,,	McNair, Alex. McK.
12955	,,	Beasley, James Oliver	13008	,,	McKenzie, Rod.
12968	,,	Biggs, Ralph	13009	,,	McQuire, Harold
12969	,,	Betteley, Arthur	13010	,,	McKenzie, Duncan
12970	,,	Clark, Ben George	13011	,,	McMullen, William
12971	,,	Colby, James Glencoe	13022	,,	McGuire, Trevor
12943	,,	Cooper, Albert Geo.	13012	,,	Murrell, Edward
12972	,,	Copping, Noel	13013	,,	Mann, James
12932	,,	Cormack, Alexander	13014	,,	Morgan, Edgar
12973	,,	Currie, John	13015	,,	Morgan, Peter R.
12974	,,	Caswell, Stephen	13016	,,	Morrison, Fred John
12975	,,	Cameron, Harold	13017	,,	Morken, Axel C.
12976	,,	Carter, Harry John	13018	,,	Muldon, Joseph
12977	,,	Clark, Alexander	13019	,,	Marlin, Walter T.
12937	,,	Connelly, Patrick	13020	,,	Muir, John
12978	,,	Deadman, William	13021	,,	Meikle, Leon. W G.
12979	,,	Edward, Andrew	12948	,,	Morris, Frank
12980	,,	Emery, James	13023	,,	Nicholls, James
12981	,,	Forsaithe, Thos. Hy.	13024	,,	Norman, George
12983	,,	Fisher, Eric	13025	,,	Neale, Albert
12982	,,	Ford, Frank Horrace	13026	,,	Neale, Charles James
12949	,,	Graham, Charles	13027	,,	Offley, Arthur Joseph
12985	,,	Gibbs, Sidney	13028	,,	Olsen, Sigmund
12986	,,	Gark, Edward	13029	,,	Orr, Ralph
12987	,,	Green,AlbertKimbell	13030	,,	Peacy,John Campbell
12988	,,	Govenlock, Thos.Geo.	13031	,,	Proven, Hall
12989	,,	Gray, Andrew	13032	,,	Porter, Philip
12990	,,	Gabbe, Albert	13033	,,	Purcer, Fred
12991	,,	Hart, Dewitt	13034	,,	Proud, Lester
12959	,,	Hill, Albert Ernest	13035	,,	Ross, James
12956	,,	Heath, Norman	13036	,,	Seeley, Ruben V.
12993	,,	Henshaw, Robert	13038	,,	Smith, Frank Ernest
12994	,,	Humphries, S. Wm.	12951	,,	Stevenson, Wm. John
12995	,,	Holland, James	13039	,,	Statham, A.
12996	,,	Hiscock, Tom	13040	,,	Shaw, J.
12997	,,	Isabelle, Ulric	13041	,,	Smith, M. K.
12998	,,	Jones, Cyril Gordon	13042	,,	Taylor, Phillip
12999	,,	Jackson, Charles	13043	,,	Wylie, George Basil
13000	,,	Kerr, Robert	13044	,,	Weir,Wm.McNaught
13001	,,	Knott, Edward	13045	,,	Weir, Robert
12957	,,	Kelly, Michael	13046	,,	Wilson, Arnold
12953	,,	Lupton, William	13047	,,	Willis, William
12938	,,	Lawson, Wm. Hoy	13048	,,	Williams, Thomas G.
13002	,,	Lawson, William	12958	,,	Watson, Kenneth

Canadian Pacific—The Empire's Greatest Railway.

5TH BATTALION, 2ND INFANTRY BRIGADE—cont.

"D" COMPANY.

Captain ... ... Innes-Hopkins, James Randolph
Lieutenant ... ... Harbord, Hugh Walter
„ ... ... Graham, Wilson Mowbray
„ ... ... Simpson, John Hilliard

Regl. No.	Rank.	Name.	Regl. No.	Rank.	Name.
13062	Col.-Sgt.	Kapadia, Kenneth P.	13105	Private	Hayes, Victor
13063	Sergt.	Crawhall, Henry F.F.	13106	„	Hamilton, Cecil Alex.
13064	„	Campbell, K. L. T.	13107	„	Honey, Herbert A.
13065	„	Hines, Fred	13108	„	Johnson, Harry
13070	„	Britton, James Capell	13109	„	King, Joseph
13067	Corpl.	Haggart, Robt.	13110	„	Kelly, Michael Jos.
13068	„	Cuthbert, Charles	13111	„	Lancaster, Harold K.
13069	„	King, Stan. Murnane	13112	„	Libby, Jack John
13173	„	Wood, Colin M.	13113	„	Lorriman, Willie B.
13071	Lce.-Cpl.	Batchelor, Alf. A. E.	13114	„	Landon, Charles
13072	„	Hamilton, John D.	13115	„	Luton, John Alfred
13073	„	McGarry, Th. Moore	13116	„	Mitchell, Fred. T.
13074	„	Nuttall, Cyril Norman	13117	„	Mitchell, John
13075	„	Dunn, Fredk. Wm.	13118	„	Morgan, Cecil M.
13076	„	Hall, Sydney Grafton	13119	„	Morris, Jos. Cowell
13061	Private	Baty, Robert	13120	„	Matheson, Alexander
13077	„	Becks, Neil	13121	„	Murphy, Walter Jos.
13078	„	Baker, Wm. Alton	13122	„	Moore, John Wm.
13079	„	Barratt, William	13123	„	Mytton, Fredk. Jas.
13080	„	Baldwin, Harold	13124	„	Manville, Edward
13081	„	Bradley, Wm. Henry	13125	„	Murchison, George
13082	„	Brown, Laurie	13126	„	McDonald, Edward A.
13083	„	Batchelor, George	13127	„	MacLaren, Millard B.
13084	„	Bennett, Isaac Wm.	13128	„	Mead, Wm. Joseph
13085	„	Brown, James	13129	„	McBean, R. Murray
13086	„	Brown, Reginald H.	13130	„	Mewburn, Wm. Henry
13087	„	Burke, Jos. Wilfred	13131	„	Neish, Stephen
13088	„	Bolous, William	13132	„	Newton, Thomas
13089	„	Clement, William	13133	„	Pickup, Wm. Hayes
13090	„	Chapman, John	13134	„	Printy, Edward Geo.
13091	„	Copus, Cyrus Walter	13135	„	Powell, Wilfred Law.
13092	„	Cudden, Cyril Thos.	13136	„	Pilkington, Geo. Sam.
13093	„	Dempster, Andrew P.	13137	„	Pennic, John August
13094	„	Deltenre, John W. F.	13138	„	Richardson, James
13095	„	Davis, Stanley Hugh	13139	„	Riehl, John George
13096	„	Eaglen, Alfred Wm.	13140	„	Rooth, Everett M.
13097	„	Everest, Robt. Edgar	13141	„	Rooth, Richard Reg.
13098	„	Edwards, Roderick Willoughby Gore	13142	„	Reid, James Allan
			13143	„	Russell, Don Bernardo Parvish
13099	„	Flynn, Michael Jos.			
13100	„	Frey, Clyde	13144	„	Richards, Wm. James
13101	„	Fitzpatrick, C. John	13145	„	Slaughter, Gordon H.
13102	„	Ford, James	13146	„	Smith, Ernest E. S.
13103	„	Glazier, Fredk. Frank	13147	„	Schaen, Leopold
13104	„	Griffiths, Reg. Mantel	13148	„	Scott, Logan Morison

Canadian Pacific—The Empire's Greatest Railway.

5TH BATTALION, 2ND INFANTRY BRIGADE—cont.

Regl. No.	Rank.	Name.	Regl. No.	Rank.	Name.
13149	Private	Sharples, John	13163	Private	Thompson, Fdk. Hen.
13150	,,	Shields, Hugh C.	13164	,,	Trowsdale, Robt. Wm.
13151	,,	Small, H. Lamerk	13165	,,	Victorian, Louis
13152	,,	Smith, Eric Bowen	13166	,,	Wallworth, John T.
13153	,,	Smith, Thomas Wm.	13167	,,	Wheatley, Jas. Edwd.
13154	,,	Stark, Frank Emerson	13168	,,	Watkin, Jack
13155	,,	Skerry, William	13169	,,	Welbelove, Geo. Robt.
13156	,,	Sandiford, Bert. E.	13170	,,	Wheldon, Fredk. Geo.
13157	,,	Scott, William	13171	,,	Walters, Edwd. Jas.
13158	,,	Thomas, Henry J.	13172	,,	Weir, John Olpherts
13159	,,	Torrance, Gordon D.	13174	,,	Wright, Cecil Medwyn
13066	,,	Tong, Richard	13175	,,	Welsh, John Hans
13160	,,	Tawn, John Richard	13176	,,	Wilson, Alexander
13161	,,	Tompkins, Wm. Hen.	13177	,,	Yeates, Charles
13162	,,	Tapp, Chas. Edmund			

"E" COMPANY.

Captain	... ...	Endacott, George Marshall
Lieutenant	... ...	Morgan, Ernest Stephen
,,	... ...	Tozer, Dugald Hamilton Adair
,,	... ...	Hill, Richard Francis Leigh

Regl. No.	Rank.	Name.	Regl. No.	Rank.	Name.
13191	Col.-Sgt.	Davies, Edwd. Buxton	13224	Private	Cranston, William
13192	Sergt.	Bowie, Geo. Pigrum	13225	,,	Cameron, Thomas
13193	,,	Colman, Geo. Alex.	13227	,,	Derbyshire, Alfred
13194	,,	Purslow, John Edw.	13228	,,	Dunne, Willoughby
13195	,,	Burgess, Albert Edw.	13229	,,	De Villiers, Corn. E.
13197	Lce.-Sgt.	McLellan, Wm. Watt	13230	,,	Eaton, Kenneth
13198	Corpl.	Horner, Harold Jas.	13231	,,	Flunder, Ralph Dan.
13199	,,	Bailey, Chris. Thos.	13232	,,	Flood, George
13200	,,	McGlashan, James S.	13205	,,	George, Douglas
13245	Lce.-Cpl.	Hunter, William J.	13209	,,	Geraty, Robert Jas.
13218	,,	Brecknell, Ernest R.	13233	,,	Groom, Ernest H.
13236	,,	Goos, Henry	13234	,,	Greer, Harry
13281	,,	Sheffield, Robt. Wm.	13235	,,	Graham, William N.
13207	,,	Hargreaves, Edwd. J.	13237	,,	Gibson, Chas. Thos.
13210	,,	Ogilvie, Thomas	13238	,,	Griffiths, Frank Wm.
13216	Private	Aspee, Wm. Stanley	13239	,,	Hemming, Leonard
13217	,,	Arnaud, August	13240	,,	Hughes, John James
13215	,,	Anderson, Andrew	13241	,,	Hanley, Clarence R.
13307	,,	Bailey, Benj. Bernard	13242	,,	Heaton, Noah
13219	,,	Bain, Forest	13243	,,	Harrison, Ernest
13220	,,	Bone, Andrew	13244	,,	Halstead, Henry
13196	,,	Bolton, Albert Hy.	13246	,,	Hayward, John
13213	,,	Cowan, James	13247	,,	Hawkins, Albert
13221	,,	Cross, David	13248	,,	Hawkins, Jesse
13222	,,	Craig, Robert	13249	,,	Johnson, Thomas P.
13223	,,	Clark, Aston A. B. M.	13250	,,	Joslyn, Edmund B.
13201	,,	Clark, George	13251	,,	King, William

Canadian Pacific—The Empire's Greatest Railway.

5TH BATTALION, 2ND INFANTRY BRIGADE—cont.

Regl. No.	Rank.	Name.	Regl. No.	Rank.	Name.
13753	Private	Keen, Cedrick M.	13276	Private	Sutherland, Herbt. P.
13304	,,	Lane, Victor John	13277	,,	Seaman, John Chas. S.
13214	,,	Lawrence, George	13278	,,	Shakes, Valentine
13252	,,	Linklater, James M.	13279	,,	Sawyer, Darwin
13253	,,	Lewendon, Edwd. V.	13280	,,	Smallwood, William
13254	,,	Lamont, John	13282	,,	Sutton, Hal
13206	,,	Miller, Wm. Murray	13283	,,	Steele, Thomas
13255	,,	Morrow, Arthur M.	13284	,,	Scott, Frederick Geo.
13256	,,	Morton, George	13285	,,	Smith, Edwin Francis
13257	,,	Mitchell, John	13286	,,	Sandieson, George
13258	,,	Morris, Thos. Arthur	13287	,,	Stowell, James
13259	,,	Murphy, Robert	13211	,,	Smith, Henry Edw.
13208	,,	McLennan, Jas. Roy	13306	,,	Simpson, Thomas N.
13212	,,	Macdonald, John	13288	,,	Tolhurst, John Thos.
13260	,,	McLaughlin, Duncan	13289	,,	Thomson, William
13261	,,	MacWilliam, Wm. A.	13290	,,	Unsworth, Ernest
13262	,,	McKenzie, William	13291	,,	Van Mill, Sander Jan
13263	,,	McLennan, John H.	13292	,,	Van Allen, Wm. H.
13264	,,	McIntosh, James	13293	,,	Valder, Percy
13265	,,	McDonald, John Wm.	13294	,,	Veale, Edward John
13266	,,	McCallum, Frank	13204	,,	White, George Avery
13267	,,	McLean, Currie Roy	13295	,,	Wilvert, Herbert N.
13268	,,	O'Donnell, Peter	13296	,,	Walmsley, James H.
13269	,,	Olsen, George Hans	13297	,,	Walker, George
13203	,,	Pontifex, Robert	13298	,,	Wright, William
13270	,,	Paquette, Eugene	13299	,,	Waters, Wm. McD.
13271	,,	Preston, Eric	13300	,,	Watret, Robert
13202	,,	Ross, Edward	13301	,,	Wallace, Clarence
13272	,,	Rolfe, Fred	13305	,,	White, Leslie
13273	,,	Reardon, Joseph	13302	,,	Young, James
13274	,,	Reid, John	13303	,,	Younie, John
13275	,,	Ramsay, Thomas M.			

"F" COMPANY.

Captain	... ...	Allen, Reginald Arthur Sinclair
,,	... ...	Davies, Frederick Macgregor
Lieutenant	... ...	Baker, James Phillip
,,	... ...	Fitzpatrick, Wilfred

Regl. No.	Rank.	Name.	Regl. No.	Rank.	Name.
13321	Col.-Sgt.	Gook, Ernest John	13432	Lce.-Cpl.	Perry, Clifford Ernest
13352	Sergt.	McKay, Alexander	13395	,,	McLocklan, Stan. R.
13406	,,	Morton, John	13385	,,	Devine, Patrick
13322	,,	Mackenzie, John	13328	,,	Clarke, Leopold
13380	Lce.-Sgt.	Coles, William	13370	,,	Ogilvie, Edgar
13341	Corpl.	McGee, John	13354	Private	Archibald, George
13353	,,	Baugh, John Henry	13355	,,	Ascott, Herbert
13381	,,	Kelly, Thomas	13324	,,	Anderson, Alexander
13407	,,	Wilkinson, Frank	13408	,,	Adamthwaite, Albert

Canadian Pacific—The Empire's Greatest Railway.

5TH BATTALION, 2ND INFANTRY BRIGADE—cont.

Regl. No.	Rank.	Name.	Regl. No.	Rank.	Name.
13325	Private	Beames, Thos. Hy.	13391	Private	Lyons, Thomas
13326	,,	Baugh, Joseph	13337	,,	Lindsay, Norman
13410	,,	Baker, Fred	13368	,,	Lemberg, Chrstphr.
12604	,,	Brierley, John	13390	,,	Lavin, Herbert
13383	,,	Bryce, William	13338	,,	Leishman, John
13327	,,	Birch, John	13340	,,	Macadams, Edward
13356	,,	Boyer, Fred William	13424	,,	Madren, George
13409	,,	Bowditch, Alf. Geo.	13425	,,	Mitchell, Adam
13411	,,	Belbin, Christopher	13396	,,	Milton, Law. Knight
13378	,,	Biro, Francis	13426	,,	McNaughton, W. K.
13412	,,	Cooke, Fred Walter	13369	,,	Macdonald, Anthony
13382	,,	Colbert, Fred	13339	,,	Macleod, Murdock
13384	,,	Conder, Wm. Joseph	13393	,,	Montgomery, Walter
13329	,,	Carlyle, Sydney	13427	,,	Moss, Chas. Clifford
13330	,,	Collison, Leonard	13394	,,	Moir, John
13357	,,	Cowell, James Done	13342	,,	Murray, William
13331	,,	Couper, Robt.	13428	,,	Newman, Peter
13359	,,	Daly, Denis	13397	,,	Norrie, Robert McK.
13358	,,	Desrosier, Joseph	13398	,,	Nelson, James Alex.
13360	,,	Davidson, Robert	13429	,,	Oliver, William
13323	,,	Dell, Robert	13430	,,	O'Halloran, Robert
13413	,,	Dowdle, John Thos.	13399	,,	O'Connor, Daniel B.
13414	,,	De la Gorgondiere, Robt. Hugh	13431	,,	Peel, Wm. Alexander
			13371	,,	Phillips, Robert
13361	,,	Drybrough, John	13433	,,	Polhill, Walter
13332	,,	Elkington, John	13372	,,	Pericho, Philip
13362	,,	Eagles, William	13343	,,	Rogers, Percy
13386	,,	Elms, Chas. Ed.	13344	,,	Robertson, Frederick
13415	,,	Eassie, Robt. McG.	13400	,,	Reilly, John Fredk.
13416	,,	Friedleben, Eric D.	13434	,,	Ross, William
13363	,,	Figgis, Herbert Art.	13345	,,	Shearer, Daniel
13417	,,	Freeman, Jos. Wm.	13373	,,	Scrim, Cecil Edward
13418	,,	Foulkes, Robt. Gerald	13346	,,	Smith, Robert
13364	,,	Gilborn, William	13404	,,	Trowell, Wm. Albert
13366	,,	Gordon, Wm. Thos.	13435	,,	Tomlinson, William
13419	,,	Goff, Frederick	13374	,,	Tomisch, Willie
13365	,,	Gillies, John James	13401	,,	Thomson, Alexander
13333	,,	Hamilton, Eric	13347	,,	Tyler, Bernard
13420	,,	Hick, Herbert	13348	,,	Thomson, John
13387	,,	Higham, John Wm.	13436	,,	Templeman, John H.
13367	,,	Horton, Raymond	13349	,,	Tunstall, Frederick
13421	,,	Holder, Geo. Henry	13377	,,	Tomkins, Henry Jas.
13388	,,	Haldane, John	13402	,,	Timbers, John Jos.
13422	,,	Heggie, George	13403	,,	Train, Wm. Austin
13334	,,	Hatton, Arthur	13375	,,	Williams, Robert J.
13335	,,	James, Arthur	13437	,,	White, Lawrence
13423	,,	Kelly, Peter	13405	,,	Wallace, Sam. Hy.
13389	,,	Kelly, Herbert Hy.	13376	,,	Wells, Albert John
13392	,,	Lamb, Cyrus Colby	13350	,,	Woods, Edward
13336	,,	Lewis, Herbert	13351	,,	Webster, Chas. Wm.

Canadian Pacific—The Empire's Greatest Railway.

5TH BATTALION, 2ND INFANTRY BRIGADE—cont.

"G" COMPANY.

Major	... ...	Pragnell, George Seabrook Thomas Joseph
Lieutenant	... ...	King-Wason, Charles George Dalegarth
,,	... ...	Tudor, Lorn Paulet Owen
,,	... ...	Ford, George Mereweather

Regl. No.	Rank.	Name.	Regl. No.	Rank.	Name.
13451	Col.-Sgt.	Brett, Thos. Alfred	13464	Private	Gordon, Cuthbert
13452	Sergt.	Daunt, Acton O'Neill	13500	,,	Gould, Robt. Edward
13453	,,	Higginbotham, Tim.	13499	,,	Gould, Arthur Fredk.
13454	,,	Blair, Robert	13501	,,	Grbich, Samuel
13455	,,	Quinan, Barrington C.	13502	,,	Haggerty, Wm. Ptrk.
13456	Lce.-Sgt.	Patton, Austin	13503	,,	Haig, Kenneth
13457	Corpl.	Keyt, Warren E.	13504	,,	Hardy, Joseph Thos.
13458	,,	McCombie, Joseph	13505	,,	Hines, Fredrick
13459	,,	Greenhalgh, B. Wm.	13506	,,	Hocking, Wm. John
13460	,,	Christie, George John	13507	,,	Hulbert, Harold John
13463	Lce.-Cpl.	Calder, George	13508	,,	Holland, PercyEdwd.
13462	,,	Kinch, Albert	13509	,,	Haydon, Charles
13461	,,	Craig, David Clark	13510	,,	Henderson, James
13465	,,	MacMahon, Ern. Ed.	13511	,,	Holloway, Alexander
13466	Private	Ammodeo, Regnld. B.	13512	,,	Jobin, Geo. Stafford
13467	,,	Anderson, Thomas	13513	,,	Keating, Patrick
13468	,,	Bailey, John Henry	13514	,,	Kennedy, Daniel
13469	,,	Brown, Wm. Whitla	13515	,,	Kinney, Thomas R.
13470	,,	Banner, Leslie	13516	,,	Kyle, William Chas.
13471	,,	Carter, George Wm.	13517	,,	Lawrence, Thos.H.K.
13472	,,	Crewe, James	13518	,,	Leach, Onebye Robt.
13473	,,	Campbell, Alexander	13519	,,	Loney, Morris F.
13474	,,	Campbell, Clifford	13520	,,	Long, George G. G.
13475	,,	Charles, George	13521	,,	Lund, SataisSebastian
13476	,,	Clarke, Frank Reeves	13522	,,	Macaulay, Malcolm
13478	,,	Coles, Frederick Jas.	13523	,,	Maggs, Fredk. Wm.
13477	,,	Clough, Bertram G.	13524	,,	McCully, Charles
13479	,,	Crawford, John Alex.	13527	,,	McLeod, Donald
13480	,,	Capps, James	13528	,,	McIntyre, WilliamW.
13481	,,	Daly, Wm. Osmond	13529	,,	McPherson, Hector
13483	,,	Dennison, Joseph	13530	,,	Melvin, James
13484	,,	Dentry, Wm. John	13531	,,	Monck, R. McIntyre
13485	,,	Dignis, John	13532	,,	Murray, Thos. Ernest
13486	,,	Dyer, John	13533	,,	Myers, Rowley B.
13487	,,	Devine, Michael John	13525	,,	McDonald, HaroldJoe
13488	,,	Eamer, Roy	13526	,,	McKay, Jas. Clifford
13489	,,	Edmonds, Thos. Peter	13534	,,	Nickisch, Otto Geo.
13490	,,	Edmondstone, A.R.B.	13536	,,	Newton, Joseph
13491	,,	Elliott, James Percy	13537	,,	Osipa, Andrew Anton
13492	,,	Ewens, George Basil	13538	,,	Parker, Arthur Wm.
13494	,,	Ellis, Wm. Arthur	13539	,,	Paskins, Fredk. Wm.
13495	,,	Foyle, Westrupp E.	13540	,,	Randall, James
13496	,,	Frechette, Fredrik	13541	,,	Reid, John Simpson
13497	,,	Grant, Ian Thorold	13542	,,	Robinson, Harry
13498	,,	Goodman, FrankEdw.	13543	,,	Rae, James Rennie

Canadian Pacific—The Empire's Greatest Railway.

5TH BATTALION, 2ND INFANTRY BRIGADE—cont.

Regl. No.	Rank.	Name.	Regl. No.	Rank.	Name.
13544	Private	Scammel, Frederick	13556	Private	Savonas, Frank
13545	,,	Sinclair, David S.	13557	,,	Trute, Arthur
13546	,,	Shiers, Frank	13558	,,	Tully, John William
13547	,,	Slaughter, Jacob Wm.	13559	,,	Tracey, Royaldana
13548	,,	Smith, Alec	13560	,,	Tedford, James
13550	,,	Snodgrass, William	13561	,,	Veale, Robert
13551	,,	Stewart, Douglas	13563	,,	Walker, Reginald
13549	,,	Smith, Stanley Craig	13564	,,	Webb, Harry
13552	,,	Straughan, Robert J.	13565	,,	Wewang, Peter
13553	,,	Stoems, Ottawa M.	13566	,,	West, William
13554	,,	Sarff, Curtis	13567	,,	Young, James
13555	,,	Shackell, Stanley S.	13568	,,	Young, John

"H" COMPANY

Major ... ... Sandeman, David Richardson
Captain ... ... Fiske, Robert Walter
Lieutenant ... ... Page, Lionel Frank
,, ... Humphreys, William Rowland Spottiswoode

Regl. No.	Rank.	Name.	Regl. No.	Rank.	Name.
13581	Col.-Sgt.	Siborne, Wm. Herbert	13609	Private	Bowyer, Jn. Higgins
13582	Sergt.	Reid, William Chas.	13610	,,	Broom, Edward
13583	,,	Dickens, Art. Herbert	13612	,,	Bromley, Clement M.
13584	,,	Yates, Goodman	13611	,,	Braidwood, David F.
13586	Lce.-Sgt.	Richmond, Edwd. C.	13613	,,	Broughton, Colin R.
13587	Corpl.	Hayward, Sidney John	13614	,,	Brown, Archibald H.
13588	,,	Warlow, Edm. J. L.	13615	,,	Burrington, Harley
13589	,,	Ryan, Daniel	13616	,,	Bryant, William
13590	,,	Ritson, Frederic W.	13617	,,	Charlton, Thomas
13585	,,	Eades, William	13618	,,	Chivers-Wilson, V.
13591	Lce.-Cpl.	Sugg, Victor Alex.	13619	,,	Clark, Edward
13592	,,	McDougall, John	13620	,,	Clark, Sidney
13593	,,	Wilkins, Henry	13621	,,	Conant, Sidney Orrin
13594	,,	Bothamley, Wm. B.	13622	,,	Cottrell, Free Henry
13595	,,	Fiske, Norman	13623	,,	Currie, Allan Rae
13596	,,	Wilcox, John Price	13624	,,	Currie, Robt. Thos.
13597	Bugler	Gore, John Henry	13625	,,	Dilworth, Norman W.
13598	Private	Abernethy, James	13626	,,	Dickson, James
13599	,,	Alcock, Raymond W.	13627	,,	Eby, Alexander
13600	,,	Agar, Daniel	13628	,,	Everett, William
13601	,,	Alexander, Oscar M.	13629	,,	Forcer, David Richd.
13602	,,	Anderson, Enar Chas.	13630	,,	Forrest, John Walter
13603	,,	Archambault, W. E.	13631	,,	Fyfe, John Roy
13604	,,	Baldwin, Andrew C.	13632	,,	Gerry, Albert John
13605	,,	Beatson, Walter Ross	13633	,,	Giles, Edward
13606	,,	Becker, Clifton John	13634	,,	Gill, Arthur William
13607	,,	Bowles, Augustine	13635	,,	Goodman, Carl H.
13608	,,	Blake, George Lionel	13636	,,	Gordon, William

Canadian Pacific—The Empire's Greatest Railway.

5TH BATTALION, 2ND INFANTRY BRIGADE—cont.

Regl. No.	Rank.	Name.	Regl. No.	Rank.	Name.
13637	Private	Green, Charles	13668	Private	Muir, John Hugh
13638	,,	Greenhalgh, James	13669	,,	Mullarney, George
13639	,,	Hamilton, Wm. C.	13670	,,	Noiles, Joseph Albun
13640	,,	Hanson, Arthur M.	13671	,,	Payne, Edgar
13641	,,	Hardy, Chas. Clarence	13672	,,	Passenger, Jn. Wm.
13642	,,	Hayward, Theo. C.	13673	,,	Patterson, Leonard
13643	,,	Henderson, Andrew	13674	,,	Purdy, Walter
13644	,,	Henderson, John B.	13675	,,	Rebbeck, Arthur P.
13645	,,	Herity, Frederick	13676	,,	Robson, Norman
13646	,,	Hinds, Roydin A.	13677	,,	Robertson, Joseph
13647	,,	Hillier, Robt. Edwd.	13678	,,	Roscoe, Albert Edwd.
13648	,,	Hollman, George	13679	,,	Ross, Francis John L.
13649	,,	Hughes, Leslie B.	13680	,,	Rush, Harlan Victor
13650	,,	James, Thomas	13681	,,	Scott, Albt. Halroyde
13651	,,	Jones, Wm. Paul	13682	,,	Scott, William Edgar
13652	,,	Kenney, Charles G.	13683	,,	Sharp, Wm. Albert
13653	,,	King, Chas. Harold	13684	,,	Shrimpton, Percy Jn.
13654	,,	Kievill, George Roy	13685	,,	Simmonds, Wm. Edw.
13655	,,	Knight, Osbert R.	13686	,,	Smith, Geo. Lauder.
13656	,,	Lewis, Ernest Wm.	13687	,,	Smithies, Jos. Barton
13657	,,	Litchfield, Oscar Wm.	13688	,,	Thomson, Adam
13658	,,	Mallory, William	13689	,,	Todd, Arthur Ernest
13659	,,	Matthews, Charles A.	13690	,,	Trumble, Frank O.
13660	,,	Masson, John	13691	,,	Wightwick, H. M.
13661	,,	McLaren, Wilmer G.	13692	,,	Whitelock, Thomas
13662	,,	Melville, Oliver R.	13693	,,	White, Alexander
13663	,,	McKenzie, John	13694	,,	Woodhall, George
13664	,,	McKenzie, Walter	13695	,,	Wright, Clark
13665	,,	McTavish, John	13696	,,	Young, Alf. Severn
13666	,,	Moore, Wm. James	13697	,,	Young, Norris Arthr.
13667	,,	Morley, Frederick E.			

BASE COMPANY.

Major ... ... Pawlett, Francis

Regl. No.	Rank.	Name.	Regl. No.	Rank.	Name.
13758	Col.-Sgt.	Latter, Ernest Henry	13712	Private	Atkins, Percy Tapling
13751	Sergt.	Jenkins, Thomas	13713	,,	Archibald, Leon
13783	,,	McIvor, Daniel	13715	,,	Baimbridge, James
12003	,,	McMahon, Robt. D.E.	13717	,,	Buchanan, John
13714	,,	Adams, Frederick	13718	,,	Bacon, Reuben Jas.
13818	Thr.-Sgt.	McKay, Alexander	13719	,,	Brown, Harold
13750	O.R.-Sgt.	Hammond, Eric Art.	13720	,,	Breidfjord, M. A. S.
13816	Lce.-Sgt.	Welch, Wm. Richard	13721	,,	Cowan, Neil Martin
13782	Corpl.	Morrison, Murdoch	13722	,,	Cowell, Norman M.
13784	,,	Nicol, David	13723	,,	Cursons, James
13796	,,	Ross, Andrew	13724	,,	Chivers-Wilson, Art.
13756	Lce.-Cpl.	King, Edward			Augs. Ewart Robt.
13711	Private	Andrew, Robert	13725	,,	Crawford, Alexander

Canadian Pacific—The Empire's Greatest Railway.

5TH BATTALION, 2ND INFANTRY BRIGADE—cont.

Regl. No.	Rank.	Name.	Regl. No.	Rank.	Name.
13726	Private	Christopherson, R. L.	13771	Private	Miller, George M. D.
13727	,,	De la Gorgendiere, Regis Fran. Fleurey	13773	,,	Miller, Nick
			13774	,,	Manson, Alexander
13728	,,	Davidson, Alb. Leslie	13775	,,	Manson, Benjamin
13729	,,	Douglas, Frank Chas.	13776	,,	Markle, Arthur A.
13730	,,	Drury-Lowe, Laurnce	13777	,,	Murray, Thomas
13732	,,	Diamond, Henry Wm.	13778	,,	Mullins, Albin Ferris
13733	,,	Eyre, Vincent	13779	,,	Murray, Allen
13734	,,	Ellis, Gordon	13780	,,	Morrison, Angus
13735	,,	Fox, Arthur Alfred	13781	,,	Mills, Maurice
13736	,,	Ferguson, Alexander	13785	,,	Nicholson, Angus
13737	,,	Freeman, Albert Ed.	13786	,,	Naylor, James
13738	,,	Field, John Wesley	13787	,,	Oke, Richard Guy
13739	,,	French, Francis Jas.	13788	,,	Pearpoint, H. F. C.
13740	,,	Fryer, Norman Moody	13789	,,	Purvis, James
13741	,,	Gill, Thomas	13790	,,	Purvis, Harold Wm.
13742	,,	Graves, Albt. Edwd.	13791	,,	Paterson, Archibld. L.
13743	,,	Hayward, John	13792	,,	Quarterman, Reg.
13744	,,	Honey, George Thos.	13793	,,	Quarterman, Alfred
13745	,,	Hartley, Edward H.	13794	,,	Rayner, Albert Edwd.
13746	,,	Hunter, Alexander	13795	,,	Robinson, Thos. Edw.
13747	,,	Harper, Geo. Buchan	13797	,,	Sentance, Richard E.
13748	,,	Hing, Horace	13798	,,	Saint, Wm. Douglas
13749	,,	Hammon, Edward	13799	,,	Sigurdson, C. G.
13752	,,	Jones, Wm. Leslie	13800	,,	Street, Harry A. L.
13754	,,	Kellett, Frank	13801	,,	Sinclair, Alexander G.
13755	,,	Kitteringham, Alfred Michael Kent	13802	,,	Sargent, Percy Jas.
			13803	,,	Stone, Walter
13757	,,	Livingstone, Herbert	13804	,,	Stade, Henry George
13759	,,	Mundle, Ernest R.	13805	,,	Spencer, Frank
13760	,,	McIvor, Neil	13806	,,	Torgerson, Carl M.
13761	,,	McIvor, Roderick	13807	,,	Throop, Clinton W.
13762	,,	McIvor, John	13808	,,	Turner, Bertram C.
13763	,,	McDonald Peter Geo.	13809	,,	Virtue, Robert Alex.
13764	,,	McDonald, Norman	13810	,,	Wilson, Howard Jas.
13765	,,	McMillan, Malcolm	13811	,,	Warren, Lindsay G.
13766	,,	McMillan, Alexander	13812	,,	Wynn, Josh. Withrow
13767	,,	McEwen, Alexander	13813	,,	Waters, William
13768	,,	Maidstone, George	13814	,,	Wade, Samuel
13769	,,	Markham, Horace C.	13815	,,	Whitfield, Fred. Jas.
13770	,,	Miller, Alexander	13817	,,	Young, Percy

Canadian Pacific—The Empire's Greatest Railway.

6th BATTALION, 2nd INFANTRY BRIGADE.
(FORT GARRYS.)
HEADQUARTERS.

Officer Commanding	Lieut.-Colonel Robert Walter Paterson
Second in Command	Major Frederick James Dingwall
Third in Command	„ Duncan Gordon Macpherson
Adjutant	Captain Edwin Maurice Fisher
Asst. Adjutant (Acting)	Lieutenant Angus Purkis Cameron
Machine Gun Officer	Prov. Lieut. Eugene Harvey Houghton
Signalling Officer	Lieutenant Hugh Ronald Selfe
Transport Officer	„ Graham Anderson Watson
Paymaster	Hon. Captain Henry Gordon Watson
Medical Officer	Captain Herbert Ernest Cummings
Quartermaster	Hon. Lieutenant Samuel L. Bedson
Chaplain	Hon. Captain Geo. Anderson Wells

Regl. No.	Rank.	Name.	Regl. No.	Rank.	Name.
14428	Sgt.-Maj.	Blaydon, R. Avey	14457	Private	Masse, David
14720	Q.M.S.	Hollingsworth, Wm.	14422	„	Richardson, E. A.
14419	Pay-Sgt.	Goodday, Norman	14426	„	Stagg, L. Thomas
14409	Sign.Sgt.	Miller, Robert Dane	14444	„	Smith, Alfred Percy
14429	Sgt.Bgl.	Dibnah, Ewart G.	14412	„	Walsh, George
14430	Pion. Sgt.	Scotland, A. Duncan	14435	„	Warren, George F.
14431	Arm. Sgt.	Burrows, Frank	14438	„	Wills, James
14432	Shoe Sgt.	Bella, J. Marshall	15579	„	Gough, Henry
14433	Cook Sgt.	Adams John James	14470	„	Carther, Wesley
14416	Sergt.	Munro, J. Robert	14471	„	Cooke, Walter E.
14441	Corpl.	Peters, Frank Ray	14475	„	Cosby, Norman W.
14462	„	Johnstone, Ralph E.	15350	„	Comstock, George
14423	Lce.-Cpl.	Ellis, Malcolm E.	14468	„	Evans, Albert E. A.
14421	„	McNally, Ernest	14472	„	Fleming, A. G. S.
14434	Private	Botterill, Frank	14463	„	Graham, R. Harold
14411	„	Duncan, R. Gowans	14474	„	Gilmour, Adam H.
14424	„	Findlay, A. Ogilvie	14466	„	Jackson, Geofrey B.
14425	„	Findlay, Stewart	14464	„	Macdonald, Neil R.
14436	„	Grant, James	14467	„	Macnab, James
14437	„	Lanigan, Joseph	14469	„	Morrow, Rupert G.
14414	„	Morrison, James D.	14465	„	Phinney, Henry H.
15578	„	Marwood, A. Joseph	14473	„	Sigg, C. Sidney
14427	„	McAvoy, M. Patrick	15186	„	Tassie, Harry
14440	„	McAlister, W. W.	15572	„	Leonard, Harry

Transport Section.

14443	Trans. Sgt.	Davis, John Austin	14446	Private	Bryan, William
14410	Sign. Cpl.	Frye, Harry	15538	„	Dunn, R. T.
14445	Private	Atcherly, Charles H.	14447	„	Dyer, Charles
14458	„	Antonio, Andy	14448	„	Fowler, Harold

Canadian Pacific—The Empire's Greatest Railway.

6TH BATTALION, 2ND INFANTRY BRIGADE—cont.

Transport Section—cont.

Regl. No.	Rank.	Name.	Regl. No.	Rank.	Name.
14413	Private	Hawkins, Thomas E.	14454	Private	Mackley, Percy
14449	,,	Hirschfield, Roland	15482	,,	McCourt, F. A.
14450	,,	Hirschfield, Max	14455	,,	McDougall, C. H.
14451	,,	Jones, Marquis	14456	,,	Reeves, Ernest
14415	,,	Lambert, George	14417	,,	Swinton, Thomas
14452	,,	La Borde, W. Henry	14459	,,	Storey, Jered
14453	,,	Lord, Frederick A.	15223	,,	Vine, A.

"A" COMPANY.

Captain	... ...	Bedson, Kenneth Campbell
Lieutenant	... ...	Dennistoun, John R.
,,	... ...	Rosa, Carl Harold
,,	... ...	Sawers, Frank

Regl. No.	Rank.	Name.	Regl. No.	Rank.	Name.
14482	Col.-Sgt.	Gadd, Claude	14510	Private	Douglas, William S.
14499	Sergt.	Stewart, Robert Dron	14531	,,	Doyle, Frank
14524	,,	Waite, Charles A. L.	14485	,,	Ferguson, Andrew
14549	,,	Dunn, Thomas H.	14511	,,	Foley, Warren P.
14575	,,	Stewart, Charles	14532	,,	Shrimpton, John
14500	Corpl.	Carter, Robert B.	14533	,,	Florence, Peter Cram
14576	,,	Mortley, Frank	14534	,,	Fletcher, Sidney
14550	,,	Curtis, Percival E.	14484	,,	Gates, Fred
14483	,,	Copeland, H. W. D.	14512	,,	Gunn, Theodore G.
14525	,,	McKay, John	14535	,,	Gahagan, Bernard M.
14502	Private	Andrews, Herbert	14536	,,	Givan, Mervyn Ross
14527	,,	Arnold, Wilfred A.	14557	,,	Gordon, Edward O.
14493	,,	Bryson, Samuel	14558	,,	Hardie, Anthony
14503	,,	Beatty, Richard	14474	,,	Humphrey, Holland
14528	,,	Barter, Herbert	14559	,,	Horn, James
14529	,,	Boby, Herbert W.	14513	,,	Harvey, John
14501	,,	Bertram, Rolf	14581	,,	Hallett, Albert L.
14552	,,	Bagrie, James	14537	,,	Jackman, Harold
14553	,,	Bradburn, Joseph	14560	,,	Jeffreys, Chris. E.
14504	,,	Charleton, David S.	14582	,,	Johnson, Erick
14505	,,	Cowan, Fred Eugene	14561	,,	Lamourie, Peter
14506	,,	Carter, Henry T.	14490	,,	Lewis, Charles
14507	,,	Cheney, Lyman G.	14562	,,	Leigh, Robert B.
14508	,,	Carrol, Laurence P.	14486	,,	Mennell, Edwin R.
14530	,,	Carter, Wilfred	14496	,,	McKee, Harry S
14554	,,	Cooper, James	14515	,,	Mickleburg, E.
14555	,,	Cumming, R. P.	14538	,,	McPherson, G. B.
14556	,,	Crofts, Thomas	14563	,,	McComb, Charles M.
14577	,,	Cox, William Bernard	14564	,,	McDonald, Albert E.
14578	,,	Campbell, A. D.	14565	,,	Maclean, Walter A.
14579	,,	Cairns, Robert G.	14583	,,	Madge, Alfred G.
14580	,,	Cox, Cecil Henry	14584	,,	Macdonald, John
14509	,,	Dobbyn, George	14585	,,	Markall, William E.

Canadian Pacific—The Empire's Greatest Railway.

6TH BATTALION, 2ND INFANTRY BRIGADE—cont.

Regl. No.	Rank.	Name.	Regl. No.	Rank.	Name.
14586	Private	McGregor, Harry A.	14595	Private	Robson, Johnston
14587	,,	Marlow, Harry A.	14487	,,	Sneddon, James K.
14514	,,	McConachy, A. F.	14488	,,	Smith, William
14526	,,	McDonald, Myles	14519	,,	Stone, Alfred T.
14588	,,	Morris, Frederick R.	14520	,,	Stevens, Reginald W.
14589	,,	Maclean, Robert B.	14521	,,	Smith, Stanley J.
14516	,,	Nunnerley, George	14522	,,	Scott, Thomas A.
14566	,,	Neill, John S.	14523	,,	Smith, Harry
14590	,,	Nyblad, Gustav M.	14543	,,	Steel, James
14591	,,	Nyblad, Frank	14544	,,	Sillman, Arthur
14540	,,	Paice, Victor H. W.	14571	,,	Scott, Clarence G.
14567	,,	Parker, Ernest J.	14572	,,	Speedie, Harry
14592	,,	Pascoe, Ernest	14596	,,	Smith, J. Sterling
14568	,,	Plumridge, Arthur L.	14597	,,	Sutcliffe, John L. R.
14593	,,	Porteous, Robert	14492	,,	Tullock, John A.
14569	,,	Powell, Frederick W.	14545	,,	Thomas, Andrew J.
14594	,,	Preece, Albert	14573	,,	Treadwell, H. W.
14489	,,	Redmond, John E.	14598	,,	Truscott, Arthur O.
14491	,,	Reid, John	14546	,,	Warde, Girton
14495	,,	Rogers, James E.	14547	,,	White, John T.
14517	,,	Robertson, Wm. E.	14548	,,	Wilson, George
14518	,,	Rankin, Cornelius	14574	,,	Waygood, James
14541	,,	Robinson, Harry A.	14497	,,	Wheeler, Arthur
14542	,,	Robertson, S. M.	14498	,,	Worlock, Henry W.
14570	,,	Roche, Basil Joseph	14551	,,	Waugh, Richard

"B" COMPANY.

Captain ... ... Dennistoun, James Alexander
Lieutenant ... ... Nation, Arthur Frederick
,, ... Ferguson, Hugh Cameron
,, ... Lewis, Reginald Cope

Regl. No.	Rank.	Name.	Regl. No.	Rank.	Name.
14603	Col.-Sgt.	Gibbs, G. S.	14620	Private	Brereton, James Hy.
14668	Sergt.	Cockerell, Frank	14701	,,	Carey, Clyde Donald
14642	,,	King, Bruce	14618	,,	Carnell, Gilbert McB.
14616	,,	O'Brien, John Robt.	14675	,,	Chaplin, Harry
14694	,,	Wilson, Alexander	14700	,,	Cliffe, Nicholas
14695	Corpl.	Bilton, George	14646	,,	Clouston, George
14669	,,	Gillis, Jock Young	14647	,,	Collie, Alan
14604	,,	Lindsay, Claude	14622	,,	Cordelle, John Hart
14617	,,	O'Hara, James	14621	,,	Cormack, Thomas
14643	,,	Wells, William	14641	,,	Cook, John
14619	Private	Archer, Charles John	14648	,,	Curle, Franklin Wm.
14671	,,	Armitage, Leslie	14703	,,	Dorward, James
14645	,,	Bartlett, Clarence	14704	,,	Dorward, Peter
14672	,,	Beulens, Robert	14702	,,	Dunbar, William
14698	,,	Bissett, Peter Wm.	14673	,,	Farquharson, Patrick
14697	,,	Birnie, John	14670	,,	Ferris, Charles
14608	,,	Birnie, David	14624	,,	Forster, Gordon
14699	,,	Blanchard, Wesley	14705	,,	Foster, James

Canadian Pacific—The Empire's Greatest Railway.

6TH BATTALION, 2ND INFANTRY BRIGADE—*cont.*

Regl. No.	Rank.	Name.	Regl. No.	Rank.	Name.
14623	Private	Francis, Fredk. Wm.	14693	Private	Neilson, James
14707	,,	Gerrard, Frank	14660	,,	Palmer, Frank Bacon
14706	,,	Gillies, James	14631	,,	Patterson, Donald
14626	,,	Hallum, Wesley B.	14713	,,	Paterson, John
14627	,,	Hallum, Stanley S.	14632	,,	Paterson, John A.
14649	,,	Harker, Edward S.	14661	,,	Pendrick, Edward
14606	,,	Harris, S.	14613	,,	Phillis, Albert E.
14650	,,	Hazel, Wilfrid John	14662	,,	Phillips, William
14696	,,	Hayes, John Fredk.	14714	,,	Phillips, James
14625	,,	Herron, Dewey McK.	14633	,,	Pike, Henry
14674	,,	Henderson, Roy	14614	,,	Povey, Frank Asker
14653	,,	Hewis, Harry	14688	,,	Prince, Charles
14644	,,	Howe, George	14663	,,	Prior, H. Thurlow
14651	,,	Howe, Henry John	14664	,,	Prior, Percy
14710	,,	Howe, Stanley L.	14635	,,	Raike, Gilbert
14652	,,	Howe, Thomas Edwd.	14665	,,	Robertson, James
14654	,,	Inkster, John	14634	,,	Rollo, James
14676	,,	Jackson, George	14615	,,	Roche, Thomas
14677	,,	Johnston, Harry	14715	,,	Roome, Roy
14709	,,	Jones, Charles	14605	,,	Ruby, Arthur Lee
14788	,,	Jorgenson, Jacob	14689	,,	Rudolph, John Fredk.
14655	,,	Kerr, James	14636	,,	Scott, Wm. Melville
14678	,,	Kernalequen, Julian	14611	,,	Sherlock, Robt. Wise
14656	,,	Kidd, Geo. Plummer	14667	,,	Sims, Edward John
14657	,,	Lainsbury, James	14666	,,	Smith, James
14711	,,	Langston, Ernest	14690	,,	Smith, Jas. Alexander
14681	,,	Langston, William	14691	,,	Starr, Walter
14679	,,	Laurie, Thos. Ramsay	14717	,,	Stewart, Harry
14680	,,	Levitsky, John Saml.	14637	,,	Stinson, Edward
14683	,,	Malcove, Nayton	14716	,,	Strachan, William
14658	,,	Martin, Ernest Rchd.	14610	,,	Sullivan, Ira
14659	,,	Martin, James	14718	,,	Taylor, Theodore
14628	,,	Mercer, Edwd. Fredk.	14692	,,	Tebbutt, Thos. Percy
14682	,,	Murray, Alfred Wm.	14638	,,	Voysey, John
14684	,,	McArthur, Edward	14719	,,	Walton, Alfred
14712	,,	McClusky, Philip	14639	,,	Warren, Edgar Cecil
14629	,,	McCallum, Andrew B.	14640	,,	Waterman, Mack
14685	,,	McDonell, Archie	14612	,,	Webster, John
14687	,,	McLean, Frank	14607	,,	Williams, Joseph
14686	,,	McLintock, William	14609	,,	Wright, Samuel
14630	,,	Neal, Frank			

"C" COMPANY.

Captain ... ... Dennistoun, Robert Maxwell
Lieutenant ... ... Wingood, Allan Charles
,, ... Hassall, Frank
,, ... Davison, Frank C. S.

Regl. No.	Rank.	Name.	Regl. No.	Rank.	Name.
14839	Col.-Sgt.	Lee, John	14785	Sergt.	Strang, Campbell S.
14731	Sergt.	Burkett, George Wm.	14733	,,	Peareth, Jno. Twisden
14757	,,	Carr, Russell	14713	Corpl.	Booth, William

Canadian Pacific—The Empire's Greatest Railway.

6TH BATTALION, 2ND INFANTRY BRIGADE—cont.

Regl. No.	Rank.	Name.	Regl. No.	Rank.	Name.
14732	Corpl.	Vickers, Albert E.	14826	Private	Huxter, William
14786	,,	Torrance, Percival V.	14728	,,	Irving, Robert
14758	,,	McKinven, Angus K.	14767	,,	Jarvis, Chas. H.
14756	,,	Wilkinson, Frank C.	14799	,,	Kelly, Ewart C.
14734	Lce.-Cpl.	Apperley, William W.	14768	,,	Kennedy, Norman H.
14787	,,	Mitchell, William W.	14828	,,	Kennedy, Mark S.
14760	Private	Aday, Harry	14800	,,	Knight, Alfred Holt
14789	,,	Anderson, A.	14743	,,	Lomer, Dudrich W.
14812	,,	Arnott, Wm.	14769	,,	Martyn, Percy A.
14791	,,	Baker, G. Hamilton	14829	,,	Martini, Harry
14815	,,	Beatty, Arthur P.	14770	,,	Moody, Harry John
14790	,,	Brydges, Chas.	14801	,,	Morse, Gerald M.
14788	,,	Burbidge, Geoffrey C.	14771	,,	Morgan, William
14735	,,	Cheswright, Fred D.	14744	,,	Montgomery, Thos. D.
14792	,,	Chipman, Hamilton B.	14772	,,	Morrison, Haslett
14722	Bugler	Christopher, Howard	14830	,,	Murdock, Alec
14817	Private	Clack, S. J. Da Millo	14745	,,	McCorquodale, D. P.
14816	,,	Cooper, Albert	14802	,,	Macdonald, John A.
14723	Bugler	Cross, Russell W.	14831	,,	McKenna, V. Jos.
14761	Private	Churchill, Harold	14803	,,	McManus, Bernard J.
14793	,,	Du Val, Paul G.	14832	,,	McKenzie, George
14794	,,	Ellis, Harold Ellerby	14833	,,	McNeill, William
14726	,,	Fidler, Peter Jasper	14746	,,	McVey, Robert R.
14818	,,	Fletcher, Owen H. L.	14834	,,	Noble, Thos. Walton
14819	,,	Fraser, Norman D.	14747	,,	Olafson, Stoney
14820	,,	Garvin, Arthur	14748	,,	Parks, Jno. Herbert
14821	,,	Gemmill, Patrick	14804	,,	Patterson, A. R. D.
14737	,,	Gibbs, George F.	14774	,,	Pickering, Herbert A.
14796	,,	Girdlestone, Robert	14775	,,	Pickering, Edward
14795	,,	Glackmeyer, Saml. B.	14773	,,	Pickering, Jno.
14736	,,	Goodman, G. Peter	14835	,,	Picknell, Charles
14738	,,	Gordon, Archibald V.	14749	,,	Reid, Jno. S.
14822	,,	Gregory, Ernest Hy.	14836	,,	Renshaw, Ernest
14797	,,	Grant, Boyd Caldwell	14776	,,	Richardson, Sidney N.
14724	,,	Gunn, James Brown	14730	,,	Robinson, John
14798	,,	Harvey, Arthur F.	14805	,,	Saunders, Alec L.
14823	,,	Harrison, Wilfrid	14721	,,	Saville, John
14814	,,	Harrison, George R.	14777	,,	Setford, Arthur
14762	,,	Hart, Henry	14837	,,	Sharman, W. Wilson
14824	,,	Hay, James	14778	,,	Shaw, Jas. Edward
14825	,,	Hatton, Jno. J.	14759	,,	Smith, Ernest B.
14729	,,	Hain, Jas. A.	14806	,,	Stanley, Chas. French
14827	,,	Hall, Jno. Godfrey C.	14750	,,	Stewart, Robt. Henry
14742	,,	Hill, William Turner	14838	,,	Stewart, Jno. Howard
14765	,,	Hine, Herbert	14808	,,	Strang, Robert S.
14739	,,	Hind, John F.	14807	,,	Sim, Ernest Fred M.
14763	,,	Holden, Reginald C.	14751	,,	Stodgill, George
14727	,,	Hollingsworth, Geo. E.	14752	,,	Sumpter, Cyril B.
14740	,,	Hoffley, Roy	14755	,,	Tollemache, Philip G.
14741	,,	Howe, Alexander E.	14754	,,	Trickett, Chas.
14764	,,	Horan, Gerald P.	14753	,,	Tucker, Chas. E.
14766	,,	Hunter, Harry G.	14725	,,	Turner, Royes L. A.

Canadian Pacific—The Empire's Greatest Railway.

6TH BATTALION, 2ND INFANTRY BRIGADE—cont.

Regl. No.	Rank.	Name.	Regl. No.	Rank.	Name.
14779	Private	Turner, Rupert	14783	Private	Williams, Reginald
14809	,,	Turner, Michael H.	14810	,,	Winslow, Hugh P.
14780	,,	Venton, William J.	14811	,,	Woodman, Francis O.
14781	,,	Whalley, James H.	14784	,,	Wright, Wilfrid C.
14782	,,	Williams, Samuel R.			

"D" COMPANY.

Captain		Wilson, Forrest Kimber
Lieutenant...		Cameron, Angus Purkis
,, ...		Coke, Edward Francis
,, ...		Woodman, Henry John

Regl. No	Rank.	Name.	Regl. No.	Rank.	Name.
14845	Col.-Sgt.	Henderson, Godfrey	14919	Private	Earnshaw, William
14860	Sergt.	Cuffe, Abram Lawsou	14893	,,	Farman, Albert
14936	,,	Hills, George	14944	,,	Faulkner, Oliver
14887	,,	Russell, Robert Aird	14920	,,	Ferguson, Donald
14910	,,	Webb, Arthur Ernest	14945	,,	Fisher, Lawrence R.
14888	Corpl.	Dones, Fred	14921	,,	Forde, William
14862	,,	Irving, George	14894	,,	Gray, Alex.
14937	,,	Kirby, Harold	14895	,,	Gregory, Olinthus L.
14861	,,	Mellard, Richard D.	14946	,,	Garbutt, W. Starr
14846	,,	Scott, William (Armourer)	14947	,,	Gearey, James
			14949	,,	Hamilton, John Wm.
14911	,,	Wright, John	14948	,,	Hartley, Henry Peel
14912	Private	Adams, Henry	14850	,,	Higgins, David A.
14913	,,	Anderson, Albert E.	14869	,,	Hills, Arthur Edwd.
14863	,,	Andrews, John D.	14896	,,	Horncastle, R. Wm.
14914	,,	Bailey, Charles Allan	14922	,,	Idle, Robert Lothian
14889	,,	Barrell, Leon. Robt.	14870	,,	Inkster, Chas. Lloyd
14938	,,	Bartlett, Hy. Thos.	14950	,,	Jackson, George Olaf
14915	,,	Beattie, Martin	14951	,,	Jackson, Hugo A. L.
14890	,,	Berryman, John	14952	,,	Jenkins, Robert
14891	,,	Berryman, Robert	14897	,,	Jones, Frank
14859	,,	Bope, Lawrence F.	14871	,,	Kewley, Benjamin H.
14916	,,	Brames, Chas.	14923	,,	Kinie, Hudson P.
14866	,,	Brew, Richard	14898	,,	La Rose, Levi
14856	,,	Brown, John Armour	14851	,,	Laughland, William
14864	,,	Buchan, J. Pulsford	14899	,,	Lemaistre, Edward
14865	,,	Buckham, A. Gilchrist	14900	,,	Lindsay, Jno. G.
14867	,,	Campbell, Collin F.	14901	,,	Lloyd, Arthur
14917	,,	Campbell, Wm. Alex.	14902	,,	Lonie, John Erskine
14892	,,	Clinie, Hugh	14872	,,	Manchester, S. J. B.
14940	,,	Cooper, John	14924	,,	Manson, Donald
14939	,,	Crabtree, Alfred	14854	,,	Mayo, Frederick Geo.
14941	,,	Craddock, Harry	14925	,,	Mellis, Robt. Hunter
14868	,,	Cumming, J. Johnsn.	14873	,,	Middleton, Arthur Z.
14942	,,	Difford, William M.	14874	,,	Miller, Alec. Lowe
14918	,,	Douglas, Harry	14840	,,	Mitchell, F. H.
14943	,,	Dyke, Edward	14875	,,	Mungall, Robert

Canadian Pacific—The Empire's Greatest Railway.

6TH BATTALION, 2ND INFANTRY BRIGADE—cont.

Regl. No.	Rank.	Name.	Regl. No.	Rank.	Name.
14853	Private	Murray, Jno.	14931	Private	Smith, Adam
14926	,,	McCorquodale, Arch.	14958	,,	Soane, Edward
14953	,,	McKenzie, Chas. G.	14930	,,	Squires, James
14954	,,	McKenzie, Sydney	14959	,,	Steenson, William
14876	,,	McTeer, Allan	14855	,,	Stoddard, Edward
14927	,,	McVarish, Daniel	14960	,,	Stokes, Chester J.
14903	,,	Newman, Geo. Stacey	14881	,,	Stovel, Edward C.
14877	,,	Newton, Arthur Jno.	14858	,,	Strachan, William
14852	,,	Ostland, Albert	14882	,,	Tuckett, George W.
14878	,,	Patterson, William	14847	,,	Tytherleigh, Percy J.
14955	,,	Pawlett, Henry Chas.	14907	,,	Underwood, George
14904	,,	Pinkstone, James	14883	,,	Vanderhargen, Geo.
14956	,,	Randith, Ralph	14908	,,	Warriner, George W.
14928	,,	Reeves, Wilfred L.	14857	,,	Waplington, Leonard
14929	,,	Reilley, Jno. Edward	14885	,,	Whyte, Gordon W.
14905	,,	Roblin, James P.	14886	,,	Whyte, Wilfred
14906	,,	Rolfe, Frederick C.	14935	,,	Wilcock, Thos.
14957	,,	Saunders, Basil H.	14961	,,	Williams, Wm. Parry
14848	,,	Schell, Sam Paul	14884	,,	Wilson, Alfred
14932	,,	Schofield, Fred	14933	,,	Wilson, Donald
14879	,,	Scrimes, Harold S.	14934	,,	Woods, Harold C.
14880	,,	Scully, Douglas	14909	,,	Wright, Robert M.
14849	,,	Shipman, David			

"E" COMPANY.

Captain	Gunning, Henry Ross.
Lieutenant	Mackenzie, John Percival.
,, ...	Rowe, Lewis Richard.
,, ...	Osborne, Richard Edgar.

Regl. No.	Rank.	Name.	Regl. No.	Rank.	Name.
15017	Col.-Sgt.	Pollexfen, Charles J.	14987	Private	Barron, Frederick G.
14985	Sergt.	Dudley, Francis G.	14984	,,	Bond, Eric
15081	,,	Andrews, Gerald	15034	,,	Carter, William A.
15057	,,	Jarvis, Herbert A.	15063	,,	Charles, Albert W.
15030	,,	Gordon, Arthur	15064	,,	Crozier, Thos. Edwin
15031	Lce.-Sgt.	Redshaw, Adolphe	15065	,,	Campbell, Fredck. K.
15032	Corpl.	Furness, Allan	14963	,,	Campbell, Hugh
15058	,,	Haig, Ronald Frank	14964	,,	Carter, Wm. Fredck.
15082	,,	Price, Walter L.	14965	,,	Chisholm, Thomas
14986	,,	Dundas, Mordaunt	14988	,,	Clarke, James W.
15050	Lce.-Cpl.	Thorburn, Robert	14989	,,	Connell, Augustus
15059	,,	Birch, Arthur Rice	14990	,,	Coote, Alfred
14979	,,	Park, Edwin F.	14991	,,	Cheney, Lawrence E.
15060	Private	Allan, William Hugh	15035	,,	Dopson, William
15033	,,	Bacon, Rudolph	15066	,,	Dunwoodey, Jas. M.
15061	,,	Bishop, George A.	15067	,,	Dodd, Albert Wm.
15062	,,	Batchelor, William H.	15068	,,	Dix, Maurice Buxton
14962	,,	Bennett, Richard T.	14992	,,	Dickenson, Arthur D.

Canadian Pacific—The Empire's Greatest Railway.

F

82 6TH BATTALION, 2ND INFANTRY BRIGADE—cont.

Regl. No.	Rank.	Name.	Regl. No.	Rank.	Name.
15069	Private	Davies, Benjamin	15046	Private	Nagy, Cecil
15036	,,	Elcock, Rolph	15074	,,	Nelson, Christian
15037	,,	Frewin, Harry	15018	,,	Pearce, William
15070	,,	Ford, Lewis Stanley	15047	,,	Pearson, George
14966	,,	Faulkner, James	15049	,,	Prince, William
14993	,,	Ferguson, Walter	15025	,,	Pratt, Frederick
14994	,,	Fleming, Gilbert P.	15075	,,	Pentland, Wm. West
14995	,,	Fraser, Aubrey C.	15000	,,	Parker, Wm. Hen.
14967	,,	Ferguson, Donald G.	15001	,,	Powers, Wm. Hen.
15038	,,	Greer, Geo. Pearson	15048	,,	Perkins, Norman
15039	,,	Gayland, Archibald	15020	,,	Price, Harold John
15071	,,	Gray, James	14980	,,	Quigley, Oliver Scott
15073	,,	Garroini, John Chas.	15076	,,	Ross, William
15027	,,	Gordon, Robert S.	15077	,,	Ryan, Math. Covell
15040	,,	Hardwick, Gerald	15028	,,	Rodger, Thos. Thyne
15041	,,	Hardwick, Donald	15002	,,	Robertson, James
15026	,,	Hirlehey, Charles E.	15024	,,	Rose, Howard Cecil
15072	,,	Hughes, Vernon M.	15003	,,	Rae, Cecil Arthur
15021	,,	Holmes, John Ernest	15004	,,	Ruisbeck, Wm. John
14968	,,	Houston, Arnold R.	15079	,,	Speight, John
14969	,,	Hunter, James	14981	,,	Shearing, Ernest
14970	,,	Hanson, Harold S.	15023	,,	Snyder, Nelson
14971	,,	Henley, Ernest Robt.	15005	,,	Standen, David
14996	,,	Hunt, Francis Scott.	15006	,,	Samson, H.
15042	,,	Kilgour, James	15080	,,	Smale, William
15012	,,	Kirkpatrick, Robert	15011	,,	Thaler, Edwin
14972	,,	Kellas, Archibald	15055	,,	Whyte, George
15043	,,	Lefley, Cyrus John	15010	,,	Webb, Albert
14973	,,	Logan, Andrew	15052	,,	Withey, George R.
14997	,,	Lawrence, Arthur	15053	,,	Wood, James
14998	,,	Large, Edward	15054	,,	Weiss, Albert
15045	,,	McLellan, Ernest	15078	,,	Walby, Wm. Thos.
15044	,,	Mabb, Victor	15029	,,	Webb, Rich. James
15022	,,	McTaggart, Gordon	14983	,,	West, Thomas
14974	,,	Moore, Geo. Avery	15007	,,	Westbrook, Maurice
14975	,,	Moore, Anthony L.	15008	,,	Wallace, Ernest
14976	,,	Mathews, Fredck. A.	15009	,,	Warren, Jhn. Gowans
14977	,,	Morris, John	15019	,,	Watts, Edgar R.
14978	,,	McCarley, Manley H.	15051	,,	Webb, Frank
14999	,,	McDonald Ken. Ger.	15056	,,	Wright, Herbert

"F" COMPANY.

Captain ... ... Lockhart, Wm. T.
Lieutenant ... ... Cunningham, Herbert D.

Regl. No.	Rank.	Name.	Regl. No.	Rank.	Name.
15083	Col.-Sgt.	Reid, Henry	15092	Corpl.	Burnell, Albert N.
15086	Sergt.	Bernas, James	15091	,,	Burnell, R. C. N.
15087	,,	Collins, Geo. Patrick	15090	,,	Peacock, John Robt.
15085	,,	Hill, George Harry	15088	,,	Sadler, Jesse
15084	,,	Martin, John	15089	,,	Taylor, Ronald

Canadian Pacific—The Empire's Greatest Railway.

6TH BATTALION, 2ND INFANTRY BRIGADE—cont. 83

Regl. No.	Rank	Name	Regl. No.	Rank	Name
15094	Private	Allen, Ph. Henry	15149	Private	Mack, Wm.
15095	,,	Arlow, Jno. McR.	15150	,,	Marriott, Fred
15103	,,	Bailey, Chas. David	15155	,,	Matthews, Chas. J.
15097	,,	Boote, Robert	15156	,,	Matthews, M. H.
15096	,,	Boulter, John H.	15147	,,	Meade, Jack
15101	,,	Broberg, Norman	15151	,,	Merrill, Lorne E.
15098	,,	Buckley, Cecil R.	15152	,,	Mooney, Stanley G.
15099	,,	Burton, Wilbert	15154	,,	Moore, David
15100	,,	Burnham, Marvin W.	15148	,,	Moore, Thos. Allan
15102	,,	Busby, Chas. Edwd.	15153	,,	Morgan, Henry A.
15108	,,	Cale, Trevor Owen	15163	,,	McCutcheon, Wm.
15111	,,	Casey, Cornelius	15160	,,	McDermott, T. M.
15106	,,	Chisholm, S. P.	15157	,,	McDonald, Peter
15109	,,	Clarke, Wm. W. E.	15162	,,	McGee, Jas.
15107	,,	Cochrane, Geo. E.	15161	,,	McKee, Donald H.
15105	,,	Cogland, Thos. Willis	15158	,,	McKnight, A. D. W.
15110	,,	Collins, Jno.	15159	,,	McLaren, S. W.
15104	,,	Crawford, Jno.	15165	,,	Napton, Syd. Francis
15117	,,	Davidson, Jack	15164	,,	Neald, Thos. Henry
15113	,,	Davies, Joe	15166	,,	Neil, Geo. E.
15114	,,	Davis, A. Brailsford	15168	,,	Olson, Carl
15116	,,	Dawson, G. Frank	15167	,,	Orley, William
15115	,,	Doyle, George	15169	,,	Preston, Victor B.
15112	,,	Dunn, Wm. Edmund	15173	,,	Reddick, Asa Stanley
15118	,,	Estlin, Alf. J. Prior	15174	,,	Reisdorf, Harold V.
15119	,,	Faulkner, Thomas	15170	,,	Reid, Chas. Allen
15120	,,	Fraser, Alex. James	15171	,,	Robertson, H. Jos.
15121	,,	Gayer, Stanley	15172	,,	Rogers, Russell J.
15123	,,	Gilmour, William	15176	,,	Scholes, John
15122	,,	Godfrey, Herbert W.	15184	,,	Selkirk, Melton L.
15126	,,	Greenhalgh, John	15175	,,	Shearer, Wm. A.
15125	,,	Goody, Kenneth H.	15183	,,	Shires, Frank
15124	,,	Graham, James	15181	,,	Sinclair, Neil A.
15132	,,	Halhead, Walter	15180	,,	Smith, James Claude
15133	,,	Hart, Francis	15179	,,	Southcombe, G. W.
15129	,,	Harvey, Jno.	15177	,,	Stanbridge, Percy C.
15131	,,	Haland, Jno. A.	15182	,,	Stawell, Ralph E.
15130	,,	Hooper, Thos. W.	15185	,,	Tallman, Stanley B.
15127	,,	Howe, Earl J.	15190	,,	Taylor, George A.
15134	,,	Innes, Thomas	15187	,,	Thistlethwaite, C. N.
15137	,,	Johnstone, J. W.	15188	,,	Thurlby, William
15136	,,	Johnson, Halfdan P.	15189	,,	Thompson, Lloyd Leo
15135	,,	Junner, William	15191	,,	Tunks. Carl W.
15140	,,	Lawrence, Robert	15199	,,	Underhill, Jno. C.
15144	,,	Leeson, James H.	15197	,,	Ward, Albert Percy
15143	,,	Lindsay, George S.	15195	,,	Warren, Chas.
15145	,,	Little, Bruce	15193	,,	Whitcombe, John
15138	,,	Logan, Peter Murray	15192	,,	Whitby, Richard J.
15146	,,	Lonsdale, Percy A.	15198	,,	Williams, Dave
15093	,,	Lovette, Francis R.	15196	,,	Woods, Walter
15142	,,	Lovette, Wm. N.	15194	,,	Wynsberg, Prosper
15139	,,	Lynn, Joseph			

Canadian Pacific—The Empire's Greatest Railway.

84 6TH BATTALION, 2ND INFANTRY BRIGADE—cont.

"G" COMPANY.

Captain	Mayes, Henry
Lieutenant	Griffin, Gerald
,, ...	Smith, Gavin
,, ...	Steeves, Roscoe

Regl. No.	Rank.	Name.	Regl. No.	Rank.	Name.
15208	Col.-Sgt.	McLaughlin, Isaac	15323	Private	Girling, Frank
15209	Sergt.	Yule, Peter	15254	,,	Girvin, John
15211	,,	Blythe, William F.	15252	,,	Greener, Colin C.
15212	,,	Limbrey, S. H. A.	15263	,,	Hamelin, Eli
15210	,,	Mathias, Chas. D.	15257	,,	Harrop, Karl
15213	Lce.-Sgt.	Price, Chas. Herbert	15258	,,	Heal, Samuel
15217	Corpl.	Logan, Alex.	15264	,,	Henderson, John
15216	,,	May, H. Wm. Hinds	15259	,,	Henry, Gordon
15215	,,	O'Sullivan, William	15266	,,	Hewitt, Reginald C.
15214	,,	Watkins, Vivian	15265	,,	Hodson, Herbert
15219	Bugler	Burke, Frederick G.	15260	,,	Horner, William
15218	,,	Onyea, Lawrence	15261	,,	Hoskins, Benjamin
15220	Pioneer	Reeve, Frank Lionel	15262	,,	Hoskins, Frederick
15222	Signaller	Humphrey, Gerald	15318	,,	Hudson, Thos. G.
15221	,,	Therien, Bruno	15267	,,	Jamieson, John
15225	Private	Allen, Wm. Alex.	15268	,,	Jones, Leonard
15226	,,	Ayvas, Sarges	15269	,,	Knowles, George H.
15228	,,	Bagshawe, John F.	15273	,,	Laverack, Sydney A.
15231	,,	Blythe, James	15270	,,	Leech, Harry
15227	,,	Boucher, John	15324	,,	Levers, John G.
15232	,,	Boyce, Henry B. G.	15271	,,	Light, Chas. Edward
15230	,,	Brettett, Frank A.	15272	,,	Long, Walter D. K.
15233	,,	Carmichael, George	15275	,,	Mallock, George
15243	,,	Carris, Thos. Henry	15284	,,	Massie, Alfred
15234	,,	Claxton, John R. T.	15274	,,	Mather, John W.
15235	,,	Cleall, Charles	15277	,,	Miller, Frederick
15236	,,	Clouston, Fred	15280	,,	Mills, Richard
15240	,,	Collie, Alex. Allen	15281	,,	Mills, William Thos.
15241	,,	Collie, Robert E.	15285	,,	Morrison, James
15242	,,	Cook, Henry	15279	,,	Mullreay, William
15238	,,	Connor, Henry	15286	,,	Munro, George Neil
15239	,,	Craig, William	15282	,,	Murphy, Francis E.
15237	,,	Croysdill, Henry	15283	,,	Murphy, Jeremiah J.
15244	,,	Currie, John L.	15278	,,	Myrthen, Frank
15245	,,	Davies, Frank	15276	,,	McKenzie, Percy
15247	,,	Destropher, Albert	15319	,,	Newton, Ivery
15322	,,	Dopson, Charles	15288	,,	Nixon, Samuel J.
15246	,,	Drouin, Eugene	15291	,,	Parkhouse, Oscar
15248	,,	Dryden, William	15309	,,	Paradice, Chas.
15249	,,	Edwards, Robert	15289	,,	Pearce, Wilfrid G.
15250	,,	Ewing, Arthur	15224	,,	Pearson, Frederick
15253	,,	Gardiner, C. M.	15320	,,	Playfoot, Sydney
15321	,,	Garvin, William	15290	,,	Poublon, Jules
15255	,,	George, Sydney	15292	,,	Quinn, James H.
15251	,,	Gibson, Horace	15293	,,	Raines, James G.

Canadian Pacific—The Empire's Greatest Railway.

6TH BATTALION, 2ND INFANTRY BRIGADE—cont.

Regl. No.	Rank.	Name.	Regl. No.	Rank.	Name.
15295	Private	Rebbits, Henry R.	15303	Private	Turner, John
15296	,,	Reid, Arthur James	15307	,,	Underhill, H. G.
15297	,,	Robertson, Peter M.	15314	,,	Walton, Frederick
15298	,,	Rose, Everett L.	15315	,,	Watson, Ernest T.
15294	,,	Ross, John	15313	,,	Werdon, Wm. G.
15302	,,	Scarrow, Frank	15310	,,	White, Richard A.
15300	,,	Simpson, Sydney H.	15311	,,	White, Samuel
15301	,,	Smith, Wm. A. R.	15312	,,	Whyte, Lachlan
15299	,,	Sufferin, James W.	15308	,,	Windsor, John
15304	,,	Taylor, Frederick T.	15316	,,	Young, Ernest
15305	,,	Taylor, Irvine	15317	,,	Young, George Wm.
15306	,,	Tillotson, Vinton			

"H" COMPANY.

Lieutenant ... ... Pigott, Augustus Chas. D.

Regl. No.	Rank.	Name.	Regl. No.	Rank.	Name.
15329	Col.-Sgt.	Britt, Albert Lewis	15364	Private	Edgar, William S.
15332	Sergt.	Fergusson, Angus E.	15362	,,	Ellis, Richard C. V.
15330	,,	Fitzgerald, John M.	15361	,,	Ellis, Thomas
15333	,,	McIlwraith, Wm. M.	15363	,,	Elliott, Jno. C.
15331	,,	McKay, Archie A. S.	15368	,,	Fairbairn, George M.
15335	Corpl.	Ellis, Thos.	15367	,,	Falconer, Wm. Lyme
15338	,,	Douglas, Tom B.	15369	,,	Favel, Alex.
15337	,,	Leary, William	15365	,,	Fettes, Robert
15336	,,	Rumball, Wilfrid G.	15366	,,	Fowler, Ezra E.
15334	,,	Turner, Harold L.	15370	,,	Fulford, Geo.
15339	,,	Smith, Gilbert J.	15374	,,	Gardiner, Thos.
15340	Private	Arter, Edward	15371	,,	Goldfinch, Wm.
15346	,,	Bate, Hugh C.	15375	,,	Gowing, Lister T.
15341	,,	Burton, Cecil Geo.	15373	,,	Graham, Robert S.
15343	,,	Birney, Geo.	15372	,,	Grundy, Arthur
15342	,,	Broughton, Kingsley	15382	,,	Hall, Frank
15348	,,	Bruce, Douglas A.	15381	,,	Harrison, James A.
15344	,,	Bruce,Alex.Leishman	15378	,,	Hawkins, Jno. R. W.
15345	,,	Byers, Jno. Kiter	15376	,,	Henderson, Roy St.C.
15347	,,	Burton, Chas.	15384	,,	Hickman, Stanley
14439	,,	Brown, E. K.	15377	,,	Hodgson, Wm.
15351	,,	Cook, Arthur Oswald	15379	,,	Howell, Jas. Henry
15353	,,	Couldrey, Ernest Alf.	15380	,,	Hunt, Francis
15352	,,	Cox, John Chas. A.	15383	,,	Hurd, Clinton C.
15355	,,	Crampton,William G.	15385	,,	Johnstone, Thomas
15354	,,	Curran, Jno. Phil	15386	,,	Kerridge, Percy L.
15349	,,	Cutting, George H.	15388	,,	King, Frank
15356	,,	Debenham, H. E.	15387	,,	King, Owen
15360	,,	Downey, Malcolm A.	15389	,,	Kirby, Francis C.
15357	,,	Dudgeon, Andrew	15391	,,	Kirby, Frederick W.
15358	,,	Duncan, John	15390	,,	Knowles, Tobie
15359	,,	Duncan, Moir Black	15392	,,	Land, Walter

Canadian Pacific—The Empire's Greatest Railway.

6TH BATTALION, 2ND INFANTRY BRIGADE—cont.

Regl. No.	Rank.	Name.	Regl. No.	Rank.	Name.
15393	Private	Laroque, Martin	15425	Private	Raper, Harold
15396	,,	Layton, Frederick G.	15421	,,	Rose, Geo. A.
15398	,,	Luck, George	15420	,,	Rose, Herbert C.
15395	,,	Lee, John	15423	,,	Robbins, Ralph B.
15399	,,	Lewis, George R.	15424	,,	Roberts, Norman C.
15394	,,	Lobb, Garnett N.	15422	,,	Rolfe, Frederick
15397	,,	Long, Hartin	15432	,,	Sharp, Joseph
15407	,,	Maconaghy, John A.	15433	,,	Sharp, William H.
15404	,,	Miller, Chas. D.	15430	,,	Simmons, Geo. A.
15403	,,	Miller, William	15428	,,	Smith, Frank
15406	,,	Mirtle, Francis W. B.	15431	,,	Smith, Geo. A.
15401	,,	Morrison, James A.	15434	,,	Stewart, Geoffrey S.
15402	,,	Morrow, Robert	15427	,,	Stocker, George
15405	,,	McClure, William	15426	,,	Sturgeon, Richd. W.
15409	,,	Macdonald, N. J.	15429	,,	Sutherland, Jas. W.
15400	,,	McIntyre, Patrick	15439	,,	Thatcher, William P.
15408	,,	McKenna, Fredk. C.	15437	,,	Thomson, James B.
15411	,,	McLeod, Dan	15438	,,	Thomson, Stuart
15410	,,	McLeod, Robert E.	15435	,,	Thompson, George
15412	,,	McQueen, Robert	15440	,,	Thompson, William
15413	,,	Onhauser, Joseph	15436	,,	Toohy, John
15417	,,	Patterson, Murray G.	15442	,,	Watson, Thos. J.
15416	,,	Patterson, William	15441	,,	Whiteford, Robert S.
15414	,,	Payne, Bernard	15443	,,	Winram, Wm. H.
15418	,,	Perkins, William	15444	,,	Winram, Wm. M.
15419	,,	Phinney, Joseph E.	15445	,,	Younghusband, Jas.

BASE COMPANY.

Captain ... ... McMeans, Vivian

Regl. No.	Rank.	Name.	Regl. No.	Rank.	Name.
15448	Sergt.	Lewis, Bert. C.	15490	Private	Cook, Albert
15511	,,	Niblett, Henry E. R.	15467	,,	Coutts, William
15574	Tlr.-Sgt.	Lavender, Gilbert H.	15491	,,	Cuthberson, Wm.
15462	Private	Agnew, William J.	15515	,,	Curtis, Walter T. C.
15484	,,	Andrews, Robert.	15492	,,	D'Eguille, Geoffrey
15513	,,	Aylesworth, McG.	15529	,,	Dallison, MacDonald
15463	,,	Bamber, Alfred	15536	,,	Dwyer, Edward
15464	,,	Barker, John R.	15493	,,	Fendon, Frank
15465	,,	Brady, Michael	15494	,,	Fetterley, Walter
15486	,,	Burton, Robert H.	15516	,,	Finigan, Harry
15451	,,	Burke, James	15526	,,	Falls, Lewis Peter
15488	,,	Baby, James	15458	,,	Graham, Duncan
15489	,,	Ballendyne, James	15468	,,	Gray, Edward
15450	,,	Barnsley, Albert	15495	,,	Goodman, Cyril
15514	,,	Bethune, Robert T.	15517	,,	Gilchrist, Robert
15455	,,	Bramley, George	15518	,,	Graham, Archibald
15466	,,	Clark, Geoffrey	15469	,,	Hames, Charles
15460	,,	Carter, Hugh Clay	15453	,,	Hedge, Cyril Edward
15459	,,	Chadwick, Geo. M.	15470	,,	Holditch, George L.

Canadian Pacific—The Empire's Greatest Railway.

6TH BATTALION, 2ND INFANTRY BRIGADE—cont.

Regl. No.	Rank.	Name.	Regl. No.	Rank.	Name.
15528	Private	Hillocks, John	15573	Private	Mitchell, Robert
15531	,,	Johnson, James	15500	,,	Newton, William
15496	,,	Jupp, Charles	15476	,,	Painter, Thomas
15576	,,	Jones, David B.	15477	,,	Pike, Percy
15575	,,	Jones, Robert A.	15501	,,	Page, James
15471	,,	Keith, James	15502	,,	Parker, Linzey
15454	,,	Killaley, Robert L.	15521	,,	Quinney, Joseph
15472	,,	Lauder, Robert	15478	,,	Rennie, John T.
15519	,,	Lynes, Albert	15504	,,	Read, Arthur
15527	,,	La Fiere, Harold	15505	,,	Roos, Edward
15537	,,	Leahy, Dan	15485	,,	Smith, Herbert
15449	,,	McGinnis, Fred. P.	15457	,,	Staines, Henry
15473	,,	McSkimming, Wm.	15479	,,	Souvie, William
		McDonald	15506	,,	Stewart, John
15452	,,	McGrath, B.	15507	,,	Stilt, David
15474	,,	McFadyen, David	15524	,,	Silvers, Irvine
15475	,,	Marshall, Frederick	15480	,,	Tench, Reginald F.
15497	,,	Marshall, Thomas	15508	,,	Truscott, Leonard
15498	,,	Mackenzie, Robert	15522	,,	Tomes, Joseph
15499	,,	McCortmick, Archie	15461	,,	Wallace, David
15487	,,	Macdonald, Geoffrey	15481	,,	Wright, Joseph
15512	,,	Mann, Anson	15509	,,	Williams, Hugh
15520	,,	Marshall, Andrew	15523	,,	Woodhall, Herbert J.
15533	,,	Murray, James	15534	,,	West, Arthur Wm.
15456	,,	Mitchell, Robert N.	15535	,,	West, George T.

SUPERNUMERARY OFFICERS AND BAND.

Captain	...	...	...	Wells, George Anderson
Lieutenant		...	...	Jackson, Ernest C.
Bandmaster		...	...	Stelges, Edwin James

Regl. No.	Rank.	Name.	Regl. No.	Rank.	Name.
15542	Corpl.	Cramp, William A.	15555	B'ndsm'n	Kelly, Frederick
15541	,,	Filer, Alfred	15556	,,	Kennedy, James
15543	B'ndsm'n	Ambrose, Robert	15558	,,	Luff, Harry
15544	,,	Braybrook, Fred.	15559	,,	Mayson, Boyd
15545	,,	Cadwallader, C. M.	15560	,,	Morris, Tom
15546	,,	Chambers, John	15561	,,	Macfarlane, John
15547	,,	Davies, Jas. Wm.	15562	,,	Nunn, Cornelius
15548	,,	Ducat, Wallace	15571	,,	Paul, Edward
15549	,,	Edwards, George	15563	,,	Robinson, Henry L.
15550	,,	Evers, Harry	15570	,,	Russell, Harry
15551	,,	Gabell, James	15564	,,	St. Lawrence, Harry
15552	,,	Hallett, Herbert G.	15565	,,	Skelton, William
15553	,,	Hayton, Clifford	15566	,,	Spicer, Arthur
15554	,,	Hills, Harry	15567	,,	Venables, Thomas D.
15557	,,	Johnston, D. W.	15568	,,	Whittingham, Wm.
			15569	,,	Wilmore, Percy

Canadian Pacific—The Empire's Greatest Railway.

7th BATTALION (BRITISH COLUMBIA REGIMENT), 2nd INFANTRY BRIGADE.

HEADQUARTERS STAFF.

Lieut.-Colonel...	Hart-McHarg, William Frederick Richard
Major ...	Odlum, Victor W.
,, ...	Byng-Hall, Percy (D.S.O.)
Adjutant ...	Capt. Gardner, Stanley Douglas Cmg mc
Asst. Adjutant ...	Capt. Humble, Gerard Maynard
Transport Officer ...	Lieut. Brothers, Orlando Frank
Machine Gun Officer ...	Lieut. Bellew, Edward Donald
Signalling Officer ...	Capt. Edmond-Jenkins, William Hart
Medical Officer ...	Capt. Gibson, George Hubert Rae
Quartermaster ...	Hon. Capt. Macmillan, John McLarty
Paymaster ...	Hon. Capt. Bayliss, Frederick
Chaplain ...	Hon. Capt. Barton, William

Attached.

Lieutenant ...	Hodgson, Reginald Drury
,, ...	Kendall, Richard A.

Regl. No.	Rank.	Name.	Regl. No.	Rank.	Name.
16201	Sgt.-Maj.	Philpot, David	16416	Private	Cramp, Carl John
16202	Q.M.S.	Young, A. F.	16296	,,	Curley, John A.
16259	,,	Welford, Herbert	16252	,,	Davidson, Geo. A.
16206	,,	Youhill, W. H.	16222	,,	Davies, V. L. G.
16203	Col.-Sgt.	Keatinge, Walter H.	16546	,,	Fudger, Geo. B.
16204	Sgt.-Dmr.	Cocroft, Frederick	16224	,,	Gilchrist, John
16208	Signl.Sgt.	Lindsay, Robert	16253	,,	Graham, Frank
16207	Trs. Sgt.	Barge, William R.	16225	,,	Hays, Geo. David
16239	M.G.Sgt.	Clark, Harry Steere	16258	,,	Hart, William L.
16439	Arm. Sgt.	Hunter, Edward	16214	,,	James, Henry
16241	Corpl.	Weeks, Herbert H.	16212	,,	Johnson, Frank W.
16965	Arm. Cpl.	Loughton, Albert H.	16240	,,	Lees, Harold Andrew
16967	Lce.-Cpl.	Anderson, D. M.	16248	,,	Loureiro, Frank
16217	,,	Cook, Joseph	16230	,,	McCarthy, Daniel
16219	Private	Andrew, Charles L.	16255	,,	McDowell, Samuel
16508	,,	Baker, Victor Albert	16250	,,	Martin, Owen
16245	,,	Blackie, Ernest J.	16243	,,	Metzler, Seymour
16235	,,	Bozson, Walter	16213	,,	Morris, A. Henry
16249	,,	Brown, Edward	16237	,,	Nicholles, Rupert
17301	,,	Brown, James	16231	,,	Nott, John Charles
16234	,,	Bruce, Alexander M.	16251	,,	O'Connor, Peter
16209	,,	Callahan, Jas. J.	16254	,,	Painting, Chas. W.
17207	,,	Carmichael, Henry	16226	,,	Parry, Frank
16263	,,	Carr, Harry	17293	,,	Pearce, Percy
16209	,,	Chambers, Jas. I.	16246	,,	Pearless, Hugh N.
16256	,,	Clark, James	16233	,,	Pode, Frank
16221	,,	Corridan, E. D. P.	16227	,,	Pryke, Herbert W.
16257	,,	Cottew, Harold	16229	,,	Raymond, Roland

Canadian Pacific—The Empire's Greatest Railway.

7TH BATTALION, 2ND INFANTRY BRIGADE—cont. 89

Regl. No.	Rank.	Name.	Regl. No.	Rank.	Name.
16236	Private	Reynardson, E. V. B.	16232	Private	Smith, William
16228	,,	Robinson, Frederick	17069	,,	Wall, Chas. Wm.
16353	,,	Robinson, Robt.	16216	,,	Walters, Albert
16242	,,	Scott, Geo. D.	16210	,,	Williams, W. J.
16244	,,	Sheppard, Walter	16218	,,	Williamson, W. D.
16264	,,	Smith, Stanley John	16373	,,	Willoughby, C. H.

"A" COMPANY.

Captain ... ... Scudamore, Thomas Venables
Lieutenant ... ... Buscombe, Robert Frederick Edwin
,, ... Latta, Robert Peter
,, ... Spencer, Austin Godwin

Regl. No.	Rank.	Name.	Regl. No.	Rank.	Name.
16265	Col.-Sgt.	Kennedy, Alexander	16305	Bugler	Faris, Andrew Y.
16266	Sergt.	Beckerson, Robt. E.	16306	Private	Ferguson, Fredk. J.
16267	,,	Diplock, Thomas B.	16307	,,	Fox, Duncan
16268	,,	Reed, William Fredk.	16309	,,	Frost, Fred
16269	,,	Robinson, James	16308	,,	Gates, James
17211	Lce.-Sgt.	Crosby, Powell S.	16310	,,	Gaskell, George
16270	,,	Sparrow, Arthur	16311	,,	Gibson, James
16276	Corpl.	Anders, Frank C.	16312	,,	Gower, John
16272	,,	Larkins, L. B. S.	16313	,,	Haire, Wm. Howard
16271	,,	Marshall, William T.	16314	,,	Harling, Ernest C.
16273	,,	Palmer, Charles F.	16315	,,	Hart, Edward
16287	Lce.-Cpl.	Burgess, Arthur	16316	,,	Henderson, James
16288	,,	Calhoun, John	16317	,,	Hunt, Robert F. C.
16279	,,	Cooper, Thos. Ernest	16318	,,	Hicks, Stewart F.
16275	,,	Forester, Edwin H.G.	17360	,,	Hill, Harold, E. O.
17318	,,	McLean, Angus	16319	,,	Hoffman, Louis Earl
16278	,,	Stroyan, Arthur L.	16320	,,	Houston, Albert E.
16281	Private	Bailey, James Edwd.	16321	,,	Iggulden, Henry R.
16282	,,	Berentsen, Sigurd	16277	,,	Johnston, Lester C.
16283	,,	Blain, John	16323	,,	Jones, Daniel
16284	,,	Blackmore, Fdk.W.G.	16322	,,	Jones, Wm. George
16285	,,	Boscott, Harold	16324	,,	Keith, John
16286	,,	Brown, John	16325	,,	Kelly, Arthur R.
16289	,,	Campbell, Jerry	16274	,,	Kemp, Hugh G. D.
16290	,,	Charlton, Fredk. C.	16359	,,	Ladd, Forrest A.
16291	,,	Clapp, Albert Ernest	17295	,,	Lamonby, Robert
16293	,,	Collom, Horace A.W.	16326	,,	Lanchester, F. H.
16292	,,	Clarke, Albert Horan	16327	,,	Langley, Stanley
16294	,,	Coleman, William	16328	,,	Leslie, William
16295	,,	Conner, Henry	16329	,,	Little, William
16297	,,	Curry, Alfred Keddie	16330	,,	Lloyd, George
16298	,,	Davenport, Wm. N.	16331	,,	Longman, Henry
16299	,,	Davies, Richard H.	16332	,,	Marshall, John
16300	,,	Duprau, Ormond H.	16333	,,	Maynard, David W.
16302	,,	Elliott, Fred Fletcher	16334	,,	Mehan, Francis E.
16303	,,	Esson, William	17361	,,	McBeath, George
16304	Bugler	Evans, Thomas L.	16335	,,	McHallam, Peter

Canadian Pacific—The Empire's Greatest Railway.

7TH BATTALION, 2ND INFANTRY BRIGADE—cont.

Regl. No.	Rank.	Name.	Regl. No.	Rank.	Name.
16337	Private	McKelvie, Fredk. R.	16357	Private	Sealy, Fredk. Wm.
16338	,,	McLaren, Finlay F.	17399	,,	Simmons, Mervin C.
16339	,,	McLean, Wm. Ernest	16358	,,	Simmons, Wm. R.
16340	,,	Milne, Robert	16360	,,	Skidmore, Andrew H.
17372	,,	Miloci, Joseph	16376	,,	Smedley, John Wm.
17248	,,	Milroy, James	16361	,,	Smith, Perley Watts
16341	,,	Morrison, Alex. C.	16362	,,	Smith, Wm. Thomas
17376	,,	Mudge, Montague F.	16363	,,	Smith, Reginald A.
16342	,,	Oram, Samuel W.	16364	,,	Somerville, Wm. N.
16343	,,	Owen, Thomas E.	16365	,,	Tait, Albert Roland
16344	,,	Parker, John H. L.	16366	,,	Teather, George
16345	,,	Paton, Robert	16367	,,	Thurgood, Wm. C.
16346	,,	Parry, Robert Bell	17286	,,	Timleck, Lee
16348	,,	Preston, Joseph	16369	,,	Todd, Alfred
16349	,,	Quinney, James L.	16370	,,	Tripp, Hubert B. H.
16350	,,	Rawlins, Alex. A.	17288	,,	Tyack, Harold L.
16351	,,	Reed, George Alfred	16371	,,	Ward, William
16352	,,	Renshaw, Rodney	17412	,,	Weller, Harold
16347	,,	Robertson, John W.	16372	,,	Wisdom, Colin M.
16354	,,	Sanderson, George	16374	,,	Woolsey, Chas. Edwin
16355	,,	Scott, John Watson	16375	,,	Yearwood, N. L.
16356	,,	Scott, Thomas Cecil			

"B" COMPANY.

Captain	... ...	Warden, John W.
Lieutenant	... ...	Scharschmidt, Howard B.
,,	... ...	Leslie, G. Herbert.
,,	... ...	Anderson, H. Graham

Regl. No.	Rank.	Name.	Regl. No.	Rank.	Name.
16377	Col.-Sgt.	Ward, Bertram	16398	Private	Beaton, John A.
16378	Sergt.	Underhill, Reginald	16399	Bugler	Bebeau, Archd. L.
16379	,,	Macgregor, Herbt. G.	16400	Private	Bell, Charles C.
16380	,,	Stafford, Harold E.	16401	,,	de Bellevue, L. C.
16381	,,	Moore, Herbert E.	16402	,,	Blackman, Joseph
16382	Lce.-Sgt.	Exton, Ernest W.	16403	,,	Bourns, Thomas W.
16383	Corpl.	Harrison, E. G. A.	16404	,,	Bowser, William J.
16384	,,	Moodie, Charles A.	16405	,,	Braiden, Robert
16385	,,	Mahood, David	16406	,,	Brew, Arthur
16386	,,	Bell, Wilfred J.	16407	,,	Burnett, Alexander
16387	Lce.-Cpl.	Lamond, John M.	16408	,,	Burrow, George D.
16388	,,	Love, Richard C.	16409	,,	Campbell, Donald F.
16389	,,	Sayer, Henry Wm.	16410	,,	Campbell, George
16390	,,	Sellars, Sydney G.	16411	,,	Carlisle, John
23443	,,	Shaw, W. H. T.	16412	,,	Carr, Frank E.
16391	,,	Twynam, William H.	16238	,,	Carter, H.
16393	Private	Archibald, K. M.	16413	,,	Chaffey, Charles R.
16394	,,	Ashcroft, Stephen	16414	,,	Charles, Sidney C.
17193	,,	Aldous, John Edwin	16415	,,	Clarke, Herbert C. R.
16395	,,	Babcock, Ernest L.	16416	,,	Cramp, Carl Jno.
16397	,,	Beaton, Charles S.	16417	Bugler	Cucksey, Charles W.

Canadian Pacific—The Empire's Greatest Railway.

7TH BATTALION, 2ND INFANTRY BRIGADE—cont.

Regl. No.	Rank.	Name.	Regl. No.	Rank.	Name.
16418	Private	Daniels, James	23423	Private	McConeghy, T. W.
16419	,,	Dodge, Clifford T.	16455	,,	McKinnell, Archd. J.
16420	,,	Dryden, William H.	16456	,,	McKinnell, Colin S.
23380	,,	Dunbar, W.	16457	,,	McNeiry, David
16421	,,	Elworthy, Fredk. B.	16458	,,	Neill, Thomas A.
16423	,,	Ensor, George C.	16459	,,	Neville, George
16422	,,	Ensor, Edward	16460	,,	Oakes, John J.
16424	,,	Farley, Harold W.	16461	,,	Paton, David
16425	,,	Farmer, John	16462	,,	Pearson, Chas. P. L.
16426	,,	Fleet, Thomas	16463	,,	Pearson, John
16427	,,	Flinn, Eric C.	16464	,,	Peter, William
16428	,,	Fraser, Cyril D. L.	16465	,,	Powell, Frank G.
16429	,,	Goyer, Daniel M.	16466	,,	Powell, Harold M.
16430	,,	Hall, Orton	23340	,,	Reece, C. A.
23392	,,	Heppel, J.	16467	,,	Robins, William
16431	,,	Hetherington, J. W.	16468	,,	Ross, John
17296	,,	Hitchings, Walter R.	17276	,,	Ryland, John
16432	,,	Hicks, Valentine R.	16469	,,	Scale, George D.
16433	,,	Hill, Arthur	16470	,,	Shanks, Francis
16434	,,	Hill, Lionel J.	16471	,,	Sherwood, Samuel H.
16435	,,	Hillesley, Charles D.	16472	,,	Sparks, George J.
16436	,,	Hodgson, W. Curtis	16473	,,	Steward, Fred
16437	,,	Honess, James	16474	,,	Temple, Charles C.
16438	,,	Hunter, Chas. H. S.	16475	,,	Thompson, Almer
16440	,,	Hutchinson, Hubt.H.	16476	,,	Thompson, Andrew
16441	,,	Huygebaert, Julius J.	16477	,,	Thompson, Harold F.
16442	,,	Jones, Charles H.	16478	,,	Thornton, Joseph H.
16443	,,	Langston, Thomas	16479	,,	Tofts, Robert C.
16444	,,	Lansdell, Ernest E.	16480	,,	Turner, William H.
16445	,,	Long, George T.	16481	,,	Underhill, Claude C.
16446	,,	Mackay, Donald H.	17297	,,	Verran, Walter
16447	,,	Martin, Samuel P.	16482	,,	Walker, James
16448	,,	Maskell, Albert	16483	,,	Weir, Robert B.
16449	,,	Meldrum, William	16484	,,	Weston, William W.
16450	,,	Moran, Thomas	16485	,,	Wharton, Stanley
16451	,,	Morrison, Roderick	16486	,,	Williams, David E.
16452	,,	Mulvany, Charles A.	16487	,,	Williams, George B.
16392	,,	Murphy, Arthur	16488	,,	Williams, Stanley G.
16453	,,	Murray, John G.	16489	,,	Withers, Charles
16454	,,	McCaffrey, James	16490	,,	Woods, Wm. Henry

"C" COMPANY.

Major	... ...	Rigby, Percy George	
Lieutenant	... ...	Thorn, John Charles	
,,	... ...	Steves, Rufas Palmer	
,,	... ...	Forshaw, S. G.	

Regl. No.	Rank.	Name.	Regl. No.	Rank.	Name.
16491	Col.-Sgt.	Moore, Walter	17308	Sergt.	Potentier, A.
16494	Sergt.	Harney, John C.	16495	,,	Trimnell, Harry W.
16493	,,	Leeson, David	16496	Lce.-Sgt.	Ross, John

Canadian Pacific—The Empire's Greatest Railway.

7TH BATTALION, 2ND INFANTRY BRIGADE—cont.

Regl. No.	Rank.	Name.	Regl. No.	Rank.	Name.
16497	Corpl.	McCabe, James	16557	Private	Halstead, Harry
16500	,,	Mitchell, Geo. F.	16559	,,	Hammond, Albert E.
17314	,,	Roe, G. S.	17358	,,	Harrison, J.
16499	,,	Vinson, John	16558	,,	Hay, Douglas
16562	Arm. Cpl.	Hillary, Chas. R. P.	16561	,,	Higgins, Harry C.
16503	Lce.-Cpl.	Collins, James Albert	17357	,,	Holmes, H. H.
17322	,,	Douglas, T.	16563	,,	Hubbard, Fredk. W.
17321	,,	Paterson, Geo,	17354	,,	Humphries, H.
16596	,,	Purvis, Albert Victor	16566	,,	Johnstone, Walter A.
16505	Bugler	Adams, Frank W. R.	16568	,,	Kelly, John
16506	Private	Allen, Henry George	16569	,,	Laws, Benjamin
16507	,,	Anderson, Hugh	16570	,,	Lee, Albert
17327	,,	Bailey, A. E.	16573	,,	Leckey, George A.
16520	,,	Baker, Charles	16571	,,	Lundy, Joseph
16517	,,	Ball, Frederick J.	17347	,,	Marshall, C.
16518	,,	Booth, Henry	16574	,,	Massy, Hugh De H.
16519	Bugler	Bowler, George	16585	,,	May, John B.
16512	Private	Brown, Harry	16580	,,	Maybin, Joseph M.
16513	,,	Bruce, John P.	17373	,,	Merry, D. B.
16516	,,	Bullock, Charles	16575	,,	Midgley, Benjamin H.
16522	,,	Burchall, Alfred E.	16576	,,	Mullins, Thomas M.
16514	,,	Burns, Robert	16577	,,	Moy, George
16526	,,	Campbell, Alec	17413	,,	Macdonald, Roderic
16530	,,	Cameron, John J.	16589	,,	McLean, Donald
16533	,,	Cheatley, Joseph	16588	,,	McPherson, Alec
17342	,,	Cleaton, A. T.	16579	,,	Mould, Harold G.
17341	,,	Clifford, C. C.	16581	,,	Metcalfe, James E.
16525	,,	Cooke, Charles S.	16587	,,	Moody, Allen
16531	,,	Crain, Otho	16582	,,	Maloney, Michael
16534	,,	Cramp, John	16583	,,	Mulligan, John
16529	,,	Crombie, Claude	17371	,,	Munroe, A. D.
16524	,,	Crutchfield, Harry E.	17474	Bugler	Nicholas, Roy
16532	,,	Cumine, Butler P.	17333	Private	Nikitovitch, M.
16528	,,	Cunningham, E. W.	17332	,,	Nikitovitch, Z.
16535	,,	Degrandmont, F.	16591	,,	Ormrod, Wm.
16536	,,	Degrandmont, T.	17391	,,	Parton, T.
16537	,,	Duffy, Arthur	16594	,,	Pickles, Henry N.
16538	,,	Dunbar, John	17349	,,	Powell, J.
16540	,,	Drummond, H. W. G.	16597	,,	Robertson, David
16539	,,	Dunwoody, David	16598	,,	Richmond, Henry O.
16543	,,	Elder, Alexander	16599	,,	Revill, John
16544	,,	Fennell, Henry C.	16600	,,	Ritchie, Alexander L.
16547	,,	Ferguson, George	17395	,,	Rakovitch, R. R.
16545	,,	Findlay, James	17401	,,	Sharp, C. B.
16548	,,	Foley, Edward B.	17403	,,	Slater, J.
17346	,,	Foot, R. W.	17400	,,	Soutar J.
16550	,,	Forbes, William	16602	,,	Stevens, George
16551	,,	Gillis, Malcolm	16368	Armr.	Tibbs, Robt.
16555	,,	Gildert, Hugh J. C.	16603	Private	Tugwell, Lawson
16556	,,	Grant, Donald	17404	,,	Turner, W. A.
16553	,,	Grindell, Arthur	17409	,,	Walker, D.
16565	,,	Hall, John	16605	,,	Weber, Sylvester G.

Canadian Pacific—The Empire's Greatest Railway.

7TH BATTALION, 2ND INFANTRY BRIGADE—cont. 93

Regl. No.	Rank.	Name.	Regl. No.	Rank.	Name.
17410	Private	Whitfield, F.	17407	Private	Wyatt, A. E.
17413	,,	Wildblood, G.	16606	,,	Wyllie, Arth. S.
16604	,,	Wilson, Thos, H.			

"D" COMPANY.

Captain	... ...	Locke, P. J.
Lieutenant	... ...	Chisholm, Gilbert Gordon
,,	... ...	McNally, A. W.
,,	... ...	Mackintosh, Arthur

Regl. No.	Rank.	Name.	Regl. No.	Rank.	Name.
17305	Col.-Sgt.	Tennant, J.	17343	Private	Dennehy, C.
16610	,,	Bushell, James	16621	,,	Flynn, George
16612	,,	Hamilton, Robert L.	16641	,,	Frost, Thomas
17306	,,	Hurst, J.	16644	,,	Gibson, William
17310	Lce.-Sgt.	Guille, E. C.	17351	,,	Goodall, H. H.
16617	Corpl.	Banks, John William	16646	,,	Gordon, Robert
16614	,,	Huggett, Charles	16647	,,	Gray, Robert Henry
17315	,,	Merry, N. C. R.	16654	,,	Hambleton, William
16608	,,	Odlum, Joseph W.	16650	,,	Hamilton, Charles
16620	,,	Whittaker, Frank	16655	,,	Harson, Percival F.
16638	Arm. Cpl.	Cosgrove, Ambrose	16652	,,	Hardman, William
17316	Lce.-Cpl.	Allen, E. C. F.	16648	Str.-B'rer.	Harmer, Walter
17317	,,	Aylmer, B. W.	16651	Private	Harrington, Charles
16640	,,	Farron, Francis B.	16653	,,	Hermon, Theophilus
16684	,,	Parkinson, Robert J.	16649	,,	Holland, Percy V.
16705	,,	Trumpour, Samuel S.	16656	,,	Hunter, James
16724	,,	Watson, John F.	17355	,,	Hurrell, E.
16619	Private	Allison, Robert M.	16657	,,	Jackson, Neil
17324	,,	Anderson, A. W.	16658	,,	Jean, William W.
16622	,,	Anderson, James A.	16659	,,	Knudson, Peter
17328	,,	Bacchus, N.	17364	,,	Krempeaux, C.
16625	,,	Barnes, George	16662	,,	Lapsansky, John R.
16624	,,	Barnes, Joseph	16660	,,	Lecky, Frederick
16631	,,	Barker, Thomas	17367	,,	Liddicoat, W.
17334	,,	Basford, F.	16665	,,	MacDonald, Hugh
17333	,,	Board, H. R.	16666	,,	MacDonald, Malcolm
17331	,,	Bowyer, W.	16668	,,	Marks, David Herbt.
16629	,,	Brazier, Alfred	16669	,,	Mason, Frank Trevor
17332	,,	Broadwood, H. C. H.	16671	,,	Milne, Walter Thos.
16626	,,	Brown, George	16670	,,	Morgan, David Chas.
16627	Pioneer	Burchnall, William	16663	,,	Morley, Robert
16623	Private	Butcher, Edward C.	17369	,,	Morrison, J.
16632	,,	Charleson, Wm. D. C.	16673	,,	Newcombe, Leslie R.
17339	,,	Clark, L.	16672	,,	Nicholas, Archid. L.
17338	,,	Coomber, H. A.	16674	,,	Nicholson, Geo. Wm.
17337	,,	Cooper, W.	17386	,,	Oatts, F. J.
16634	,,	Craig, James	16676	,,	O'Brien, Frank
16633	,,	Cross, Arthur Leslie	16675	,,	O'Brien, John Michl.

Canadian Pacific—The Empire's Greatest Railway.

94 7TH BATTALION, 2ND INFANTRY BRIGADE—cont.

Regl. No.	Rank.	Name.	Regl. No.	Rank.	Name.
16679	Private	Odlum, Howard	16702	Private	Sprogue, John
17384	,,	Oliver, S.	16699	,,	Squirrell, Ernest
17385	,,	Oliver, W. E.	16701	,,	Sugden, Walter
16677	,,	Olver, Albert Bernard	16691	,,	Sutherland, Walter
16678	Signaller	Overs, Arthur Fredk.	16696	,,	Svendson, Conrad
16683	Private	Parks, Henry Heath	16706	,,	Taggart, Nathaniel F.
17388	,,	Paterson, D.	16707	,,	Tannahill, John S.
16680	,,	Patrick, Alec	16708	,,	Taylor, James
16682	,,	Plater, Bert	16710	,,	Thompson, Joe
16616	,,	Poulter, Donald E.	16704	,,	Trumpour, James
16681	,,	Price, George Fredk.	16709	,,	Turner, Leonard R.
16685	,,	Quinn, Alec Filmore	16712	,,	Valentine, Albert
17394	,,	Reid, W. E.	16711	,,	Vanstone, Wm. J.
16686	Signaller	Rogers, George Jos.	16717	,,	Waldener, George
16690	Private	Romer, Charles	16718	Str.-B'rer	Walker, Samuel A.
16687	,,	Ronahan, Walter	16720	Private	Watkins, William
16688	,,	Ronald, James	16721	,,	Webb, Robert
16689	,,	Rowland, F. H. J. M.	16719	,,	Whitworth, Ernest
16693	,,	Scott, Angus	16716	,,	Whyte, James
16692	,,	Sears, Robert	16615	,,	Williams, William
16694	,,	Shoesmith, Robt. H.	16713	,,	Wilson, Alfred
16695	,,	Smith, Dana	16723	,,	Wilson, Andrew H.
17397	,,	Smith, L. C.	16722	,,	Wright, Fred
16697	,,	Smith, Sydney	17408	,,	Wrightson, A.
16703	,,	Spence, David			

"E" COMPANY.

Captain	...	Cooper, Richard Clive
Lieutenant	...	Bromley, Herbert Assheton
,,	...	Barton, Walter Shepherd
,,	...	Boggs, Herbert Beaumont

Regl. No.	Rank.	Name.	Regl. No.	Rank.	Name.
16239	Col.-Sgt.	Clarke, —	16742	Private	Atknson, George M.
16727	Sergt.	Carroll, James Victor	16743	,,	Alker, Samuel
23313	,,	Paul, —	16744	,,	Arthur, Hugh
16613	,,	Wilson, D.	16747	,,	Bagnall, F.
16731	,,	Bateman, Edward W.	16746	,,	Baker, Hugh Glynn
23307	Corpl.	Holland, —	16755	,,	Beevor-Potts, Lionel
23309	,,	Jones, —	23370	,,	Beaumont, H.
17299	,,	Madore, Henry J.	16750	,,	Bennett, Syd. C. S.
16734	,,	Pilkington, W. A. C.	23364	,,	Blakeman, H.
16733	,,	Wylie, Robert	23371	,,	Bolton, R.
23359	Lce.-Cpl.	Crowther, —	16748	,,	Brignall, Frank
16737	,,	Milligan, Alex. W.	16752	,,	Brodie, Kenneth D.
16739	Private	Abraham, Edwd. W.	16753	,,	Brooke-Smith, E. C.
16740	,,	Abraham, Arthur T.	16754	,,	Bryant, Harry H.
23361	,,	Anderson, C. F.	16756	,,	Carter, Nicholas M.
16741	,,	Appleby, Harold L.	16757	,,	Childs, James A.

Canadian Pacific—The Empire's Greatest Railway.

7TH BATTALION, 2ND INFANTRY BRIGADE—cont.

Regl. No.	Rank	Name	Regl. No.	Rank	Name
16760	Private	Clarke, Thomas A.	23422	Private	McIvor, M.
16759	,,	Corfield, William E.	16797	,,	McMullen, Martin
23372	,,	Cooper, J. G. W.	16799	,,	Meyerstein, Wm. C.
16761	,,	Dunn, Edmund C.	16800	,,	Moore, Robert
23382	,,	Dickinson, W. S.	16795	,,	Murphy, Joseph V.
16762	,,	Evans, Edward	16801	,,	Nation, Philip B.
16765	,,	Farquharson, A. R.	16802	,,	Nelson, Beauvoir
16767	,,	Ford, Edgar Norton	16803	,,	Nicks, Ernest
16769	Bugler	Foster, Leonard	16804	,,	Norman, Wilfrid E.
16763	Private	Franklin, Albert	16805	,,	Oakes, Arthur E.
16764	,,	Fraser, Norman			(alias Alex.McD. May)
16768	,,	Fry, Pat	16807	Bugler	Parkinson, Leonard
16771	,,	Gallighan, William	16811	Private	Patterson, Donald
17298	,,	Geernahrt, Edwd. D.	23435	,,	Phillips, G.
16773	,,	Godley, John	16233	,,	Pode, F.
16770	,,	Grant, George C.	16806	,,	Porter, Geoffrey L.
16774	,,	Greaves, Harry P.	23436	,,	Porter, J,
16772	,,	Green, John	16809	,,	Puddiphatt, George
23387	,,	Griffiths, R. A.	16812	,,	Ravenhill, Horace L.
16775	,,	Hay, William F.	23438	,,	Reeves, I. C.
16777	,,	Hickling, Horace R.	23437	,,	Roberts, F.
16776	,,	Hill, Francis C.	16818	,,	Salter Donald
16779	,,	Holmes, Cedric C.	16814	,,	Scott, Matthew
16781	,,	Holroyd, Harold	16834	,,	Shaw, Thos. E.
23391	,,	Horan, G.	16819	,,	Shinner, William H.
16778	,,	Howe, Lewis Parker	16816	,,	Smith, Enos
23401	,,	Hume, H. T.	16817	,,	Smythe, John Wm.
16783	,,	Hutchinson, Thomas	16820	,,	Stevens, Charles G.
16785	,,	Jaynes, Jno. Neville	16821	,,	Taylor, H. W.
16784	,,	Jaynes, Percy C.	16823	,,	Thurburn, A. E. C. S.
16787	,,	Jarrett, Randall	16822	,,	Trendell, Cecil H.
16786	,,	Jennings, John S.	16824	,,	Turton, John
23402	,,	Jenson, A.	16831	,,	Wachter, Peter Le R.
16788	,,	Kerry, Joseph R.	16825	,,	Waldie, Adam Short
16789	,,	Lawrence, G ald W.	16826	,,	Walker, Lawrence H.
16791	,,	Laybourne, John	23459	,,	Waters, S.
23406	,,	Laycock, S.	16828	,,	Webb, Harry V.
16790	,,	Letts, Archibald F.	16829	,,	Webb, William H.
23407	,,	Levy, A.	16830	,,	Webb, Frank Joseph
23409	,,	Lyons, T.	23454	,,	Wellspring, W. G.
16796	,,	Mantach, Thomas	16836	,,	Weston, Albert
16794	,,	Mason, Walter R.	16838	,,	White, John Stanley
16792	,,	Martin, A. D'Arcy	16832	,,	Williams, Arthur W.
23418	,,	Martindale, J.	16833	,,	Williams, Frederick
23412	,,	Matheson, J.	16837	,,	Wolfe, Roy C.
16793	,,	Maynard, Harry	16840	,,	Woodley, Lorne A.
16798	,,	McLagan, W. E. G.	16835	,,	Woodman, S. T.
23431	,,	McLean, A.	16839	,,	Wright, Reuben B.
23420	,,	McLellan, B.			

Canadian Pacific—The Empire's Greatest Railway.

7TH BATTALION, 2ND INFANTRY BRIGADE—*cont.*

"F" COMPANY.

Captain	... ...	Harvey, Robert Valentine.
Lieutenant	... ...	Holmes, Carleton Colquhoun.
,,	... ...	Macdowall, Henry Charles Victor.
,,	... ...	Shaw, George Edward.

Regl. No	Rank.	Name.	Regl. No	Rank.	Name.
16843	Sergt.	Casey, Wm. Archer	16881	Private	Davey, James Henry
16844	,,	McIllree, John R.	16882	,,	Doughty, George
16842	,,	Newberry, Fredk. W.	16883	,,	Drummond, William
16845	,,	Sapsted, Thos. Wm.	16884	,,	Edginton, Lewis
16611	,,	Wiltshire, Arthur	16885	,,	Elliott, George Wm.
16846	Corpl.	Collison, Henry	16886	,,	Fisher, John
16848	,,	Hibberd, John S.	23386	,,	Fitz, George Janson
16847	,,	McVie, William	16887	,,	Foyster, Kenneth B.
23351	,,	Strudwick, Edward	17300	,,	Freeman, Edwin
16849	,,	Thomas, Harold Eric	16888	,,	Fretwell, Herbert
16850	,,	Wilson, Lewis	16889	,,	Fry, Sidney Walter
23352	,,	Wood, Frank	16890	,,	Garland, George L.
16956	Arm. Cpl.	Scriver, Wm. Daily	16891	,,	Gill, Keith Elmer
16851	Lce.-Cpl.	Anthony, John C.	16892	,,	Gillander, Warren
16855	,,	Chaine, Harry	16893	,,	Glazan, Louis
16853	,,	Christy, Norman	16894	,,	Griffin, Chas. Edm.
16856	,,	Geddes, William	16895	,,	Guthrie, Archibald C.
16852	,,	Lahiff, Robert	16896	,,	Haikala, Arvo
16854	,,	Thomas, Charles	23396	,,	Hall, Albert Edward
16857	Private	Andrews, Oscar Cecil	16897	,,	Harnham, Abdiel L.S.
16858	,,	Ashby, Herbert	16898	,,	Harris, William
16860	,,	Bell, Dudley Hayes	16953	,,	Haynes, David H.
16861	,,	Bevan, Gordon F.	16899	,,	Helmer, Abner
23365	,,	Bickley, Ellis	23399	,,	Hicks, Francis James
16862	,,	Bone, Frank T. F.	16900	,,	Himes, Alanson
16863	,,	Bouch, Wilfrid	16905	,,	Hodge, Alfred
16865	,,	Brierton, William	16901	,,	Holland, Alwin
16866	,,	Brown, Albert H.	16903	,,	Howland, Harry
16867	,,	Buckley, Arthur M.	16902	,,	Howard, George Kerr
16868	,,	Buckley, Joseph	16904	,,	Husband, W.
16864	,,	Buxton, Edgar B.	16906	,,	Ingram, William H.
16869	,,	Cannon, Thomas	16907	,,	Ivey, Frederick R.
16870	,,	Chandler, Roy D.	16908	,,	Jackson, Arthur F.
16871	,,	Chisholm, Arthur	16909	,,	Johnson, Roger A.
16954	,,	Clarke, Peter	16910	,,	Kay, Robert
16872	,,	Cleeves, Vincent	16911	,,	King, Geoff. Victor
16873	,,	Cook, Wm. John	16912	,,	Lever, Reuben A.
16874	,,	Corker, Arthur D.	16916	,,	McCune, Wm. H.
16875	,,	Corker, Frank A.	16913	,,	McDonald, James
16876	,,	Cresswell, Warneford Henry	16917	,,	McKinney, John
			16918	,,	McKinnon, Ernest
16877	,,	Currell, William	16919	,,	McLean, Neil
16878	,,	Dalgas, Agner Emile	16920	,,	McMillan, Robert G.
16879	,,	Darley, Harry	16921	,,	McQueen, Daniel R.
16880	,,	Davey, John	16922	,,	McQueen, William A.

Canadian Pacific—The Empire's Greatest Railway.

7TH BATTALION, 2ND INFANTRY BRIGADE—cont. 97

Regl. No.	Rank.	Name.	Regl. No.	Rank.	Name.
16923	Private	McVie, Robert	16936	Private	Sivell, Alfred Gilbert
16924	Bugler	McVie, James	16937	,,	Smyth, Heyland
16914	Private	Martin, James	23453	,,	Taylor, Percy Edw.
16915	,,	May, Arthur Douglas	16940	,,	Waddington, A. H.
16925	,,	Menear, John W. R.	16941	,,	Waddington, J. F.
16926	,,	Miller, Frank	16955	,,	Wallis, Edgar
16927	,,	Oliver, Sydney M.	16942	,,	Wallis, Walter
17417	,,	Peters, Jn. Franklyn	16943	,,	Walker, Gerald Cecil
16928	,,	Purdy, George	16944	,,	Warner, George
16929	,,	Rickard, Hugh Percy	16945	,,	Webb, Sidney
16930	,,	Robinson, Harry	16946	,,	White, Frank Samuel
16931	,,	Rowe, Charles E. G.	16947	,,	Whitaker, Wm. Edw.
16932	,,	Salmon, Leonard R.	16948	,,	Willey, Frank
16933	,,	Scott, Leslie Gordon	16949	,,	Wood, Walter H. H.
16934	,,	Senior, Edward	16950	,,	Wood, William Jas.
16935	,,	Shaw, Douglas Carl	16951	,,	Woods, Sidney
16938	,,	Shepherd, Herbert F.	16952	,,	Woodham, Thomas

"G" COMPANY.

Major ... ... Moberly, Guy
Lieutenant ... ... Ford, William Lowry
,, ... Jessop, Napier Arnott
,, ... Ashton, William

Regl. No.	Rank.	Name.	Regl. No.	Rank.	Name.
16957	Col.-Sgt.	Gilson, Wm. Forbes	16981	Private	Bradner, Earle M.
16958	Sergt.	Swindells, William	16982	,,	Bramwell, William
16959	,,	Saunders, A. L. W.	16983	,,	Browne, Samuel J.
16960	,,	Taylor, John	16984	,,	Butterworth, Frank
16961	,,	Allan, George Albert	16985	,,	Cameron, John L.
17030	A.S.Bchr	Maundrell, F. E.	16986	,,	Candy, Ernest James
16962	Lce.-Sgt.	Lloyd, Douglas D.	16987	,,	Carter, Robert R.
16963	Corpl.	Kelly, Wallace Scott	16988	,,	Chawner, F. H. D.
16964	,,	Castle, Donald R.	16989	,,	Cony, Joseph Nelson
16966	,,	Morcombe, Ernest G.	16990	,,	Cowling, Walter S.
17015	Arm. Cpl.	Hodges, George A.	16991	,,	Creighton, James O.
16972	Lce.-Cpl.	Atkins, John	16992	Bugler	Dance, William
16968	,,	Lucas, Clifton Malet	16993	Private	Davis, William R.
16970	,,	Matthias, Wm. J.	16994	,,	Dolling, H. H. R.
16969	,,	Mitchell, Gordon A.	16995	,,	Downing, Richard L.
16971	,,	Wilson, James M.	16996	,,	Doyle, Alfred E.
16973	Private	Adam, John	16997	,,	Duck, Albert George
16974	,,	Allwood, Ernest G.	16998	,,	Edgar, John
16975	,,	Anderson, John C.	16999	,,	Egan, Thomas M.
16976	,,	Armes, Alfred Wm.	17000	,,	Field, William A.
16977	,,	Barrett, William	17001	,,	Field, Clifford E.
16978	,,	Belli, Greig Antonio	17002	,,	Fisher, Frederick T.
16979	,,	Bolton, Maitland	17343	,,	Ford, A. J.
16980	,,	Boyle, John	17003	,,	Foster, Harold James

Canadian Pacific—The Empire's Greatest Railway.

7TH BATTALION, 2ND INFANTRY BRIGADE—cont.

Regl. No.	Rank.	Name.	Regl. No.	Rank.	Name.
17004	Private	Fraser, Robert	17040	Private	Murphy, Frederick
17005	Bugler	Fulton, Alexander Y.	17042	,,	Newton, Samuel T.
17349	Private	Gammer, A.	17041	,,	Nipius, George
17006	,,	Gardner, Albert S.	17043	,,	Odling, Vere Gordon
17007	,,	Goldish, Frank	17044	,,	Palmer, Percy Geo.
17009	,,	Gowanlock, Wm. J.	17045	,,	Pendergast, Joseph
17010	,,	Gray, Dave	17046	,,	Phillips, Joseph
17011	,,	Greer, William	17048	,,	Quinton, Edward
17012	,,	Halley, Andrew P.	17049	,,	Ralph, Arthur
17013	,,	Hamilton, Guy D.	17050	,,	Reede, Cecil Francis
17014	,,	Hayes, Thomas Cook	17051	,,	Reid, Robert Andrew
17016	,,	Howson, Joseph H.	17052	,,	Rose, James Frank
17017	,,	Inglis, James	17053	,,	Sands, Harold Frank
17018	,,	Jessop, Rupert Harry	17054	,,	Sanderson, Wm. C.
17020	,,	Labovich, Milo	17055	,,	Saunders, Harry
17021	,,	Lamble, Robert	17057	,,	Smith, Thomas Jones
17022	,,	Langford, Alfred	17058	,,	Stapleton, Henry
17023	,,	Lawson, Frederick	17059	,,	Still, Geoffrey
17024	,,	Leggatt, Edward W.	17060	,,	Stonestreet, George
17025	,,	Legge, Arthur Dallas	17402	,,	Sunderland, D. C.
17026	,,	Little, Robert	17061	,,	Sutliff, William
17027	,,	Loader, William	17062	,,	Tapner, George J.
17028	,,	Lucas Lucas, R. W.	17063	,,	Tattrie, Harry A.
17029	,,	Matthews, H. G. V.	17064	,,	Taylor, Alexander G.
17030	,,	Maundrell, F. E.	17065	,,	Thacker, William
17031	,,	Maylor, Henry	17066	Str.-B'rer	Thompson, Charles
17032	,,	McAllister, G. A.	17067	Private	Tinson, Arthur
17033	,,	McConnell, A.	17068	,,	Tozer, Edward J.
17034	,,	Macpherson, P. Cook	16715	,,	Walker, N.
17035	,,	Millar, Thomas	17070	Str.-B'rer	Watson, Charles G.
17036	,,	Miller, Albert George	17071	Private	Wilkey, William J.
17038	,,	Mitchell, Charles	17072	,,	Winslow, Frank W.
17037	,,	Mitchell, James	17073	,,	Wright, Jesse
17039	,,	Morrison, John H.			

"H" COMPANY.

Captain	Haines, Leslie Earls
Lieutenant	Hornby, Geoffrey
,, ...	Diamond, John Herbert
,, ...	Thomas, Lionel John

Regl. No.	Rank.	Name.	Regl. No.	Rank.	Name.
17074	Col.-Sgt.	Hepburn, Thomas G.	17080	Corpl.	McClelland, John C.
17076	Sergt.	Griffiths, Roderick F.	17081	,,	Wheeler, Albert H.
17077	,,	Dolphin, James E.	23467	Arm.Cpl.	Ashby, G. K.
17078	,,	Langley, William H.	17087	Lce.-Cpl.	Barnes, Albert
17075	,,	O'Reilly, Jacob F.	17088	,,	Beatty, Arthur P.
17079	Lce.-Sgt.	Wells, Frederick F.	17089	,,	Frost, Benjamin W.
17083	Corpl.	Bundy, Lenord	17085	,,	Postlethwaite, F. L.
17082	,,	Fergusson, William A.	17092	Private	Adamson, Maurice L.

Canadian Pacific—The Empire's Greatest Railway.

7TH BATTALION, 2ND INFANTRY BRIGADE—cont.

Regl. No.	Rank.	Name.	Regl. No.	Rank.	Name.
17090	Private	Alcock, George	17140	Private	Lonsdale, John
17091	,,	Anderson, John	17141	,,	Mackie, James Oscar
17093	,,	Arnold, Fredk. C. E.	17142	,,	Martin, John Ernest
17095	,,	Benge, Henry R.	17143	,,	Mavius, Cecil
17188	Bugler	Bowden, C. John	17368	,,	Maynard, H. F.
17096	Private	Braithwaite, Arth. J.	17144	,,	McCabe, Frank E.
17097	,,	Brown, Horace G.	17145	,,	McCombe, Stanley R.
17098	,,	Bunnett, Alfred	17146	,,	McInnes, Daniel
17099	,,	Cairnduff, John	17147	,,	McKenzie, John T.
17101	,,	Campbell, Kenneth M.	17148	,,	McLeod, Malcolm C.
23376	,,	Carter, H. W.	17149	,,	Monk, Joseph
17102	,,	Cave, Bertram	17150	,,	Mortison, Stanley R.
17103	,,	Chamberlin, C. C.	17187	Bugler	Mortison, Walter F.
17104	,,	Clarke, Basil Edward	17151	Private	Noyes, Thomas R.
17105	,,	Cleghorn, Walter S.	17152	,,	O'Connor, Leslie A.
17106	,,	Dancy, William B.	17153	,,	Olliver, Harry Alban
17107	,,	Darke, Cecil Robert	17154	,,	Orr, James Douglas
17108	,,	Davidson, James W.	17155	,,	Orr, George Evans
17109	,,	Day, William McLean	17156	,,	Patten Fred
17110	,,	Drumm, Joel Adam	17157	,,	Pearson, Harry E.
17111	,,	Dudden, Arthur C.	17158	,,	Pettigrew, Thomas P.
17112	,,	Dunford, Ernest F.	17159	,,	Pitts, George C.
17113	,,	Eastman Edward F.	17160	,,	Purser, Albert E.
17116	,,	Farrant, Lionel E.	17161	,,	Reynolds, Albert
17117	,,	Featherstone, G. W.	17162	,,	Rice, Nathan
17118	,,	Finnie, Frederick	17163	,,	Robertson, Alexander
17119	,,	Fitzgerald, W. F.	17164	,,	Robertson, James C.
17120	,,	Fletcher, Cecil A.	17084	,,	Royds, Nowell Bond
17121	,,	Fletcher, Walter R.	17165	,,	Ruddock, Richard F.
17122	,,	Flummerfelt, Edger	17166	,,	Shaw, Harold Martin
17123	,,	Foote, Alexander	17167	,,	Sherwood, Clifford H.
17125	,,	Garroway, L. R. H.	23444	,,	Skelly, D.
17124	,,	Gardiner, John A.	17168	,,	Smale, Bertram
23389	,,	Gately, F.	17169	,,	Solomon, Stanley A.
17126	,,	Goseltine, Percy A.	17170	,,	Spicer, Roy Hartley
16215	,,	Gracey, T.	17171	,,	Stacey, Herbert J.
17127	,,	Graham, David J.	17172	,,	Sutherns, Bernard W.
17128	,,	Gray, Charles T.	17173	,,	Sutton, Thomas
17129	,,	Guy, Harold Russell	17174	,,	Tait, William Gunn
17130	,,	Hamilton, W. R.	17175	,,	Talbot, Arthur
17131	,,	Hardman, James D.	17176	,,	Theobald, Nigel D.
17132	,,	Harrison, Fred	17177	,,	Thompson, James
17133	,,	Hughes, Peter A.	17178	,,	Tull, Albert William
17134	,,	Jones, Robert Elfyn	17179	,,	Wamsley, Albert E.
23404	,,	Kirby, H.	17180	,,	Webber, Vaughan H.
17135	,,	Kirk, Donald	17181	,,	Wells, William A.
17136	,,	Laird, John Malcolm	17086	,,	Whitehouse, W.
17137	,,	Langstaffe, Edward	17182	,,	Whiter, Bertram T.
17189	,,	Lambert-Pegram, H.	17183	,,	Williams, Fairflax N.
17138	,,	Leech, Norman B.	17184	,,	Williams, Henry W.
17294	,,	Little, Thomas C.	17185	,,	Wintemute, Harry L.
17139	,,	Lloyd, Henry Edward	17186	,,	Young, John

Canadian Pacific—The Empire's Greatest Railway.

7TH BATTALION, 2ND INFANTRY BRIGADE—cont.

BASE COMPANY.

Captain ... ... Carleton, David Elmer

Regl. No.	Rank.	Name.	Regl. No.	Rank.	Name.
17190	Sergt.	Regan, Jas. Francis	16641	Private	Frost, T.
17191	,,	Muir, D. McNicol	17228	,,	Garrett, Richard
17192	Sgt. Tlr.	Flack, Robert Jas. B.	17227	,,	Gandy, William
17232	,,	Hall, Ernest Lewis	16552	,,	Gardner, Frank
17233	,,	Harvey, G. Dawton	17229	,,	Geddes, Alexander
17230	,,	Goodridge, J. C. B.	16643	,,	Gingell, Wilfred E.
17270	,,	Parker, Robert	17231	,,	Godson, J. Evelyn
17194	Private	Appa, Patsy	16554	,,	Gordon, James
17195	,,	Arnold, Russell K.	17008	,,	Goulet, Albert
17196	,,	Askew, Edmund	16645	,,	Green, Harold
17197	,,	Babcock, W. Lester	16501	,,	Hamilton, Grover
17198	,,	Bailey, W. John	16652	,,	Hardman, H.
16628	,,	Bamford, Wm. Jas.	16654	,,	Hogg, Geo. C.
17199	,,	Bampton, E. C. S.	16560	,,	Hurst, Robert
16630	,,	Beaton, M.	17234	,,	Hopper, Arthur W.
17201	,,	Beattie, Reginald	17235	,,	Humphreys, William
17202	,,	Bentley, W. Clive	17236	,,	Johns, Frederick
17204	,,	Blackburn, Percy D.	17019	,,	Joseph, Lewis
16509	,,	Boseley, Ernest Geo.	17237	,,	Jurgens, Adolph D.
16504	,,	Boyce, A.	17239	,,	Keith, James M.
17205	,,	Bryant, Aubrey	17238	,,	Keith, Austin M.
17206	,,	Campbell, Joseph	17240	,,	Killick, Stuart
16637	,,	Carter, Robt. G.	16661	,,	Latham, James
17244	,,	Cherry, Harold C.	17241	,,	Lawrence, A. H.
16527	,,	Conlin, Michael A.	16572	,,	Lawrie, Vernon
16635	,,	Cook, Wm. Henry	17242	,,	Leacock, Arthur
17210	,,	Cooter, Ernest F.	17243	,,	Linton, James S.
17209	,,	Crawford, John	17245	,,	Mallows, George
16636	,,	Crolse, A. G.	16667	,,	Malone, Joseph
17212	,,	Daines, John	17246	,,	Martin, Alec.
17213	,,	Davis, William	17247	,,	Martin, Frank David
17214	,,	Denton, David S.	16586	,,	Mayer, William
17217	,,	Diamond, Andrew	16584	,,	Miller, Robert
17215	,,	Dickson, John Noble	17249	,,	Mitchell, Rowland
17216	,,	Dickson, W. Keith	17250	,,	Moore, Alfred
17218	,,	Douglas, George	17251	,,	Mumford, Thomas
16541	,,	Dunthorne, Arthur	16578	,,	Munger, Ralph C.
16542	,,	Edwards, H.	17252	,,	McArthur, Henry
17219	,,	Emes, Clare Silas	17253	,,	McArthur, John
17220	,,	Everett, L. Rayman	17254	,,	McCormack, R. P.
16642	,,	Ferguson, John R.	17255	,,	McCreight, Thomas
17222	,,	Fern, Sidney N.	17256	,,	McDermott, Richard
17221	,,	Fermor, Albert A.	16502	,,	McDonald, Donald
17223	,,	Fetterly, Charles	17257	,,	McDonnell, Leo
17226	,,	Fetterly, Norman	17258	,,	McGillis, Donald J.
17224	,,	Ford, George Marvin	17265	,,	McGiveran, Bruce
16549	,,	Foster, Edward	17259	,,	McInnes, Arthur
17225	,,	Fowler, Joseph	17260	,,	MacKay, R. Angus.

Canadian Pacific—The Empire's Greatest Railway.

7TH BATTALION, 2ND INFANTRY BRIGADE—cont. 101

Regl. No.	Rank.	Name.	Regl. No.	Rank.	Name.
17262	Private	McKenzie, Norman	17280	Private	Smethurst, John H.
17261	,,	McKenzie, Joseph	17279	,,	Smith, Joseph
17263	,,	McLaughlin, Milton	16601	,,	Smith, Wm.
17264	,,	McMillan, John G.	17281	,,	Sommerville, John
17266	,,	Noble, Ernest A.	16618	,,	Steele, Robt.
17267	,,	Oberg, Remhold	17282	,,	Storr, James
17268	,,	Osborne, William J.	16698	,,	Stuart, Robert B.
17269	,,	Palmer, Roy	17284	,,	Sutton, Francis
16595	,,	Pike, Harry	17283	,,	Sutherland, Daniel
16596	,,	Purvis, Albert V.	17285	,,	Thornton, William
17271	,,	Quinn, Edward J.	17287	,,	Townsend, J. G. F.
17272	,,	Ramage, William A	17289	,,	Vigor, Charles
17273	,,	Reber, Gordon	17290	,,	Vivian, Herbert
17274	,,	Richards, Edward	16714	,,	Wallace, Thos.
17275	,,	Russell, Francis W.	17292	,,	Walsh, Thomas A.
17278	,,	Simpson, Robert	17291	,,	Williams, Harry
16760	,,	Sinclair, John	17200	,,	White, Frederick
17277	,,	Sedore, Percy	17208	,,	Young, Charles

8th BATTALION (90th RIFLES), 2nd INFANTRY BRIGADE.

HEADQUARTERS.

Officer Commanding	Lieut.-Colonel Louis James Lipsett
Sr. Major	Major William Aird Munro
Jr. Major	,, H. H. Matthews
Adjutant	Major James Kirkcaldy
Asst. Adjutant	W. A. Bertram
Quartermaster	Lieut. William Ernest Firmstone
Transport Officer	Captain Henry Ambrose Wise
Signalling Officer	Lieut. Wallace Alexander MacKenzie
Machine Gun Officer	,, Thomas Head Raddall D S O

Attached.

Medical Officer	Major George Sydney Mothersill
Chaplain	Captain the Rev. Albert W. Wood
Scoutmaster	,, George William Andrews
Paymaster	Hon. Captain H. M. Cherry

Regl. No.	Rank.	Name.	Regl. No.	Rank.	Name.
1058	Sgt.-Major	Robertson, Wm.	1610	Signallers	Carter, James Geo.
	Qr.M.Sgt.	Blurton, Jno. F.	1611	Corpl.	Cotching, William
1605	Pion'r Sgt.	Nicholson, Thomas	1615	Signallers	Sparhan, Arthur D.
1606	Sgt. Cook	Cameron, William	1616	,,	Thornton, James
1607	Trans. Sgt.	Myles, Frank Wm.	1613	,,	Johnston, Chas. W
1608	Sgt.Shoemr.	Sartin, Albert Ed.	1617	,,	Toft, Thomas
1140	O.Rm.Cpl.	Simpson, Jack O.	1612	,,	Grant, William
411	A.Sgt.Dr.	Shields, John Miller	1614	,,	Rowe, Frank

Canadian Pacific—The Empire's Greatest Railway.

8TH BATTALION, 2ND INFANTRY BRIGADE—cont.

Orderlies for Medical Officer.

Regl. No.	Rank.	Name.	Regl. No.	Rank.	Name.
1619	Lce.-Cpl.	Angus, George	1618	Private	Thompson, Robt. Wltr.

Drivers (1st line transport).

Regl. No.	Rank.	Name.	Regl. No.	Rank.	Name.
1625	Lce.-Cpl.	Latham, James	1622	Private	Godfrey, Arthur W.
1638	Private	Tinsley, Arthur	1623	Groom	Garner, Geo.
1637	,,	Walters, Thos.	1671	Batman	Strachan, Alexander
1636	,,	Martin, Jno.	1672	,,	Marshall, John
1635	,,	Pritchard, James	1673	,,	Feeney, John
1634	,,	Spyker, John C.	1640	,,	Kirkcaldy, John Alex.
1633	,,	Roy, Fredk.	1641	,,	Carrol, Fred
1632	,,	Cuthill, Thomas	1642	,,	Green, Thomas
1631	,,	Hill, Charles Henry	1644	,,	Blackburn, Ernest
1630	,,	Wismer, Russell D.	1674	,,	Webster, Frank
1628	,,	Hadden, William	1646	,,	Dickens, Harry
1627	,,	Watson, David Henry	1654	S.M.Talr.	Milne, Geo.
1626	,,	McLeod, John	436	Batman	Bullock, James Chas.
1624	,,	Blackhurst, Frank J.			

Attached.

Regl. No.	Rank.	Name.	Regl. No.	Rank.	Name.
1664	Armourer (Sgt.)	Davidson, Wm.	1668	Private	Wilcox, George
1665	Pay Sgt.	Fisher, Aubrey H.	1669	,,	Crampton, William
1666	Corpl.	McKinnon, William S.	1670	,,	Chaplin, Maxwell H.
1667	Private	Kelly, James France	92	Ar.S.Maj.	Northover, Harry R.

Machine-Gun Section.

Regl. No.	Rank.	Name.	Regl. No.	Rank.	Name.
1647	Sergt.	Houghton, Alfred	457	Private	Hamilton, James L.
1650	Private	Handley, Wm. Edwd.	1651	,,	Watkins, Wallace
1652	,,	Leeson, William C.	1653	,,	Peterson, Joel
1655	,,	Flower, Wm. Horace	1656	,,	Ferguson, Wm. Jarnes
1657	,,	Jackson, Harry	1658	,,	Jonasson, Peter
1660	,,	Schoefield, Waltr. Wm.	1662	,,	Daintry, Chas. Stewart
1648	,,	McAulay, Alex. S.	429	,,	Andrews, Archibald A.
673	,,	Gumm, Alexander	747	,,	Reed, George Henry
1485	,,	Thickett, Walter D.			

"A" COMPANY.

Captain ... ... Watson, Geo. Kelsey Wm.
Lieutenant ... ... Weld, Geo. Hammond
,, ... Durrand, Geo.
,, ... O'Grady, Wm. De Courcy

Regl. No.	Rank.	Name.	Regl. No.	Rank.	Name.
1	Col.-Sgt.	Bawden, Alex. Reginald	6	Corpl.	Pozer, Wm. Secord
2	Sergt.	Simpson, Wm. Henry	8	,,	Ness, Garnett Valentine
3	,,	Beken, Horace Carl	9	,,	Jones, Jos. Horace
4	,,	Higgs, Leslie	10	Private	Scott, John Armstrong
71	,,	Mobberley, John H.	49	Bugler	Godwin, Jack Ralph
25	Lce.-Sgt.	Alldritt, Wm. Alex.	12	,,	Maskell, Thomas
5	Corpl.	Gray, Nathaniel	13	Str. B'rer.	Shannon, Thos. Luke

Canadian Pacific—The Empire's Greatest Railway.

8TH BATTALION, 2ND INFANTRY BRIGADE—cont.

Regl. No.	Rank	Name	Regl. No.	Rank	Name
14	Str. B'rer.	Kirkwood, Alex. S.	67	Private	McBride, Adam
23	Private	Absetz, Jos. Anthony	68	,,	Mullin, Jas. Smith
24	,,	Arnold, Franklin Geo.	69	,,	Mutimer, Chas. H. G.
26	,,	Attwood, Charles	70	,,	Mitchell, William
131	Arm.-Cpl.	Harris, Robert Whinry	72	,,	McCormack, Chas.
27	Private	Burch, Arthur Thomas	73	,,	McKay, Wm.
28	,,	Barugh, Walter	74	,,	McKenzie, James
29	,,	Bignell, Herbert Henry	75	,,	McKinven, Angus K.
20	,,	Brady, Matthew Ellard	76	,,	McNiell, Alex. Lorne
21	,,	Brown, Herbert Alfred	77	,,	McQuat, Stanley
15	Pioneer	Bridge, Alexander	78	,,	McCallum, John
126	Private	Butland, Frederick L.	79	,,	McKenzie, Geo. C
30	,,	Bender, George P.	80	,,	McLean, Wm.
31	,,	Burge, Clifford	81	,,	McLean, Duncan Jas.
32	,,	Brown, Robert McG.	82	,,	McQuilty, Geo. Alex.
33	,,	Ballantyne, John	83	,,	McRae, Alexander
34	,,	Brown, Patrick F.	84	,,	Naylor, Herbert V.
35	,,	Button, Mason	85	,,	Naslund, Arthur Oscar
36	,,	Capner, John Wm.	86	,,	Nicholson, Matthew
38	,,	Clossett, Adolph E.	87	,,	O'Connor, Daniel
39	,,	Colville, Jas. M.	88	,,	Partridge, Harold R.
40	Corpl.	Clifton, Philip Jas.	89	,,	Peacock, Geo. James
41	Private	Colville, Henderson A.	90	,,	Poole, Reginald
42	,,	De Courcey, Thos. Jos.	91	,,	Parliament, John
43	,,	Edwards, Richard B.	92	,,	Palmer, Arthur James
44	,,	Evans, Rees Ivor	128	,,	Price, Alfred Thomas
22	,,	Elsey, Chas. Edward	93	,,	Pryce, Chas. Frederick
45	,,	Field, Edgar	94	Lce.-Cpl.	Quinn, Herbert Victor
46	,,	Frazer, Wm.	95	Private	Rivard, Napolen Alric
47	,,	Fulker, Howard E.	127	,,	Rands, Benjamin John
48	,,	Fawcett, Albert E.	17	,,	Rhind, James
18	,,	Foreman, Stanley W.	97	,,	Repchinsky, Jacob A.
50	,,	Green, John Wm.	98	,,	Robertson, Duncan
130	,,	Green, Sidney	99	,,	Savage, Geo. Percy
51	,,	George, Ernest F.	100	,,	Sanders, Wm.
52	,,	Gurevitch, Simon	101	,,	Scarrow, Wm. Irvine
53	,,	Halcrow, David	102	,,	Sigurdson, Stonie Holm
54	,,	Hermanson, Mack	103	Lce.-Cpl.	Simpson, John Ernest
55	,,	Hanson, Peter Ejler	104	Private	Sears, Robt. Samuel
56	,,	Heriot, Geo. Archibald	105	,,	Spalding, Henry Ernest
129	,,	Harriman, John G. G.	106	,,	Strother, Paul Franklin
57	,,	Iriam, Frank Stanley	107	,,	Turriff, Robt. Gilles
58	,,	Johnston, Arthur H.	108	,,	Weaver, Leonard
59	,,	Jenking, Herbert L.	109	,,	Webb, Walter
60	,,	Johnceline, Edwin A.	110	,,	Walling, Sidney John
61	,,	Johnston, Chris. D. T.	111	,,	Wallace, Ernest E.
62	,,	Jolly, William	112	,,	Wambolt, Bert
16	,,	Keen, Frederick John	113	,,	Williams, Geo. Burton
64	,,	Lethbridge, Harry	114	Lce.-Cpl.	Williamson, Nelson S.
65	,,	Morley, Robert E.	115	,,	Wood, Horace V. M.
66	,,	Mitchell, Albert E.	116	Private	Welsh, Frederick Jos.
19	,,	Marshall, John Niel	7	,,	Wright, Wm. Henry

Canadian Pacific—The Empire's Greatest Railway.

8TH BATTALION, 2ND INFANTRY BRIGADE—cont.

"B" COMPANY.

Captain	... ...	McMeans, Ernest D'Harcourt
Lieutenant	... ...	Passmore, Harold Egbert
„	... ...	Paget, Richard James
„	... ...	Kaine, Alex. J.

Regl. No.	Rank.	Name.	Regl. No.	Rank.	Name.
201	Col.-Sgt.	McDonell, Wm. Chas.	241	Private	Cotter, Thomas
202	Sergt.	Godsmark, Harry S.	242	„	Coture, Alfred
204	„	Christopher, William	243	„	Curtis, Russell Frank
205	„	Halliday, Walter M.	244	„	Davies, Evan Cyril
203	„	Bishop, Frederick J.	245	„	Dimmock, Phillip L.
206	Corpl.	Scott, Hugh D. H.	246	„	Dowling, Barney
207	„	Maitland, Wm. John	247	„	Doherty, Hugh
208	„	Harris, Sidney	248	„	Eaton, Harry
209	Private	Marchant, George	249	„	Evans, Charles Arthur
210	Lce.-Cpl.	Figsby, Wm. Harry	805	„	Gardiner, Fredk.
279	Corpl.	McLeod, Geo. Alex.	251	„	Godwin, Arthur Magg
301	„	Symes, William	252	„	Green, Geo. Leonard
211	Bugler	Coward, Frederick J.	304	Arm. Cpl.	Thorton, William
212	„	Livingstone, Stanley J.	254	Private	Garrett, Ernest Chas.
213	Private	Wilson, William	255	„	Garett, Harry
214	„	Sanderson, John M.	256	„	Greenwood Chris. H.
215	„	Bowman, Hugh	257	„	Goodmanson, Minty
216	Str.B'rer.	La Ferla, Chas. W. W.	218	„	Harrison, Arthur Ross
217	„	Norris, Frederick T.	258	„	Harris, Thomas Dennis
308	Driver	Vowles, Thomas	261	„	Hacker, Norman Oliver
219	„	Sexton, Bert	262	„	Hallwood, Charles B.
220	Batman	O'Connor, Roland L.	263	„	Hamilton, Chas. Roy
221	„	Barker, Harry	264	„	Hartwell, William
331	„	Forsyth, Campbell	265	„	Henderson, John
289	„	Orr, George Syme	266	„	Jesson, Albert V.
223	Private	Anderson, Arthur N.	267	„	Johns, Ernest Wm.
224	„	Anderson, Oliver N.	268	„	Keeling, Thomas
320	„	Archer, Samuel	269	„	Kilvert, Henry Braum
225	„	Barlow, Albert Edward	270	„	Lyons, John
226	„	Bell, James	317	„	LeMoin, Louis
227	„	Birkett, Norman W.	271	„	Markall, Fred. Wm. T.
228	„	Bradshaw, Charles	272	„	Marr, Alexander
229	„	Brady, John	273	„	Matheson Murdock A.
230	„	Brayfield, Hugh C.	274	„	McLean, Rodrick M.
231	„	Britton, John Sidney	276	„	McCallum Howard R.
232	„	Budd, Clarence Alex.	277	„	McCallum, Thos. M.
233	„	Bruce, George	278	„	McClung, Hugh Ross
234	„	Buck, Walter Keith	280	„	McNamara, Lyall
222	„	Bears, John Wesley	282	„	Milne, Alexander John
235	„	Campbell, Henry P.	283	„	Mitchell, James
236	„	Caron, Edward	285	„	Mole, John Robert
237	„	Chapman, Dave	286	„	Moyse, Gordon Ernest
238	„	Combe, Charles Victor	287	„	Munnock, Alex. Wm.
239	„	Cornell, Athol A.	288	„	O'Brien, Donald
240	„	Cossar, Norman	290	„	Oxby, Roland George

Canadian Pacific—The Empire's Greatest Railway.

8TH BATTALION, 2ND INFANTRY BRIGADE—cont.

Regl. No.	Rank.	Name.	Regl. No.	Rank.	Name.
291	Private	Phillips, Wm. C.	305	Private	Thorsteinson, K.
292	Pioneer	Powell, Frank	306	,,	Townsend, Fred. B.
293	Private	Ryan, Osborne Edmond	307	,,	Underwood, John
294	,,	Sanders, Howard R.	309	,,	Walsh, Matheson
295	,,	Sanders, Montague A.	310	,,	Wearne, Hugh
296	,,	Scotland, Alexander	311	,,	White, Richard
297	,,	Smith, Harry	312	,,	Wilesmith, Jos. Wm.
298	,,	Sommerville, Geo. C.	313	,,	Wilson, Douglas G.
299	,,	Stiles, John Thomas	314	,,	Williams, George
300	,,	Sutherland, Martin	315	,,	Wither, David Alfred
302	,,	Thrasher, John Mangan	319	,,	Wilcox, Richard P.
303	,,	Thornley, Stanley F.	316	,,	Yeats, Clarence G.

"C" COMPANY

Captain	Morley, Arthur William
Lieutenant	Hargraft, Stuart Alexander
,,	Eadie, Shaver
,,	Bell, John Kidd

Regl. No.	Rank.	Name.	Regl. No.	Rank.	Name.
1539	Col.-Sgt.	Hall, Fredk.	432	Lce.-Cpl.	Bird, Richard de Berghs Molyneux
402	Sergt.	Noyes, Geo. Wm.			
403	,,	Jasper, Chas. Edward	433	,,	Bligh, Charles H.
404	,,	Rose, Alfred Edward	434	Private	Bourne, Walter Wm.
405	..	Gillatt, Alfred	435	,,	Bovill, Robert Dudley
406	Corpl.	Newland, Francis P.	437	,,	Carrol, Fred.
407	,,	Fowler, Robt. Geo.	438	,,	Carruthers, Wm. A.
408	,,	Aldworth, Oscar H.	440	Batman	Clark, James McNair
409	,,	Savage, Robert	441	Private	Cornwall, John
410	Lce.-Cpl.	Christian, Wm. Henry	442	,,	Cox, William James
412	Bugler	Morgan, Lewis Thos.	443	,,	Densley, Chas. Fredk.
413	Private	Brown, Lawrence E.	444	,,	Dick, Arthur
414	Signaller	Rice, Walter Cody	445	,,	Dyer, Royce Colman
415	Str.B'rer.	Bowles, Geo.	446	Batman	Eadie, Reginald W.
416	,,	Currie, Walter Henry	447	Private	Emmonds, Henry
417	Driver	McEwan, James	448	,,	Erskine, Thomas
418	Private	Knox, Thos. Robt.	449	,,	Falconer, Albert
419	Batman	Davis, Hilliard	450	,,	Fidler, Wilfred Tait
420	,,	Drummond, Thos. R.	1123	,,	Foster, Robert Geo.
421	,,	Freeman, Leslie	451	,,	Fowler, Frederick
422	Pioneer	Noiles, John Alex.	452	,,	Garroway, Percy G.
423	Private	Alderson, Wm. Jos.	453	,,	Gloag, John
424	,,	Allen, Geo.	454	,,	Gordon, Donald
425	,,	Allingham, Sydney	455	,,	Green, Herbert
426	,,	Anderson, Chas.	458	,,	Holland, John
427	Lce.-Cpl.	Anderson, Edwin F.	459	,,	Hoskins, Henry H.
428	Private	Anderson, Harry Cecil	460	Lce.-Cpl.	Kemp, Edward Wm.
430	,,	Bailey, Chas.	1150	Private	Lamontagne, Rene L.
431	Driver	Batchelor, Walter G.	461	,,	Laurie, Robert James

Canadian Pacific—The Empire's Greatest Railway.

106   8TH BATTALION, 2ND INFANTRY BRIGADE—cont.

Regl. No.	Rank.	Name.	Regl. No.	Rank.	Name.
462	Private	Little, Samuel	488	Private	Rogerson, John Wm.
463	,,	Logan, John Mitchell	489	,,	Rowan, James Grant
464	,,	Lovell, James Geo.	·490	,,	Rowan, Harry Butler
465	,,	Lytle, Alex. Clifford	492	,,	Scott, Hugh Gault
466	,,	MacDonald, Wm.	493	Corpl.	Slater, William
467	,,	Mathias, Leonard S.	494	Lce.-Cpl.	Sharp, Frank Leonard
1661	,,	Monto, Herman	495	Private	Smith, Howard S.
468	,,	McBride, Leslie	496	,,	Smith, Reginald G.
469	,,	McCaw, Hugh H.	497	,,	Smith, Stanley
470	,,	MacConnell, James A.	498	,,	Smith, Walter John A.
471	Arm.Cpl.	McKay, Hen. Stewart	499	,,	Stainsby, Wm. John
472	Private	McKenna, Damien	500	,,	Stanton, David
473	,,	McKenzie, Donald	501	,,	Steel, James
1528	Batman	McRae, Norman	502	,,	Stevenson, Alex. Chas.
474	Private	Minchinton, Reg. Alf.	503	,,	Stimpson, Chas. Hen.
475	,,	Morgan, David Emlyn	504	,,	Stroud, Hubert Ernest
1649	,,	Neish, James	505	,,	Taylor, Leslie
476	Lce.-Cpl.	O'Sullivan, Eugene	506	,,	Towse, Cecil
477	Private	Owen, James Wilson	507	,,	Uprichard, John
478	,,	Payne, John A. K.	508	,,	Walters, Howard
479	,,	Perkin, Henry Ernest	530	,,	Veriker, Jeffrey
480	,,	Platt, Edwin	510	,,	Watt, Robert
481	Lce.-Cpl.	Proudfoot, Sydney	511	,,	Way, Samuel Percey
482	Private	Puddy, Victor Thomas	512	,,	Webb, Fred. Montague
483	,,	Reeves, Herbert	513	,,	Whelan, John
484	,,	Reidy, John Patrick	514	Signaller	Wiggins, John Keble
485	,,	Riley, Percival	515	,,	Wilson, Chas. Henry
486	,,	Robins, Jos. Henry	516	Batman	Wilson, Thomas
487	,,	Rodenhiser, Jno.Percy	517	,,	Wood, James

"D" COMPANY:

Captain ... ... O'Grady, Gerald Francis
Lieutenant ... ... Harris, Guy Newburn
,, ... Denison, Richard Lippincott
,, ... Scott, James Nimmo m c

Regl. No.	Rank.	Name.	Regl. No.	Rank.	Name.
601	Col.-Sgt.	Hay, John	631	Private	Alexander, Gabriel
602	Sergt.	Parfitt, David George	634	,,	Baizenett, Emile C.
604	,,	Cook, Michael	644	Batman	Baker, Percival James
605	,,	Pilley, Frank Lindley	637	Private	Bassett, Robt. Thaden
608	,,	Moir, John	635	,,	Beckworth, Arthur M.
606	Corpl.	Davidson, C. Taylor	633	,,	Bernhardt, C. Nelson
610	,,	Niblett, Arthur	636	,,	Betts, Jas. Wilfred
612	,,	McDonald, James	613	,,	Bradley, Joseph A.
616	,,	Neighbor, Hendry	638	,,	Burns, Roy
1118	Arm. Cpl.	Hartley, Herman	632	,,	Boyd, George Thomas
630	Private	Allen, Robert Hendry	766	,,	Boyce, Robert

Canadian Pacific—The Empire's Greatest Railway.

8TH BATTALION, 2ND INFANTRY BRIGADE—cont.

Regl. No.	Rank	Name	Regl. No.	Rank	Name
639	Private	Brown, John Chalmers	712	Private	Massey, Herbert S.
640	,,	Berry, Arthur Cooper	714	,,	Moffitt, Robt. Lindsay
641	,,	Brownlee, Hugh Edw.	715	,,	Mitchell, Arthur
642	,,	Barker, Ernest B.	716	,,	Mitchell, Frank
1659	,,	Buckley, Edmund H.	717	,,	Mackie, Wm. Gowan
659	,,	Carphin, George	719	,,	Mortimer, Patrick F.
611	Lce.-Cpl.	Coad, Oscar Sidney	720	Prov. Cpl.	Murray, Robert Harry
648	Private	Cormack, James	721	Private	Minty, Fred Francis
651	,,	Coleman, Arthur F.	705	,,	McDonald, John Ed.
652	,,	Cooke, Edward L.	709	,,	McBride, J. Franklin
647	,,	Cooper, William Geo.	724	,,	Mathews, Wm. McG.
655	,,	Cochrane, Alexander J.	730	,,	Nash, Arthur
656	,,	Cook, Ernest Victor	729	,,	Nuttall, Ernest
657	Driver	Cassells, George A. G.	732	,,	O'Brien, John Edgar
654	Private	Coture, Edgar Stanley	731	,,	Osborne, William
623	Bugler	Davidson, H. A.	734	,,	Parker, Harry Derby
664	Private	Dawson, William	735	,,	Perkins, Leslie Noel
661	,,	Dempster, Thomas	736	,,	Purcel, Arthur
662	,,	Drew, John	737	,,	Rackley, William
666	,,	Evans, Charles	738	,,	Roberts, Rene Jeffrey
670	,,	Greenland, Lwrnce. W.	739	,,	Robinson, John Wm.
671	Lce.-Cpl.	Grigg, Wm. James	740	,,	Robinson, Fred Wm.
674	Private	Godwin, Charles	741	,,	Robson, John
672	,,	Godall, Herbert Jos.	742	,,	Ross, Norman
676	,,	Hutchinson, John G.	743	,,	Rowe, Fred
677	,,	Hughes, Gordon S.	744	,,	Ross, Alexander
679	,,	Hall, Bert	745	,,	Rose, Matthew
680	,,	Hurley, Dennis	746	,,	Read, David Richard
681	,,	Hartley, Edward	751	,,	Stevenson, John
683	Lce.-Cpl.	Higgins, George G.	615	,,	Sharpe, John
768	Private	Higgins, Fred Wm.	748	,,	Shaw, William
684	,,	Hay, Adam Cramond	749	,,	Shore, Hubert
687	,,	Hanniman, Ernest C.	750	,,	Scott, David Angus
689	,,	Hunt, Russell William	753	,,	Smith, Percy
690	,,	Ingalls, Allan Grannis	754	,,	Spalding, Lister L.
692	,,	Jackson, Ruben C.	625	Signaller	Stewart, Leo Joseph
693	,,	Johnson, Ralph	626	,,	Stoker, Robt. Ernest
695	,,	Jones, William W.	757	Private	Tate, Hamilton
691	,,	Jones, Clement Chas.	756	,,	Taylor, Walter
696	,,	Jepson, Russell	758	,,	Thorne, Marlborough
698	,,	Kennedy, William	767	,,	Vincent, John
699	,,	Kinch, William	759	,,	Winram, James Clark
701	,,	Lightfoot, George W.	760	,,	Winkworth, Chas. W.
702	,,	Little, Lionard Wm.	763	,,	Wallace, Guy
710	,,	McDonald, Phillip	765	,,	Wallace, Alfred Geo.
723	,,	Maxwell, Robt. Birch	761	,,	Watson, Joseph Hy.
711	,,	McKenzie, Chas. A.	621	Bugler	Wilson, Robt. B. K.
1663	,,	McMahon, Charles P.	1119	Private	Wilson, Christopher B.

Canadian Pacific—The Empire's Greatest Railway.

8TH BATTALION, 2ND INFANTRY BRIGADE—cont.

"E" COMPANY.

Captain ... ... Northwood, George Wm.
Lieutenant ... ... Andrews, George Frank
    ,, (Transport) ... Maurice, John K.

Regl. No.	Rank.	Name.	Regl. No.	Rank.	Name.
801	Col.-Sgt.	Mitchell, William H.	848	Private	Graham, Walter John
802	Sergt.	Chiswell, Percy M.	849	,,	Gyles, Gerald Henry
803	,,	Ward, Charles Cyril	259	Lce.-Cpl.	Harvey, Charles
804	,,	Jones, Thomas	850	Private	Haywood, John
806	Act. Sgt.	Ronaldson, Thomas S.	851	,,	Haydock, Arthur
807	Corpl.	Wolfe, Howard C.	852	,,	Hayes, John
808	,,	Smith, Charles	853	,,	Halward, Frederick
810	,,	Jones, Edward L.	854	,,	Halcombe, Ronald F.
809	Lce.-Cpl.	Meyers, Arthur Wm.	945	,,	Hendrickson, J.
811	Bugler	Buckells, William	857	,,	Hughes, Joseph
812	Arm. Cpl.	Austman, Joseph V.	858	,,	Holloway, Edwin Cecil
813	Drummer	Lang, Robert Dodds	859	,,	Herron, Leonard
814	Private	Acheson, Weir Henry	860	,,	Hurman, John Thos.
815	,,	Allman, George Arthur	862	,,	Huestes, Wilfred W.
816	,,	Allman, Ernest H.	864	,,	Kenyon, Levi
817	,,	Allen, John	865	Lce.-Cpl.	Lewis, William
818	,,	Barnes, John Ernest	866	Private	Love, William
819	,,	Breckon, Fred Ernest	867	,,	Lape, Frank
820	,,	Burns, Walter	869	,,	Moore, Julian
821	,,	Badgley, James C.	870	,,	Masters, Wm. Fredk.
822	,,	Black, John Clark	871	,,	Meyers, Frank Spencer
823	,,	Brown, Wm. Archibald	872	Batman	Monahan, Thomas
824	,,	Baker, Frederick P.	873	Private	McDonald, John Alex.
825	,,	Butler, Earl Reid	874	,,	McDonald, John Allen
826	,,	Banks, Gilbert	875	,,	McInnerny, Wm. James
827	Str. B'rer.	Brown, Oliver Henry	876	,,	McIlroy, John
829	Private	Campbell, Robert	877	,,	McGilvray, Alexander
830	,,	Cameron, Alex. Donald	878	,,	McNeil, David
946	,,	Carson, Thornton McC.	879	,,	Morgan, Charles.
831	,,	Clement, Geo. Wm.	880	,,	Mahood, Wm. James
832	Post Cpl.	Currie, Wm. Ward	881	,,	Nicholas, John
439	Private	Clark, George	882	,,	Nelson, August
834	,,	Coulter, George	884	,,	O'Dowd, Robert
835	,,	Dougherty, Charles G.	885	,,	O'Neill, James Donnell
836	,,	Davidson, Henry	886	,,	O'Brian, Geo. Henry
837	,,	Dusatoy, Ernest	887	,,	Patterson, Wm. John
838	,,	Eikrem, Walter	888	Str. B'rer.	Parke, Hume Orlaff
839	,,	Ferris, Samuel James	889	Private	Paul, Charles Marr
840	,,	Ferg, Ed. Charles	890	,,	Pierce, Wm. George
841	,,	Fonsales, Fk. Jean	891	,,	Peake, Norman A.
842	,,	Ford, Chas. Edward	892	,,	Pottage, Herman
843	,,	Fenety, Ernest	893	,,	Peden, Ernest John
844	,,	Felton, Cornelius T.	894	,,	Radcliffe, Chester W.
845	Lce.-Cpl.	Forrester, Chas. C.	895	,,	Ruddell, Robt. James
846	,,	Graham, Wm. John	896	,,	Roberts, Basil Gilbert
847	Private	Garth, Wm. James	897	,,	Russell, Joseph

Canadian Pacific—The Empire's Greatest Railway.

8TH BATTALION, 2ND INFANTRY BRIGADE—cont.

Regl. No.	Rank.	Name.
898	Lce.-Cpl.	Saunderson, Henry
899	Private	Stott, Percy Gladstone
924	,,	Sambrook, Alfred
937	Corpl.	Sandford, Arthur Geo.
900	Private	Saword, Algernon L.
901	,,	Spankie, Hugh Vernon
902	,,	Snell, Lount
903	,,	Squires, Joseph
926	,,	Stanley, Allen
904	,,	Stubbs, Donald Marsh
905	,,	Sandells, Thomas
908	Lce.-Cpl.	Tebb, Wm. Albert
909	Private	Thornley, John Edwin
910	,,	Taylor, James
911	,,	Treilhard, Stanley B.
912	,,	Vickery, William
913	,,	Vance, Samuel George
914	,,	Ward, Albert Edward
936	,,	Ward, Wm. John
915	,,	Weston, Arthur Leslie
916	,,	Williamson, B. Y.
917	,,	Weir, Thomas Victor
944	Bugler	Wrigley, Hadley

"F" COMPANY.

Lieutenant ... ... Neale, William
,, ... McLeod, Norman George Morison
,, ... Muirhead, George Beverley Grey

Regl. No.	Rank.	Name.
1227	Col.-Sgt.	Evans, Thos. Kelly
1088	Sergt.	Mears, Joseph Wm.
1059	,,	Millar, James Fulton
1002	Act. Sgt.	Rae, Charles Ed. B.
1031	Private	Walters, Albert Ed.
1089	Sergt.	Whyte, William
1060	Act. Sgt.	Hackett, John
1003	Corpl.	Kennedy, Archie J.
1117	Arm. Cpl.	Hackett, Charles J.
1061	Corpl.	Chapman, Guy
1032	,,	Basing, Albert Hy.
1006	Lce.-Cpl.	King, Jack
1091	Corpl.	Martin, James Reid
1028	Bglr.Cpl.	Few, Wm. Ernest
1048	Bugler	Underhill, Harry
1121	Private	Adams, George Bruce
1093	,,	Addison, Fred
1007	,,	Baldwin, Wm. Ed.
1034	,,	Beach, Jas. Herbert
1008	,,	Bonny, Sidney
1095	,,	Brayley, Archibald H.
1063	,,	Bridger, Reginald
1064	Cook	Brodie, Archie
1062	Private	Brommell, Robt. B.
1035	,,	Brumwell, Robert
1005	Lce.-Cpl.	Bunt, Hugh Albert
1065	Private	Cairns, George
1036	,,	Caister, Walter V.
1097	,,	Carlton, Ross
1098	,,	Caswell, Ernest
1009	,,	Clare, James
1066	Lce.-Cpl.	Cookman, Geo. Alfred
1011	Private	Corrigal, Wm. Chas.
1037	,,	Corrigan, Thomas H.
1038	,,	Cosh, Robert M.
1012	,,	Courtice, Robt. C.
1130	,,	Crook, Herbert John
1067	,,	Dodds, Henry H.
1068	,,	Dolling, John Henry
1099	Driver	Donohoe, Alexander
1013	Private	Douglas, Duncan
1039	,,	Duncan, Andrew
1077	,,	Dwyer, Munden
1100	,,	Eccleston, George
1101	,,	Fenton, Thomas
1040	,,	Ferguson, James
1102	,,	Fleming, William
1014	,,	Fletcher, Fredk. Geo.
1033	Lce.-Cpl.	Foley, Thomas Odo
1041	Private	Garrioch, Stanley
1069	,,	Gibbs, James
1042	,,	Gibson, Herbert
1070	,,	Gray, Wm. Edwin
1103	,,	Griffiths, David T.
1104	,,	Hall, Arthur Godfrey
1071	,,	Hall, Edgar Montague
1072	,,	Hansford, Edwin
1052	,,	Hanson, Albert
1043	,,	Hickling, Benjamin E.
1073	,,	Holiday, Clarence M.
1074	,,	Hoskin, Fredk. A.
1105	,,	Howell, Harry

Canadian Pacific—The Empire's Greatest Railway.

110   8TH BATTALION, 2ND INFANTRY BRIGADE—cont.

Regl. No.	Rank.	Name.	Regl. No.	Rank.	Name.
1106	Private	Johnson, Fredk. Wm.	1024	Private	Prout, John Wm.
1044	,,	Kelly, James	1113	Lce.-Cpl.	Robertson, Alex. P.
1075	Lce.-Cpl.	Kilshaw, Gradwell	1004	Private	Robertson, Bertram
1015	Private	Knox, John	1079	,,	Roach, John
1045	,,	Lamb, John Edward	1080	,,	Rogers, Walter
1016	,,	Larkin, James	1053	,,	Saunders, Fred
1076	Cook	Leigh, Fredk. Wm.	1081	,,	Sargent, Chas. Wm.
1017	Private	Linklater, Frank	1082	Lce.-Cpl.	Simmins, Richard G.
1046	,,	McBain, Alexander	1054	Private	Smith, Albert
1078	,,	McCallum, Frank A.	1114	,,	Smith, Arthur
1107	,,	McCulloch, Frank	1083	,,	Smith, Alexander W.
1018	,,	McCulloch, Jack P.	1115	,,	Smith, John T.
1019	,,	McDonald, Albert	1055	,,	Smith, Wm. Isaac
1047	,,	McDonald, Arthur N.	1084	,,	Stagg, Ernest George
1108	,,	McIntosh, Charles	1025	,,	St. John, James A.
1020	,,	McKenzie, Fred A.	1026	Signaller	Stone, William
1010	,,	McKenzie, Geo. Y.	1085	Private	Sturrock, George
1021	,,	McLean, Roderick	1056	,,	Tapp, George Rupert
1022	,,	Meek, Fred	1096	,,	Taylor, George
1049	,,	Moore, Frank Preston	1116	,,	Tunbridge, Fredk. C.
1110	,,	Murphy, Thomas	1027	,,	Tyrrell, William
1050	,,	O'Byrne, John Ed.	1057	Lce.-Cpl.	Wallace, William
1111	,,	Oldaker, Bernard G.	1086	Private	Watson, Fredk. Roy
1112	Driver	Peck, Frank	1029	,,	Wilson, John
1023	Private	Peden, William	1087	,,	Winstone, Scarlet H.
1051	,,	Pettitt, Sidney	1090	,,	Young, George
1109	,,	Pouchet, Frank			

"G" COMPANY.

Captain	... ...	Bingay, Lloyd Woolsey
Lieutenant	... ...	Owen, Henry Ernest Lloyd
,,	... ...	Lewis, Stanley Ed.

Regl. No.	Rank.	Name.	Regl. No.	Rank.	Name.
1202	Col.-Sgt.	Bradbury, Robert W.	1213	Private	Boutet Ernest
1252	Sergt.	Johnson, Francis G.	1206	,,	Brown, Joseph
1602	,,	Mercer, Wm. Thos.	1212	,,	Boa, Archibald
1204	,,	Brown, Gordon S.	1217	,,	Boynton, Clifford
1268	,,	Murray, John	1207	,,	Barrett, James
1305	Corpl.	Tassell, Fredk. Geo.	1253	Bugler	Baddeley, Archibald
1203	,,	Brown, Archibald J.	1218	Private	Christopher A. H.
1225	,,	Edmondson, Arthur	1222	,,	Conroy, Patrick
456	Arm.Cpl.	Gridley, John Howard	1221	,,	Collins, Daniel
1308	Private	Vorster, Christian J.	1220	,,	Clark, George Fredk.
1201	,,	Anderson, Thomas	1219	,,	Clark, Richard H.
1205	,,	Brown, John	1223	Lce.-Cpl.	Daley, William
1210	,,	Blake, David	1231	Private	Daggett, James
1211	,,	Boyce, Herbert Geo.	1224	,,	Deegan, Wm. Michael
1215	,,	Burk, Thomas Howell	1226	,,	Edgar, James
1216	,,	Burke, James Jerrie	1228	Corpl.	Eccles, Thomas

Canadian Pacific—The Empire's Greatest Railway.

8TH BATTALION, 2ND INFANTRY BRIGADE—cont.

Regl. No.	Rank.	Name.	Regl. No.	Rank.	Name.
1229	Private	Frith, William	1270	Private	Mains, Thomas
1233	,,	Gaul, Horace Joseph	1271	,,	McGarry, James
1232	,,	Gallagher, James J.	1279	,,	McEvoy, James
1234	,,	Getliffe, Ed. Thos.	1274	,,	McMillan, David
1230	,,	Grundy, Sydney	1275	,,	McKechnie, Wm.
1250	,,	Hogarth, Henry H.	1273	,,	McLeod, John
1247	,,	Higgins, Thos. Adrian	1278	,,	McRae, John
1245	,,	Hewittson, Lawrence	1277	,,	McRae, Daniel
1248	,,	Hills, Alfred Thos.	1272	,,	McChristie, Henry A.
1244	,,	Headland, Walter	1276	,,	McKay, James
1240	,,	Harvey, William	1286	,,	Nicholson, John P.
1237	,,	Hanson, Frederick J.	1290	,,	Piper, Geo. Wm.
1242	,,	Henry, George	1287	Lce.-Cpl.	Pain, Coard Henry
1239	,,	Hartling, Thomas	1291	Batman	Pringle, Richard
1246	,,	Houle, Arthur	1288	Private	Phillips, Harry
1238	,,	Harris, Arthur	1293	,,	Purcell, Daniel
1249	,,	Holmes, David	318	,,	Peters, Wm.
1243	,,	Heale, James	1292	Batman	Proudfoot, Thos. R.
1235	,,	Hall, Alfred Lanyon	1317	Private	Robinson, Malcolm
1236	,,	Hampshire, Thomas	1296	,,	Rickhard, John
1251	,,	Innis, John	1295	,,	Riel, Patrick
1254	,,	Kemp, Ernest Wm.	1297	Signaller	Sandall, Thos. C.
1256	,,	Kellagher, John	1298	Private	Sawyer, Henry
1255	,,	Kelly, Patrick	1301	,,	Stephens, James
1258	,,	Knobel, Harry Ed.	1303	,,	Slack, Mayward
1259	,,	Keine, Denis	1302	,,	Stevens, Albert
1257	,,	Kimberley, George	1306	,,	Tichener, Harold
1264	,,	Lilley, Horner Beech	1307	,,	Tracey, Patrick
1265	,,	Long, Geo. Robert	1313	,,	Wilson, Albert
1262	,,	Leslie, Thos. Stewart	1310	,,	Watts, John Edward
1260	,,	L'Abbe, Phillip	1309	,,	Walker, James W.
1263	Lce.-Cpl.	Le Mesurieur, George	1311	,,	Walsh, Peter
1284	Private	Munroe, Keith	1312	,,	Wilson, James
1280	,,	Marshall, Albert	1314	,,	Wyatt, Robert
1285	,,	Maloche, Joseph	1316	,,	Yeoll, Edward
1282	,,	Murphy, Edward			

"H" COMPANY.

Captain		Prower, John Mervyn
Lieutenant		Burton, Robert Bruce Stocker
,, ...		Dear, Lionel Sexters
,, ...		Dinsdale, Harry Hamblin

Regl. No.	Rank.	Name.	Regl. No.	Rank.	Name.
1401	Col.-Sgt.	Stewart, Thomas	1409	Corpl.	Angus, James Robert
1402	Sergt.	Townsend, Gordon J.	1411	,,	Farden, Fred
1404	,,	Parkinson, George V.	1609	,,	Stevens, Jas. Lester
1406	,,	Brown, James	1482	Arm.Cpl.	Seeley, Alex. Storey
1407	,,	Parkinson, Clement H.	1426	Private	Allan, Austin Ed.
1410	Lce.-Sgt.	Parkinson, Alex. C.	1494	,,	Allen, Norman
1408	Corpl.	Halliday, Alex. H.	1495	,,	Augusta, John B.

Canadian Pacific—The Empire's Greatest Railway.

112   8TH BATTALION, 2ND INFANTRY BRIGADE—cont.

Regl. No.	Rank.	Name.	Regl. No.	Rank.	Name.
1424	Private	Batchelor, Thos. Ed.	1461	Private	McDermott, William
1417	,,	Ball, Richard	1462	,,	McDonald, William
1427	,,	Barnard, Leopold	1463	,,	Meddings, William
1428	,,	Bain, Thomas	1477	,,	McKay, Charles
1429	,,	Brooks, William	1478	,,	McKay, James
1450	,,	Ballock, John	1412	Lce.-Cpl.	McKinnon, John C.
1451	,,	Buttler, William	1504	Private	Murray, John
1472	,,	Bow, Norman	1505	,,	Murray, Malcolm
1492	,,	Burke, Harry	1506	,,	McAuley, Alexander
1496	,,	Bridger, Arthur K.	1464	,,	Nicholls, Charles
1497	,,	Bridger, Dennis H.	1465	,,	Oxley, Gordon
1498	,,	Bowes, Thos. Watson	1416	,,	Pottinger, George
1499	,,	Bruce, Harry	1423	,,	Playford, Hugh
1414	Bugler	Collyer, Charles	1442	Lce.-Cpl.	Petty, Reginald
1452	Private	Caren, Chas. Andrew	1443	Private	Pratt, Charles
1473	,,	Carmody, Wm. John	1444	,,	Pilford, Harry
1493	,,	Chapman, Albert	1466	Lce.-Cpl.	Parker, Harold E.
1519	,,	Carson, Joseph	1419	Private	Pearson, Arthur
1538	,,	Craik, James	1467	,,	Pilon, Eady
1430	,,	Dennis, John Anthony	1479	,,	Platt, Henry John
1453	,,	Darke, Alfred	1507	,,	Pierce, Robt. Henry
1474	,,	Drummond, John J.	1518	Lce.-Cpl.	Stoddart, Stewart
1502	,,	Dewer, Hugh Malcolm	1418	Private	Sandbrook, Alex. J.
1480	,,	Eddy, George	1405	Lce.-Cpl.	Stetham, Henry A.
1458	,,	Fairbairn, Thomas	1420	Private	Slocombe, Joseph
1431	,,	Fenn, Arthur	1421	,,	Stewart, Peter
1432	,,	Follett, George	1445	,,	Searle, Harold Allen
1481	,,	Findlayson, Donald	1446	,,	Scotton, Francis E.
1500	,,	Flaherty, Jas. Patrick	1468	,,	Sheppard, Herbert C.
1422	,,	Galpin, Healey Sidney	1483	,,	Sunderland, Angus
1433	,,	Gooding, George H.	1508	,,	Scobie, Glenn
1434	,,	Goater, Chas. Richard	1509	,,	Stone, Victor Augusta
1435	,,	Geddes, Peter Muirgo	1488	,,	Thompson, Robert
1454	,,	Gordon, James	1447	,,	Towers, Albert
1491	,,	Girard, Joe	1469	Lce.-Cpl.	Twist, John
1501	,,	Giles, Arthur	1484	Private	Tanner, Frederick
1415	Bugler	Hussey, Chas. Francis	1510	,,	Turner, Percy
1455	Private	Howlett, Horace	1511	,,	Tucker, Sidney
1526	,,	Heron, James Jeffrey	1512	,,	Taylor, Fredk. Wm.
1475	,,	Hamilton, John	1513	,,	Taylor, Stanley Chas.
1476	,,	Irwin, William James	1471	,,	Varlow, Herbert A.
1503	,,	Irvine, James	1490	,,	Vennear, Walter
1436	,,	Johnston, Alec Smith	1425	,,	Walker, Arthur
1437	,,	Jones, Henry Joseph	1448	Lce.-Cpl.	Wilson, Talbert E.
1456	,,	James, David	1449	Private	Webster, Robert
1532	,,	Kiely, James	1470	,,	Williams, Townsend H.
1438	,,	Lavender, James	1486	,,	Walker, Thomas
1459	,,	Le Bean, Oscar	1487	,,	Whiteside, Robert
1460	,,	Leuvin, Eusebe	1489	,,	Wilson, Harry C.
1439	,,	McKenzie, Malcolm	1515	,,	Welsh, Herbert
1440	,,	Mason, William John	1516	,,	Wilson, Wilfred G.
1441	,,	Morrison, Donald			

Canadian Pacific—The Empire's Greatest Railway.

8TH BATTALION, 2ND INFANTRY BRIGADE—cont.

"K" COMPANY.

Lieutenant ... ... Blake, Charles

Regl. No.	Rank	Name	Regl. No.	Rank	Name
327	Band Sgt.	Farrell, James	1331	Private	Johnston, Herbert D.
609	Sergt.	Bovill, Charles Albert	527	,,	Jennings, Leonard A.
918	,,	Thomas, Wm. Geoffrey	1327	,,	Knott, Henry K.
1603	O.R.Sgt.	Jackson, Geo. Airey	1544	,,	Kerr, Jas. Alex. Green
330	Lce.-Cpl.	Beardmore, Chas. E. A.	1131	,,	Lynch, James
1540	,,	Stanton, Peter Owen	1545	,,	Lockhart, Herbert
1519	Private	Adams, Geo. Frederic	1325	,,	Lampen, Harold M.
326	,,	Akerstream, Neil Jas.	700	,,	Lawrence, Herbert
629	,,	Atkinson, Thomas	1330	,,	Lacelle, James Emile
628	,,	Arkwell, William	333	,,	Lemoine, Fred Victor
1318	,,	Amos, George	1130	,,	Levine, John
321	,,	Bissel, John Alexander	118	,,	Lewis, Wm. Edward
329	,,	Beardmore, Stanton Milo Knight	706	,,	McDougall, George T.
927	,,	Bell, David Ernest	942	,,	McMillan, John Earl
1535	,,	Burley, Thomas.	718	,,	Milicent, John
1523	,,	Bacchus, Harry	1326	,,	McNally, Hugh
1534	,,	Bailey, Walter George	1520	,,	McLennan, James
1324	,,	Crowder, William	1133	,,	MacHugh, John
658	,,	Carslake, Arthur	713	,,	Moffat, Robert
1322	,,	Cardy, Louis Davidson	1029	,,	McLeod, John
649	,,	Curley, William	324	,,	Mullins, Roy Sidney
1122	,,	Clarkson, Arthur E.	1334	,,	McNally, Joseph
322	,,	Duchane, Frederick	335	,,	Mitchell, James Wm.
941	,,	Daligianis, Arthur	610	,,	McDonald, Kenneth
523	,,	Drumps, John Arthur	707	,,	McDougall, Alex. W.
522	,,	Dillon, Edward	1135	,,	Mills, Fred Conroy
521	,,	Eadie, Wilfred	1132	,,	McCormack, Frank
524	,,	Eatwell, Wm. John	518	,,	Norris, Thos. Wm.
1639	,,	Flannigan, James	833	,,	Nurse, Albert Henry
1627	,,	Frame, George	1522	,,	O'Malley, Lawrence
328	,,	Frazer, Fred	1525	,,	Parker, Wm. Murray
928	,,	Frenette, Emery Jos.	1413	,,	Pitt, Cecil
668	,,	Furnell, Jack	618	,,	Palmer, Arthur
1530	,,	Green, Jas. Alexander	1052	,,	Reynolds, Ernest
1521	,,	Goddike, Charles	1321	,,	Rhind, Hubert Henry
1124	,,	Gazzana, Ronald C. H.	1138	,,	Randall, Hbt. Phillip
121	,,	Greenwood, Ralph	125	Lce.-Cpl.	Rand, Geo.
1126	,,	Gunston, Chas.	923	Private	Scott, John Sydney
1125	,,	Gregson, Samuel	1142	,,	Swaffer, Chas. Ronald
1531	,,	Gibson, William	922	,,	Scott, John
120	,,	Grey, Claude William	1141	,,	Spavins, Walter
1524	,,	Gibson, Ruthvian	1329	,,	Siddall, Wm.
332	,,	Hamilton, David	1139	,,	St. Germain, Louis
1542	,,	Hudson, E. (Butcher)	752	,,	Stevens, Walter
921	,,	Horne, David	1332	,,	St. Louis, Albert
681	,,	Hill, Thomas	1144	,,	Tarling, Charles
1129	,,	Jenkins, Wm.	123	,,	Torrence, George
			920	,,	Trayford, Albert

Canadian Pacific—The Empire's Greatest Railway.

8TH BATTALION, 2ND INFANTRY BRIGADE—cont.

Regl. No.	Rank.	Name.
1145	Private	Trewella, Fred Leslie
1320	,,	Trotter, Lewis M.
925	,,	Vickers, Ernest Geo.
620	,,	Williams, Arthur E.
336	,,	Wilson, David
943	,,	White, Thomas
1147	Private	Walker, Robert
124	,,	Wood, Arthur J. R.
325	,,	Walters, Charles
1323	Lce.-Cpl.	Wilkinson, Hbt. Geo.
1148	Private	Woods, James
1527	Lce.-Cpl.	Worth, Jesse

3rd INFANTRY BRIGADE.

HEADQUARTERS.

Brigadier...	Colonel R. E. W. Turner, V.C., D.S.O.
Brigade Major ...	Lieut.-Colonel G. B. Hughes
Staff Captain ...	Captain E. W. Pope
Orderly Officer ...	,, C. B. Costin
Clerk ...	Hon. Lieutenant J. P. McPeake
Staff Captain ...	Captain G. N. Weekes
Orderly Officer ...	Lieutenant H. F. McDonald
Veterinary Officer ...	,, E. Souter

Regl. No.	Rank.	Name.
29900	Q.M. Sgt.	Birch, G. R.
29901	Act. O.R.S.	Sutherland, David
29903	Private	Marcott, Edmond
29904	,,	Connolly, John
29905	,,	Laing, Alex.
29907	,,	Hatfull, Chas. S.
29906	,,	Kendall, Clifford
29918	,,	Gilman, Wm. C.
29908	,,	Harland, Edward
29911	Lce.-Cpl.	Duffield, F. W.
30405	Private	Moore, John
30398	,,	Johnson, W. M.
30395	,,	Hayward, W. A.
29902	,,	Roselle, Victor
29913	,,	Harrison, H. E.
30400	,,	Kinsey, Thomas
30414	,,	Scott, John C.
25527	Private	Bennet, Jos. S.
28785	,,	Rodolph, Frank
29914	Prov. Sgt.	Day, Chester R.
29916	Prov. Cpl.	Kewley, Robt. W.
29915	,,	Nelson, Cecil H.
25674	,,	Leslie, John
28636	,,	Hill, Frank L.
29910	Private	Parkinson, S.
29919	,,	Chagnon, F. C. (Postal).
12005	,,	Livingston, H. W. (Postal).
29920	Corpl.	Wallis, G. T. (Postal).
28549	Arm. S.-M.	Gibson, P. B. (W.O.)
29912	Private	McKane, W. J.

Canadian Pacific—The Empire's Greatest Railway.

13th BATTALION, 3rd INFANTRY BRIGADE.

(ROYAL HIGHLANDERS OF CANADA.)

Lieut.-Colonel	Loomis, Frederick Oscar Warren
Major	Norsworthy, Edward Cuthbert
,, ...	Buchanan, Victor Carl D S O
Adjutant	Captain George Eric McCuaig
Asst. Adjutant	,, Alexander George Cameron
Transport Officer	,, Edmund John Carthew
Signalling Officer	,, Gilbert Donald McGibbon
Surgeon Major	Brown, Ernest Rudolf
Paymaster	Hon. Captain William John Taylor
Chaplain	,, ,, Alex. McLellan Gordon
Quartermaster	,, ,, John Handley
Machine Gun Officer... ...	Lieutenant James Gordon Ross

Regl. No.	Rank.	Name.	Regl. No.	Rank.	Name.
24001	Sgt.-Maj.	Jeffery, John	24029	Private	Blythe, William
25000	Q.M.Sgt.	Tweedie, W. R.	24030	,,	Cawthorne, F.
24003	O.R.Clk.	Smith, Frederick C.	24031	,,	Foot, W.
24004	Drm.Sgt.	McGeagh, A. H.	24032	,,	Hampson, William S.
24005	Pion.Sgt.	Ford, Percy	24033	,,	Harding, Charles
24006	Cook Sgt.	Harriman, Alfred	24034	,,	Howlett, George
24007	Trns. Sgt.	Colls, Edward Joseph	25118	,,	Down, R. A. R.
24008	Sgnl. Sgt.	Blake, Frederick H.	24036	,,	Miles, James
25121	Shoe Sgt.	Ayling, J. A.	24038	,,	Wilson, William
24010	Pipe Sgt.	Burns, James	24684	,,	Pritchard, J.
24011	Piper	Dyce, John	24039	,,	Braley, R. E.
24012	,,	Lawson, William	24040	,,	Geary, J.
24013	,,	McDonald, Alex. J.	24685	,,	Wardle, J.
24014	,,	Sinclair, Neil	24041	,,	Read, Frank A. G.
24015	,,	Singer, Alex.	24043	Batman	Brenchley, G. B.
24016	Sgnl. Pte.	Williams, George	24044	Private	Clark, David
24017	Sgnl. Cpl.	Claridge, Welton, J.	24045	,,	Doran, Samuel
24447	,,	Brown, J.	24046	,,	Fairley, William F.
24212	,,	Sutherland, M. C.	24047	,,	Fletcher, Allan
24020	,,	Lapraik, Thomas	24092	,,	Hadfield, T.
24680	,,	MacCartney, J.	24048	,,	Holt, Samuel
24022	,,	Ritson, Howell	24049	,,	McNicol, William
24023	Lce.-Cpl.	Splatt, William F.	24051	,,	Towns, William
24024	Med. Sgt.	Vickers, John	24053	,,	Wood, Thomas
24025	Med. Pte.	Burns, James	24415	,,	Wright, N. H.
24026	Drv. Cpl.	McCormick, Robert	24189	,,	Wright, R.
24027	Private	Anderson, R.			

Attached.

24054	Corpl.	Mowatt, Alex.	24058	C.A.M.C.	Shaw, James
24055	C.A.M.C.	Brown, Robert Henry	24583	Pay. Sgt.	Campbell, J. J.
24056	,,	Gerrard, George	24060	Arm. Sgt.	McMillan, William
24057	,,	McLonney, William			

Canadian Pacific—The Empire's Greatest Railway.

13TH BATTALION, 3RD INFANTRY BRIGADE—cont.

Machine Gun Section.

Regl. No.	Rank.	Name.	Regl. No.	Rank.	Name.
24061	Col.-Sgt.	Trainor, John	24070	Private	Hincks, George W.
24062	Corpl.	Garrick, Robert L.	24071	,,	Mooney, John R.
24063	Driver	Gowdy, William O.	24072	,,	Morrison, William
24064	,,	Whetter, Richard	24073	,,	Reaume, Stanley
24065	Private	Barrie, George R.	24074	,,	Stewart, John
24066	,,	Fisher, Fred	24075	,,	Watt, Robert I.
24067	,,	Goldsmith, Charles A.	24076	,,	Wand, Edward W.
24068	,,	Grimwood, William	24077	Batman	Arnold, Bertram
24069	,,	Hammell, Sidney H.			

"A" COMPANY.

Major	... ...	McCuaig, Douglas Rykert
Captain	... ...	Walker, Herbert F.
Lieutenant	... ...	Stephens, Francis Chattan
,,	... ...	Smith, Walter Dugald McK.

Regl. No.	Rank.	Name.	Regl. No.	Rank.	Name.
24078	Col.-Sgt.	Morrison, John	24109	Private	Beach, William
24079	Sergt.	Imrie, George E. W.	24110	,,	Bissett, David
24086	,,	Ableson, F.	24111	,,	Biddulph, Phillip
24085	,,	Thomson, J. H.	24112	,,	Boland, George
24084	,,	Townsend, F.	25119	Pioneer	Bennett, J. A.
24177	Corpl.	Stewart, R. E.	24114	Private	Carr, Henry Wilfred
24081	,,	Small, W.	24115	Lce.-Cpl.	Carr, Joseph Horace
24113	,,	Curwen, F.	24116	Private	Copeman, Henry
24083	,,	McIntyre, E.	24118	,,	Cooper, Walter A.
24194	,,	Young, S.	24119	,,	Campbell, Sidney
24089	Drummer	Laing, Robert	24120	,,	Crichton, Robert
24090	Pioneer	Harvel, Frank	24121	,,	Cartwright, Alfred
24091	Private	Robertson, D. A.	24122	Lce.-Cpl.	Day, Harry
24105	,,	Baxter, Charles	24123	Private	Douglas, Alexander
24094	Str.-B'rer	Armstrong, J. B.	24124	,,	Evans, William
24095	,,	Bell (Corp.) L.	24125	,,	Elphick, Thomas
24096	P.Cb.Dr.	Kent, George	24715	,,	Eldridge, J.
24097	,,	McCahon, George	24126	,,	Fothergill, Lawrence
24098	Batman	Hamilton, John H.	24127	Lce.-Cpl.	Fraser, George A.
24099	,,	Wilkins, Charles	24128	Private	Feather, James
24100	,,	Fergus, William	24129	,,	Ferguson, Duncan J.
24101	Private	Herber, Arthur S.	24130	,,	Grant, William
24019	,,	Harding, J.	24131	,,	Giveen, Butler
24102	,,	Allan, Andrew	24132	Cook	Glidden, Ernest
24103	,,	Ayre, William	24133	Private	Goodyear, William
24104	,,	Bayliss, Harold	24134	Lce.-Cpl.	Green, Harry R.
24106	,,	Bennett, Edward	24135	Private	Heney, Francis
24107	,,	Bowman, Percy	24136	Arm. Cpl.	Hughes, Thomas
24108	,,	Brown, George L.	10539	Private	Hamilton, W. W.

Canadian Pacific—The Empire's Greatest Railway

13TH BATTALION, 3RD INFANTRY BRIGADE—cont. 117

Regl. No.	Rank.	Name.	Regl. No.	Rank.	Name.
24137	Private	Harper, Harry	24163	Private	McCuaig, Arch. D.
24138	,,	Holden, Mitchell	24164	,,	McArthur, Neil
24139	,,	Isherwood, Richard	24165	,,	Mitchard, Frederick
24140	,,	Johnston, Charles	24166	,,	McPherson, R. N.
24141	,,	Jones, W. E.	24050	,,	Murphy, J.
24142	,,	Kranchel, Otto	24167	Lce.-Cpl.	Nimmo, Robert C.
24143	,,	Keay, George N.	24168	Cook	Olsen, Peter
24144	,,	Knight, Gordon	24169	Private	Patterson, Thos. R.
24080	,,	Lawson, H. Y.	24170	Lce.-Cpl.	Poole, Robt. J. M. S.
24145	Cook	Lewis, Arnold S.	24171	Private	Roberts, Claude J.
24146	,,	Leigh, William A.	24173	,,	Ruston, Arnold W.
24147	Private	Lawson, James	24174	,,	Smith, Andrew W.
25069	,,	Leon, Harry V.	24175	,,	Sampson, James E.
24148	,,	Magee, Robert J.	24176	Lce.-Cpl.	Stewart, James
24149	,,	Mathieson, Wm. R.	24178	Private	Stringer, Dixon
24150	,;	Marshall, Anthony	24179	,,	Snowdon, Robert
25018	,,	Moon, T. H.	24180	,,	Spencer, Kenneth
24151	,,	Moran, Patrick	24181	,,	Sawyer, Gilbert G.
24152	,,	Mitchener, Thos. H.	24182	,,	Skuce, Richard
24153	,,	Maltby, Charles	10164	,,	Seabrook, H. J.
24154	,,	McCahon, Chas. P.	24184	,,	Thyer, James Asta
24155	,,	Macdonald, Neil W.	24185	,,	Wilson, Harold
24087	,,	MacArthur, W.	24186	,,	Wilson, Ernest W.
24156	,,	MacFarlane, Hugh	24187	,,	Wilkinson, Cust L.
24157	,,	McLeod, John	24188	,,	Wallace, William B
24158	Lce.-Cpl.	McConachie, John A.	24190	,,	Ward, William T.
24159	Private	McDougall-Forbes,J.	24191	,,	Willis, W. Ingram
24160	,,	Maclure, Thomas	24192	,,	Williams, John
24161	,,	McNeilage, Neil	24193	,,	Wells, Douglas
24162	,,	McGrory, Frank			

"B" COMPANY.

Captain ... ... Smith, Charles John
,, ... Drummond, Guy Melfort
Lieutenant ... ... Horsey, Clifton Maubank
,, ... Cantley, Charles Lang

Regl. No.	Rank.	Name.	Regl. No.	Rank.	Name.
24195	Col.-Sgt.	Harris, Charles	24219	Private	Anderson, John T.
24196	Sergt.	Black, Charles G.	24218	,,	Aldridge, Robert
24202	,,	McLeod, P.	24042	,,	Bird, J. H. (alias Addley, J. H.)
24199	,,	Hall, Charles F. E.			
24203	,,	Boothby, G. W.	24224	,,	Baker, Charles W.
24200	Private	Reid, David L.	24225	Lce.-Cpl.	Banks, Albert J.
24201	Corpl.	Bailey, Hugh R.	24222	Private	Banning, S. Henry
24255	,,	Glithero, J. H.	24214	,,	Bartlett, Charles N.
24204	,,	Osborne, Neil	24223	,,	Beverley, John L.
24245	,,	Edge, F. C.	24206	Drummer	Blackwell, George E.

Canadian Pacific—The Empire's Greatest Railway.

118 13TH BATTALION, 3RD INFANTRY BRIGADE—cont.

Regl. No.	Rank.	Name.	Regl. No.	Rank.	Name.
24220	Private	Brown, William B.	24277	Private	McKenzie, John
24221	,,	Burrows, Arthur	24278	,,	McLean, John F.
24229	,,	Campbell, John	24274	,,	McLennan, David
24234	,,	Campbell, R. J.	24276	,,	McNaught, John
24226	,,	Carter, Guy B.	24197	,,	McCaskill, M.
24227	,,	Carney, Michael	24269	,,	Mennie, James D.
24237	,,	Cassel, George	24267	,,	Montanelli, John
24235	,,	Chandler, Sidney	24271	,,	Morgan, Charles W.
24228	Arm. Cpl.	Clarke, Edwin	24268	,,	Morgan, Thomas A.
24236	Cook	Clarkson, John	24270	,,	Moyes, J. McQueen
24238	Private	Clements, W. A.	24272	,,	Murdoch, John L.
24230	,,	Clover, Alfred	24273	,,	Murney, Henry J.
24240	,,	Coleman, Ernest W.	24280	Corpl.	Nolton, Stanley H.
24239	,,	Craig, Robert A. M.	24281	Private	O'Connell, G. B.
24232	,,	Croally, James	24282	Cook	O'Hara, Victor
24231	Lce.-Cpl.	Cunliffe, W. J.	24284	Private	Palmer, Albert E.
24233	Private	Cuthbert, George	24283	,,	Palmer, John
24241	,,	Daly, Michael D.	24288	,,	Parnaby, W. F.
24244	,,	Dalziel, John	24286	Corpl.	Petrie, Alexander
24205	Bugler	Daniels, W. James	24285	Private	Pocock, Charles A.
24242	Private	Duberges, Valmor	24287	,,	Proudfoot, Arthur
24243	,,	Durden, F. George	24289	,,	Quinn, William
24246	,,	Ferguson, Daniel	24292	,,	Reid, John
24207	Pioneer	Ferguson, James C.	24291	,,	Reid, Francis John
24247	Private	Findlay, Alexander	24293	,,	Robertson, Gabriel
24250	,,	Finnie, A. Flemming	24290	,,	Robinson, T. W.
24254	,,	Fitzgerald, T. B.	24295	,,	Rochester, John J.
24252	,,	Fleury, Arthur	24294	,,	Rosselli, F. E. J.
24249	,,	Fordyce, John	24296	,,	Ryan, Henry Edward
24253	,,	Fowler, James	24297	,,	Scott, William A.
24248	,,	Fox, Harry	24301	,,	Sheldon, Lewis R.
24251	,,	Fraser, Francis T.	24217	P.C.Driv.	Shergold, Stanley E.
24009	,,	Grant, S.	24302	Private	Sinclair, Daniel G.
24256	,,	Gallagher, John W.	24303	,,	Sinnett, Milton C.
24257	,,	Gibb, George	24300	,,	Smith, Thomas
24258	,,	Grangel, W. J.	24209	Batman	Smith, William J.
24211	Batman	Green, George	24208	Private	Southwick, Henry J.
24259	Lce.-Cpl.	Hegarty, Cecil John	24298	,,	Stephens, W. C.
24263	Private	Haines, James	24299	,,	Stuart, John D.
24262	,,	Hammon, Robert	24305	Lce.-Cpl.	Taylor, George H.
24215	,,	Harrison, F. R.	24304	Private	Teffer, F. G.
24260	,,	Heavyside, John	24213	,,	Trew, Robert E. H.
24261	,,	Hogan, James John	24306	,,	Vincent, John W.
24264	,,	Holland, F. C. V.	24309	,,	Walker, Alexander
24265	,,	Hore, Enos Edward	24311	,,	Warren, Ernest
24266	,,	Hyslop, James	24310	,,	Watson, John
24216	P.C.Driv.	Ibbotson, I. W. H.	24307	,,	Weir, William J.
24279	Private	McDonald Albert	24308	,,	Wellman, A. Thomas
24275	,,	McKellar, John	24210	,,	Wilson, John

Canadian Pacific—The Empire's Greatest Railway.

13TH BATTALION, 3RD INFANTRY BRIGADE—cont. 119

"C" COMPANY.

Captain	Jamieson, Robert H.
Lieutenant	Fisher, Alastair M.
,, ...	Sellon, Ernest M.
,, ...	Greenshields, Melville

Regl. No.	Rank.	Name.	Regl. No.	Rank.	Name.
24312	Col.-Sgt.	McMillan, Charles J.	24364	Private	Hannan, John
24315	Sergt.	Anderson, Walter J.	24363	,,	Harland, George
24316	,,	Howard, Albert T.	24327	,,	Harrison, John
24317	,,	Anderson, Geo. M. G.	24365	Lce.-Cpl.	Hartnell, Reginald E.
24318	,,	Joliceour, Ernest	24331	Private	Henderson, Cyril
24319	Corpl.	Benson, Allan H.	24362	,,	Hodgson, Thomas
24320	,,	Lee, Howard F.	24422	,,	Howard, John M.
24397	,,	Smith, C. M.	24326	,,	Irvine, Louis J.
24401	,,	Steel, J.	24366	,,	Irvine, Robert
24323	,,	Earle, Gerard L.	24313	,,	Jamieson, Lyle W.
24334	Cook	Adams, Thomas R.	24369	,,	Jarrett, Edward
24335	Private	Armstrong, F. H.	24367	,,	Johnson, William H.
24330	,,	Ash, Reginald A.	24368	,,	Johnston, Duncan
24339	,,	Bain, James	24372	,,	Kane, Lawrence J.
24420	,,	Barker, Thomas H.	24370	Lce.-Cpl.	Lowe, Robert
24328	,,	Beard, James	24371	Private	Lucas, Sidney
24336	,,	Beggs, Patrick J.	24386	,,	Lockwood, Sidney S.
24341	,,	Berry, Arthur	24329	,,	MacDonald, Ken. N.
24337	,,	Blanchard, A.	24421	,,	MacLucas, Kenneth
24338	,,	Boyer, Edgar M.	24385	,,	MacRae, Murdoch T.
24340	,,	Brown, Alexander L.	24059	,,	Monsarrat, H. R.
24325	Bugler	Burns, Edward	24387	,,	Maguire, Owen W.
24332	Private	Campbell, Robert	24374	,,	Martin, Samuel D.
24343	,,	Carson, Ambrose	24377	,,	Matheson, Frank
24342	Lce.-Cpl.	Carstairs, David L.	24378	,,	Matheson, James F
24464	Private	Chandler, S.	24373	,,	Maxwell, Thomas
24345	,,	Charlton, William T.	24375	,,	McAuley, Alexander
24344	,,	Cockburn, Robert	24383	,,	McDermot, Arthur
24324	,,	Davies, Frederick	24384	,,	McMillan, John A.
24346	,,	Delaney, Martin	24382	,,	McPherson, John
24349	,,	Dickerson, Ernest	24381	,,	Millward, Chris.
24348	,,	Drew, Daniel	24379	,,	Moores, Ernest
24347	,,	Druett, George A.	24376	,,	Moulder, Aubry C.
24351	,,	Eadle, George W.	24333	,,	Morrison, William C
24350	,,	Edsell, Harold S.	24380	,,	Muir, Charles B.
24352	,,	French, Alexander	24427	Lce.-Cpl.	O'Donnell, Cornelous
24355	Cook	Gaffney, Hugh	24390	Private	Parsons, George H.
24358	Private	Gardner, Horace P.	24389	,,	Pegram, Michael
24357	,,	Gardner, William H.	24388	,,	Pemberton, George
24360	,,	Goodwin, Thomas A.	24426	Far. Sgt.	Prince, H. B.
24359	,,	Gougeon, Joseph	24408	Private	Reekie, John G.
24356	,,	Gray, Charles	24391	,,	Reeve, Robert
24354	,,	Green, Henry T.	24314	Lce.-Cpl.	Renateau, Lewis
24353	,,	Grimsdale, Harry	24424	Private	Riddoch, Jock
24361	,,	Gordon, Samuel	24392	,,	Robertson, Hay

Canadian Pacific—The Empire's Greatest Railway.

120 13TH BATTALION, 3RD INFANTRY BRIGADE—cont.

Regl. No.	Rank.	Name.	Regl. No.	Rank.	Name.
24393	Private	Robertson, Robert M.	24322	Private	Thompson, J.
24394	,,	Scott, James	24425	,,	Talbot, James
24428	P.C.Driv.	Seivwright, Henry	24409	,,	Walker, Thomas
24404	Private	Sims, Arthur	24414	Lce.-Cpl.	Walters, John P.
24407	,,	Sladen, Joseph D.	24418	Private	Watson, Alexander
24395	Arm. Cpl.	Smallridge, Mark	24417	,,	Watson, Walter
24406	Private	Stephenson, Chas. G.	24419	,,	Wild, John
24405	,,	Stephenson, Leslie	24411	,,	White, Philip
24402	,,	Stratton, George	24410	,,	White, Robert R.
24396	,,	Strefford, Albert	24412	,,	Williams, John H.
24403	,,	Sykes, Thomas	24413	Lce.-Cpl.	Wilson, Leslie C.
24400	,,	Smith, Frank C.	24321	Private	Ward, W.
24398	,,	Smith, John R.	24416	,,	Wylie, Robert H.
24399	,,	Smith, Robert H.			

"D" COMPANY.

Captain	... ...	Perry, Kenneth Meikle
Lieutenant	... ...	Reford, Andrew
,,	... ...	Chipman, Leverett de V.
,,	... ...	Peterman, Wilfred Ferrier

Regl. No.	Rank.	Name.	Regl. No.	Rank.	Name.
24429	Col.-Sgt.	Wayman, Henry	24458	Private	Bagnall, Harold
24437	Sergt.	Caslake, A. J.	24459	,,	Barlow, George F.
24902	,,	Evans, E.	24460	,,	Bedford, Percy
24172	,,	Robinson, A.	24461	,,	Bell, James Bertram
24844	,,	Chanter, H. H.	24462	,,	Beaver, Robert G.
24506	Corpl.	McGregor, R.	24463	,,	Brooks, Thomas C.
24434	,,	Wilson, M. C.	24433	Corpl.	Bailey, H.
24436	,,	Robinson, Samuel	24465	Private	Creak, William F.
25096	,,	Buckley, J. H.	24466	,,	Conn, George D.
25097	Lce.-Cpl.	Line, H.	24468	,,	Cowan, Joseph
24439	Drummer	Adair, L. P.	24469	,,	Davidson, George
24440	Bugler	Ozon, Louis	24470	,,	Davidson, Charles N.
24441	Pioneer	Parkinson, Ralph G.	24471	,,	Davis, Orville C.
24442	Batman	Heggie, John	24472	,,	Dobson, Henry
24444	,,	Kiddie, Thomas	24473	,,	Dyer, Henry Seth
24445	,,	Gray, Alexander	24474	,,	Dyce, John
24446	Signaller	McLeish, William M.	24475	,,	Ducker, James W.
24018	,,	Dick, P.	24476	Cook	Dahlmann, B. J.
24448	Str. B'rer	Lowe, Alfred	24477	Private	Eccles, Michael V.
24449	P.C.Driv.	Hendry, James H.	24438	,,	Fothergill, C. G.
24450	,,	Keith, Stephen W.	24478	,,	Fielding, Arthur
24451	,,	Wall, Michael J.	24479	,,	Field, Percy
24452	Private	Allen, William	24480	Lce.-Cpl.	Ferguson, William
24453	,,	Allan, Robert	24481	Private	Fox, Thomas G.
24454	,,	Armet, Robert	24482	,,	Fisher, William C.
24455	,,	Alexander, George	24484	,,	Gracey, William
24456	,,	Astbury, Albert	24485	,,	Hiscock, George T.
24457	,,	Bryant, Hezekiah A.	24486	,,	Huggan, James D.

Canadian Pacific—The Empire's Greatest Railway.

13TH BATTALION, 3RD INFANTRY BRIGADE—cont. 121

Regl. No.	Rank.	Name.	Regl. No.	Rank.	Name.
24487	Private	Hewitt, Samuel A.	24517	Private	Olney, Herbert E.
24488	,,	Hamilton, Wilbert G.	24518	,,	Osborne, James S.
24489	,,	Hamilton, William	24519	Lce.-Cpl.	Piché, James H.
24490	,,	Hayward, Stanley A.	24520	Private	Piché, Basil R.
24491	,,	Hay, Thomas	24521	,,	Paterson, Arthur L.
24492	,,	Hall, Joseph	24432	,,	Palmer, W. G.
24493	,,	Hutchison, James B.	24522	,,	Palmer, Edward G.
24494	,,	Hicks, Francis G.	24435	,,	Pearce, H. G.
24495	,,	Herring, Reginald F.	24523	Cook	Quigg, Edward
24496	,,	Inglis, Alexander	24524	Private	Rainey, Edward
24497	,,	Jones, Walter	24525	Cook	Rankin, Thomas
24498	,,	Kelly, Clarence	24526	Private	Rankin, James
24499	,,	Kirker, Walter H.	24527	Lce.-Cpl.	Robb, Robert
24500	,,	Knights, Albert T.	24528	Private	Riley, Francis J.
24501	,,	Latto, Mathew	24529	,,	Russell, David M.
24502	,,	Lindsay, John	24530	,,	Sellick, William
24503	,,	Lilly, Walter G.	24531	,,	Sweeney, Bertram K.
24504	,,	Lee, James	24532	,,	Smith, Edmund J.
24505	,,	Lapierre, Harry	24533	,,	Stewart, Norman C.
24507	,,	MacInnes, Harry	24534	,,	Stonard, William J.
24443	,,	McLeod, Angus	24535	,,	Steel, Alexander
24508	,,	Morton, Robert	24536	Lce.-Cpl.	Sullivan, William M.
24509	,,	Carruthers, John	24431	Private	Tucker, C. E.
24510	,,	Marsh, Thomas	24537	,,	Thorpe, Harry
24511	,,	Midgley, Thomas	24538	,,	Thomas, Henry
24512	,,	Muirhead, Thomas	24539	,,	Wilson, Adam
24513	,,	Murphy, Wilson	24540	,,	Wright, Henry
24514	,,	Mann, Charles	24541	,,	White, Francis E.
24545	,,	MacAskill, Percy M.	24542	Arm. Cpl.	Withinshaw, David
24516	,,	Mell, Walter	24543	Private	Wilson, John H.
24515	,,	Myles, Fred			

"E" COMPANY.

Captain	Whitehead, Lionel Ward
Lieutenant	Crowdy, Charles Hutton
,, ...	Pitblado, Charles Bruce
,, ...	Ferguson, Peter George

Regl. No.	Rank.	Name.	Regl. No.	Rank.	Name.
24549	Col.-Sgt.	Wood, Henry James	24559	Drummer	Orr, William Wright
24550	Sergt.	Crawford, Thomas N.	24560	Bugler	Blake, James F.
24551	,,	Deeks, Clifford H.	24561	Pioneer	McKenzie, Andrew
24552	,,	Gibbon, Edward	25562	Batman	Peters, Charles C.
24553	,,	Brown, Daniel McN.	24563	Private	McCombie, John
24554	Corpl.	Alexander, Colin	24564	,,	O'Hara, Patrick
24614	,,	Lang, T.	24565	,,	Taylor, Jack
24556	,,	Saunders, Eric G.	24566	Signaller	Chambers, Wm. F.
24557	,,	Black, Albert R.	24567	Lce.-Cpl.	Ross, John
24558	,,	Reid, James Leslie	24568	Str. B'rer	Alford, Harry

Canadian Pacific—The Empire's Greatest Railway.

122   13TH BATTALION, 3RD INFANTRY BRIGADE—cont.

Regl. No.	Rank	Name	Regl. No.	Rank	Name
24569	Str. B'rer	Turnbull, Wm. A.	24617	Private	McKenzie, Kenneth
24546	P.C.Driv.	Piche, Albert	24618	,,	McGuinness, F. W.
24547	,,	Scott, William	24619	Batman	McDonald, Wm. M.
24570	Private	Adam, Alexander F.	24620	Private	McNeil, Duncan
24571	Lce.-Cpl.	Anderson, James	24621	Lce.-Cpl.	McNeil, Donald J.
24572	Private	Boyle, Austin Hugh	24622	Private	McInally, Michael
24573	,,	Benoy, Francis John	24623	,,	McCowan, Charles A.
24574	,,	Bigland, Ronald C.	24624	,,	McAuley, Murdo M.
24575	,,	Brogden, Frederick	24625	,,	Maloney, Michael
24576	,,	Bullock, Charles A.	24626	,,	Mott, Herbert Basil
24577	,,	Byrne, Gerald F.	24627	,,	Milloy, Andrew
24578	Lce.-Cpl.	Brown, Frederick	24628	,,	Michelson, Walter
24555	Private	Christopher, J. F.	24629	,,	Muncaster, A. J.
24579	,,	Campbell, George W.	24630	,,	Marsh, Jack
24580	Lce.-Cpl.	Chopin, Aloysius J.	24631	,,	Moore, Henry
24581	Cook	Clarke, Thomas W.	24632	,,	Mellowes, William O.
24582	Private	Cowan, George F.	24633	,,	Murphy, Joseph
24584	,,	Cameron, Fred	24634	,,	Mayhew, Arthur
24585	Cook	Cadieux, Eugene	25061	,,	Nixon, R.
24586	Private	Coones, Alfred W.	24635	,,	Neil, William C.
24587	,,	Cuin, Walter Martin	24636	,,	O'Sullivan, Patrick
24588	,,	Carley, Donald John	24637	,,	Peoples, James H.
24589	,,	Cameron, John	24638	,,	Peet, William John
24590	,,	Dand, Matthew G.	24639	,,	Pierce, John Preston
24591	,,	Dunsmore, Charles	24640	,,	Quin, James Edward
24592	Lce.-Cpl.	Dupre, Thomas	24641	,,	Ross, James Donald
24593	Private	Dunbar, Alex. F.	24642	Lce.-Cpl.	Ryan, Patrick J.
24594	,,	Fairley, Thomas	24643	Private	Reilly, James
24595	,,	Fisher, James A. B.	24644	,,	Riley, James
24596	,,	Fitzgerald, Jack	24645	,,	Reid, Wilfred
24597	,,	Gill, George	24646	,,	Robertson, George
24598	,,	Glad, Konghard	24647	,,	Senior, Horace
24599	,,	Goulding, James	24548	,,	Strutt, Derek Henry
24600	,,	Garrett, John T.	24648	,,	Story, Nevil
24601	Lce.-Cpl.	Gyde, Edward	24649	,,	Stephen, John Mason
24602	Private	Hollingsworth, Wm.	24650	,,	Stanley, Arthur
24603	,,	Hindle, James M.	24651	,,	Smith, William
24604	,,	Hollands, John	24652	,,	Smith, William John
24605	,,	Holden, Harry	24653	,,	Smith, John
24606	,,	Hunt, John James	24654	,,	Stanfield, Israel
24607	,,	Hunter, Thomas	24655	,,	Smillie, William J.
24608	,,	Jenson, Philip	24656	,,	Sockett, Alfred
24609	,,	Jones, William	24657	,,	Templeman, H. W.
24610	,,	Kealey, Chauncey	24658	,,	Wise, Herbert
24611	Lce.-Cpl.	Kerr, Alexander W.	24659	,,	Winter, George S.
24612	Private	Legault, Paul	24660	,,	Wilson, Isaac
24613	Lce.-Cpl.	Laurie, William	24661	,,	Wallace, Victor A. J.
24615	Private	McDonald, Donald J.	24662	,,	Young, William J.
24616	Arm. Cpl.	McTaggart, Henry			

Canadian Pacific—The Empire's Greatest Railway.

13TH BATTALION, 3RD INFANTRY BRIGADE—cont.

"F" COMPANY.

Captain	Morrisey, Thomas Sydney
Lieutenant	Molson, Francis Stuart
,, ...	McCuaig, Clarence Norman
,, ... /o.	Morrow, James Curzon

Regl. No.	Rank.	Name.	Regl. No.	Rank.	Name.
24667	Col.-Sgt.	Logan, Edward	24708	Private	Connolly, Peter
24663	Sergt.	Morrison, George P.	24709	,,	Cosh, Rex Frederick
24665	,,	Morrison, William C.	24710	,,	Cunningham, F. J.
24666	,,	Dowie, Robert	24711	,,	D'Arcy, Alfred J. K.
24669	,,	Dougall, Sydney D.	24712	,,	Deans, William D.
24668	Corpl.	Taunton, Robert T.	24713	,,	Dixon, Thomas C.
24670	,,	Grieve, David Clark.	24714	Lce.-Cpl.	Eagle, Richard
24671	,,	Hossick, Kenneth C.	24716	Private	Gardner, James
24672	,,	Knight, Herbert J.	24720	,,	Goodwin, James E.
24733	,,	Kinnear, Campbell O.	24717	,,	Ganson, Wm. J. S.
24673	Bugler	McMillan, James D.	24719	,,	Glover, Francis C.
24674	Drummer	Ballantyne, Walter	24718	Arm.Cpl.	Gibb, George
24675	Private	Donaldson, Alexander	24721	Private	Grant, Charles D.
24676	Batman	Morrison, John McH.	25065	,,	Grant, Donald
24677	,,	Campbell, D. McD.	24722	,,	Hare, Charles
24679	,,	Morrish, Albert	24723	,,	Hatter, Harold
24678	Pioneer	Brennan, Andrew	24724	,,	Hawkings, W. C.
25075	Signaller	Gubbins, H. P. N.	24725	,,	Hayes, Ernest E.
24681	,,	Rust, Benjamin H.	24726	,,	Henderson, James H.
24682	Str.-B'rer	Bailes, George	24727	,,	Hesketh, James E.
24683	,,	Fisher, John Weston	24728	,,	Higginbottom, Jos.
24777	Private	Wood, B.	24729	,,	Holmes, George A.
24028	,,	Armstrong, J.	24730	,,	Johnson, Clifford H.
24686	,,	Adams, John Baptist	24731	,,	Jones, George
24687	,,	Addison, Adam	24732	,,	Kidd, William
24688	,,	Ash, George	24734	,,	Knight, Maurice
24689	,,	Armstrong, Kenneth	24735	Lce.-Cpl.	Macartney, And. A.
24690	,,	Armstrong, Leslie	24736	Private	McEldownie, G.
24691	,,	Auld, Alexander	24737	,,	Macfarlane, W. E.
24692	,,	Bishop, Gilbert	24021	,,	McCarthy, J.
24693	,,	Black, William F.	24738	Lce.-Cpl.	MacKay, John
24694	,,	Boland, George C.	24739	Private	McKim, William
24695	,,	Bowen, Charles S.	24740	,,	MacKinnon, Daniel
24696	,,	Bradgate, Geoffrey	24741	,,	MacLean, N. McL.
24697	,,	Brittan, Stanley V.	24742	Lce.-Cpl.	MacLean, Wm. S.
24698	,,	Brookes, William	24743	Private	MacLeod, Alexander
24699	Cook	Burke, Joseph A.	24744	,,	MacLeod, John
24700	Lce.-Cpl.	Butters, George M.	24745	Lce.-Cpl.	MacNeil, Nicholas
24701	Private	Byatt, Geoffrey P.	24746	Private	MacNeish, John S.
24702	,,	Calvert, John Cyril	24747	,,	MacQuade, James P.
24703	,,	Caine, John	24748	,,	MacRae, Donald
24704	,,	Campbell, David	24749	,,	Marriott, Fred
24705	,,	Campbell, John	24750	,,	Miller, Frank M.
24706	,,	Chipps, Herbert G.	24751	,,	Miller, James A.
24707	,,	Clarke, Frederick E.	24752	Batman	Milne, Lewis G.

Canadian Pacific—The Empire's Greatest Railway.

124 13TH BATTALION, 3RD INFANTRY BRIGADE—cont.

Regl. No.	Rank.	Name.	Regl. No.	Rank.	Name.
24753	Corpl.	Neilson, Alan	24765	Private	Simpson, G. W. R.
24754	Private	Oborn, John	24766	,,	Skillen, Harry R.
24755	,,	Ogilvie, Charles Scott	24767	,,	Slessor, Peter
24756	,,	Potter, Guy Ralph L.	24769	,,	Stott, Raymond
24757	,,	Powell, Haynes R.	24770	,,	Taylor, Russell
24758	,,	Putt, Harry	24771	,,	Townsend, John
24664	,,	Ramsay, Allan D.	24772	,,	Waller, Horace W.
24759	,,	Reynolds, Fredk. G.	24773	,,	Watkinson, John
24760	,,	Rowan, Frederick J.	24774	,,	Webster, John N.
24791	,,	Strudwicke, M. A.	24775	,,	Wilson, David
24761	Cook	Saggers, Charles	24776	Lce.-Cpl.	Wilson, John W.D.M.
24762	Private	Sanderson, J.	24778	Private	Yaldwyn, C. E. G.
24763	,,	Stracey, Harry	24779	,,	Yarnell, Llewellyn R.
24764	,,	Sherwood, Richard			

"G" COMPANY.

Captain	Lees, Gerald Oscar
Lieutenant	Worthington, Alan N.
,, ...	Ives, Hubert Douglas
,, ...	Hastings, John Ogilvie

Regl. No.	Rank.	Name.	Regl. No.	Rank.	Name.
24430	Sergt.	Adams, A.	24806	Private	Baker, William W.
25008	,,	Wilson, E. W. D.	24807	,,	Barber, Douglas F.
24781	,,	Tulley, E. H.	24808	,,	Barton, Allan Gordon
24782	,,	Metcalfe, A.	24809	,,	Beaconsfield, James
24783	,,	Race, G. E.	24810	,,	Bole, John James
24784	Corpl.	Scott, W. G.	24811	Lce.-Cpl.	Bowen, Richard L.
24787	,,	Hammond, J.	24812	Private	Bowman, Charles
24789	,,	Key, R.	24813	,,	Boyle, Henry
24785	,,	Davidson, H. M.	24814	,,	Bradley, Geo. H. R.
24786	,,	Gray, D. H.	24815	,,	Brown, Alexander
24878	Lce.-Cpl.	Simpson, J.	24816	,,	Buchanan, Ernest J.
24790	Drummer	Rodden, Edward	24817	,,	Campbell, Thomas J.
24792	Pioneer	Cavanagh, James	24818	,,	Cecil, William
24793	Batman	Hall, Spencer	24819	,,	Collins, Edward J.
24794	Private	Jackson, William C.	24820	,,	Connell, Robert
24795	Batman	O'Keeffe, Dennis	24821	,,	Connor, Bertie James
24796	,,	Stratton, George H.	24822	,,	Cook, George
24798	Signaller	Farquharson, J. M.	24823	,,	Craig, Cameron D.
24851	,,	Livingstone, M. A.	24825	,,	Clark, Charles B.
24799	Str.B'rer	Abercrombie, J. D.	24824	,,	Clark, Alexander C.
24800	,,	McLeod, John Angus	24826	,,	Dickie, John George
24801	Private	Eastwood, Oliver W.	24828	,,	Doyle, William B.
24802	,,	Wallace, James	24827	Cook	Dougall, Robert
24803	,,	Anderson, John	24829	Private	Duncan, David
24804	,,	Anning, Harry	24830	,,	Gallagher, James
24797	,,	Brokenshire, L.	24832	,,	Godfrey, Harold
24805	,,	Baker, Wilson S.	24833	,,	Gullett, James M.

Canadian Pacific—The Empire's Greatest Railway.

13TH BATTALION, 3RD INFANTRY BRIGADE—cont.

Regl. No.	Rank	Name	Regl. No.	Rank	Name
24831	Private	Gayner, Walter R.	24868	Private	Munro, Harry
24834	,,	Gyde, Norman	24867	,,	Muncey, Edwin
24836	,,	Harpell, Herbert H.	24869	,,	Murdock, John A.
24835	,,	Hallam, Thomas	24870	,,	Murray, Charles R.
24837	,,	Harvey, Arthur	24866	,,	Mowat, George
24841	,,	Hickey, Leon	24871	,,	O'Neil, Martin
24842	,,	Hill, Ruby Charles	24872	,,	Owen, William E.
24840	Batman	Herlihy, Thomas	24873	,,	Parks, Stanley
24839	Private	Haynes, Howard A.	24544	,,	Read, Thos. W.
24845	,,	Howell, Frederick	24874	,,	Reid, David Barclay
24843	,,	Holdway, Charles H.	24875	,,	Revel, Albert Benj.
24838	Arm.Cpl.	Hawley, Carlton B.	24876	,,	Richardson, A. E.
24788	Private	Jarman, A.	24877	,,	Sim, Thomas
24846	,,	Kevins, William	24879	,,	Slavin, Richard
24847	Cook	Kimmins, John	24880	,,	Southgate, Lewis M.
24848	Private	Latour, Emile	24881	,,	Spencer, Charles
24849	,,	Lefebvre, Louis V.	24882	,,	Stirling, David S.
24852	,,	Lovett, Albert E.	24883	,,	Tate, Herbert
24850	,,	Leggett, Reginald J.	24884	,,	Thomson, Walter
24853	,,	Macdonald, Rich. F.	24886	,,	Toovey, Ernest V. H.
24854	,,	MacFarlane, Norman	24885	,,	Todd, Alexander B.
24856	,,	MacLaurin, Doug. C.	24887	,,	Twamley, John B.
24858	,,	McCready, John	24888	,,	Wakelin, Fredk. J.
24860	,,	McKay, Alexander J.	24889	,,	Walker, Fredk. J.
24857	,,	McCallum, W. T.	24890	,,	Westerman, John E.
24859	,,	McDowell, James	24891	,,	White, Eric W. McK.
24855	,,	MacKay, John B.	24892	,,	Williams, Wm. J.
24861	,,	Matte, George	24893	,,	Woodstock, William
24862	,,	Mileham, William	24894	,,	Wylie, John McLean
24863	,,	Milne, Robert L.	24895	Lce.-Cpl.	Yates, Clement O.
24864	,,	Morgan, Stanley B.	24896	Private	Young, Ronald
24865	Lce.-Cpl.	Mould, Leonard S.			

"H" COMPANY.

Captain ... ... Clark-Kennedy, William H.
Lieutenant ... ... Lindsay, Stanley B.
,, ... MacTier, W. Stewart M.
,, ... Sinclair, Ian M. R.

Regl. No.	Rank	Name	Regl. No.	Rank	Name
24897	Col.-Sgt.	Chalmers, William	24923	Corpl.	Bromley, W. H.
24898	Sergt.	Caryer, William E. S.	24907	Lce.-Cpl.	Gibson, Gilbert W.
24899	,,	Crighton, James	24908	,,	Orr, John
24900	,,	Millar, Samuel	24909	,,	Mathewson, Frank S.
24906	,,	Bennett, W. H. D.	24911	Private	Anderson, John
24903	Corpl.	Taylor, Richard B.	24912	Cook	Britton, William
24904	,,	MacGregor, John	24913	,,	Bolt, Robt. H.
24905	,,	Mather, Edward	24914	Private	Boyce, E. Archibald
24910	,,	Macpherson, J. D.	24915	,,	Bailey, Arthur

Canadian Pacific—The Empire's Greatest Railway.

126   13TH BATTALION, 3RD INFANTRY BRIGADE—cont.

Regl. No.	Rank.	Name.	Regl. No.	Rank.	Name.
24916	Private	Ballard, Albert E.	24964	Private	Maxwell, C. M.
24917	,,	Breslin, Peter	24965	,,	Melluish, William A.
24918	,,	Bonner, Joseph	24966	,,	Murray, John R.
24919	,,	Byars, Henry	24967	,,	Mitchell, Donald M.
24920	,,	Brown, Alexander	24968	,,	Minton, Harold E.
24921	,,	Bingham, Frederick	24969	,,	McDonald, Daniel A.
24922	,,	Barker, Benson	24970	,,	McDermott, Patrick
24117	Arm.Cpl.	Cooper, H.	24971	,,	McKay, Robert
24901	Private	Cockburn, J. W.	24972	,,	McLean, John F.
24924	,,	Crozier, Joseph	24973	,,	McDonald, George
24925	Drummer	Campbell, Wm. J.	24974	,,	McKeown, Stephen
24926	Private	Cottrell, William	23975	Lce.-Cpl.	McNamee, Wm. H.
24927	,,	Cameron, James B.	24976	Private	O'Donnell, Abraham
24928	,,	Clarkson, John	24977	,,	O'Connell, Patrick
24930	,,	Connock, John J.	24978	,,	Purves, David
24931	,,	Carson, William O.	24979	,,	Petrie, James
24932	,,	Cornwall, Charles W.	24980	,,	Pearce, W. C.
24933	,,	Clarkson, George	24981	,,	Pizzy, Frederick
24934	,,	Dougherty, Charles	24982	,,	Rowe, James J.
24467	,,	Cunningham, A.	24983	,,	Robson, Henry
24935	,,	Eaton, William	24984	,,	Reay, James
24936	,,	Easson, John	24985	,,	Russell, John
24937	,,	Evans, Thomas J.	24986	,,	Robinson, John R.
24938	,,	Fisher, Arthur	24987	Lce.-Cpl.	Reynolds, John
24939	,,	Fraser, David S.	24988	Private	Ryan, James J.
24940	,,	Finn, Daniel J.	24989	Lce.-Cpl.	Slater, Andrew
24941	,,	Gallagher, Anthony	24990	Private	Swan, John
24929	,,	Gowans, Stephen	24991	,,	Storrier, Melville
24942	,,	Godbeer, Henry A.	24992	,,	Sandison, James
24943	,,	Gould, Roy S.	24993	,,	Stewart, James
24944	,,	Garnett, Errol R.	24994	,,	Sparks, William
24945	,,	Godwin, Edward J.	24995	,,	Seymour, William J.
24946	,,	Hardman, Herbert	24996	,,	Smith, John
24947	,,	Huntley, Herbert	24997	,,	Skeen, Oswald
24948	,,	Halifax, Reuben	24998	,,	Sharples, Frederick
24949	,,	Howes, Charles A.	24999	,,	Spenceley, Herbert
24950	,,	Ingram, Charles	25001	,,	Tipson, Morris J.
24951	,,	James, Harry H.	25002	,,	Tate, Arthur K.
24952	,,	Johnston, Thomas	25003	,,	Vokey, George
24953	,,	Johnson, Desmond	25004	,,	Thompson, William
24954	,,	Jones, William J.	25005	,,	Wright, David T.
24955	,,	Kelly, Patrick	25006	,,	Wafer, Thomas
24956	,,	Keith, Peter	25007	,,	Walker, George
24957	,,	Loveridge, Harold D.	25009	,,	Wilson, Joseph
24958	,,	Lovelock, Robert H.	25010	,,	Watt, William
24959	,,	Loomis, George A.	25011	,,	Wood, Herbert C.
24960	,,	Maclachlan, Robt. H.	25012	,,	Wood, Samuel
24961	,,	Mackenzie, Robert A.	25013	,,	Wells, Samuel W.
24962	,,	MacArthur, David S.	24052	,,	Williamson, J. H.
24963	,,	Morrison, John			

Canadian Pacific—The Empire's Greatest Railway.

13TH BATTALION, 3RD INFANTRY BRIGADE—cont. 127

BASE COMPANY.

Captain ... ... Buchanan, Fitz-Herbert Price

Regl. No.	Rank.	Name.	Regl. No.	Rank.	Name.
24780	O.R.Sgt.	McDonell, G. O.	25108	Private	Hogg, George S.
24002	Band Sgt.	Manson, D.	25062	,,	Hudson, John Wm.
25122	S.M.Tlr.	Stuart, J.	25038	,,	Ingalls, Fred
24198	Sergt.	Scott, W. H.	25089	,,	Irving, Robert
25018	Private	Moon, Thomas H.	25098	,,	James, Walter A.
25025	,,	Adamson, Ernest	25087	,,	Jay, William A.
25074	,,	Anderson, Robert	25039	,,	Johnson, Ben
25026	,,	Annetts, Arthur G.	25111	,,	Jacobs, H.
25103	,,	Annon, John Francis	25086	,,	Keen, George C.
25085	,,	Barlow, George	25040	,,	Ketteridge, Merton E.
25014	,,	Bell, James	25083	,,	Kelly, James E.
25023	,,	Birnie, Alexander	25070	,,	Lamey, William
25117	Lce.-Cpl.	Brazier, F.	25088	,,	Langan, Michael
25081	Private	Budding, John T.	25044	,,	Larin, Gilbert
25027	,,	Brais, William	25042	,,	Leadbetter, Robert
25024	,,	Baker, William	25043	,,	Leger, Arthur
25017	,,	Craig, W. A.	25069	,,	Leon, Harry Victor
25104	,,	Caine, Carstairs	25100	,,	Little, George
25028	,,	Charette, John E.	25068	,,	Lecky, George R.
25015	,,	Cheval, Albert E.	25109	,,	Macdonald, Allan
25094	,,	Clarke, William	25045	,,	Macdonald, James W.
25079	,,	Clarke, John Miller	25032	,,	McGuire, James T.
25029	,,	Clarson, Harry T.	25092	Lce.-Cpl.	McKinnon, Malcolm
25019	Lce.-Cpl.	Coop, Henry	25046	Private	MacLean, Alex. McM.
25030	Private	Courchaine, Oscar	25047	,,	McNulty, Edward J.
25031	,,	Craig, David	25076	,,	Marshall, Archibald
25022	,,	Connelly, Daniel	25048	,,	Minskip, Charles R.
25033	,,	Cairns, James	25049	,,	Morrell, Edward
25077	,,	Davidson, Emanuel	25107	,,	McLean, Athol A.
25034	,,	Davies, David	25101	,,	Moore, Allan
25073	,,	Dickinson, Edwin	24088	,,	Morby, Wm.
25080	Lce.-Cpl.	Easson, John	24037	,,	Penfold, J. W.
25093	Private	Edwards, Harry	25095	,,	Phillips, Ernest
25020	,,	Ette, Harry	25050	,,	Pickup, Harold
25035	Lce.-Cpl.	Evans, Richard	25064	,,	Pyke, Frank Wm.
25084	Private	Ellis, William	25051	,,	Quinnett, Henry
25099	,,	Fitzpatrick, M. E.	25052	,,	Reeves, Joseph
25021	,,	Fryer, Harry	25110	,,	Roberts, George J.
25078	,,	Garrick, David	25054	,,	Rodgers, William J.
25091	,,	Gee, William H.	25072	,,	Ross, Archibald
25036	,,	Glover, Herbert	25055	,,	Rowley, Thomas
25106	,,	Goodman, Richard	25090	,,	Richardson, Wm. A.
24483	,,	Gordon, J.	25113	,,	Rose, Walter James
25063	,,	Grigg, Bertie	25053	,,	Roberts, James
25105	,,	Galvin, David	25056	,,	Somerville, Wm. F.
25037	,,	Holliday, Richard	25057	,,	Schofield, George
25114	,,	Howles, Albert	25016	,,	Sheldon, Alfred
25041	,,	Hunt, Henry G.	25120	,,	Stearn, W. H.

Canadian Pacific—The Empire's Greatest Railway.

128 13TH BATTALION, 3RD INFANTRY BRIGADE—cont.

Regl. No.	Rank.	Name.	Regl. No.	Rank.	Name.
25071	Private	Stead, George Wm.	25115	Private	Vickers, James
25058	,,	Tipson, John J.	25116	,,	White, George
25082	,,	Thomas, William S.	25112	,,	Whyte, William
25066	,,	Thompson, William	25067	,,	Wood, Gilbert
25102	,,	Thornton, F. J.	25059	,,	Walters, David
24082	,,	Venables, W. R. B.	25060	,,	Workman, John

14th BATTALION, 3rd INFANTRY BRIGADE.
(ROYAL MONTREAL REGIMENT.)

HEADQUARTERS.

Officer Commanding	Lieut.-Colonel Frank S. Meighen
Major	,, W. W. Burland
Junior Major	,, Frederick H. Hopkins
Adjutant	Lieutenant Andrew Paton Holt
Assistant Adjutant	,, Henry A. Thompson
Quartermaster	Captain Herbert Hamilton Smith
Transport Officer	Lieutenant James Fellows Adams
Signalling Officer	,, Kenneth L. McCuaig
Machine Gun Officer	,, R. de V. Terroux

Attached.

Medical Officer	Captain F. A. C. Scrimger
Paymaster	Hon. Captain A. F. C. Winslow
Chaplain	,, ,, Adolphe L. Sylvestre
,, ...	,, Major Frederick George Scott

Headquarters Subordinate.

Regl. No.	Rank.	Name.	Regl. No.	Rank.	Name.
25540	Sgt.-Maj.	Stephenson, John M.	26652	Pnr. Sgt.	Bach, R. C.
25541	BandSgt.	Salmon, H. (Q.M.S.)	26653	Sgt. Cook	McLeod, G. H.
26649	Q.M.Sgt.	Duncan, H. St. Clair	25502	Tspt.Sgt.	Butcher, H. Cecil
26677	O.R.Sgt.	Lukeman, Frank L.	26614	Sig. Sgt.	Stelfox, J. C.
26650	O.R.Clk.	Smith, H. R. (Sgt.)	26654	Shoe Sgt.	Kalabza, W.
26651	Sgt. Dmr.	Ivimey, James			

Signallers.

Regl. No.	Rank.	Name.	Regl. No.	Rank.	Name.
26620	Corpl.	Madden, A.	26618	Private	Cronk, W. J.
26622	Private	Swift, G.	26615	,,	Barltrop, A. H.
26619	,,	Lawton, R. M.	26679	,,	Caldwell, G.
26621	,,	McLean, A. L.	26680	,,	Close, G.

Orderlies for Medical Officer.

26655	Lce.-Sgt.	Bethell, Charles	25537	Private	Gowan, Alex. Milton

Canadian Pacific—The Empire's Greatest Railway.

14TH BATTALION, 3RD INFANTRY BRIGADE—cont.

Transport Drivers.

Regl. No.	Rank.	Name.	Regl. No.	Rank.	Name.
25503	Lce.-Cpl.	Davidson, R. H.	25511	Private	Woolley, S. V.
25533	Private	Smith, G. C.	25534	,,	George, W.
25504	,,	Fearon, Edward	25535	,,	Sheriff, W.
25505	,,	Rogers, A. F.	25510	,,	Wallace, Thomas
25506	,,	Millan, J. K.	25543	,,	Langevin, Ovile
25507	,,	Jones, L. V.	25512	,,	Havelin, William
25508	,,	Forsyth, Robert	25528	,,	McIvor, Samuel
25509	,,	Peat, A. N.	25514	,,	Goult, Austin C.

Batmen.

26663	Private	Molt, Charles Maltby	26644	Private	Fournier, O.
25515	,,	Endersby, E. A.	25891	,,	Soady, George, P.
26666	,,	Wright, P.	25536	,,	Baker, William
25518	,,	Greenwood, W. G.	26665	,,	Singleton, J. M.
26662	,,	Hartwick, Herbert	26664	,,	Ormerod, A. S.
26658	,,	Duncan, B. J.	26657	,,	Chippendale, L.

Attached Subordinate.

26674 Arm.Sgt. Parnell, Alexander | 26675 Pay.Sgt. Robinson, H. P.

Machine Gun Section.

26624	Sergt.	Bremner, F. E. A.	26633	Private	Pattman, E. A.
26626	Private	Bradbury, P. R.	26634	,,	Robertson, R. W. S.
26627	,,	Gould, W. G.	26635	,,	Scott, R.
26628	,,	Halfhide, R. G.	26636	,,	Sinclair, R.
26629	,,	Humphreys, A. E.	26637	,,	Swann, H. H.
26630	,,	Kerr, R.	26638	,,	Tivey, W.
26631	,,	Nesbitt, J. K.	26639	,,	Waller, R. S.
26632	,,	Nesbitt, S. V.	26640	,,	Bond, A. M.

Water Detail.—Attached.

26668	Corpl.	Boyd, Robert J.	26671	Private	Knill, R.
26669	Private	Baker, W. E.	26672	,,	Wright, A. W.
26670	,,	Bailey, H. L.			

" A " COMPANY.

Captain	Warmington, John Nicoll
Lieutenant	Williamson, George Massey
,, ...	Frost, Reginald W.
,, ...	Pearce, William M.

Regl. No.	Rank.	Name.	Regl. No.	Rank.	Name.
25544	Col.-Sgt.	Burgess, W. G. E.	25550	Corpl.	Lunn, Albert E.
25545	Sergt.	Evans, William	25551	,,	Barraclough, Thomas
25546	,,	Bonshor, William A.	25552	,,	Fryatt, William
25547	,,	Wallis, William	25553	,,	Little, Percy
25548	,,	Oram, Wilmot Plant	25554	Private	Allan, John
25549	Corpl.	Whiteman, H. H.	25555	,,	Anderson, G.

Canadian Pacific—The Empire's Greatest Railway.

I

130   14TH BATTALION, 3RD INFANTRY BRIGADE—cont.

Regl. No.	Rank.	Name.	Regl. No.	Rank.	Name.
25556	Private	Amyot, Delphis	25610	Private	Maxim, William L.
25557	,,	Alexander, William	25611	,,	Mornan, Robert C.
25558	,,	Bullick, Andrew	25612	,,	Morley, Harold
25559	,,	Barker, William	25613	,,	McCann, William
25560	,,	Brunt, S. E.	25614	,,	McLennan, G. A.
25561	,,	Bellord, James G.	25615	,,	Mann, Samuel
25562	,,	Burns, Frederick W.	25616	,,	McCulley, Clarence
25563	,,	Boon, Samuel	25617	,,	Murray, Alexander
25564	,,	Budgen, John	25618	,,	Mackay, Andrew
25565	,,	Bownes, Ernest	25619	,,	McAtameny, A.
25567	,,	Coldwell, William	25620	,,	Mercer, George H.
25568	,,	Crack, William C.	25621	,,	McCarthy, R. G.
25569	,,	Carpenter, W. H.	25622	,,	Middlemore, Thomas
25570	,,	Chapman, Wm. P.	25623	,,	Norman, William
25571	,,	Claus, David Frank	25624	,,	Outerson, George G.
25572	,,	Clark, Alexander	25625	,,	Officer, William
25573	,,	Cooley, Leonard W.	25626	,,	Oakes, Edward
25574	Bugler	Clarkson, J.	25627	,,	Plow, Arthur
25575	Private	Crawford, Joseph	25628	,,	Parker, Alfred S.
25576	,,	Cullum, W. J.	25629	,,	Penman, Matthew
25577	,,	Demme, Ludwig	25630	,,	Quick, Harold Ewart
25578	,,	Davidson, John	25631	,,	Ralphs, Frank
25579	,,	Dodd, Albert	25632	,,	Robertson, Ian
25580	,,	Elderkin, Vernon	25633	,,	Rait, James Malcolm
25581	,,	Few, James	25634	,,	Russon, John
25582	,,	Flannigan, Frank	25635	,,	Rowe, Joseph Ewart
25583	,,	Farnworth, Percy	25636	,,	Reddington, James
25584	,,	Flynn, Alfred	25637	,,	Shill, H. E.
25585	,,	Galbraith, Neil	25638	,,	Skanes, William
25586	,,	Guthrie, Frederick	25639	,,	Scott, Albert E.
25588	,,	Gray, Austin	25640	,,	Sheriff, Robert
25589	,,	Gocking, Philip S.	25641	,,	Syder, Sydney
25590	,,	Hallet, R.	25642	,,	Sambell, Thomas G.
25591	,,	Hossack, J.	25643	,,	Sprague, Nelson
25592	,,	Hayward, James	25644	,,	Snow, Augustus R.
25593	,,	Hetu, James	25660	,,	Smith, Harvey
25594	,,	Howie, John James	25645	,,	Stewart, George A.
25595	,,	Herrick, A.	25646	,,	Stokes, William
25596	,,	Johnstone, James	25647	,,	Swindly, Douglas
25597	,,	Jennings, Frederick	25648	,,	Saunders, F.
25598	,,	Keenan, William J.	25649	,,	Strangward, Edward
25599	,,	Kenyon, George	25650	,,	Townsend, Hugh V.
25600	,,	Kirby, Richard	25651	,,	Tollerton, Leonard
25601	,,	Knight, Reginald G.	25652	,,	Turner, William
25602	,,	Lomas, Harry G.	25653	,,	Woodhouse, Walter
25603	,,	Lomax, Cyril Charles	25654	,,	Wright, Hugh
25604	,,	Lindsay, Frank	25655	,,	Wylie, William
25605	,,	Lambourne, W. J.	25656	,,	Wallis, Albert
25606	,,	Lane, Edward	25657	,,	Welsh, John
25607	,,	Lee, J.	25658	,,	Wallis, Thomas J.
25608	,,	Matheson, Kenneth	25659	,,	Yaxley, Eric Cecil
25609	,,	Matheson, J. M.			

Canadian Pacific—The Empire's Greatest Railway.

14TH BATTALION, 3RD INFANTRY BRIGADE—cont. 131

"B" COMPANY.

	Captain	...	...	...	Steacie, Richard
	,,	...	...	...	Larkin, Frank Dudley Bate
	Lieutenant	...	...	...	English, A. Soden
	,,	...	...	...	Stairs, Gavin Lang

Regl. No.	Rank.	Name.	Regl. No.	Rank.	Name.
25666	Col.-Sgt.	Rooke, James Arthur	25716	Private	Gould, Michael
25667	Sergt.	McCaffery, William	25717	,,	Griffiths, Thomas
25668	,,	Edwards, William H.	25718	,,	Gyde, Harold Stephen
25669	,,	Worral, Richard	25719	,,	Hann, William
25670	,,	Lang, Daniel George	25724	,,	Higginson, F.
25671	Corpl.	Flood, Arthur Henry	25725	,,	Higginson, Harry
25672	,,	Weaver, John Rex	25726	,,	Hodgson, Thomas
25673	,,	Marshall, Charles	25727	,,	Hughes, William
25675	,,	Lock, Leonard E.	25728	,,	Hunt, Charles E.
25678	Private	Allan, John George	25729	,,	Hawkins, R. H.
25683	,,	Bottle, Ernest	25730	,,	Harding, Ford
25684	,,	Bell, John William	25682	,,	Hampson, E. E.
25685	,,	Betts, Reginald	25676	,,	Harrison, F. A.
25686	,,	Bagnall, Fred Wm.	25721	,,	Harrison, Robert B.
25687	,,	Berry, Harry	25720	,,	Harmer, Chas. W.
25688	,,	Blackett, William C.	25722	,,	Harvey, Frederick
25689	,,	Bolton, J.	25723	,,	Heighes, Wilford
25690	,,	Bolwell, Albert E.	25731	,,	Johnston, Alex. L.
25691	,,	Bowman, Isaac	25732	,,	Jones, Arthur
25692	,,	Boucher, John	25733	,,	Jones, Gordon
25693	,,	Boyle, Edward D.	25734	,,	Kearney, John Harry
25694	,,	Brown, Hal Hareward	25735	,,	Kidd, John
25695	,,	Boyce, Arthur	25736	,,	Kirtland, Allan F.
25696	,,	Bush, William Geo.	25737	,,	Lawrence, T. F. W.
25697	,,	Cleaver, Charles	25738	,,	Lawton, Eustace A.
25698	,,	Conroy, Michael	25739	,,	Leighton, Douglas J.
25699	,,	Coughlin, William	25740	,,	Lennan, Collin R.
25700	,,	Crowther, Ronald	25741	,,	Lockett, Levy
25701	,,	Cummings, Alfred	25742	,,	Loup, Alec
25702	,,	Dabate, David	25743	,,	Lawrie, David
25662	,,	Dashwood, H. G.	25680	,,	Lane, Charles F.
25703	,,	Davey, Sydney S.	25752	,,	Morgan, Frank M.
25704	,,	Dooley, Harry	25744	,,	Morgan, E. F.
25705	,,	Dunn, James	25745	,,	May, James
25706	,,	Dwyer, John	25746	,,	Martin, Berchemin
25707	,,	Drake, R. H.	25747	,,	McGurk, James
25708	,,	Evans, Ellis	25748	Bugler	McLaughlin, R. L.
25709	,,	Evans, William E.	25749	Private	Meulman, John
25710	,,	Fisher, Henry	25750	,,	McKenna, John
25711	,,	Fletcher, Albert	25751	,,	Miller, Edgar
25712	,,	Forster, John Phillip	25753	,,	Norton, Alfred
25713	,,	Fraser, Frank Wm.	25754	,,	Palin, Francis
25714	,,	Fry, William Henry	25755	,,	Perkins, C. Wm.
25677	,,	Fowler, Alfred	25756	,,	Picthall, Wm. R.
25715	,,	Goodfellow, A. S.	25681	,,	Rexford, Volney G.

Canadian Pacific—The Empire's Greatest Railway.

132   14TH BATTALION, 3RD INFANTRY BRIGADE—*cont.*

Regl. No.	Rank.	Name.	Regl. No.	Rank.	Name.
25757	Private	Rees, Ernest	25769	Private	Stanton, James R.
25758	,,	Roberts, James	25770	,,	Stevenson, Hollis S.
25759	,,	Rodgers, George	25771	,,	Thomas, John R.
25760	,,	Shanks, Alexander	25772	,,	Thompson, Edgar
25679	,,	Smith, Ernest S.	25773	,,	Trupnell, Donald
25761	,,	Sampson, Phillip	25774	,,	Turner, William
25762	Bugler	Sanchez, W.	25775	,,	Tutt, Frederick H.
25763	Private	Schulze, C. F. L.	25777	,,	Wakefield, Walker
25764	,,	Scott-Proctor, R.	25778	,,	Wallis, Albert
25765	,,	Sharkie, F. W.	25779	,,	Will, David
25766	,,	Shergold, Frederick	25780	,,	Williams, Nathaniel
25767	,,	Silke, Joseph Henry	25781	,,	Winters, J. J.
25768	,,	Sinclair, W.	25782	,,	Yates, J.

"C" COMPANY.

Captain	...	...	...	Hanson, Paul Renard
Lieutenant	...	...	...	Knubley, Walter Kirkwood
,,	...	...	...	Brotherhood, Wilfred Cashel
,,	...	...	...	Stairs, George William

Regl. No.	Rank.	Name.	Regl. No.	Rank.	Name.
25787	Col.-Sgt.	Tod, George	25815	Private	Coombs, Edwd. Jas.
25788	Sergt.	Volkert, Wm. Chas.	25816	,,	Chadwick, Ernest
25789	,,	Donnaghy, William	25817	,,	Cunningham, F.W.T.
25790	,,	Hawkins, Albt.Edwd.	25818	,,	Crosier, Charles
25792	,,	Green, John William	25819	,,	Cowen, Edwin
25793	Corpl.	Randall, Sydney	25820	,,	Drew, Noble Reekie
25794	,,	Urquhart, Donald	25821	,,	Dewar, James Kirk
25795	,,	Tucker, Edward	25822	,,	Devine, Russell Reed
25796	,,	Bailey, R. C.	25823	,,	Duffin, Tom
25797	Private	Anderson, Carl Johan	25824	,,	Daly, Daniel
25798	,,	Allcorn, Bernard F.	25825	,,	Edward, John Wm.
25799	,,	Allan, Alexander	25826	,,	Elliott, Saml.Hughes
25800	,,	Bennett, Richard W.	25827	,,	Emigh, George
25801	,,	Bowes, James Wm.	25828	,,	French, Esmond
25802	,,	Bowman, Chas.Edwd.	25829	,,	Field, John
25803	,,	Brennan, Wm. Henry	25830	,,	Finder, Charles
25804	,,	Bellingham, Herbert	25834	,,	Finlay, R. W.
25805	,,	Bolton, Patrick R.	25904	,,	Finlay, H.
25806	,,	Bird, Thomas	25831	,,	Finn, Henry
25807	,,	Burns, Harry	25832	,,	Fournival, Eugene
25808	,,	Browne, Edgar	25836	,,	Gleave, George
25809	,,	Cahill, John Thomas	25837	,,	Glendinning, John
25814	,,	Campbell, S. D.	25838	,,	Greenwood, Edward
25810	,,	Chambers, Percy	25839	,,	Goodman, Bert
25811	,,	Coleman, Thomas W.	25840	,,	Gifford, Allan
25812	,,	Connors, Wm.Patrick	25841	,,	Hack, George Wm.
25813	,,	Cornick, William	25842	,,	Haynes, George Wm.

Canadian Pacific—The Empire's Greatest Railway.

14TH BATTALION, 3RD INFANTRY BRIGADE—cont.

Regl. No.	Rank	Name	Regl. No.	Rank	Name
25843	Private	Haynes, Harry A.	25872	Private	Morgan, George
26661	,,	Hardacre, H.	25873	,,	Nicholls, C. J.
25845	,,	Hallett, Wm. Thos.	25874	,,	O'Shaughnessy, Thos.
25846	,,	Ince, Wm. Henry	25875	,,	O'Sullivan, James
25847	,,	Jones, Thomas	25876	,,	Osgoode, Wilfred
25848	,,	Jones, James	25877	,,	Phillips, Arthur
25849	,,	Johnston, Duncan J.	25878	,,	Poulton, Albert Jas.
25850	,,	Kelly, Geo. Raynond	25879	,,	Pulling, William
25851	,,	Kennedy, James	25880	,,	Pimblett, Alfred
25852	,,	Kavanagh, William	25881	,,	Rees, Eaneas
25853	,,	Kellaway, Harold	25882	,,	Russell, Charles
25855	,,	Lewis, Wm. Geo. C.	25883	,,	Regan, Vaughan
25856	,,	Logan, Charles	25885	,,	Russell, E. S.
25857	,,	Lennard, Fred	25886	,,	Sinfield, Alfred
25858	,,	Labelle, Joseph	25887	,,	Slater, Richard
25854	,,	Lothian, W. B.	25888	,,	Salmon, Wm. Charles
25859	,,	Lindley, Ross	25889	,,	Simpson, George
25860	,,	Lardie, James	25892	,,	Smith, Herbert
25861	,,	Mack, Henry John	25893	,,	Spencer, Wilton W.
25862	,,	Maugham, Claude H.	25894	,,	Sparrow, Walter Fred
25863	,,	Maugham, Edgar E.	25895	,,	Sutherland, James
25864	,,	Mattingly, William	25896	,,	Thompson, George
25865	,,	Matthews, Regnld. E.	25897	,,	Tilt, Frederic Geo.
25866	,,	MacNaughten, Perry	25898	,,	Taylor, Frederic
25867	,,	McCoy, John Henry	25899	,,	Underwood, J. W.
25868	,,	McRae, James	25900	,,	Wells, Alex.
25869	,,	Mitchell, Fras. Edwd.	25902	,,	Wingard, Hume S.
25870	,,	Montague, Michael	25903	,,	Wood, John
25871	,,	Morgan, Jacob			

"D" COMPANY.

Captain	... ...	McCombe, Gault
Lieutenant	... ...	Grant, Seaward
,,	... ...	Whitehead, Edward Ashworth
,,	... ...	Major, Albert Frederick

Regl. No.	Rank	Name	Regl. No.	Rank	Name
25908	Col.-Sgt.	Handcock, Arthur	25919	Private	Baber, George C.
25909	Sergt.	Armstrong, Harold	25920	,,	Baby, Lucien
25910	,,	Smith, Wm. W. C.	25921	,,	Bacque, Fredk. H.
25911	,,	Arundell, J. d'A. H.	25922	,,	Barbour, William G.
25912	,,	Beswick, Archer N.	26616	,,	Bastable, Maurice A.
25913	Corpl.	Hood, Richard H.	35923	,,	Bickley, Herbert P.
25914	,,	Hardwick, Albert V.	25924	,,	Biggs, Frank
25915	,,	Common, William C.	25925	,,	Bremner, Reg. O.
25916	,,	Burns, William B.	25926	,,	Brewer, Hugh G.
25917	,,	Mitchell, Thomas	25927	,,	Brown, John Spencer
25918	Private	Atkinson, Alex. F. B.	25928	,,	Brown, Albert Victor

Canadian Pacific—The Empire's Greatest Railway.

14TH BATTALION, 3RD INFANTRY BRIGADE—cont.

Regl. No.	Rank.	Name.	Regl. No.	Rank.	Name.
25929	Private	Butler, Alphonse E.	25978	Private	Moran, John F.
25930	,,	Callaghan, Matt. J.	25979	,,	Myles, Thos. J. E. B.
25931	,,	Cameron, Evan S.	25980	,,	Nantel, Joseph L. A.
25932	,,	Cameron, Francis B.	25981	,,	Napier, Robert J.
25933	,,	Campbell, Henry	25982	,,	Noad, James A. L.
25934	,,	Campbell, John D.	25983	,,	Norton, Cecil H.
25935	,,	Chandler, John K.	25984	,,	O'Brien, Charles L.
25936	,,	Chevalier, Pierre	25985	,,	Odell, Oliver H. C.
25937	,,	Chevalier, Phillipe	25986	,,	Oliver, Frederick C.
26617	,,	Clark, Melville Roy	25987	,,	Orr, Archie
25938	,,	Cleghorn, Andrew G.	25988	,,	Osborne, Samuel
25939	,,	Constable Fredk. W.	25989	,,	Page, H. A. S.
25940	,,	Cooke, George	25990	,,	Patman, Valentine
25941	,,	Corrigan, James W.	25991	,,	Peate, William S.
25942	,,	Cooke, Herbert G.	25992	,,	Perfrement, Fdk. B.
25943	,,	Denning, James R.	25993	,,	Planche, Norman E.
25944	,,	Denman, Clarence B.	25994	Bugler	Pollard, William
25945	,,	Dugan, Patrick J.	25995	Private	Poole, George
25946	,,	Duncan, Ellery S.	25996	,,	Racey, Baron R.
25947	,,	Dupuy, Harry L.	25997	,,	Rattigan, Patrick
25948	,,	Fafard, Alfred C.	25998	,,	Robertson, N. H.
25949	,,	Forneri, David A.	25999	,,	Robertson, Alex. G.
25950	,,	Green, Ernest	26000	,,	Runte, William H.
25952	,,	Heather, Fredk. W.	26001	,,	Sanders, Richard I.
25953	,,	Henry, Alfred S.	26002	,,	Saunders, Alex. L.
25954	,,	Hollaley, William A.	26003	,,	Savage, Ivan Burke
25955	,,	Howell, William P.	26004	,,	Slubicki, John
25956	,,	Ince, Arthur D.	26005	,,	Roach, Albert E. V.
25957	,,	Jackson, William H.	26006	,,	Simpson, Robert J.
25958	,,	Johnson, Cuthbert J.	26007	,,	Southin, John W.
25959	,,	Johnson, R. A.	26008	,,	Steeves, Gordon A.
25960	,,	Jones, Arthur S.	26009	,,	Stevens, William G.
25961	,,	Kavanagh, William	26010	,,	Summers, George W.
25962	,,	Knight, Joshua	26011	,,	Swift, Frederick
25963	,,	Lajoie, George Leo	26012	,,	Symonds, Herbert B.
25964	,,	Lister, Robert W.	26013	,,	Taylor, Leonard W.
25966	,,	Mackenzie, Robt. C.	26014	,,	Taylor, Cuthbert S.
25967	,,	Mallett, William	26015	,,	Taylor, Milton, J.
25968	,,	Malone, Charles S.	26016	,,	Taylor, Wm. W. S.
25969	,,	Manfield, Henry J.	26017	,,	Thwaites, Arthur P.
25970	,,	Martin, William A.	26018	,,	Turley, George E. H.
25971	,,	Marshall, Ernest	26019	,,	Van Someren, E. C.
25972	,,	McTurk, John G.	26020	,,	Wales, Roland
25973	,,	McGilton, George A.	26021	,,	Weir, William J.
25974	,,	Mercier, Leslie P.	26022	,,	Whitby, Chas. D. B.
25975	,,	Moffitt, William H.	26023	,,	White, Lionel
25976	,,	Monte, Edward	26024	Bugler	Wright, William
25977	,,	Morrison, William			

Canadian Pacific—The Empire's Greatest Railway.

14TH BATTALION, 3RD INFANTRY BRIGADE—cont.

"E" COMPANY.

Captain	... ...	Shaw, Allan Crawford
Lieutenant	... ...	Porteous, Charles Frederick Claustan
,,	... ...	O'Brien-Twohig, Michael Joseph
,,	... ...	Hueston, Francis Robert

Regl. No.	Rank.	Name.	Regl. No.	Rank.	Name.
26648	Col.-Sgt.	Price, Chas. Basil	26076	Private	Fallen, Gordon J.
26029	Sergt.	Rankin, Richard W.	26078	,,	Fleming, John
26031	,,	Sullivan, Chris. H.	26077	,,	Fitzgerald, Joseph
26032	,,	Duncan, Wm. Reid	26080	,,	Gartshore, Neil
26033	,,	Young, Ralph Stuart	26079	,,	Garvey, Edward E.
26030	Corpl.	Howe, John	26081	,,	Gibson, Arthur
26034	,,	Boothby, John N.	26082	,,	Godsall, Alfred F.
26035	,,	McMahon, Benj. F.	26083	,,	Gough, Ernest C
26036	,,	Jeffery, Chas. E. A.	26084	,,	Hall, George Edwd.
26037	,,	Burlinson, M. A.	26085	,,	Hartwick, John W.
26039	Bugler	Thomson, William	26560	,,	Huxley, Ernest Wm.
26040	,,	Blair, George A.	26086	,,	Hebert, Joseph
26041	Pioneer	Strickland, John	26087	,,	Heron, William
26042	Signaller	Lalor, Robert C.	26088	,,	Hirshorne, Saml. L.
26043	,,	Daniel, Thomas S.	26089	,,	Howe, W. H.
26044	Str.B'rer	Lee, William	26090	,,	Hoare, John Wm.
26045	,,	Patch, Chas. Norman	26091	,,	Hone, Ernest
26048	Batman	Johnson, Eric Chas.	26092	,,	Hopkins, Arthur E.
26049	,,	Andrews, David J.	26093	,,	Hughes, William
26051	,,	Swindlehurst, Arthur	26094	,,	Hunter, Frank
26052	Private	Anderson, Alfred G.	26145	,,	Hoby, C. B.
26053	,,	Baker, Thomas S.	26095	,,	Jeffery, Edward
26054	,,	Ball, John	26096	,,	Jennings, S. F. T.
26055	,,	Barker, Richard J.	26097	,,	Jones, George
26056	,,	Barnett, Sydney G.	26144	,,	Jones, William
26057	,,	Bayliss, Wm. James	26098	,,	McBurney, Fdk.Wm.
26055	,,	Biggs, George E.	26099	,,	McKeegan, James
26059	,,	Board, Fred Charles	26100	,,	McMartin, Henry G.
26060	,,	Bolton, Jacob	26101	,,	Marsh, Chas. Edwd.
26061	,,	Brewer, Aubrey D.	26103	,,	Mason, George
26062	,,	Brown, Lorne	26102	,,	Martin, John
26064	,,	Charlebois, L. J.	26104	,,	Matchett, Edwd. H.
26065	,,	Clewley, William	26105	,,	Muncaster, Percy H
26066	,,	Coady, Arthur J.	26106	,,	Murphy, Arthur
26063	,,	Copeland, Phillip J.B.	26107	,,	Nelson, Henry
26068	,,	Craggs, William	26109	,,	Newcombe, Walter U.
26067	,,	Craig, Alex. M. J.	26108	,,	Nicholls, Percy H.
26069	,,	Cross, William	26110	,,	O'Grady, John J.
26070	,,	Curtis, William	26114	,,	Pearson, Frank La C.
26071	,,	Deere, Chas. Thos.	26113	,,	Platt, Richard
26072	,,	Doherty, James	26111	,,	Pounden, John Robt.
26073	,,	Douglas, Edward J.	26112	,,	Pratt, Bertie James
26074	,,	Douglas, George J.	26117	,,	Raby, Arthur George
26075	,,	Dundas, James H.	26115	,,	Rooke, Charles E.
26038	,,	Eaton, Kenneth A.	26118	,,	Runte, Edward

Canadian Pacific—The Empire's Greatest Railway.

14TH BATTALION, 3RD INFANTRY BRIGADE—cont.

Regl. No.	Rank.	Name.	Regl. No.	Rank.	Name.
26116	Private	Rogers, Eunice Jay	26130	Private	Volume, Edward D.
26119	,,	Shelton, Hector C.	26131	,,	Wall, Matthew Jas.
26120	,,	Sheridan, Wm. John	26133	,,	Warner, Sidney Jas.
26121	,,	Shirley, John Fredk.	26135	,,	Watson, James
26122	,,	Smith, Albert	26134	,,	Watters, James
26123	,,	Smith, Leonard	26136	,,	Webb, Fredk. Wm.
26124	,,	Smith, Stanley	26137	,,	Webster, Charles
26126	,,	Tastard, William	26138	,,	Wilson, Richard S.
26125	,,	Taylor, William	26141	,,	Woolley, Norman E.
26128	,,	Turner, Alfred N.	26142	,,	Wyatt, Gordon J.
26127	,,	Thatcher, James G.	26143	,,	Wyatt, Howard John
26129	,,	Vidler, Carlos John			

"F" COMPANY.

Captain	...	...	...	Curry, Victor G.
Lieutenant	...	...	...	Adams, Wm. D.
,,	...	...	...	Draper, Wm. H.
,,	...	...	...	Kirkconnell, Walter Allison

Regl. No.	Rank.	Name.	Regl. No.	Rank.	Name.
26150	Col.-Sgt.	Sharp, Wylie	26181	Private	Conway, Joseph
26151	Sergt.	Gregson, Jas. Harold	26182	,,	Corry, Fred
26152	,,	Armstrong, George	26183	,,	Coulson, Percy
26153	,,	D'Aragon, Hubert	26184	,,	Cox, Charles
26154	,,	Neilson, Frank K.	26185	,,	Crump, Edward
26157	Corpl.	Hunt, George G.	26177	,,	Crann, Norman
26223	,,	Leighton, Gordon E.	26186	Bugler	Darge, Joseph John
26159	,,	Pain, Alex.	26187	Private	Davidson, James
26158	,,	Mitchell, Ernest S.	26188	,,	Davin, Henry A.
26160	Private	Albin, Ross	26189	,,	Dionne, Joseph F.
26161	,,	Anstey, William	26155	,,	Dods, Lorimer
26162	,,	Arnold, Chris. John	26156	,,	Dolling, William A
26164	,,	Binks, Joseph A. S.	26190	,,	Dower, Edward
26165	,,	Blair, Hugh James	26191	,,	Duffin, Norman A.
26167	,,	Blair, Samuel	26192	,,	Dunlop, Robert
26169	,,	Blomfield, Geo. A.	26193	,,	Edwards, David J.
26170	,,	Boulanger, Frank	26194	,,	Elliott, Robert
26166	,,	Brayton, Bertram	26195	,,	Ensum, Edward W.
26172	,,	Brown, John	26196	,,	Fenton, Herbert J.
26168	,,	Burt, John	26197	,,	Finlay, John C.
26173	,,	Bushell, Charles A.	26200	,,	Freeman, Douglas
26171	,,	Bulger, Harold	26198	,,	Gallacher, John
26174	,,	Call, John	26199	,,	Gilbert, John Oliver
26175	,,	Cantin, John B.	26265	Bugler	Ginley, Anthony
26176	,,	Capper, Cawthorne	26203	Private	Girvan, Thos. D.
26178	,,	Carr, Albert Edward	26201	,,	Golden, Jas. Gerald
26179	,,	Chadwick, Benjamin	26202	,,	Goskar, Herbert J.
26180	,,	Clark, Charles	26205	,,	Haldeman, Fred

Canadian Pacific—The Empire's Greatest Railway.

14TH BATTALION, 3RD INFANTRY BRIGADE—cont.

Regl. No.	Rank.	Name.	Regl. No.	Rank.	Name.
26681	Private	Hanley, Ernest	26236	Private	Page, Henry John
26206	,,	Harrison, Wm. F.	26238	,,	Pate, Sidney
26207	,,	Harrington, Geo. H.	26239	,,	Pike, Edwin James
26208	,,	Harleigh, Cyril. A.	26237	,,	Presant, Bert
26209	,,	Haylock, Geo. Edw.	26241	,,	Racicot, Alphonse
26210	,,	Herring, Wm. James	26242	,,	Raggett, Sidney
26212	,,	Hinton, Wilfred	26243	,,	Reid, Harry
26211	,,	Hunt, Albert Henry	26240	,,	Riggs, Robert V.
26213	,,	Imray, Alexander B.	26244	,,	Roberts, John
26214	,,	Keane, Philip	26245	,,	Rogers, Levi
26216	,,	Kemp, Cyril	26246	,,	Russell, John Joseph
26217	,,	King, Ernest Wm.	26247	,,	Russell, George F.
26215	,,	Kinghorn, Chas. F.	26249	,,	Smith, Edward Wm.
26218	,,	Kirby, William	26250	,,	Soanes, Victor
26219	,,	Kyte, William	26248	,,	Stewart, George
26220	,,	Laliberte, Alexander	26251	,,	Stuart, Robert C.
26221	,,	Larock, Paul	26252	,,	Sullivan, Thos. F.
26222	,,	Larose, Lorenzo R.	26253	,,	Tasker, Thos. Edw.
26224	,,	Manks, George	26257	,,	Terroux, Henry C.
26225	,,	March, Herbert	26255	,,	Taylor, Richard G.
26226	,,	McCowan, John C.	26256	,,	Topham, Bertram J.
26228	,,	McKimm, John R.	26254	,,	Trant, Frederick
26229	,,	McNulty, Chas.	26258	,,	Urwin, Alexander
26230	,,	Mitchell, William	26259	,,	Vaughan, Joseph
26231	,,	Moore, Samuel	26260	,,	Wilde, William
26232	,,	Morrison, Thos.	26261	,,	Wilson, James
26233	,,	Murray, Geo.	26262	,,	Wilson, Geo. B. A.
26266	,,	Nesbit, Thos.	26263	,,	Williams, Fred. S.
26234	,,	Newman, Albert	26264	,,	Williamson, William
26235	,,	Odesky, Max			

"G" COMPANY.

Captain	...	...	...	...	Barre, Hercule
Lieutenant	...	...	...	...	Des Rosiers, Marie Joseph Romeo H.
,,		...	...	...	Quintal, Henri
,,		...	...	...	Deserres, Rodolphe

Regl. No.	Rank.	Name.	Regl. No.	Rank.	Name.
26271	Col.-Sgt.	Giard, Pierre Charles	26282	Private	Alexandre, J. H. M.
26272	Sergt.	Martin, Joseph A. E.	26281	,,	Arpin, E.
26274	,,	Thomas, Edmond	26284	Bugler	Barrette, Armand
26275	,,	Gauthier, Origene	26286	Private	Beland, Joseph U.
26278	,,	Lapointe, J. L. G.	26300	,,	Bertrand, Joseph H.
26277	Corpl.	Andre, Rene	26285	,,	Bourget, M. O.
26283	,,	Aubin, Napoleon	26287	,,	Beaudricault, Ernest
26279	,,	Charbonneau, Felix O.	26288	,,	Belisle, Joseph Alfred
26305	,,	Cyr, Joseph Damase	26289	,,	Boudreault, Henri
26314	,,	Dechesne, Albert	26290	,,	Barrette, Arthur

Canadian Pacific—The Empire's Greatest Railway.

138   14TH BATTALION, 3RD INFANTRY BRIGADE—cont.

Regl. No.	Rank	Name	Regl. No.	Rank	Name
26291	Private	Belanger, F. X. L.	26343	Private	Lapierre, Antoine E.
26292	,,	Bercier, Joseph N.	26344	,,	Lariviere, Pierre
26293	,,	Billen, Jean H. J.	26345	,,	Lafleur, Henri A.
26294	,,	Bonnin, Albert Joseph	26346	Lce.-Cpl.	Langelier, Charles E.
26295	,,	Bourbonnais, D. J. A.	26347	Private	Lefebvre, Wilfred L.
26296	,,	Bernier, Georges	26348	,,	Levesque, J. P. T.
26297	,,	Beriault, Georges, N.	26349	,,	Laurendeau, W. W. J.
26298	,,	Blanchet, Joseph A.	26350	,,	Labelle, Joseph A.
26299	,,	Bernard, J. N. H.	26351	,,	Lapointe, Henri
26301	,,	Bond, Arthur	26352	,,	Leclerc, Joseph F. X.
26385	,,	Burns, Joseph A.	26341	,,	Leveille, F. X. A.
26273	,,	Carbonneau, J. E. E.	26353	,,	Moreau, Joseph D.
26302	,,	Christoffel, E. G. A.	26354	,,	Mallette, Joseph R.
26386	,,	Crevier, Seraphin E.	26355	,,	Morvan, Henri
26303	,,	Cote, Joseph A. E.	26356	Bugler	Mathieu, Josephat
26304	,,	Carriere, Joseph L.	26357	Private	Patry, Joseph N.
26306	,,	Dion, Julien Louis P.	26276	,,	Paquette, Antonio
26307	,,	Deschene, Pierre	26358	,,	Poirier, Auguste A.
26308	,,	Dubeau, Joseph A. N.	26359	,,	Patry, Adelard Henri
26309	,,	Desjardins, Wilfrid	26360	,,	Pichette, Stanislas
26310	,,	Deseve, Joseph Avila	26361	,,	Portugaels, H. A. C.
26311	,,	Daigle, Camille	26362	,,	Potvin, Louis Victor
26312	,,	Dufresne, William	26363	,,	Porchon, Marcel L. P.
26313	,,	Delongchamps, J. X.	26364	,,	Quintal, Alfred
26315	,,	Desroches, C. E. A.	26365	,,	Robillard, Arthur
26316	,,	De Nevers, Henri	26366	,,	Roy, Charles Aurele
26317	,,	Deguise, Joseph A.	26367	,,	Robillard, Jean B.
26318	,,	Dextrase, J. A. R.	26368	,,	Rochon, Joseph A.
26319	,,	Desnoyers, J. W. A. L.	26369	,,	Raymond, J. V. E.
26320	,,	Ethier, Leandre H.	26338	,,	Sirois, Charles E.
26321	,,	Fournier, Emile	26323	,,	St. Hilaire, Joseph A.
26322	,,	Fortier, R.	26373	,,	St. Jacques, Edouard
26325	,,	Giroux, Jos. A.	26374	,,	Simard, Joseph M.
26326	,,	Garceau, Joseph	26370	,,	St. Onge, Clovis A. J.
26324	,,	Gendreau, A.	26371	,,	Suberville, Auguste
26327	,,	Guitard, Alfred	26372	,,	Scraire, Joseph A.
26328	,,	Gauthier, Joshaphat	26376	,,	Ternisien, E. C. S. A.
26329	,,	Guyot, Louis Alfred	26375	,,	Thibodeau, Joseph A.
26330	,,	Godard, Delphis	26379	,,	Tetreault, Joseph W.
26331	,,	Gauthier, Joseph F.	26387	,,	Trudeau, Charles A.
26332	,,	Gauthier, Phillippe	26377	,,	Theriaut, Isidore
26334	,,	Huron, Eugene C. R.	26378	,,	Trudel, Donat
26335	,,	Hurtuibise, Joseph A.	26280	,,	Turcotte, Joseph A.
26336	,,	Houle, Romeo	26381	,,	Varin, Joseph F. A.
26333	,,	Honnay, Lionel A.	26382	,,	Vigneaut, Theophile
26337	,,	Jobel, A.	26380	,,	Vaillant, Joseph H.
26340	,,	Kenney, Cleophas	26383	,,	Williams, Joseph E.
26342	,,	Letourneau, J. W.	26384	,,	Wiseman, Henri E.

Canadian Pacific—The Empire's Greatest Railway.

14TH BATTALION, 3RD INFANTRY BRIGADE—cont.

"H" COMPANY.

Captain	... ...	Ranger, Emile
Lieutenant	... ...	Roy, Robert
,,	... ...	Leprohon, Edmond
,,	... ...	de Kappell, William

Regl. No.	Rank.	Name.	Regl. No.	Rank.	Name.
26392	Col.-Sgt.	Marion, Rene	26438	Private	Gendron, Joseph
26394	Sergt.	Duhamel, Ludovic	26439	,,	Godin, J.
26395	,,	Laurent, Pierre	26440	,,	Gendron, Herve
26396	,,	Charbonneau, E.	26441	Corpl.	Guertin, Joseph A.
26399	,,	Thibault, Henri	26442	Private	Goudreau, Arthur
26397	Corpl.	Dugas, Theodore	26443	,,	Gauthier, Raymond
26398	Private	Bernard, Amedee	26444	,,	Gratton, Antoine
26400	,,	Belisle, Joseph	26445	,,	Handfield, Jules
26401	Corpl.	Prudhomme, Adrien	26446	,,	Hetu, Napoleon
26402	Private	Allard, Albert	26447	,,	Hardy, Victor
26403	,,	Arial, Antonio	26448	,,	Hurtubise, Alphonse
26404	,,	Beaulieu, Ephrem	26449	,,	Houle, Henri
26405	,,	Boulard, Emile	26451	,,	Jarry, Delphis
26406	,,	Blais, Rosario	26452	,,	Jerome, J.
26407	,,	Bousquet, Philippe	26453	,,	Juteau, Arthur
26408	,,	Benoit, Edmond	26450	,,	Jubinville, E.
26409	,,	Brady, James	26454	,,	Klein, Pierre
26410	,,	Brisebois, Elphege	26455	,,	Lavigne, Elzear
26411	,,	Brissette, Georges	26456	,,	Lacroix, Adolphe
26412	,,	Beauchemin, N.	26457	,,	Lecompte, Gaston
26414	,,	Bourcier, Eugene	26458	,,	Lacroix, Joseph
26415	,,	Bissonnette, Wilfrid	26459	,,	Lacroix, Charles
26416	,,	Bellieres, Albert	26460	Corpl.	Lepine, Paul
26417	,,	Bernier, Joseph	26461	Bugler	Laferriere, Samuel
26418	,,	Bourgault, Emile	26462	Private	Lepine, Eugene
26419	Bugler	Coallier, Antone	26463	,,	Lapointe, Lucien
26420	Private	Chapadeau, J. E.	26464	,,	Lescarbeau, Emile
26421	,,	Crevier, Charles	26465	,,	Lacroix, Ovila
26422	,,	Cote, Emile	26466	,,	Laine, Romeo
26423	,,	Charbonneau, C.	26467	,,	Lacerte, Wilbray
26424	,,	Cote, Norbert J.	26468	,,	Laurent, Georges
26425	,,	Carrier, Joseph	26469	,,	Ligonnet, Albert
26426	,,	Cherrier, Raymond	26470	,,	Leduc, Donat
26427	,,	Collerette, Theophile	26471	,,	Lachaine, Alfred
26413	,,	Delisle, Henri	26472	,,	Lafond, Albert
26428	,,	Dupil, Raoul	26473	,,	Lajeunesse, Alfred
26429	,,	D'Astous, Amedee	26474	,,	Messier, Hector
26430	,,	Desloges, Raymond	26475	,,	Martin, Paul
26431	,,	Deslongchamp, J.	26476	,,	Marion, Antoine
26432	,,	De Vreese, Gustave	26477	,,	Mireault, Richard
26433	,,	Dufresne, Pierre	26478	,,	Martin, Joseph
26434	,,	Dube, Joseph	26479	,,	Messier, Joseph
26435	,,	Favreau, Alexandre	26480	,,	Ouimet, Albert
26436	,,	Gagnon, Henri	26481	,,	Pelletier, Rosario
26437	,,	Girard, Charles E.	26482	,,	Poncelet, Eugene

Canadian Pacific—The Empire's Greatest Railway.

14TH BATTALION, 3RD INFANTRY BRIGADE—cont.

Regl. No.	Rank.	Name.	Regl. No.	Rank.	Name.
26483	Corpl.	Pichette, J. Albert	26497	Private	Racette, Jean B.
26484	Private	Potvin, Rene	26498	,,	Roy, Henri
26485	,,	Parent, Stanislas	26499	,,	St. Marie, Lucien
26486	,,	Poitras, Anthime	26500	,,	Sasseville, Saul
26487	,,	Pelletier, A.	26501	,,	Seguin, Antonio
26488	,,	Poirat, Eugene	26502	,,	Steben, Georges
26489	,,	Paris, Victor	26393	,,	Tetu, Eugene
26490	,,	Paradis, Joseph	26503	,,	Theoret, Antoine
26491	,,	Panneton, Ivanhoe	26504	,,	Villeneuve, Arthur
26492	,,	Raymond, Joseph	26505	,,	Van Meulebroeck, H.
26493	,,	Rose, Gaston	26506	,,	Vallee, Adelard
26494	,,	Rioppel, Lucien	26507	,,	Valin, Gilbert
26495	,,	Racette, Alphonse	26508	,,	Wouters, France

BASE COMPANY.

Major ... ... Woodside, Henry Joseph

Regl. No.	Rank.	Name.	Regl. No.	Rank.	Name.
26513	Col.-Sgt.	Morgan, Walter	26539	Private	Croteau, Albert
26518	Sergt.	Robideau, Frank	26540	,,	Clifford, Herbert
26519	,,	Fegan, William P.	25522	,,	Clayton, Robert
26520	,,	Hanratty, John	26514	,,	Caddy, Charles
26522	Corpl.	Sevard, Albert A.	26517	,,	Day, Thomas Henry
25791	,,	Moore, Thomas	26541	,,	Devlin, Archibald
26521	,,	Phillip, James	26542	,,	Ellery, James
26568	,,	Kirkwood, Thomas J.	26543	,,	Fournier, A. M. J.
26554	,,	Gray, Thomas	26545	,,	Finnigan, Gustave
26608	,,	Wilson, Martin John	26546	,,	Foley, John H.
26523	Private	Anderson, Joseph J.	26547	,,	Flynn, Francis P.
26510	,,	Adams, William G.	26548	,,	Franklin, W. V. J.
26511	,,	Barton, Harold G.	26549	,,	Gagnon, Henry
26524	,,	Branchaud, Adelard	26550	,,	Gravelle, Fardinand
26525	,,	Brooks, Alfred	26551	,,	Gaudreau, Alfred J.
26526	,,	Baker, Alexander	26552	,,	Gaudreau, Isidore
26527	,,	Beck, Lester Charles	26553	,,	Gaudreau, Josephat
26528	,,	Bues, George W.	26555	,,	Gardner, William A.
26529	,,	Bellanger, Lewis A.	25523	,,	Gandy, Robert B.
26530	,,	Blythe, Adam.	26556	,,	Hopwood, Fred
26512	,,	Blake, George J.	26557	,,	Hamelin, Peter
26611	,,	Bowles, Thomas	26558	,,	Harrigan, Thomas P.
26612	,,	Boyle, John	26559	,,	Hills, Horace
25513	,,	Briere, Armand	26561	,,	Johnston, Lionel W.
26533	,,	Chanu, Henri	26562	,,	Jordan, Edward
26534	,,	Chittleburg, George	26563	,,	Jarry, Charles E. M.
26535	,,	Clouthier, Harvey J.	26564	,,	Kenny, Joseph A.
26536	,,	Chenard, Thomas	26565	,,	Keenan, Kieran J.
26610	,,	Chouinard, Joseph	26566	,,	Kirkwood, Andrew
26148	,,	Conroy, John	26567	,,	Kirkwood, William
26537	,,	Creagh, Thomas P.	26515	,,	Largan, James
26538	,,	Cusson, Arthur	26569	,,	Lewis, William J. F.

Canadian Pacific—The Empire's Greatest Railway.

14TH BATTALION, 3RD INFANTRY BRIGADE—cont.

Regl. No.	Rank.	Name.	Regl. No.	Rank.	Name.
26570	Private	Lewis, George	26590	Private	Paquet, Joseph W.
25965	,,	Lloyd, Leslie	26591	,,	Parry, John George
26572	,,	Lapointe, Charles	26592	,,	Robinson, William
26573	,,	Lalonde, Osias J.	26593	,,	Rhamey, Edward J.
26574	,,	Maunder, F. G.	26594	,,	Ryan, John
26575	,,	Morrison, George W.	26595	,,	Roy, Rosario
26576	,,	Martel, Joseph L. E.	26596	,,	Rogers, Claude P.
26577	,,	Mireault, Leo	26597	,,	Regan, Thomas
26578	,,	Mitchell, Patrick	26598	,,	Smith, Harold B.
26579	,,	McCormack, John S.	26599	,,	Smith, James
26580	,,	Murphy, Thomas P.	26600	,,	Smith, Lewis George
26581	,,	McCartney, William	26602	,,	Sawyer, Arthur J.
26582	,,	McKenzie, William	26603	,,	Sherborne, Oliver J.
26583	,,	Mundy, Thomas	26604	,,	St. Laurent, B. A.
26584	,,	Noble, Nelson Albert	26605	,,	Tapp, Adolphis
26585	,,	Owen, Norman	26606	,,	Thivierge, Joseph
26586	,,	Owen, Matthew	26607	,,	Tracy, John Stewart
26587	,,	O'Neill, John P.	26625	,,	Vosburgh, E.
26588	,,	Post, James J. M.	26139	,,	Winterton, Isiah
26589	,,	Parker, Edward	25526	,,	Woods, John Henry

15th BATTALION, 3rd INFANTRY BRIGADE.

(48th HIGHLANDERS OF CANADA.)

Officer Commanding ...	Lieut.-Col. John Allister Currrie
Second in Command ...	Major William R. Marshall ᴅᴊᴇᴏ
Adjutant ...	Captain Robert Clifford Darling
Asst. Adjutant ...	,, Trumbell Warren
Signalling Officer ...	Lieutenant Walter B. Lawson
Machine Gun Officer ...	,, Richard R. McKessock
Quartermaster ...	Hon. Captain Robert C. M. Donaldson
Paymaster ...	,, ,, Oliver Hugel Mabee
Chaplain ...	,, ,, Samuel W. Moffitt
Medical Officer ...	Major Alexander J. MacKenzie
Officer for Base Company ...	Lieutenant Godfrey Taylor

Attached (A.M.C.).

Regl. No.	Rank.	Name.	Regl. No.	Rank.	Name.
33671	Corpl.	Cross, Herbert Victor	33674	Private	Byron, Milford
33672	Private	Benson, Charles	33675	,,	Saunders, Clarence G.
33673	,,	Binstead, George F.			

Canadian Pacific—The Empire's Greatest Railway.

142 15TH BATTALION, 3RD INFANTRY BRIGADE—cont.

"A" COMPANY.

Captain ... ... McGregor, Archibald Robert.
Lieutenant ... ... Davidson, Robert Hay
  ,, ... Mavor, Wilfred
  ,, ... Jago, Walter Whitaker

Regl. No.	Rank.	Name.	Regl. No.	Rank.	Name.
27001	Col.-Sgt.	Keith, James	27060	Private	Dallon, Donald
27002	Sergt.	Burness,Chas. Stuart	27061	Lce.-Cpl.	Delaney, John J.
27003	,,	Annand, James	27062	Private	Edmondson, John
27005	,,	Allison, Peter M.	27063	,,	Edwards, Walter
27004	,,	Hunter, David	27064	,,	Fisher, John
27057	Lce.-Sgt.	Checkley, Albert	27065	,,	Flaxman, Reuben
27009	Corpl.	Anderson, Louis D.	27066	,,	Flanagan, John
27008	,,	Purser, Harold	27067	,,	Garden, Charles J.
27006	,,	Robertson, James	27068	,,	Gibbs, George H.
27007	,,	Brownlee, Archibald	27027	,,	Gillespie, Alexander
27013	Lce.-Cpl.	May, William John	27069	,,	Grant, Leonard G.
27010	,,	Dring, Sidney W.	27070	,,	Gowans, John Walter
27011	,,	Wyatt, William Geo.	27071	,,	Girvan, John P.
27012	,,	Boyd,PhilipBentinck	27072	,,	Gilchrist, Frank J.
27021	Sergt.	Keith, Alexander R.	27073	,,	Gibbs, Albert C.
27030	Private	Ailles, John	27018	,,	Hodges, Edgar B.
27032	,,	Alexander, James	27074	,,	Hogg, John W.
27033	,,	Archer,Rbrt. Gordon	27075	,,	Husband, Albert Roy
27034	,,	Archibald, Samuel	27076	,,	Henderson, William
27035	,,	Armstrong, Fred	27077	,,	Henson, Harry
27036	,,	Bryce, George W.	27078	Lce.-Cpl.	Hobbes, Percy Victor
27037	,,	Bennet, Walter	27079	Private	Hewetson, George
27038	,,	Bergin, John	27080	,,	Jones, Harry
27039	,,	Baker, Thomas G. St. Barbe	27024	,,	Jones, William
			27081	,,	Kelly, George A.
27040	,,	Brooks, Warren C.	27019	,,	Laird, William
27041	,,	Beattie, Joseph H.	27082	,,	Lunney, Christopher
27042	,,	Brown, Herman C.	27083	,,	Lewis, David
27043	,,	Bernard, Lionel	27084	,,	McKeogh, Thomas
27044	,,	Binny, Walter J.	27085	,,	McLean, Alexander
27045	,,	Briscoe, Phillip H.	27087	,,	McColl, Duncan
27046	,,	Carr, Roy	27086	,,	McColl, J. Duncan
27047	,,	Clapp, Ernest	27088	,,	McArthur, Horace H.
27048	,,	Cassels, John	27089	,,	McClay, Walter
27049	,,	Cantley, Alexander	27090	,,	McMillan, Wm. Fred.
27050	,,	Cummings, John	27091	,,	McLeod, Alexander
27051	,,	Chivas, Edwin J.	27092	,,	McLeod, Malcolm
27052	,,	Cleal, George	27093	,,	McLeod, Duncan
27053	,,	Campbell, Hugh	27094	,,	McGillivray, Angus
27056	,,	Campbell, Robert	27095	,,	McGrath, John
27054	,,	Crosby, Emerson	27096	,,	Macaulay, Edward
27055	,,	Coats, Robert	27023	,,	Miller, Kenneth
27058	,,	Cowan, Fred. A.	27097	,,	Munroe, Donald M.
27022	,,	Cox, James Thomas	27098	,,	Munro, James
27059	,,	Donald, John	27099	,,	May, William Joseph

Canadian Pacific—The Empire's Greatest Railway.

15TH BATTALION, 3RD INFANTRY BRIGADE—cont. 143

Regl. No.	Rank.	Name.	Regl. No.	Rank.	Name.
27101	Private	Moore, Norman D.	27121	Private	Stephens, William
27100	,,	Moore, James A.	27123	,,	Smith, Albert E.
27102	,,	Mutimer, Joseph	27122	,,	Smith, George W.
27103	,,	Mutimer, James	27124	,,	Sim, George
27104	,,	Marshall, John	27125	,,	Shields, Alexander
27105	,,	Mann, John	27126	,,	Spaul, Wilbert H.
27106	,,	Martin, James W.	27127	,,	Spence, Lewis P.
27107	,,	Notley, John	27128	,,	Spindler, Lawrence C.
27108	,,	Nathan, Lewis W.	27129	,,	Tait, Reginald E. R.
27109	,,	Nagle, James	27105	,,	Tait, Robert
27110	,,	Nicholson, Malcolm A.	27017	,,	Thistle, Ralph
27111	,,	Paramore, William	27130	,,	Tushingham, W. R.
27112	,,	Prior, Henry	27131	,,	Thomas, William A.
27025	,,	Pressy, Fred	27020	,,	Venner, Wm. Bent.
27113	,,	Preston, Thomas	27132	,,	Vine, George Herbt.
27114	,,	Robertson, John	27133	,,	Walsh, John
27115	,,	Robertson, Thomas	27134	,,	White, Charles R.
27117	,,	Robertson, George D.	27135	,,	Wauchope, William
27116	,,	Robertson, George	27136	,,	Wilkings, C. Roy
27014	,,	Sanson, Robert	27137	,,	Whalley, Thomas
27016	,,	Sculley, Arthur A.	27138	,,	Warren, William
27118	,,	Sparks, Douglas E.	27139	,,	Whyte, William
27119	,,	Stewart, John A.	27140	,,	Winks, Edwin G.
27120	Lce.-Cpl.	Stewart, R. Gordon C.	27029	,,	Wall, Charles E.
27031	Private	Stephen, George M.			

"B" COMPANY.

Captain	... ...	Cory, Robert Young
Lieutenant	... ...	Campbell, Peter G. C.
,,	... ...	Malone, Willard Park
,,	... ...	Muir, Arthur Edward

Regl. No.	Rank.	Name.	Regl. No.	Rank.	Name.
27141	Col.-Sgt.	Ratcliffe, William	27148	Corpl.	Baxter, James G.
27143	Sergt.	Harcombe, Fredk. J.	27175	Private	Bowerbank, Herbert
27144	,,	Hooper, Henry Wm.	27165	,,	Beith, John
27145	,,	Macdonald, Alex. A.	27174	,,	Bone, Frederick
27142	,,	McMaster, Wm. L.	27168	,,	Blake, Louis
27157	Private	Atkin, Thomas	27160	,,	Balmer, Walter
97158	,,	Ault, Jas. Thos. Wm.	27170	,,	Brady, James T.
27166	,,	Boisse, Herman	27173	,,	Booth, Harold
27147	Lce.-Sgt.	Brown, John J. E. C.	27167	,,	Boyce, Barney
27171	Private	Brown, Harry	27180	,,	Coats, Robert
27172	,,	Brown, James Wm.	27178	,,	Cooper, Reginald S.
27163	,,	Baron, Thomas	27177	,,	Carson, Roswell
27161	,,	Barlow, Herbert	27181	,,	Connolly, James J.
27159	,,	Bailey, John Bell	27155	Corpl.	Calder, John M.
27169	,,	Branciere, Robert R.	27149	,,	Cameron, John F.
27164	,,	Baxter, Wm. Clark	27150	,,	Campbell, Allen

Canadian Pacific—The Empire's Greatest Railway.

144 15TH BATTALION, 3RD INFANTRY BRIGADE—cont.

Regl. No.	Rank.	Name.	Regl. No.	Rank.	Name.
27179	Private	Cook, Ernest R.	27229	Sergt.	Miller, William
27176	,,	Carroll, Dennis	27231	Private	Morris, Arthur E.
27182	,,	Cuthbert, Fred	27238	,,	Macleod, Donald
27183	,,	Dean, William J.	27230	,,	Moncton, Harvey
27184	,,	Dowey, John J.	27232	,,	McConnell, Charles
27186	,,	Ellins, Harold F. A.	27234	,,	McDaniel, Samuel
27187	,,	Ellins, Harry F.	27239	,,	McLaughlin, Alfd. J.
27185	,,	Elliott, Alfred	27236	,,	McDonald, Angus
27188	,,	Fieldwick, Fred	27241	,,	McNeill, James
27156	,,	Fisher, Wilfred W.	27131	,,	McMaster, Alexander
27190	,,	Flowers, John F.	27237	,,	Mackenzie, Albert E.
27192	,,	Fraser, John	27233	,,	McCrae, Nicholas
27152	Lce.-Cpl.	Fellows, John T.	27240	,,	McLeish, Alexndr. N.
27189	Private	Foster, Walter	27242	,,	McGowan, William
27191	,,	Ferguson, Douglas	27235	,,	McDougall, Allan
27193	,,	Fortier, Alfred	27244	,,	Prettyman, Percy A.
27195	,,	Griffin, George	27243	,,	Perrot, Alfred H.
27196	,,	Gutcher, John J.	27245	,,	Quinn, Thomas R.
27154	Lce.-Cpl.	Glass, Edward M.	27146	Sergt.	Russ, William
27194	Private	Gibbons, William T.	27252	Private	Rutherford, Matthew
27201	,,	Heald, Walter	27247	,,	Ratcliffe, Alfred W.
27205	,,	Howard, Victor G.	27246	,,	Rae, Alfred
27200	,,	Hannah, Thomas	27251	,,	Reid, Matthew M.
27198	,,	Hardacre, Alex. K.	27248	,,	Read, Alexander H.
27203	,,	Horton, Steve	27249	,,	Robertson, Charles
27204	,,	Howitt, Frank	27250	,,	Robertson, James
27197	,,	Halliday, Thomas	27259	,,	Spalding, Thomas
27199	,,	Hastings, John M.	27254	,,	Sinclair, Colin M.
27202	,,	Hodder, Joseph A.	27255	,,	Sinclair, Gordon M.
27206	,,	Irvine, James	27260	,,	Stephens, Henry A.
27207	,,	Jolliffe, John H.	27263	,,	Strachan, John
27209	,,	Jones, George E.	27261	,,	Stevenson, Albert
27208	,,	Jones, Charles S.	27256	,,	Shurety, Ralph P.
27216	,,	Kirk, Wilfred	27257	,,	Skene, Forbes M.
27210	,,	Kerr, Matthew K.	27258	,,	Smith, Joseph
27211	,,	Kerr, Donald E.	27262	,,	Stodart, John
27212	,,	Kearns, Milford S.	27268	,,	Tyler, Clement
27213	,,	Kehoe, Joseph	27264	,,	Tait, William
27214	,,	Kensett, John	27266	,,	Terry, William
27224	,,	Lewis, William C.	27265	,,	Terry, Everett A.
27226	,,	Long, William J.	27267	,,	Todd, George
27217	,,	Lane, Albert	27269	,,	Urquhart, Robert
27220	,,	Lickers, William F.	27274	,,	Wilkinson, Chas. H.
27153	Lce.-Cpl.	Lamerton, Alfred F.	27271	,,	Watson, James
27222	Private	Lewis, Percy T.	27276	,,	Williams, Henry H.
27225	,,	Logan, David B.	27272	,,	White, Harry
27221	,,	Ling, Leonard L.	27273	,,	White, James A.
27218	,,	Laing, Cecil R.	27275	,,	Wilford, Hugh
27219	,,	Leal, Archibald	27270	,,	Walker, William
27223	,,	Lewis, Clifford H.	27277	,,	Wilson, Frank
27228	,,	Maskell, Lovell	27278	,,	Young, James
27227	,,	Marsden, John			

Canadian Pacific—The Empire's Greatest Railway.

15TH BATTALION, 3RD INFANTRY BRIGADE—cont. 145

"C" COMPANY.

Captain	... ...	McLaren, George Hagarty
Lieutenant	... ...	Shoenberger, William Hamilton
,,	... ...	Bath, Edward Osler
,,	... ...	Acland, Perigine Palmer

Regl. No.	Rank.	Name.	Regl. No.	Rank.	Name.
27280	Q.M.S.	Wilkinson, Chas. R.	27325	Private	Churchill, Charles
27281	Col.-Sgt.	Jackson, James	27327	,,	Danks, Sidney
27283	Sergt.	Burley, Edward	27330	,,	Dewar, James
27284	,,	Wells, Wm. Forester	27331	,,	Devlin, John
27285	,,	Gridley, Wm. Ernest	27332	,,	Devlin, William
27286	,,	Band, Harry	27329	,,	Dallas, Wm. Morse
27287	Lce.-Sgt.	Barker, Thomas	27328	,,	Dzwonkowski, Anthy.
27386	Sergt.	Newlands, A. Austin	27335	,,	Edwards, Wm. Alex.
27282	Lce.-Cpl.	Noble, Leonard	27334	,,	Edwards, Arthur
27289	,,	McCulloch, Wm. A.	27333	,,	East, Percy Charles
27290	,,	Patton, George H.	27336	,,	Forbes, John
27292	Corpl.	Covill, Arthur	27337	,,	Forbes, Alex. Smith
27293	Lce.-Cpl.	Lockhart, Wm. S. B.	27340	,,	Freeman, Wm. Geo.
27294	,,	Howes, William H.	27339	,,	Fothergill, C. R. P.
27295	,,	Gray, James Shirra	27338	,,	Fulton, Edgar
27296	Private	Adkins, Thomas	27342	,,	Gillespie, Norman A.
27297	,,	Ashfield, Herbert	27343	,,	Guy, Herbert
27298	Corpl.	Anderson, Thomas	27341	,,	Goode, William
27299	Private	Anderson, David S.	27351	,,	Hannay, John
27317	,,	Belfield, John W.	27352	,,	Hopley, Herbert
27318	,,	Bush, William	27354	,,	Hannah, Douglas
27302	,,	Barnard, Cyril M.	27350	,,	Humphries, Ralph S.
27300	,,	Barry, William Jas.	27353	,,	Honsberger, Thos. F.
27307	,,	Black, William R.	27346	,,	Howarth, Fred Geo.
27308	,,	Beavis, Fred Victor	27347	,,	Hodges, Harry
27309	,,	Bradley, William	27344	,,	Haley, Albert
27310	,,	Brooks, Augustus	27345	,,	Houston, John
27311	,,	Buick, Joseph	27348	,,	Hodges, Roy Bowen
27312	,,	Botterell, Edward S.	27349	,,	Hodges, Wm. Benj.
27313	,,	Bacon, William Geo.	27357	Lce.-Cpl.	Ingram, John Wm.
27314	,,	Ball, William Henry	27745	Private	Ireland, C. E.
27303	,,	Bean, Delbert	27355	,,	Irving, Wm. Adam
27304	,,	Brown, Henry	27356	,,	Irwin, Robert John
27305	,,	Brown, Myron	27360	,,	Jamieson, Robert C.
27306	,,	Biglow, Ellard	27361	,,	Jamieson, John D.
27315	,,	Bunston, Melvin	27358	,,	Journeaux, Henry
27316	,,	Bell, Alex. W. R.	27362	,,	Johnson, Alfred
27301	,,	Brodie, Thomas	27363	,,	Johnston, Wm. H.
27322	,,	Carruthers, Bruce	27359	,,	Jarman, Joseph Hy.
27323	,,	Cowie, William	27369	,,	Ledingham, Geo. F.
27320	,,	Cole, Clifford	27368	,,	Liscombe, Russell
27324	,,	Crockford, Alf. Wm.	27366	,,	Lawrence, Wm. J.
27319	,,	Cummings, Jn. Dean	27365	,,	Loosely, Alfred
27326	,,	Cruxton, John Patrick	27367	,,	Lang, Burnie
27321	,,	Crawford, Chas. Wm.	27370	,,	Lloyd, William H.

Canadian Pacific—The Empire's Greatest Railway.

K

146 15TH BATTALION, 3RD INFANTRY BRIGADE—cont.

Regl. No.	Rank.	Name.	Regl. No.	Rank.	Name.
27378	Private	Miller, David	27398	Private	Robertson, George
27375	,,	McGuire, Joseph P.	27397	,,	Rickard, Harry T.
27382	,,	Marshall, Sidney H.	27396	,,	Raven, William
27376	,,	McNaughton, John	27407	,,	Stowell, John James
27374	,,	McDowell, Charles	27405	,,	Sangster, Edgar
27371	,,	McDonald, Murdoch	27404	,,	Sinclair, Hugh
27372	,,	McLachlan, David S.	27400	,,	Skinner, Wilfred
27373	,,	McGregor, George	27399	,,	Symon, Alexander L.
27377	,,	Mahon, Michael	27403	,,	Sholert, Fred Wm.
27379	,,	Morris, Dyson	27401	,,	Strickland, Gerald F.
27383	,,	Meikle, Alexander	27402	,,	Sutton, William
27380	,,	Murphy, Thomas	27406	,,	Spreadbury, John
27381	,,	Murray, Alexander	37409	,,	Truss, Peter G.
27384	,,	Noon, Thomas Jas.	27408	,,	Tellier, Fred Russell
27388	,,	Neil, Robert	27410	,,	Vandervoort, W. C.
27385	,,	Neville, James Dean	27413	,,	Walker, John Alex.
27387	,,	Newland, Albert L.	27412	,,	Wickens, Frederick
27389	,,	Ogden, Albert	27416	,,	Williams, Sidney
27394	,,	Pond, James Roy	27417	,,	Weymouth, Ernest W.
27393	,,	Peters, John	27414	,,	Wishart, James
27391	,,	Page, Frank	27415	,,	Wood, Fred Charles
27390	,,	Pilkington, Alfred	27411	,,	Walsh, Ernest Jas.
27392	,,	Powell, Ernest John	27418	,,	Young, Albert H.
27395	,,	Robertson, Rollo W.			

"D" COMPANY.

Captain ... ... Osborne, James Ewart
Lieutenant ... ... Fessenden, Charles V.
,, ... Bickle, Edwards W.
,, ... Kay, John

Regl. No.	Rank.	Name.	Regl. No.	Rank.	Name.
27419	Col.-Sgt.	Goodfellow, Adam	27437	Private	Blundell, Roland C.
27420	Sergt.	Ashling, Harold	27438	,,	Barrett, Fred W.
27421	,,	Ashling, Claude V.	27440	,,	Bell, Neil
27422	,,	Rodgers, Edward	27436	,,	Bell, Robert J.
27423	,,	Wink, James	27441	,,	Bickle, Wilfred N.
27424	Corpl.	Cameron, George	27442	,,	Boland, Sidney
27425	,,	Cavanagh, Thos. F.	27443	,,	Ball, Frederick
27426	,,	Campbell, Phillip	27444	,,	Begley, James
27427	,,	Gibbs, Alford	27445	,,	Boulton, Thomas
27428	,,	Staunton, Harry J.	27446	,,	Bethley, Charles
27429	Lce.-Cpl.	Lusted, Thomas J.	27447	,,	Bethley, Fred
27430	,,	Matthews, Harvey O.	27448	,,	Barkey, Alfred
27431	,,	Sinclair, Charles T.	27449	,,	Barnes, B.
27432	,,	White, John Cowan	27450	,,	Bradley, Thomas A.
27433	Private	Arnott, Thomas	27451	,,	Brown, George A.
27434	,,	Alexander, Andrew	27453	,,	Callighan, Ernest O.
27435	,,	Armstrong, Roy	27454	,,	Campbell, Arch. P.
27439	,,	Bell, David Gray	27455	,,	Chatfield, Thomas

Canadian Pacific—The Empire's Greatest Railway.

15TH BATTALION, 3RD INFANTRY BRIGADE—cont. 147

Regl. No.	Rank.	Name.	Regl. No.	Rank.	Name.
27456	Private	Cochrane, Robert	27507	Private	Lennox, William
27457	,,	Cochrane, James R.	27508	Sergt.	Macpherson, Stanley
27452	Sergt.	Cormack, H.	27509	Private	Melluish, Alexander
27458	Private	Corson, Archibald W.	27510	,,	McAllister, George F.
27459	,,	Cushway, George W.	27511	,,	McIvor, Benjamin
27460	,,	Chaplin, Arthur W.	27512	,,	McRobbie, Charles
27461	,,	Craighead, Charles	27513	,,	McBride, Archibald C.
27462	,,	Carmichael, Thomas	27514	,,	McCallum, Archibald
27463	,,	Coleman, Frank W.	27515	,,	McCluskey, Albert
27464	,,	Clement, Arthur W.	27516	,,	McIntyre, William J.
27465	,,	Coventry, Andrew	27517	,,	McCormick, Ernest
27466	,,	Comber, Albert H.	27518	,,	Magill, James
27467	,,	Cobb, Victor L.	27519	,,	MacKenzie, Chas. R.
27468	,,	Carr, James E.	28064	,,	McKnight, W.
27469	,,	Dutton, Fred C.	27521	,,	Miller, John R.
27470	,,	Dickson, Charles	27522	,,	Milligan, George D.
27471	,,	Donaldson, G. W.	27523	,,	Muir, John
27472	,,	Earl, Charles	27524	,,	Moule, William
27473	,,	Foster, Leonard	27525	,,	Milton, Edward
27474	,,	Foster, Gordon	27526	,,	Nixon, Melville W.
27475	,,	Green, Norman L.	27527	,,	Oswald, William
27476	,,	Green, Elmer M.	27528	,,	Parker, Stanley E.
27477	,,	Goodfellow, Jas. W.	27529	,,	Prior, F. H.
27478	,,	Gallimore, Thomas	27530	,,	Parker, William
27479	,,	Gordon, J.	27531	,,	Pirt, Richard
27520	Sergt.	Graham, Stuart W.	27532	,,	Price, Gordon J.
27480	Private	Hooper, Gordon	27533	,,	Pearce, Clifford
27481	,,	Harvey, John G.	27534	,,	Ross, Charles
27482	,,	Heard, Arthur	27535	,,	Ross, Walter
27483	,,	Hubbard, Frank	27536	,,	Roberts, Daniel J.
27484	,,	Hunter, Allan	27537	,,	Richardson, Frank
27486	,,	Hannam, Albert V.	27538	,,	Rigby, Herbert
27487	,,	Hopkins, Ernest W.	27539	,,	Sutton, Stephen E.
27488	,,	Haley, Frank	27544	,,	Smith, Sidney R.
27489	,,	Hannan, Barney W.	27541	,,	Stamps, Roy
27490	,,	Hester, William	27542	,,	Simons, Robert
27491	,,	Holmes, James L.	27543	,,	Smith, Frederick
27492	,,	Horsfield, Herbert	27540	Corpl.	Smith, Harry Elmer
27493	,,	Hill, John R.	27545	Private	Sutherland, William
27494	,,	Henderson, Alex. A.	27546	,,	Scott, Walter C.
27495	,,	Jackson, Thomas	27547	Corpl.	Thompson, John
27496	,,	James, Walter H.	27548	Private	Thorn, William
27497	,,	Jones, Morgan	27549	,,	Tweedie, Osborne
27498	,,	Johnson, Joseph	27550	,,	Webster, William
27499	,,	Kane, James	27551	,,	Wells, Reginald P.
27500	,,	Kennedy, Thomas	27552	,,	Whelan, William J.
27501	,,	Lewis, John C.	27553	,,	Webb, Thomas
27502	,,	Lusted, Walter H.	27554	,,	Wilson, Earle J.
27503	,,	Lusted, George F.	27555	,,	White, George
27504	,,	Luck, Lewis E.	27556	,,	Young, Donald
27505	,,	Lundius, William	27557	,,	Yetman, Alexander
27506	,,	Layton, Arthur H.			

Canadian Pacific—The Empire's Greatest Railway.

K 2

148 15TH BATTALION, 3RD INFANTRY BRIGADE—cont.

"E" COMPANY.

Captain ... ... Alexander, George MacKenzie
Lieutenant ... ... Barwick, Hugh Atkinson
„ ... ... Jones, Frederick Vernon
„ ... ... Livingstone, John A. M.

Regl. No.	Rank.	Name.	Regl. No.	Rank.	Name.
27558	Sgt.-Maj.	Grant, William Hay	27611	Private	Coyde, Charles
27559	Col.-Sgt.	Hermitage, George T.	27696	„	Chalk, Richard
27560	„	Rigby, Hubert J. S.	27659	„	Crosby, Kenneth W.
27561	Sergt.	Page, Henry William	27600	„	Daubert, Alexander
27660	„	Ralph, Henry	27604	„	Davies, Charles
27595	„	Mould, John	27639	„	Day, Charles Edw.
27629	„	Fraser, William	27676	„	Dawson, John Chas.
27596	Lce.-Sgt.	Pay, Ernest Albert	27647	„	Dall, Harry
27562	Corpl.	Lowndes, John	27648	„	Dall, David
27661	„	Cunningham, Thos.	27692	„	Durward, Alex. Kerr
27630	„	Lee, Morris	27644	„	Dugan, Cyril
27631	Lce.-Cpl.	Logan, Albert	27609	„	Dillon, Leo John
27662	Corpl.	McLean, Wallace A.	27685	„	Drummond, Albert
27563	Lce.-Cpl.	House, Fredk. Thos.	27616	„	Eyles, George Henry
27598	„	Eyles, Charles Daniel	27649	„	Edmonds, Charles L.
27615	Private	Adams, Geo. J.	27587	„	Ferland, Frank
27643	„	Alston, James	27617	„	Fleming, Geo. Wm.
27588	„	Atwell, Ernest	27629	„	Fraser, W.
27684	„	Austin, Henry David	27591	„	Gower, William Jas.
27583	„	Baker, Austin	27581	„	Gold, F.
27613	„	Barrett, Sidney W.	27634	Lce.-Cpl.	Gledhill, Fred Chas.
27614	„	Barrett, James	27586	Private	Guy, William Jas.
27589	„	Barrett, Hugh H. G.	27658	„	Green, Frederick
27625	„	Bedford, Alfred C.	27686	„	Frudemacher, Alfred
27666	„	Bell, William	27633	„	Hart, Alfred
27619	„	Bennet, Lionel John	27669	„	Head, Thomas
27657	„	Bodker, Cecil Chas.	27691	„	Hargreaves, Chris.
27593	„	Boyce, James C.	27678	„	Husband, Alfred D.
27679	„	Brown, Alvin W.	27624	„	Insley, Percy
27636	„	Brown, John	27566	„	Jackson, Charles R.
27572	„	Brobyn, Samuel J.	27571	„	Johnston, Robert
27695	„	Bradley, Sidney	27664	„	Johnston, Josiah A.
27612	„	Blunt, Harry	27651	„	Johnston, Wilfred
27627	„	Blunt, Walter A.	27642	„	Jordan, Henry
27667	„	Brookes, Bernard L.	27594	„	Kent, Harry
27665	„	Carpenter, Digby R.	27579	„	Kirkpatrick, W. G.
27654	„	Cameron, Donald	27628	„	Kingscott, Walter A.
27607	„	Campbell, Hugh S.	27626	„	Ladd, Frederick G.
27641	„	Chadwick, John	27680	„	Laceby, George Edw.
27584	„	Coe, Cecil Ardagh	27635	„	Longstaff, C.
27621	„	Clark, Edward Thos.	27622	„	Lowe, Norman
27623	„	Corey, Rowan	27687	„	Ludgate, Dawson J.
27675	„	Clappison, Edw. W.	27580	„	Meek, Harry
27638	„	Cox, F.	27575	„	Meredith, Harold S.
27574	„	Coyle, William	27637	„	Milloy, David C.

Canadian Pacific—The Empire's Greatest Railway.

15TH BATTALION, 3RD INFANTRY BRIGADE—cont. 149

Regl. No.	Rank.	Name.	Regl. No.	Rank.	Name.
27590	Private	Mooney, Harold W.	27671	Private	Sharp, John
27599	,,	Miller, J. Malcolm	27673	,,	Seear, Oliver
27577	,,	Miller, Peter	27606	,,	Saunders, Leonard J.
27605	,,	McReynolds, James	27672	,,	Tucknott, Christpher
27693	,,	Macdonald, Allan	27603	,,	Thorpe, Harold
27640	,,	Olsen, Frederick L.	27578	,,	Twells, Joseph
27592	,,	Parnham, Verna	27576	,,	Tickner, Douglas B.
27570	,,	Phillips, Roscoe L.	27569	,,	Tuck, William Henry
27655	,,	Quinn, David Patrick	27568	,,	Tuck, Thomas Geo.
27620	,,	Ramey, Lyman	27567	,,	Tuck, ArthurOscar B.
27601	,,	Rowley, John	27564	,,	Turner, Almor C.
27682	Lce.-Cpl.	Rose, Hugh	27610	,,	Trueman, Melville
27674	Private	Ross, William Allan	27690	,,	Thompson, Charles J.
27573	,,	Robertson, William	27683	,,	Varney, Albert Edw.
27646	,,	Robertson, Fdk. D. S.	27670	,,	Wallace, Stephen
27602	,,	Sinclair, John Craig	27688	,,	Watts, Edward Reg.
27645	,,	Sinclair, Horace V.	27582	,,	Williams, Arthur C.
27632	,,	Smith, Joseph.	27663	,,	Williams, John H.
27681	,,	Shaw, Benj. Albert	27565	,,	Wilmot, Scott M.
27656	,,	Styan, Charles	27653	,,	Wilson, Geo. Shine
27694	,,	Stone, Samuel Lord	27585	,,	Whale, Percy Francis
27652	,,	Smith, Sidney	27650	,,	Worsley, Wm. Henry
27618	,,	Skimins, Walter M.	27689	,,	Winn, John William
27668	,,	Stanley, Irvin Edwd.	27608	,,	Wormington, Robert
27677	,,	Stanley, George			

"F" COMPANY.

Captain	Marshall, Kenneth Rudd
Lieutenant	Perry, Frank M.
,, ...	Gibson, Frank M.
,, ...	Langmuir, Gavin Ince.

Regl. No.	Rank.	Name.	Regl. No.	Rank.	Name.
27697	Col.-Sgt.	Stephens, John T.	27701	Private	Adamson, Robert
27703	Sergt.	Bradshaw, Joseph	27795	,,	Bacon, Francis G.
27711	,,	Crane, George A.	27788	,,	Barrington, Albert
27698	,,	Walker, William	27793	,,	Bass, Leviro A.
27801	,,	Williams, Duncan	27804	,,	Bissett, Thomas
27736	,,	Ball, Charles	27805	,,	Blundy, Isidore G.
27768	,,	Stevens, Alfred	27739	,,	Bouldry, William
27722	Lce.-Sgt.	Leitch, James	27702	,,	Billson, John Edward
27707	,,	Campbell, John H.	27835	,,	Brooks, Samuel J.
27802	Corpl.	Evans, William H.	27797	,,	Browley, William M.
27699	,,	Uden, Arthur	27767	,,	Brackenborough,B.J.
27769	,,	Gleed, James	27704	,,	Browne, Cedric M.
27715	,,	Freeland, Gordon C.	27705	,,	Browne, Russell M.
27700	Lce.-Cpl.	Matches, William	27740	,,	Brown, Fred
27803	,,	Jackson, James	27706	,,	Bunch, Bert
27770	,,	Louden, Albert	27778	,,	Bussell, Frank
27737	,,	Bailey, Leonard	27788	,,	Cairns, Harry
27776	,,	Murray, James	27806	,,	Carter, Fred Nelson

Canadian Pacific—The Empire's Greatest Railway.

15TH BATTALION, 3RD INFANTRY BRIGADE—cont.

Regl. No.	Rank.	Name.	Regl. No.	Rank.	Name.
27708	Private	Carter, Gilbert	27818	Private	McIntyre, Wilson H.
27807	,,	Carter, Harry	27798	,,	Martin, William
27808	,,	Clarke, William J.	27726	,,	Millard, Arthur G.
27709	,,	Conway, Lawrence A.	27725	,,	Millard, William Hy.
27710	,,	Cooper, Edward	27787	,,	Mitchell, James A.
27809	,,	Cornhill, Lewis	27817	,,	More, Angus
27782	,,	Curtis, Edward J.	27754	,,	Morris, Allard
27800	,,	Campbell, Gordon	27727	,,	Morris, Kenneth
27741	,,	Cotterill, Gordon	27751	,,	Morrison, John
27811	,,	Davidson, Archibald	27728	,,	Muir, John
27712	,,	Davis, Frederick J.	27752	,,	Murison, Charles W.
27742	,,	Davis, Harold V.	27724	,,	Macleod, James
27713	,,	Delahaye, Charles N.	27821	,,	Neil, Edward J.
27810	,,	Dennis, Kenneth	27784	,,	O'Keefe, James T.
27834	Corpl.	Duff, Robert John	27783	,,	O'Keefe, L.
27799	Private	Fielding, Eli	27823	,,	Pollock, John
27714	,,	Fontaine, Morris	27822	,,	Porter, William G.
27716	,,	Frith, Walter	27786	,,	Powers, Grant R.
27779	,,	Gazey, Alfred	27836	,,	Price, Cecil
27785	,,	Gibson, Robert	27729	,,	Reading, Gordon
27792	,,	Griffin, George	27757	,,	Reid, Herbert G.
27288	Corpl.	Hall, Geo.	27824	,,	Robinson, John
27814	Private	Hawes, Frank	27755	,,	Roscoe, William
27743	,,	Hart, Milburn M.	27730	,,	Rowan, Thomas
27717	,,	Harrigan, Alfred B.	27756	,,	Rowe, Heydon
27718	,,	Hibbard, Hartley	27759	,,	Scott, Frank M.
27777	,,	Hudson, Basil	27758	,,	Scott, John K.
27744	,,	Husson, Harry	27760	,,	Scott, Robert
27812	,,	Holtby, Arthur W.	27761	,,	Shaw, Harry
27813	,,	Hyde, Harry	27731	,,	Simpson, Richard
27719	,,	Ingle, Harry	27790	,,	Singleton, James H.
27774	,,	James, Samuel H.	27827	,,	Slim, Alfred
27720	,,	Jamieson, Alexander	27825	,,	Shearman, Harold
27721	,,	Jamieson, Thomas A.	27732	,,	Smith, Thomas
27747	,,	Keais, Michael	27789	,,	Smyth, David
27749	,,	Kelsall, Frank	27794	,,	Stephens, Frederick
27746	,,	Kirk, Andrew	27826	,,	Stuckey, Charles
27748	,,	Kritzer, Harry	27791	,,	Taylor, George W.
27775	,,	Lacey, Hollis C.	27733	,,	Thomas, Albert
27815	,,	Lambie, Andrew A.	27829	,,	Thomas, Thomas H.
27780	,,	Lavelle, Edward C.	27763	,,	Thompson, Alexander
27723	,,	Leach, Charles B.	27734	,,	Thompson, John C.
27796	,,	Levick, John	27762	,,	Tilley, Robert
27750	,,	Litchfield, Reg. C.	27828	,,	Tyler, John W.
27771	,,	Love, Andrew	27833	,,	Ward, Arthur G.
27819	,,	Mackie, Charles S.	27764	,,	Warden, George
27753	,,	Mankey, Thorold	27766	,,	Warren, William
27820	,,	Malyon, Frederick	27830	,,	Watson, Frank
27816	,,	Marks, William	27735	,,	Weeks, Ernest
27773	,,	McEwen, William	27765	,,	Whitehead, Robert
27772	,,	McKean, Peter	27831	,,	Wilson, Robt. Walter
27781	,,	McInture, Hugh	27832	,,	Woods, John

Canadian Pacific—The Empire's Greatest Railway.

15TH BATTALION, 3RD INFANTRY BRIGADE—cont.

"G" COMPANY.

Captain	... ...	Musgrove, George Henry ᴅꜱᴏ
Lieutenant	... ...	Smith, Frank, J.
,,	... ...	Scott, H. Maxwell
,,	... ...	Dansereau, Joseph Adolph

Regl. No.	Rank.	Name.	Regl. No.	Rank.	Name.
27836	Col.-Sgt.	De Hart, Lewis E.	27882	Private	Domaille, Charles F.
27837	,,	Goodwin, Hugh Hy.	27883	,,	Donaldson, Alex.
27838	,,	Browne, Harry Fred	27884	,,	Duncan, Bruce Thos.
27839	,,	Edmunds, Geo. Rbt.	27885	,,	Dunn, Albert
27840	,,	Duguid, W. Geo. B.	27886	,,	Durant, Fred Edwd.
27841	Corpl.	Gillespie, Milo John	27887	,,	Ellis, Geo. Shanley
27842	,,	Cochrane, Mack	27888	,,	Everitt, Alex. James
27843	,,	Newman, Geo. W. B.	27889	,,	Fairbairn, Angus
27844	,,	Yates, Clifford F.	27890	,,	Falkner, Henry
27845	,,	Hannah, John D.	27891	,,	Falkner, Walter F.
27846	Lce.-Cpl.	Reid, Thos. Wilson	27892	,,	Flood, Wm. James
27847	,,	Halley, Peter	27893	,,	Ford, John
27848	Sergt.	Stockley, James A.	27894	,,	Fortnum, Charles
27849	Lce.-Cpl.	Walsh, William Hy.	27895	,,	Franks, John Sidney
27850	,,	Williams, Wm. John	27896	,,	Gilpin, Robt. Fredk.
27852	Private	Pyke, Clarence E.	27897	,,	Goodrich, Frank E.
27853	,,	Aikenhead, Robert	27898	,,	Gorwell, Wm. Henry
27854	,,	Austin, Geo. Lewis	27899	,,	Goyette, Eugene
27855	,,	Baldwin, Wm. Henry	27900	,,	Gray, Alex. John
27856	,,	Beane, Bert Stanley	27901	,,	Griesbach, Arthur
27857	,,	Berry, Albert John	27902	,,	Haldane, Ewen M.
27858	,,	Beverly, Henry Ezra	27903	,,	Hanlon, Ernest
27859	,,	Bolton, Frank W.	27904	,,	Harris, Albert Wm.
27860	,,	Brigden, Percival J.	27905	Corpl.	Hendry, John Adam
27861	,,	Brindley, Chas. Ed.	27906	Private	Hogean, Charles W.
27862	,,	Broley, Frank H.	27907	,,	Hunt, Walter Fredk.
27863	,,	Browne, Robt. Offord	27908	,,	Hurley, John H.
27864	,,	Bruce, Allan	27909	,,	Johnson, David
27865	,,	Burr, Wm. Henry	27910	,,	Jones, Andrew Haley
27866	,,	Cameron, Donald	27911	,,	Jones, Morris
27867	,,	Campbell, Arch. S.	27912	,,	Jones, Robert
27868	,,	Carroll, Joseph E.	27913	,,	Jordan, Robert D.
27869	,,	Cawood, Joseph	27914	,,	Jucksch, Arno
27870	,,	Choles, Frederick H.	27915	,,	Kells, David Wesley
27871	,,	Clarke, George Thos.	27916	,,	Laroque, Arthur
27872	,,	Coleman, Vincent	27917	,,	Leacock, Geo. Edwd.
27873	,,	Collins, Neville L.	27918	,,	Lewis, Owen S.
27874	,,	Colquhoun, John L.	27919	,,	Lewis, William Robt.
27875	,,	Conibear, Philip S.	27920	,,	Long, Clarence A.
27876	,,	Coombs, William	27921	,,	Lothian, David E.
27877	,,	Crane, Joseph G. E.	27922	,,	Lynch, Michael Thos.
27878	,,	Dare, Thomas	27923	,,	MacDonald, Arch.
27879	,,	Davis, William	27924	,,	MacDonald, Fred. B.
27880	,,	Davison, William N.	27925	,,	MacDonald, Chas. H.
27881	,,	Desjardins, Emile	27926	,,	May, Vivian

Canadian Pacific —The Empire's Greatest Railway.

15TH BATTALION, 3RD INFANTRY BRIGADE—cont.

Regl. No.	Rank.	Name.	Regl. No.	Rank.	Name.
27927	Private	Maybin, William	27951	Private	Scott, John Simpson
27928	,,	McKellar, James	27952	,,	Scrimgeour, Wm. A.
27929	,,	McInnis, George Jas.	27953	,,	Shevlin, Peter
27930	,,	McCall, Thomas	27954	,,	Smith, William Geo.
27931	,,	McMillan, Alexander	27955	,,	Smith, Wilfred M.
27932	,,	McMillan, Alfred	27956	,,	Stanley, Harold
27933	,,	McMaster, Robert	27957	,,	Stuart, James
27934	,,	Merry, Edward	27958	,,	Sweet, John L. Leslie
27935	,,	Moores, William	27959	,,	Swift, Alfred Victor
27936	,,	Nicolson, Peter O.	27960	,,	Thompson, Edward
27937	,,	Noble, Frederick W.	27961	,,	Thoms, Frederick
27938	,,	Nokes, Albert Chas.	27962	,,	Turnbull, William
27939	,,	North, Thomas A.	27963	,,	Wallace, William
27940	,,	Pennington, Albert	27965	,,	Watson, Robert Sam.
27941	,,	Potts, John Ramsay	27964	,,	Watson, Clarence H.
27942	,,	Rae, William James	27966	,,	Weaver, Thomas S.
27943	,,	Raper, Frederick A.	27967	,,	Welsh, James
27944	,,	Rice, Ephraim	27968	,,	Weston, Henry
27945	,,	Richards, Wilmot	27969	,,	Wheeler, Thomas J.
27946	,,	Roche, Charles W.	27970	,,	White, Albert Ed.
27947	,,	Royal, Stanley	27971	,,	Wickham Edward G.
27948	,,	Ruddock, George	27972	,,	Wishart, George R.
27949	,,	Rumsey, Allan	27973	,,	Woollard, Fredk. J.
27950	,,	Sayers, Edward	27974	,,	Young, William B.

"H" COMPANY.

Captain		Daniels, Albert Murdoch
Lieutenant		Macdonald, Frederick Wyld
,, ...		Sinclair, Alexander
,, ...		Wilson, Harold Mackenzie

Regl. No.	Rank.	Name	Regl. No.	Rank.	Name.
27975	Col. Sgt.	Vernon, Harold	27992	Private	Allan, Wellington
27981	Sergt.	Grattan, Paul	27993	,,	Allan, George
27976	,,	Jones, Walter	27994	,,	Allen, William
27977	,,	Milne, James	27995	,,	Bacon, Arthur B.
27978	,,	Shield, James	27996	,,	Best, Cecil H.
27979	,,	Thompson, John A.	27997	,,	Bonin, Oliver B.
27980	Sig. Sgt.	Arthur, William	27998	,,	Bowen David
27982	Lce.-Sgt.	Baldwin, John	27999	Lce.-Cpl.	Breach, George E.
27983	Corpl.	Christie, Campbell	28000	Private	Brown, Albert Sid.
27984	,,	Cresswell, George H.	28001	,,	Brown, Douglas
27985	Private	Dancks, Gustave C.	28002	,,	Brown, George A.
27986	Corpl.	Derbyshire, Wilfred	28003	,,	Budd, Charles
27987	Private	Cockburn, Ross C.	28004	,,	Byiers, Peter
27988	Lce.-Cpl.	Keddie, James L.	28005	,,	Calcott, Arthur C.
27989	Corpl.	Marshall, Harry	28006	,,	Campbelton, William
27990	Private	Adam, John	28007	,,	Carter, Christopher
27991	,,	Alek, Michel	28008	,,	Clark, John E.

Canadian Pacific--The Empire's Greatest Railway.

15TH BATTALION, 3RD INFANTRY BRIGADE—*cont.*

Regl. No.	Rank.	Name.	Regl. No.	Rank.	Name.
28009	Private	Clayton, Harold M.	28060	Private	McDonald, James
28010	,,	Clifford, Arthur F.	28061	,,	McClelland, Herbert
28011	,,	Colley, Peter	28062	,,	McIntosh, James
28012	Lce.-Sgt.	Connell, Eric McI.	28063	,,	McKinnon, Alf. Neil
28013	Private	Cumming, H. W. S.	28065	,,	McLaughlin, John
28014	,,	Davidson, John A.	28066	,,	McNeill, Archibald
28015	,,	Dennett, William J.	28067	,,	MacNeill, Jas. Cleary
28016	,,	Drane, Ernest Wm.	28068	,,	McSorley, Walter
28017	,,	Douglas, Daniel	28113	,,	McCurdie, Harry
28018	,,	Dunbar, Alvin Percy	28069	,,	Nelson, Harry James
28019	,,	Dupont, Emile	28070	,,	O'Connor, Daniel Jas.
28111	,,	Dudley, Morgan	28071	,,	Odd, Frank
28020	,,	Faultless, Wm. E.	28072	,,	Oliver, George R. C.
28021	,,	Feeney, James	28073	,,	Palmer, Stephen A.
28022	Lce.-Sgt.	Ferguson, Angus	28074	,,	Paxton, Edwin M.
28023	Private	Filce, Joseph E.	28075	,,	Peasley, John Henry
28024	,,	Frost, Alfred Arthur	28076	,,	Peck, Thomas
28112	,,	Fraser, John	28077	,,	Pearce, George
28025	,,	Gauthier, F. X.	28078	,,	Phillip, John Forbes
28026	Lce.-Cpl.	Gold, Arthur Fife	28079	,,	Provencher, Dolphis
28027	Private	Good, Richard Geo.	28080	Corpl.	Richards, Hy. Dudley
28028	,,	Greenwood, Mat. H.	28081	Private	Ritchie, James
28029	,,	Hamilton, George G.	28082	,,	Robinson, William
28030	,,	Hamilton, John H.	28083	,,	Robson, Robert Chas.
28031	,,	Hart, Thomas	28084	,,	Ross, Edward F.
28032	,,	Harvey, James H.	28085	,,	Ross, John Patterson
28033	,,	Henderson, John M.	28086	,,	Shaw, Alexander
28034	,,	Hill, William Geo.	28087	,,	Skelton, Thomas
28035	,,	Hilton, Harold	28088	,,	Smith, Samuel L.
28036	,,	Hunter, David	28089	,,	Stark, William
28037	,,	Hunter, Robert D.	28090	,,	Strombtz, Joseph
27485	,,	Hunter, Archie C.	28091	,,	Somerville, Cecil A.
28038	,,	Holt, John George	28092	,,	Syrett, Arthur
28039	,,	Imlach, George Aleck	28093	,,	Syrett, Barry
28040	,,	Irwin, John	28094	,,	Tillotson, Hugh Law
28041	,,	Irwin, Arthur Veral	28095	,,	Todd, Leslie George
28042	,,	James, Stanley P.	28096	,,	Towner, Samuel
28043	,,	Jezeph, James A.	28097	Lce.-Cpl.	Tweddle, James
28044	,,	Jones, George Aleck	28110	Private	Tomalin, Harry
28045	,,	Keele, Walter Wm.	28098	,,	Vartinian, Chanas
28046	,,	Kerrigan, Charles	28099	,,	Wallace, Archibald L.
28047	,,	Kirkaldy, Chas. Adie	28100	,,	Walters, John E.
28048	,,	Knowles, John	28101	,,	Watson, George S.
28050	,,	Leake, Erick Gilbert	28102	,,	Watson, John
28051	,,	Leclerc, Joseph	28103	,,	White, George Stan.
28052	,,	Lothian, Norman B.	28104	,,	Weir, Frederick
28053	,,	Lyness, Thomas	28105	,,	Weir, Peter
28054	,,	Marsh, Robert John	28106	,,	Wilder, Edward J. A.
28055	,,	Moore, William Hy.	28107	,,	Wilson, James S.
28056	,,	McCracken, William	28108	,,	Wilson, John
28058	,,	Macdonald, Peter	28109	,,	Wright, Ernest T.
28059	,,	McDonald, John			

Canadian Pacific—The Empire's Greatest Railway.

16th BATTALION, 3rd INFANTRY BRIGADE
(THE CANADIAN SCOTTISH).

Staff Officers.

Lieut.-Colonel	Leckie, Robt. Gilmour Edwards
Major	Leckie, John Edwards, D.S.O.
,,	Roberts, Henry Lucas
Adjutant	Major Godson-Godson, Gilbert
Assistant Adjutant	Captain Ross, Geo. Huntington
Signalling Officer	,, Markham, Ralph Farrar
Medical Officer	,, Gillies, B. W. D.
Chaplain	Hon. Captain Beattie, John Alex.
Transport Officer	Lieutenant Ward, E. M. Picton
Maxim Gun Officer	,, Tupper, Reg. Hibbert
Quartermaster	Hon. Captain Browne, Beverly W.
Paymaster	,, ,, McGregor, J. Herrick

Staff.

Regl. No.	Rank.	Name.	Regl. No.	Rank.	Name.
28501	Sgt.-Maj.	Nelson, D.	28551	Cpl. A.M.C.	Price, W. J.
28502	Q.M.Sgt.	Skinner, G.	28561	Cpl. Piper	Park, J.
28503	O.R. Sgt.	Masson, J. S.	28557	Pte. Piper	McGillivray, Alex.
28504	Drum Sgt.	Graham, J. H.	28560	,,	McKellar, Hugh
28550	Pay. Sgt.	Dey, C. E.	28559	,,	McDonald, Hugh
28505	Pion. Sgt.	McLennan, D. T.	28558	,,	McDonald, Ronald
28509	Shoe. Sgt.	Boyd, J. A.	28553	Pte. A.M.C.	Dunn, J.
29566	Tlr. Sgt.	Fitzgerald, W.	28552	,,	Findlay, Thos. W.
28556	Piper Sgt.	McLeod, D. L.	28554	,,	Wood, H.
29618	O.R. Sgt.	Steele, G. W.	28555	,,	Kilpatrick, S.
29529	O.R.Act.Sgt.	Heakes, S. R.	28884	Cook Sgt.	McMillan, J. C.
28518	Med. Sgt.	Robertson, R. T.			

Machine Gun Section.

28562	Sergt.	Bennett, V. E.	28765	Private	Moore, F. E.
28563	Corporal	Brooker, E. O.	28761	,,	Mansford, G.
28564	Private	Bevan, C.	28576	Driver	Walker, J.
28565	,,	Barlow, F.	28568	Private	Lockerby, J. D.
28566	,,	Ball, Frank F.	28567	,,	Langhorne, H. J.
28577	Batman	Clayton, F.	28570	,,	McIlwaine, J. B.
28520	Private	Donald, H.	28573	,,	O'Sullivan, Patrick
28569	,,	Ryder, J. H.	29607	,,	Tripp, Harold
28575	Driver	Fyson, E.	28730	,,	Fyffe-Johnson, A. J.
28796	Private	Sandy, W. E.	28747	,,	Hart, R. C.

Transport.

28507	Sergt.	McRae, G. A.	28524	Private	Kentley, W.
28521	Private	Herriott, A. M.	28526	,,	Edwards, A.
28522	,,	Crafer, W. G.	28527	,,	Thompson, T. S.

Canadian Pacific—The Empire's Greatest Railway.

16TH BATTALION, 3RD INFANTRY BRIGADE—cont.

Transport—cont.

Regl. No.	Rank.	Name.	Regl. No.	Rank.	Name.
28528	Private	Hunter, H. D.	28541	Servant	Williamson, Wm.
28529	,,	Newling, A.	28545	Private	Smith, W. Jas.
28530	,,	Robertson, W.	28542	,,	Goult, H. G.
28531	,,	Bain, J.	28538	,,	Byewell, C. N.
28532	,,	Ingram, W.	28540	,,	Martin, W.
28534	,,	Douglas, Frank	28544	,,	Mackie, Jno.
28535	,,	Ford, John	28543	,,	Hall, John
28537	,,	Mungo, Tom	28519	,,	Freeman, C. J. W.
28533	,,	Mennie, W.	28523	,,	Weatherstone,Cmbll.
28536	,,	Smith, D.	28539	,,	Brown, Wm.
28548	,,	McDonald, Neil	28547	,,	Rabjohn, G. S.
28546	,,	Mulvin, V. W.			

Signalling Section.

Regl. No.	Rank.	Name.	Regl. No.	Rank.	Name.
28508	Sergt.	Marshall, F.	28514	Private	McEwen, J.
28510	Private	Stewart, D.	28515	,,	Newton, J.
28511	,,	Taylor, L. H.	28516	,,	Bloomfield, G. C.
28512	,,	Fraser, J. C.	28517	,,	Smith, G.
28513	,,	Urie, G. V.			

"A" COMPANY.

Major ...	...	Ross, Lorne
Lieutenant ...	...	Ager, George S.
,, ...	...	McClure, James H. S.
,, ...	...	Rochfort, D'O. T.

Regl. No.	Rank.	Name.	Regl. No.	Rank.	Name.
28581	Col.-Sgt.	Sutton, A. C.	28597	Private	Busk, G. L.
28582	Sergt.	Mathisen, P.	28598	,,	Butler, H.
28583	,,	Dewar, J. A.	28599	,,	Cameron, K. McL.
28584	,,	Cooney, George A.	28600	,,	Campbell, C.
28585	,,	Tuck, E. S.	28601	,,	Campbell, R. H.
28587	Lce.-Sgt.	Hollett, F. L.	28602	,,	Charlton, H. A.
28588	Corpl.	Gamble, R. B.	28603	,,	Collinson, E. O.
28589	,,	Fyvie, D.	28605	,,	Coulson, T. A.
28590	,,	James, A.	28606	Lce.-Cpl.	Court, S. C.
28628	,,	Hall, C. J.	28604	Private	Ross, Corbit
28631	Arm. Cpl.	Hayhurst, D. J.	28607	Lce.-Cpl.	Cowen, J. C.
28655	Bugler	Marrs, G. L.	28608	Private	Crookston, A. S.
28658	Pioneer	Moffit, A. H.	28609	,,	Davey, A. F.
28710	Private	Aves, E. O.	28610	,,	Davies, J. T.
28592	,,	Baldwin, R. J.	28611	,,	Denny, H. A. M.
28593	,,	Barton, John	28612	,,	Denny, R. E.
28594	,,	Beams, W.	28613	,,	Dickson, George
29529	,,	Bell, Wallace	28614	,,	Evans, H. A.
28595	,,	Birnie, G. W.	28615	Signaller	Fahrni, W. W.
28596	,,	Brawn, H.	28616	Private	Fergusson, J. G.

Canadian Pacific—The Empire's Greatest Railway.

16TH BATTALION, 3RD INFANTRY BRIGADE—cont.

Regl. No.	Rank.	Name.	Regl. No.	Rank.	Name.
28617	Private	Fish, Walter	29579	Private	McLeod, W.
28618	,,	Fletcher, C.	28653	,,	McNicol, D.
28619	,,	Forster, J. G.	28654	,,	McPhee, J.
28620	,,	Forster, Robert	28695	,,	McPherson, D. M.
28621	,,	Fyvie, R.	28662	,,	Nixon, H.
28622	,,	Gallon, T. H.	28661	Signaller	Neilson, G.
28623	,,	Gardener, A. J.	28663	Private	Norton, R.
28624	,,	Gilbert, C. A.	28664	,,	Oliver, Philip
28625	,,	Glover, J.	28665	,,	Parry, E.
28626	,,	Griffiths, J. O.	28666	,,	Payze, A. R.
28627	,,	Guilbride, S. A.	28667	,,	Rees, L. A.
28629	,,	Hamilton, H. E.	28668	,,	Reid, A.
28630	,,	Harding, W. N.	28669	,,	Rideout, R.
28632	,,	Hayhurst, S. G.	28670	,,	Scott, J. C.
28633	,,	Hayward, H. B.	28671	,,	Shawyer, W.
28635	,,	Hick, T. J. W.	28672	,,	Shrewsbury, W. B.
28636	,,	Hill, Frank L.	28673	,,	Smith, W. H.
28637	,,	Horne, W. G. F.	28674	,,	Soden, J. B.
28638	,,	Howie, R. J.	28675	,,	Souper, N. B.
28639	,,	Jenkins, M. G.	28676	,,	Southern, H. E.
28640	,,	Jones, E. M. A.	28677	,,	Stein, A.
28642	,,	Kersey, A. H.	28678	Lce.-Cpl.	Stone, J. R.
28643	,,	Lloyd, S. V.	28679	Private	Straker, C. E.
28644	,,	Long, E. E.	28680	,,	Swannell, C. E.
28656	Lce.-Cpl.	Mitchell, James	29605	,,	Stewart, J. H. A.
28659	,,	Morley, H. A.	28682	,,	Tisseman, J. A. J.
28657	Private	Moffatt, W.	28681	Batman	Thomas, S. R.
28660	,,	Murphy, W. T.	28694	Private	Thomson, Jas.
28693	Str.-B'rer	McBryer, James	28683	,,	Truin, W. G.
28648	,,	McCarter, D.	28684	,,	Uden, A.
28649	Batman	McCue, W. D.	28685	Lce.-Cpl.	Walker, W. H.
28650	Private	McDonald, D.	28686	Private	Waters, D. J.
28651	,,	McEachern, J.	28688	Batman	Wilkinson, H.
28652	,,	McIlroy, S.	28687	Private	Williams, Thomas
28645	,,	McLeod, Alec	28690	,,	Wilson, J. B.
28646	,,	McLeod, Angus	28691	,,	Wood, A.
28647	,,	McLeod, H. J.	28692	,,	Young, T. J.

"B" COMPANY.

Captain	...	...	...	Villiers, P. F.
Lieutenant	...	...	...	Wallis, P. R. M.
,,	...	...	...	Gray, A. J.
,,	...	...	...	Gordon, M. L.

Regl. No.	Rank.	Name.	Regl. No.	Rank.	Name.
28698	Col.-Sgt.	Forbes, D. G. P.	28703	Lce-Sgt.	Wilkinson, E. A.
28699	Sergeant	Hardy, H.	28704	Corporal	McPherson, J. P.
28700	,,	MacDonald, G.	28705	,,	Lyons, A.
28701	,,	Crockett, C. J.	28706	,,	Herdman, T.
28702	,,	Clark, R. M.	28707	,,	Hawley, E. S.

Canadian Pacific—The Empire's Greatest Railway.

16TH BATTALION, 3RD INFANTRY BRIGADE—cont. 157

Regl. No.	Rank.	Name.
28708	Private	Anscomb, B.
28709	,,	Anderson, D. L.
28749	,,	Bedbrook, C. A.
28711	,,	Birns, C. G.
28712	,,	Brown, J. P.
28713	,,	Brown, P. W.
28714	,,	Bridges, W. H.
28715	,,	Bruce, J. C.
28716	Lce.-Cpl.	Cook, A.
28717	Private	Campbell, D. N.
28718	,,	Campbell, T. M.
28719	,,	Campbell, D.
28720	,,	Croxford, H. E.
28721	,,	Cameron, A.
28722	,,	Chester, R. M.
28723	,,	Dunlop, C. M.
28724	,,	Dix, B. F.
28725	,,	Davis, L. G.
28726	,,	Dunn, R.
28727	,,	Dicks, A.
28728	,,	Forsyth, J. M.
28729	,,	Frampton, B. E.
28731	,,	Gammon, K. W.
28732	,,	Gahan, A. C.
28733	,,	Gravlin, G. A.
28734	,,	Goodlet, R.
28735	,,	Guthrie, W.
28736	,,	Gardner, J. A.
28737	Lce.-Cpl.	Hill, P. J.
28738	,,	Hardman, G. W.
28739	,,	Hill, C. H.
28740	Private	Haines, A. L.
28741	,,	Hodder, E. W.
28742	,,	Heyland, D.
28743	,,	Hill, B. T.
28744	,,	Hill, L.
28745	,,	Holt, H.
28746	,,	Heal, F. G.
28747	,,	Hart, R. C.
28748	,,	Hincks, B.
28750	,,	Hudson, A. F.
28751	Signaller	Hardwick, E. F.
28752	Lce.-Cpl.	Julier, L.
28753	Private	Kennedy, N. A.
28754	,,	Kirk, J.
28917	Arm.Cpl.	Leighton, A.
28756	Private	Leigh, C. F.
28757	,,	Logan, D.
28758	,,	Law, J.
28759	,,	Mann, J. U.
28760	,,	Minnis, G.
28762	,,	Milloy, C. A.
28763	Private	Moysey, J. S.
28764	,,	Mathewson, C.
28765	,,	Moore, F. E.
28766	,,	Moore, R. J.
28767	,,	Mason, J. F.
28768	,,	McNeill, J.
28769	,,	McRae, D. C.
28770	,,	McKenzie, J. K.
28771	,,	McMillan, A.
28772	,,	Macmillan, Alex.
28773	,,	McPhee, D.
28774	,,	McPhail, M. C.
28775	,,	McHattie, A.
28776	Signaller	Macarthur, A.
28777	Bugler	McCreadie, A. R.
28778	Private	McGregor, D.
28779	Piper	McIvor, W.
28780	Private	Neill, C. E. S.
28781	,,	North, J.
28782	,,	Paul, A. S.
28783	,,	Punnett, S.
28784	,,	Pickard, R. P.
28785	,,	Rodolph, F.
28786	,,	Ricketts, S. L.
28787	,,	Ricketts, L. O.
28788	,,	Richardson, J. H.
28789	,,	Schloesur, A.
28790	,,	Sol, D.
28791	,,	Smith, A. M.
28792	,,	Stinson, R. G.
28793	,,	Sharrock, J. W.
28794	,,	Shaw, H. A.
28796	,,	Sandy, W. E.
28797	,,	Salt, T.
28798	,,	Storer, S. A.
28799	Lce.-Cpl.	Stonor, A. F.
28800	Private	Skae, M. A.
28801	,,	Tanner, R. A.
28802	,,	Turney, J. A.
28803	,,	Watt, A. A.
28804	,,	Wilkinson, T.
28805	,,	Warnock, J. B.
28806	,,	Wilson, J. L.
28807	,,	Weir, D. D.
28809	,,	Wrath, F. C.
28810	,,	Waage-Mott, R. W.
28811	,,	Welsh, W. J.
28812	Piper	Wilson, C. R.
28813	Private	Williams, F. J.
28689	,,	Willyams, H. V.
28814	,,	Yard, B. J.

Canadian Pacific—The Empire's Greatest Railway.

158 16TH BATTALION, 3RD INFANTRY BRIGADE—cont.

"C" COMPANY.

Captain	Rae, W
Lieutenant	Armour, S. D.
,, ...	Kenworthy, J. G.
,, ...	McLean, V. A.

Regl. No.	Rank.	Name.	Regl. No.	Rank.	Name.
28815	Col.-Sgt.	Robertson, R. W.	28881	Private	Grant, R. M.
28874	Sergeant	Dougall, J.	28859	,,	Grant, H.
28816	,,	Pawsey, A. J.	28860	,,	Gunning, J. S.
28902	,,	Sutherland, B.	28861	,,	Glegg, R. C. E.
28846	,,	Wrightson, C. B.	28910	,,	Hamilton, A. F.
28817	Lce.-Sgt.	Le Maistre, W.	28862	,,	Herald, R. E.
28847	Corpl.	Bressey, F. M.	28911	,,	Hermon, J. W.
28903	,,	Dougans, D. W. Y.	28912	,,	Holbrooke, G. H.
28845	,,	Fiddes, W. F.	28873	,,	Huggard, E.
28875	,,	Henry, E. H.	28899	,,	Hunt, R. F.
28818	,,	McLennan, W. N.	28914	,,	Harkness, H. T. B.
28849	Private	Adam, J. G.	28827	,,	Jenkins, F.
28820	,,	Allan, A. W.	28863	,,	Johnston, S. B.
28821	,,	Anderson, A.	28913	,,	Johnston, W. A.
28877	,,	Armstrong, S. M.	28929	,,	Johnstone, P.
28850	,,	Attrel, A.	28870	,,	Jones, C.
28851	,,	Blair, G.	28828	,,	Kirk, F.
28869	,,	Bancroft, K. G.	28829	,,	Landry, H. L.
28852	,,	Barton, W. B.	28915	,,	Leslie, C. H.
28905	,,	Beley, W.	28841	,,	Main, W. S.
28878	,,	Bing, W. C.	28842	,,	Mattix, D. J.
28879	,,	Buchan, G.	28916	,,	Maltby, T.
28844	,,	Burdette, E. E.	28882	,,	Middleton, A.
28898	,,	Calvert, H. W.	28919	,,	Mossman, J. N.
28822	,,	Chaffey, W. F.	28832	,,	Molliott, T. M.
28823	,,	Chandler, R.	28833	,,	Molliott, E. L.
28906	,,	Chapman, G.	28834	,,	McCurragh, W.
28853	,,	Chiverall, S. J.	28900	,,	McDonald, N.
28824	,,	Clarke, S. L.	28835	,,	McDougall, C. N.
28907	,,	Clucas, J. H.	28919	,,	McFarlane, W.
28854	,,	Conley, F.	28871	,,	McKinlay, J. G.
28925	,,	Cowley, J. P.	28525	,,	McKenna, J.
28880	,,	Craddock, E. W.	28872	,,	McLeod, G. A. N.
28855	,,	Cream, C. B. C.	28864	,,	McLennan, A.
28876	Lce.-Cpl.	Donaldson, A. C.	28883	,,	McLennan, H.
28928	Private	Dickson, A.	28920	,,	McPhee, J.
28825	,,	Dunlop, J.	28885	,,	McRoberts, N. de P.
28856	,,	Evans, J.	28831	,,	Mitchell, R.
28857	,,	Forrest, R.	28917	,,	Moore, S. V.
28826	,,	Forsyth, A. A.	28836	,,	Ogilvie, R. W.
28858	,,	Forward, C. B.	28886	,,	Owen, P. W.
28904	Lce.-Cpl.	Gray, G. K.	28865	,,	Orchard, F. T.
28908	Private	Games, W.	28848	Lce.-Cpl.	Peel, A. E.
28909	,,	Gardiner, F.	28887	Private	Prentice, A. H.
28927	,,	Grant, G. A.	28921	,,	Purdie, J.

Canadian Pacific—The Empire's Greatest Railway.

16TH BATTALION, 3RD INFANTRY BRIGADE—cont. 159

Regl. No.	Rank.	Name.	Regl. No.	Rank.	Name.
28930	Private	Richardson, J.	28867	Private	Speirs, L. M.
28866	,,	Ragborne, H. W.	28924	,,	Stephenson, J.
28931	,,	Robertson, S.	28891	,,	Stroyan, H. G.
28922	,,	Rodger, W. A.	28840	,,	Sutherland, F.
28923	,,	Rouse, A. E.	28892	,,	Swanston, C.
28819	Lce.-Cpl.	Stewart, P. D. F.	28890	,,	Stark, W. H.
28888	Private	Savage, C. F.	28893	,,	Tait, D. B.
28889	,,	Sanders, F.	28894	,,	Taylor, C.
28837	,,	Scott, R.	28868	,,	Todd, R.
28838	,,	Smith, D. P.	28895	,,	Turner, A. B.
28830	,,	Smith, J. H.	28869	,,	Walker, D. B.
28843	,,	Stacey, F. W.	28896	,,	Whittaker, R. D.
28901	,,	Stanford, P. N.	28925	,,	Young, J.
28839	,,	Sterling, G.	28897	,,	York, N. S.

"D" COMPANY.

Captain ... ... Fleming, H. M.
Lieutenant ... ... Davis, Gavin Hardwicke
,, ... Lindsay, A. L.
,, ... Reid, J. M.

Regl. No.	Rank.	Name.	Regl. No.	Rank.	Name.
29049	Col.-Sgt.	Johnstone, D. M.	29077	Private	Bellamy, Frank
29050	Sergt.	Digby, Albert Henry	29078	,,	Burke, Patrick T.
29051	,,	Biddlecombe, Geo. A.	29079	,,	Blott, Charles MacG.
29052	,,	Calderwood, A. T.	29080	,,	Burns, Robert
29053	,,	Barnard, Thomas W.	29081	,,	Craig, Robert
29054	Corpl.	Loughnan, David	29082	,,	Carley, John J.
29055	,,	Botham, Harry G.	29083	,,	Cucksey, Walter L.
29056	,,	Stewart, R. McLean	29084	,,	Cowdy, Donald B.
29057	,,	Buist, William D.	29085	,,	Campbell, Donald
29058	,,	James, Walter J.	29086	,,	Chamberlain, Jos. R.
29059	,,	Russell, Robert	29087	,,	Chaplain, L. F. C.
29060	,,	Rolston, Leonard	29202	,,	Creery, K. A.
29061	,,	Airy, James O.	29088	,,	Dunn, Eric J.
29062	Lce.-Cpl.	Edwards, Henry	29089	,,	Dunn, Douglas A. J.
29063	,,	Harris, Claude L.	29090	,,	Dunlop, Raymond
29064	,,	Gibbs, H. C. St. Clair	29091	,,	Digby, Fred. W.
29065	,,	Symes, Harry H.	29092	,,	Downs, Percy
29066	Private	Avery, John Henry	29093	,,	Day, Robert B.
29068	,,	Angus, John R.	29094	,,	Elliott, John
29069	,,	Asher, William M.	29095	,,	Ekman, Oscar
29070	,,	Breese, William L.	29096	,,	Freeman, Stephen J.
29071	,,	Barclay, Charles	29097	,,	Ferguson, Arthur J.
29072	,,	Bushnell, Lucius H.	29546	,,	Fyson, Oliver
29073	,,	Bigsby, J. Herbert	29127	,,	Frisby, Robt.
29074	,,	Bullock, Cecil H.	29098	,,	Green, Denmilne
29075	,,	Black, Ronald	29099	,,	Gillis, John R.
29076	,,	Beattie, John	29100	,,	Goodall, Gordon B.

Canadian Pacific—The Empire's Greatest Railway.

160 16TH BATTALION, 3RD INFANTRY BRIGADE—cont.

Regl. No.	Rank.	Name.	Regl. No.	Rank.	Name.
29101	Private	Harris, Henry J.	29135	Private	McDonnell, E. J. R.
29102	,,	Hunter, Alexander	29136	,,	Newson, Percy H.
29103	,,	Holder, James B.	29137	,,	Osborne, Henry
29104	,,	Holmes, Alfred E.	29138	,,	Olliver, Thomas H.
29105	,,	Hay, Andrew L.	29139	,,	Powell, Cyril
29106	,,	Hoggarth, Thos. E.	29140	,,	Philbin, John
29107	,,	Huggett, George E.	29141	,,	Park, Stewart G.
29108	,,	Innes, James	29142	,,	Parker, W. B. H.
29109	,,	Johnston, Chas. C.	29143	,,	Rae, Andrew S.
29110	,,	Kirkwood, Archie	29144	,,	Ryder, John
29111	,,	Lidiard, Fred. H.	29145	,,	Robertson, John
29113	,,	Long, Frank W.	29146	,,	Rayner, Charles
29112	Signaller	Long, Fred.	29147	,,	Redmond, Frederick
29114	Private	Lynch, Edward	29149	Piper	Ross, Gordon
29115	,,	Marshall, Thomas	29150	Private	Spencer, William
29116	,,	Morrison, David A.	29151	,,	Sinclair, Francis L.
29117	,,	May, P. B.	29152	,,	Stevenson, John
29119	,,	Mayes, Frank R.	29153	,,	Shearer, James
29120	,,	McNeill, Alex. G.	29154	,,	Sloan, Alexander W.
29121	,,	McNeil, William B.	29155	,,	Staniland, George
29122	,,	McDonald, Alec	29156	,,	Scott, Guy
29123	,,	Muir, Frank V.	29157	,,	Thomson, Ernest A.
29124	,,	Meadows, Ernest G.	29158	,,	Turnbull, David W.
29125	,,	McKenzie, Harry	29159	,,	Taylor, Eumund F.
29126	,,	McQuoid, Urell	29160	,,	Van der Stegen, T.
29128	,,	McDonell, Duncan J.	29161	,,	Watt, Maurice J.
29129	,,	McPherson, Ian	29162	,,	Welsh, Alexander W.
29130	,,	McLennan, Alex.	29163	,,	Watson, George A.
29131	,,	McLennan, Alex,	29164	,,	Wylie, James
29132	,,	McKeown, John	29067	,,	Westall, Denis
29133	,,	McIvor, James	29148	,,	Weeks, Ernest
29134	,,	McGregor, James C.			

"E" COMPANY.

Captain ... ... Merritt, C. M.
Lieutenant ... ... Marshall, C.
    ,, ... Cotton, R. P.
    ,, ... Gilliat, E. N. mc

Regl. No.	Rank.	Name.	Regl. No.	Rank.	Name.
28932	Col.-Sgt.	Ramsay, H. V.	28940	Corpl.	Thomson, Jno.
28933	Sergt.	Paton, Jno. R.	28941	,,	Downs, Jno. E.
28934	,,	Smith, J. H.	28942	Lce.-Cpl.	Dibbs, Wm. A.
28935	,,	Spear, W. E.	28943	,,	Allison, Walter
28936	,,	Malcolm, E. C.	28944	,,	Ross, Alex.
28937	Corpl.	Palmer, Geo. F.	28945	,,	Robinson, W. J.
28938	,,	Nicholson, N.	28946	,,	Cook, Thos. C.
28939	,,	Burney, Geo. W.	28947	,,	Bird, Henry I.

Canadian Pacific—The Empire's Greatest Railway.

16TH BATTALION, 3RD INFANTRY BRIGADE—cont.

Regl. No.	Rank.	Name.	Regl. No.	Rank.	Name.
28948	Lce.-Cpl.	Tupper, Victor G.	28992	Private	Lund, Oscar
28949	,,	Sawyer, W. P.	28993	,,	Laing, Andrew
28950	Private	Armour, Angus D.	28994	,,	Leese, A. R.
28951	,,	Amos, Charles B.	28995	,,	Le Mesurier, A. S.
28952	,,	Alsdorf, Wm.	28996	,,	McConnell, Wm. B.
28953	,,	Beatson, R. S. M.	28997	,,	McKenzie, Jas.
28954	,,	Beck, Marshall	28998	,,	McKenzie, Geo.
28955	,,	Bruce, Wm.	28999	Arm.Cpl.	McGregor, Donald G.
28956	,,	Berry, Robt. T.	29000	Private	McDonald, J. W.
28957	,,	Brock, Jno. R.	29001	,,	McDonald, W. J.
29037	,,	Black, Arthur A.	29002	,,	Mosse, Wm. S.
29046	,,	Bandy, Geo. B.	29003	,,	Myson, Frank
29044	,,	Barker, Leonard A.	29005	,,	Marsh, Eddie
29041	,,	Beaton, Jas.	29006	,,	Macdonald, A. G.
29185	,,	Bell-Irving, A. D.	29047	,,	Minchin, A. W.
29039	,,	Burmeister, C. M.	29048	,,	MacNab, Allan C.
28959	,,	Chilcott, Jno. W.	29007	,,	Neale, A. R.
28960	,,	Crofton, Thos. H.	29038	,,	Oughten, B. O.
28961	,,	Cox, Hiram B.	29008	,,	Peden, Hugh A.
28962	,,	Cummings, Jas.	29009	,,	Perry, Alex. S.
28963	,,	Campbell, Donald E.	29010	,,	Perkins, G. G.
28964	,,	Caie, Alex.	29011	,,	Puddy, Edward
28965	,,	Douglas, Hector	29012	,,	Pearson, Jas.
28966	,,	Duchesnay, Frank A.	29013	,,	Perks, Arthur W.
28967	,,	Dunsford, G. C.	29014	,,	Popham, Jno. C.
29036	,,	De Paivo, J. H.	29015	,,	Royston, R. C.
28969	,,	Edgar, Thos.	29016	,,	Redmond, C. D.
28970	,,	Fraser, Wilfrid D.	29004	,,	Raine, S. J.
28971	,,	Grim, W. A. E.	29017	,,	Rourke, M. W.
28972	,,	Green, Herbert B.	29018	,,	Sceales, J. A. C.
28973	,,	Gibson, Jno. P.	29019	,,	Sarel, C. W.
28974	,,	Gray, Jno. H.	29022	,,	Siddall, Geo.
28975	,,	Griffin, Stanley	29023	,,	Smith, H. D. A.
28976	,,	Grant, Peter M.	29024	,,	Southern, Robt.
28977	,,	Gibson, Percy B.	29025	,,	Smith, Wm. A.
28978	,,	Glencross, Fredk. A.	29020	,,	Strangeways, H.
28979	,,	Gillespie, Robt. M.	29045	,,	Sutton, Fred
28980	,,	Hunter, Wm. A.	29026	,,	Townsley, Bryan H.
28981	,,	Harrold, Francis W.	29027	,,	Taylor, Robt.
28982	,,	Herrmann, Frank A.	29028	,,	Taylor, A. R.
29558	,,	Herne, A. D. C.	29029	,,	Turner, G. J.
28983	,,	Inglis, Wm. L.	29035	,,	Urquhart, Jas.
28984	,,	Jorgenson, Peter O.	29030	,,	Wright, Uriah
29040	,,	Johnson, S. N.	29031	,,	Walker, G. W.
28985	,,	Kinnear, Jno.	29032	,,	Williams, E. J.
28986	,,	Kinred, S. W.	29033	,,	Wood, Alan K.
28987	,,	Kent, Herbert S.	29034	,,	Withers, Alex. K.
28988	,,	Kent, Jno. S.	29042	,,	Wilson, N. G.
28989	,,	Kirby, Wm. H.	29043	,,	Wolff, Mark A.

Canadian Pacific—The Empire's Greatest Railway.

16TH BATTALION, 3RD INFANTRY BRIGADE—cont.

"F" COMPANY.

Captain	Morison, Frank
Lieutenant	Kemp, W. F.
,, ...	Duncan, H. A.
,, ...	Colquhoun, H. A.

Regl. No.	Rank.	Name.	Regl. No.	Rank.	Name.
29400	Col.-Sgt.	Mitchell, Geo.	29447	Private	Goffin, F.
29401	Sergt.	Stewart, Jno.	29448	,,	Hamilton, A.
29402	,,	Slessor, Geo. H.	29449	,,	Hamilton, J. E.
29403	,,	Cochrane, J.	29450	,,	Heath, C.
29404	,,	Steel, Jno. T.	29451	Lce.-Cpl.	Hickmott, T.
29405	Corpl.	Almond, E. A.	29452	Private	Howard, J.
29406	,,	Jackson, W. H.	29453	,,	Howie, G. F. P.
29407	,,	Haynes, J.	29454	,,	Henderson, W. J.
29408	,,	Ryder, A. E.	29455	,,	Ireland, J.
29409	,,	Bryant, F.	29456	,,	Irvine, G. C.
29410	Private	Appleton, E.	29457	,,	Jackson, A. C.
29411	,,	Adamson, J. S.	29458	,,	Johnstone, A.
29412	,,	Aitken, H.	29459	,,	Kean, W.
29413	,,	Barr, A.	29460	,,	Keeton, S.
29414	,,	Binkley, R.	29461	,,	Keeton, R.
29416	,,	Black, H.	29619	,,	Keeton, H.
29417	Lce.-Cpl.	Bleakley F. C.	29462	,,	Kelley, J.
29418	Private	Bizley, J. W.	29463	,,	Lake, W.
29419	,,	Booker, J.	29464	,,	Lambe, J. W.
29420	,,	Boyes, J. G.	29465	,,	Law, J.
29421	,,	Brown, E. E.	29466	,,	Lytle, S.
29422	,,	Brighton, T. C.	29467	,,	Matthews, A.
29423	,,	Buckley, E.	29468	Piper	Morrison, A.
29424	,,	Burrell, P. A.	29469	Private	McClenaghan, J.
29426	,,	Campbell, A.	29470	,,	McIntosh, W.
29427	,,	Campbell, J. C.	29471	,,	McFarlane, A.
29428	,,	Campbell, J. S.	29472	,,	McFarlane, R.
29429	Lce.-Cpl.	Campbell, D.	29473	,,	McIntyre, A.
29430	Private	Carroll, P. J.	29474	,,	McKay, M.
29431	,,	Carroll, J.	29475	Lce.-Cpl.	McLay, J.
29432	,,	Crewe, T.	29476	Private	McMillan, A.
29433	,,	Cutler, H. G.	29477	,,	McMillan, J.
29434	,,	Davidson, A.	29478	Lce.-Cpl.	McRitchie, G.
29435	,,	Dean, R.	29479	Private	Nivin, J.
29436	,,	Decker, J. J.	29480	,,	Parsons, A. E.
29437	,,	Duffy, J.	29481	,,	Payne, C.
29438	,,	Dunbar, H. M.	29482	,,	Picton, E. J.
29439	,,	Dunbar, R. C.	29483	,,	Porter, O.
29440	,,	Findlater, N.	29484	,,	Purcha, B. J.
29441	,,	Flook, F. G.	29485	,,	Read, S. H.
29442	,,	Foord, A.	29486	,,	Rees, W.
29443	,,	Gallagher, E. J.	29487	,,	Ritchie, S.
29444	Lce.-Cpl.	Gemmell, J.	29488	,,	Ritchie, A.
29445	Private	Galloway, R. W.	29489	,,	Roberts, Dudley T.
29446	,,	Giles, Frederic	29490	,,	Rowland, S. S.

Canadian Pacific—The Empire's Greatest Railway.

16TH BATTALION, 3RD INFANTRY BRIGADE—cont.

Regl. No.	Rank.	Name.	Regl. No.	Rank.	Name.
29491	Private	Ridley, A.	29504	Private	Tourtel, W.
29492	,,	Russell, J.	29505	,,	Tribeck, W. G.
29493	,,	Ryder, W. G.	29506	,,	Trezise, Wm.
29494	,,	Stamford, A. R.	29507	,,	Tugnett, F. R.
29495	,,	Shaw, A. McK.	29508	,,	Turnbull, J.
29496	,,	Sherwood, J.	29509	,,	Valentine, T.
29497	,,	Shutt, Arthur	29510	,,	Vyse, W.
29498	,,	Smart, Jas. A.	29511	,,	Watson, W. L.
29499	,,	Smith, Wm.	29512	,,	White, W.
29500	,,	Stokes, W.	29513	,,	Wilson, R. B.
29501	,,	Sugden, H.	29514	,,	Wyatt, A.
29502	,,	Taylor, R. S.	29515	,,	Warrick, E.
29503	,,	Taylor, F. W.	29516	,,	Whiskin, J. A.

"G" COMPANY.

Captain	... ...	Jameson, G. W.
Lieutenant	... ...	Hastings, V. J.
,,	... ...	Ainslie, G. M.
,,	... ...	Williams, E. M. W.

Regl. No.	Rank.	Name.	Regl. No.	Rank.	Name.
29166	Col.-Sgt.	Kay, J.	29196	Private	Clementson, J. F.
29167	Sergt.	Denholm, A.	29197	,,	Cormack, J. S.
29168	,,	Dowsett, E. C.	29198	,,	Collie, J. S.
29169	,,	McPherson, R. A.	29199	,,	Cameron, D.
29170	,,	Craig, J. G.	29200	,,	Carter, S.
29171	Corpl.	Grant, I.	29201	,,	Cooter, J.
29172	,,	Wanbon, Jas.	29242	,,	de Montmorency, H. B.
29173	,,	Henderson, D.			
29174	,,	Duff, W. D.	29203	,,	Dickie, J. S.
29175	,,	Gall, E.	29204	,,	Donald, J.
29176	,,	Annand, A.	29205	,,	Douglas, G.
29177	Private	Allison, S.	29206	,,	Dean, C. A. W.
29178	,,	Adams, C. J.	29207	,,	Duthoit, A. G.
29179	,,	Brown, G. R.	29208	,,	Didsbury, W. H.
29180	,,	Brown, W. J.	29209	,,	Edwards, H. J.
29181	,,	Bennett, A. V.	29210	,,	Esplin, S.
29182	,,	Barron, W.	29211	,,	Edwards, W.
29183	,,	Barry, J.	29212	,,	Evans, R. E.
29184	,,	Black, A.	29213	,,	Fraser, W. B. J.
29186	,,	Binnie, A.	29214	,,	Fraser, G. W.
29187	,,	Boyd, R.	29215	,,	Fulton, W. R.
29188	,,	Burrell, F. H.	29216	,,	Gillespie, D.
29189	,,	Chappell, E.	29217	,,	Gulliford, H.
29190	,,	Cousins, W. H.	29218	,,	Gray, R. B.
29191	,,	Collins, H. P.	29219	,,	Greig, H. G.
29192	,,	Caton, D. T.	29220	,,	Hull, W.
29193	,,	Cruickshank, J. D.	29221	,,	Huston, O. A.
29194	,,	Carswell, R.	29222	,,	Hain, D.
29195	,,	Cornes, W.	29223	,,	Haines, Ernest E.

Canadian Pacific—The Empire's Greatest Railway.

16TH BATTALION, 3RD INFANTRY BRIGADE—cont.

Regl. No.	Rank.	Name.	Regl. No.	Rank.	Name.
29224	Private	Hislop, W. R.	29253	Private	McIntyre, J.
29225	,,	Hay, James	29254	,,	McKeand, S. B.
29226	,,	Hamilton, J.	29255	,,	McDermott, C. G.
28506	,,	Howard, R. C.	29256	,,	McDermid, A.
29227	,,	Hudson, W. P. N.	29257	,,	Middlemass, T.
29228	,,	Ingraham, W. St. C.	29258	,,	McAulay, F. G.
29229	,,	Johnston, J. M.	29259	,,	MacKay, J. Q.
29230	,,	Johnston, J. H.	29260	,,	McManus, P. A.
29231	,,	Kerr-Wilson, R. H.	29261	,,	Parker, F. W.
29232	,,	Lawrie, H.	29262	,,	Ross, D. Stewart
29233	,,	Low, John	29263	,,	Stafford, John
29234	,,	Lovett, J. H.	29264	,,	Steele, Herbert H.
29235	,,	Little, R.	29265	,,	Smith, H. Thomas
29236	,,	Lowe, James M.	29266	,,	Smith, A. Tristam
29237	,,	Lewis, C.	29267	,,	Sneath, W. Henry
29238	,,	Lloyd, S. J. T.	29268	,,	Siberry, Richard
29239	,,	Leitch, S. L.	29269	,,	Sutton, Benjamin
29240	,,	Lisney, E.	29270	,,	Smith, G. White
29241	,,	Leitch, L.	29271	,,	Stocks, Geo.
29243	,,	Mowatt, A. B.	29272	Corpl.	Smith, Richard
29244	,,	Mowatt, W.	29273	Private	Scott, D. J.
29245	,,	McDonald, D.	29274	,,	Thorburn, Jno.
29246	,,	McNeill, J. C.	29275	,,	Wallis, J. Harold
29247	,,	McKenzie, A.	29276	,,	Walton, Herbert
29248	,,	Morris, F. W.	29277	,,	Wallis, H. McD.
29249	Arm.Cpl.	Menzies, J.	29278	,,	Woollat, Philip
29250	Private	McLain, C. F.	29279	,,	Walker, W. Morris
29251	,,	Martin, A. D.	29280	,,	Warwick, George
29252	,,	McKean, H. A.	29281	,,	Wattie, Jas.

"H" COMPANY.

Captain	... ...	Geddes, J.
Lieutenant	... ...	Urquhart, H. M.
,,	... ...	McKerrell, R. J. M.
,,	... ...	Chambers, S. W. G.

Regl. No.	Rank.	Name.	Regl. No.	Rank.	Name.
29283	Col.-Sgt.	Burns, G.	29298	Private	Aitken, H.
29284	Sergt.	White, A.	29299	,,	Aitkens, G.
29285	,,	Ridge, M.	29300	,,	Aitkens, J.
29286	,,	McKane, A.	29301	,,	Ahier, W.
29287	,,	Mackenzie, N. J.	29302	,,	Aird, J.
29288	Lce.-Sgt.	Steele, W. J.	29303	,,	Allan, R. M.
29289	Corpl.	Mackie, W. D.	29304	,,	Baker, A.
29290	,,	Cameron, A.	29305	,,	Bean, L. M.
29291	,,	Stewart, R.	29306	,,	Begg, A.
29292	,,	McVicar, D.	29307	,,	Bethune, H. E.
29118	Arm.-Cpl.	Mattatal, —	29294	Lce.-Cpl.	Bryce, P.

Canadian Pacific—The Empire's Greatest Railway.

16TH BATTALION, 3RD INFANTRY BRIGADE—cont.

Regl. No.	Rank.	Name.	Regl. No.	Rank.	Name.
308	Private	Cameron, N.	29356	Private	McPhail, E.
309	,,	Cameron, R.	29357	,,	McSloy, W.
310	,,	Caine, J. G.	29358	,,	Manson, G. C.
311	,,	Charlton, C. O.	29359	,,	Mathieson, C. S.
312	,,	Chisholm, F. T.	29361	,,	Medcalfe, J. H.
313	,,	Cleary, E.	29362	,,	Meikle, I.
314	,,	Donald, W.	29360	,,	Mathieson, E. H.
315	,,	Donald, W. M.	29363	,,	Miller, R. M.
316	,,	Denholm, J.	29364	,,	Millar, A.
317	,,	Don, R.	29365	,,	Michie, A.
318	,,	Elliott, S.	29366	,,	Munro, D.
319	,,	Dustan, G.	29367	,,	Moffat, R.
320	,,	Ferrier, J.	29368	,,	Moir, R.
321	,,	Field, J. W.	29369	,,	Mowatt, A.
322	,,	Fraser, J.	29370	,,	Murray, J.
323	,,	Greaves, B. W.	29371	,,	Neal, J. I.
324	,,	Greene, A.	29372	,,	Nicolle, R. J.
325	,,	Grierson, J.	29293	Lce.-Cpl.	Paterson, D.
326	,,	Gillespie, J.	29373	Private	Patterson, F. D.
327	,,	Groat, J.	29374	,,	Paterson, N. W.
328	,,	Harrold, D.	29375	,,	Pollock, G.
330	,,	Hobbs, S.	29376	,,	Purvis, W.
331	,,	Holmes, A.	29377	,,	Richardson, T.
332	,,	Houston, R.	29378	,,	Rodgers, Jas.
333	,,	Houston, W. B.	29379	,,	Rymall, A.
334	,,	Hunter, A. J.	29380	,,	Ross, A.
335	,,	Hunter, G.	29381	,,	Ross, G. O.
336	,,	Inglis, G.	29382	,,	Ross, J.
337	,,	Irvine, W.	29383	,,	Ross, J. N.
338	,,	Jones, H.	29384	,,	Robb, H. F.
339	,,	Kelly, D.	29385	,,	Scott, J. P.
340	,,	Lamb, T. J.	29386	,,	Simpson, C.
297	Lce.-Cpl.	Laidlaw, W. J.	29387	,,	Scougall, W. J.
341	Private	Lewis, P. E.	29388	,,	Smith, F.
342	,,	Liddle, C. D.	29389	,,	Steele, R.
343	,,	Lindsay, D.	29390	,,	Stewart, G.
344	,,	Lindsay, T.	29391	,,	Sutherland, J.
345	,,	Love, J.	29392	,,	Taylor, T. C.
346	,,	McDonald, A.	29393	,,	Thomas, H.
347	,,	MacDonald, D.	29394	,,	Thom, J.
348	,,	MacDonald, F.	29295	Lce.-Cpl.	Thompson, J. G.
349	,,	MacDonald, J. A.	29395	Private	Torrance, J.
350	,,	MacKenzie, D.	29296	Lce.-Cpl.	Torrance, W.
351	,,	MacLennan, A. M.	29396	Private	Waugh, T.
352	,,	MacLean, D.	29397	,,	Watson, J. C.
353	,,	McLauchlan, J.	29398	,,	Waller, J.
354	,,	McMurdy, A.	29399	,,	White, Andrew
355	,,	McOnie, R. J.			

Canadian Pacific—The Empire's Greatest Railway.

16TH BATTALION, 3RD INFANTRY BRIGADE—cont.

BASE COMPANY.

Captain ... ... Goodall Sydney, H.
Lieutenant ... ... Bell-Irving, R. O.
„ ... ... Powis, Paul P.

Regl. No.	Rank.	Name.	Regl. No.	Rank.	Name.
29517	Col.-Sgt.	Southey, W. H.	29556	Private	Hanscombe, E. W. C.
29518	Sergt.	Forbes, H. W.	29557	„	Henderson, G. D.
29519	„	Lunn, B. C.	29560	„	Hyatt, P.
29520	„	Bailey, A. J.	29561	„	Innes, W. J.
29521	„	Hubbard, T. S.	29562	„	Jollie, R. O.
29618	O.R.S.	Steele, G. W.	29563	„	Jones, A.
29566	Sgt. Tlr.	Fitzgerald, W.	29564	„	Knight, A.
29522	Corpl.	Ruttle, R.	29565	„	Kiloh, J.
29523	„	Bernard, A.	29567	„	Lambert, O. F.
29524	„	Heath, G. C.	28755	„	Linge, W. G.
29615	„	Camm, J. H.	29568	„	Lloyd, J. E.
29525	Private	Aitken, J.	29569	„	Lipsham, C. W.
29617	„	Bate, S. C.	29570	„	Legate, H.
29526	„	Baker, A. P.	29571	„	Menzies, W.
29625	„	Baker, Julius	29572	„	McAdam, J.
29527	„	Baker, W. B.	29573	„	McKay, J.
29528	„	Bell, D. H.	29574	„	McGaan, J.
29530	„	Baston, J. P.	28570	„	McIlwaine, J. B.
29531	„	Bean, C. A. S.	29575	„	McSweyn, D. G.
29532	„	Bailey, C. E.	29576	„	McGugan, D.
29534	„	Bullman, L.	29577	„	McNair, J.
29535	„	Bowstead, T.	29578	„	McTavish, I. F.
29536	„	Casella, C.	29580	„	McFitridge, J.
29537	„	Campbell, A. W.	29581	„	McNutt, C.
29538	„	Campbell, L. H.	29582	„	McLennan, K. B.
29539	„	Campbell, H.	28574	„	McLeod, G.
29540	„	Clarkson, C. E.	29583	„	Mahon, T. C. G.
29541	„	Cadenhead, J. F.	29584	„	Mowatt, J.
29626	„	Crawford, R. M.	29585	„	Murray, J.
29542	„	Dixon, A. T.	29586	„	Oakley, F. E.
29543	„	Douglas, W.	28571	„	Oldaker, H. H.
29544	„	Devlin, J.	29587	„	Palmer, F. E.
28968	„	Duncan, J.	29588	„	Pettit, J. W.
29545	„	Ellis, J. R.	29589	„	Penberthy, F.
29547	„	Findley, H.	29590	„	Phillip, S. J.
29548	„	Fail, W.	29591	„	Rigg, B. H.
29549	„	Ferry, E. M.	29620	„	Ritchie, J.
29550	„	Gibb, J. B.	29618	„	Robb, A. C.
29559	„	Glendinning, W.	29592	„	Robb, J.
29551	„	Goodser, T.	29593	„	Rourke, W. M.
29533	„	Gower, M. F.	29594	„	Robertson, W.
29614	„	Graves, L.	29595	„	Russell, J.
29616	„	Grant, A.	29596	„	Rutherford, M.
29552	„	Homan, J. S.	29624	„	Snider, R. M.
29553	„	Harris, A. D.	29598	„	Spears, J.
29555	„	Hamilton, R. P.	29599	„	Swanston, J. B.

Canadian Pacific—The Empire's Greatest Railway.

16TH BATTALION, 3RD INFANTRY BRIGADE—cont. 167

Regl. No.	Rank.	Name.	Regl. No.	Rank.	Name.
29613	Private	Smith, J. Y.	29607	Private	Tripp, H.
29600	,,	Smith, W. McB.	29608	,,	Taylor, R. D.
29601	,,	Sachs, R. L. S.	29609	,,	Thomas, A.
29602	,,	Stevens, F. S.	29610	,,	Watson, C. R.
29603	,,	Stirling, J. H.	29611	,,	Waugh, A.
29604	,,	Smith, H. W.	29612	,,	Yardley, F. G.
29606	,,	Soule, W. M.			

4th INFANTRY BRIGADE.

Staff Officers.

Brigadier... ... ... Lieut.-Colonel John Edward Cohoe
Brigade Major ... ... Major Chalmers Jack Mersereau
Staff Captain ... ... Captain Chas. Herman Vandersluys
Intelligence Officer ... ... Major Arthur Baring Snow
Orderly Officer ... ... Captain Joseph Chaballe
Veterinary Officer ... ... ,, Harry Elliott
Chaplain (Rev. Father) ... ... ,, Edward Gordon Doe (attached)

Subordinate Staff.

Regl. No.	Rank.	Name.	Regl. No.	Rank.	Name.
19476	Q.M.Sgt.	Barbour-Mercer, Wm.	19492	P'lice Sgt.	Paxton, Walter
19477	O.R.Sgt.	Raymond, Charles Alfred Harold	23466	Police	Hunter, James D.
			19486	Batman	Lamothe, Oscar
19478	,,	Proctor, Bascom Palmer	19491	,,	Bloxham, Charles
			19483	,,	Grubb, Walter
19481	Batman	McDonald, Henry	19480	,,	Winters, Joseph
19482	,,	Weston, Samuel	19489	,,	Binns, John
19485	Driver	Renison, Geo. Wm.	19484	,,	Hembroff, Thos. M.
19488	Batman	Morrison, Moses	19500	Driver	Hill, Thomas Hooten
19490	,,	Davies, John	23644	Batman	Dugre, Joseph A.
19493	Police	Blackwell, William	19497	,,	Townend, George
19494	,,	Brooks, Wm. Herbert	20151	Cook	Short, Henry
19495	,,	Hiscott, Clement	22166	Driver	Booth, Samuel
19496	Corpl.	Witham, Wm. James	22158	,,	Pearce, Wm. A. V.
19479	Far. Sgt.	Varley, Thos.	21190	,,	Cullis, John

P.O. Attached.

21366	Corpl.	Gorman, Geo. Wm.	18941	Private	England, Henry E.
		21160 Private Heys, Walter			

Canadian Pacific—The Empire's Greatest Railway.

9th BATTALION, 4th INFANTRY BRIGADE.

Headquarters.

Lieutenant-Colonel	Rogers, S. Maynard
,, ,,	Osborne, Frank A.
Major	Anderson, Peter
Adjutant	Captain Allister C. Gillespie
Assistant Adjutant	Lieut. James A. Turner
Signalling Officer	,, Henry C. L. Gillman
Machine Gun Section	,, N. Arthur Sparks
Transport	Hon. Major William H. Watts
Quartermaster	Hon. Captain Frederic W. Utton
Paymaster	Hon. Major Bryce J. Saunders
Medical Officer	Captain Earl A. Neff
Chaplain	Hon. Captain Thomas L. Bruce

Regl. No.	Rank.	Name.	Regl. No.	Rank.	Name.
19249	Sgt.-Major	Carpenter, Fredk. N.	19208	Signalling Sgt.	Mattingly, Alfred G.
19201	Q.M.Sgt.	Clarke, Rbt. D.	19246	Arm. Sgt.	McInnes, Dougald
19202	Sergt.	Adamson, Wm.			
19203	O.R.Sgt.	Parker, Ernest	18907	Provost Sgt.	Gale, Charles G. W.
19245	P.M.Sgt.	Farrell, Eustace L.	18906	Str.-Br. Ac. Sgt.	Bradford, Wm.
19204	Sgt. Drummer	Creighton, Geo.	19239	Acting Sgt.	Kyle, Fredk. J.
19205	Pioneer Sgt.	McLean, John	19236	Private	Cairns, Joseph
19207	Transport Sgt.	Schell, Joseph (Transport)	19235	,,	Hornby, Ernest
			19234	,,	Webster, Chas.
19206	Sgt. Cook	Chiverton, Fredk.			

Signallers.

19210	Private	Haddow, William	19215	Private	Penn, William C.
19211	,,	Jones, John H. R.	19209	,,	Dungate, Arthur E.
19212	,,	Miller, Alexander	19216	,,	Roberts, William H.
19213	,,	North, George H.	19265	,,	Brown, George C.
19214	,,	Parsons, Arthur F. C.	19247	,,	Allbright, Ernest R.

Machine Gun Section.

19250	Corpl.	Cherry, Philip A. B.	19260	Private	Meikle, James C.
19251	Private	Ogilvie, Henry	19257	,,	Mayne, Leonard E.
19253	,,	Winser, Arthur C.	19256	,,	Slade, William
19258	,,	Adams, Harry	19254	,,	Schmidt, James
19252	,,	Duncan, Thomas	19264	,,	Scott, Reginald A.
19261	,,	Hogg, Thomas	19255	,,	Stephen, John A.
19262	,,	Irvine, John C.	18470	,,	Bragg, Edward C. F.
18348	,,	Gowan, Anthony	18007	,,	Jacques, Henry B.

Canadian Pacific—The Empire's Greatest Railway.

9TH BATTALION, 4TH INFANTRY BRIGADE—cont. 169

Transport.

Regl. No.	Rank.	Name.	Regl. No.	Rank.	Name.
19225	Private	Blondheim, Frncs. H.	19268	Private	Dolhenty, Frank
19226	,,	Blower, Herbert	19269	,,	Martin, Thomas
19219	,,	Dimoline, Stanley	19273	,,	Christensen, George
19228	,,	Freeman, William	19274	,,	Crouse, Joseph
19218	Corpl.	Graham, Gordon	19275	Groom	Murphy, Thomas
19224	Private	Hughes, Frank	19276	,,	Green, James E.
19220	Corpl.	Hughes, William	19277	,,	Ison, John E.
19233	Private	LeCleche, John	19237	,,	Black, John
19223	,,	Lyon, James	19272	Private	Navestad, Thomas
19227	,,	Smith, John	18786	,,	Clark, John D.
19229	,,	Wilson, Herbert	18185	,,	De Paiva, Rawdon
19230	,,	Zall, Peter	19003	,,	Soular, Albert
19221	,,	Radford, Thomas	18943	,,	Foster, Edward
19266	,,	Doheney, James	19143	,,	Riddell, William
19267	,,	Miller, Michael			

C. A. M. C.

19217	Lce.-Cpl.	Whipple, Arthur V.	33644	Private	Bastow, William A.
33641	Private	Reynolds, Rufus	33645	,,	Shannon, James G.
33643	,,	Meaby, Arthur H.	33642	,,	Else, William G.

"A" COMPANY.

Captain ... ... Mulvey, Victor C.
Lieutenant ... ... Relph, H. Spencer
,, ... Leonard, Dennis J.
,, ... Simpson, Robert

Regl. No.	Rank.	Name.	Regl. No.	Rank.	Name.
18001	Col.-Sgt.	Bell, Benjamin T.	18023	Private	Blaine, William W.
18005	Sergt.	Stewart, William	18024	,,	Browne, Joseph E.
18002	,,	Maclean, Alex.	18025	,,	Bailey, William J.
18003	,,	Fraser, Thomas, A.	18113	,,	Bishop, Richard
18004	,,	Key, Mark	18026	,,	Curtis, Daniel
18006	Corpl.	Thomasson, Edwin W.	18027	,,	Coker, John S.
18009	,,	Jex, William	18028	,,	Comrie, John
18085	,,	Sheeran, Edward	18029	,,	Crerar, John C.
18110	,,	Clarke, George	18030	,,	Candy, Leonard C.
18010	Private	Aspinwall, Alfred W.	18031	,,	Curry, Alfred H.
18109	Lce.-Cpl.	Lees, Edward	18032	,,	Daley, James
18111	,,	Griffin, Baldwin, W.	18033	,,	Donovan, Frank
18012	Bugler	Nelson, Horace A.	18034	,,	Drolet, Roy
18013	,,	Worsley, Eric	18035	,,	Dales, Noel
18016	Private	Baraneck, Joe	18036	,,	Davis, John
18017	,,	Bennett, Joseph	18037	,,	Densmore, Albert
18018	,,	Burns, Thomas	18116	,,	Fergusson, Llewellyn
18019	,,	Bonnell, Henry A.	18117	,,	Fyfe, Harold
18020	,,	Badcock, Alfred S.	18038	,,	Fletcher, Harry F.
18021	,,	Belley, Patrick	18039	,,	Frame, James
18022	,,	Black, Robert	18040	,,	France, Charles H.

Canadian Pacific—The Empire's Greatest Railway.

9TH BATTALION, 4TH INFANTRY BRIGADE—cont.

Regl. No.	Rank.	Name.	Regl. No.	Rank.	Name.
18041	Private	Fitzgerald, Gerald	18074	Private	Person, Edward
18042	,,	Fairbairn, James	18075	,,	Pinkerton, Edward
18043	,,	Fraser, Peter	18076	,,	Paton, John
18120	,,	Fry, Arthur G.	18077	,,	Peltier, Peter
18044	,,	Grey, Robert	18078	,,	Pyne, Edward
18111	,,	Gould, Alfred	18079	,,	Powers, John J.
18045	Corpl.	Graham, George	18080	,,	Rutherford, Alex. S.
18046	Private	Hall, Evan	18081	,,	Ruffles, Sidney
18114	,,	Hopkins, Richard	18082	,,	Rigby, Frederick J.
18047	,,	Ingold, Adolph	18083	,,	Salisbury, Ernest
18049	,,	Jones, William	18084	,,	Semko, Tares
18050	,,	Jones, Edward	18086	,,	Stapleton, Benj. A.
18051	,,	Jessen, Martin S.	18087	,,	Scott, Henry
18052	,,	Jamieson, Harry B.	18088	,,	Smith, Robert
18118	,,	Johnstone, William H. T.	18089	,,	Smith, Leonard
			18090	,,	Smith, Alexander
18053	,,	Kingston, William J.	18091	,,	Smith, Charles F.
18054	,,	Lind, Charles	18092	,,	Stewart, John
18055	,,	Lord, Henry S.	18093	,,	Sorenson, Harold
18056	,,	Lescamure, Andrew	18094	,,	Stephen, Alexander
18057	,,	Leat, William J.	18095	,,	Stoddart, Alexander
18058	,,	Littrell, Louis	18115	,,	Swainson, John
18059	,,	Le Brocq, Philip	18096	,,	Theobald, Ernest
18060	,,	Lodge, Edward	18097	,,	Thomson, Rupert A.
18061	,,	Lyons, Archibald	18098	,,	Thomas, David G.
18062	,,	Moen, Martin	18099	,,	Vance, John
18063	,,	Milne, James K.	18100	,,	Vaisey, Guy
18064	,,	Miller, Fred	18101	,,	Wilson, Thomas
18065	,,	Miles, Albert W.	18102	,,	Wilson, William H.
18066	,,	McNish, Harris H.	18112	,,	Wilson, Charles
18067	,,	McAllister, Marshall	18103	,,	Welch, Charles
18068	,,	McNeil, Daniel	18104	Lce.-Cpl.	Woodward, Fred. W.
18069	,,	McAskill, Alexander	18105	Private	Wrenn, Frank F.
18070	,,	Newell, Stewart	18106	,,	Wrenn, Reginald
18071	,,	Oliver, Harry D.	18107	,,	Winser, William S.
18072	,,	Orischenko Ajanaza	18108	,,	Woodley, William E.
18073	,,	Perkins, Frederick P.	19263	,,	Wilkins, William G.

"B" COMPANY.

Major	...	...	...	...	Marriott, Guy W.
Lieutenant	...	...	...	...	de Balinhard, John
,,	...	...	...	...	Briscoe, Ross, D.
,,	...	...	...	...	Howe, Gordon G.

Regl. No.	Rank.	Name.	Regl. No.	Rank.	Name.
18151	Col.-Sgt.	Gibbins, Frederick	18155	Corpl.	Blanchard, George B.
18152	Sergt.	David, C. Robertson	18156	,,	Swedinbank, John E.
18153	,,	Ashworth, Archibald W. R.	18158	,,	Inglis, Louis A. B.
			18160	,,	Robitaille, Joseph
18154	,,	Griesbach, Henry H.	18157	Private	Potter, George H.
18159	,,	Blanchett, Chrstphr.	18161	Corpl.	Agar, Archie A.

Canadian Pacific—The Empire's Greatest Railway.

9TH BATTALION, 4TH INFANTRY BRIGADE—cont.

Regl. No.	Rank.	Name.
18163	Lce.-Cpl.	Cheale, Walter
18162	,,	Thomas, William A.
18164	Private	Andrews, Alexander
18166	,,	Archer, Ernest
18167	,,	Arnull, C. Thomas
18168	,,	Anderson, John D.
18169	,,	Brady, Patrick
18170	,,	Bertrand, Ray
18171	,,	Bodell, John
18172	,,	Brown, Austin L.
18173	,,	Barker, George
18174	,,	Baynham, Maxwell
18266	,,	Bell, Peter D.
18175	,,	Burger, Elisha T.
18176	,,	Clayton, Joseph
18177	,,	Collinge, Robert
18178	,,	Cheney, George
18179	Lce.-Cpl.	Campbell, Thomas
18180	Private	Charlesworth, John
18181	,,	Cooper, James A.
18182	Lce.-Cpl.	Day, Frederick A.
18183	Private	Davidson, John
18184	,,	Dayes, Walter
18265	Lce.-Cpl.	Digby, John K.
18260	Bugler	Erickson, Eric
18187	Private	Fournier, Alfred
18188	,,	Foster, Ernest
18189	,,	Fowler, Clarence
18190	,,	Ferron, Fred
18191	,,	Fox, William E.
18192	,,	Gray, Arthur W.
18193	,,	Gannon, James
18194	,,	Goldsworthy, Alfred
18195	,,	Guild, Walter
18196	,,	Grisdale, John
18197	,,	Gordon, William
18198	,,	Gow, John
18202	,,	Hauff, Gordon
18199	,,	Hammond, Charles
18200	,,	Happer, Robert
19271	,,	Hazzey, Alf
19402	,,	Haynes, Cyril A.
18201	,,	Holmes, Frank
18203	,,	Hoy, James
18204	,,	Hunter, Cecil
18206	,,	Hanrahan, Harry
18205	,,	Hanrahan, William
18207	,,	Jones, Samuel
18261	,,	Johnson, George
18208	,,	Johnston, Willis D.
18209	,,	Jones, Robert E.
18210	,,	Kennedy, John
18211	Private	Kirkpatrick Percy
18212	,,	Knight, Laurel
18213	,,	Lindsay, Edward
18214	,,	Lucas, Mervyn
18215	,,	Levey, Mark
18216	,,	Lowden, Charles
18217	,,	Lyle, Archibald
18219	,,	Marr, John
18218	,,	MacDonald, Alex.
18220	,,	Morrison, David
18221	,,	MacDonald,ArchieR.
18222	,,	Munro, Archibald
18223	,,	Nash, Ernest
18224	,,	Nichols, Harry B.
18225	,,	Nalty, Reginald E.
18226	,,	Olson, Thovald
18227	,,	Ownsworth, Louis
18231	,,	Pigot, Horace
18228	,,	Patton, S. Porter
18229	,,	Pratt, Joseph B.
18230	,,	Perrow, John
18232	,,	Piquet, Arthur F.
18233	,,	Puley, Percy
18235	,,	Ranger, Walter
18266	,,	Reeve, George W.
18234	,,	Rouby, Pierre
18236	,,	Robertson, Richard
18237	,,	Ruthven, Herbert C.
18238	,,	Sanders, Albert H.
18239	,,	Selwyn, Christopher
19447	,,	Seely, Harry
18240	,,	Spillman, Alexander
18241	,,	Stickney, John
19358	Lce.-Cpl.	Storrier, George
18242	Private	Scott, Daniel E.
18243	,,	Suttell, Norman
18244	,,	Stanesby, George
18245	,,	Salter, Leonard
18246	,,	Salter, Oscar
18247	,,	Stevens, Ernest W.
18248	,,	Simpson, George M.
18249	,,	Somerford, Harold
18250	,,	Sproule, Robert
18251	,,	Tingle, Wilson
18252	,,	Taylor, Alexander
18253	,,	Tory, Charles H.
18254	,,	Vincent, Jess
18257	,,	Wylie, John
18255	,,	Walker, Archibald A.
18256	,,	Williams, William
18258	,,	Worsley, Thomas
18259	,,	Young, Roland

Canadian Pacific—The Empire's Greatest Railway.

172 9TH BATTALION, 4TH INFANTRY BRIGADE—cont.

"C" COMPANY.

Captain	Hayne, Arthur N.	
Lieutenant	Young, James C. L.	
,, ...	Pike, Howard H.	
,, ...	Sheffield, Robert H.	

Regl. No.	Rank.	Name.	Regl. No.	Rank.	Name.
18301	Col.-Sgt.	Eston, John H.	18344	Lce.-Cpl.	Foster, Thomas
18302	Sergt.	Laxdal, John A.	18410	Private	Foxen, William E.
18303	,,	Shillabeer, John B.	18345	,,	Fry, Alfred
18309	,,	Stockton, John	18352	,,	Gough, William
18306	Corpl.	Huggins, Cyril G. G.	18349	,,	Gordon, John
18310	,,	Henderson, George	18346	,,	Gregor, Daniel
18305	Private	Tyldesley, John	18350	,,	Greenwood, Harry W.
18308	Corpl.	Mugridge, Charles	18347	,,	Grimes, Henry
18307	Sergt.	Taggart, Herbert	18356	,,	Haigh, William G.
18359	Lce.-Cpl.	Johnston, John	18357	,,	Howarth, Percy
18351	Private	Green, Percival A.	18353	,,	Hill, Frederick
19363	,,	Antonenko, Michael	18358	,,	Higgins, James E.
18312	,,	Atherton, Robert	18355	,,	Helloway, George
18311	Lce.-Cpl.	Audrey, Arthur G.	18354	,,	Hunke, Wasyl
18314	Private	Bell, Ralph	18361	,,	Jones, Sidney A.
18322	,,	Benke, Roman	18360	,,	Johnston, James D.
18316	,,	Blackford, John	18362	Lce.-Cpl.	Johnsen, Einar H.
18324	,,	Blackburn, Grdnr. B.	18363	Private	Knowles, Anthony H.
18317	,,	Blissett, William	18412	,,	Koster, Harry J. M.
18321	,,	Bill, Frank	19412	,,	Kuberchuk, Cuzmoc
18318	,,	Broome, Frank	18364	,,	Lawson, John K.
18323	,,	Broder, William	18366	,,	Larson, John L.
18325	,,	Bradt, Charles E.	18365	,,	Linberg, Olaf
18315	Bugler	Bradburn, Walter C.	19422	,,	Lucas, William
18319	Private	Buchanan, Angus	18367	,,	Lyons, William
18320	,,	Burke, William J.	18368	,,	McNaughton, Ross
18327	,,	Carson, Leslie M.	18413	,,	McConnell, Hugh
18410	,,	Chate, William T.	18371	,,	McGovern, Thomas
19380	,,	Chickel, Michael	18373	,,	McNeil, John W.
18330	Lce.-Cpl.	Clarke, Harry	18370	,,	Mather, Frederick
18326	Private	Colvin, George	18374	,,	Madson, Christian
18328	,,	Colwell, Fredk. F. G.	19424	,,	Masseuk, Eylet
18329	Drmr.	Cooke, John W.	18376	,,	Medcraft, Harry J.
18331	Private	Cuzmachuck, Bill	18369	,,	Messent, Cuthbert W.
18332	,,	Davenport, C. N. C. C.	18372	,,	Morling, William P.
18335	,,	Davies, Percy V.	18414	Lce.-Cpl.	Moore, George
18333	,,	Davies, Frederick H.	18375	Private	Munroe, Donald
18334	,,	Davies, Anthony	18377	,,	Nyhus, Ingvald
18337	,,	Donald, William	18378	,,	Nicholls, Fredk. C.
19389	,,	Dobrek, Jacob	18379	,,	Orman, Jacob
18338	,,	Duffin, William	18415	,,	O'Brien, George J.
18339	,,	Ellis, Alfred W.	18416	,,	Palmer, Ernest T.
18340	,,	Elvidge, Alfred W.	18380	,,	Parrack, Edward
18342	,,	Fieldhouse, Harold	18382	,,	Peattie, George R.
18343	,,	Fountain, Harmidas	18386	,,	Peattie, Alexander P.

Canadian Pacific—The Empire's Greatest Railway.

9TH BATTALION, 4TH INFANTRY BRIGADE—cont. 173

Regl. No.	Rank	Name	Regl. No.	Rank	Name
18383	Private	Preston, John	18394	Private	Silverton, Edward J.
18384	,,	Prudius, John	18399	,,	Shea, John
18381	,,	Preston, Roger	18398	,,	Sproule, John
18387	,,	Rochon, John E.	18402	,,	Tinkess, Alfred
18388	,,	Roberts, Albert L.	18400	Corpl.	Tucker, Charles
18385	,,	Ross, James G.	18401	Private	Turner, George
18389	,,	Rigby, Joseph	18403	,,	Ward, Albert
18390	,,	Shanahan, Harry	18405	,,	West, Alfred J.
18391	,,	Sparks, William	18406	,,	West, Percy
18393	,,	Spedding, Robison	18408	,,	Waugh, David
19450	,,	Sperka, Michael	18404	,,	Wilson, Gilmour H.
18392	,,	Smith, Thomas	18409	,,	Wilson, Robert
18395	,,	Steel, Robert	18407	,,	Wilton, Herbert
18396	,,	Salmon, Alex. B.	18850	,,	Woolcock, Harold
19446	,,	Seemsha, John	19464	,,	Yakolecky, Mike
18397	,,	Seymour, Albert J.			

"D" COMPANY.

Captain ... ... Parks, John H.
Lieutenant ... ... Horsley, Gordon F.
,, ... McComb, Harold A.
,, ... Adams, Henry J. M.

Regl. No.	Rank	Name	Regl. No.	Rank	Name
18451	Col.-Sgt.	Buchanan, Neil G.	18477	Private	Burberry, Fredk. C.
18452	Sergt.	Jones, David E.	18478	,,	Burke, Thomas
18453	,,	Murray, John J. T.	18479	,,	Campbell, John A.
18454	,,	MacDonald, James A.	18480	Arm. Cpl.	Campbell, Thomas
18455	,,	Davies, Louis B.	18481	Private	Carberry, Fredk. J.
18564	Private	Beck, Herbert A.	18482	,,	Cheshire, Arthur
18456	Corpl.	Lawson, Charles W.	18484	,,	Clibbery, John C.
18457	,,	Martin, William J. B.	18485	,,	Clubb, Maxwell
18458	,,	Cook, William	18486	,,	Condor, Joseph F.
18459	,,	Dobbie, Alexander	18487	,,	Cunningham, Joseph
18460	,,	Richards, William J.	18488	,,	Carter, Hume E.
18461	Lce.-Cpl.	Pringle, John	18489	,,	Deakin, Arthur S.
18462	,,	Furry, Basil D.	18490	,,	Delouche, Jean B.A.
18463	,,	Kinnell, George	18566	,,	Dobson, William R.
18464	Private	Allbut, Frederick J.	18491	,,	Down, Henry W.
18465	,,	Alberts, Frederick J.	18492	,,	Doherty, John
18466	,,	Allan, Oliver	18493	,,	Farrant, Frank S.
18467	,,	Andrews, Reginald S.	18494	,,	Ficht, Herbert R.
18468	,,	Ashton, Thomas	18495	,,	Flaherty, Roy L.
18469	,,	Barnes, Francis B.	18496	Pnr. Cpl.	Ford, Alexander A.
18471	,,	Bend, Charles A.	18497	Private	Foster, John
18472	,,	Bewsher, Frank	18498	,,	Fulford, Charles
18473	,,	Birse, John	18499	,,	Gallichan, Alfred J.
18474	,,	Boolsen, Carl S.	18500	,,	Gardner, William D.
18475	,,	Bruce, Neil S.	18565	,,	Genicot, Philemon
18476	,,	Buntin, Frederick J.	18501	,,	Gerrie, Russell D.

Canadian Pacific—The Empire's Greatest Railway.

9TH BATTALION, 4TH INFANTRY BRIGADE—cont.

Regl. No.	Rank.	Name.	Regl. No.	Rank.	Name.
18502	Bugler	Gonon, Peter	18536	Private	Peddieson, Chas. F.
18503	Private	Gordon, David	18537	,,	Pratt, Harry
18505	,,	Goss, Samuel A.	18538	,,	Pye, Charles
18506	,,	Gunn, George A.	18539	,,	Ramsey, James
18504	,,	Gordon, George F.	18540	,,	Raphael, James
18507	,,	Hart, Myrl	18541	,,	Ravenscroft, Wm.
18508	,,	Harvey, Roland H.	18543	,,	Robertson, Arch. W.
18510	,,	Hollands, Thomas	18542	,,	Robson, Arthur
18509	,,	Holtum, Fredk. J.	18544	,,	Scott, William H.W.
18511	,,	Iley, Thomas	18545	,,	Salice, Peter
18512	,,	James, William	18546	,,	Seal, John K.
18513	,,	Jensen, Silius	18569	,,	Shaw, William T.
18514	,,	Johnston, Hugh N.	18547	,,	Smith, Leigh R.
18516	,,	Johnstone, James W.	18548	,,	Smith, William F.
18517	,,	Jones, John E.	18549	,,	Spackman, Charles E. W.
18520	,,	Kerr, John E.			
18518	,,	Keeler, Albert E.	18550	,,	Sumner, Edward
18521	,,	King, William H.	18551	,,	Sutcliffe, Harold
18522	,,	Kitto, Richard H.	18552	,,	Thorn, William
18523	,,	Landsborough, John	18553	,,	Tongs, Reginald
18524	,,	Lauchlan, William J.	18554	,,	Tuck, John W. D.
18525	,,	Lawson, Lewis D.	18555	,,	Turnbull, Walter B.
18526	,,	Lundby, Rudolph	18556	,,	Tyner, John W.
18527	,,	Mayer, Frank	18557	,,	Walker, Herbert N.
18531	,,	Maxwell, Robert	18559	,,	Ward, Henry P.
18567	,,	McLellan, Gordon D.	18558	,,	Watts, John
18528	,,	McKinnon, Angus	18568	,,	Weir, Elias F.
18529	,,	McPherson, Charles	18560	,,	Whelpley, Howard S.
18533	,,	Murray, John G.	18561	,,	Williams, Henry
18534	,,	Pearce, Freeman G.	18562	,,	Windsor, Edwin
18535	,,	Peat, Harold R.	18563	,,	Windsor, Eli

"E" COMPANY.

Captain	Bowen, Peter E.
Lieutenant	Day, George S.
,, ...	McDiarmid, John H.

Regl. No.	Rank.	Name.	Regl. No.	Rank.	Name.
18601	Col.-Sgt.	Marr, William B.	18611	Corpl.	Telford, Thomas H.
18603	Sergt.	Delaney, Fred	18645	Lce.-Cpl.	Gibson, William S.
18605	,,	Oldcroft, Robert	18641	Private	Allingham, Joseph
18602	,,	Samuel, Albert E.	18608	Corpl.	de Grouchy, Joshua
18604	,,	Mount, Wilfrid	18700	Lce.-Cpl.	Williams, Richard
19356	Corpl.	Baker, Martin	18612	Private	Allen, William A.
18709	,,	Calcheff, T. Sanco	18613	,,	Alexander, George B.
18609	,,	Carson, Walter E.	18617	,,	Baldwin, Charles T.
18606	,,	Chatterton, Will. E.	19375	,,	Begoff, Alex.
18607	,,	Sylvester, John B. A.	18618	,,	Budge, Thomas
18707	,,	Donald, Charles W.	18619	,,	Blair, Harry F.

Canadian Pacific—The Empire's Greatest Railway.

9TH BATTALION, 4TH INFANTRY BRIGADE—cont. 175

Regl. No.	Rank.	Name.	Regl. No.	Rank.	Name.
18620	Private	Burt, Charles E.	18658	Private	Merkley, George
18614	,,	Barrie, Jack	18657	,,	Mason, William
18615	,,	Bruce, Thomas	18666	,,	Massey, John
18616	,,	Black, George E.	19426	,,	Medalsky, Thos.
18621	,,	Bond, John	18660	Bugler	Muckleston, Fredk.
19366	,,	Borlick, Michael	18663	Private	Middlebrough, Frank
18622	,,	Barrow, Frederick L.	18665	,,	Muir, John L.
18715	,,	Burns, Magnus	18667	,,	Michealoff, George
18710	,,	Cummings, George	18659	,,	McKinnon, Arch. W.
18708	,,	Clover, Robert	18664	,,	McKenzie, Peter
18709	,,	Coleman, Francis C.	18669	,,	McAlpine, Hugh
18624	,,	Coombs, Harold H.	18670	,,	McLaren, John
18668	,,	Crapper, Newman L.	18662	,,	McKinlay, Alex.
18628	,,	Cunningham, John	18661	,,	McDougall, Archd.
18627	,,	Clarke, James	18671	,,	McPhail, Peter
18610	,,	Courtney, William H.	18672	,,	Nightingale, Alb. E.
18714	,,	Cuthbertson, Robt. M.	19431	,,	Oberadovich, Milon
18626	,,	Cuthbert, James	18675	Lce.-Cpl.	Patrick, Gordon
18625	,,	Church, Hugh H.	18676	,,	Pedersen, Paul
18623	,,	Craig, Robert	18674	,,	Publicover, Rich. J.
18629	,,	Chase, Rose C.	18677	,,	Parsons, James W.
18630	,,	Campbell, Finlay	18673	,,	Pecknold, Alfred A.
18683	,,	Clarke, John	18678	Private	Royle, James H.
18635	,,	Davidson, Walter W.	18679	,,	Reynolds, Claude H.
18637	,,	Devins, Erskin	18680	,,	Rassmuss, Raymond
18634	,,	Drakolich, Daniel L.	18682	,,	Roggeveen, Paul A.
18631	,,	Dunn, James W.	18681	,,	Range, William
18636	Lce.-Cpl.	Dixon, Thomas	18690	,,	Smith, George
18633	Private	Donald, Duncan S.	18684	,,	Stevenson, George H.
18716	Corpl.	Davies, Arthur	18685	,,	Sennitt, Archie F.
18638	Private	Edwards, Edward	18686	,,	Stoodley, George
18640	,,	Emmerson, Frederick	18687	,,	Strugar, Blazo I.
18639	,,	Engall, John K.	18688	,,	Starley, Richard
18644	,,	Fowler, William T.	18689	,,	Smith, William
18643	,,	Ford, Phillip	18691	,,	Sonaheim, Louis
18642	,,	Fuller, Walter H.	18692	,,	Silverlock, Arthur F.
18646	,,	Grant, Colin	18693	,,	Saren, Victor
18647	,,	Hodgson, Harold	18694	,,	Sheppard, H. E.
19408	,,	Holstinin, Jacob	18695	,,	Trotter, William
18648	,,	Huston, Claud	18696	,,	Viau, Adolpha
18649	,,	Hurley, Edward P.	18697	,,	Watson, Edward
18650	Bugler	Jones, Llewellyn	18698	,,	Wells, Harry
18651	Private	Johnston, Joshua R.	18699	,,	Wolfe, Hermann
18652	,,	Johnston, Wilburn S.	18701	,,	Woods, George H.
18653	,,	Jordison, Jack	18702	,,	Woodard, Henry
19413	,,	Kosovitch, Eli	18703	,,	Woodcock, Donald
18654	,,	Lacombe, Henry N.	18705	,,	Watts, John E. P.
18655	,,	Lattin, Edward C.	18706	,,	Wait, John
18656	,,	Lang, Elmore R.	18704	,,	Young, William

Canadian Pacific—The Empire's Greatest Railway.

9TH BATTALION, 4TH INFANTRY BRIGADE—cont.

"F" COMPANY.

Captain ... ... Stewart, Robert H.
Lieutenant ... ... Brooks, Allan

Regl. No.	Rank.	Name.	Regl. No.	Rank.	Name.
18751	Col.-Sgt.	Lafferty, Alex. M.	18815	Private	Gilmour, Cephus D.
18752	Sergt.	Boyce, Llewelyn	18793	,,	Gray, Percy
18754	,,	Campbell, William J.	18773	,,	Green, Arthur G.
18753	,,	Lucas, Henry	18814	,,	Grieve, Allan
18810	,,	Worester, Fredk. T.	18772	,,	Groves, Hubert S.
18837	Corpl.	Allison, John	18846	,,	Hampton, Benjamin
18824	,,	Arkless, Oswald P.	18795	,,	Haldane, Roy
18783	,,	Burford, Sidney J.	18775	,,	Hall, Archie C.
18756	Private	Fraser, Harold G.	18819	,,	Hardman, Samuel
18797	Corpl.	Tilley, Arthur B.	18776	,,	Hickman, B.
18827	Lce.-Cpl.	Richmond, Oliver C.	18796	,,	Hill, Douglas
18770	Corpl.	Scobie, Samuel M.	18798	,,	Hill, Gordon
18771	Lce.-Cpl.	Winter, Harry	18799	,,	Hinkle, Marion W.
18811	Private	Adams, Albert E.	18818	,,	Holst, Olus N.
18838	,,	Adzich, Vuko	18817	,,	Hughes, Edward S.
18784	,,	Aitken, William	18816	,,	Hutton, Alexander G.
18769	Bugler	Ash, John E.	18800	,,	Johnson, Hugh
18757	Private	Bainbridge, Charles	18847	,,	Johnston, John
18839	,,	Barrett, Edward A.	18820	,,	Jones, Edward
18840	,,	Barrie, William	18801	,,	Kelly, James W.
18813	,,	Bechervaise, B.	18802	,,	Kennedy, Hugh D.
18759	,,	Bishop, John A.	18821	,,	King, John J. A.
18812	,,	Blain, John	18836	,,	Knowles, Harry W
18760	,,	Brown, John G.	18848	,,	Kostich, Sam.
18758	,,	Bray, Eugene	18849	,,	Lowe, William
18761	,,	Burns, John J.	18855	,,	Martinovich, John
18785	,,	Calder, William	18782	,,	Marinskee, Kosta
18762	,,	Cameron, Alexander	19238	,,	McArthur, Fred.
18791	,,	Carroll, Tim	18778	,,	Macdonell, Charles E.
18787	,,	Cowley, Philip H.	18853	,,	McDowall, John
18763	,,	Clements, Jesse	18777	,,	McHale, Clarence A.
18764	,,	Clifford, Fred	18852	,,	McLeod, Alexander A.
18765	,,	Coholan, William J.	18854	,,	McMillan, Angus
18841	Bugler	Collister, David	18803	,,	Miller, Walter J.
18842	Private	Crane, George	18822	,,	Mockler, Edwd. C.W.
18788	,,	Crick, Edmund	18856	,,	Needham, John
18789	,,	Cumbleton, Wm. L.	18857	,,	Nightingale, Thos. B.
18766	Lce.-Cpl.	Cummings, C. W.	18779	,,	Nord, Peter
18792	Private	Dale, William	18780	,,	O'Sullivan, John
18790	,,	Davis, John H.	18823	,,	Parlette, Al.
18844	,,	Day, Walter	18804	,,	Peterson, Henry A.
18767	,,	Dexter, William	18781	,,	Pilgrim, Henry H.
18843	,,	Donald, William O.	18859	,,	Radoman, Blazo
18768	,,	Duff, Henry D.	18858	,,	Radford, Sidney H.
18774	,,	Edler, Charles	18805	,,	Rault, Peter M.
18794	,,	Fergus, John K.	18825	,,	Reid, Alfred J.
18845	,,	Fraser, Hugh	18828	,,	Richards, Harry

Canadian Pacific—The Empire's Greatest Railway.

9TH BATTALION, 4TH INFANTRY BRIGADE—cont.

Regl. No.	Rank.	Name.	Regl. No.	Rank.	Name.
18826	Private	Ritchie, George	18807	Private	Sumner, David
18851	,,	Saidler, John	18830	,,	Tait, Randolph C.
18860	,,	Sampson, Frank T.	18863	,,	Thomas, David
19475	,,	Serejos, Alexander	18833	,,	Thorold, George W.
18861	,,	Sargeant, Gordon	18832	,,	Tracy, Henry
18806	,,	Sheehan, Daniel J.	18809	,,	Visser, George H. J.
18829	,,	Shorthouse, H. de W.	18834	,,	Wherry, Arthur R.
18862	,,	Sjklosha, Blazo	18835	,,	Wherry, Frank A.
18831	,,	Smeathers, Alfred F.	18808	,,	Wolstenholme, W. A.

"G" COMPANY.

Captain ... ... McInnis, Carlyle W.
Lieutenant ... ... Willson, Harvey L.
,, ... Crawford, Richard G.
,, ... Black, Fergus N.

Regl. No.	Rank.	Name.	Regl. No.	Rank.	Name.
18901	Col.-Sgt.	Cowie, James	18934	Private	Dunbar, James
18902	Sergt.	Lyons, William H.	18935	,,	Doyle, James
18903	,,	Sinclair, Alex. G.	18936	,,	Dain, William
18904	,,	Rusk, Harry	18937	,,	Duncan, Ross
18905	,,	Adamson, Alexander	18938	,,	Elliott, John D.
18908	Corpl.	Rule, Walter	18939	,,	Edwards, Stuart
18909	Private	Walthall, B. James	18940	,,	Edwards, Robert
18910	Corpl.	Ferguson, JohnWood	18942	,,	Exelby, Lionel
18911	,,	McKnight, Harry B.	19398	,,	Ferrier, Walter
18912	,,	MacLean, George M.	19396	,,	Firman, Frank H.
18913	Lce.-Cpl.	Barthelemy, William	18944	,,	Gifford, Thomas
18914	Private	Murphy, John	18945	,,	Gooder, William A.
18915	,,	Davies, Herbert	18946	Lce.-Cpl.	Godber, Robert P.
18916	Bugler	Martin, Arthur E.	18947	Private	Graham, Allan
19376	Private	Barnes, Joseph	18948	,,	Graham, Peter
18918	,,	Burns, Samuel	18949	,,	Green, William
18919	Lce.-Cpl.	Barthelemy, Maurice	18950	Lce.-Cpl.	Gregory, Windle W.
18920	Private	Boulton, Robert V.	18951	Private	Haworth, John
18921	,,	Brown, George	18952	,,	Hanson, Peter
18922	,,	Bunkall, Alfred	19409	,,	Heatherington,W. G.
18923	,,	Bootle, Edwin	18953	,,	Hodgson, Augustas
18924	,,	Bagot, Harold C.	19407	,,	Hopkinson,Theodore
19382	,,	Camche, George	18954	,,	Hutton, Robert
18926	,,	Cathcart, Francis D.	18955	,,	Hern, Loftus R.
18927	,,	Chamberlain, Ernest	18957	,,	Jamieson, John R.
18928	,,	Cheeseman, Fred	18956	,,	Jamieson, John G.
18929	Lce.-Cpl.	Clark, Francis	18958	,,	Jansen, Homer
18930	Private	Cooper, Charles T.	18959	,,	Jones, David
18931	Corpl.	Cooper, Alfred F.	18960	,,	Jones, David Lloyd
19359	Private	Cornelius, Geo.	18961	,,	Jakes, Harry
18932	,,	Cowley, Herbert C.	19415	,,	Kubanek Joseph
19377	,,	Craik, William	19417	,,	Laboucan, Sam.
18933	,,	Curtis, William H.	19420	,,	Laterneau, H.

Canadian Pacific—The Empire's Greatest Railway.

178 9TH BATTALION, 4TH INFANTRY BRIGADE—cont.

Regl. No.	Rank.	Name.	Regl. No.	Rank.	Name.
19416	Private	Lochin, Filimon	18987	Private	Ringrose, Charles
18962	,,	Lodge, Jack E.	19441	,,	Rugg, William
18963	,,	Lion, Charles S.	18988	,,	Saunders, Thomas
18964	,,	Longmuir, William A.	18989	,,	Sheppard, Henry
19419	,,	Lothian, James	19016	,,	Stratford, William
18965	,,	Loutit, Henry	18992	,,	Sadzak, Mike
18966	,,	Loubovich, Mike	19448	,,	Salenko, Geo.
18967	,,	Maloy, John W.	18993	,,	Shorney, Richard
18968	,,	McKenzie, George	19443	,,	Serette, H.
18969	,,	McLean, Harry	18994	,,	Sevigny, Omer
18970	,,	McAughtrie, Thomas	18995	,,	Smith, Howard G.
18971	,,	McBrinn, Joseph	18996	,,	Sproule, Samuel
18972	,,	McCarty, Daniel	18997	,,	Steele, Ross
18973	,,	McCormick, William	18998	,,	Stevenson, Ole
18974	,,	McDonald, Murdoch	18999	Corpl.	Stewart, Allan
18975	,,	McKay, Alex. R.	19000	Private	Stewart, Frederick R.
18976	,,	McNaught, Wm. J.	19002	,,	Sturdy, Frank
18977	Lce.-Cpl.	McWilliams, Wm.	19001	,,	Stuer, Octave
19231	Private	Marguard, Martin	19005	,,	Tarratt, Charles W.
18978	,,	Michaloff, Alexander	19006	,,	Taylor, Frederick W.
18979	,,	Mitchell, James F.	19007	,,	Thompson, Frank A.
18980	,,	Morton, James M.	19008	,,	Wilson, Arthur
18981	,,	Monk, Robt.	19461	,,	Watson, Dalton
18982	,,	Morin, Joseph	19009	Corpl.	Watson, Percy
18983	,,	Parris, Andrew	19010	Private	Wilcox, Ernest H.
19428	,,	Naumoff, Lewis	19011	,,	Warren, Dennis M.
18984	,,	Pearce, Newton	19012	,,	Winterbourne, G. H.
19437	,,	Parsons, Charles	19013	,,	Wright, Hugh
18985	,,	Petrie, William	19014	,,	Wyman, Harold
19438	,,	Pennington, Frank	19015	,,	Young, John Moir
18986	,,	Richards, Henry	19466	,,	Zorich, Bob

"H" COMPANY.

Captain	... ...	Cookson, Percy S.
Lieutenant	... ...	Sims, Tweedie C.
,,	... ...	Tate, Simon M.
,,	... ...	Finn, Edward A.

Regl. No.	Rank.	Name.	Regl. No.	Rank.	Name.
19051	Col.-Sgt.	Nevin Thomas	19061	Lce.-Cpl.	Pidd, Cyril
19052	Sergt.	Cole, Ernest G.	19063	,,	Bailey, Charles
19053	,,	McCann, William	19062	Private	Haney, Andrew W.
19055	,,	Kranz, Harry	19064	,,	Armstrong, Wm. W.
19058	Corpl.	Henderson, James	19065	,,	Anderson, Charles H.
19059	Private	Crocombe, George	19066	,,	Adlam, Douglas H.
19057	,,	Beaton, George	19067	,,	Aimes, William H.
19056	,,	Carter, James	19068	,,	Ashby, Charles
19060	,,	Seymour, Geo. E.	19069	,,	Burnes, Carlton

Canadian Pacific—The Empire's Greatest Railway.

9TH BATTALION, 4TH INFANTRY BRIGADE—cont. 179

Regl. No.	Rank.	Name.	Regl. No.	Rank.	Name.
19070	Private	Bradley, John	19088	Private	Julien, Octave
19071	,,	Berteau, Louis	19089	,,	Keates, Robert C.
19073	,,	Batten, William	19090	,,	Maloney, Frank
19072	,,	Brenner, Arnold	19091	,,	Moore, William M.
19074	,,	Bateson, Fred	19092	,,	Matthews, Geo. W.
19104	,,	Buchanan, Wm. H.	19093	,,	Mowat, Malcolm
19162	Bugler	Boughey, Terence A.	19094	,,	Mildon, Herbert A.
19105	Private	Broughton, Ernest	19095	,,	Martin, Thomas H.
19103	,,	Bloomfield, Daniel J.	19096	,,	Munn, Donald
19106	,,	Bilsland, James	19097	,,	McLennan, Allan
19107	,,	Brogden, Robert	19098	,,	Mac Donald,McIntosh
19108	,,	Brader, Harold	19099	,,	McCallum, Wm. A.
19109	,,	Cole, Louis	19100	,,	McIntosh, Peter
19168	,,	Chapman, Benjamin	19101	,,	McIntosh, Tracy W.
19110	,,	Charles, Frederick J.	19102	Lce.-Cpl.	McLetchie, Arthur
19111	,,	Czajkowski, Walter	19130	Private	McLean, Edward
19112	,,	Carrier, Magloirer	19131	,,	McIvor Angus
19113	,,	Caminer, Harry H.	19132	,,	McPherson, William
19114	,,	Conlin, James	18304	,,	McWiggen, J. M.
19115	,,	Cussen, Thomas	19133	,,	Not, Charles
19116	,,	Dolman, William	19134	,,	Oldershaw, Harry
19117	,,	Davidson, Robert	19270	,,	Owen, Eric
19118	,,	Dixon, Percy	19135	,,	Persons, Koln
19119	,,	Dimond, W.	19136	,,	Pierce, Stewart
19120	,,	Deugau, Robert V.	19137	,,	Rathie, Walter R.
19121	,,	English, Howard	19138	,,	Ramsey, Thomas C.
19122	,,	Easton, George	19139	,,	Rankin, William
19123	,,	Elliott, Ernest	19140	,,	Redfern, Harry
19124	,,	Ely, Robert	19141	,,	Rutter, James
19125	,,	Ford, William	19142	,,	Rail, William
19126	,,	Fraser, Hugh	19144	,,	Roxburgh, CharlesA.
19166	,,	Foster, Charles	19145	Corpl.	Sims, John
19128	,,	Gilmour, Andrew	19146	Private	Smith, George
19129	Lce.-Cpl.	Graham, Wendall	19147	,,	Smith, George F.
19127	Private	France, Cyrille	19167	Corpl.	Slevin, Michael
19075	,,	Gates, Ernest	19148	Private	Sinclair, James
19076	,,	George, David	19149	,,	Sharp, George
19077	,,	Gibson, Robert S.	19150	,,	Townsend, Arthur
19078	Lce.-Cpl.	Holmes, Cecil	19151	,,	Thompson, Robert
19079	Private	Hawley, Robert H.	19160	,,	Vanderhouten, Leo
19080	,,	Halliday, Matthew	19152	,,	Walton, Frederick S.
19081	,,	Haney, William	19153	,,	Wheatley, Charles
18304	,,	McWiggen, J. M.	19154	Arm. Cpl.	Watt, John
19082	,,	Hobson, Sidney	19155	Private	Webb, William H.
19083	,,	Hutchinson, David	19156	,,	Williams, John D.
19084	,,	Harkness, John	19157	,,	Williams, Thomas
19085	,,	Jessop, Donald	19158	,,	Walker, Thomas
19086	,,	Jeffery, William	19159	,,	Wood, Gordon
19087	,,	Jones, Gamer	19161	Bugler	Walker, Joshua

Canadian Pacific—The Empire's Greatest Railway.

M 2

9TH BATTALION, 4TH INFANTRY BRIGADE—cont.

"K" COMPANY.

| | Lieutenant | ... ... | Brunton, Harold G. |
| | „ | ... ... | Pace, William J. |

Regl. No.	Rank.	Name.	Regl. No.	Rank.	Name.
19352	Sergt.	Stafford-Bush, John	19397	Private	Fechuck, Fred
19353	„	Dart, John	19399	„	Fauque, August
18755	„	Larkman, John	19402	„	Haynes, Cyril A.
19354	„	Simeonoff, Nicholas	19403	„	Herbert, Walter
19355	„	Poole, William	19404	„	Henningsen, Leon
19357	Private	Motovillo, Michael	19405	„	Hancock, Charles
19360	„	Watson, Dalton	19406	„	Holtorf, Henry
19362	„	Anderson, John	19410	„	Julian, Louis
19364	„	Anderton, Benjamin	19411	„	Joroff, Daniel
19365	„	Addy, Charles E. R.	19418	„	Lizotte, Dacite
18867	„	Blackburn, Edward	19421	„	Luft, Edgar
19368	„	Baronin, Bagdaser	19425	„	Micallof, Emanuel
19369	„	Bakum, Ildcom	19429	„	Nastero, William
19367	„	Browne, George H.	19430	„	Neilson, Paul
19370	„	Barrett, William	19433	„	Panomar, Komon
19371	„	Belanger, Henri	19434	„	Perovich, Samuel
19373	„	Begbie, Peter	19435	„	Plachic, George
19374	„	Bohutenko, Joseph	19439	„	Paull, Theodore
19378	„	Caruana, Leona	19440	„	Richer, Eulic
19379	„	Cremona, Frank	19442	„	Romano, August
19381	„	Cooling, Jesse	19444	„	Sheykin, Fred
19383	„	Churich, Joseph	19445	„	Sivick, Frank
19384	„	Carlo, Simon	19449	„	Stackoff, Spas
19385	„	Chonomod, Nicholas	19451	„	Tickich, Radal
19386	„	Day, Thomas	19453	„	Tomlinson, Walter
19388	„	Deweydenka, George	19351	Sergt.	Tompkins, Philip F.
19387	„	Dickran, Koumogian	19455	Private	Woodley, Thomas A.
19390	„	Dematti, Paul	19454	„	Woodley, George B.
19391	„	Dubich, Michael	19457	„	Wright, H. Roy
19392	„	Enever, Thomas	19459	„	Wills, Jesse H.
19393	„	Eastman, James	19460	„	Wein, David
19394	„	Evanoff, Velko	19462	„	Yesenchuk, Joseph
19395	„	Ellis, Kenneth	19465	„	Yaskavotich, Peter

Band.

Regl. No.	Rank.	Name.	Regl. No.	Rank.	Name.
19004	Sergt.	Timberlake	18711	Private	Novelli, Eugene
18262	Private	Armstrong, Albert	18712	„	Patston, John A.
18263	„	Berry, William	18713	„	Pears, Frank
18264	„	Brenton, Harry J.	18864	„	Pilling, Alfred M.
18014	„	Coutts, James S.	18865	„	Ross, Chas. E.
18015	„	Dewhurst, Geo. T.	18866	„	Senior, Charles A.
18336	„	Dredge, Percy	18990	„	Senior, Wilfred
18341	„	Elliott, John H.	18265	„	Southwood, James
18411	„	Irwin, Donald	18991	„	Stowe, John
18515	„	Johnson, W. A.	19163	„	Thomas, Chas. W.
18519	„	Kennedy, Francis P.	19164	„	Welsh, Robert
18532	„	Mosher, Robt. G.	19165	„	Wheeler, Fred.

Canadian Pacific—The Empire's Greatest Railway.

10th BATTALION, 4th INFANTRY BRIGADE.

HEADQUARTERS.

Lieut.-Colonel...	Boyle, R. L.
Major ...	McLaren, J.
,, ...	Lightfoot, J.
Adjutant ...	Ormond, Captain D. M.
Assistant Adjutant ...	Suydam, Captain H. C.
Quartermaster	Ross, Hon. Lieut. E.
Transport Officer	Lowry, Lieutenant W.
Signalling Officer	Sinclair, Lieutenant D. H.
Machine Gun Officer...	Yates, Lieutenant C. R.

Attached.

Medical Officer	Glidden, Lieutenant G. C.
Paymaster	Houston, Hon. Captain A. M.
Chaplain	Elmsley, Hon. Major Rev. W. H.

Company Officers.

Major	Nasmyth, W. W.
Captain	Howell, E. L.
,,	Arthur, C. J.
,,	Robinson, C. W.
,,	Meikle, A. F. T.
,,	Cook, H.
,,	Redman, D. L.
,,	Pott, F.
,,	Wallace, H. A. C.
Lieutenant	Suydam, H. C.
,,	Nasmyth, G. T.
,,	Morgan, A. N.
,,	Coldwell, W. R.
,,	Duncan, G. G.
,,	Critchley, W. R.
,,	Collins, J.
,,	Simpson, J. D.
,,	Norton-Taylor, S.
,,	Thomson, A. T.
,,	Harrison, A. E.
,,	Snelgrove, H. P.
,,	Cookshutt, W. A.
,,	Forneret, G. R.
,,	Hoskins, R.
,,	McColl, D. C.
,,	Fryer, C.
,,	Craggs, S.
,,	Ball, A. R.
,,	Watson, C. H. D.
,,	Knowles, W. N.
,,	Glanfield, S. L.
,,	Bell, A. L.

Canadian Pacific—The Empire's Greatest Railway.

182   10TH BATTALION, 4TH INFANTRY BRIGADE—cont.

Regl. No.	Rank.	Name.	Regl. No.	Rank.	Name.
19576	Sgt.-Maj.	Good, R. (W.O.)	20878	Sergt.	Rutherford, T. G.
19578	Q.M.Sgt.	Haylett, J. G.	20588	,,	Cox, H. S.
20278	Col. Sgt.	Stuart, D.	19831	,,	Hardy, G. R.
19826	,,	Winter, G. E.	20148	,,	Rayfield, E.
19976	,,	Sharland, H. E.	20350	,,	Murrey, G.
20272	,,	Nesbit, T. O.	20095	Lce.-Sgt.	Eccles, E. J.
20275	,,	Jacobs, S. J.	20282	,,	Hopkins, G.
20426	,,	Rickard, E.	20433	,,	Goodfellow, W.
20576	,,	Watson, J.	19832	,,	Right, W. D. F.
20726	,,	Alexander, W.	20879	Actg. Sgt.	Knights, F. W.
20876	,,	Grant, J.	19802	,,	Forbes, M.
19579	O.R. Sgt.	Baker, S. H.	20271	Arm. Cpl.	Mann, D. G.
19577	Sgt.Bugler	Barton, F.	19985	,,	Billings, H. S.
19580	Pn'r Sgt.	Clarke, L. A.	20390	,,	Grant, G.
19581	Cook Sgt.	Alderton, W.	20919	,,	Smith, L. G.
19626	Pay Sgt.	Dacre, C. V.	20578	Corpl.	Welch, W.
20581	Sgt. Tailor	Aitcheson, A.	19745	,,	Massey, J.
26434	Arm. Sgt.	Dube, J.	19690	,,	Bennet, J. G.
20838	,,	Scott, E. J.	19770	,,	Roots, J.
19936	Shoe Sgt.	Still, J.	19782	,,	Shaw, G. B.
19683	Sergt.	Banks, E. C.	19981	,,	Grimshaw, G. F.
19799	,,	Cattanach, A. M.	19982	,,	Forman, A.
19788	,,	Scriven, G.	19983	,,	Spencer, E.
19786	,,	Thatcher, W. J.	20167	,,	Menzies, W.
19827	,,	Steel, A. K.	20207	,,	Greenaway, T.
19830	,,	Moss, J. M.	20242	,,	Williams, C. W. C.
19828	,,	Evans, G. H.	20283	,,	Parks, C.
19829	,,	Hand, F. J.	20284	,,	Jones, T. G.
19977	,,	Couchman, W. G.	20285	,,	McCabe, J. D.
19978	,,	Martin, A. N.	20432	,,	Burton, P.
19979	,,	Green, W.	20434	,,	Mortimer, F.
19980	,,	Frances, W.	20435	,,	Smith, B. B.
20241	,,	Marks, R. J.	20585	,,	Linekar, S.
20206	,,	Williams, P.	20587	,,	Lockheart, P.
20155	,,	Belshaw, T.	20667	,,	Sparks, J. W.
20248	,,	Clare, C.	20731	,,	Scott, R.
20277	,,	Giles, J.	20732	,,	Washford, H. J.
20279	,,	Miller, J.	20733	,,	Matheson, J. C.
20280	,,	Scarrot, A.	20734	,,	Wiffen, H. A.
20281	,,	Bixcoe, V. H. R.	20735	,,	Lee, T. F.
20427	,,	Davies, W. E.	20880	,,	Edwards, M.
20428	,,	Wilson, W. W.	19605	,,	Forbes, D.
20429	,,	Glover, N. R.	19946	,,	Young, S. J.
20430	,,	Miller, J.	19987	,,	Stephenson, C. J.
20577	,,	Larkin, J.	20287	,,	Rafetary, J.
20579	,,	Ford, F.	20288	,,	King, R.
20580	,,	Taylor, A. E.	19899	,,	Bird, C. E.
20727	,,	Knights, F. A.	20483	,,	Foster, F. A.
20728	,,	Mathers, B.	19741	,,	Kennedy, W. J.
20729	,,	Norton, C. W.	20219	,,	Lloyd, F. O.
20730	,,	Walsh, E.	20345	,,	Marrifield, H. C.
20877	,,	Rolfe, H.	20654	,,	Nicholls, C.

Canadian Pacific—The Empire's Greatest Railway.

10TH BATTALION, 4TH INFANTRY BRIGADE—cont. 183

Regl. No	Rank	Name	Regl. No	Rank	Name
20522	Corpl.	Ryman, A. H.	19696	Private	Beard, T.
20678	,,	Whyte, A.	19798	,,	Burns, J.
20881	O.R. Cpl.	Sydenham, S.	19838	,,	Beauchamp, G.
19685	Lce.-Cpl.	Bates, E.	19839	,,	Bendall, H. H.
19834	,,	McIntosh, D.	19840	,,	Bennett, J.
19835	,,	McDonald, J. A.	19990	,,	Brereton, C. S.
19836	,,	Robotham, S.	19991	,,	Barnes, F. F.
19860	,,	Graham, J.	19992	,,	Bronsdon, S. G.
19881	,,	Lewis, F.	19993	,,	Bradford, H.
19986	,,	Jones, E. H.	19994	,,	Brooks, H.
19988	,,	Morrison, A. E.	19995	,,	Brown, A.
20286	,,	Moir, A.	19996	,,	Browne, R. E.
20289	,,	Robertshaw, F.	19997	,,	Bell, T. E.
20736	,,	Sculthorpe, E. J.	19998	,,	Branch, H. E.
20797	,,	Mackinnon, S.	19999	,,	Beeton, G.
20754	,,	Clift, A.	20137	,,	Berg, H.
19682	Private	Arthurs, J.	20243	,,	Bell, D.
19676	,,	Adams, C. H.	20244	,,	Bomford, A. R. G.
19677	,,	Allison, H.	20245	,,	Bull, W. I.
19679	,,	Antony, D.	20246	,,	Balchin, W. H.
19680	,,	Apperley, F. J.	20208	,,	Barnes, G.
19681	,,	Atnott, J.	20169	,,	Ballance, G.
19797	,,	Alcock, H.	20171	,,	Bristow, Frank
19837	,,	Abbott, S. L.	20172	,,	Broadhurst, F. E.
19989	,,	Atherton, H.	20173	,,	Bicknell, W.
20008	,,	Adshead, H. P.	20131	,,	Bell, H.
20138	,,	Ager, R.	20136	,,	Bristow, Fred.
20168	,,	Alexander, D.	20141	,,	Beasley, J.
20150	,,	Andrews, H.	20143	,,	Bryan, G.
20139	,,	Adamson, R.	20151	,,	Bell, G.
20290	,,	Acheson, S.	20294	,,	Balfour, W.
20291	,,	Adair, W. H.	20295	,,	Bennet, S
20292	,,	Armstrong, A. P.	20296	,,	Bonna, G.
20293	,,	Andrews, A.	20297	,,	Boultbee, J. M.
20436	,,	Adams, T. A.	20298	,,	Brett, E¹
20437	,,	Atwell, S. G.	20299	,,	Brown, J. D.
20438	,,	Atherton, E. J.	20439	,,	Barritt, G.
20590	,,	Annand, C.	20441	,,	Boyd, J. B.
20591	,,	Armstrong, W.	20442	,,	Birrel, A.
20738	,,	Abbott, T. C.	20443	,,	Bunyan, J. A.
20739	,,	Aikenhead, J.	20444	,,	Bibby, L.
20740	,,	Allen, P. H.	20445	,,	Bramwell, J.
20741	,,	Allingham, J. R. E.	20446	,,	Baker, H.
20882	,,	Arthur, J.	20447	,,	Burrow, T.
20883	,,	Asifat, W.	20448	,,	Burrows, J. H.
19678	,,	Ansen, T,	20449	,,	Baird, H.
19684	,,	Barlow, C.	20450	,,	Brown, E.
19687	,,	Bandains, S. P.	20451	,,	Bailey, L. H.
19688	,,	Bean, H. N.	20702	,,	Boag, J.
19691	,,	Boyden, J. G.	20686	,,	Bailey, W.
19692	,,	Bryan, G.	20592	,,	Black, A.
19694	,,	Burns, W.	20593	,,	Blake, P. W.

Canadian Pacific—The Empire's Greatest Railway.

10th BATTALION, 4th INFANTRY BRIGADE—cont.

Regl. No.	Rank.	Name.	Regl. No.	Rank.	Name.
20596	Private	Boyden, W.	20211	Private	Cooper, T.
20597	,,	Brown, F.	20212	,,	Cartwright, J.
20684	,,	Bloomfield, F. E.	20196	,,	Chappelow, E.
20692	,,	Bennet, E.	20175	,,	Cheeseman, H. A.
20742	,,	Babbage, J. B.	20301	,,	Cabeldue, H.
20743	,,	Baker, H.	20302	,,	Cameron, W. K.
20744	,,	Barb, G.	20304	,,	Coats, A.
20745	,,	Bingham, C.	20305	,,	Coats, J. E.
20746	,,	Bridge, J. T.	20306	,,	Crosby, G. C.
20748	,,	Burns, R.	20452	,,	Clarke, A. B.
20884	,,	Baker, B. F.	20453	,,	Conley, H.
20887	,,	Burns, H.	20454	,,	Courtney, A.
19686	,,	Batten, T.	20455	,,	Cooper, F.
20598	,,	Bury, J.	20456	,,	Connah, A. L.
20000	,,	Belshaw, W.	20457	,,	Cecil, E. E.
20595	,,	Bowman, R.	20458	,,	Cox, W. G.
19141	,,	Bloxham, C. H.	20459	,,	Cudmore, C.
20300	,,	Bell, B.	20460	,,	Conybeare, B.
20001	,,	Brothers, R. A.	20461	,,	Clarke, J. S.
19600	,,	Bell, J. D.	20599	,,	Cadman, T.
34430	,,	Boward, P. R.	20600	,,	Cann, W.
20594	,,	Bolton, J.	20601	,,	Chester, S. D.
19597	,,	Barrs, C. J.	20602	,,	Clack, C.
20193	,,	Brownlee, J.	20603	,,	Cottam, A.
19635	,,	Bull, G. W.	20604	,,	Cullum, W.
20096	,,	Brangan, F.	20689	,,	Costello, R.
19833	,,	Berry, J.	20749	,,	Cameron, G.
19698	,,	Campbell, T.	20750	,,	Ching, H.
19701	,,	Cox, A.	20751	,,	Chipperfield, W.
19702	,,	Critchely, J.	20752	,,	Clarke, M. T.
19703	,,	Crook, R.	20753	,,	Clarke, C. H.
19704	,,	Cross, D.	20755	,,	Colin, B. P.
19800	,,	Coyle, W.	20756	,,	Congdon, W. R.
19842	,,	Carver, L.	20757	,,	Cooke, E.
19844	,,	Challinor, J. J.	20758	,,	Cox, R.
19845	,,	Challinor, W. J.	20759	,,	Cumming, G.
19846	,,	Clarke, J.	20760	,,	Cumming, P.
19847	,,	Clarke, R.	19700	,,	Cope, J.
19848	,,	Clayton, H. P.	20926	,,	Clutterbuck, S.
19849	,,	Connell, D.	19603	,,	Campbell, G.
19942	,,	Campbell, J.	20689	,,	Clawson, W.
19943	,,	Campbell, N.	19841	,,	Carr, J.
20002	,,	Carrington, R.	19984	,,	Campbell, J.
20003	,,	Cairns, J.	20093	,,	Chaplain, H.
20004	,,	Cook, J.	19706	,,	Deally, J.
20005	,,	Cooper, E. L.	19707	,,	Douglas, R.
20006	,,	Curtiss, J. R.	19708	,,	Drayton, G.
20007	,,	Campbell, T.	19850	,,	Dickenson, P.
20009	,,	Curtiss, W. E.	19851	,,	Dolan, E.
20247	,,	Crosbie, H.	19852	,,	Daven, J. A.
20209	,,	Clarke, F.	19944	,,	Dumais, J. B.
20210	,,	Cranston, G.	20010	,,	Davidson, T.

Canadian Pacific—The Empire's Greatest Railway.

10TH BATTALION, 4TH INFANTRY BRIGADE—cont. 185

Regl. No.	Rank	Name	Regl. No.	Rank	Name
20011	Private	Duff, J. T.	20128	Private	Ellis, W. G.
20012	,,	Duff, J.	20476	,,	Evans, P. J.
20013	,,	Devenport, J.	20611	,,	Ellis, C.
20014	,,	Dyke, A. R.	20612	,,	Emmeck, J.
20214	,,	Davidson, J.	20683	,,	Elton, W. J.
20307	,,	Davis, T.	20766	,,	Erickson, V.
20308	,,	Denholm, W.	19631	,,	Eden, H.
20309	,,	Dewar, E. L.	19601	,,	Edwards, J.
20310	,,	Donaldson, C.	20767	,,	Evans, C. B.
20463	,,	Dowty, A. B.	20613	,,	Fantley, A.
20464	,,	Davies, F. A.	20614	,,	Fillmore, H.
20465	,,	Davies, A.	20615	,,	Flannigan, W.
20466	,,	Davies, J. A.	20616	,,	Fox, T.
20467	,,	Durham, G. C.	20617	,,	Fraser, A.
20468	,,	Deakin, T.	20687	,,	Frendo, J.
20469	,,	Drew, C.	19712	,,	Fitzgerald, J.
20470	,,	Drew, A.	19713	,,	Flowers, E.
20471	,,	Dunn, J.	19801	,,	Farrington, W.
20472	,,	Drown, G. H.	19718	,,	Fenn, F. C.
20473	,,	Dooty, J.	19717	,,	Foley, M.
20474	,,	Doirion, E.	19714	,,	Foote, G. S.
20475	,,	Denney, J.	19715	,,	Frampton, C.
20605	,,	Davies, T.	19716	,,	Fraser, J. S.
20606	,,	Doherty, E. P.	19719	,,	Fry, A. H.
20608	,,	Douglass, J.	19855	,,	Fox, S. M.
20609	,,	Drysdale, J.	19856	,,	Fox, A.
20610	,,	Duncan, A.	20019	,,	Furber, W.
20630	,,	Don, C.	20020	,,	Finnigen, H.
20697	,,	Dick, J.	20021	,,	Fairweather, A.
20763	,,	Degan, F. G. W.	20022	,,	Frizzel, R.
20764	,,	Dowd, L.	20023	,,	Franklin, W. B.
20765	,,	Dier, W.	20024	,,	Fullerton, W. M.
20888	,,	Darling, J. R.	20236	,,	Ford, C. W.
20889	,,	Darley, C. B.	20177	,,	Ferris, G.
20891	,,	Denyer, W.	20896	,,	Fenn, W. J.
20892	,,	Dubois, J.	20311	,,	Foster, H.
20893	,,	Donald, T. W.	20477	,,	Frost, G. W.
20894	,,	Dennis, A.	20478	,,	Fitzbibben, A. G.
20895	,,	Deuchman, A. L.	20479	,,	Farmer, A. C.
20607	,,	Dougherty, L. D.	20480	,,	Furmstone, S. C.
20015	,,	Dick, C. G.	20481	,,	Farley, R.
20762	,,	Dent, S.	20482	,,	Findley, W. H.
20462	,,	Daniels, A.	20545	,,	Forbes, J. F.
19710	,,	Ellis, A.	20768	,,	Fraser, P. R.
19711	,,	Ellis, E.	20769	,,	Faulkner, G. K.
19853	,,	Enderton, H. F.	20484	,,	Goddard, W.
19854	,,	Esterbrook, F. H.	20485	,,	Gregory, R. A.
20016	,,	Elliott, W.	20486	,,	Gow, J. S.
20017	,,	Eggleston, A. H.	20487	,,	Grasby, R.
20018	,,	Embree, H. J.	19721	,,	Gardiner, W.
20249	,,	Earl, W.	19722	,,	Gerrard, E.
20176	,,	Ellis, H. A.	19723	,,	Ginn, H.

Canadian Pacific—The Empire's Greatest Railway.

10TH BATTALION, 4TH INFANTRY BRIGADE—cont.

Regl. No.	Rank.	Name.	Regl. No.	Rank.	Name.
19803	Private	Good, J.	19870	Private	Hawksworth, A. R.
19804	,,	Green, J.	19871	,,	Hilliam, W. M.
19857	,,	Gates, R.	19872	,,	Hallard, J.
19859	,,	Gold, C. W.	19873	,,	Hartman, W.
19861	,,	Griffiths, V. S.	19874	,,	Higginson, J.
19862	,,	Griffiths, N.	19875	,,	Hogg, J. E.
19863	,,	Gregor, W.	19943	,,	Hobbs, G. J.
19864	,,	Gilles, A.	20030	,,	Hunt, E.
19865	,,	Gryner, N.	20031	,,	Hudgins, J.
19866	,,	Gorse, B.	20032	,,	Horner, R.
19940	,,	Guy, E.	20033	,,	Herold, R.
20025	,,	Goodwin, G. A.	20034	,,	Hicky, W.
20027	,,	Gillies, W.	20035	,,	Houle, N.
20028	,,	Glover, J. G.	20036	,,	Hardy, J.
20029	,,	Genest, A.	20037	,,	Hassal, A. H.
20250	,,	Gilbert, F.	20251	,,	Hood, A. W.
20145	,,	Gunn, H.	20215	,,	Hewer, F. C.
20133	,,	Goodham, J.	20217	,,	Hulme, A.
20313	,,	Gerrish, H.	20178	,,	Howard, W.
20314	,,	Grassie, W. W.	20134	,,	Howard, F.
20315	,,	Gray, J.	20126	,,	Harries, A. R.
20316	,,	Greentree, G. D.	20127	,,	Hunt, F. C.
20391	,,	Goodall, H.	20132	,,	Horn, W. C.
20618	,,	Gilbert, J.	20217	,,	Henderson, J.
20621	,,	Gregory, T.	20317	,,	Hayman, A.
20622	,,	Gribben, T.	20318	,,	High, C.
20696	,,	Gorden, J.	20319	,,	Hurst, A.
20699	,,	Gold, D.	20320	,,	Hodges, C. W.
20770	,,	Gibb, F. S. M.	20321	,,	Horton, W. H.
20771	,,	Goddard, S. H.	20322	,,	Hughes, A.
20772	,,	Goodall, J.	20323	,,	Hutchinson, J.
20773	,,	Gorden, H.	20488	,,	Heron, A.
20774	,,	Gray, F. H.	20489	,,	Hansford, H.
20775	,,	Gwynn, C.	20490	,,	Hewett, B. L.
20897	,,	Galvin, J.	20491	,,	Hutchinson, C. G.
20899	,,	Gilmore, G.	20492	,,	Hughes, E. R.
19720	,,	Goldsworthy, J.	20495	,,	Hastings, W.
20026	,,	Googay, W. A.	20623	,,	Hague, W.
20925	,,	Gibb, G.	20624	,,	Hall, A. B.
19583	,,	Griffiths, W. J.	20625	,,	Hall, J. W.
19724	,,	Hadden, G. T.	20626	,,	Hall, E.
19725	,,	Hall, A. G.	20627	,,	Houlden, T.
19805	,,	Hall, H. C.	20628	,,	Hughes, A.
19726	,,	Hanna, W.	20629	,,	Hughes, G.
19727	,,	Harris, G.	20631	,,	Hunter, A.
19728	,,	Hayes, G.	20632	,,	Hayter, A.
19730	,,	Higgins, R.	20634	,,	Harkness, J.
19729	,,	Hill, E. A.	20635	,,	Hutton, J.
19732	,,	Hughes, A.	20776	,,	Henderson, A.
19867	,,	Hall, J. E.	20777	,,	Henderson, J.
19868	,,	Hatcher, C. F.	20778	,,	Henderson, J. R.
19869	,,	Hartling, R.	20779	,,	Holland, G.

Canadian Pacific—The Empire's Greatest Railway.

10TH BATTALION, 4TH INFANTRY BRIGADE—cont. 187

Regl. No.	Rank	Name.	Regl. No.	Rank	Name.
20780	Private	Holmes, J. S.	20494	Private	Knack, E.
20781	,,	Hoyer, N.	20496	,,	Kidd, T.
20900	,,	Howe, W. J.	20497	,,	Keeling, S. R.
20901	,,	Henry, J. E.	20498	,,	King, W.
20902	,,	Horne, R.	20638	,,	Karn, A.
20903	,,	Huxtable, H. J.	20639	,,	Keith, T.
19731	,,	Howard, J.	20640	,,	Keith, W. J.
20904	,,	Hammond, C.	20641	,,	Kennedy, T.
20273	,,	Hardy, G. H.	20642	,,	Kinman, G.
19634	,,	Hunt, L. W.	19743	,,	Latter, R. B.
20782	,,	Huston, M. S.	19806	,,	Leverton, J.
20431	,,	Hale, H.	19744	,,	Liveridge, J. F.
19876	,,	Irvine, D.	19883	,,	Little, W. J.
19734	,,	Johnson, F. W.	19884	,,	Lovatt, J.
19736	,,	Johnson, P.	19885	,,	Lovell, W.
19735	,,	Johnson, B.	20044	,,	Leeming, J. E.
19737	,,	Jones, F. T.	20045	,,	Lane, L.
19738	,,	Jones, T.	20253	,,	Less, P.
19877	,,	Johnson, H.	20254	,,	Lyons, A. D.
19935	,,	Jacons, W. H.	20235	,,	Lane, M. H.
19938	,,	Jennings, W.	20154	,,	Lee, G.
20038	,,	Jay, W.	20182	,,	Lamb, M.
20039	,,	Janoe, W.	20129	,,	Lawton, W.
20218	,,	Johnston, J.	20223	,,	Lewis, S. E.
20179	,,	Jorden, P.	20393	,,	Lewis, V.
20325	,,	Jackson, J. M.	20329	,,	Lindsay, J.
20326	,,	Johnstone, C. H.	20330	,,	Lipsett, W. A.
20493	,,	Jarvis, H. J.	20331	,,	Lowe, H.
20636	,,	Johnson, A. D.	20332	,,	Lunn, E. H.
20637	,,	Johnson, E. E.	20499	,,	Lane, W. G.
20783	,,	Jameson, E.	20500	,,	Lawrence, R.
20784	,,	Jeffray, W.	20502	,,	Leeman, L.
20785	,,	Jeffrey, W. W.	20503	,,	Lynch, J. C.
20786	,,	Johnstone, W.	20643	,,	Leahy, M.
20787	,,	Johnstone, W. H.	20691	,,	Lloyd, G.
20788	,,	Jackson, G.	20789	,,	Lawrence, A. E.
20905	,,	James, W.	20790	,,	Lennon, W. F.
20906	,,	Jackson, H.	20791	,,	Lever, W. F.
19739	,,	Kay, G. L.	20792	,,	Landen, W.
19740	,,	Kelly, W. H.	20907	,,	Lowe, W.
19742	,,	Kerr, A.	20501	,,	Lockart, G. M.
19878	,,	Keers, F.	19598	,,	Lawless, R.
18879	,,	Kiddie, A.	19882	,,	Lennie, R. F.
18880	,,	Kirkham, W.	19746	,,	Maxwell, A. W.
20041	,,	Kerss, J.	19749	,,	McCall, W. P.
20042	,,	Kennedy, A.	19750	,,	McDonald, Alex.
20043	,,	Koller, F. B.	19752	,,	MacDonald, R. M.
20252	,,	Komick, J.	19753	,,	McIvor, M.
20180	,,	Kearns, T.	19754	,,	McMaster, J.
20181	,,	Kneale, J.	19755	,,	McPherson, A. H.
20327	,,	Kerr, G.	19756	,,	McWilliams, F.
20392	,,	Kennedy, W.	19747	,,	Middleton, H.

Canadian Pacific—The Empire's Greatest Railway.

188　10TH BATTALION, 4TH INFANTRY BRIGADE—cont.

Regl. No.	Rank.	Name.	Regl. No.	Rank.	Name.
19748	Private	Mount, J. A.	20505	Private	McNiven, C. H.
19886	,,	Madge, W.	20506	,,	McGregor, P.
19889	,,	Martin, A. H.	20507	,,	Magee, A. M.
19888	,,	Marshall, S.	20508	,,	Moncrief, H.
19898	,,	Moore, G.	20509	,,	Moore, J. H.
19900	,,	Miller, J.	20510	,,	Morris, D. H.
19901	,,	Middleton, P.	20511	,,	Marshall, H.
19936	,,	Middleton, J.	20512	,,	Mangin, J.
19887	,,	MacRae, A.	20513	,,	Murray, A.
19890	,,	McCullough, A. H.	20703	,,	McKibben, J.
19891	,,	McFarlane, A.	20704	,,	McKew, E. J.
19892	,,	McGregor, R.	19937	,,	Marshall, A.
19893	,,	McGregor, W. R.	20645	,,	Martin, J.
19894	,,	McKenzie, D.	20646	,,	Martin, T. J.
19895	,,	McLachlan, W.	20647	,,	McClintock, J.
19897	,,	McNaughton, D.	20648	,,	MacDonald, W.
20046	,,	McFarlane, H. N.	20650	,,	McNeice, A.
20047	,,	McGovern, P.	20651	,,	Mills, G.
20048	,,	Marchant, F.	20652	,,	Murray, D. S.
20049	,,	Moore, R. E.	20694	,,	Maxwell, S.
20050	,,	Moorhouse, F.	20697	,,	Morish, C. R.
20255	,,	McGee, W. E.	20700	,,	Minshall, H.
20222	,,	McCormick, C. V.	20793	,,	McAllister, W. F.
20223	,,	McNaughton, H. P.	20794	,,	McCallum, J.
20157	,,	McVicar, J.	20795	,,	McClain, J. W.
20152	,,	McGaffin, H.	20796	,,	MacRae, G.
20220	,,	Melville, N.	20798	,,	Madsen, R.
20221	,,	Mertens, F.	20799	,,	Middleton, C.
20225	,,	Moore, A. H.	20800	,,	Mollison, A.
20226	,,	Morrison, T. J.	20801	,,	Morris, E.
20256	,,	Mead, G.	20909	,,	Morrison, D. W.
20257	,,	Maughan, W.	20910	,,	McDermott, J.
20183	,,	Montgomery, C. H.	20911	,,	Morrish, S.
20184	,,	Matthews, G.	20912	,,	McDonald, G.
20146	,,	Mack, C.	20913	,,	McMahon, R.
20333	,,	McAusland, R.	19808	,,	Moran, D.
20334	,,	McBride, J.	19751	,,	McDonald, A.
20335	,,	McDonald, M. D.	19896	,,	McDonald, J.
20336	,,	McDonald, N.	19594	,,	McWhirter, J.
20337	,,	McLean, A. J.	19640	,,	Marshall, A.
20338	,,	McLean, K.	19222	,,	McIntosh, J.
20339	,,	McLeod, G.	20737	,,	McLoughland, T.
20340	,,	McPherson, A.	19902	,,	Niven, B.
20341	,,	MacKenzie, D.	19903	,,	North, G.
20342	,,	Malcolm, S.	20051	,,	Niven, J.
20343	,,	Mansfield, T.	20052	,,	Noddle, M.
20344	,,	Matheson, J.	20185	,,	Nelson, E. E.
20346	,,	Miller, R.	20351	,,	Newcombe, F. C.
20347	,,	Milne, A.	20352	,,	Nicoll, W.
20348	,,	Monk, W.	20514	,,	Nash, F. H.
20349	,,	Morgan, M.	20653	,,	Neale, W. A.
20504	,,	McGuire, J.	20802	,,	Neale, W.

Canadian Pacific—The Empire's Greatest Railway.

10TH BATTALION, 4TH INFANTRY BRIGADE—cont.

Regl. No.	Rank.	Name.	Regl. No.	Rank.	Name.
19606	Private	Nickle, T. J.	19775	Private	Rowley, L.
19607	,,	Newn, D.	19908	,,	Riley, C.
19904	,,	Ogilvie, J.	19909	,,	Rigby, E. F.
19905	,,	Outham, W.	19910	,,	Ross, T. O.
20053	,,	Oddell, G.	19911	,,	Revell, G.
20054	,,	O'Dell, F.	20060	,,	Rideberg, R. W.
20055	,,	Oldridge, W.	20061	,,	Richards, G.
20259	,,	O'Brien, R.	20062	,,	Ross, J. G.
20260	,,	Ososky, H.	20063	,,	Ross, D.
20186	,,	O'Brien, J.	20261	,,	Ross, J.
20515	,,	O'Connell, J.	20262	,,	Rainez, J.
20655	,,	Old, A.	20263	,,	Rasmussen, O.
20656	,,	O'Leary, J. J.	20264	,,	Ricketts, L. J.
20803	,,	Osborne, H.	20153	,,	Ross, A.
20804	,,	Owen, S.	20189	,,	Ross, F.
19757	,,	Paradise, F. G.	20188	,,	Royce, A. E.
19758	,,	Park, C.	20358	,,	Rabone, S.
19759	,,	Peterson, G. L.	20359	,,	Rafferty, T. P.
19761	,,	Portch, E. J.	20360	,,	Ramsden, W.
19762	,,	Prince, W.	20361	,,	Renton, S.
19906	,,	Patton, S. H.	20362	,,	Richardson, D. A.
19907	,,	Peck, R. G.	20389	,,	Richardson, G.
19939	,,	Pennec, A.	20363	,,	Robins, C.
20056	,,	Pascoe, H.	20364	,,	Robins, J. F.
20057	,,	Patton, J. S.	20365	,,	Roy, J.
20058	,,	Porter, J. E.	20366	,,	Russell, O. S.
20059	,,	Prew, A.	20518	,,	Reynolds, J.
20227	,,	Pinnock, W.	20519	,,	Roughton, C. G.
20228	,,	Poulton, E.	20520	,,	Roughton, B. P.
20187	,,	Purmal, W.	20523	,,	Rosenroll, A. S.
20354	,,	Peterson, C.	20657	,,	Ramsey, A.
20355	,,	Pope, C.	20658	,,	Roulston, W. G.
20356	,,	Porter, J. L.	20809	,,	Rees, J. V.
20357	,,	Prandy, F. D.	20810	,,	Reid, W. J.
20516	,,	Pearce, E.	20811	,,	Rimmer, L. J.
20517	,,	Prince, N.	20812	,,	Robinson, A. W.
20805	,,	Pack, A. B.	20813	,,	Robison, N. J.
20806	,,	Phillips, A.	20814	,,	Rocher, D. A.
20807	,,	Pearson, G. W. R.	20815	,,	Roy, R. W.
20808	,,	Price, G. F.	20916	,,	Ritchie, E. G.
19760	,,	Pinkerton, R.	20917	,,	Reynolds, S.
20094	,,	Page, G.	20918	,,	Rutledge, W. J.
20533	,,	Perdian, E. D.	19766	,,	Rickner, S.
20534	,,	Parker, R.	19771	,,	Rottenberg, M.
20535	,,	Parsons, W.	19599	,,	Richards, H.
19763	,,	Quay, J.	19627	,,	Ringrose, F.
19765	,,	Reid, F. J.	19776	,,	Sangsetr, J. W.
19767	,,	Robertson, A.	19777	,,	Sexton, F. J.
19768	,,	Robertson, J.	19809	,,	Shaw, J.
19769	,,	Robinson, J. A.	19783	,,	Simpkin, J.
19773	,,	Rockwell, W.	19784	,,	Simpson, J.
19774	,,	Ross, J. H.	19779	,,	Stevens, H.

Canadian Pacific—The Empire's Greatest Railway.

190   10TH BATTALION, 4TH INFANTRY BRIGADE—cont.

Regl. No.	Rank.	Name.	Regl. No.	Rank.	Name.
19780	Private	Stevenson, S.	20544	Private	Smith, J.
19781	,,	Stockall, F. A.	20524	,,	Shaver, E. W.
19912	,,	Sherlock, W. J.	20525	,,	Stone, E.
19913	,,	Sixby, F.	20526	,,	Sinclair, A. G.
19916	,,	Simpson, H.	20527	,,	Smith, A. G. H.
19914	,,	Smylie, R.	20528	,,	Simpson, R.
19915	,,	Smith, H. R.	20529	,,	Sattin, A.
19917	,,	Steele, L.	20530	,,	Smith, J. W.
19918	,,	Stewart, R.	20543	,,	Starky, C. S.
19919	,,	Stone, H.	20166	,,	Small, S.
19920	,,	St. Pierre, J.	20659	,,	Selby, G.
19921	,,	Secord, G.	20660	,,	Sergeant, J. H.
20064	,,	Simmons, G.	20661	,,	Sharrah, R. W
20065	,,	Sutherland, W.	20662	,,	Shoesmith, F.
20066	,,	Scott, E.	20663	,,	Smith, B.
20067	,,	Sharratt, F.	20664	,,	Sharp, J.
20068	,,	Simpson, H. J.	20665	,,	Smith, R.
20069	,,	Slater, F.	20666	,,	Skelton, J.
20070	,,	Spalding, C.	20668	,,	Stair, H. J.
20071	,,	Slye, P.	20669	,,	Standring, G.
20072	,,	Saville, T.	20706	,,	Smith, E. G.
20073	,,	Sheard, A.	20816	,,	Shiels, R.
20074	,,	Swann, H. B.	20817	,,	Simmonds, W. R.
20075	,,	Stephens, E.	20818	,,	Smith, A. H.
20076	,,	Smith, W.	20819	,,	Stinson, W. H.
20077	,,	Shelden, L. I.	20820	,,	Stirling, J. B.
20265	,,	Smith, D.	20821	,,	Street, C. M.
20266	,,	Stevenson, A.	20822	,,	Stubbs, J. P.
20229	,,	Sewell, S.	20823	,,	Swanson, J. W.
20232	,,	Sharp, F.	20761	,,	Smith, A.
20190	,,	Shipp, W.	20747	,,	Smith, E. L.
20191	,,	Springett, C.	19778	,,	Spectre, N.
20192	,,	Salmon, A. P.	19604	,,	Spalding, G. B.
20149	,,	Scott, A.	19595	,,	Stephenson, G. L.
20142	,,	Schofield, G.	19596	,,	Stephenson, V. E.
20135	,,	Starfield, S.	20531	,,	Tonkin, F. S.
20194	,,	Sherman, P.	20532	,,	Towers, J. A.
20367	,,	Samson, W. E.	20546	,,	Toole, A. M.
20368	,,	Sawers, O. C.	20701	,,	Trout, W.
20369	,,	Scott, J.	20690	,,	Tawse, W.
20370	,,	Secord, W.	20670	,,	Tallents, G.
20371	,,	Sherman, Albert	20671	,,	Thomson, A.
20372	,,	Sloan, R.	20673	,,	Tozer, W.
20373	,,	Soman, L. A.	19787	,,	Trebble, W.
20374	,,	Somers, J.	19922	,,	Terriss, J.
20375	,,	Somerset, V. H.	19923	,,	Thurston, J.
20376	,,	Stokes, H.	19924	,,	Thomas, D. R.
20377	,,	Smith, G.	19925	,,	Thomas, E.
20378	,,	Smith, H. R.	19926	,,	Travis, D. H.
20379	,,	Smythe, L. W.	19927	,,	Turner, W.
20380	,,	Stephens, W. J.	20078	,,	Taylor, N. V.
20381	,,	Sutton, P. V.	20079	,,	Taylor, A.

Canadian Pacific—The Empire's Greatest Railway.

10TH BATTALION, 4TH INFANTRY BRIGADE—cont.

Regl. No.	Rank	Name	Regl. No.	Rank	Name
20080	Private	Taylor, G.	20088	Private	White, S. W.
20081	,,	Tunnicliffe, H.	20089	,,	Whyte, M.
20082	,,	Tucker, W.	20090	,,	Watson, W.
20083	,,	Thirwell, H.	20091	,,	Wauchope, R. F.
20140	,,	Totton, W.	20092	,,	Watts, C. C.
20144	,,	Taylor, R. W.	20268	,,	Williams, A. E.
20233	,,	Thomson, W.	20269	,,	Wheatley, E. A.
20267	,,	Thomas, W. H.	20270	,,	Wood, C. M.
20382	,,	Tait, J.	20156	,,	Walpole, W. C.
20383	,,	Thompson, H.	20147	,,	Williams, W.
20824	,,	Taylor, J. C.	20384	,,	Watson, H. A.
20825	,,	Trim, G. K.	20385	,,	White, R.
20827	,,	Tilley, A.	20386	,,	Wilson, R. C.
20826	,,	Trimm, F. W.	20387	,,	Wooley, W.
20828	,,	Turnbull, J. H.	20537	,,	Watson, J. D.
20920	,,	Tasker, L.	20538	,,	Wilson, G.
20672	,,	Torrington, C. D. W.	20539	,,	Wilson, S.
19811	,,	Tee, H.	20541	,,	Wright, A.
19602	,,	Thompson, R. A.	20542	,,	Webb, W. G.
19608	,,	Templeton, N.	20674	,,	Walker, E. T.
20839	,,	Upton, F.	30675	,,	Walker, R.
19788	,,	Valentine, W. R.	20676	,,	Webster, T.
19810	,,	Van Achter, P.	20677	,,	West, G.
19789	,,	Vincent, G.	20681	,,	Wyness, G.
20084	,,	Van Beeston, J.	20688	,,	West, A. C.
20085	,,	Vowell, G. A.	20693	,,	Whitney, W.
20536	,,	Viner, H.	20830	,,	Wade, W.
20695	,,	Vernon, W.	20831	,,	Watson, W. S.
20829	,,	Vincent, D. G.	20832	,,	Watson, F. G.
19928	,,	Vieullemier, A.	20680	,,	Winters, C.
19792	,,	Walsh, G.	20833	,,	Walkner, H.
19812	,,	Walpole, W.	20834	,,	Warner, W. E.
19796	,,	Webb, J. T.	20835	,,	Williams, A.
19791	,,	Wennerold, J.	20836	,,	Wills, J. G.
19792	,,	Whitmarsh, T. H.	20837	,,	Wisdom, P. W.
19793	,,	Willmore, C.	20921	,,	Wheelan, A.
19794	,,	Wilson, J.	20922	,,	Waller, J.
19929	,,	Watson, P.	20923	,,	Wilson, M.
19930	,,	Wells, E.	19790	,,	Woods, A.
19931	,,	Wheatley, R.	20540	,,	Wilson, L. R.
19932	,,	White, S.	20679	,,	Wibrow, D.
19933	,,	Watkins, M.	19592	,,	Wright, C. H.
19934	,,	Williams, R. E.	20388	,,	Williams, J.
19945	,,	Willingham, R. A.	20234	,,	Younghusband, J.
20086	,,	Williams, D. B.	19593	,,	Young, N. T.
20087	,,	Wilson, C.	20924	,,	Zuidema, L.

Water Detail.

Regl. No.	Rank	Name	Regl. No.	Rank	Name
33646	Corpl.	Lockington, W.	33649	Private	Tribe, H.
33647	Private	Mills, R.	33650	,,	Buchanan, W.
33648	,,	Dale, T.			

Canadian Pacific—The Empire's Greatest Railway.

10TH BATTALION, 4TH INFANTRY BRIGADE—cont.

Batmen.

Regl. No.	Rank.	Name.	Regl. No.	Rank.	Name.
19628	Private	Foster, R.	19633	Private	Workman, F.
19629	,,	Kaves, J. H.	19636	,,	Davidson, R. W.
19630	,,	Smith, R. P.	19637	,,	Schultz, S.
19632	,,	Van Skipdale			

Machine Gun Section.

19610	Sergt.	Swayne	19618	Private	Bennett, A. W.
19609	Corpl.	Colomb, H.	19619	,,	Brown, W.
19611	Private	Marshall, S. W.	19620	,,	Carnell, W.
19612	,,	O'Rourke, D.	19621	,,	Hogarth, G.
19613	,,	Higgins, C. F.	19622	,,	Dobbs, S. H.
19614	,,	Foss, A.	19623	,,	Howard, P.
19615	,,	Lay, F.	19634	,,	McLaughland, A
19616	,,	Allen, S. W.	19635	,,	Harrison, A.
19617	,,	Palmer, J.			

Signallers.

19582	Sergt.	Turner, S.	19588	Private	Perry, E. C.
19584	Private	Morrison, C.	19589	,,	King, H. W.
19585	,,	Wilson, R.	19690	,,	Nive, C.
19586	,,	Nowell, A.	19691	,,	Burley, G.
19587	,,	Doig, C. L.			

Buglers.

20588	Fairhurst, R.	20362	Roberts, W. G.
20237	Somerset, S. A.		

11th BATTALION, 4th INFANTRY BRIGADE.

HEADQUARTERS.

Officer Commanding ...	Lieut.-Colonel Royal Burritt
Second-in-Command ...	,, Anson Dulmage
Major ...	Major Joseph George Wayne
Adjutant ...	,, Daniel William Bigelow Spry
Asst. Adjutant ...	Captain John McAughey
Machine Gun Officer ...	Lieutenant Stanley Peter Stewart Capt
Chaplain ...	Hon. Captain Alfred B. Payne
Transport Officer ...	Lieutenant Stanley Hall Mitchell
Paymaster ...	Hon. Captain Theodore Tyson Kirkby
Signalling Officer ...	Lieutenant Frederick Thomas Nichol
Quartermaster ...	,, George Stephen Spindler
Medical Officer ...	,, Stanley Gordon Chown

Canadian Pacific—The Empire's Greatest Railway.

11TH BATTALION, 4TH INFANTRY BRIGADE—cont.

Subordinate Staff.

Regl. No.	Rank.	Name.	Regl. No.	Rank.	Name.
21054	Sgt.-Maj.	Boston, Joseph H.	21101	Cook Sgt.	Thorpe, William J.
21077	Q.M.Sgt.	Morris, William	21093	Trs. Sgt.	Sutherland, John
21078	O.R.Sgt.	Morris, H. B.	22160	Sgl. Sgt.	Stubbington, Wm.
21079	Sgt.-Dmr.	Morley, William D. E.	21784	Shoe Sgt.	Waite, R.
21197	Pnr. Sgt.	Wilson, Charles			

Signallers.

21332	Private	Ashton, Samuel	22157	Private	Longley, E. F.
21058	,,	Craig, Andrew A.	21084	,,	Norris, J.
21068	,,	Jarvis, Frank	22156	,,	Thomas, William
21069	,,	Kosakoski, W. O.	21104	,,	Vose, E.

Orderlies to Medical Officer.

21100	Corpl.	Tait, Andrew	21062	Private	Dunsmore, J.

Drivers 1st Line Transport.

21797	Private	Balfour, R. E.	21087	Private	Page, John
21315	,,	Campbell, R.	21089	,,	Peyton, Charles G.
21812	,,	Currie, W.	21090	,,	Powers, Thomas W.
21064	,,	Garvie, Parker	22110	,,	Sherwood, H.
21065	,,	Hunt, John William	21097	,,	Sherwood, Henry F.
22170	,,	Irwin, Thomas K.	21096	,,	Spence, Thomas H.
22177	,,	McLean, Donald	21206	,,	Stringer, J. H.
21493	,,	McKie, S. R. J	21913	,,	White, John S

Batmen and Grooms.

21053	Private	Baxter, William F.	21081	Private	Mann, Alexander
21055	,,	Bouvier, George S.	21083	,,	McAughey, Alex. B.
21057	,,	Chisholm, Charles W.	21080	,,	McLean, Charles
21059	,,	Croucher, Charles	21103	,,	Tiplady, John W.
21149	,,	Flanagan, D. L.	22195	,,	Wilson, James
21070	,,	Knight, George H.	21106	,,	Whitnell, William
21071	,,	Leviston, James	21915	,,	Wright, H. H.

Machine Gun Section.

21095	Sergt.	Sanders, Horace R.	21082	Private	McLeod, John K.
21098	Corpl.	Travis, Charles Lea	21085	,,	Nicholson, Ewen
21052	Private	Bentley, William H.	21091	,,	Randle, Samuel J.
21061	,,	Donaldson, John	21094	,,	Sinclair, John M.
21066	,,	Hall, Albert Charles	21102	,,	Tamkin, Charles E.
21073	,,	Martin, Samuel H. C.	21099	,,	Taylor, Wilfrid V.
21076	,,	Miles, Robert	22190	,,	Kelly, John

Canadian Pacific—The Empire's Greatest Railway.

11TH BATTALION, 4TH INFANTRY BRIGADE—cont.

Drivers.

Regl. No.	Rank.	Name.	Regl. No.	Rank.	Name.
21067	Private	Henderson, John T.	21088	Private	Perry, Charles Henry

Batman.

21072 Private Lockett, Walter

C.A.M.C.

33651	Corpl.	Holmes, Arthur E.
33655	Private	Harding, W. M. G.
33653	,,	Jackson, William
33654	,,	Sharp, James E.
33652	,,	Turner, Richard J.

Watermen.

21105	Arm.Sgt.Maj.	Wünsch, G. S.
21060	Pay Sgt.	Cottam, James M.
21075	Prov. Sgt.	Munn, Victor H.
21074	Sgt.Mr.-Tr.	Moffatt, Walter
21122	O.R. Sgt.	Bent, L. L.

Band.

22149	Band Sgt.	Vail, Sidney
22125	Lce.-Cpl.	Haynes, Wm. (Bass Drummer)
22163	Bands'n.	Alexander, William (Drummer)
22153	,,	Andrews, Leonard H.
22152	,,	Atherton, H. (Bugler)
22151	,,	Behde, William
22150	,,	Bosworth, Ernest
22121	,,	Carlile, Albert D.
22123	,,	Cartwright, Thomas
21126	,,	Crouch, Albert Victor (Bugler)
22120	,,	Cumbers, William J.
22148	,,	Denholme, John
22124	,,	Eden, Harry
22127	,,	Gavin, James D. M.
22126	,,	Harrow, Sidney
22128	,,	Hill, Hedley
22129	,,	Hill, John Edward
22130	Bands'n.	Kay, Stanley
22131	,,	Kerr, James
22132	,,	Kerr, John Robertson
22133	,,	Knowles, Wm. A. G. (Bugler)
22134	,,	Lucas, G. W. (Bugler)
22135	,,	Moore, Thomas
22138	,,	Moore, Walter Edw.
22139	,,	McBurnie, John
22136	,,	McKenzie, John H. (Bugler)
22137	,,	McPherson, Wm. C.
22141	,,	Phythian, Douglas G.
22140	,,	Pottinger, Stanley Victor (Bugler)
22143	,,	Sullivan, P.
22144	,,	Swain, Edgar
22145	,,	Whitley, F. (Bugler)
22146	,,	Wood, David

"A" COMPANY.

Major ... ... McClelland, Samuel
Lieutenant ... ... Oulster, Gordon Dixon
,, ... Macfarlane, William George

Regl. No.	Rank.	Name.	Regl. No.	Rank.	Name.
21121	Col.-Sgt.	Brander, Alastair Ian	21163	Sergt.	Hunt, F. J.
21110	Sergt.	Alderson, Francis	21132	Corpl.	Cox, John
21118	,,	Brown, Ernest R.	21155	,,	Geddes, Benjamin
21063	,,	Ford, R. A.	21125	,,	Ball, Charles Edward
21171	,,	Lesser, Paul Fredk.	21133	,,	Coulling, Frederick

Canadian Pacific—The Empire's Greatest Railway.

11TH BATTALION, 4TH INFANTRY BRIGADE—cont.

Regl. No.	Rank	Name
21219	Corpl.	Wood, John
22119	Bugler	Crouch, Alfred J.
21218	Lce.-Cpl.	Windle, Richd. H. C.
21196	,,	Smith, Richd. Walter
21166	,,	Joiner, Percy
21215	,,	Woolston, Alfd.Thos.
21158	,,	Harrison, Wm. R. C.
21114	,,	Van Buskirk, Frank
21111	Private	Adams, A. H.
21123	,,	Beaton, Percy
21124	,,	Bannister, Harry
21120	,,	Brearley, Ernest V.
21119	,,	Brown, Charles
21117	,,	Brown, Thos. Howard
21116	,,	Buckley, Ernest
21115	,,	Bulmer, Leslie Thos.
21113	,,	Byers, Fredk. Chas.
21112	,,	Byers, Thomas Wm.
21138	,,	Campbell, Gordon H.
21137	,,	Chamberlain, Albert
21136	,,	Chislett, Arthur J.
21135	,,	Coleman, Walter L.
21134	,,	Cooper, Arthur
21131	,,	Cramb, George T.
21129	,,	Crampton, Walter
21130	,,	Cranmer, William J.
21128	,,	Cranwell, V. A. B.
21127	,,	Croasdell, Edward S.
21139	,,	Dailley, C. P.
21142	,,	Daly, Edward Thos.
21141	,,	Dewar, Joseph
21140	,,	Dodwell, Geo. P. V.
21145	,,	Eakins, Arth. Henry
21144	,,	Eaton, Frank Herbt.
21143	,,	Evans, James
21151	,,	Fairhurst, Albert
21150	,,	Ferguson, Arth. J. D.
21148	,,	Fournier, Edwd. R.
21147	,,	Fowler, Robert Geo.
21146	Signaller	Foxley, John
21154	Private	George, Alex.
21153	,,	Gibson, Jas. Belford
21152	,,	Gorringe, Thomas
21156	,,	Hardy, Harold Wm.
21157	,,	Harrison, Ralph C.
21159	,,	Heaslip, David
21162	,,	Holdsworth, Harold
21161	,,	Hooper, Albert
21164	,,	Hunt, Frank Wm.
21165	,,	Illingsworth, H. E.
21167	,,	Kingsley, Percy L.
21168	Private	Knight, Arth. Ernest
21169	,,	Knowles, Wm. Henry
21170	Arm.Cpl.	Lawrence, C.
21172	Private	Lewis, J. H.
21223	,,	Lines, Wm. George
21173	,,	Lintott, Cuthbert W.
21180	,,	Martin, George
21178	,,	Martin, Harry
21174	,,	Miles, Herbert Jas.
21177	Lce.-Sgt.	McDerment, Wm.
21176	Private	McGillivray, Angus
21179	,,	McKenzie, Thomas
21181	,,	Newport, Walter
21182	,,	Noble, Albert Victor
21183	,,	Nolan, John Patrick
21175	,,	Murphy, Michael
22179	,,	O'Mara, John Walter
21184	,,	Pargeter, Bruce
21185	,,	Parsons, Owen
21186	,,	Payne, Percy Chas.
21187	,,	Potter, George Jas.
21188	,,	Pritchard, Chas. A.
21189	,,	Purdy, Jas. Ringland
21190	Signaller	Quigley, Harry S.
21194	Private	Reynolds, Geo.Edwd.
21195	,,	Richardson,Fredk.H.
21191	,,	Riley, Harry
21192	,,	Robertson,John Wm.
21193	,,	Ryall, Thomas Geo.
21198	,,	Saunders, Salter A.
21197	,,	Savoy, Joseph M.
21199	,,	Scott, Morly Victor
21200	,,	Sellar, Gerald
22191	,,	Shinn, Max Robert
21201	,,	Simpson, Harry
21203	,,	Stewart, George
21204	,,	Stoddard, Wm. John
21205	,,	Strachan, Edward M.
21207	,,	Sudds, Fredk.Stanley
21208	,,	Swain, Thomas
21209	,,	Talbot, Ernest Arth.
21210	,,	Teer, John Mark
21211	,,	Thoday, Fras. H. A.
21213	,,	Vicary, Thos. Alex.
21212	,,	Voysey, Albt. Sidney
21216	,,	Walton, Harry
21217	,,	Wermig, Sidney
21220	,,	Worsey, Thos. Arthr.
21214	,,	Wright Daniel
21221	Bugler	Wright, Fred. G.
21222	Private	Young, Thomas

Canadian Pacific—The Empire's Greatest Railway.

11TH BATTALION, 4TH INFANTRY BRIGADE—cont.

"B" COMPANY.

Captain ... ... Lindsay, Charles D.
Lieutenant ... ... Carey, Leo Joseph
,, ... Warner, Gerald Lyman
,, ... Hudson, E. A.

Regl. No.	Rank.	Name.	Regl. No.	Rank.	Name.
21302	Col.-Sgt.	Guest, Ralph	21299	Private	Grey, Alfred Ewing
21255	Sergt.	Perriam, Harold	21298	,,	Green, Reginald J.
21259	,,	North, Frederick J.	21301	,,	Groves, Vaughan
21297	,,	Henderson, Percy E.	21293	,,	Hadman, Alfred
21295	,,	Hammersley, F. G.	21291	,,	Hall, Christopher W.
21300	Corpl.	Grills, Norman H.	21294	,,	Harris, Walter John
21296	,,	Harris, George W.	21289	,,	Hicks, Percy Alec
21412	,,	Neve, Albert James	21288	,,	Hives, Herbert
21230	,,	Wheatland, A. J.	21292	,,	Howard, Gunlangur
21224	Lce.-Cpl.	Edmonds, F. A.	21290	,,	Hudson, Leslie
21329	,,	Bruce, John Alex.	22159	,,	Humphrey, J. Geo.
21225	,,	Cundal, William J.	21287	Str.B'rer.	Hutton, Charles P.
21312	,,	Dukelow, Jack	21286	Private	Jack, Edward R.
21237	,,	Thompson, Harry M.	21285	,,	Jamison, Frederick
21231	,,	Webb, Harold R.	21284	,,	Johnson, Walter
22122	Bugler	Carey, Joseph M.	21283	,,	Johnston, Albert V.
21330	Private	Allen, James Alfred	21108	,,	Jones, Charles E.
21331	,,	Arnold, Edward	21282	,,	Kennett, George A.
21326	,,	Bass, Francis John	21281	,,	King, Samuel
21226	,,	Balfour, Fred W.	21280	Bugler	Leafe, Thomas
22192	,,	Beatty, William T.	21279	Private	Legg, Percy B.
21327	,,	Bowen, William	21278	,,	Leydon, James J.
21328	,,	Bradley, William	21277	Signaller	Little, Donald A. D.
22118	,,	Budd, Clement	21276	Private	Logan, William
21313	,,	Caldwell, Robert	21275	,,	Lucas, Frederick C.
21314	,,	Cameron, F. J.	21267	,,	Maguire, Edward E.
21056	Signaller	Carey, P.	21264	,,	Markusson, T. E.
21316	Private	Carleton, Hugh J.	21274	,,	Menzies, William
21317	,,	Chalk, Alfred H.	21273	,,	Merritt, Robert
21318	,,	Charles, Daniel	21271	,,	Mills, Frederick E.
21321	,,	Coulton, George	21272	,,	Mills, Percy William
21322	,,	Cowley, Albert E.	21262	,,	Mortimer, Herbert G.
21319	,,	Cober, Albert H.	21270	,,	Moss, Arthur
21323	,,	Cox, Roland J.	21269	,,	Mullin, Robert J.
21324	,,	Craig, John Bishop	21268	,,	Muschik, Percy
21325	,,	Currie, Thomas A.	21263	,,	McAllister, Samuel
21309	,,	Dickenson, C. E.	21266	,,	McCarthy, Patrick J.
21310	,,	Dixon, George	21265	,,	McKinnon, D. E.
21311	,,	Downie, Thomas	21261	,,	McMullin, Robert
21308	,,	Ellison, Joseph	21260	,,	Nickle, William
21305	,,	Fox, James	21258	,,	Page, Walter F.
21304	,,	Foster, Reginald L.	21257	,,	Pearce, William J.
21306	,,	Fricker, Arthur J.	21256	,,	Perkin, George B.
21307	,,	Frith, L. E. C.	21249	,,	Phillips, Charles H.
21303	,,	Garrison, William R.	21254	,,	Pinnette, Joseph R.

Canadian Pacific—The Empire's Greatest Railway.

11TH BATTALION, 4TH INFANTRY BRIGADE—cont.

Regl. No.	Rank.	Name.	Regl. No.	Rank.	Name.
21253	Private	Piper, John	21240	Private	Spencer, Albert
22161	,,	Potts, William M.	21241	,,	Stevens, Augustus G.
21252	,,	Preston, John	21239	,,	Tait, Frank Lionel
21251	,,	Pritchard, Harry	21238	,,	Teulon, E.
21250	,,	Proctor, Sydney	21235	,,	Thompson, Herbert
21248	,,	Rock, Robert Henry	21236	,,	Tilbrook, William H.
21246	,,	Rodriguez, R. M.	21234	,,	Urquhart, James
21247	,,	Rose, Harold	21233	,,	Waterhouse, Fred
21245	Arm. Cpl.	Russell, William J.	21232	,,	Watts, Thomas A.
21243	Private	Seager, Frank W.	21229	,,	Wheatland, T. H.
21242	,,	Simmonds, P. C. K.	21228	,,	White, Edgar H.
21244	,,	Simpson, A. R.	21227	,,	Wilkinson, Albert

"C" COMPANY.

Captain	... ...	Walker, Phillip
,,	... ...	Fairbrother, R.
Lieutenant	... ...	Seller, Raymond
,,	... ...	Kirby, Walter Lennard

Regl. No.	Rank.	Name.	Regl. No.	Rank.	Name.
21436	Col.-Sgt.	West, Edward Lynn	21355	Private	Capatos, Phillip
21401	Sergt.	Nicholas, Griffith	21353	,,	Chignell, Stephen
21354	,,	Casey, David	21345	,,	Clayson, James C.
21404	,,	Playfair, George S.	21352	,,	Coleman, Roy R.
21377	,,	Jilks, James Edwin	21351	,,	Colin, Ralph
21416	Corpl.	Robbins, Roy Russell	21350	,,	Coulter, Albert
21407	,,	Peaty, Fred Albert	21349	,,	Coulter, Samuel S.
21397	,,	McAllister, Archie	21346	,,	Cox, Sidney Percival
21418	,,	Scott, John	21348	,,	Curmi, Alfred
21419	,,	Stocker, William V.	21347	,,	Currell, Ernest A.
21368	Lce.-Cpl.	Glen, William F.	21361	,,	Davison, Samuel M.
21376	,,	James, John	21360	,,	Dean, Frank
21417	,,	Saunders, James A.	21358	,,	Delacour, Edward B.
21427	,,	Tease, Finlay Gregg	22045	,,	Duckworth, James
21435	,,	Watson, Daniel G.	21357	,,	Duncan, Roy McD.
21335	Private	Algeo, Luther	21356	,,	Duval, Merlin K.
21334	,,	Allan, William	21362	,,	Ford, Jeremiah
21333	Str.-B'rer	Amison, Thomas	21363	,,	Faircloth, John T.
21343	,,	Barnes, Richard G.	21836	,,	Gendron, Albert J.
21344	Private	Barratt, Henry G.	21367	,,	Goodman, Sigurdur
21342	,,	Bathie, William	21364	,,	Gowenlock, C. P.
21340	,,	Bennett, George T.	21365	Scout	Gosling, William
21341	,,	Bennett, Arthur S.	21371	Private	Halliday, Alfred
21446	Pioneer	Bennetts, R. W.	21370	,,	Harbour, C. Wm.
21339	Private	Booth, Frederick L.	21369	,,	Harbour, Edward V.
21338	,,	Booth, Thomas	21372	Scout	Hay, Campbell S.
21336	,,	Bradshaw, John F.	21373	Private	Horsfield, Roderick
21359	,,	Brown, Clifford	22197	,,	Horsfield, R. S.

Canadian Pacific—The Empire's Greatest Railway.

198 11TH BATTALION, 4TH INFANTRY BRIGADE—cont.

Regl. No.	Rank.	Name.	Regl. No.	Rank.	Name.
21374	Private	Howlett, Benjamin J.	21408	Arm. Cpl.	Paquette, George E.
22154	,,	Hunter, Robert Swan	21410	Str.-B'rer	Richmond, A. Wm.
21375	,,	Inman, Edward	21411	Private	Roberts, Victor
21378	,,	James, Sidney Chris.	21413	,,	Roberts, William
21384	,,	Kitchen, John	21414	,,	Robertson, Allen S.
21382	,,	Kirk, Sidney Arthur	21415	Bugler	Russell, Charles
21380	Signaller	Kerr, Peter Robertson	21420	Private	Scott, William J.
21381	Private	Kerr, William Alfred	21421	Signaller	Seller, Harold Lorne
21383	,,	Kirkwood, Rex O.	21422	Private	Skelton, Chas. G. G.
21385	,,	Law, James	21423	,,	Skillicorn, Douglas
21386	,,	Law, William	21424	,,	Smith, Marshall G.
21387	,,	Lockhart, James	21425	,,	Speers, Thomas
21388	,,	Lucas, Charles S.	21426	,,	Sutherland, Hugh
91393	,,	Mackey, James O.	21428	Scout	Thompson, John
21400	,,	Main, Arthur	21429	Private	Thompson William
21389	,,	Matthews, James E.	21430	,,	Thorogood, T. F.
21390	,,	Moore, Herbert E.	21431	Corpl.	Tomlin, E. (Mtd. Pol.)
21391	,,	Moore, Percival P.	21432	Private	Towns, Archibald
21396	,,	McDonald, John D.	21433	,,	Trotter, George A.
21395	,,	McGimpsie, James C.	21441	,,	Wells, Jack Warren
21394	,,	McGregor, Peter	21438	,,	Walters, Donald
21392	,,	McKee, James P.	21437	,,	Walker, Thomas
21398	,,	McLean, Robt. Alex.	21434	,,	Warn, Reginald A.
21399	Bugler	McPherson, Harold	21439	,,	Watson, John Robt.
21402	Private	Ollard, Francis D.	21442	,,	Westwood, William
21405	,,	Pearce, Arthur	21443	,,	White, Arthur B.
21406	,,	Peebles, Andrew A.	21445	,,	Williamson, Fred O.
21409	,,	Pether, Ernest Paul	21444	,,	White, Charles S.
22189	,,	Polaski, Sam	21447	Str.-B'rer	Young, Archibald
21403	,,	Pollard, Walker B.			

"D" COMPANY

Captain	...	MacLean, Archibald
Lieutenant	... ...	Clinskill, James Thomas
,,	... ...	MacDermid, John Edgar
,,	... ...	Sparling, A. W.

Regl. No.	Rank.	Name.	Regl. No.	Rank.	Name.
21483	Col.-Sgt.	Henderson, John L.	21550	Lce.-Cpl.	Beveridge, John F.
21525	Sergt.	Tait, James M.	21515	,,	Robinson, Frederick
21505	,,	O'Brien, Harold	21518	,,	Shaw, Horace F.
21478	,,	Hay, William Reid	21531	,,	Ward, Robert
21526	,,	Tinkess, Ivan W.	21535	,,	Webster, Arthur E.
21557	Private	Anderson, John	22164	Private	Adamson, Roland F.
21546	Corpl.	Baker, J. S.	21560	,,	Armstrong, Cecil
21453	,,	Costello, Francis Geo.	21561	,,	Austin, T. C. Bert
21528	,,	Tressider, Geo. Hen.	21549	,,	Balfe, Lewis N.
21537	,,	Winchurst, Arthur	21553	,,	Beattie, William J.

Canadian Pacific—The Empire's Greatest Railway.

11TH BATTALION, 4TH INFANTRY BRIGADE—cont.

Regl. No.	Rank.	Name.
21552	Private	Bimson, George
21555	,,	Bissett, James
21545	,,	Boddington, Wm. F.
21548	,,	Brannan, Peter R.
21547	,,	Brinton, Lyle
21556	,,	Bloxam, George B.
21551	,,	Brown, George
21554	,,	Byers, R.
21457	,,	Calder, David
21459	,,	Campbell, William
21449	,,	Chambers, Stanley W.
21541	,,	Code, J. H.
21456	,,	Cobbin, Frank B.
21454	,,	Coffin, Chas. Leland
21542	,,	Collins, Ernest W. F.
21543	Signaller	Cooling, Chris. L.
21544	Private	Couchman, Gerald E.
21455	,,	Caunter, Henry
21451	,,	Coverly, Philip W.
21458	,,	Cowley, Harry R.
21452	,,	Cox, Frank Stanley
21450	,,	Cutter, Charles J.
21460	,,	Davis, Wilson
21462	,,	Dempsey, Otto L.
21461	,,	Desjarlais, George
21463	,,	Dowling, Timothy
21464	,,	English, George Wm.
21468	,,	Field, George
21467	,,	Fifield, Roy M.
21465	,,	Franklin, Chas. W. H.
21466	,,	Frederickson, W. F.
21469	,,	Gabbitas, Joseph
21471	,,	Gagen, Guy S.
21472	,,	German, John H.
21476	,,	Gibson, James
21475	,,	Giroux, Jos. Homer
21474	,,	Godfrey Frank L.
21473	,,	Gordon, David E.
21470	,,	Guy, Frederick J.
21481	,,	Hallamm, Arthur G.
21479	,,	Henshall, Fred Brown
21484	Bugler	Hill, James
21480	Private	Hopkins, Frances E.
21477	,,	Houghland, William
21482	,,	Howell, Phillip J.
21486	,,	Jameson, Sydney
21485	,,	Jones, Llewelyn W.
21487	Private	Kellie, Franklin
21490	,,	Lawrence, Orton B.
22073	,,	Lane, Victor P.
21448	,,	Lea, John
21489	,,	Lea, William
21497	,,	McBain, John
22176	,,	MacBrayne, Duncan
21499	,,	McDonald, Alex. G.
21494	,,	MacDonald, William
21500	,,	McDonald, M. M.
21492	,,	MacLaren, Walter R.
21491	,,	McTurk, James D.
21496	,,	Marr, Andrew
21501	Str.B'rer.	Martin, Wm. Henry
21498	Sergt.	May, Emil August F.
21495	Private	Mays, Jess
21502	,,	Newland, Laurence J.
21503	,,	Newton, Robert
21504	,,	Ogilvie. Robert
21508	,,	Pearson, Donald
21558	,,	Phillips, Arthur
21507	,,	Prince, Frederick J.
21511	,,	Rippengale, George
21512	,,	Ritchie, James H.
21513	,,	Redmond, Moses A.
21510	,,	Robertson, Daniel
21517	,,	Robertson, Thos. L.
21514	,,	Robinson, Frank B.
21509	,,	Ross, Albert Edw. Jas.
21516	,,	Rothwell, Norman
21523	,,	Scott, George Henry
21522	,,	Scott, John Johnson
21521	,,	Smedley, William
21519	,,	Stelfox, E.
21524	Groom	Steptoe, Shadrach
21520	Private	Stuart, Spencer
21530	,,	Taylor, Walter
21529	,,	Templeton, Arch. J.
21527	,,	Trickett, Joseph Geo.
21539	,,	Walsh, John Robert
21536	,,	Warren, Henry Wm.
21540	,,	Warwick, H.
21532	,,	Webb, George Walter
21534	,,	Wescomb, Herbert J.
21669	,,	Wilson, Harold Geo.
21538	,,	Williams, E.

Canadian Pacific—The Empire's Greatest Railway.

11TH BATTALION, 4TH INFANTRY BRIGADE—*cont.*

"E" COMPANY.

Captain	... ...	McGee, Charles Edward
Lieutenant	... ...	McIlwaine, William Robert
,,	... ...	Scatcherd, Edwin C.
,,	... ...	Smith, Sholto.

Regl. No.	Rank.	Name.	Regl. No.	Rank.	Name.
21605	Col.-Sgt.	Guild, George D.	21584	Private	Crawford, Wm. M.
21636	Sergt.	Muir, John	21590	,,	Crawley, Cuthbert
21629	,,	Lockman, Lewis A.	21588	,,	Crouch, Thomas R. S.
21606	Private	Guilfoyle, John	21593	,,	Eldridge, Reginald G.
21610	Sergt.	Hartnett, James	21596	,,	Farrell, John B.
21592	,,	Dominy, James	21597	,,	Fawcett, Archibald
21661	Corpl.	Steeves, R. J.	21598	,,	Ferguson, James
21649	,,	Neil, Charles W.	21599	,,	Ford, Ernest W.
21662	,,	Stewart, James	21600	,,	Fowler, William G.
21591	Lce.-Cpl.	Davies, William G.	21607	,,	German, Thomas
21595	,,	Fowler, John G.	21608	,,	Gibson, Charles W.
21625	,,	Kilpatrick, Herbert	21609	,,	Gillis, Gamaliel
21587	,,	Crabtree, Owen	21601	,,	Graham, James
21594	,,	Edington, Samuel P.	21602	,,	Greenman, F. M.
21639	,,	Melville, Paul	21603	,,	Greentree, F. A.
22165	Private	Adamson, Frederick	21604	,,	Griffiths, George C.
21559	,,	Agar, Bernard	21611	,,	Hallsworth, David
21674	,,	Alexander, John	21617	,,	Hewitt, George
22025	Batman	Allen, Joseph James	21616	,,	Hill, Evan
21563	Private	Anderson, William	21615	,,	Hobin, William
21564	,,	Andrews, F.	21614	,,	Hood, Eric
21562	,,	Arseneault, John B.	21613	,,	Hood, Robert
21567	,,	Bambridge, Harry J.	21612	,,	Hopkins, John J.
21566	,,	Bambridge, William	21618	,,	Hawarth, James
21578	,,	Banyard, Robert E.	21619	Bugler	Ingram, Charles L.
21579	,,	Barker, Frank	21620	Private	Jarvis, John E.
21568	,,	Buchanan, Alex.	21621	,,	Johnson, William
21577	,,	Bevan, Joseph	21622	,,	Kennedy, John C.
21574	,,	Beetlestone, Harry	21623	,,	Kidd, Thomas W.
21570	,,	Biggam, Andrew	21624	,,	Kiernan, Michael C.
21571	,,	Bird, Harry G. D.	21626	,,	Knox, William
21573	,,	Beckett, Reid E.	21627	,,	Kyle, Oliver S.
21572	,,	Bishop, Arthur H.	21628	,,	Leach, Joseph H.
21576	,,	Bodkin, John	21631	Str.B'rer	Lee, Robert J.
21569	,,	Britton, John	21630	,,	Loughland, Andrew
21565	,,	Brooks, Thomas A.	21642	Private	Mallon, Matthew
21580	Signaller	Burdon, Burt Allan	21641	,,	Markle, Walter
21581	Private	Burleton, Arthur V.	21640	,,	Martin, Frederick L.
21585	,,	Cameron, Alec.	21632	,,	Melville, John
21586	,,	Cameron, Ewen N.	21638	,,	Morgan, Thomas
21589	,,	Cawthorne, Charles	21637	,,	Morrow, Frederick
21815	,,	Cooper, Ernest S.	21635	,,	Mullen, Charles H.
21583	,,	Coulson, F. G. W.	21634	,,	Munro, Hugh A.
21582	,,	Craig, John A.	21633	,,	Murphy, Henry

Canadian Pacific—The Empire's Greatest Railway.

11TH BATTALION, 4TH INFANTRY BRIGADE—cont. 201

Regl. No.	Rank.	Name.	Regl. No.	Rank.	Name.
21646	Private	McCullough, H. W.	21658	Private	Smith, Frederick
21647	,,	McKay, James	21659	,,	Smith, Hector G.
21648	,,	McKerracher, J. D.	21660	,,	Smith, William
21645	Batman	McLardie, Hugh	21663	,,	Storr, Henry L.
21643	Private	McMillan, John L.	21664	,,	Sweeny, Henry
21644	Batman	McMillan, James	21666	,,	Templeton, E. C.
21650	Private	Oreste, Zucco	21667	,,	Upex, Percy B.
21652	,,	Pullan, Thomas R.	21668	,,	Waldron, F. G.
21651	,,	Pye, Edwin	21670	Signaller	Ward, Ernest Arthur
21654	Bugler	Rainbird, Harold	21672	Private	Wilkie, Joseph R.
21653	Private	Rogers, William L.	21673	,,	Wilkie, John
21665	,,	Sanders, James H.	21533	Arm. Cpl.	Wilson, Gavin
21656	,,	Smith, Barney A.	21671	Private	Wood, Arthur L.
21657	,,	Smith, Charles V.			

"F" COMPANY.

Captain	... ...	Anderson, Stanley John
Lieutenant	... ...	Bothwell, William H.
,,	... ...	Reid, Robert R. T.
,,	... ...	Finn, Ivan

Regl. No.	Rank.	Name.	Regl. No.	Rank.	Name.
21729	Col.-Sgt.	McKenzie, C. J. M.	21678	Private	Buchan, William
21703	Sergt.	Gilbert, Willoughby	21685	,,	Clarke, Arch. D. P.
21745	,,	Phillips, Charles H.	21686	,,	Clark, Albert
21725	,,	McDonald, Alec	21688	,,	Clark, William
21787	,,	Goddard, Cecil H.	21687	,,	Cook, Henry Penman
21786	Corpl.	Boyle, James	21689	Str. B'rer	Cross, William
21704	,,	Gilmore, Eric McRea	21690	Private	Davis, John T.
21707	,,	Hampshire, Wyatt	21691	,,	Deeks, Arthur E.
21779	,,	Whitfield, Harry	21693	,,	Eady, Albert L.
21700	,,	Gentles, Herbert E.	21692	,,	Emard Joseph Wm.
21682	Arm.Cpl.	Brown, Lewis G. H.	21694	,,	Galpin, Sidney
21767	Lce.-Cpl.	Thompson, Horace	21701	,,	Gerry, James
21759	,,	Scott, Frances Wm.	21702	,,	Gibson, B.
21732	Private	Menzies, John	21705	,,	Graham, William F.
21696	Lce.-Cpl.	Griffin, Mansell J.	21695	Signaller	Gray, Joseph
21697	,,	Grant, Kenneth	21698	Bugler	Good, Harold M.
21675	Private	Alder, Ernest	21699	Private	Goodson, Arthur
21676	,,	Andrews, Herbert	21706	,,	Gourlay, John T.
21677	,,	Appleton, Thomas E.	21709	,,	Hart, George Henry
21796	,,	Bailey, Frederick C.	21711	,,	Hinchey, Ernest R.
21684	,,	Beaumont, James	21710	Str.B'rer	Hitchcock, George
22196	,,	Bird, J. A.	21708	Private	Hynds, George F.
21683	,,	Bolding, C. E.	21712	,,	Irwin, Frederick
21680	,,	Braybrooke, Frank	21713	,,	Jardine, James
21681	,,	Brown, John A.	21714	,,	Jones, David
21679	Bugler	Brown, Charles R.	21715	,,	Jones, Thomas

Canadian Pacific—The Empire's Greatest Railway.

202   11TH BATTALION, 4TH INFANTRY BRIGADE—cont.

Regl. No.	Rank.	Name.	Regl. No.	Rank.	Name.
21716	Private	Jackson, Thomas	21754	Private	Richards, Claude F.
21717	,,	Kerr, Thomas C.	21755	Bugler	Richardson, R.
21718	,,	Kielly, LeRoy Bell	21749	Private	Riddle, John P. T.
21719	,,	Knox, Harvey	21751	,,	Robertson, Wm. S.
22070	,,	Lewis, Arthur R.	21761	,,	Sears, George
21721	,,	Loney, Edward G.	21760	,,	Sharp, Thomas
21722	,,	Lowe, George A.	21762	,,	Sinclair, William T.
21724	,,	Mantle, Bertram	21758	,,	Statia, Harold E.
21743	,,	Malcolm, James	21763	,,	Steane, Percy
21735	,,	Martin, Frank	21764	,,	Stephen, James
21734	,,	Menker, John	21756	,,	Strachan, Frank P.
22186	,,	Miller, Oliver Lyle	21765	,,	Symon, George
21723	,,	Moore, Joseph	21757	,,	Sykes, Thomas
21731	,,	Morgan, Harry E.	21766	,,	Tanner, Frederick
21921	,,	Morris, A. W.	21770	,,	Taylor, Harry
21733	,,	Mudge, Albert B.	21768	,,	Titmus, Charles Wm.
21739	,,	McCutcheon, E. P.	21771	,,	Trafford, James
21726	,,	McCutcheon, Roy	21788	,,	Travers, Ernest W.
21737	,,	McDonald, Hugh	21769	,,	Turner, W. C.
21742	,,	McDonald, Malcolm	21772	,,	Vye, Charles H.
21738	,,	McDonald, Robert	21781	,,	Walker, William
21740	,,	McGill, Arthur S.	21789	,,	Webb, Albert Edwin
21741	,,	McGregor, Alexander	21775	,,	West, Edward
21728	,,	McIntyre, William	21777	,,	Wickens, Alfred J.
21736	,,	McLaughlin, John	21776	,,	Whiteway, Lewis
21730	,,	McLeod, Duncan	21780	,,	Whittaker, Frederick
21744	,,	Norris, Henry John	21778	,,	Weston, Harry V.
21746	,,	Paget, Ferrand	21773	,,	Wilton, Frederick
21748	,,	Patterson, Andrew	21782	,,	Wimbush, Henry A.
21747	,,	Preston, Lewis	21774	,,	Wolfe, William
21753	,,	Rake, Charles	21785	,,	Wride, Robert
21752	,,	Reid, Ormond R.	21783	,,	Wood, Lewis Richard
21750	,,	Reardon, Blake			

"G" COMPANY.

Captain	...	...	...	...	Anderson, Percy Mendall
Lieutenant	...	...	...	...	Dawson, James Wright
,,		...	...	...	Murdie, R.
,,		...	...	...	Bailey, H. M.

Regl. No.	Rank.	Name.	Regl. No.	Rank.	Name.
21871	Col.-Sgt.	O'Brien, Frank	21862	Corpl.	Moffatt, Robert
21863	Sergt.	Metcalfe, Richard E.	21855	,,	Joslyn, Robt. Wray
21837	,,	Jarrett, Samuel F. A.	21826	Arm.Cpl.	Dunk, Herbert W.
21890	,,	Shield, James C.	21793	Lce.-Cpl.	Brooks, Joseph Lyle
21885	,,	Straight, Marshall S.	21886	,,	Scrivener, Harry L.
21819	Corpl.	Chapman, Percy	21867	,,	McRorie, Charles K.
21818	,,	Clarke, St. George S.	21831	,,	Ferguson, James

Canadian Pacific—The Empire's Greatest Railway.

11TH BATTALION, 4TH INFANTRY BRIGADE—cont.

Regl. No.	Rank.	Name.	Regl. No.	Rank.	Name.
21821	Lce.-Cpl.	Dale, Clarence R.	21847	Private	Hood, Stewart Clink
21859	,,	Moss, Cecil Fredk.	21845	,,	Horne, John
21791	,,	Anderson, Robert M.	21844	,,	Hunter, Thomas G.
21790	Private	Allen, William Levi	21843	,,	Hutcheon, Alexander
21792	,,	Armour, George H.	21853	,,	I'Anson, Charles W.
21795	,,	Baird, Robert John	21854	,,	Jeffs, Wilfred A.
21804	,,	Baxter, Patrick Jas.	21379	,,	Kidd, Percy Clifton
21794	,,	Beardsworth, Reg. J.	21856	,,	Kohl, Peter Jacob
21803	,,	Bertrand, Lancelot J.	21906	,,	Lancaster, Alfred
21806	,,	Bewsher, John	21857	,,	Lavender, Lewis
21801	,,	Binns, Albert G.	21858	,,	Lowinge, Horace
21802	,,	Blois, George	21866	,,	Mann, Robert Wm.
21799	,,	Bond, William A.	21865	,,	Markell, Elben Alex.
21800	,,	Bremner, Robert H.	21861	,,	Muirhead, James W.
21907	,,	Broughton, Wm. J.	21860	,,	Musgrave, Gothorp P.
21798	,,	Brown, D. P. McN.	21869	,,	McKay, John Allan
21805	,,	Bull, James Robert	21864	,,	McKinnon, Hector
21807	,,	Burch, Arthur Hy.	21868	,,	McNair, Hugh John
21811	,,	Carter, George	21870	,,	Nind, James
21817	Signaller	Clarke, Edwin Cedric.	21872	,,	O'Toole, Alfred
21809	Private	Collier, Albert John	21873	,,	Preece, John V.
21816	,,	Collier, William	21874	Str. B'rer	Probert, Frederick
21814	,,	Cook, Edward H. P.	21875	Private	Quick, Charles A.
21813	Signaller	Cowlishaw, William	21879	,,	Rawlinson, Robt. J.
21808	Private	Cox, Alexander	21878	Bugler	Renton, A. W.
21810	,,	Cunning, Nicholas H.	21880	Private	Richardson, Robt. H.
21820	,,	Cunning, Walter A.	21876	,,	Roberts, Harry
21822	,,	Delahay, John Alec	21877	,,	Robson, Raymond
21823	,,	Dewer, William	21887	,,	Scanlon, William M.
21824	,,	Dickson, Alec Bruce	21891	,,	Shawcross, Charles
21825	,,	Ducross, Walter P.	21889	,,	Simpson, Walker
21827	,,	Durham, Garnett W.	21888	,,	Sissons, Ernest E.
21829	,,	Eccles, Seth	21882	,,	Smith, Arthur
21830	,,	Edwards, Wm. Jas.	21883	,,	Stockwood, Wm. B.
21828	,,	Evans, Frank V.	21881	,,	Swann, Walter H.
21832	,,	Flannigan, John G.	21897	,,	Taylor, Roswell E.
21835	,,	Ford, Maurice	21892	,,	Townhill, John Wm.
21833	,,	Frost, James S.	21893	,,	Travers, Alfred G.
21834	,,	Froud, Percival W.	21894	,,	Travis, Herbert G.
21838	,,	Gaval, George Wm.	21895	,,	Trotter, Austin S.
21840	,,	Gilbert, Hedley Roy	21896	,,	Turnley, Frobile D.
21841	,,	Gillespie, Andrew	21900	,,	Warwick, Benjamin
21852	,,	Hay, Peter Charles	21905	,,	Watt, Charles
21851	,,	Healy, Andrew	21904	,,	Warr, Horace M.
21846	,,	Hassell, Thomas	21901	,,	West, Gordon B.
21850	,,	Hazell, Albert Edwd.	21902	,,	Whiskin, Frank
21848	,,	Hine, Harold	21903	,,	Williams, Frank M.
21842	,,	Hindle, David S.	21898	,,	Wood, Albert Edwd.
21839	,,	Hilbert, Ronald	21899	,,	Woods, Henry John
21849	,,	Hilliard, Harvey C.			

Canadian Pacific—The Empire's Greatest Railway.

11TH BATTALION, 4TH INFANTRY BRIGADE—cont.

"H" COMPANY.

Lieutenant ... ... Ferguson, G. A.
,, ... Goodwillie, Frederick B.
,, ... Romeril, Wilfrid
,, ... Holmes, James Elliott

Regl. No.	Rank.	Name.	Regl. No.	Rank.	Name.
21939	Col.-Sgt.	Pearne, Richard	21989	Bugler	Dyer, James
21919	Sergt.	Tressider, Thomas	21988	Private	Engen, Ole P.
21987	,,	Evered, Herbert G.	22051	,,	Fuller, Robert
22003	,,	Crofton, George T.	21984	,,	Gale, Duane B.
21985	Corpl.	Fordham, Richard	21983	,,	Gray, George Shaw
21993	,,	Delaney, William	21977	,,	Graham, Arthur
21926	,,	Seath, Alec Ferguson	21978	,,	Gorringe, Frank C.
21980	,,	Gane, Herbert W.	21982	,,	Green, Albert Robert
21979	,,	Goldsworthy, A. W.	21981	,,	Grimes, Thomas A.
21995	Arm.Cpl.	Crowthers, Frederick	21973	,,	Halcro, George
21934	Lce.-Cpl.	Risbey, Albert	21975	,,	Hale, William G.
21986	,,	Frost, Charles John	22065	,,	Harvey, George
21997	,,	Crockford, C. E. J.	21968	,,	Heatley, John J.
22013	,,	Brownbridge, C. H.	21969	,,	Henderson, Walter
21911	,,	Williams, Leonard	21976	,,	Hewitson, Richard
21927	,,	Slinn, William	21970	,,	Hilsenter, Joseph
22020	Private	Anderson, Edwin T.	21971	,,	Holbrook, James B.
22019	,,	Archibald, William	21972	,,	Howrie, William J.
22021	,,	Arsenau, James	21966	,,	Kennard, Walter E.
22023	,,	Ashton, Arthur J.	21967	,,	Kostenko, Max
22022	,,	Ashton, William V.	21965	,,	Lang, Francis A.
22016	,,	Bain, William S.	21964	,,	Livingstone, Lachlan
22015	,,	Bannerman, Angus	21963	,,	Lloyd, Thomas
22018	,,	Baptist, David Yale	21962	,,	Lyne, Ernest James
22008	,,	Barnard, Lewis H.	21961	,,	Lyne, John
22011	,,	Beames, Robert T.	21950	,,	Malcolmson, G. W.
22010	,,	Benard, Frederick	21951	,,	Maller, Hubert C.
22009	,,	Berger, William	21952	,,	Mann, Herbert John
22012	,,	Biner, Reginald A.	21081	,,	Mann, A.
22014	,,	Brown, William	21953	,,	Manson, Nelson
22017	,,	Butler, William R.	21954	,,	Martin, Percy
22006	,,	Carter, Henry Astor	21955	,,	Matthews, Henry
22005	,,	Carter, William G.	21960	,,	Miller, George
22004	,,	Chambers, Arthur E.	21956	Str.B'rer.	Mellor, John
21998	,,	Christy, Amos B.	21957	Private	Murphy, William T.
21908	,,	Cook-Watson, L. S.	21958	,,	Myers, Henning
22002	,,	Cooper, Henry	21959	,,	Mylie, Robert Carter
21999	,,	Conlon, Arthur L.	21947	,,	McDonald, Hanford
22001	,,	Corrigal, Thomas	21946	,,	McGill, Archibald R.
21996	Str.B'rer.	Creasey, George E.	21948	,,	McLauchlan, A.
22007	Private	Curry, Charles W.	21949	,,	McPherson, John
21994	,,	Dawes, George	21945	,,	Owen, Cecil Clarkson
21992	,,	Dickson, James P.	21938	Bugler	Paine, Edwin
21991	,,	Deane, Melville R.	21940	Private	Pells, John Street
21990	,,	Dow, Robert C.	21941	,,	Pepper, Vivian J.

Canadian Pacific—The Empire's Greatest Railway.

11TH BATTALION, 4TH INFANTRY BRIGADE—cont.

Regl. No.	Rank	Name	Regl. No.	Rank	Name
21942	Private	Philo, Charles Phillip	21929	Private	Street, Edward L.
21943	,,	Pickering, Geo. W.	21928	,,	Stewart, George
21944	,,	Pickering, Thos. F.	21922	,,	Taylor, Thomas T.
21936	,,	Pither, Arthur H.	21921	,,	Thomas, George A.
21937	,,	Porter, Frederick	21920	,,	Thompson, Samuel J.
21931	,,	Randel, Francis E.	21918	,,	Tulloch, John R.
21935	,,	Relf, Herbert	21917	,,	Turner, Stanley
21932	Signaller	Reach, Albert Victor	21909	,,	Way, Wilfrid James
21933	Private	Richards, Richard R.	21916	,,	Walker, Astley J.
21925	,,	Samm, James L.	21912	,,	Widdows, Clifford
21924	,,	Sirwinski, Joseph	21910	,,	Wingham, G. W.
21923	,,	Slater, Percy	21914	,,	Wright, Sidney
21930	,,	Spencer, George E.			

BASE COMPANY.

Lieutenant ... ... Graham, J.
,, ... Manahan, R. N.

Regl. No.	Rank	Name	Regl. No.	Rank	Name
22058	Sergt.	Graham, William	22103	Private	Finch, Lawrence L.
21575	,,	Beer, William T.	22055	,,	Gale, Joseph Edward
22024	Private	Ashe, William H.	22060	,,	Gillings, John
22194	,,	Anderson, John Mac	22059	,,	Gordon, George
22035	,,	Bareham, Arthur H.	22054	,,	Gray, Alexander B.
22030	,,	Bee, Carl	22057	,,	Gray, Ernest Calder
22029	,,	Bell, Herbert	22052	,,	Gray, John
22026	,,	Bidwell, William	22053	,,	Gray, Lionel Victor
22033	,,	Blatch, Harry	22056	,,	Green, Albert
22027	,,	Boyd, Edward R.	22169	,,	Griffin, Arthur W.
22109	,,	Bradbury, Frank M.	22061	,,	Hallgarth, Lionel
22032	,,	Brayman, George W.	22064	,,	Head, Charles Edw.
22034	,,	Brickell, G.	22062	,,	Holloway, John
22031	,,	Brown, Arthur	22066	,,	Henry, William Jas.
22028	,,	Brown, John	22063	,,	Hurlburt, Joseph
22038	,,	Cardy, John	22067	,,	Jenner, Thomas S.
22040	,,	Childs, Henry James	22193	,,	Jones, E.
22102	,,	Clark, Reginald H.	22068	,,	King, Graham Guy
22042	,,	Cleghorn, David	22069	,,	Kirby, George Henry
22036	,,	Cliner, John Barnard	22105	,,	Kirby, Thomas V. J.
22043	,,	Coleman, Fredk. H.	22172	,,	Kresko, Mike
22041	,,	Cooper, James H.	22074	,,	Latham, Ernest R.
22037	,,	Corbett, John H.	22072	,,	Lees, Sidney
22044	,,	Cryer, Sidney	21720	,,	Lewis, Roy A.
22039	,,	Cumming, David A.	22071	,,	Locke, Arnold Victor
22115	,,	Dempster, W. R.	22075	,,	Luttman, Frederick
22048	,,	Desmereaux, Jas. A.	22076	,,	Lynn, Cyril Lionel B.
22047	Signaller	Dow, Walter Charles	22175	,,	Manson, D. A. R.
22046	Private	Durham, Arthur W.	22078	,,	MacLennan, Duncan
22049	,,	Ellery, George John	22081	,,	Martin, Herbert
22050	,,	Ellison, Ray Deve	22080	,,	Martindale, Percy E.

Canadian Pacific—The Empire's Greatest Railway.

11TH BATTALION, 4TH INFANTRY BRIGADE—cont.

Regl. No.	Rank.	Name.	Regl. No.	Rank.	Name.
22077	Private	Murray, Alex. R.	22093	Private	Smith, Reuben
22079	,,	Menzies, Fred. C.	22094	,,	Smithers, Robert
21727	,,	McDougall, John A.	22107	,,	Stansfield, Gilbert
22183	,,	McKinnon, Hugh	22143	,,	Sullivan, Patrick
22178	,,	McNally, Henry H.	22185	,,	Sutton, Charles S.
22099	,,	O'Donoghue, Tim.	22100	,,	Thomas, Ernest J.
22084	,,	Parker, Frank	22096	,,	Tomlinson, Robert
22083	,,	Pauline, John	22097	,,	Turner, Thomas
22088	,,	Peel, Walter Edm.	22098	,,	Tyler, Henry
22087	,,	Poulton, John	22113	,,	Waller, Richard C.
22106	,,	Port, William	22115	,,	Walters, Frank
22086	,,	Powell, Harold A.	22112	,,	Ward, Fred
22085	,,	Powell, Morris A. C.	22147	,,	Warnock, J. W.
22082	Pioneer	Pyper, Bertram	22111	,,	Wender, Louis
22089	Private	Quayle, Daniel	22104	,,	Windle, Francis H.
22091	,,	Rein, Jack W.	22116	,,	Webb, James W.
22090	,,	Ridgway, Joseph	22117	,,	Wells, Robert
22092	,,	Roche, Thomas	22114	,,	Wightman, Thomas
22108	,,	Shaw, Alfred A.	22101	,,	Witherington, Wm.
22180	,,	Sinclair, Albert	22182	,,	Wyatt, James A. G.
22181	Signaller	Smith, Alfred Wm.	21440	,,	Weldon, John
22095	Private	Smith, Montague S.			

12th BATTALION, 4th INFANTRY BRIGADE.

HEADQUARTERS.

Officer Commanding	Lieut.-Colonel Harry Fulton Macleod
—	Major Albert Edward Swift
—	,, Percy Albert Guthrie
Asst. Adjutant	Lieut. E. Owen Greening
Transport Officer	Captain Norman Craik Ogilvie
Machine Gun Officer	,, Harry F. Caulfeild
Signalling Officer	,, Horace Hume Van Wart
Paymaster	Hon. Captain Arthur Lorne Hamilton
Quartermaster	Captain Ronald A. McAvity
Medical Officer	,, Robert Sutherland

Company Officers.

Captain Harry G. Deedes	Lieut. John W. Hupt. Vandenberg
,, Harold C. Sturdee	,, Hercule Lefebvre
,, William Leopold McWilliams	Capt Jasper Andrew Winslow CFA D. 22/3
,, Henry P. D. Gowen	,, John Maurice Scott 33AC
,, Charles K. Fraser	,, Louis Philip Ormond Pickard
,, Harry A. Sampson	,, Charles Auguste Brousseau
,, Fred Hayes Mersereau	,, W. H. Key-Jones
,, Harry McDonald	,, Arthur Cleveland Kelley

Canadian Pacific—The Empire's Greatest Railway.

12TH BATTALION, 4TH INFANTRY BRIGADE—cont.

Company Officers—cont.

Lieut. G. Stewart Ryder
,, Frank Eason
,, G. E. Theodore Roberts
,, Ernest H. Welch (K/1, 30/9/16 26&)
,, Cuthbert J. Morgan
,, Cecil Mersereau
,, Robert A. Sterling
,, Theodore Rand McNally
,, Charles William Wiggs
,, D. Allan Laurie

Lieut. H. Forsythe Hall
,, Frank B. MacRae
,, Edward H. Bowen
,, Ian L. Crawford
,, Milton K. Adams
,, Ernest William Sansom
,, Eric MacDonald
,, Arthur Blake
,, Douglas C. Jennings

Regl. No.	Rank.	Name.
23215	Cpl. M.G.	Adams, Albert A.
23487	Private	Adams, Ernest
22541	,,	Adams, George H.
23231	Lce.-Cpl.	Adams, Victor
22704	Private	Addison, Joseph
23097	Lce.-Cpl.	Aldridge, Arthur
23132	Private	Alexander, Earl
22833	,,	Allan, Creswell John
22963	,,	Allen, James
23476	Sergt.	Allen, Ronald
22964	Private	Allke, Nicholas
22705	,,	Alward, Wm. Alex.
23486	Corpl.	Anderson, Enoch M.
23088	,,	Anderson, John F.
22542	Private	Andrews, John Geo.
22706	,,	Appleby, Joseph H.
23222	,,	Archambault, Louis George
23488	,,	Ashford, William
23622	,,	Ashworth, Joseph
22543	,,	Atkinson, Charles
22707	,,	Atkinson, Sydney H.
22834	,,	Auger, Oliva Joseph
22835	,,	Auger, Wilfred
23621	,,	Augur, Fortunat
23620	,,	Audette, Arthur
23098	,,	Baiette, Angelo
23232	,,	Bailey, Thomas S.
22531	Lce.-Cpl.	Bailey, Cecil H.
22715	Private	Bailey, Edwin
23099	,,	Baird, Alexander
23239	,,	Baker, George Fred.
22544	,,	Ball, George
23491	,,	Balser, William
23235	,,	Banks, Henry
23493	,,	Barden, Norman
23241	,,	Barlow, Edward
23496	,,	Barnes, Morley
23245	Bugler	Barnett, Archie

Regl. No.	Rank.	Name.
23102	Private	Barsto, Harold
22844	,,	Batchlor, Charles W.
22545	,,	Bateman, Walter
22712	,,	Bates, Hugh
23073	Arm.Cpl.	Bathe, William H.
22563	Private	Bearisto, Frank
22546	,,	Beatty, Ernest E.
22547	,,	Beatty, George M.
22564	,,	Beatty, Henry E.
23618	Corpl.	Beaudry, Louis P.
23242	Private	Beaulieu, Armand
23243	,,	Beaulieu, Henry
22710	,,	Beckwith, John
23100	,,	Bedard, Albert
23102	,,	Beirsto, Alfred
22843	,,	Belanger, Alfred
23624	,,	Belanger, Wilfrid
23237	,,	Belisle, Joseph
23627	,,	Benoy, Arthur
23238	,,	Bentley, Leslie E.
23629	,,	Berard, Albert
23628	,,	Berard, Delphis
23626	,,	Bernier, Hector
23475	Sergt.	Berry, Jas. Balfour
23233	Private	Berwick, Willard L.
23495	,,	Betts, Magnus
23489	,,	Bickerton, Herbert
22838	,,	Bickford, Norman
23103	,,	Biggs, Henry R.
22969	,,	Binet, Alfred
22836	,,	Birdseye, Roger Wm.
22837	,,	Bishop, Arthur L.
23234	,,	Blackburn, Charles
22652	Pn'r.Sgt.	Blair, Charles E.
22942	Private	Blair, Stewart C.
22830	,,	Blais, Edward
23104	,,	Blanchette, Arthur
23718	,,	Blanchette, Paul
22971	,,	Blaney, David J.

Canadian Pacific—The Empire's Greatest Railway.

208 12TH BATTALION, 4TH INFANTRY BRIGADE—cont.

Regl. No.	Rank.	Name.	Regl. No.	Rank.	Name.
23631	Private	Blaxall, Joseph	23108	Private	Burns, Thomas
22839	,,	Blaxell, James	22941	,,	Burns, William
23492	,,	Bloomfield, George	23240	,,	Burrows, Arthur
22974	,,	Blondin, Osias	22532	Corpl.	Burtt, Osborn G.
23609	,,	Blouin, Joseph	22841	Private	Butler, Ben. Oswald
23497	,,	Blue, Donald R.	22823	Sergt.	Byrne, Robert E.
22549	,,	Boby, Jack M.	22842	Private	Byrne, Walter
22708	,,	Bonnevie, Hypolite	22661	Arm.Cpl.	Cadieux, Louis R.
22713	,,	Boone, George W.	23109	Private	Cairns, William
23105	,,	Boucher, Lucien	22846	,,	Calder, Thomas B.
23623	,,	Boulanger, Arthur	23500	,,	Caldwell, John
23101	,,	Boulanger, Donald	22982	,,	Cameron, Andrew
22714	,,	Boulanger, Rosaire Gedeon	22722	,,	Cameron, Hector
			22557	,,	Cameron, Morton A.
23244	,,	Boulich, Anthony	22723	,,	Carlson, Christian
23630	,,	Bourbonnais, Edward	23110	,,	Carrier, Joseph C.
22966	,,	Bourdage, Joseph	23638	,,	Carriere, Joseph
22973	,,	Bourdon, Louis	22986	,,	Cartlidge, Albert
23490	,,	Bourgeois, Mark F.	23633	,,	Castonguay, Felix
23625	,,	Bourque, Joseph	23111	,,	Chabot, Joseph A.
22550	,,	Boyd, Edwin J.	22654	,,	Chalu, S. Arthur
22972	,,	Bradshaw, John H.	22959	Corpl.	Chambers, Walter
22961	Lce.-Cpl.	Braik, John	23260	Private	Champagnot, Eugene
22551	Private	Brander, Arthur G.	23252	,,	Chandler, Albert
22967	,,	Bratt, Sydney Wilson	22558	,,	Chandler, Richard
22709	,,	Brennan, William J.	23248	,,	Chapman, Charles
22552	,,	Brewer, Alfred B.	23251	,,	Chapman, George
22565	,,	Brewer, John L.	23249	,,	Chapman, John
22970	,,	Brewster, George G.	23250	,,	Chapman, Oscar B.
22934	,,	Bridgeford, Thomas Arthur	23636	,,	Charette, Cyprien
			23254	,,	Charron, Lorenza
22703	Lce.-Cpl.	Briggs, David Henry	23502	,,	Charters, David I.
22965	Private	Briggs, Tracey W.	22559	,,	Chase, Hartley
33656	Corpl.	Brierly, Walter	22976	,,	Chedgey, Thos. Geo.
23608	Private	Brisebois, Gustave	23634	,,	Chevalier, Adolphe
22845	,,	Brouard, Arthur.	22727	,,	Chittick, William
23106	,,	Brown, Charles	23112	,,	Cinq-Mars, Paul
23107	,,	Brown, Henry	23256	,,	Choat, Williams.
22566	,,	Brown, Robert	22856	,,	Clare, Edward
23236	,,	Brown, Ronald	22721	,,	Clark, Christopher
22956	,,	Bruce, Ronald B.	22584	,,	Clark, William J.
22239	,,	Buchan, Alexander	23259	,,	Clark, Charles
22554	,,	Buchanan, W. Arthur	33657	,,	Clarkson, Harry E.
23465	,,	Buckley, John	23503	,,	Clay, Henry George
22555	Lce.-Cpl.	Budd, Arnold O.	22526	Sergt.	Claydon, Fred. John
23494	Corpl.	Bunnell, Albert L.	22635	Private	Clement, Edward
23481	Private	Bunnell, Geo. Allen	23114	,,	Clermont, Phillipe
22556	,,	Burdon, Walter McF.	22981	,,	Clifford, Frank
22840	,,	Burke, John	22720	,,	Clifford, Joseph C.
22711	,,	Burlock, Charles L.	23113	,,	Clifford, Thomas
22968	,,	Burnell, Thomas W.	22847	,,	Clint, Albert Henry
23246	,,	Burns, John	23501	,,	Cochran, Hamilton

Canadian Pacific—The Empire's Greatest Railway.

12TH BATTALION, 4TH INFANTRY BRIGADE—cont.

Regl. No.	Rank.	Name.
23637	Private	Codresco, Richard
23091	,,	Coleman, William
23115	,,	Collett, Arthur L.
23257	,,	Collier, Percy
22855	,,	Collins, John James
23247	,,	Conlon, Thomas
23069	,,	Conway, John Joseph
23640	,,	Cook, Thomas
23116	,,	Cook, Joseph
22848	,,	Cooper, Charles
22985	,,	Cooper, William
23506	,,	Copp, Hiram A.
22717	,,	Corbin, Harold J.
23258	,,	Cork, Herbert Foster
23546	,,	Cormier, Edgar
22979	,,	Corner, Otto H.
23119	,,	Corney, Arthur
22984	,,	Corrison, Cecil Daniel
22983	,,	Corrigan, John
22724	,,	Coughlan, Walter
23074	,,	Cossette, Emile
23632	,,	Courcie, George
22718	,,	Coutts, Andrew
22719	,,	Coutts, James
22850	,,	Couture, Napoleon
23639	,,	Couture, Eugene
22980	,,	Cox, Thomas
22560	,,	Craig, Leonard
23504	,,	Craigs, Walter Ray
23229	Lce.-Cpl.	Crawford, Harry Geo.
23083	Sergt.	Creighton, Wilden C.
22725	Private	Cripps, George D.
23117	,,	Crockett, Parker H.
22978	Lce.-Cpl.	Croft, Cyril
22977	Private	Crook, Alfred
23118	,,	Crosby, William C.
23505	,,	Crossman, Frank
23253	,,	Crothers, George
23255	,,	Crump, Albert
22726	,,	Cullen, Charles
23338	Sgl. Sgt.	Cunningham, Chas. S.
22851	Lce.-Cpl.	Cunningham, Harold Wilbert
22561	Private	Cuthbertson, Sam. A.
22728	,,	Coté, Ernest
22853	,,	Coté, Edouard
22852	,,	Coté, George Fredk.
23121	,,	Daley, John Daniel
23109	,,	Daley, Thomas
22857	,,	D'Armour, John
23650	,,	Dancause, Thomas
22562	,,	Dando, Percy Henry

Regl. No.	Rank.	Name.
23648	Private	D'Aoust, Romeo
22563	,,	Darcus, Solomon Jno.
22653	Act. Sgt.	Darnell, William
23227	Lce.-Cpl.	Davidson, Albin
22660	Private	Davis, David V.
22992	,,	Dawson, Peter
23507	,,	Dawson, Michael
22946	,,	Davis, Wm. Jos. Pat.
23642	,,	Dechantel, Ernest
22691	Col.-Sgt.	De Fallot, Carl
23122	Private	Delaney, William L.
23646	,,	Descary, Georges
22991	,,	Descharme, Raymond
23123	,,	Descôuteaux, Arthur
23649	,,	Desjardin, Sylveo
22807	Arm. Cpl.	Desjarlais, Jos. Omer
23511	Private	Dequetteville, Alfred
23124	,,	Desroche, Joseph
22564	,,	Devoo, John W.
23508	,,	Dewar, Leslie
23509	,,	Dewar, Oliver
23131	,,	Devore, Robert H.
22987	,,	Dickson, John
22858	,,	Dillon, Michael Jos.
23261	,,	Dionne, Ovila
23510	,,	Dixon, Henry
22730	,,	Donnell, James L.
22729	,,	Donohue, John Jos.
22988	,,	Donovan, Mich. Jos.
23125	,,	Douville, Eloi
22859	,,	Doo, Louis John
22945	,,	Doyle, Michael A.
23263	,,	Dorman, Chas. Hy.
23643	,,	Dufort, Oscar
23126	,,	Duffy, Charles
22861	,,	Dufresne, Jacques T.
23644	,,	Dugré, Joseph Art.
23337	Arm. Sgt.	Duggan, A. R.
22989	Private	Duggan, Rich. Hen.
22860	,,	Dunbar, Fredk. Art.
23262	,,	Duncan, William
23127	,,	Duncan, Oliver
23477	,,	Dunhill, Edgar
22990	,,	Dunn, William John
23383	,,	Dunnett, William
23719	,,	Dupré, Henri
23130	,,	Duplissea, Harold
23128	,,	Dupuis, Arthur
23129	,,	Dupuis, Alphonse
23645	,,	Dupuis, Horace
23651	,,	Durocher, Oscar
23641	,,	Duseigne, Armand

Canadian Pacific—The Empire's Greatest Railway.

o

12TH BATTALION, 4TH INFANTRY BRIGADE—cont.

Regl. No.	Rank.	Name.	Regl. No.	Rank.	Name.
23647	Private	Dutillieu, Pierre M.	23137	Private	Fournier, Henry
23133	,,	Earle, John	22736	,,	Fraser, James Alex.
23514	,,	Easterbrooks, Parker	23516	,,	Fraser, James Benj.
22995	,,	Eaton, Richd. Carter	22864	,,	French, Leonard
23220	Sergt.	Edgell, Geoffrey S.	23720	,,	Frenette, Joseph
22996	Private	Edgley, Wm. John	23656	,,	Frerot, Fernand
22733	,,	Edwards, Frederick J.	23654	,,	Frick, Louis
22565	,,	Edwards, Phillip S.	22865	,,	Fritze, William
22731	,,	Ellick, Joseph	23525	,,	Gagnon, Lewis Albert
23512	,,	Ellis, Alfred	22743	,,	Gallagher, Bernard
22993	,,	Elnetsky, Constantine	22999	,,	Gallagher, John
23653	,,	Emond, Alexander	23138	,,	Gallon, John
22695	Sergt.	Emslie, Jas. Gordon	23524	,,	Galloway, Fred
23513	Private	Englehart, Benjamin	23001	,,	Gammon, Lee
22994	,,	Eustache, George	22744	,,	Ganter, Hubert Jas.
22732	,,	Evans, Robert L.	22745	,,	Gardner, Charles A.
23086	,,	Everitt, Albert	23002	,,	Gareau, Raoul
23339	,,	Estabrooks, Geo. H.	23270	,,	Gaskins, Walter H.
23517	,,	Fairley, Chester	23139	,,	Gaudet, Francis
23656	,,	Falardeau, Oscar	23657	,,	Gauthier, Arthur
22862	,,	Fanning, Wm. John	23216	Sgt. M.G.	Gauvreau, Leo
22734	,,	Farquharson, Wm.	23140	Private	Genest, Odilon
23518	,,	Farrer, Claude	22868	,,	Genois, Alexander
23267	,,	Faulkner, Albert	22825	Lce.-Cpl.	Gibault, Alf. Phillip
22950	Col.-Sgt.	Fawcett, Herbt. Wm.	22701	,,	Gibbs, Edward P.
23134	Private	Felix, Thomas	23141	Private	Giguere, Arthur
22827	Lce.-Sgt.	Fellows, Wm. Alf. Hy.	23522	,,	Gilbert, Grantley
22867	Private	Ferguson, John Dan.	22742	,,	Gill, John W.
23135	,,	Ferguson, Patrick	23142	,,	Gillis, Harold
22866	,,	Fernie, Frank	22947	San.-Sgt.	Giltinan, Joseph
23520	,,	Filion, Joseph	22871	Private	Glass, Frank Kenneth
22566	,,	Fillimore, John A.	23660	,,	Glidden, George
22997	,,	Finch, Gerald W.	23531	,,	Godsoe, Stanley
22567	,,	Findley, Alfred E.	23659	,,	Golding, George
22568	,,	Findley, Sidney	23658	,,	Golding, Harry
22697	C. B. Sgt.	Finley, Harold D.	23336	R.S.M.	Good, J. J. (W.O.)
23515	Private	Finno, Joseph	22739	Private	Gorman, Louis W.
22735	,,	Fisher, Charles D.	23000	,,	Gosselin, Peter A.
23266	,,	Fisher, Frank	22569	,,	Gough, Percy J.
23519	,,	Fisher, Henry W.	22570	,,	Graham, Everett
22649	Q.M.Sgt.	Fitten, Richard C.	22737	,,	Graham, James Knox
23268	Private	Fitzgerald, Maurice	22738	,,	Graham, John W.
23092	Lce.-Cpl.	FitzPatrick, Jos. A.	22869	,,	Grant, Benj. Disraeli
22863	Private	Fletcher, Russell H.	23271	,,	Grant, George Edwd.
22824	Sergt.	Fletcher, Ernest R.	23269	,,	Gray, Arthur Frank
22998	Private	Flynn, John Paul	23528	,,	Gray, Chesley
23136	,,	Foley, Daniel	22740	,,	Gray, Frank
23264	,,	Foley, James	22571	,,	Grearson, Henry I.
23617	Corpl.	Ford, Thomas	22741	,,	Greer, Byron P.
23213	Private	Ford, Herbert	23146	,,	Gregoire,
23265	,,	Fournier, Edouard	22949	,,	Grenier, Henri
23090	,,	Fournier, Frank	23143	,,	Grier, John

Canadian Pacific—The Empire's Greatest Railway.

12TH BATTALION, 4TH INFANTRY BRIGADE—cont. 211

Regl. No.	Rank.	Name.	Regl. No.	Rank.	Name.
22572	Private	Griffin, Harry	22678	Private	Horncastle, J. Roy
23612	Sergt.	Griffith, John Jacob	22746	,,	Horner, Joseph
22698	Corpl.	Griggs, Douglas V.	22975	Arm. Cpl.	Horsfield, Allen J.
23523	Private	Grimes, Wm. George	22800	Private	Horton, Wm. Altward
22573	,,	Grindlay, Walter	23275	,,	Horwood, Alfred
22821	Col.-Sgt.	Gudgeon, Stephen E.	22655	,,	Howe, John
23527	Private	Guidry, Odon	22747	Lce.-Cpl.	Howard, Alfred
23526	,,	Guimond, Earnest	23462	Private	Howard, Dennis,
22870	,,	Gunnip, George	23278	,,	Hudd, Leslie C.
22579	,,	Hacquoil, John P.	23529	,,	Hughes, James
22749	,,	Haines, Daniel B.	22877	Lce.-Cpl.	Hughes, William Jno.
22872	,,	Haines, John Henry	23280	Private	Humphries, Ernest
22951	Sergt.	Haines, Thomas Edw.	22878	Lce.-Cpl.	Hunt, Arthur John
23219	,,	Hall, Thomas C.	23004	Private	Hunt, John Walter
23474	Col.-Sgt.	Hall, Wm. Harris	22583	,,	Hunter, Robert
22574	Private	Hallett, Arden Roy	22748	,,	Hunter, Rufus
22575	,,	Hallett, Greely Budd	23478	Sergt.	Huntingford, Ralph
22873	,,	Halligan, Jas. Chris.	22879	Private	Hustwick, William
23272	,,	Hamilton, James H.	23009	,,	Ironside, Wemyss
23145	,,	Hanlon, Dennis E.	23531	,,	Irving, James
22752	,,	Hanlon, Harry	22882	,,	Isaacs, Ernest
22667	,,	Hanlon, Walter	23010	,,	Jackson, Reginald
22576	,,	Hanson, Earle	22585	,,	James, Thomas Wm.
22577	,,	Hanson, Hedley C.	22832	Lce.-Cpl.	James, Robert
22874	,,	Hanson, John	23535	Private	Jardine, John
22578	,,	Hanson, Lawson	22883	,,	Jefferson, Bertram D.
23007	,,	Harper, Archie A.	23151	,,	Jenkins, Louis L.
23005	,,	Harris, William	23011	,,	Jenkins, William
23273	,,	Harris, William A.	23532	,,	Jimmo, William
23218	,,	Harrison, Arthur	22753	,,	John, Charles
23274	,,	Harrison, Cameron	22586	,,	Johnson, Charles
23093	Lce.-Cpl.	Hart, Henry D.	22587	,,	Johnston, Frederick
22826	Sergt.	Hawkins, Stanley H.	22588	,,	Johnston, Harry G.
23530	Private	Heard, Alfred	22589	,,	Johnston, Martin S.
23003	,,	Heason, Joseph	23152	,,	Johnston, William
23148	,,	Hebert, Hector A.	23281	,,	Jolin, Arthur
23149	,,	Hedlund, Hilding	22754	Lce.-Sgt.	Jones, Idriss George
23150	,,	Henderson, A. Cecil	23153	Private	Jones, George
23276	,,	Henry, Joseph	22590	,,	Jones, John
22875	,,	Henshall, Harry	22755	,,	Jones, Geo. Cameron
23008	,,	Hewton, James Neven	23403	,,	Jones, William Hen.
23361	,,	Hildebert, Leon	22591	,,	Jones, Samuel
22751	,,	Hill, Fred	23230	Lce.-Cpl.	Jones, Wm. Sydney
22876	,,	Hill, James	23012	Private	Joule, John Trafford
22582	Lce.-Cpl.	Hitchings, William	23662	,,	Jungblut, Ernest
23006	Private	Hixon, James Joseph	22854	,,	Katchefamas, James
22580	,,	Hodges, Arthur J.	22680	,,	Kavanagh, Alex.
23279	,,	Hoffenden, Arthur John Fuller	22885	,,	Keating, Daniel
			23154	,,	Keens, Austin
23277	,,	Hollings, Arthur	22582	,,	Kelly, Allan
22581	,,	Homewood, John	22583	,,	Kelly, James D.
22750	,,	Hopey, Edmund E.	23081	Col.-Sgt.	Kelly, Edward L.

Canadian Pacific—The Empire's Greatest Railway.

o 2

212　12TH BATTALION, 4TH INFANTRY BRIGADE—cont.

Regl. No.	Rank.	Name.	Regl. No.	Rank.	Name.
23084	Sergt.	Kelly, Osborne	23676	Private	Le Brun, Wilfrid
22884	Private	Kelly, J. Dennison	23286	,,	Leduc, Victor
22948	,,	Kelly, Thomas John	23547	,,	Leeman, Edward
22756	Corpl.	Kenney, Clarence E.	23721	,,	Lefebvre, Hyacinthe
23282	Private	Kensit, Edward A.	23544	,,	Legere, Vincent Jos.
23535	,,	Keoughan, James	23285	,,	Lemay, Carolus
22757	,,	Kerley, Peter	23665	,,	Lemay, Eugene
22962	Lce.-Cpl.	Ketteringham, E. A.	23666	,,	Lemay, Alfred
23732	Private	Kettle, A.	23017	,,	Lemessurier, Chas. S.
23537	,,	King, Berard	22952	C.P. Sgt.	Lemessurier, Garnet Wolsley
22584	,,	King, James			
22585	,,	King, Lee	23671	Private	Lemieux, Harry
22669	,,	King, Robert	23204	,,	Lemoil, Ernest
23536	,,	Kinnear, William	22759	,,	Lenihan, John C.
23068	Arm. Cpl.	Kipling, Harold	22758	,,	Lennox, Charles
22668	Private	Kitchen, Elwood	23016	,,	Lenzo, James
23283	,,	Knapp, William H.	23015	,,	Lesage, Napoleon P.
22886	,,	Knight, Charles	23667	,,	Lescournac, Norbert
22887	,,	Knight, Rupert	22955	Cook Sgt.	Lewis, Joseph
22596	,,	Knox, William	22888	Private	Lewthwaite, Cornelius William
23463	,,	Kubler, Walter			
23287	,,	Labaree, Arthur O.	23203	,,	Levesque, Alfred F.
23284	,,	Labbé, Joseph	23722	,,	Levesque, Charles
22890	,,	Labbé, M. Holland	22570	,,	Lifford, Joseph
23499	Lce.-Cpl.	Lacharité, Morris	22958	Corpl.	Lingard, Arthur
23664	Private	Lachat, Ernest	23221	,,	Lloyd, William Henry
23156	,,	Lackin, William Jos.	23014	Private	Llewelling, Harold B.
23157	,,	Lacroix, Joseph	22760	Sergt.	Lodge, Frederick
23672	,,	Lagace, Eugene	23538	Private	Long, Edward
23019	,,	Lajoie, Alcide	23020	,,	Long, William
23158	,,	Lajoie,	23539	,,	Long, Irven
23159	,,	Laline, Louis de Q.	23663	Lce.-Cpl.	Logeot, Armand
23673	,,	Lamoreux, Henri	23541	Private	Lorette, Joseph
22891	,,	Lamplough, Syd. L.	23484	Lce.-Cpl.	Lorette, William
23205	,,	Langford, Elmer G.	22601	Private	Love, Cecil J. D.
23464	,,	Langhorne, Fran. H.	22536	Corpl.	Lovely, Bruce
22599	,,	Langley, John Edw.	23018	Private	Lukka, Harry
23670	,,	Langlais, Gratien	23540	,,	Lund, Daniel
23723	,,	Langlois, Desiré	23545	,,	Lutes, Stanley
23543	,,	Langtagne, Jerry	23542	,,	Lynch, Joseph
22892	,,	Langton, Edwin R.	22894	,,	Lynch, Luke
22597	,,	La Pointe, Clement	23209	,,	Mackey, Thomas
23289	,,	Lavallé, Joseph	23164	,,	Mackins, Charles
23669	,,	Laverdiere, Joseph	23293	,,	Madden, Fred
23668	,,	Laverdure, Edward	22950	,,	Maguire, Frank
23013	,,	Lawlor, John Jos.	22602	,,	Maguire, James
22598	,,	Lawrie, James G.	22774	,,	Mahoney, Joseph P.
22761	,,	Lawson, Lowell	23028	,,	Malcolm, Ernest
23288	,,	Learmouth, Lester L.	22773	,,	Manderson, Robt. F.
22893	,,	Learmouth, Okill M.	23555	,,	Mann, John W. D.
23155	,,	Lebeau, Albert Jos.	23096	Bugler	Manning, Edwin A.
23482	Lce.-Sgt.	Le Blanc, Arthur P.	23686	,,	Mansfield, Joseph

Canadian Pacific—The Empire's Greatest Railway.

12TH BATTALION, 4TH INFANTRY BRIGADE—cont. 213

Regl. No.	Rank.	Name.	Regl. No.	Rank.	Name.
22694	Sergt.	Manson, Candlish G.	23095	Lce.-Cpl.	Munroe, Hamilton
22899	Private	Mantle, William	23550	Private	Munroe, Ernest
22603	,,	Manzer, Francis E.	23170	,,	Murphy, William
22900	,,	Marchant, Joseph S.	22829	Corpl.	Murphy, Thos. Geo.
22604	,,	Markey, John	23034	Private	Murray, Alexander
22761	,,	Markham, G. Harold	22775	,,	Murray, Barnard
22828	Corpl.	Marquis, Geo. Arth.	33658	,,	Murray, Frank Jos.
22778	,,	Marr, John D.	23551	,,	Murray, Harry S.
23087	,,	Marshal, James L.	22776	,,	Murray, Peter
23171	Private	Martel, Ernest	23296	,,	Murray, Robert
23206	,,	Martel, Joseph J.	23556	,,	McAllister, Howard L.
23298	,,	Martin, Raymond B.	22762	,,	McArthur, William C.
23299	,,	Martin, Joseph	23029	,,	McAuley, Malcolm A.
23725	,,	Martin, Alphonse	22896	,,	McCallum, Arch. S.
22777	,,	Mascoll, Thomas	23291	,,	McCarley, Charles G.
23558	,,	May, Edward	23160	,,	McCarthy, Jeremiah
23025	,,	Mead, Daniel	22763	,,	McCollum, Earnest
22772	,,	Medford, Fredk. A.	23031	,,	McCool, Chas. Austin
23548	,,	Meehan, James	23297	O.R.Cpl.	McCord, Geo. Rankine
23033	,,	Melarkey, Hugh	22897	Private	McCormick, Jn. Jos.
23211	,,	Mercier, Arthur	23030	,,	McCosh, Allen P.
23685	,,	Mercier, Georges	22768	,,	McDonald, Alexander
23687	,,	Mennier, Jos. Arth.	22681	,,	McDonald, Edward
22614	,,	Metcalf, Wm. H.	23557	,,	MacDonald, Edward
23682	,,	Methot, Arthur	22606	,,	McDonald, John D.
23172	,,	Meyers, Warren	22533	Sergt.	MacDonald, George
23166	,,	Michaud, John	23021	Private	McDonald, James
22902	Lce.-Cpl.	Michaud, Thomas	23161	,,	McDonald, John
23023	Private	Miedema, Peter	23162	,,	McDonald, Malcolm
23679	Bugler	Miles, Frederick	22769	,,	McDonald, Thomas J.
23689	Private	Miller, Joseph	22605	,,	MacDonald, Walter
23688	,,	Miller, Fredk. John	23553	,,	McDonald, Whitney
22616	,,	Miller, Kenneth	23677	,,	McGuire, Joseph
23552	,,	Miller, Stanley	22528	Sergt.	McKay, Christphr. A.
22954	Sergt.	Milne, James	22771	Private	McKee, Thomas M.
22895	Private	Minchin, Robert S.	22764	,,	McKeil, Rudolph
23724	,,	Miner, G.	23292	,,	McKenna, Peter Jos.
23684	,,	Mitchell, George	22898	,,	McKenzie, Chas. Hy.
23683	,,	Mitchell, Henri	23022	,,	McKeown, Robert J.
23027	Lce.-Cpl.	Mitchinson, Thomas	22903	,,	McElroy, James
33660	Private	Mock, Richard Ira	23554	,,	McKinnon, Archibald
22779	,,	Mofford, Cuthbert G.	22765	,,	MacKinnon, Bruce
23026	,,	Montgomery, Wm. Jn.	23163	,,	McLaren, John
23167	,,	Moon, Stanley	22607	,,	McLaughlin, Beryl
23294	,,	Moore, Thomas	22608	,,	McLaughlin, Chester
23615	Corpl.	Moran, Thomas	22609	,,	McLaughlan, Wm.
23035	Private	Morgan, Chas. Henry	22767	,,	McLaughlin, George
23169	,,	Morin, Leon	22612	,,	McLay, Edward
23549	,,	Morris, Richard	23024	,,	McLean, Alexander
22615	,,	Morris, Henry	23483	Corpl.	McLean, Gordon A
23678	,,	Mouvet, Lucien	22936	Private	McLean, Daniel
23226	Corpl.	Muir, Andrew	22766	,,	McMahon, Howard

Canadian Pacific—The Empire's Greatest Railway.

214   12TH BATTALION, 4TH INFANTRY BRIGADE—cont.

Regl. No.	Rank.	Name.	Regl. No.	Rank.	Name.
22679	Private	McMillan, Harry	23082	Sergt.	Pelletier, René A.
22537	Lce.-Cpl.	McNairn, Addison L.	23693	Private	Pepin, Donat
23032	Private	McNally, Stephen J.	22802	,,	Perring, Thomas J.
23290	,,	McNamara, Thomas	23303	,,	Perusse, Lucien
22901	,,	Macrae, Donald F.	23067	Arm. Cpl.	Peters, Herbert
22613	,,	McWha, Albert M.	23567	Private	Peterson, Frank
23690	,,	Nadreau, Louis	22624	,,	Peterson, Stephen
22617	,,	Nash, Ernest	23566	,,	Philpot, Jerry
23036	,,	Newman, Alfred	23040	,,	Piggott, Alfred
23560	,,	Nichol, Boyd	23041	,,	Piggott, Daniel Wm.
23559	,,	Nickerson, Cecil	22910	,,	Pincock, John Wm.
23301	,,	Noble, Joseph	23214	,,	Player, Ernest
23726	,,	Noel, Napoleon	23728	,,	Plamondon, Joseph
23037	,,	Normand, Phillipe	23729	,,	Plamondon, Raoul
23300	,,	Norwood, John V.	23570	,,	Poirier, Arthur
22780	,,	Nuttall, Jack	23302	,,	Poole, Austin, Albert
23611	Sergt.	Normandin, Clodomir	23219	Cook Sgt.	Poling, Thomas
23610	Col.-Sgt.	Normandin, Leopold	22672	Private	Pond, Dorien
23073	Private	Norris, James	23564	,,	Porter, Fred
22781	,,	O'Brien, Charles	22782	,,	Porter, Gardner
22618	,,	O'Brien, John H.	22912	,,	Postolos, John
22619	,,	O'Brien, Wm. James	23304	,,	Potter, James
23173	,,	Ockenden, Ernest P.	22918	,,	Powell, Herbert D.
22830	Lce.-Cpl.	O'Connor, Arthur F.	23220	,,	Powell, Albert
22534	Private	O'Dell, William	22911	,,	Power, William
22904	,,	Odgers, Rich. Batten	23224	Corpl.	Pratt, Thos. George
23727	,,	O'Donnell, John	22919	Private	Prescott, William J.
23561	,,	O'Keefe, Arthur	23044	,,	Price, Henry John
23562	,,	O'Keefe, Daniel	22937	,,	Proctor, Frederick
22620	,,	Oldenburg, Maurice	23176	,,	Provost, Morris
22905	,,	Oliver, Thos. Henry	23177	,,	Pullen, John
22951	,,	Orkney, Donald Duke	23605	,,	Quentin, Francois J.
23038	,,	Osborne, Jas. Arthur	23178	,,	Racine, Jos. Gaston
22906	,,	Oswald, Edgar	23606	,,	Racine, Médéric
23174	,,	Oulette, Ernest	23312	,,	Randall, Elias John
23691	,,	Oulette, Omer	23571	,,	Reading, Edward
23039	,,	Oulton, Thos. Edwin	22627	,,	Reddall, Frank
22621	,,	Owens, David M.	22784	,,	Regan, Thomas
22622	,,	Page, Elijah	22628	,,	Reed, Thomas
23568	,,	Pammenter, George	22783	,,	Reid, Ellsworth J.
23175	,,	Paquet, Adelard	23075	,,	Reid, John
23692	,,	Parent, Raymond	22809	,,	Reynar, Joseph
23222	Arm.Cpl.	Parfitt, Charles	23179	,,	Reynolds, Charles
22623	Private	Parsons, Ernest	22813	,,	Rhade, Foster W.
23043	,,	Passmore, Francis Eden Leonard	23572	,,	Rhodes, Ernest
			23309	,,	Rice, Harry C.
23217	Sergt.	Paterson, John	23575	,,	Richardson, Harry
22907	Private	Patton, Harold Rupert	22629	,,	Richardson, Wm. J.
			23223	Corpl.	Rigby, Fred
23042	,,	Pearce, Chas. Ratley	23180	Private	Riley, Michael
22535	,,	Pearson, Henry	23049	,,	Riley, William
23694	,,	Peck, Jack	23700	,,	Riopel, Zephirin

Canadian Pacific—The Empire's Greatest Railway.

12TH BATTALION, 4TH INFANTRY BRIGADE—cont.

Regl. No.	Rank.	Name.	Regl. No.	Rank.	Name.
22913	Private	Roach, Leonard	23314	Private	Scanlon, Charles
23701	,,	Robert, Armand	23707	,,	Schellink, Charles
23306	,,	Roberts, John	23188	,,	Scollard, William F.
23311	,,	Roberts, John B.	23313	,,	Scott, Arthur
22700	Corpl.	Robertson, Charles C.	22650	O.R. Sgt.	Scott, Meville Stewart
23181	Private	Robertson, Chester E.	22957	Corpl.	Scott, Wm. Bridges
22944	,,	Robertson, George	23317	Private	Searle, Austin E. T.
23182	,,	Robinson, Albert	23576	,,	Secord, Ralph Nelson
23183	,,	Robinson, David M.	23707	,,	Seed, Ernest R.
23046	,,	Robinson, Harry B.	23613	Sergt.	Senecal, Henry
23045	,,	Robinson, Peter H.	23070	Private	Sewell, Jos. Algernon
22915	,,	Robinson, Edward	22788	,,	Sharkey, Louis
23048	,,	Rochester, Herman	23583	,,	Sharpe, George
22916	,,	Rochette, Joseph	22656	,,	Sharpe, John
23696	,,	Rochon, Albert	22789	,,	Sheilds, Geo. Kingsley
23207	,,	Rogers, Joseph	22673	,,	Sheldon, Rupert
23699	,,	Rodgers, Samuel	23580	,,	Sherwood, Dudley S.
23698	,,	Roland, Joseph	22922	,,	Sheppard, Norman L.
22785	,,	Rolston, Fred H.	23705	,,	Sicard, Henri
22648	,,	Rolston, George A.	23208	,,	Simard, Arthur
23730	,,	Rouleau, Albert	23185	,,	Simmonds, Joseph J.
22917	,,	Rousseau, Joseph	23318	,,	Sims, George William
23731	,,	Routier, Wilfrid	23733	,,	Sirois, Charles
23308	,,	Rowley, George	22943	,,	Sinclair, Fredk. John
23573	,,	Roy, Thomas	23578	,,	Slater, Thomas
23047	,,	Royer, Wilfred	23579	,,	Slipp, George L.
23574	,,	Rushton, Fred	22674	,,	Sloat, Theodore
23480	Corpl.	Russell, Arthur	22632	,,	Smith, Archie Flmg.
23697	Private	Russell, Edward	22647	,,	Smith, Arnold Art.
23307	,,	Russell, Fred.	22692	Sergt.	Smith, Bartholomew
23310	,,	Russell, Jas. Stvnsn.	23704	Private	Smith, Aime
23616	,,	Russell, James	22919	,,	Smith, Gordon Hugh
22786	,,	Ryan, Herman	22920	Corpl.	Smith, Herbert Wm.
23050	,,	Ryan, James Patrick	22657	Private	Smith, John
22914	,,	Ryan, John	23057	,,	Smith, John
22538	Corpl.	Ryder, Frank Herbert	23320	,,	Smith, John E.
22621	Bglr. Sgt.	Ryder, John P.	23055	,,	Smith, John Henry
23305	Private	Rye, Walter	22699	Corpl.	Smith, Thomas J.
23706	,,	Sadowinsky, Victor	23056	Private	Smith, Thomas
23619	Corpl.	Saint Germain, A.	22790	,,	Snelgrove, Ephraim
23333	Private	Saint Hilaire, Alfred	23054	,,	Soane, George
23053	,,	Saint Onge, Joseph John Leo	23051	,,	Southall, Fredk. Jas.
			22923	,,	Soutter, John
22918	,,	Sangster, John Herbert Thomas	22921	Corpl.	Spargo, Reginald Jos.
			22787	Private	Speight, Edward
22631	,,	Sanson, Hbrt. Rymd.	22792	,,	Spellman, John Fltr.
22630	,,	Sansom, Hrbt. Klbn.	22539	Corpl.	Spencer, Frank P.
23582	,,	Sargent, Edmund	22634	Private	Starkey, Joseph
23581	,,	Sargent, Leonard	23319	,,	Stedman, Wm. Hen.
23316	,,	Saunders, Geo. Aylmr.	23315	,,	Stevens, William
23577	,,	Sawyer, Gale	22924	,,	Stewart, Alick Ross
23614	Sergt.	Sauvage, Phillipe	23340	Sergt.	Stuart, Herbert Jas.

Canadian Pacific—The Empire's Greatest Railway.

216 12TH BATTALION, 4TH INFANTRY BRIGADE—cont.

Regl. No.	Rank.	Name.	Regl. No.	Rank.	Name.
23702	Private	Stuart, Florant	23587	Private	Ullock, Frank
23058	,,	Stewart, William	23713	,,	Valandry, Theodore
23703	,,	Stoffin, Leon	23195	,,	Verrett, Alphonse
22791	,,	Steward, Chas. Edw.	23062	,,	Verette, Alfred
22793	,,	Stuart, Lawrence	22927	,,	Vezina, Armand
23188	,,	Sudsbury, Whylie	23225	Corpl.	Vickers, John
23187	,,	Sudbury, A. James	22678	Private	Vicary, William
23052	Lce.-Cpl.	Sullivan, Thomas	23196	,,	Viens, Herbert
22635	Private	Sutherland, Robert	23595	,,	Vauture, Fred
22633	,,	Sutton, William	22926	,,	Vyse, Eric Thomas
22831	Lce.-Cpl.	Styants, Walter John	22527	,,	Wade, Fred
23217	Private	Staymond, George	22529	Sergt.	Walker, Alan
22795	,,	Tait, Chesley R.	22659	Lce.-Sgt.	Walker, Victor E.
22530	Sgt.-Maj.	Tait, Joseph John	23591	Private	Wallace, Alexander
22675	Private	Tapley, Edwin	23592	,,	Waller, Charles
23218	Sergt.	Tate, Harold Glen	22639	,,	Waller, John G.
23585	Private	Taylor, William Jas.	22930	,,	Walmsley, William
22797	,,	Taylor, Robert D.	22804	,,	Walsh, Edward
22796	,,	Thatcher, Robert H.	22928	,,	Walsh, Herbert Jos.
23189	Lce.-Cpl.	Therrien, Alphonse	23197	,,	Walsh, John G.
23332	Private	Therion, Florian	22929	,,	Warburton,Geo.Wm.
23060	,,	Thibault, Alcide	23198	,,	Ward, John
23228	Lce.-Cpl.	Thomas, William	23334	,,	Ward, John E.
23324	Private	Thompson, Charles	23064	,,	Ward, James Ernest
23071	,,	Thompson,CyprianA.	23335	,,	Warren, William
23059	,,	Thompson, Fredk. A.	23715	,,	Waselash, John
22637	,,	Thompson, William	22802	,,	Watling, Archie
22810	,,	Thompson, Fred	22658	,,	Watson, John
23313	,,	Thuot, Eugene	23331	,,	Watts, John Thomas
22798	,,	Tippett, Samuel C.	22642	Far. Sgt.	Weazel, Jacob
23325	,,	Tite, William	22641	Private	Webb, Arthur
23190	,,	Tobin, Edward	22540	Corpl.	Webb, James. W.
22925	,,	Todd, Arthur G.	23341	Private	Webb, Robb
22794	,,	Toher, Frank E.	22643	,,	Webster, Charles
23321	Lce.-Cpl.	Tolson, George H.	22640	,,	Weir, Adam
23450	Private	Townsend, Fredk. C.	22702	Lce.-Cpl.	Weldon, Stewart
23711	,,	Trepannier, Alphonse	22676	Private	White, George
23712	,,	Trepannier, Arthur	23063	,,	White, George
33659	,,	Trebilcock, Roy C.	22662	Sergt.	White, James
23584	,,	Trites, Ohad	23199	Private	White, John Francis
23192	,,	Trudell, Louis	22677	,,	White, John
23322	,,	Tucker, Percy	22644	,,	White, Oscar
23709	,,	Turcotte, J. Albert	22931	,,	White, Stanley H.
23061	,,	Turcotte, Leo	22693	Sergt.	Whitehead, Alex. W.
23479	Sergt.	Turner, Chas. Edw.	22805	Private	Whitehouse, John
23194	Private	Turner, William H.	22806	,,	Wigney, Maurice
23193	,,	Turner, Alfred W.	23593	,,	Williams, John
22799	Post.Cpl.	Twist, Thomas	22953	Sergt.	Williams, John
22800	Private	Twaites, William V.	23327	Private	Williams, Alf. Allen
23586	,,	Tyler, Chas.	22645	,,	Willis, John
22960	Corpl.	Underhill,Alfd. Thos.	23200	,,	Wilson, Alex. A.
23085	Sergt.	Ussher, Benjamin	23328	,,	Wilson, Fredk. Ed.

Canadian Pacific—The Empire's Greatest Railway.

12TH BATTALION, 4TH INFANTRY BRIGADE—cont. 217

Regl. No.	Rank.	Name.	Regl No.	Rank.	Name.
22803	Private	Wilson, George	22811	Private	Wolf, Patrick J.
23201	,,	Wilson, Robert W.	23065	,,	Woodward, Fredk.
23589	,,	Wilson, Thomas	23329	,,	Wooten, Fredk. E.
23216	Col.-Sgt.	Wilson, Th. Cawood	22646	,,	Worth, Charles O.
22932	Lce.-Cpl.	Wilson, Walter Leslie	23326	,,	Wright, Herbert
23590	Private	Williston, Clay	23202	,,	Young, Joseph G.
23716	,,	Wing, Ernest	23717	,,	Young, William
23714	,,	Wistaff, William	22822	Sergt.	Young, Charles A.
23330	,,	Witchell, Wm. Geo.	23066	Private	Zinck, Leo

17th BATTALION—NOT BRIGADED.

(NOVA SCOTIA HIGHLANDERS.)

Headquarters.

Officer Commanding	Lieut.-Colonel Robertson, S. G.
Senior Major	Cameron, D. D.
Junior Major	Murray, D.
Adjutant	Major Bent, C. E.
Assistant Adjutant 28n (*K/n)* 5/6/16	Captain Cutten, L. R.
Quartermaster	,, McMeekin, R.
Transport Officer	,, Catty, Hamilton
Signalling Officer	Lieutenant McKee, N. F.
Chaplain	Hon. Captain Pringle, John
Medical Officer	Captain Morell, H.
Paymaster	Hon. Captain McKay, A.
Machine Gun Section	Lieutenant Bamfield, T. C.

Company Officers.

Captain	Allan, W. H.
,,	Archibald, G. C.
,,	Bentley, L. O.
,,	Coulter, W. B.
,,	Forbes, J. W.
,,	Reed, T. C.
,,	Sheppard, D. C.
,,	Watson, A. C.
Lieutenant	Bartlett, J.
,,	Bell, J. R.
,,	Bentley, F. M.
,,	Christie, J. E.
,,	Donald, B.
,,	Eager, G. E. C.

Canadian Pacific—The Empire's Greatest Railway.

17TH BATTALION—NOT BRIGADED—cont.

Company Officers—cont.

Lieutenant	...	...	...	Fraser, A.
"	...	...	...	Gillis, J. M.
"	...	...	...	Goforth, P.
"	...	...	...	Groggett, C. J.
"	...	...	...	Harris, G. W.
"	...	...	...	McDonald, F. G.
"	...	...	...	Marlowe, G. E.
"	...	...	...	Mingo, E.
"	...	...	...	Moran, P.
"	...	...	...	Peerless, A. N.
"	...	...	...	Ross, G. A. R.
"	...	...	...	Russell, J. R.
"	...	...	...	Walker, W. G.

Regimental Staff.

Regl. No.	Rank.	Name.	Regl. No.	Rank.	Name.
46001	R.Sgt.-Maj.	Maxwell, W.	46044	Transpt. Sergt.	Chipman, T.
46002	Q.M.S.	Francis, W.	46025	Sig. Sergt.	Mills, R. C.
46004	Pipe Maj.	Bailee, K. McK.	46008	Shoemakr. Sergt.	Joysey, J.
46003	O.R. Sgt.	Richards, Dick	46006	Pay Sergt.	Cadoux, B. T.
46012	Sgt. Dmr.	Wray, W. H.	46007	Mess Sergt.	Hillyer, T.
46005	Pnr. Sgt.	Leroy, Wm.	46009	Provost Sergt.	Leslie, W.
46010	Cook Sgt.	Cavanagh, G.	46011	Arm. Sergt.	Myers, E. E.

Signallers.

46027	Private	Fowlie, H.	46028	Private	Hyde, W.
46026	"	Davison, J.	46029	"	Leonard, R.
46030	"	Lester, G.	47028	"	McDonald, W. R.
46804	"	Atkinson, Chas.	46031	"	Stewart, F.

Orderlies for M.O.

| 46622 | Lce.-Cpl. | Fraser, A. | 47056 | Private | McKenzie, D. |

Batmen.

| 47010 | Private | Hughes, Geo. | 46877 | Private | Puddington, Chas. |
| 47051 | " | Traynor, Rbt. | | | |

Transport.

46045	Farrier	O'Connell, W.	46056	Private	Cook, J.
46073	Corpl.	Reed, J.	46055	"	Colburn, Wm.
46047	Private	Bradshaw, S.	46058	"	Dukeshire, C.
46048	"	Bushey, T.	46057	"	De Mille, R.
46049	"	Beech, C.	46059	"	Fraser, J.
46052	"	Bell, R.	46060	"	Grant, H. G.
46050	"	Bigney, J.	46061	"	Grey, H.
46051	"	Bridgeman, T.	46063	"	Goodwin, Wm.
46053	"	Cairns, W.	46064	"	Harlow, R.
46046	"	Calvin, J.	46065	"	Johnson, P.
46054	"	Casey, B.	46066	"	Mills, F.

Canadian Pacific—The Empire's Greatest Railway.

17TH BATTALION—NOT BRIGADED—cont.

Transport—cont.

Regl. No.	Rank.	Name.	Regl. No.	Rank.	Name.
46067	Private	Mills, M.	46075	Private	Rice, J.
46069	,,	Muzzar, M.	46076	,,	Rushton, O.
46068	,,	Morris, J.	46077	,,	Sacritch, H.
46071	,,	Noiles, F.	46078	,,	Saunders, W.
46070	,,	Negus, T.	46079	,,	Van Tuill, C.
46072	,,	Porter, T.	46080	,,	Winslow, R.

"A" COMPANY.

Regl. No.	Rank.	Name.	Regl. No.	Rank.	Name.
46101	Col.-Sgt.	Blakeney, H.	46143	Private	Eldridge, A.
46102	Sergt.	Bryson, E.	46144	,,	Elliott, G.
46103	,,	Manners, G.	46145	,,	Eyres,
46104	,,	Melvin, H.	46146	,,	Finalyson, H.
46105	,,	Smith, W.	46119	Cook	Frizzel, F.
46106	Lce.-Sgt.	Lawrence, P.	46147	Private	Gazeley, G.
46110	Corpl.	Kay, F.	46148	,,	Gargin, W.
46107	,,	Layton, F. B.	46149	,,	Greggs, W.
46111	,,	McDowell, C.	46150	,,	Giles, H.
46108	,,	Walters, D.	46151	,,	Greenough, L. M.
46109	,,	Wright, N. R.	46153	,,	Haley, L.
46112	Lce.-Cpl.	Blakeney, R.	46152	,,	Harris, G.
46114	,,	Burris, D.	46158	,,	Harrison, H.
46115	,,	Campbell, W.	46157	,,	Harvey, W.
46113	,,	Leek, R.	46156	,,	Henderson, G.
46120	Private	Anthony, A.	46154	,,	Higney, J.
46121	,,	Benvie, A.	46159	,,	Hopkirk, J.
46122	,,	Betts, R.	46155	,,	Hutchinson, P.
46123	,,	Blanchard, B.	46160	,,	Iler, R.
46124	,,	Blaikie, A.	46161	,,	Joy, F.
46125	,,	Bruce, J.	46162	,,	Knowles, F.
46126	,,	Brown, E. C.	46164	,,	Laffin, G.
46118	Cook	Brown, N. E.	46165	,,	Lockhart, F.
46127	Private	Buchanan, W.	46166	,,	Lockhart, W.
46116	Bugler	Burke, Jas. E.	46163	,,	Loomer, N.
46128	Private	Chapman, C.	46167	,,	Lynds, B. D.
46129	,,	Chamberlain, E. C.	46170	,,	McAdams, G.
46135	,,	Callan, D.	46172	,,	McCabe, C.
46130	,,	Carter, A. F.	46169	,,	McCallum, R.
46133	,,	Carswell, W. M.	46168	,,	McKenzie, C. R.
46136	,,	Carson, E.	46176	,,	McLeod, H. T.
46132	,,	Coulter, F.	46177	,,	McLeod, V.
46134	,,	Cowek, F.	46174	,,	Mawson, F.
46131	,,	Currie, J.	46173	,,	Merriweather, R.
46137	,,	Dakin, F.	46175	,,	Mounce, A.
46138	,,	Dickson, R.	46171	,,	Munroe, D.
46139	,,	Doane, R.	46178	,,	Nickerson, W.
46140	,,	Dupuis, R.	46179	,,	O'Brien, Geo.
46141	,,	Ellsworth, E.	46188	,,	Payne, R.
46142	,,	Ellicott, J.	46181	,,	Pentz, R.

Canadian Pacific—The Empire's Greatest Railway.

17TH BATTALION—NOT BRIGADED—cont.

Regl. No.	Rank.	Name.	Regl. No.	Rank.	Name.
46183	Private	Petcoff, A.	46196	Private	Tucker, D.
46182	,,	Pinch, A.	46200	,,	Warr, O.
46184	,,	Probert, W.	46205	,,	Wallbridge, J.
46187	,,	Reddin, S. J.	46204	,,	Watson, S.
46188	,,	Reid, P.	46202	,,	White, J.
46185	,,	Robertson, F.	46210	,,	Wickham, J.
46186	,,	Robertson, J.	46207	,,	Wicks, W. E.
46193	,,	Salmon, D.	46208	,,	Wicks, W. H.
46195	,,	Selon, C.	46206	,,	Wiley, J.
46192	,,	Skerry, P.	46211	,,	Wilmot, P.
46189	,,	Smith, P.	46212	,,	Winnard, J.
46190	,,	Smith, W.	46203	,,	Woods, D.
46194	,,	Steeves, H.	46201	,,	Woodworth, R.
46191	,,	Stratford, J.	46199	,,	Wyatt, F.
46198	,,	Thompson, G.	46213	,,	Yorke, E.
46197	,,	Tolmey, James			

"B" COMPANY.

Regl. No.	Rank.	Name.	Regl. No.	Rank.	Name.
46273	Col.-Sgt.	Daley, P. G.	46304	Private	Glenn, G.
46274	Sergt.	Goucher, F.	46308	,,	Garon, L. A.
46275	,,	Harmon, J. W.	46305	,,	Harris, T.
46276	,,	Peck, C.	46846	,,	Hefferman, M.
46283	Corpl.	Milner, E.	46307	,,	Hunter, R.
46277	,,	Poole, E.	46306	,,	Hilshey, F.
46278	,,	Simpson, F.	46309	,,	Hervey, B.
46279	Arm.-Cpl.	Bennett, R. G.	46310	,,	Jones, D.
46280	Corpl.	Kane, G. W.	46311	,,	Jodrie, A.
46281	Lce.-Cpl.	Green, T.	46312	,,	Joudry, E.
46282	,,	Jones, W.	46313	,,	Joudry, H.
46284	,,	Olson, E.	46314	,,	Kane, J. H.
46805	Private	Annan, R.	46286	Cook	Kane, M. A.
46288	,,	Alying, W. H.	46315	Private	Knox, J.
46290	,,	Berry, C. L.	46317	,,	Layte, H.
46289	,,	Baker, L.	46318	,,	Lynch, A. J.
46292	,,	Bond, H.	46856	,,	Mayre, R.
46293	,,	Burden, H.	46319	,,	Marriott, J.
46291	,,	Borden, F.	46320	,,	Mitchell, W.
46294	,,	Burt, D. G.	46323	,,	Mitchell, J. W.
46295	,,	Clarke, E.	46324	,,	Mitchell, L.
46296	,,	Cossman, C.	46321	,,	McLoughlin, R.
46297	,,	Coldwell, E. J.	46322	,,	McLoughlin, S.
46298	,,	Cameron, B.	46325	,,	Messenger, R.
46299	,,	Cameron, J.	46326	,,	Meister, O.
46302	,,	Churchill, B. J.	46327	,,	Mader, W.
46817	,,	Curley, D.	46328	,,	Mills, C.
46300	,,	Dundale, K.	46329	,,	McLellan, L.
46301	,,	Duke, T.	46330	,,	Nearing, N.
46303	,,	Francis, M.	46331	,,	O'Connor, A. G.

Canadian Pacific—The Empire's Greatest Railway.

17TH BATTALION—NOT BRIGADED—cont.

Regl. No.	Rank.	Name.	Regl. No.	Rank.	Name.
46332	Private	Parker, R.	46340	Private	Spurr, A.
46876	,,	Powers, J.	46341	,,	Stafford, W.
46333	,,	Rowe, J.	46342	,,	St. Lewis, J.
46334	,,	Ritchie, W.	46343	,,	Savoir, F.
46335	,,	Roberts, A.	46344	,,	Scott, W.
46336	,,	Ruffee, G.	46287	Cook	Wrenott
46338	,,	Sanders, O.	46345	,,	Wile, J. B.
46339	,,	Selig, M.	46043	,,	Van Buskirk, F.

"C" COMPANY.

Regl. No.	Rank.	Name.	Regl. No.	Rank.	Name.
46443	Col.-Sgt.	Hall, C.	46476	Private	Emmett, J.
46445	Sergt.	Black, J. W. E.	46477	,,	Eggins, J.
46446	,,	Cupiss, F.	46478	,,	Emery, T.
46615	,,	Harkness, L. C.	46479	,,	Evans, H. S.
46447	,,	McFayden, K.	46480	,,	Fox, A. W.
46444	,,	Wilson, J.	46481	,,	Foster, S.
46455	Corpl.	Atkinson, S.	46485	,,	Foyle, R.
46562	,,	Durkin, R.	46482	,,	Fry, W.
46450	,,	Fidler, C.	46483	,,	Franklin, A.
46561	,,	Jardine, W.	46484	,,	French, H.
46554	,,	Whelon, E.	46489	,,	Gardner, J.
46451	,,	Whiley, H.	46486	,,	Green, A.
46452	Arm.-Cpl.	Davis, J.	46487	,,	Grant, J.
46456	Lce.-Cpl.	Bellamy, W. O.	46488	,,	Govain, J.
46453	Private	Alderson, T.	46493	,,	Hiam, W.
46455	,,	Atkinson, R.	46491	,,	Higgins, P.
46457	,,	Blackburn, R.	46492	,,	Hussey, H.
46458	,,	Broadwood, J.	46494	,,	Jackson, R.
46459	,,	Boyd, H. O.	46495	,,	Johnson, J. E.
46460	,,	Barnes, P.	46497	,,	Knight, W.
46466	,,	Beesley, J.	46498	,,	Kennedy, E.
46461	,,	Bremner, A.	46503	,,	Lamb, H.
46462	,,	Brown, W.	46500	,,	Larmour, D.
46464	,,	Burcey, R.	46488	,,	Lawson, A.
46463	,,	Brown, V.	46501	,,	Lewis, D.
46465	,,	Burley, J.	46502	,,	Leddingham, G.
46469	,,	Clarke, J. A.	46504	,,	Linnington, H.
46560	,,	Chittick, H.	46499	,,	Luscombe, A. H.
46470	,,	Cholmondeley, R.	46510	,,	Maxfield, F.
46468	,,	Connelly, P.	46505	,,	Mercer, J. C.
46471	,,	Cootes, R.	46506	,,	Moore, E. H.
46472	,,	Creedon, J.	46507	,,	Morris, W.
46467	,,	Crockford, J.	46508	,,	Murray, G.
46473	,,	Dayment, W. H.	46509	,,	Murphy, J.
46285	Bugler	Dean, G.	46517	,,	McArthur, D.
46474	Private	Devally, J.	46512	,,	McDonnell, J.
46475	,,	Dickson, C.	46520	,,	McDougall, V. H.

Canadian Pacific—The Empire's Greatest Railway.

17TH BATTALION—NOT BRIGADED—cont.

Regl. No.	Rank	Name	Regl. No.	Rank	Name
46521	Private	McKenzie, F.	46543	Private	Shaw, T.
46516	,,	McKenzie, D.	46538	,,	Sherlock, T.
46518	,,	McLean, E. S.	46539	,,	Smith, F.
46511	,,	McLeod, A.	46541	,,	Smith, P. J.
46515	,,	McNeil, H. S.	46540	,,	Spriggs, A. E.
46519	,,	McIvor, P.	46542	,,	Stroud, R.
46514	,,	McQuarrie, J.	46545	,,	Swane, A. W.
46524	,,	Nesbitt, F.	46547	,,	Train, W.
46525	,,	Newman, C.	46549	,,	Wakeland, L.
46522	,,	Nunn, R. J.	46551	,,	Walker, S.
46523	,,	Nolan, J. J.	46556	,,	Walsh, P.
46529	,,	O'Grady, T.	46555	,,	Watts, G. E.
46527	,,	Old, F.	46449	,,	Warren, R. M.
46528	,,	Oliver, James	46550	,,	Webb, C.
46526	,,	Onley, A.	46553	,,	White, P.
46530	,,	Pass, G.	46558	,,	Williams, H.
46531	,,	Peters, A.	46557	,,	Williams, J. A.
46533	,,	Peterson, B.	46454	,,	Wise, J.
46532	,,	Pullen, A.	46552	,,	Wood, C. L.
46535	,,	Reid, A.	46907	,,	Woolston, E.
46536	,,	Richardson, R.	46548	,,	Woolston, W.
46544	,,	Scutner, F.	46559	,,	Yell, C.
46537	,,	Sharman, W. J.			

"D" COMPANY.

Regl. No.	Rank	Name	Regl. No.	Rank	Name
46614	Col.-Sgt.	Clark, E. W.	46643	Private	McCulloch, H.
46617	Sergt.	Thorpe, H.	46631	,,	MacDougall, F.
46632	Private	Anderson, J. M.	46642	,,	McKellar, T. B.
46633	,,	Cameron, W R.	46634	,,	MacMaster, J.
46636	,,	Connacher, Jas.	46641	,,	Miller, Jos.
46629	,,	Fernie. D.	46639	,,	Noble, P. F.
46627	,,	Gordon, Geo.	46640	,,	Phillips, G. H.
46628	,,	Hepburn, W.	46630	,,	Seggir, J.
46635	,,	Lamont, W.	46637	,,	Simpson, E. A.
46638	,,	Lemon, C. R.			

"E" COMPANY.

Regl. No.	Rank	Name	Regl. No.	Rank	Name
46785	Col.-Sgt.	McInnes, J. E.	46852	Corpl.	King, T. W.
46786	Sergt.	Donovan, P. J.	46790	,,	Webb, A. J.
46789	,,	Meades, Henry	46793	,,	Willey, Geo.
46788	,,	Mont, John	46794	Arm.-Cpl.	Lister, Earl
46787	,,	Sowden, Geo.	46797	Lce.-Cpl.	Davidge, F.
46792	Corpl.	Curtis, H.	46795	,,	Markham, H.
46791	,,	Dale, Jerry	46796	,,	McKay, H.

Canadian Pacific—The Empire's Greatest Railway.

17TH BATTALION—NOT BRIGADED—cont.

Regl. No.	Rank.	Name.	Regl. No.	Rank.	Name.
46798	Lce.-Cpl.	Watling, A.	46853	Private	Livingstone, J.
46803	Private	Ashley, Thos.	46855	,,	Lowther, S.
46816	,,	Bailey, R.	46856	,,	Luck, J. H.
46806	,,	Barkhouse, G.	46859	,,	Mann, A.
46815	,,	Barrett, A.	46912	,,	Mann, Chas.
46908	,,	Best, W.	46860	,,	Meekins, J.
46809	,,	Boreham, F.	46801	,,	Millington, J.
46811	,,	Boss, N.	46861	,,	Mountford, T.
46810	,,	Bradley, E.	46866	,,	McDonald, R.
46812	,,	Brodie, P.	46869	,,	McFeeters, D.
46813	,,	Buchanan, J.	46864	,,	McIsaac, Pat.
46807	,,	Burnley, F.	46865	,,	McIsaac, Frank
46814	,,	Burnstein, J.	46868	,,	McKinnon, Neil
46818	,,	Cameron, H.	46867	,,	McLeod, J.
46800	Bugler	Campbell, J.	46870	,,	McPherson, H.
46819	Private	Chapman, R.	46863	,,	McTague, J.
46823	,,	Churchill, D.	46871	,,	Nicholls, Hugh
46820	,,	Coates, R.	46873	,,	Oakley, J. S.
46825	,,	Cook, F. C.	46875	,,	O'Brien, J.
46821	,,	Cook, G.	46872	,,	O'Kane, D.
46824	,,	Cook, Gordon	46909	,,	Orr, Chas.
46822	,,	Crosson, J.	46874	,,	Oxnard, J.
46799	Bugler	Danson, H.	46878	,,	Phillips, H.
46830	Private	Davis, H.	46879	,,	Pippin, C.
46826	,,	Davison, F.	46880	,,	Pierce, C.
46827	,,	Dewar, H.	46802	,,	Porter, Wm.
46828	,,	Doncaster, J.	46881	,,	Rees, C.
46829	,,	Doncaster, F.	46882	,,	Rees, Gus
46834	,,	Ellis, H.	46883	,,	Reilly, Gordon
46831	,,	Ellsworth, M.	46884	,,	Roach, W.
46832	,,	Embree, W.	46885	,,	Ryan, T.
46833	,,	Everson, H.	46893	,,	Sloan, J.
46835	,,	Fenton, W.	46887	,,	Sloss, R. G.
46838	,,	Ferdinand, H.	46890	,,	Smith, F.
46837	,,	Foster, A.	46891	,,	Smith, R.
46836	,,	Friend, G.	46912	,,	Smith, T. M.
46840	,,	Gallagher, L.	46886	,,	Spencer, C. L.
46062	,,	Garrison, H.	46892	,,	Stephenson, E.
46839	,,	Goddard, E.	46896	,,	Tabor, Roy
46841	,,	Goldrick, W.	46897	,,	Taylor, S.
46842	,,	Goodwin, A.	46895	,,	Temple, J.
46843	,,	Grimley, H.	46898	,,	Terriss, D.
46844	,,	Higgs, L.	46899	,,	Thompson, J.
46845	,,	Holt, T.	46894	,,	Touchet, A.
46847	,,	Inderwick, B.	46900	,,	Townshend, G.
46848	,,	Jennings, W.	46901	,,	Warren, F.
46849	,,	Judge, A. L.	46906	,,	Webb, J. E.
46851	,,	Kent, J.	46904	,,	White, H.
46850	,,	Kingsley, C.	46902	,,	Wilson, J. W.
46854	,,	Langill, D.	46905	,,	Winship, M.
46857	,,	Lawrence, Wm.	46903	,,	Wynn, L.

Canadian Pacific—The Empire's Greatest Railway.

17TH BATTALION—NOT BRIGADED—cont.

"F" COMPANY.

Regl. No.	Rank.	Name.	Regl. No.	Rank.	Name.
46956	Col.-Sgt.	Louth, C. E.	47011	Private	Holland, J. J.
46957	Sergt.	Fraser, S. M.	47009	,,	Hynd, R.
46958	,,	Seaman, G. A.	47012	,,	Johnson, G.
46960	Private	Seymour, J.	47014	,,	Kennedy, J.
46959	Sergt.	Simpson, E.	47013	,,	Kirk, G.
46965	Corpl.	Burt, F.	47015	,,	Lamming, G.
46963	,,	Coulter, F. W.	46974	Cook	Livingstone, J.
46964	,,	Grant, A. G.	47017	Private	Long, W.
46961	,,	McDonald, B.	47016	,,	Luscombe, J.
46962	,,	Taylor, J. E.	47018	,,	Mason, L.
46966	Arm.-Cpl.	McFarlane, W.	47057	,,	Miller, R. L.
46967	Lce.-Cpl.	McLeod, W.	47053	,,	Morris, F. H.
46968	,,	McKenzie, A. J.	47034	,,	Murphy, J.
47048	,,	Turner, W. A.	47029	,,	McArthur, A.
47052	,,	Urquhart, E.	47036	,,	McDonald, D.
46976	Private	Ainsworth, W.	47027	,,	McDonald, G. B.
46975	,,	Armour, J.	46971	Bugler	McDonald, J. G.
46977	,,	Armstrong, W.	47033	Private	McDonald, R.
46978	,,	Baigent, A.	47026	,,	McDonald, W. R.
46979	,,	Betts, N.	47020	,,	McGillvray, D.
46983	,,	Bishop, A.	47030	,,	McIntosh, J.
46980	,,	Bower, H.	46970	,,	McKay, N.
46981	,,	Bowran, W.	47035	,,	McKenzie, A.
46982	,,	Brawn, J. D.	47056	,,	McKenzie, D.
46989	,,	Canham, R. S.	47023	,,	McKinnon, S.
46988	,,	Cantley, J.	47031	,,	McLaren, E.
46992	,,	Carberry, T.	47022	,,	McLaughlin, A.
46993	,,	Carrigan, G.	47021	,,	McLaughlin, W.
46995	,,	Chisholm, C.	47024	,,	McLennon, F.
46994	,,	Clark, G.	47025	,,	McNeil, H.
46984	,,	Classen, E.	47019	,,	McNeil, J.
46990	,,	Cook, O. S.	47032	,,	McPherson, J.
46991	,,	Cox, A. H.	47040	,,	Patterson, B.
46985	,,	Curley, D.	47039	,,	Payton, J.
46986	,,	Currie, John	47037	,,	Penny, J.
46987	,,	Curry, Joe	47038	,,	Pollard, H.
47000	,,	Dawson, R. W.	47972	Bugler	Rees, D.
46996	,,	Day, W.	47047	Private	Richards, C.
46999	,,	Dinnie, D.	47054	,,	Ritchie, J.
46997	,,	Dixon, E.	47041	,,	Robertson, A.
46998	,,	Dewar, J.	47042	,,	Robinson, A.
47001	,,	Fleod, J.	47055	,,	Rogers, J. H.
47005	,,	Forbes, H.	47043	,,	Rogers, N. W.
47003	,,	Forsythe, E.	47044	,,	Ross, M.
47002	,,	Fry, H.	47045	,,	Ross, H.
47004	,,	Graham, R.	47046	,,	Ross, A. R.
47006	,,	Grossart, A.	47050	,,	Smith, M.
47059	,,	Hall, F.	47060	,,	Thompson, E.
46973	Cook	Hallam, J.	47049	,,	Tudy, J. R.
47008	Private	Hicken, S.			

Canadian Pacific—The Empire's Greatest Railway.

17TH BATTALION—NOT BRIGADED—cont. 225

"G" COMPANY.

Regl. No.	Rank.	Name.
47127	Col.-Sgt.	Mulholland, J.
47129	Sergt.	Groshaw, W.
47128	,,	Hands, C.
47131	,,	Nussey, W.
47130	Lce.-Sgt.	Watts, M.
47132	Corpl.	Wilson, J.,
47153	,,	Johnstone, S.
47347	,,	Eversfield, T.
46209	Arm.-Cpl.	Waldorf, W.
47133	Lce.-Cpl.	Hexter, H. C.
47170	Private	Andrews, A.
47136	,,	Axford, T.
47172	,,	Baldock, E.
47171	,,	Baxter, A.
47173	,,	Beeching, T.
47135	Cook	Binns, J.
47174	Private	Bourne, A.
47137	,,	Broadway, S.
47138	Cook	Broadway, M.
47139	Private	Bronquist, G.
47177	,,	Calloway, S.
47175	,,	Caney, W.
47142	,,	Challenger, F.
47140	,,	Chapple, J.
47176	,,	Coley, C.
47141	,,	Corbett, J.
47178	,,	Craig, W.
47179	,,	Dadson, H.
47144	,,	Dann, J.
47143	,,	Davis, J.
47204	,,	Davis, W.
47145	,,	Ellerback, F.
47146	,,	Fleming, H.
47180	,,	Francis, R.
47181	,,	Geer, G.
47183	,,	Gibbons, F.
47182	,,	Goldsmith, T.
47148	,,	Hammond, C.
47185	,,	Hanon, A.
47205	,,	Harkness, G.
47147	,,	Hawker, G.

Regl. No.	Rank.	Name.
47184	Private	Hay, F.
149	,,	Hearson, J.
47187	,,	Hollandy, A.
47186	,,	Horton, F.
47152	,,	Jenkins, J. A.
47150	,,	Jones, E.
47151	,,	Jones, T.
47189	,,	Kenley, K.
47188	,,	Kemp, A.
47190	,,	Lambden, G.
47154	,,	Linton, P.
47157	,,	Martin, F.
47191	,,	Mason, G.
47192	,,	Maver, W.
47155	,,	Mills, J.
47156	,,	Mitchell, R.
47193	,,	Moon, P.
47202	,,	Mynott, A. F.
47206	,,	McGuiness, A.
47160	,,	Priaulx, A.
47194	,,	Prior, R.
47195	,,	Quinnell, F.
47196	,,	Rich, R.
47165	,,	Riley, J.
47161	,,	Rodgers, W.
47163	,,	Ruse, R.
47162	,,	Ryan, T.
47199	,,	Sanders, E.
17168	,,	Simmonds, F.
47167	,,	Smith, C.
47169	,,	Stewart, G.
47166	,,	Stroud, F.
46888	,,	Sullivan, J.
47197	,,	Sykes, A.
47200	,,	Taylor, W.
47409	,,	Trethewey, H.
47201	,,	Usherwood, J.
47203	,,	Vankoughnet, P.
47411	,,	Waide, P.
47198	,,	Wyles, S.

"H" COMPANY.

Regl. No.	Rank.	Name.
47298	Col.-Sgt.	Langtry, L.
47299	Sergt.	Appleton, H. A.
47302	,,	Bullock, H.

Regl. No.	Rank.	Name.
47301	Private	Ellis, P. H.
47300	,,	Riddle, J. J.
47303	Lce.-Sgt.	Mallory, H. R.

Canadian Pacific—The Empire's Greatest Railway.

P

17TH BATTALION—NOT BRIGADED—cont.

Regl. No.	Rank.	Name.	Regl. No.	Rank.	Name.
47305	Corpl.	Allsopp, W. H.	47365	Private	Hendy, F.
47306	,,	Bliss, E.	47316	,,	Henthorn, T. G.
47308	Arm.Cpl.	Gibson, A.	47359	,,	Holdsworth, W.
47313	Lce.-Cpl.	Charles, L.	47362	,,	Howard, H.
47311	,,	House, E.	47360	,,	Hudgin, E. A.
47309	,,	Leedham, W. L.	47361	,,	Hunt, S. H.
47312	,,	Porritt, J. M.	47363	,,	Hutcheson, J.
47310	,,	Raisbeck, Geo.	47366	,,	Irons, T.
47321	Private	Aimes, J.	47367	,,	Jackson, E. H.
47317	,,	Aithie, G.	47368	,,	Lacey, A.
47319	,,	Andrews, L. J.	47369	,,	Lawton, A. E.
47423	,,	Andrews, R.	47370	,,	Leitch, J. F.
47320	,,	Ashton, L.	47371	,,	Lewis, F.
47318	,,	Austin, L.	47373	,,	Ling, G.
47326	,,	Bailey, F.	47372	,,	Lucas, R. H.
47327	,,	Barnard, A.	47376	,,	McCartney S.
47328	,,	Barnett, W.	47377	,,	McConnell, E.
47329	,,	Bell, F.	47380	,,	Mallinson, W.
47322	,,	Bennett, F.	47379	,,	Marney, R.
47324	,,	Berry, G.	47375	,,	Martin, H.
47330	,,	Bliss, E.	47381	,,	Mason, J.
47331	,,	Boyle, P.	47384	,,	Miller, T. E.
47332	,,	Bradley, E.	47383	,,	Miller, R.
47333	,,	Brannigan, T. P.	47374	,,	Mills, S.
47334	,,	Brown, W.	47385	,,	Molloy, J.
47325	,,	Burgess, C.	47386	,,	Monkman, S. C.
47323	,,	Butler, F.	47382	,,	Moore, G. H.
47335	,,	Caine, W.	47378	,,	Muirhead, E. F.
47336	,,	Castle, A.	47424	,,	Nagle, H. A.
47337	,,	Chalmers, F.	47387	,,	Nokes, W. J.
47338	,,	Corfield, S.	47389	,,	O'Brien, G.
47339	,,	Cowie, W,	47388	,,	Owen, F.
47340	,,	Cross, L. W.	47390	,,	Pavier, F.
47341	,,	Cullen, J.	47391	,,	Perkes, G.
47343	,,	Dalton, F.	47392	,,	Purdy, J.
47344	,,	Davis, S.	47393	,,	Rafferty, F.
47345	,,	Doidge, A. J.	47395	,,	Raisbeck, Thos.
47342	,,	Dunn, J.	47398	,,	Reece, R.
47346	,,	Eastwood, D.	47396	,,	Renwick, T.
47348	,,	Essex, J. W.	47394	,,	Richards, R.
47350	,,	Fernie, A.	47397	,,	Rigby, J.
47349	,,	Finn, O.	47422	,,	Rigby, Joe
47351	,,	Fisher, A. F.	47399	,,	Robertson, G.
47352	,,	Fowle, A.	47400	,,	Robinson, W.
47353	,,	Gallagher, J.	47401	,,	Rowland, H.
47358	,,	Garrett, A. G.	47402	,,	Scott, A.
47355	,,	Goode, A. C.	47403	,,	Short, J.
47354	,,	Grant, J.	47404	,,	Spinks, J.
47356	,,	Graver, G.	47405	,,	Stevenson, J.
47357	,,	Gray, G.	47406	,,	Tighe, J.
47315	,,	Green, W. G.	47407	,,	Torrance, E. A.
47364	,,	Hawkins, S. E.	47410	,,	Turley, W. C.

Canadian Pacific—The Empire's Greatest Railway.

17TH BATTALION—NOT BRIGADED—cont.

Regl. No.	Rank.	Name.	Regl. No.	Rank.	Name.
47408	Private	Tyrrell, G. G.	47415	Private	Wilson, J.
47314	,,	Wallace, W.	47417	,,	Wisoner, W.
47411	,,	Walsh, R.	47420	Act.-Sgt.	Wells, J.
47413	,,	Walt, J.	47419	Private	Wheeler, R.
47414	,,	Wardell, E.	47418	,,	Whitney, P.
47421	,,	Watson, H.	47416	,,	Wood, T.

PRINCESS PATRICIA'S CANADIAN LIGHT INFANTRY.

Headquarters.

Lieut.-Colonel	Farquhar, Francis Douglas, D.S.O.
Major	Gault, Andrew Hamilton
Captain and Adjutant	Buller, Herbert Cecil DSO
Surgeon-Major	Keenan, Campbell Brown
Hon. Lieut. and Quartermaster	Wake, Charles Alexander
Hon. Captain and Paymaster	Bennett, George Horace

No. 1 COMPANY.

Major	Pelly, Raymond Theodore
Captain	Smith, Cuthbert Fairbanks
,,	Colquhoun, William Gourlay
,,	Cornish, Philip Victor
,,	Minchin, Frederick Frank
,,	Eardley-Wilmot, Frederick Lawrence

Regl. No.	Rank.	Name.	Regl. No.	Rank.	Name.
3	R.S.M.	Fraser, Alexander	203	Lce.-Sgt.	Martin, Stanley
2	C.Q.M.S.	Bradley, Joseph H.	204	Corpl.	Abram, Thomas
193	C.S.M.	Smith, Harry Geo. L.	236	,,	Cordery, Albert
292	Q.M.S.	Lake, Richd. Shepherd	155	,,	Franks, Arthur
267	,,	Hoad, Albert Joseph	23	,,	Dean, Thomas
38	Sergt.	Lee, James	115	,,	Linnington, Alfred
50	,,	Philpotts, James	58	Private	Allen, Harry Thomas
136	,,	Carvell, George Cecil	70	,,	Aiken, Robert
201	,,	Brown, John George	72	,,	Ashton, William
150	,,	McBrearty, Robert	79	,,	Anderson, James
151	,,	Lofts, Herbert	92	,,	Armstrong, Henry
29	,,	Stamper, Walter	133	,,	Air, Robert
213	,,	Lloyd, Walter	198	,,	Austin, George
262	,,	Laing, Henry	233	,,	Arnold, William E.
48	,,	Benham, John	246	,,	Astley, Harry
9	,,	Wigney, Clarence R.	40	,,	Barrett, Edward
142	Lce-Sgt.	Brock, Edwin Gordon	5	,,	Boulter, Robert
286	,,	Laing, Robert	30	,,	Brassell, Albert
8	,,	Mansfield, Robert	34	,,	Buzzacott, Arthur

Canadian Pacific—The Empire's Greatest Railway.

228 PRINCESS PATRICIA'S CANADIAN LT. INFANTRY—cont.

Regl. No.	Rank.	Name.
73	Private	Bliss, Thomas
93	,,	Brock, George
106	,,	Buchanan, Robert
121	,,	Bleakley, James
143	,,	Beattie, Samuel
146	,,	Burns, Joseph
163	Lce.-Cpl.	Bowness, James
168	,,	Betts, William
175	Private	Bassinger, Frederick
185	,,	Boswell, Henry
199	,,	Burdett, Francis
208	,,	Bowie, William
235	,,	Burton, Frank
258	,,	Blackman, John
259	,,	Barrett, Sidney
280	,,	Bishop, William
1018	,,	Brydon, George
11	,,	Cavanagh, Frederick
22	,,	Campbell, John
55	,,	Clarke, Henry
61	,,	Cooper, Harry
63	,,	Cosh, Harold
78	,,	Cross, Peter
98	,,	Crane, Harry
108	,,	Collinge, John
123	,,	Connor, William
249	,,	Conway, John
135	,,	Cork, Alfred
140	,,	Campbell, Thomas
194	,,	Coleby, Frederick
160	,,	Crokey, George Fredk.
166	,,	Clifford, Frank
225	,,	Carr, Robert
240	,,	Chappell, George H.
248	Lce.-Cpl.	Cope, John
251	Private	Craig, Charles Henry
271	,,	Cundiff, Arthur
296	,,	Cripps, Alfred
153	,,	Connaughton, Charles
6	,,	Dursley, William
16	,,	Ducker, Arthur E.
18	,,	Dedman, William
43	,,	Donald, John
59	,,	Downey, Robert
68	,,	Doyle, James
81	,,	Dicker, William
91	,,	Don, Peter Stuart
114	,,	Dunning, James
118	,,	Daffern, Albert
159	,,	Driver, Alfred
195	,,	Dempster, Alexander
237	,,	Dorney, Arthur Jas.
218	Private	Dawson, Chris. H. L.
21	,,	Evans, Herbert
24	,,	Everett, William
33	,,	Emery, Thomas
39	,,	Edwards, Edward
102	Lce.-Cpl.	Elson, William
124	Private	Eastham, Hy. George
269	,,	Easton, George
75	,,	Fry, Henry
147	,,	Fox, George
183	,,	Foreman, Frederick
191	,,	Frith, Thomas
1312	Act. Sgt.	Finnemore, Charles
209	Private	Foster, James
223	,,	Finlay, James
252	,,	Fry, Norman
17	,,	Gee, Philip
20	,,	Geekie, David
26	,,	Gillies, Henry
95	,,	Gilpin, John
56	,,	Green, John
65	,,	Gilbey, George
83	,,	Gardner, William
99	,,	Grant, Arthur S.
117	,,	Graham, Robert
134	Lce.-Cpl.	Gordon, James
157	Private	Gillen, Frank
158	,,	Gallagher, Bernard
181	,,	Gough, William
229	,,	Griffiths, Samuel
257	,,	Grey, John
276	,,	Gillen, Charles
1145	,,	Garvey, Patrick
13	,,	Horton, Albert
19	,,	Horner, Charles Ed.
37	,,	Haslett, Robert
47	,,	Harrison, Harry
52	,,	Harmon, Arthur
53	,,	Hill, Arthur
207	,,	Horn, Walter
62	,,	Hennings, Oscar
80	,,	Hannan, John
82	,,	Hicks, William
87	,,	Hogg, George
129	,,	Hubbard, John
130	,,	Hubbard, Frederick
154	Lce.-Cpl.	Hayes, Robert Cecil
173	Private	Huntington, Harry
179	,,	Harrison, James
222	,,	Hawke, Herbert
227	,,	Harding, Charles
250	,,	Higgins, William

Canadian Pacific—The Empire's Greatest Railway.

PRINCESS PATRICIA'S CANADIAN LT. INFANTRY—cont.

Regl. No.	Rank.	Name.	Regl. No.	Rank.	Name.
253	Private	Hayes, Harry	186	Private	Nash, Charles
263	,,	Herrick, John	231	,,	O'Neill, Thomas
273	,,	Hatchman, John	127	,,	Ottaway, Arthur
285	,,	Harness, Alfred	88	,,	Porter, Frank
101	,,	Jermy, Thomas	178	,,	Pearson, George
138	,,	Jackson, Henry	180	,,	Proudfoot, Bennett
171	,,	Johnson, Frank	27	,,	Patten, Thomas
284	,,	Jerred, Samuel	294	,,	Proctor, Frederick
299	,,	Jackson, John	71	,,	Quinn, William
109	,,	Kennedy, Adam	89	,,	Rees, Daniel
111	,,	Kelso, John	96	,,	Roberts, Edward
164	,,	Kirby, Herbert Ed.	301	,,	Roberts, Joseph
210	,,	Knevett, Jas.	104	,,	Rudolph, Leslie
245	,,	Knight, John	113	,,	Ruddigan, Thomas
31	Lce.-Cpl.	Leach, Harry	148	,,	Ross, Donald
46	Private	Lilley, Daniel	177	,,	Ross, Allister Cameron
51	,,	Lang, Alexander, Wm.	182	,,	Richardson, William
74	,,	Larkin, Frederick	261	,,	Rippin, John
105	,,	Lawrie, James	264	,,	Ritchie, John
112	,,	Lavery, Samuel	265	,,	Robertson, Wm. McB.
125	,,	Last, Frank	279	,,	Ratcliffe, William
152	,,	Lewis, Samuel	32	,,	Stevens, Arthur
141	,,	Lee, Charles	64	,,	Sowden, Walter
200	,,	Lancaster, Henry	77	,,	Scarfe, Charles
221	,,	Lewthwaite, John	84	,,	Skinner, Albert Victor
238	,,	Leith, William G.	85	,,	Sweetland, George
303	,,	Logan, David	119	,,	Smith, Richard
243	,,	Logue, Robert	170	,,	Stock, Albert
219	,,	Leach, John	184	,,	Shepherd, George
161	,,	Lindop, George	187	,,	Sheriff, Lorne
1034	,,	Little, Alfred	188	,,	Souch, William
1777	,,	Lee, Frank Edward	211	,,	Skinner, Henry
28	,,	Marchant, Samuel D.	212	,,	Smith, John
66	,,	Morley, George	232	,,	Scott, William
122	,,	Mannion, Thomas	239	,,	Simpson, Harold
128	,,	Moore, John	254	,,	Stanborough, Walter
162	,,	Masson, John	278	,,	Sibthorpe, James
169	,,	Marsh, George	270	,,	Stanner, Charles
228	,,	Matthews, Percy	1100	,,	Simpson, Robert
234	,,	Montgomery, William	7	,,	Tilley, Frederick
256	,,	Murphy, Bartholomew	76	,,	Taylor, Samuel
281	,,	Matthews, Graham	107	,,	Taylor, Oliver B.
295	,,	Mickleburgh, Ernest	131	,,	Taylor, George
300	,,	Manser, George	165	,,	Thomas, Harry
15	,,	McArthy, John	174	,,	Todd, Herbert
41	,,	McManus, Joseph	189	,,	Taylor, James
167	,,	McDermott, Thomas	217	,,	Tomlinson, Charles
255	,,	McAllum, Leigh	220	,,	Trindell, Edward
266	,,	McLean, Charles	241	,,	Thorburn, William
86	,,	Nixon, Charles	4	,,	Woodhams, William
126	,,	Nelson, Harry	35	,,	Wing, William
172	,,	Nourse, Charles	42	,,	Woods, Frederick

Canadian Pacific—The Empire's Greatest Railway.

230 PRINCESS PATRICIA'S CANADIAN LT. INFANTRY—cont.

Regl. No.	Rank.	Name.	Regl. No.	Rank.	Name.
54	Private	Watterson, James	214	Private	Walden, Joseph
90	,,	White, Joseph	224	,,	Warren, Alfred E.
94	,,	Webb, Charles	226	,,	Wells, Frederick
100	,,	Walker, Charles	242	,,	Wolstenholme, John L.
116	,,	Waylett, Joseph	268	,,	Wiltshire, James
144	,,	Warner, Frederick	275	,,	West, William
149	,,	Wassell, Maurice	44	,,	Wright, George
206	,,	Wing, John	196	,,	Young, Frederick

No. 2 COMPANY.

Major	...	...	...	...	McKinery, John William Herbert
Captain	...	...	...	...	Adamson, Agar
Lieutanant	...	...	...	...	Jones, Stanley Livingstone
,,		...	...	...	Niven, Hugh Wilderspin
,,		...	...	...	Bainsmith, Bruce Fred
,,		...	...	...	Sulivan, Henry Ernest

Regl. No.	Rank.	Name.	Regl. No.	Rank.	Name.
1315	C.S.M.	Dames, James Wm.	753	Private	Bateson, Henry L.
500	C.Q.M.S.	Foden, Wm. John	642	,,	Beech, Albert H. S.
667	PipeMaj.	Colville, John	755	,,	Beken, William Henry
777	Sergt.	Iles, Wm. Robert H.	760	,,	Bell, Thomas
624	,,	Stirling, David	629	,,	Bertram, Reginald J.
830	,,	Grattan, Andrew	637	,,	Blane, William James
829	,,	Parker, James	712	,,	Blees, Jack
751	,,	Aldridge, George C.	558	,,	Blitch, Alfred
852	,,	Watkins, Donald McG.	531	,,	Boundy, Charles
833	,,	Bevington, Ernest J.	837	,,	Boyer, David
640	,,	Scott, Louis	807	,,	Brettell, James E.
651	,,	Soley, Fred Henry	825	Lce.-Cpl.	Brown, Gerald H.
635	,,	Stone, Arthur M.	589	Private	Brown, George Henry
623	Corpl.	McDonald, George	709	,,	Bruce, William
745	,,	Holmes, Fredk. Wm.	550	,,	Buchan, Harry
665	,,	Irwin, James Henry	763	Lce.-Cpl.	Bullen, William
804	,,	Straker, Ernest J.	785	Private	Burnett, Marshall Y.
824	,,	Burrell, John Percy	518	,,	Burns, Stephen W.
774	,,	Fleming, Ernest W. B.	758	,,	Burns, Thomas
618	,,	Gillingham, Frederick	850	,,	Cadogan, Richard T.
695	,,	Connor, Harry	803	,,	Campbell, Alex. H.
539	,,	Batten, Albert	839	,,	Campbell, Frederick
672	Pipe Cpl.	McIntosh, Duncan	647	,,	Carling, Gordon B.
748	Private	Agar, Harold	811	,,	Carson, George A.
708	,,	Albrow, Archibald	878	,,	Carter, Herbert H.
662	,,	Allen, Thomas	1797	,,	Chalmers, James
810	,,	Armishaw, Percy M.	746	,,	Cheyne, William
773	,,	Almon, John Egan	759	,,	Coetzee, John
874	,,	Attwell, Walter H.	537	,,	Colborne, David
514	,,	Badley, Sidney	513	Lce.-Cpl.	Coleman, Frederick C.
764	Lce.-Cpl.	Baldock, Arthur	519	Private	Cooke, William
510	Private	Barker, Francis C. C.	517	,,	Cowley, Charles B.

Canadian Pacific—The Empire's Greatest Railway.

PRINCESS PATRICIA'S CANADIAN LT. INFANTRY—cont. 231

Regl. No.	Rank.	Name.
568	Private	Crumb, William B.
683	,,	Davey, John
572	,,	Davis, Arthur S.
569	,,	Davis, John
727	,,	Dempsey, Thomas
823	Lce.-Cpl.	Dove, Arthur Le Neve
794	Private	Dove, Andrew Amos
610	,,	Drake, Alfred
737	,,	Duncan, George
547	,,	Dunn, James P.
595	,,	Dwyer, Guy
507	Lce.-Cpl.	Edgar, James Nesbitt
704	Private	Elliott, Andrew
703	,,	Farrell, Frank
791	,,	Ferguson, Norman
541	,,	Fisher, Duncan
645	,,	Flintoft, Thomas
853	Lce.-Cpl.	Forrest, Guy A.
656	Private	Fowler, Richard T.
713	,,	Francis, Thomas
659	,,	Frend, William
521	,,	Gibson, Albert A.
700	,,	Gibson, Robert A.
511	,,	Giles, Thomas
714	,,	Goodall, Henry
602	,,	Grant, George
770	,,	Grant, Robert
710	,,	Hall, Alfred Edward
796	,,	Hampson, Albert
769	,,	Hance, William R.
699	,,	Harris, James
721	,,	Harrison, John Henry
644	,,	Harry, Wilmot Earl
1086	,,	Havelock, Fred C.
522	,,	Hawkridge, Sydney
754	,,	Hawley, Edward B.
655	,,	Hoey, Thomas S. H.
854	,,	Horner, Archibald H.
788	,,	Howell, Edward T.
840	,,	Hudson, Charles
799	,,	Humphreys, Sydney
616	,,	Hunt, Henry
795	Lce.-Cpl.	Huston, Wm. John
787	Private	Hustwayte, Henry
784	,,	Jameson, George
506	,,	Jeandron, Philip G.
806	,,	Jennings, Edward S.
877	,,	Jennings, Sydney
693	,,	Jervis, William
834	,,	Johnson, Gerald A.
838	,,	Johnston, Alfred
869	,,	Johnston, William

Regl. No.	Rank.	Name.
552	Private	Johnston, William G.
686	,,	Jones, John
591	,,	Jones, Sidney
798	,,	Joslin, James Alfred
674	,,	Joyce, Charles
757	,,	Kay, John
691	,,	Kerr, William
863	,,	King, Charles Henry
45	,,	King, John Douglas
868	,,	Kysh, William B.
584	,,	Laing, Robert A.
605	,,	Langford, William
786	,,	Lawson, Walter G.
634	,,	Lewis, Albert John
772	,,	Little, Charles
780	,,	Lloyd, Samuel
873	,,	Love, Henry
599	,,	Madison, Horace
528	,,	Magee, Robert Henry
769	,,	Marchant, Henry G.
685	,,	Martin, Charles
836	,,	Masters, Thomas
702	,,	Mayor, Arthur
596	,,	Meachem, Albert G.
730	,,	Meiklejohn, James
502	,,	Miller, John William
677	,,	Miller, William
866	,,	Mohan, Joseph Percy
789	,,	Montgomery, James A.
765	,,	Morgan, Herbert
761	,,	Morrison, Val H. B.
813	,,	Mould, Arthur
601	,,	Mowat, James A.
828	,,	Mulvey, William
697	,,	Murdoch, John
619	,,	Murray, George
578	Lce.-Cpl.	Murray, Neil
802	Private	Macartney, Donald H.
676	,,	McCloy, John
690	,,	McConnell, Samuel
783	,,	McCullough, Samuel
535	,,	McCusker, Charles
859	,,	Macdonald, Archie
705	,,	MacDonald, Donald
860	,,	Macdonald, John
545	,,	McEachran, James G.
561	,,	McIntyre, Alexander
812	,,	McIntyre, James
817	,,	McIntyre, Lloyd
579	,,	MacKay, Mackay
711	,,	McKenzie, George
848	,,	MacLachlan, Angus

Canadian Pacific—The Empire's Greatest Railway.

232 PRINCESS PATRICIA'S CANADIAN LT. INFANTRY—cont.

Regl. No.	Rank.	Name.	Regl. No.	Rank.	Name.
658	Private	McLeod, Norman	657	Private	Sims, James
762	,,	McLeod, Percy	534	,,	Simpson, Cecil Jas. S.
664	,,	McMahon, Thomas	603	Lce.-Cpl.	Sinclair, Neil Francis
621	,,	McMorris, George	801	Private	Small, James
858	,,	McNish, James	530	,,	Smith, Carl
800	,,	McPhee, Angus	192	,,	Smith, Colin C. D.
526	,,	Needes, Sydney	790	,,	Smith, Ernest
633	,,	Neilans, John	835	,,	Smith, Gilbert
625	,,	Nelson, William H.	631	,,	Smith, Harry Russell
567	,,	Newton, Arthur F.	882	,,	Snowden, Edgar
767	,,	Nicol, Wenley	792	,,	Spurgeon, Christopher
814	,,	Nicholson, Reginald A.	881	,,	Starke, Robert T.
875	,,	O'Connell, Herbert F.	831	,,	Staples, Robert
862	,,	Odams, Ernest	587	,,	Stewart, George
701	,,	Owens, David	503	,,	Sturrock, Alex. M.
734	,,	Page, George	1236	,,	Sutherland, Fred
857	,,	Page, Henry	805	Lce.-Cpl.	Sweeney, Joseph E.
871	,,	Palmer, Harry	808	Private	Sykes, Arthur Darrell
654	,,	Parke, Edmund F.	716	,,	Tallamy, Wilfred
842	,,	Parry, Owen	643	,,	Tansley, Henry
652	,,	Peplar, Roger Crook	549	,,	Tate, John William
692	,,	Phillips, George R.	818	,,	Taylor, Fredk. W. J.
782	,,	Picton, Thomas Hy.	622	,,	Todd, John
533	,,	Pollock, Andrew T.	815	,,	Towler, Frank
532	,,	Poole, Irvine	666	,,	Trump, John
771	,,	Pritchett, Fredk. A.	529	,,	Tunnicliffe, Samuel
749	,,	Pryke, George Henry	536	,,	Tyler, Richard Owen
636	,,	Purvis, Robert	706	,,	Underdown, John E.
849	,,	Quinn, John	872	,,	Urquhart, Henry T.
682	,,	Rainsbury, Edward	816	,,	Vincent, Frank
768	,,	Ramage, Andrew	653	,,	Virtue, Ronald M.
793	,,	Rawsthorne, Wm. J.	627	,,	Wakeling, George A.
689	,,	Rennie, Alexander B.	1074	,,	Walsh, Maurice T.
766	,,	Richards, William A.	607	,,	Waters, James
865	,,	Richardson, Tracy	638	,,	Watson, Henry Geo.
820	,,	Riley, William	743	,,	Watson, James
879	,,	Rock, Frank R.	797	,,	Welsh, William H.
880	,,	Roeth, Michael T. O.	715	,,	Wesley, Charles
626	,,	Roffey, William	752	,,	Western, Robert Wm.
826	,,	Rooks, Lester George	1284	,,	Wheatley, Jas. G. B.
570	,,	Rowley, John	832	,,	Wheeler, Charles E. S.
559	,,	Roy, Frederick David	609	,,	Whistlecroft, John
512	Lce.-Cpl.	Ryan, Daniel	747	,,	White, Thomas
551	Private	Salsbury, Lloyd	809	,,	Williamson, Frank J.
615	,,	Sanders, Arthur	845	,,	Wilson, Arthur
614	,,	Sanders, James	639	,,	Wilson, Archibald J.
876	,,	Sawer, James	688	,,	Wilson, George Alex.
600	,,	Shannon, Alex. G.	718	,,	Worthington, James
844	,,	Shaughnessey, Michael	736	,,	Wylie, Robert
822	,,	Simmons, Arthur H.	524	,,	Young, John
819	,,	Simmons, George	641	,,	Yourston, George

Canadian Pacific—The Empire's Greatest Railway.

PRINCESS PATRICIA'S CANADIAN LT. INFANTRY—cont. 233

No. 3 COMPANY.

Captain	... ...	Ward, John Simeon
,,	... ...	Newton, Denzel Onslow Cochrane
Lieutenant	... ...	Stewart, Charles James
,,	... ...	Cameron, Donald
,,	... ...	de Bay, Michel Spruyt
,,	... ...	Papineau, Talbot Mercer
,,	... ...	Carr, John Lewis

Regl. No.	Rank.	Name.	Regl. No.	Rank.	Name.
650	C.S.M.	McDonnell, G. L.	1058	Private	Birt, Cyrus Beaumont
1316	C.Q.M.S.	Guerin, James W.	1021	,,	Borthwick, William
1000	Sergt.	Champion, Alfred G.	1059	,,	Bull, Frank
1193	,,	Rose, Harold Alfred	244	,,	Blatchford, Alfred
1311	,,	Workman, Edward C.	1094	,,	Baker, Alfred Edw.
1224	,,	de Volpi, Paul B. W.	1092	,,	Baker, William A.
1157	,,	Leach, Frederick	1110	,,	Bell, Thomas
1120	,,	Palmer, Arthur	1105	,,	Box, William
1003	,,	Hanley, Gerald Victor	1109	,,	Boath, James
1184	,,	Burgess, George J.	1288	,,	Bosc, Leon
1046	,,	Pike, Geoffrey	1108	,,	Brockbank, Henry
1199	,,	Jordan, William	1180	Lce.-Cpl.	Brider, Andrew John
1246	,,	Brown, Frank Smith	1159	,,	Bain, James William
1135	,,	Lowe, William	1167	,,	Bishop, Alfred
1001	Corpl.	Bramhall, Wm. J. J.	1122	Private	Bell, John
1270	,,	Brittain, Alfred E.	1292	,,	Bingle, Hamilton
1161	,,	Leach, Philip Wm.	1183	,,	Borland, John
1005	,,	Whitmore, Richard D.	1257	,,	Blackburn, John
1280	,,	Robins, Archibald J.	1178	,,	Burgess, Francis
1186	,,	Anderson, John	1262	,,	Burns, Harry
1195	,,	Godwin, Francais E.	1323	,,	Brown, William
1004	,,	Ridley, Mark C. W.	1338	,,	Brown, H.
1147	,,	Saunders, Frederick	1264	,,	Bellinger, Henry G.
1045	,,	Pascoe, Leslie	1267	,,	Bryant, William H.
1214	Private	Ashbee, Herbert	1247	Lce.-Cpl.	Bowler, Ernest
1175	,,	Arnaud, Ernest	720	Private	Bourne, Fred
1028	,,	Adams, Joseph L.	1008	Lce.-Cpl.	Bennett, Henry S.
1019	,,	Arnold, Albert	1126	,,	Chubb, Robert N.
1133	,,	Armitage, Henry	1012	Private	Coke, Charles
1243	,,	Appleton, Cedric	1091	,,	Complisson, Charles E.
1244	,,	Appleton, Raymond J.	1134	,,	Cooper, Frank
1156	,,	Adams, Joseph	1104	,,	Crook, Richard
1283	,,	Anderson, Leland	1289	,,	Coughlin, James
1219	,,	Anderson, George L.	1237	Lce.-Cpl.	Craig, Nathaniel
1329	,,	Allingham, James H.	1087	,,	Clarke, William
1049	,,	Bayliss, Harry	1330	Private	Clarke, Arthur R.
1011	,,	Bayliss, Stanley	1185	,,	Cairns, Robert
1022	,,	Benson, Frederick	1163	,,	Cameron, Archibald F.
1073	,,	Beard, Frank Almer	1146	,,	Chapman, Percy
1040	,,	Bligh, Percival	1294	,,	Chubb, Ralph H.
1054	,,	Bishop, John	1307	,,	Chew, Henry
1055	,,	Bigland, Richard K.	1149	,,	Cross, Charles H.

Canadian Pacific—The Empire's Greatest Railway.

234 PRINCESS PATRICIA'S CANADIAN LT. INFANTRY—cont.

Regl. No.	Rank.	Name.	Regl. No.	Rank.	Name.
1160	Private	Clarson, Alexander	1164	Private	Jaggs, Maurice W.
1238	,,	Callan, Frank	1079	,,	Jordan, Arthur B.
1242	,,	Cooper, John	1101	,,	Jury, James
1233	,,	Cunningham, Elson P.	1222	,,	Jarvis, Lewis J. E.
49	,,	Dunlop, John W.	1337	,,	Jones, W. T. S.
1276	,,	Darby, Claude S.	1230	,,	Johnston, Thomas S.
1119	,,	des Forges, Arthur	1081	Arm.Sgt.	Keble, Frederick E.
1150	,,	Dickie, John	1179	Private	Kay, Albert
1141	,,	Dowling, Horace	1144	,,	Kerr, Thomas
1249	,,	Dunhill, Francis	1152	,,	Keats, Alfred Allan
1155	,,	Duchesnay, Antoine	1755	,,	Knight, Abel
1308	,,	Davis, Gerald David	1053	,,	Lacey, William
1324	,,	Deverson, Ernest J.	1069	,,	Lake, Stuart William
1075	,,	Elliott, John	1153	,,	Lang, Arthur
1190	,,	Edge, Harold Henry	1174	,,	Logan, Henry John
1010	,,	Findlow, Harry	1013	,,	Mason, Alexander
1170	,,	Fuller, Leonard	1062	,,	McAllister, James
1103	,,	Fleming, Stanley	1287	,,	McCallum, Witney S.
1042	,,	Gillett, Moris	1098	,,	Mason, Thomas
1297	,,	Govan, John	1112	,,	Mosely, William
1050	Lce.-Cpl.	Georgelin, Harry	1138	,,	Mousir, G. E.
1154	Private	Galbraith, Wm. H.	1166	,,	Mason, Edward
1256	,,	Gilvear, George H.	1158	,,	Mann, Daniel
1252	Lce.-Cpl.	Garwood, Charles	1171	,,	Mangin, Henry R. F.
1229	Private	Gill, Frederick	1260	,,	McKelvie, Robert
1310	,,	Gordon, Erskine	1158	,,	McKenzie, Hugh
1127	,,	Goodwin, Albert	1255	,,	Maurice, Thomas
197	,,	Greenaway, Frank	1261	,,	Mitchell, George
1084	Lce.-Cpl.	Goldsworthy, E. C.	1266	,,	Martin, Alexander G.
1020	Private	Hamilton, George	1231	,,	Morgan, Pierce
1325	,,	Hookey, Arthur	1273	,,	Meaker, Charles H.
1125	Lce.-Cpl.	Harflett, John T.	1217	,,	Munroe, Murdock J.
1271	,,	Hewitt, Harry M.	1321	,,	Mitchell, Edward
1096	Private	Hancox, George T.	1071	,,	Meiklejohn, Percival
1107	,,	Hall, Isaac	756	,,	Morphy, Charles
1336	,,	Hayes, Henry	1303	,,	Niven, Gilbert
1121	,,	Heddick, Leonard	1064	,,	Nairn, Robert Colgan
1245	Lce.-Cpl.	Hetherington, H. G.	1173	,,	Nicholson, Archibald
1191	Private	Harrison, John	1235	,,	O'Brien, Patrick
1259	,,	Hardman, William E.	1196	Lce.-Cpl.	Potts, Arthur Taylor
1300	,,	Hammer, Arnold	1116	Private	Peacock, Charles
1306	,,	Hinton, Thomas	1285	,,	Pountney, E. Wm.
1168	,,	Hodgson, James S.	1142	,,	Penswick, Edward
1189	,,	Hughes, William H.	847	,,	Pemberton, Wm.
1215	,,	Hoskin, Walter A.	1151	,,	Perry, George Horace
1240	Lce.-Cpl.	Horner, Hugh	1143	,,	Picher, Clarence O.
1182	Private	Hacking, Samuel	1299	,,	Pritchard, Thomas
1076	,,	Howard, Harry	1220	,,	Payce, George
1061	,,	Inglee, Jack	1322	,,	Park, Albert Edward
1047	,,	Jacobs, Sydney S.	1038	,,	Reece, Stephen
1035	,,	Jordan, Bertrand S.	1026	,,	Richardson, F. T.
1064	,,	Joyner, Walter C.	1065	,,	Ridley, Stanley John

Canadian Pacific—The Empire's Greatest Railway.

PRINCESS PATRICIA'S CANADIAN LT. INFANTRY—cont. 235

Regl. No.	Rank.	Name.	Regl. No.	Rank.	Name.
1024	Private	Roberts, Thomas N.	1097	Private	Taylor, George Wm.
1106	,,	Reid, William James	1080	,,	Thomas, Charles
1128	,,	Rosher, John Henry	1177	,,	Temple, Alexander
1241	,,	Richardson, Herbt. W.	1302	,,	Turner, John Henry
1253	,,	Richardson, George A.	1317	,,	Tilleard, John Henry
1002	,,	Rainey, Charles E.	1228	,,	Thomas, Clement D.
1263	,,	Roper, Geoffrey S. R.	1226	,,	Thorpe, Martin
1332	,,	Rose, James Stuart	1318	,,	Trezise, Sydney
1296	,,	Robertson, John McI.	1015	,,	Uncles, Bertie
1031	,,	Scott, John Leslie	1136	,,	Venables, Herbert
1023	,,	Slevin, James Catrick	1044	,,	Walsh, Gerald Wm.
1281	,,	Smith, Henry	1051	,,	Walters, Lawrence E.
1275	,,	Sommers, Harry	1254	,,	Watson, Earl Bazil K.
1029	,,	Stevenson, Louis B.	1052	,,	White, Stanley Victor
1111	Lce.-Cpl.	Scott, John	1033	,,	Woodcock, Henry
1162	,,	Shuter, Hugh R. S.	1139	Lce.-Cpl.	Williams, Frederick A.
1102	,,	Shutt, Richard	1093	Private	Walsh, William Geo.
1282	,,	Stewart, Harry Aicken	1099	,,	Watts, William Eli
1117	,,	Stephens, William J.	1082	,,	Williams, John Dorset
1328	,,	Sutton, James Herbt.	1132	,,	White, George Edward
1291	,,	Scott, Keith	1114	,,	Wright, Frederick
1320	,,	Shillam, Frank	1290	,,	Walker, John Gordon
1313	,,	Smithson, George	1181	,,	Wilkinson, Robert
1293	,,	Stocks, George	1188	,,	Whitehouse, Thomas
145	,,	Sheppard, Frederick	1279	,,	Wybrow, William
1208	Lce.-Cpl.	Sunderland, William	1213	Lce.-Cpl.	West, John Langlands
1090	Private	Scott, Fergus Alex.	1272	Private	Ward, James
1221	,,	Shields, John	1070	,,	Webb, Thomas
1234	,,	Smither, Frank	1113	,,	Webb, Edward
1286	,,	Smith, Arthur	1265	,,	Ware, Alfred James
1298	,,	Stevens, Bertram	617	,,	Wildman, Thomas
1066	Lce.-Cpl.	Tylee, Ernest	679	,,	Wood, James
1169	Private	Taylor, William	1032	,,	Wright, Thomas
1055	,,	Thompson, George R.	1209	,,	Willey, Alfred
1025	,,	Thornton, Chas. Pryce	1140	Lce.-Cpl.	Young, Edwin
1067	,,	Turner, Robert Henry			

No. 4 COMPANY.

Lieutenant ... ... Fitzgerald, Frederick
,, ... Gray, Donald Fairlie Branston
,, ... Crabbe, Colville Eyre
,, ... Price, Charles Heritage

Regl. No.	Rank.	Name.	Regl. No.	Rank.	Name.
1615	R.Q.M.S.	Paterson, Stewart	1600	Sergt.	Keith, John Reid
1500	C.M.S.	Sampson, Percy L.	1683	,,	Mackay, John
1589	C.Q.M.S.	Godfrey Stuart	1713	,,	Forman, Harry
1501	Sergt.	Lloyd, Conway	1503	Lce.-Sgt.	Patterson, Samuel V.
1763	,,	Clarke, Dameral A.	1559	,,	Sharp, James
1765	,,	Crawford, John	1695	,,	Stewart, Thomas

Canadian Pacific—The Empire's Greatest Railway.

236 PRINCESS PATRICIA'S CANADIAN LT. INFANTRY—cont.

Regl. No.	Rank	Name
1729	Lce.-Sgt.	Webb, George Henry
1705	Act. Sgt.	Dudley-Ward, F. W.
1711	Corpl.	Adams, George L.
1505	,,	Phillips, Leonard
1730	,,	Patterson, George D.
1622	,,	Smith, George Duncan
1572	,,	Beaton, William J.
1513	,,	Fruen, Roland Chas.
1762	,,	Cooper, Edwin
1708	,,	Wilson, Kerridge
1519	Lce.-Cpl.	Batchelor, George A.
1510	,,	Stevens, William Jas.
1514	Private	Alcock, Robert
1527	,,	Allen, John George
1569	,,	Allen, Henry David
1635	,,	Aitchison, William D.
1636	,,	a'Court, Wm. A. R. H.
1637	,,	Ashby, Frederick T.
1742	,,	Allan, Melville
1643	,,	Blower, Chas. Ed.
1504	,,	Bristowe, Arthur H.
1522	,,	Birnie, Charles
1536	,,	Bain, William Donald
1553	,,	Burton, Eric Frank
1562	,,	Bradley, Albert James
1570	,,	Bailey, Alexander
1571	,,	Barry, Patrick Joseph
1573	,,	Burton, Julius Henry
1638	,,	Byrne, Isaac
1639	,,	Bowlt, Thomas
1640	,,	Barlowe, Joseph Edw.
1641	,,	Baker, Charles
1642	,,	Boothroyd, William
1721	,,	Bryant, John
1731	,,	Bullock, Arthur
1734	,,	Bisbee, Olando Arthur
1744	,,	Bett, Stewart
1523	,,	Clason, Thomas Ross
1524	,,	Collins, Henry Andrew
1541	,,	Candy, Gilbert Walker
1547	,,	Clarke, James Albert
1552	,,	Crook, Charles
1574	,,	Carver, Arthur Stanley
1575	Lce.-Cpl.	Caw, John Lewis
1576	Private	Christie, James Mdk.
1577	,,	Colville, Edward McD.
1578	,,	Coffee, Samuel Wbstr.
1579	Lce.-Cpl.	Cooper, William
1581	Private	Cuthbert, David Wood
1582	,,	Clafton, Thomas
1644	,,	Clementson, George
1645	,,	Carr, Thomas Edwd.
1646	Private	Chalmers, Thomas K.
1647	,,	Cook, Edward Herbt.
1648	,,	Charie, Fred
1649	,,	Crook, Harry
1714	,,	Cowie, John
1722	,,	Cooke, Thomas
1756	,,	Cruly, Alfred Melvin
1764	,,	Cuthbert, Thomas
1776	,,	Campbell, John W. R.
1783	,,	Carr, Harry Camden
1800	,,	Clayton, Arthur G.
1712	,,	Davey-Thomas, E. L.
1651	,,	Doresa, Hector
1561	,,	Dixon, Julian
1566	,,	Dunnett, David
1583	,,	Daniels, Ernest Edwd.
1584	,,	Davidson, Ernest Alf.
1585	,,	Davison, Norman L.
1586	,,	Dover, Crawford
1724	,,	Dalby, William
1757	,,	Davey, William B.
1778	,,	Day, Charles
1557	,,	Earls, Walker, R.
1551	,,	Forrest, James
1558	,,	Foote, James Archbld.
1565	Lce.-Cpl.	Fox, George Robert
1587	Private	Forster, James
1588	,,	Fraser, Arthur
1654	,,	Farrer, Sidney
1007	,,	Guthrie, Henry Walter
1525	,,	Goodwin, Esmond
1529	,,	Gallacher, John
1548	,,	Gardner, Daniel
1555	,,	Greer, Francis E. G.
1656	,,	Gray, John
1658	,,	Gower, Lewis
1752	,,	Grieve, Andrew
1518	,,	Handson, George
1539	,,	Hughes, Hugh Stanley
1591	,,	Holloway, Walter
1592	,,	Hill, Alfred
1659	,,	Hall, Frank
1660	Lce.-Cpl.	Harrison, George E.
1662	,,	Hodges, Thomas Henry
1663	Private	Haddock, Thomas B.
1665	,,	Herbert, George Henry
1666	,,	Horwood, Harry
1725	,,	Hill, Wm. Geo. Chas.
1767	,,	Hector, Alexander, O.
1768	,,	Haggard, Rider L.
1770	Lce.-Cpl.	Hunter, John
1771	Private	Harvie, George Hume

Canadian Pacific—The Empire's Greatest Railway.

PRINCESS PATRICIA'S CANADIAN LT. INFANTRY—cont. 237

Regl. No.	Rank.	Name.	Regl. No.	Rank.	Name.
1780	Private	Herbert, Herbert Rd.	1680	Private	Millan, Martin
1785	,,	Holt, Benjamin	1681	,,	Marion, Joseph Alfred
1793	,,	Hartley, Ernest	1682	,,	Moore, Edgar
1593	,,	Inkster, George	1735	,,	McKay, Thos.
1667	,,	Ivall, Gerald	1740	,,	Murphy, John Henry
1668	,,	Irving, John Peel	1743	,,	MacLeod, John Arch.
1669	,,	Innes, James	1747	,,	Matthews, Matthew
1760	,,	Ingram, John	1750	Lce.-Cpl.	MacFarlane, James
1786	,,	Jenkin, Harry	1758	Private	Monaghan, Joe A.
1532	,,	Johnston, Kenric A.	1769	,,	Munroe, John Alex.
1594	,,	Joy, Charles	1772	,,	Miller, George Alex.
1595	Lce.-Cpl.	Jacques, John Robert	1790	,,	Mundell, Wm. Geo. R.
1596	Private	Johnson, Ernest H.	1792	,,	Marks, James
1597	,,	Johnson, Robert Geo.	1799	,,	Matcham, Sidney H.
1598	,,	Jones, Bert	1732	,,	Malone, John
1670	,,	Jackson, Richard	1613	,,	Nash, Robert Arth. S.
1753	,,	Jennings, William H.	1614	,,	Newton, Harry
1599	,,	Keeley, Thomas	1684	,,	Novis, Charles
1601	,,	Kelly, John	1710	,,	Nicholls, Sydney
1671	,,	Killoh, Charles	1784	,,	Neale, George
1672	,,	Keenie,PieterTheymac	1738	,,	Orrick, Joseph
856	,,	Leach, Douglas	1685	,,	Povey, Lionel
1715	,,	Legge,George Stafford	1686	.,	Phillipson, Alfred
1508	,,	Ladler, Chas. Herbert	1716	,,	Popey, William James
1516	,,	Lilburn, Harry K.	1727	,,	Pacano, Nicholas
1602	,,	Laird, John	1746	,,	Peterson, Walter
1603	,,	Lyons, Wm. James	1774	,,	Patterson, Athol Scott
1673	,,	Lees, George	1521	,,	Richards, Walter A.
1674	,,	Litster, George	1616	,,	Robinson, John
1675	,,	Leahy, John	1617	,,	Ross, Alexander
1739	,,	Linley, Sidney	1618	,,	Ruston, Samuel
1779	,,	Lever, James	1619	,,	Rothwell, John Alston
1789	,,	Lane, Percy Ernald	1687	,,	Robinson, Harry
1788	,,	Leatherby, Jas. Thos.	1688	,,	Rowley, Joseph Stoker
1787	,,	LeSueur, Harold Payn	1689	,,	Read, James Frederick
1507	,,	Michelmore, Erik	1741	,,	Roper, Ernest
1512	,,	MacDonald, Robert G.	1748	,,	Russell, John
1515	,,	McGowan, Herbert W.	1794	,,	Roberts, Horace
1517	,,	McLaughlin, John	1528	,,	Simpson Alex. Noble
1531	,,	Morshead, John	1533	,,	Stewart, George
1554	,,	Murphy, Francis Hy.	1540	,,	Swain, Cyril George
1567	,,	Mullaly, Thomas Jas.	1546	,,	Storey, Frederick
1604	,,	McDonald, Peter	1549	,,	Stevenson, James S.
1606	,,	McMillan, Dougald	1556	,,	Shaw, Robert
1607	,,	Morden, Hubert	1560	,,	Sloane, Robert Henry
1609	,,	Muddeman, Sidney T.	1621	,,	Skinner, George Henry
1610	,,	Murphy, Andrew	1623	,,	Smith, Percy Arthur
1612	,,	Morrison, George	1624	,,	Snider, Barnet
1676	,,	Mitchell, John	1625	,,	Stewart, Geo. Blaikley
1677	,,	Moon, William	1626	,,	Stewart, William A.
1678	,,	Miller, Cecil	1627	,,	Stripp, Austin John
1679	,,	Murray, Hugh	1628	,,	Sullivan, James

Canadian Pacific—The Empire's Greatest Railway.

238 PRINCESS PATRICIA'S CANADIAN LT. INFANTRY—cont.

Regl. No.	Rank.	Name.	Regl. No.	Rank.	Name.
1629	Private	Swan, Charles John	1759	Private	Toyne, James Joseph
1690	,,	Shears, Ellias	1766	,,	Triggs, Guy
1691	,,	Shuttleworth, Chas. A.	1544	,,	Vivian, Arthur
1692	,,	Simmonds, Henry	1718	,,	Vale, William E.
1693	,,	Sharman, Elijah	1795	,,	Viets, Alex. Griswold
1694	,,	Shepherd, Wallace	1509	,,	Walker, Thomas
1696	Lce.-Cpl.	Shine, John	1511	,,	Wernick, Michael
1697	Private	Shea, Howard Wm.	1526	,,	Ward, Alfred John
1698	,,	Sclanders, Robert	1530	,,	Waller, Horace E.
1699	,,	Serjeant, Frederick	1537	,,	Williamson, Fredk. A.
1745	,,	Scott, Edward	1563	,,	Wilson, George
1754	,,	Spanswick, John	1564	,,	Watkins, John
1781	,,	Smith, Sinclair B.	1632	,,	Watson, James Henry
1791	,,	Sealey, Frederick	1634	,,	Walker, Ernest Robt.
1796	,,	Skene, Archibald J.	1704	,,	Winder, John Wm.
1801	,,	Sheridan, Wm. Pat.	1717	,,	Wright, George
1520	,,	Trocme, Alexander F.	1720	,,	Watson, Oswald
1550	,,	Thompson, Frank W.	1707	,,	Watts, John
1631	Lce.-Cpl.	Thomson, William S.	1761	,,	Ward, Fred
1700	Private	Taylor, Robert	1706	,,	Williams, Ernest
1701	,,	Thomson, Thomas M.	1751	,,	Wilson, George
1702	,,	Tabor, John	1798	,,	White, Herbert Hy.
1703	,,	Tabernacle, Percy B.	1506	,,	Yelf, Edward George
1733	,,	Turner, Alfred	1709	,,	Young, Wm. Phillip

DIVISIONAL SIGNAL COMPANY.

Major	Lister, F. A.
Captain	Kilburn, F. C.
Lieutenant	Powers T. E.
,, ...	Ford, E.
,, ...	Cline, G. A.
? Paymaster (K().CE 3/10/16 ...	Hon. Captain Wilson, W. W.
Hon. Capt. and Chaplain ...	Rev. Dunne, L.

Supernumerary Attached.

Major	Hennessy, J. T.
Captain	Fox, F. G.
Lieutenant	McCready, C. A.
,, ...	Leavitt, A.
,, ...	Underhill, E. L.

Canadian Pacific—The Empire's Greatest Railway.

DIVISIONAL SIGNAL COMPANY—cont. 239

Regl. No.	Rank	Name
5807	S.M.I.	Birbeck, G. C.(W.O.)
5601	C.S.M.	May, H. T.
5654	C.Q.M.S.	Delain, J. W.
5608	Sergt.	Carpenter, C. O.
5644	,,	Clout, H.
5610	,,	Davison, H.
5603	,,	Harrop, J. R.
5605	,,	Henderson, W. D.
5602	,,	Massey, G. C.
5776	,,	McMinn, W.
5752	,,	Skinner, F. W.
5763	,,	Thompson, E. O.
5779	,,	Thompson, W.
5628	Corpl.	Buttle, G.
5674	,,	Gale, T.
5684	,,	Howell, A. R.
5777	,,	Lush, F. P.
5741	Sergt.	Shaw, F.
5767	Corpl.	Waterfield, J. G.
5604	,,	Weeks, E. G.
5646	2nd Cpl.	Castles, E.
5607	,,	Collins, J. L.
5702	,,	Le Lacheur, L.
5611	,,	Norton, G.
5768	,,	Watson, M. B.
5645	Lce.-Cpl.	Carney, F.
5665	,,	Faulkner, H. J.
5715	,,	McMenamin, L.
5806	Cpl. SS.	Brown, C. W.
5693	Lce.-Cpl.	Jeanes, C. F.
5614	Private	Anderson, E. H.
5615	,,	Adams, H.
5616	,,	Appleby, I. D.
5617	,,	Anderson, R. E.
5618	,,	Allan, J. R.
5619	,,	Appleby, E.
5792	,,	Bates, H. A.
5788	,,	Brown, W. H.
5620	,,	Bateman, J. J.
5221	,,	Bain, A.
5622	,,	Barr, J.
5624	,,	Bartlett, A. F.
5625	,,	Brosnan, M. E.
5626	,,	Brown, A.
5627	,,	Burton, H.
5630	,,	Butler, H. J.
5631	,,	Blair, J. R.
5632	,,	Brown, E.
5781	,,	Brownlee, W. B.
5784	,,	Betts, F. C.
5606	,,	Butler, L. A.
5609	,,	Church, A. J.
5633	Private	Carroll, R. R.
5634	,,	Craven, T. R.
5636	,,	Conibear, W.
5637	,,	Cunningham, J.
5638	,,	Crozier, D.
5639	,,	Craft, G. F.
5803	,,	Crosby, H. D.
5640	,,	Creighton, L.
5641	,,	Campbell, J. K.
5642	,,	Carson, J.
5643	,,	Charles, L.
5647	,,	Cartier, J. N.
5648	,,	Coutts, H.
5649	,,	Curran, G.
5650	,,	Cronshaw, G.
5651	,,	Douglas, R. T.
5652	,,	Dent, N.
5653	,,	Dyce, H.
5655	,,	Daley, C.
5656	,,	Dryden, J.
5657	,,	Dick, A. G.
5658	,,	Dickens, T.
5659	,,	Draper, S. G.
5660	,,	Duffey, J. T.
5783	,,	Dow, S. A.
5804	,,	Delisle, A. J.
5661	,,	Eyre, E. R.
5662	,,	Emmons, C. V.
5663	,,	England, S.
5664	,,	Fullerton, W.
5666	,,	Field, A.
5667	,,	Fryer, H. J.
5668	,,	Fryer, W.
5789	,,	Frampton, G.
5669	,,	Grieve, G. R.
5670	,,	Gardner, W. J.
5671	,,	Graham, T.
5672	,,	Gardiner, G. W.
5675	,,	Gair, H.
5676	,,	Goodenough, H. J.
5775	,,	Gossling, G.
5786	,,	Graves, H.
5795	,,	Grant, W. W.
5567	,,	Hammond, G.
5678	,,	Hudson, J. C.
5679	,,	Hudson, H.
5680	,,	Howard, T.
5681	,,	Harrington, P. L.
5682	,,	Humphrey, C.
5685	,,	Hawes, W. T.
5686	,,	Hughes, J.
5687	,,	Hurst, H. A.

Canadian Pacific—The Empire's Greatest Railway.

DIVISIONAL SIGNAL COMPANY—cont.

Regl. No.	Rank.	Name.	Regl. No.	Rank.	Name.
5780	Private	Humphrey, G. A.	5729	Private	Porter, A. W.
5793	,,	Henderson, J.	5730	Lce.-Cpl.	Pflug, J.
5691	,,	Jones, W.	5731	Private	Parks, K.
5688	,,	Jones, A.	5732	,,	Parker, T.
5689	,,	Jordan, T. A.	5733	,,	Pearce, S. H.
5690	,,	Johnston, T. A.	5798	Trumpt'r	Philp, H. W.
5692	,,	Johnston, R.	5734	Private	Quigg, L. G.
5695	,,	Kellett, C.	5735	,,	Randall, C. W.
5696	,,	Kennedy, B.	5736	Cpl. Art.	Reimer, J. B.
5697	,,	Keegan, C. F.	5737	Private	Robinson, J. K.
5778	,,	Keating, E.	5738	,,	Robinson, A.
5698	,,	Ketnor, C. C.	5794	,,	Ross, A. R.
5699	,,	Kane, F.	5740	,,	Spruit, J. W.
5700	,,	Kearon, P.	5742	,,	Sharp, H. D.
5701	,,	Leonard, J.	5743	,,	Swale, F. A.
5704	,,	Lloyd, W.	5744	,,	Seymour, F.
5705	,,	Large, H. R.	5745	,,	Southern, H.
5706	,,	Lewin, F.	5746	,,	Southern, E.
5796	,,	Lister, W. R.	5747	,,	Saunders, S. C.
5707	,,	Munden, S.	5749	,,	Spencer, F. T.
5708	,,	Mathews, C.	5750	,,	Somerville, W.
5709	,,	Mack, A.	5751	,,	Schooling, P. H.
5710	,,	Miller, T.	5753	,,	Stewart, H. R.
5711	,,	Murphy, J.	5754	,,	Simms, P. M.
5712	,,	Mahany, W. J.	5756	,,	Shaw, C. S.
5713	,,	McDonald, C.	5757	,,	Shepherd, E.
5714	,,	McLeod, V. H.	5759	,,	Stuart, J.
5716	,,	McNaughton, T. D.	5760	,,	Sargeant, W.
5717	,,	McLeod, R.	5761	,,	Savage, J.
5718	,,	McLoughlin, H.	5791	,,	Smith, J. M.
5719	,,	McMurray, A. H.	5797	,,	Selfe, E.
5720	,,	Matheu, C. V. W.	5801	,,	Storey, W. R.
5694	,,	McIlroy, S. A.	5802	,,	Sprague, C. M.
5721	,,	Nuttall, G. A.	5762	,,	Taylor, R. J.
5722	,,	North, W. H.	5764	,,	Townsend, S.
5723	,,	Norman, A.	5765	,,	Twaite, H. W.
5724	,,	Nicholson, H.	5766	,,	Turner, F. D.
5612	,,	Norton, J. G.	5769	,,	Wilkins, S.
5787	,,	Nash, R. E.	5770	,,	Wade, N.
5725	,,	Ord, J. W.	5771	,,	Whitlock, H.
5726	,,	O'Donnell, J.	5774	,,	Wilson, J.
5727	,,	Olive, A. D.	5799	,,	West-Jones, H.
5728	,,	Pryce, W. H.			

Attached.

| 5785 | Pay Sgt. | French, H. H. | 33719 | Private | Palmer, R. V. |
| 33718 | Private | Adams, G. (A.M.C.) | | | (A.M.C.) |

Canadian Pacific—The Empire's Greatest Railway.

DIVISIONAL CAVALRY.

Lieutenant-Colonel ... ... Jamieson, F. C.
Veterinary Officer ... ... Captain W. G. Stedman
Paymaster ... ... Hon. Captain R. Thomson
Lieutenant ... ... Watson, W. F.
,, ... Tipton, J. W.
,, ... Edmiston, K. W.
,, ... Ferris, D. N.
,, ... Dawson, H. M.

Regl. No.	Rank.	Name.	Regl. No.	Rank.	Name.
1901	S.S.-M.	King, W. D. M.	2015	Trooper	Caswell, J. P. J.
1902	S.Q.M.S.	MacKay, A. R.	1987	,,	Copping, F. G.
1903	Sergt.	Thieme, S.	1964	,,	Church, J. A.
1904	,,	Taylor, W.	1979	,,	Chutter, T. S.
1909	,,	Langley, J. B.	2082	Lce.-Cpl.	Cook, S.
1910	,,	Cavanagh, O.	1988	Trooper	Cranley, H.
1911	,,	Thompson, J. H.	2081	,,	Cottrell, J. C.
1919	,,	Claxton, J.	1984	,,	Cuthbert, C. R.
1923	,,	Matthews, W. T.	2042	,,	Currie, N. T.
1908	,,	Caws, S. W.	2069	,,	Cummings, G.
1906	,,	Harrison, J.	1969	,,	Cameron, F. S.
1907	Far. Sgt.	MacDonald, A. W.	1932	,,	Carrick, J.
1912	Lce.-Sgt.	Balfour, J.	1945	,,	Duncan, G.
1926	Corpl.	Bissett, J.	1997	,,	Dewar, A.
1914	,,	Pugh, J.	2055	,,	Dann, R.
1915	,,	Pryce, W. H.	2009	,,	Drummond, F. A.
1916	,,	Martin, C A.	1938	,,	Davis, E.
1917	,,	Wilson, C. A.	1990	,,	Davis, R.
1918	,,	Ford, B. St. V.	1992	,,	Dempsey, O.
1920	,,	Goodlands, C.	1950	,,	Dayton, A.
1943	,,	Vallocott, W. F.	1986	,,	Day, E.
1922	Lce.-Cpl.	Healing, J.	1935	,,	Day, F. S.
1925	,,	Needham, H.	2088	,,	Derbyshire, T. L.
1927	,,	Jackson, J. A.	1955	,,	Durham, C. G.
1913	Far. Cpl.	Latham, J.	1951	,,	Evans, H. C.
1928	Lce.-Cpl.	Bell, S. W.	1968	,,	Exham, L. A.
1929	,,	Franklin, L. K.	1994	,,	Frayne, R. C.
1949	,,	Watson, H.	2094	,,	Ferguson, H. M.
1969	Trooper	Alford, S. P.	2038	,,	Fisher, R. W.
1978	,,	Adshead, J.	1983	,,	Fullerton, F.
1944	,,	Aitken, G. T.	2000	,,	Finlay, J.
2067	,,	Anderson, R. T.	1982	,,	Fortier, J. E.
1958	,,	Anderson, J. G.	1934	,,	Gray, W. J.
2079	,,	Airth, H.	2047	,,	Gibson, H. H.
2037	,,	Barnett, H. A.	2060	,,	Gomer, T. C.
1993	,,	Browning, J. S.	1956	,,	Gough, G. C.
1936	,,	Bush, J. W.	2076	,,	Hartree, T
2084	,,	Bouck, C. R.	1966	,,	Hyland, F.
2044	,,	Bryan, S. O.	2049	,,	Hepburn, W. H.
1942	,,	Brickman, R.	1991	,,	Hardy, C.
1924	Lce.-Cpl.	Butler, F. C.	2092	,,	Harvie, T.

Canadian Pacific—The Empire's Greatest Railway.

DIVISIONAL CAVALRY—cont.

Regl. No.	Rank.	Name.	Regl. No.	Rank.	Name.
1933	Trooper	Hutchison, H.	2070	Trooper	Pritchard, W.
2078	,,	Heric, F. T.	2087	,,	Richard, H.
1937	,,	Hutchison, J. A.	1948	,,	Rourke, D. M.
2017	,,	Hunter, J.	1953	,,	Robertson, N. L.
2064	,,	Hornby, J.	1980	,,	Robinson, H.
2018	,,	Ingolby, R.	2065	,,	Robinson, D. L.
2001	,,	Ingram, Z. V.	2095	,,	Robinson, N. L.
2034	,,	Jenkins, R. H.	1975	,,	Rindland, L. S.
2058	,,	Jackson, J. J.	1971	,,	Scott, W.
2077	,,	Koch, A.	1930	,,	Shepherd, H. W. R.
2005	,,	Kelly, D. R.	1962	,,	Spier, A.
2073	,,	Kent, S. H.	2032	,,	Stacey, A. T.
2071	,,	Kitchen, C. R.	2080	,,	Stannard, A. G.
2004	,,	Kelly, N. P.	1973	,,	Stevens, J. J.
1989	,,	Lavalle, H. W.	2090	,,	Street, W.
1965	,,	Leader, R. A.	2091	,,	Street, H.
2014	,,	Lansdown, C. V.	1981	,,	Smith, W.
1959	,,	Long, D.	2072	,,	Sutton, W. E.
1995	,,	Madill, B. C.	2026	,,	Seccombe, H. C.
2028	,,	Marlow, N. G.	1977	,,	Smith, J.
2035	,,	Melbourne, L. E.	2016	,,	Scanlon, P. D.
2027	,,	Murphy, C. H.	1960	,,	Tibbles, J. T.
2024	,,	Morris, E.	2031	,,	Tomlinson, J. R.
2019	,,	Middlemas, W.	1952	,,	Toole, E. T.
2050	,,	Munroe, W. D.	1939	,,	Tooley, R.
2003	,,	Macklin, J. W.	2030	,,	Trotter, C.
1998	,,	McNamara, W. J.	2013	,,	Tallack, R. C.
1963	,,	McCurdy, J. F.	1985	,,	Vautibault, J. de
2008	,,	McMillan, J.	1961	,,	Vanbuskirk, Le R.
2086	,,	McNulty, D. A.	2020	,,	Victor, H. B.
1976	,,	McLean, V. T.	2033	,,	Woods, W. S.
2068	,,	McLennan, T. D.	2093	,,	Wilson, J. L.
2002	,,	McKibbon, W. S.	1972	,,	Whillans, W. T.
1957	,,	McRobert, A. A.	1974	,,	Whitlock, C.
2085	,,	McLaurin, S.	1967	,,	Wallace, L.
2089	,,	Nixon, H.	2039	,,	Wall, F. E.
1954	,,	Nixon, W.	2066	,,	Westgate, C. D.
1946	,,	O'Connor, T.	2010	,,	Wilson, A. L.
1999	,,	Ottewell, R.	2056	,,	Walker, R. A.
2011	,,	Price, C.	2007	,,	Warwick, W.
1931	,,	Pointon, F.	1996	,,	Yeomans, J.
2074	,,	Phillips, H. B.	1941	,,	Younger, S.
2006	,,	Pilkington, G.			(Attached from
2012	,,	Potter, R.			C.A.M.C.)
1946	,,	Pirie, A. S.	33717	,,	Campbell, John
2075	,,	Perkins, R. J.	33716	,,	Craig, John Logan

Canadian Pacific—The Empire's Greatest Railway.

DIVISIONAL CYCLIST COMPANY.

Captain ... ... Robinson, Robert Sheriff
Lieutenant ... ... Child, Cecil George
,, ... Everall, William M.
,, ... Bush, Clayton Elden
,, ... Chadwick, Francis Joseph Guy

Regl. No.	Rank.	Name.
2117	C.S.M.	Delavigne, Fred
2118	C.Q.M.S.	Dow, William E.
2119	Sergt.	Harvey, Rufus
2120	,,	Freeman, Thomas
2121	,,	Henderson, Edward J.
2122	Corpl.	Brown, William A.
2123	,,	Willson, Arthur G.
2124	,,	Montgomery, H. L.
2125	,,	MacFarlane, R. G.
2126	,,	Alexander, F. Wm.
2127	,,	Good, Harry
2128	,,	Manning, Robert C.
2130	Private	Atkinson, Joseph
2131	,,	Ayliffe, Frederick R.
2132	,,	Barron, John Bernard
2133	,,	Barraclough, Thomas
2134	Lce.-Cpl.	Basinette, Charles P.
2135	Private	Beaudry, George
2136	,,	Brown, Joseph B.
2137	,,	Britton, Frederick C.
2138	,,	Bramwell, Alfred
2139	,,	Blume, Charles
2140	,,	Bubb, William C.
2141	,,	Carruthers, Robert
2142	,,	Conlon, Sidney
10745	,,	Cook, Leslie C.
2143	,,	Cotton, George
2144	,,	Daniel, Frank E.
2145	Lce.-Cpl.	Dennis, Frank
2146	Private	Dixon, William
2147	,,	Donaldson, Laurence P.
2148	,,	Dunham, Laurence J.
2149	,,	Eagles, James
30606	,,	Elias, Arthur E.
2150	,,	Faulkner, Allan C.
2151	,,	Fleiger, Charles C.
2152	,,	Gallagher, Louis
2153	,,	Goldberger, Cecil G.
2154	,,	Gray, Edward Y.
2155	,,	Harris, Ernest Arthur
2156	,,	Hayhurst, James O.
2157	Lce.-Cpl.	Hedge, Fred
2158	Private	Hillier, Stanley
2159	,,	Hughes, William

Regl. No.	Rank.	Name.
2160	Private	Hurst, George Henry
2161	Lce.-Cpl.	Irvine, Earle
2162	Private	Jacobson, William
2114	,,	James, Arthur W.
2163	,,	James, Francis A.
2164	,,	Jenkinson, Edward A.
2165	,,	Johnson, James G.
2166	,,	Kelly, James Joseph
2167	,,	Kenworthy, Fred
2168	,,	Laderoute, Joseph
2169	,,	Lane, Clement
2170	,,	Ling, Walter
2171	,,	Longhta, William
2172	,,	Luxford, Fred
2173	,,	Maher, W. B.
2174	,,	Martin, Gordon H.
2175	,,	McCann, William
2176	,,	McCluskey, James
2177	,,	Miller, John Andrew
2178	,,	Moate, Herbert A.
2179	,,	Murphy, James J.
2180	,,	Nelle, Herman
2181	,,	Parry, John
2182	,,	Quin, Patrick
2183	,,	Reid, Wallis Austin
2184	,,	Read, Clifford B.
2185	,,	Ross, Oswald Burdett
2186	,,	Salter, George
2116	,,	Shane, William A.
2187	,,	Smith, Thomas M.
2188	,,	Spring, Victor G.
2189	,,	Stretch, Oscar
2190	,,	Stevens, Victor K.
2191	,,	Stinson, Wm. T.
2192	,,	Tinguey, George
2193	,,	Tomlinson, Albert C.
2194	,,	Unwin, Laurence B.
2195	,,	Wadhams, Joseph
2196	,,	Walpole, Olley
2197	,,	Watson, Fred
2198	,,	White, Harry V.
2115	,,	Williams, Sidney L.
2199	,,	Webber, Harold
2200	,,	Wingfield, Fredk. C.

Canadian Pacific—The Empire's Greatest Railway.

ROYAL CANADIAN DRAGOONS.

HEADQUARTERS STAFF.

Lieut.-Colonel	Nelles, Charles M.
Major	Elmsley, James H.
Captain	Gilman, Frederick
Quartermaster	Hon. Captain Edward A. Williams
Transport Officer	Lieutenant Nathan Medhurst

Attached.

Veterinary Officer	Major T. J. Taschereau
Medical Officer	Captain J. Harvey Todd
Paymaster	Hon. Captain George C. Drury

Regl. No.	Rank.	Name.	Regl. No.	Rank.	Name.
35	R.S.-M.	Steer, E. A. (W.O.)	20	Private	Lawrence, John T.
36	S.-M.Ar.	Patton, J. A. (W.O.)	21	„	Winters, Melvin
1	R.Q.M.S.	Dore, George	22	„	Bragg, William Q.
2	Q.M.S.F.	Galway, Philip	25	„	Bailey, William
3	S.S.M.I.	Dee, Francis J.	26	„	Simpkin, Albert *alias* Reardon, Eugene
4	Staff Sgt.	Mountford, Joseph			
5	„	Ackerman, Fredk.	27	„	Simpkin, George C.
6	„	Travers, John	30	„	Cook, William
7	Sergt.	Sutton, Henry	122	„	Squarebriggs, Wesley
8	„	Churchward, Gerald	128	„	Wicks, Robert
9	Private	Probert, Robert	602	„	Price, Lee
10	„	Hilton, Arthur	107	„	Crouter, Harry C.
11	„	Atkinson, Robert	106	„	Crabbe, Arthur Ellis
12	„	Roach, William	312	„	Montgomery, Hilliard
13	„	Laker, Stephen	119	„	Patterson, Edgar V.
14	„	Martin, Arthur S.	126	„	Webb, Thomas
16	„	Dadswell, Gilbert	599	„	Perkins, Fredk. H.
17	„	Payne, Joseph Albert	117	„	Mintram, Charles
18	„	Payne, Henry G.	124	„	Towers, Harry E.
19	„	Gill, George	109	„	Devonport, Philip G.

Attached.

31	Sergt.	Marshall, George	33708	Private	Carrell, John
33726	Corpl.	Walton, George M.	33709	„	Foret, Henry

Machine Gun Section.

Lieutenant ... ... Stethem, Hubert.

51	Sergt.	Scott, Fred. Veasey	56	Private	Blackwell, Thomas
52	Corpl.	Lunn, William	57	„	Griffin, Philip G.
53	Private	Ball, Arthur	58	„	Harden, William G.
54	„	Burton, Norman S.	59	„	Jones, William R.
55	„	Breed, George	60	„	Kennedy, Samuel

Canadian Pacific—The Empire's Greatest Railway.

ROYAL CANADIAN DRAGOONS—cont. 245

Machine Gun Section—cont.

Regl. No.	Rank.	Name.	Regl. No.	Rank.	Name.
61	Private	Knighton, Charles H.	71	Private	Veckins, Frederick C.
62	,,	Matthews, John D.	72	,,	Franklin, Alfred
63	,,	More, Colin	73	,,	Lattimer, Edwin Jas.
64	,,	McKay, William	570	,,	Hatton, Charles
65	,,	Palmer, James C.	652	,,	Mackinnon, John A.
66	,,	Pottier, Harry	945	,,	Ward, Henry
67	,,	Powney, Willett R.	899	,,	Maigret, John A.
68	,,	Sheere, James F.	352	,,	Wolfe, Herb. Stuart
69	,,	Willett, Richard	229	,,	Beardsley, George F.
70	,,	Mather, Robert A.			

Base Details.

Captain ... ... Kingsford, William R.

Regl. No.	Rank.	Name.	Regl. No.	Rank.	Name.
101	S.Q.M.S.	Hammond, L. D.	129	Private	White, Robert W.
102	Sergt.	London, Whiley, A.	130	,,	Willis, Albert
103	,,	Walker, Frederick	131	,,	Young, John Wm.
104	Private	Brown, James Percy	15	,,	Allen, Frank S.
105	,,	Bennett, John James	28	,,	Turton, Walter
108	,,	Craven, George	563	,,	Griffin, H. E. F.
111	,,	Fay, Harry	234	,,	Bobby, Thomas
112	,,	Grahams, George H.	331	,,	Schenenker, Charles
113	,,	Harrison, David G.	133	,,	Margerison, Fredk. W
114	,,	Hansen, Henry L.	134	,,	Howarth, Herbert
115	,,	Hubbard, John B.	135	,,	Johnson, James
116	,,	Marsden, Thomas	136	,,	Crossley, Emanuel
118	,,	Mounce, Reginald	137	,,	Fawcett, Fred.
120	,,	Roberts, James	138	,,	Isherwood, Percy
121	,,	Rogers, Clifford	325	,,	Cote, Charles Aine
123	,,	Soloman, Samuel	908	,,	Penny, Steven
125	,,	Wade, Arthur H.	530	Trumpt'r	Hamilton, Harold
127	,,	Walters, David H.			

"A" SQUADRON.

Major Lt. Col. (K(A) 3/6/18 ... Van Straubenzee, Charles T.
Captain ... ... Bowie, Douglas Bain
Lieutenant ... ... Caldwell, Eugene Lloyd
,, ... Le Blanc, Beaudry R.
,, ... McCarthy, John Francis
,, ... Wilkes, Frank Hilton
Captain ... ... Garon, Marie M. L.

Regl. No.	Rank.	Name.	Regl. No.	Rank.	Name.
201	S.S.-M.	Bull, George Leonard	204	Sergt.	Deane, Desmond
205	S.Q.M.S.	Osborne, Elijah	206	,,	Snape, John
202	S.S.Far.	Hogan, Patrick	207	,,	Benskin, Leonard
203	Sergt.	Merrix, Albert E.	208	,,	Campbell, William

Canadian Pacific—The Empire's Greatest Railway.

ROYAL CANADIAN DRAGOONS—cont.

Regl. No.	Rank.	Name.	Regl. No.	Rank.	Name.
209	Sergt.	Ellis, William T. C.	260	Private	Fairlie, John
210	,,	Karcher, Harry E.	261	,,	Feighen, George C.
212	,,	Goodall, Andrew F.	262	,,	Ferrie, Richard
213	Corpl.	Hollowell, Walter	263	,,	Fraser, George
214	,,	Legge, David St. C.	265	,,	Gilbert, William
216	,,	Shortill, John	266	,,	Goldsmith, Charles
217	,,	Beaumont, George	269	,,	Greenaway, Joseph
218	,,	Jones, John F.	270	,,	Grisley, Ernest
219	,,	Shand, Albert	271	,,	Hargreaves, Ernest
220	,,	Hardaker, Samuel	272	,,	Harfleet, Charles A.
221	,,	Pym, John	273	,,	Hathaway, Harold
342	,,	Vowles, James F.	29	,,	Hartland, Benjamin
356	Lce.-Cpl.	Wheeler, William	274	,,	Hay, Angus
264	,,	Gardner, David	275	,,	Herrick, Elliott
248	,,	Cosby, Bert	276	,,	Holtby, Arthur
345	,,	Webb, Harry S.	277	,,	Hood, Charles
237	,,	Bullock, Alfred	278	,,	Hope, Oliver
267	,,	Granson, Thomas	279	,,	Hunter, Charles E.
257	,,	Davidson, Robert	354	,,	Huff, Gordon E.
324	,,	Michie, George	280	,,	Izon, Hubert
251	,,	Cooke, Cyril A.	281	,,	Jalbert, Ralph
327	,,	Rowe, Frederick	282	,,	Jauncey, Frederick
225	Cpl.S.S.	Wright, Walter	283	,,	Johnson, Alfred J.
222	L.C.Trpr.	Bowles, George H.	284	,,	Judd, John H.
223	Trumpt'r	Rice, Victor Hugo	285	,,	Keeley, Leo
224	Sh'sm'th	Freeman, Caroll	286	,,	Kelley, Michael
226	,,	Falconer, William	287	,,	Kirby, Leonard
211	,,	Nicholas, Alfonso	288	,,	Langford, Frank
228	Private	Austin, Kenneth G.	289	,,	Laverty, Mathew
230	,,	Becker, Charles	290	,,	Lewis, James F.
231	,,	Bankhart, Arthur	291	,,	Lindsay, Allan
232	,,	Birch, Harry	292	,,	Linstead, George H.
233	,,	Blaker, Alfred	293	,,	McDonald, C. S.
235	,,	Booth, Leslie	294	,,	Macpherson, Charles
236	,,	Bray, Harold	295	,,	MacQueen, Alex.
238	,,	Bush, Herbert	296	,,	Martin, John
239	,,	Carroll, James	297	,,	McCawley, Peter
240	,,	Chard, Norman C.	298	,,	McGinley, Joseph
241	,,	Chesley, Albert	299	,,	McLachlan, Robert
242	,,	Chataway, Charles	300	,,	McNab, Elmer
243	,,	Coles, Herbert	301	,,	McKercher, Archie
244	,,	Collins, Charles	302	,,	McVey, David
245	,,	Collins, Thomas	303	,,	McVickor, Frederick
246	,,	Code, William Willis	355	,,	McQuinn, Frank
247	,,	Colsbrook, Kent	305	,,	Mitchell, Stewart
249	,,	Cairns, Joseph	306	,,	Mathews, Frederick.
250	,,	Cook, William	307	,,	Masey, Thomas D.
252	,,	Childs, James G.	308	,,	Moore, Charles
253	,,	Crompton, Thomas	309	,,	Moore, Harry
255	,,	Curtiss, Clarence W.	310	,,	Morris, George
258	,,	Duff, Thomas	311	,,	Morris, Lemuel
259	,,	Edwards, Hugh	313	,,	Munson, Neville

Canadian Pacific—The Empire's Greatest Railway.

ROYAL CANADIAN DRAGOONS—cont. 247

Regl. No.	Rank.	Name.	Regl. No.	Rank.	Name.
314	Private	Murray, Benjamin	332	Private	Shields, Robert W.
315	,,	Nadeau, Victor	333	,,	Shearer, John B.
316	,,	Needham, John	334	,,	Simmons, Frank
317	,,	Nicolls, George	335	,,	Sonnenburg, Edward
318	,,	Norquay, Frank	336	,,	Smith, Andrew
319	,,	Penfold, Alfred	337	,,	Sullivan, Timothy
320	,,	Pickering, Albert E.	215	,,	Sparkes, George
321	,,	Powell, Duncan	338	,,	Taylor, Edward
322	,,	Pudifin, Arthur	339	,,	Tregening, Archelaus
356	,,	Pyke, W. Herbert	340	,,	Turkington, Jas. S.
227	,,	Perrins, Frank	341	,,	Vincent, Arthur J.
323	,,	Ramsay, William	343	,,	Wadsworth, Alfonso
324	,,	Redgate, Albert	346	,,	Wetmore, David
325	,,	Robertson, George	347	,,	Wilkinson, Wilfred
326	,,	Rose, Walter	348	,,	Wiltshire, Charles
328	,,	Salto, Benedict	349	,,	Wilkins, Charles
329	,,	Sawyer, William	351	,,	Whittle, Arthur
330	,,	Searle, George A.	353	,,	Worfolk, Frank

"B" SQUADRON.

Major	...	...	...	Young, Douglas David
Captain	...	...	...	Bell, Walker H.
,,	...	...	...	Timmis, Reginald S.
Lieutenant	...	...	...	Newcomen, Terence
,,	...	...	...	Fisher, Donald Shrives
,,	...	...	...	Nordheimer, Roy
,,	...	...	...	Jarvis, Aemilius

Regl. No.	Rank.	Name.	Regl. No.	Rank.	Name.
501	S.S.-M.	James, Thomas A.	647	Corpl.	Mayman, George
502	S.Q.M.S.	Morgan, Percy	521	,,	Anderson, Walter
503	Sergt.	Mathews, John	523	Lce.-Cpl.	Parkinson, Thomas
504	,,	Fletcher, James	597	,,	Oakes, George
505	,,	Smith, Charles W.	642	,,	Elder, Frank C.
507	,,	Spalding, Frank	623	,,	Tamlyn, William
509	,,	Cox, Frederick	598	,,	Othen, Charles
510	,,	Copeland, John	525	Sh'sm'th	Cooper, John
511	,,	Norman, Sydney G.	526	,,	Warbrick, John A.
516	,,	Martin, Cuthbert	527	,,	Cortman, Harry
646	Far. Sgt.	Madden, Arthur	528	Saddler	Oliver, Frank
512	Shoe Cpl.	Brindle, Alf.	529	Trumpt'r	Smith, Alfred
514	Corpl.	Anstee, George	553	,,	Dempsey, James
517	,,	Melville, Francis	531	Private	Allam, George Wm.
518	,,	Atkins, Kinward G.	532	,,	Armstrong, Charles
519	,,	Sayger, Charles	648	,,	Ackerstrean, Bertil J.
520	,,	Easthorpe, Thomas	533	,,	Baker, Alfred R.
524	,,	Sharp, Mathew G.	534	,,	Banbury, Charles
522	,,	Henry, Harold	535	,,	Bailey, Daniel
573	,,	Hopkins, Bernard	536	,,	Bissett, Fred

Canadian Pacific—The Empire's Greatest Railway.

ROYAL CANADIAN DRAGOONS—cont.

Regl. No.	Rank	Name	Regl. No.	Rank	Name
537	Private	Bowes, Robert	585	Private	Mackenzie, Donald S.
539	,,	Brown, Edward T.	586	,,	Marshall, Thomas
540	,,	Brown, Frederick A.	587	,,	McCordick, Thomas
23	,,	Brown, Thomas H.	588	,,	Merrick, Alfred
541	,,	Butler, Alexander	589	,,	Miller, John B.
649	,,	Barge, Lee	590	,,	Millward, William
515	,,	Blair, Hugh Ramsay	591	,,	Muir, Thomas
542	,,	Caswell, Arthur E.	592	,,	Murray, Alexander J.
543	,,	Churchill, Arthur H.	644	,,	Macdonald, George
544	,,	Clark, Leslie	24	,,	Merritt, Charles
657	,,	Clark, Fred Batt	593	,,	Naden, William
545	,,	Cockerill, John	594	,,	Nelson, Frederick
546	,,	Calthorpe, Max.	595	,,	Norquay, Alexander
547	,,	Conroy, Richard	596	,,	Norris, Andrew
548	,,	Conroy, Frank	653	,,	Ogden, Charles
550	,,	Corry, Samuel	513	,,	Pritchard, George
551	,,	Courtney, George	645	,,	Powell, Francis S.
650	,,	Dawe, James S.	600	,,	Picken, Edward K.
552	,,	Davidson, George T.	601	,,	Preece, William
554	,,	Dempster, Douglas	603	,,	Pybus, George W.
508	,,	Ellis, William	604	,,	Reid, Andrew
555	,,	Evans, Alfred	605	,,	Reeve, Edgar A.
556	,,	Evans, Alexander G.	606	,,	Repton, Charles E.
643	,,	Evans, Roland E.	607	,,	Roberts, Charles L.
557	,,	Ewart, Edward	608	,,	Robertson, Eric A.
641	,,	Earl, Lawrence	609	,,	Robinson, James P
110	,,	Elsbury, John	610	,,	Robinson, John
558	,,	Fetterley, Silas	611	,,	Roy, John
559	,,	Foster, Bernard	654	,,	Robinson, Colin B.
560	,,	Foster, Harry James	612	,,	Salter, Alfred John
561	,,	Fraser, Stanley	613	,,	Salvador, Fred
562	,,	Gordon, John	614	,,	Sampson, Charles
564	,,	Grummett, William	615	,,	Savage, Francis
565	,,	Guthrie, Arthur	616	,,	Sharpe, Frederick
868	,,	Higham, Robert	617	,,	Sharpe, Samuel M.
566	,,	Hallett, James	618	,,	Sprately, Alfred
568	,,	Harrison, John	619	,,	Stanford, Walter
569	,,	Hare, Edward	620	,,	Stewart, Robert
571	,,	Haydon, Russell	621	,,	Stone, Albert E.
572	,,	Hazel, Alfred	622	,,	Stonely, John
574	,,	Jessett, Edward	656	,,	Trayler, William V.
575	,,	Jenkinson, Thos. B.	132	,,	Thomson, William
576	,,	King, Edward A.	624	,,	Theobald, Charles W.
577	,,	King, Edgar Gowan	625	,,	Thomas, Jesse P.
578	,,	King, Frederick	626	,,	Thompson, Foster C.
579	,,	King, John	627	,,	Tyner, Henry R.
580	,,	Kelly, Charles	628	,,	Vince, Alfred A.
581	,,	Kennedy, Roderick S.	629	,,	Waddell, Robert
582	,,	Learmond, James	630	,,	Watson, Robert W.
583	,,	Lees, Benjamin J.	631	,,	Webb, George
584	,,	Lighthall, William S.	632	,,	West, Robert
651	,,	Lightwood, Frank	633	,,	Weston, Charles W.

Canadian Pacific—The Empire's Greatest Railway.

ROYAL CANADIAN DRAGOONS—cont.

Regl. No.	Rank.	Name.	Regl. No.	Rank.	Name.
634	Private	White, Richard	638	Private	Wiltshire, Francis J.
635	,,	Whitworth, Thomas	639	,,	Wodehouse, Alfred P.
336	,,	Wilkinson, Ernest G.	640	,,	Wren, Sydney
637	,,	Wilson, Norman W.	506	,,	Wardell, Frank

"C" SQUADRON.

Major	... ...	McMillan, Alexander
Captain	... ...	Morrison, Frank Stanley
Lieutenant	... ...	Codville, Frank H. M.
,,	... ...	Sherwood, Lewis Percy
,,	... ...	Broome, Douglas F.
,,	... ...	Irving, Arthur B.
,,	... ...	Muirhead, William H.

Regl. No.	Rank.	Name.	Regl. No.	Rank.	Name.
801	S.S.-M.	Berteau, Gerald	821	Private	Amos, Ernest
802	S.Q.M.S.	La Rose, Valmas H.	822	,,	Adamsky, Joe
803	Sergt.	Doyle, Arthur	823	,,	Atkins, William
954	,,	Spalding, Victor	824	,,	Bailey, Alfred B.
804	,,	Walshe, Patrick	827	,,	Barber, Alfred H.
805	,,	Hopkinson, George C.	828	,,	Bott, Douglas
806	,,	Adlam, Horace	829	,,	Brown, Hugh
807	,,	Cookson, Gerald R. S.	830	,,	Brown, Charles
808	,,	Doxey, William	831	,,	Beckett, Albert H.
909	,,	Olmstead, Charles	832	,,	Bates, Robert
810	Far. Sgt.	Reese, William J.	833	,,	Banner, Claude E.
811	Sgl. Cpl.	Earnshaw, George	834	,,	Bruce, Alexander
814	Shoe Cpl.	McLeod, Hugh	835	,,	Clark, William Horace
817	Corpl.	McCutcheon, James	836	,,	Charlton, William
818	,,	Teahan, John P.	837	,,	Cochrane, John
819	,,	Parker, Robert	838	,,	Clarke, James D.
895	,,	Murphy, Hugh	839	,,	Connolly, Harry
892	,,	Macklem, William H.	840	,,	Cummiskey, A. W.
873	,,	James, Ernest	841	,,	Carroll, Christphr. J.
926	,,	Smith, Harry S.	842	,,	Clarke, William
887	,,	Meikle, John	843	,,	Cook, George
812	Sh'sm'th	Ianson, Herbert	845	,,	Devlin, Russell H.
813	,,	Blair, John A.	846	,,	Duffy, Leo
815	Trumpt'r	Holmes, George	847	,,	De Groot, William
816	,,	Green, Emmanuel G.	848	,,	Davies, Richard
826	Lce.-Cpl.	Blackwell, Clar. B.	849	,,	Darnboro, Walter
857	,,	Gorse, Alfred	850	,,	Erickson, Edwin
880	,,	Legge, William	852	,,	Fisher, Walter John
881	,,	Lightbody, Robert E.	853	,,	Fortier, Adelard
894	,,	M'Kinley, John	854	,,	Fennimore, James W.
911	,,	Parry, Ernest	855	,,	Gray, Charles H.
844	,,	Corbett, Arthur F.	861	,,	Gray, James Morrison
910	,,	Porter, Sidney A.	856	,,	Grant, Thomas A.
851	Saddler	Emmerson, Lyman C.	858	,,	Gutterez, Alfred

Canadian Pacific—The Empire's Greatest Railway.

ROYAL CANADIAN DRAGOONS—cont.

Regl. No.	Rank.	Name.	Regl. No.	Rank.	Name.
860	Private	Greux, Arthur	912	Private	Phillips, Willis H.
862	,,	Gillespie, Allan	913	,,	Proulx, William L.
863	,,	Humphrey, Fredk. G.	914	,,	Peterson, Carl
864	,,	Hopkins, John R.	915	,,	Preston, Milford W.
865	,,	Houston, Ivan	916	,,	Pope, Charles
866	,,	Harris, Richard Fred	917	,,	Pearson, George
867	,,	Holloway, Charles	918	,,	Rogette, Alfred
567	,,	Harbour, Thomas	919	,,	Ralph, Edmund R.
869	,,	Ingham, Frank	920	,,	Rigg, Thomas
859	,,	Julius, James	921	,,	Rowe, Trevalyn
870	,,	Jones, Harry	922	,,	Ross, James
871	,,	Jackson, Edward	923	,,	Rutledge, Joe
872	,,	Jebb, William F.	924	,,	Reid, Charles
874	,,	Jones, John	925	,,	Saunders, William B.
955	,,	Jones, Ellis	927	,,	Smith, Francis C.
875	,,	Kinder, Henry E.	928	,,	Smith, Alex. F.
876	,,	Kinder, Gilbert Hugh	929	,,	Smith, Ben.
877	,,	Liggins, Leonard	930	,,	Stothart, James
878	,,	Lefurgey, Archie	820	,,	Sutton, Joseph
879	,,	Lewis, Harry	931	,,	St. Hiliare, Gideon
882	,,	Libby, Albert G.	932	,,	Smith, Albert
883	,,	Lawson, Thomas	933	,,	Sheppard, Cecil Louis
884	,,	McHugh, Edward	934	,,	Scholey, William A.
885	,,	Manning, Horace R.	935	,,	Swift, Cecil
886	,,	McCall, Archibald	936	,,	Stretton, William
888	,,	Menish, Wilbert W.	937	,,	Squires, Walter
889	,,	Montgomery, W. F.	938	,,	Turner, Alex.
890	,,	Muller, Robert Victor	939	,,	Tuxworth, Albert A.
891	,,	McKean, Kenneth	940	,,	Timmins, Frederick
893	,,	Martell, Howard	941	,,	Twine, Henry A.
896	,,	Memory, John	942	,,	Thompson, John
897	,,	Marquis, Achille	943	,,	Vickers, Ernest
898	,,	McGregor, James	944	,,	Volks, Alfred J.
900	,,	McKenzie, Gordon	946	,,	Wilson, Ernest A.
901	,,	Manning, William D.	947	,,	West, Clarence
902	,,	Martin, Andrew B.	948	,,	Wood, Robert
903	,,	Nadeau, William H.	949	,,	Wood, James
904	,,	Nash, John	950	,,	Walsh, William
905	,,	Newby, Gordon	951	,,	Warring, Richard
906	,,	Ormiston, James	952	,,	Walsh, Frederick
907	,,	Pearse, John	953	,,	Wilson, Alex.
909	,,	Paul, Elmer G.			

Canadian Pacific—The Empire's Greatest Railway.

LORD STRATHCONA'S HORSE (R.C.)

HEADQUARTERS STAFF.

Commanding	Lieut.-Col. A. C. Macdonell, D.S.O.
Second in Command	Major E. F. Mackie, D.S.O.
Adjutant	Lieutenant M. Docherty
Signalling Officer	,, J. R. Sparks
Quartermaster	Hon. Lieutenant F. C. Rush
Paymaster	,, Captain H. Hill
Scout Officer	Captain W. T. Lawless
Transport Officer	Lieutenant C. W. Devey
Specially Employed	,, I. C. Macdonell

Attached.

Medical Officer	Captain C. E. Fortin
Veterinary ,,	,, J. R. J. Duhault
Chaplain	,, C. M. Ambrose

Regl. No.	Rank.	Name.	Regl. No.	Rank.	Name.
2287	R.S.M.	Tomkins, F.	2426	Private	Howe, W.
2283	R.Q.M.S.	Stillwell, W.	2762	,,	Jackson, J.
1602	F.Q.M.S.	Milne, A.	2715	,,	Jardine, W.
1977	Sergt.	Macdowell, T.	2801	,,	Kendall, E. J.
2410	Sgt.Cook	Deall, G. W.	2847	,,	Lawson, A. H.
1894	Sgt.Tptr.	Jacques, C.	2631	,,	Lennon, P.
2024	Sergt.	Corson, A. L.	2845	,,	Lynch, J.
2824	Corpl.	Turnbull, W	2829	,,	Murphy, J.
2454	Private	Baker, E.	2831	,,	Okell, S.
2839	,,	Brown, A.	2769	,,	Oppenheim, A. E.
2779	,,	Ellison, J.	2755	,,	Price, T.
2887	,,	Clarke, E. G.	2813	,,	Ritchie, W.
2439	,,	Foster, J. R.	2794	,,	Smith, J.
2884	,,	Farrant, E. G	2713	,,	Steer, H. R. C. H. H.
2830	,,	Glawson, E.	2636	,,	Turner, J.
2770	,,	Hawthorne, J.	1619	,,	Thorne, W.
2375	,,	Harding, L. J.	2765	,,	Vidal, M. H.
2385	,,	Hadley, C.			

Attached—Water Detail A.M.C.

33705 Corpl. Marriott, T
33707 Private Ackery, C.

33706 Private Butt, H.

Canadian Pacific—The Empire's Greatest Railway.

LORD STRATHCONA'S HORSE (R.C.)—cont.

"A" SQUADRON.

Officer Commanding	Major F. L. Cartwright, D.S.O.
Second in Command	Captain T. L. Arnott
Subalterns	Lieutenant D. C. Davis
,, ...	,, G. Rothnie
,, ...	,, A. H. Bostock
,, ...	,, L. H. Beer

Regl. No.	Rank.	Name.	Regl. No.	Rank.	Name.
2145	S.S.M.	Connolly, C. E.	2547	Private	Campbell, M.
2005	S.Q.M.S.	Fairbrother, P. G.	2373	,,	Calverley, G. W.
1758	Far. Sgt.	Durham, G. W.	2396	,,	Clayton, G.
2357	Sergt.	Austin, G. R.	2777	,,	Clarke, C. E.
1969	,,	Bicknell, R. F.	2262	,,	Cordell, W.
2267	,,	Burton, P. W.	2832	,,	Corneil, W.
2210	,,	Brown, R. J.	2871	,,	Crawford, A. M.
1916	,,	Brown, D. C.	2530	,,	Curwen, C. E.
2592	,,	George, H. B.	2885	,,	Cross, R. C.
2623	,,	Green, A. A. L.	2424	,,	Dale, A.
2878	,,	Howell, R. B.	2834	,,	Darlington, E.
2418	Lce-Sgt.	Foster, A. E.	2540	,,	Demers, M. N.
2129	Corpl.	Binnie, A. D. W.	2434	,,	Debenham, D. C.
2466	,,	Blair, R. M.	2277	,,	Dixon, G. H.
1707	,,	Henry, T.	2539	,,	Doyle, J.
2011	,,	Richmond, R.	2543	,,	Doherty, E.
2236	,,	Sutton, J. R.	2372	,,	Dyson, V. R.
2443	,,	Woodiwiss, A. R. B.	2787	,,	Dyer, A. H.
2735	,,	Willan, A. R.	2172	,,	Duncan, J.
2506	Cpl.S.S.	Frost, C. A. E.	2409	,,	Eliot, L. C. D.
2446	Lce.-Cpl.	Ash, J. C.	2536	,,	Endacott, D.
2527	,,	Cameron, G. D.	2503	,,	Ferguson, W. J.
2535	,,	Fraser, R.	2504	,,	Ferguson, A.
2436	,,	McNeill, A. D.	2531	,,	Forster, H. B.
2605	,,	Middleton, J. R.	2423	,,	Francis, D. R.
2614	,,	Shand, G. M.	2502	,,	Francis, H. C.
2740	,,	Webster, C. M.	2431	,,	Garnett, W. M.
2213	Trumpt'r	Allen, W. G.	2392	,,	Gale, J. E.
2444	,,	Clarke, G. H.	2428	,,	Gibbs, W. J.
2510	Private	Adam, J. A.	2864	,,	Godfrey, A. E.
2509	,,	Anderson, S. L.	2468	,,	Goodale, W. H.
2202	,,	Baker, A.	2363	,,	Green, J. F.
2237	,,	Barrett, C. H.	2627	,,	Green, M. L.
2462	,,	Barclay, D. F.	2499	,,	Grestock, H.
2445	,,	Bitton, C. G.	2274	,,	Gray, W.
2275	,,	Black, J.	2593	,,	Guy, G. B.
2432	,,	Bolan, F. S.	1986	,,	Harrison, R. W.
2465	,,	Bolton, W. E.	2674	,,	Harris, R. I.
2463	,,	Bowden, N. H.	2701	,,	Hardy, H. F.
2464	,,	Boddy, G. G. D.	2675	,,	Heath, W. H.
2371	,,	Burley, J. E.	2702	,,	Hitchcock, R. F.
2874	,,	Boultbee, E. F.	2697	,,	Hodgson, C. McD.
2415	,,	Capnerhurst, A.	2266	,,	Houghton, W.

Canadian Pacific—The Empire's Greatest Railway.

LORD STRATHCONA'S HORSE (R.C.)—cont. 253

Regl. No.	Rank	Name	Regl. No.	Rank	Name
2873	Private	Hewetson, J. S.	2628	Private	Nevile, J. F.
2857	,,	Ianson, W.	2629	,,	Oswell, G. C.
2601	,,	Jones, G.	2587	,,	Parkinson, W. S.
2599	,,	Jones, J. S.	2415	,,	Player, A.
2596	,,	Johnson, G. A.	2586	,,	Powell, F. C.
2597	,,	Johnson, C.	2585	,,	Powell, G. B.
2660	,,	Knowles, A. E.	2688	,,	Priest, J. S.
2651	,,	Leighton, R. F.	2649	,,	Roberts, E. J.
2656	,,	Lang, F.	2647	,,	Roberts, G. F.
2634	,,	Lewall, B. C.	2708	,,	Sandys, W. E.
2438	,,	Lewis, F.	2707	,,	Shore, T. T.
2653	,,	Lewis, M.	2738	,,	Smith, D. W.
2657	,,	Lewis, T.	2430	,,	Steer, P. M.
2652	,,	Ligat, R. L.	2394	,,	Stewart, S.
2802	,,	Matthews, W.	2401	,,	Stuart, J. J. M.
2233	,,	Mckay, J.	2612	,,	Stevenson, W. H.
2414	,,	Macdonald, D. M.	2554	,,	Strachan, A.
2398	,,	McLeod, D.	2615	,,	Surtees, S.
2609	,,	Mason, H.	2635	,,	Thomas, M.
2606	,,	Mahan, G. H.	2362	,,	Tooth, R.
2692	,,	Mair, J. A.	2355	,,	Underwood, O.
2608	,,	MacLeod, J. A.	2866	,,	Upton, G. C.
2611	,,	MacPhadyen, C. N.	2684	,,	Vincenzi, L.
2279	,,	McManus, G. E.	2486	,,	Ward, A. A.
2626	,,	Mellor, J. R.	2703	,,	Watson, R. G.
2858	,,	Mitchell, F.	2181	,,	White, W. P.
2860	,,	Missler, J. J.	2207	,,	White, H.
2663	,,	Mitchell, E. J.	2704	,,	Wilson, J. H. H.
2435	,,	Mitchell, J. B.	2699	,,	Willes, H. W. H.
2607	,,	Miller, D.	2369	,,	Wright, D. H. C.
2376	,,	Morse, W. H.	2877	,,	Wright, C.

'B' SQUADRON.

Officer Commanding ... ... Major J. A. Hesketh
Second in Command ... ... Captain A. C. Critchley
Subalterns ... ... Lieutenant A. D. Cameron
,, ... ,, R. E. Paget
,, ... ,, J. Galt
,, ... ,, W. G. Tennant

Regl. No.	Rank	Name	Regl. No.	Rank	Name
1517	S.S.-M.	Collins, G. S.	2179	Sergt.	Newlands, R. J.
1718	S.Q.M.S.	Marsden, G. W. T.	2624	,,	Nicol, H.
1985	Far.Sgt.	Bambridge, W.	2028	,,	Reeder, G. C.
1893	Sergt.	Brown, C. G.	1857	,,	Trotter, J. B.
2621	,,	George, B.	2700	Lce.-Sgt.	Wilkinson, E. R.
2442	,,	Grell, N.	2459	Corpl.	Burkholder, E. P.
2650	,,	Loyd, E. B. K.	2528	,,	Clarke, M. H.

Canadian Pacific—The Empire's Greatest Railway.

LORD STRATHCONA'S HORSE (R.C.)—cont.

Regl. No.	Rank.	Name.	Regl. No.	Rank.	Name.
2505	Corpl.	Flowerdew, C. M.	2533	Private	Frakes, R.
2591	,,	Goodbrand, J.	2722	,,	Franklin, H. C.
2741	,,	Sworder, N.	2479	,,	Gass, G.
2575	,,	Whitford, J.	2494	,,	Gibb, A.
2733	,,	Witten, G. W. B.	2726	,,	Golden, T. L.
2452	Cpl. S.S.	Baillie, T.	2758	,,	Good, J.
2451	Lce.-Cpl.	Billett, F. B.	2577	,,	Gray, E. T.
2563	,,	Cobham, H. B.	2473	,,	Graham, G. L.
2863	,,	Evans, A. M.	2835	,,	Hatch, J. W.
2507	,,	Fry, H.	2440	,,	Hayes, D. E.
2658	,,	Kidd, T.	2619	,,	Haldane, W.
2731	,,	Mott, R.	2620	,,	Haldane, D. G. M.
2646	,,	Roberts, W.	2766	,,	Herron, G.
2725	,,	Ross, A. J.	2711	,,	Holberton, T. E.
2742	,,	Sworder, M.	2618	,,	Howitt, F. L.
2460	Trumpt'r	Burt, W. G.	2712	,,	Howse, C. A.
2616	,,	Herve, C.	2467	,,	Holland, F. R.
2448	Private	Aynsley, W. C.	2774	,,	Hunter, A.
2449	,,	Bartlett, T.	2816	,,	Irving, H.
2763	,,	Barlow, L. H.	2600	,,	Jacobs, A. G.
2786	,,	Baxter, F.	2727	,,	Johnson, C.
2526	,,	Benson, R. A.	2778	,,	Jongh, F. de
2469	,,	Blake, G.	2500	,,	Kemp, H. O.
2461	,,	Bonser, E. T.	2773	,,	Kearney, J.
2489	,,	Bolton, W. M.	2868	,,	King, G.
2453	,,	Boyer, C. B.	2661	,,	King, R. L.
2724	,,	Bowles, P.	2836	,,	Lamb, H.
2351	,,	Brown, W. E.	2834	,,	Lindsay, J. R.
2558	,,	Bradley, E.	2803	,,	Lamacraft, P.
2458	,,	Brousseau, C.	2383	,,	Mason, W.
2730	,,	Brownell, H. V.	1828	,,	McGregor, R.
2513	,,	Carlile, J. E.	2604	,,	McCluckie, D.
2490	,,	Carter, W. E.	2603	,,	McCulloch, W. L.
2787	,,	Carter, C. E.	2594	,,	McCarthy, A. W.
2515	,,	Choate, F. H.	2480	,,	McCann, J.
2516	,,	Church, E. Z.	2673	,,	McDermid, G. D.
2493	,,	Clarke, L. N.	2776	,,	McGoldrick, P.
2517	,,	Clark, T.	2732	,,	McGowan, D.
2261	,,	Clive, A.	2750	,,	McKenzie, K.
2488	,,	Clarke, A. A.	2568	,,	McKay, H.
2749	,,	Clarkin, J. E.	2670	,,	McLeod, A. D.
2562	,,	Coyne, J.	2723	,,	Miles, T. H.
2520	,,	Cooper, J.	2788	,,	Mitchell, A. W.
2487	,,	Coakley, L. H.	2844	,,	Milsom, H. G.
2806	,,	Crawford, G.	2865	,,	Moreau, C.
2521	,,	Cummer, J. W.	2397	,,	Morrison, P.
2522	,,	Currie, W. A.	2862	,,	Mullins, C. de C. C.
2795	,,	Dent, S.	2666	,,	Mudie, R. L.
2566	,,	Donald, W. L.	2764	,,	Neilson, R. A.
2799	,,	Dominick, N.	2625	,,	Noble, E. S.
2538	,,	Edgar, M.	2827	,,	O'Brien, R. P.
2843	,,	Fernie, F.	2687	,,	Parry, R.

[Canadian Pacific—The Empire's Greatest Railway.

LORD STRATHCONA'S HORSE (R.C.)—cont.

Regl. No.	Rank.	Name.	Regl. No.	Rank.	Name.
2496	Private	Parr, W. H.	2481	Private	Shaw, T.
2582	,,	Pinder, B. D.	2804	,,	Shaw, R.
2584	,,	Poole, E.	2736	,,	Street, H. J.
2837	,,	Penrose, J.	2752	,,	Strang, G. W.
2728	,,	Rear, J.	2739	,,	Sworder, G. H.
2805	,,	Ritchie, T.	2639	,,	Taylor, L. C.
2648	,,	Rodaway, C. W.	2846	,,	Thomas, J.
2632	,,	Ross, J. A.	2772	,,	Topping, J.
2643	,,	Ross, D.	2393	,,	Vernon, T. F.
2678	,,	Rose, H.	2641	,,	Vaillancourt, C. L.
2231	,,	Robinson, W.	2548	,,	Vidler, A. G. A.
2677	,,	Robinson, G. C.	2709	,,	Wick, W. H.
2747	,,	Russell, L. L.	2789	,,	Wilson, A. R.
2681	,, .	Sinclair-Smith, R.	2710	,,	Wood, B. A.
2767	,,	Size, H.	2437	,,	Zuern, J. A.

"C" SQUADRON.

Officer Commanding	Major F. C. Turner, D.S.O.
Second in Command	Captain W. R. Russell
Subalterns	Lieutenant J. A. Critchley
,,	,, D. J. McDonald
,,	,, C. Goodday
,,	,, J. C. Clarke

Regl. No.	Rank.	Name.	Regl. No.	Rank.	Name.
2358	S.S.-M.	Collins, H.	2550	Lce.-Cpl.	West, S. W.
2455	S.Q.M.S.	Bishop, S. W.	2841	,,	Wildig, B. P.
2679	Far. Sgt.	Shaw, W. T.	2456	Trumpt'r	Bradley, S. E.
2260	Sergt.	Crane, H. A.	2545	,,	Denton, P.
2406	,,	Hayter, C. N. C.	2447	Private	Andrew, J.
2581	,,	Kirby, R.	2790	,,	Ashby, T.
2672	,,	Macdonell, D. R.	2501	,,	Avery, J.
2381	,,	Malcolm, D. K.	2876	,,	Bance, A. J.
2588	,,	Paul, C. A.	2821	,,	Barff, J. B.
2705	,,	Prior, B. G.	2450	,,	Bell, H. B.
1987	,,	Smith, E.	2756	,,	Bithell, J. C.
2745	Lce.-Sgt.	Lee, H. A.	2433	,,	Broadbent, S.
2222	Corpl.	Garrett, J.	2555	,,	Brown, E. W. A.
2698	,,	Hutchinson, F. F.	2810	,,	Brown, V. R.
2552	,,	O'Reilly, T. A.	2484	,,	Burden, A. N.
2395	,,	Squibb, L. M.	2491	,,	Burke, J. C.
2682	,,	Street, F. A. H.	2782	,,	Bryant, J.
2640	,,	Trigg, J. H.	2855	,,	Batten, J.
2476	,,	Tripp, H. V.	2471	,,	Carter, A.
2511	Lce.-Cpl.	Cade, F. W.	2402	,,	Carter, C.
2544	,,	Dodd, A. P.	2474	,,	Cave, J.
2676	,,	Harvey, R.	2721	,,	Cavey, M.
2598	,,	Judd, W. S.	2477	,,	Cave, J. E. M.
2757	,,	Ross, J. R.	2814	,,	Carberry, S.
2737	,,	Smith, H. C. B.	2514	,,	Chiddy, C. W.

Canadian Pacific—The Empire's Greatest Railway.

LORD STRATHCONA'S HORSE (R.C.)—cont.

Regl. No.	Rank.	Name.	Regl. No.	Rank.	Name.
2561	Private	Chapman, W.	2823	Private	McCauley, E. A.
2792	,,	Charles, W.	2567	,,	McDonald, J. W.
2808	,	Charlton, W.	2671	,,	McLellan, C. F.
2829	,,	Chase, G.	2833	,,	McLeod, W. H.
2560	,,	Clarke, G. E.	2716	,,	McMillan, R.
2564	,,	Clendinnen, B. W.	2556	,,	McRitchie, D. M.
2519	,,	Cooper, F. A.	2785	,,	Mercer, T. W.
2518	,,	Cooper, E. G.	2668	,,	Miles, E. S.
2818	,,	Cox, W. F.	2822	,,	Miller, F.
2559	,,	Croney, T.	2811	,,	Mulligan, W. R.
2875	,,	Cobb, C.	2664	,,	Murdock, T.
2565	,,	Davies, L. S.	2665	,,	Mullins, L.
2411	,,	Dickens, C.	2690	,,	Osler, T.
2783	,,	Digby, W.	2869	,,	Parrington, P.
2812	,,	Dixon, W. de H.	2571	,,	Palmer, G. H.
2542	,,	Duford, A. F.	2815	,,	Poore, C.
2537	,,	Evans, H.	2853	,,	Pritchard, I.
2492	,,	Eisenmann, E. O.	2483	,,	Quinn, J.
2534	,,	Flowerdew, E. S.	2644	,,	Randall, W.
2842	,,	Fraser, M. D.	2495	,,	Rees, J.
2590	,,	Gordon, T. G.	2714	,,	Reid, D. J.
2576	,,	Grady, W. H.	2475	,,	Roberts, P. J.
2557	,,	Grier, J.	2759	,,	Robida, A.
2622	,,	Grierson, W. J.	2570	,,	Scheer, G.
2403	,,	Grillot, W.	2572	,,	Scougall, W. M.
2784	,,	Hards, N.	2498	,,	Sillis, V. A.
2807	,,	Hartely, G.	2720	,,	Sharp, M. H.
2852	,,	Harris, A. E.	2754	,,	Smith, W.
2384	,,	Henley, E. C.	2832	,,	Smith, P. J.
2771	,,	Heuer, T. C.	2854	,,	Smith, V. O.
2831	,,	Herbert, A.	2680	,,	Stapleton, L. C.
2617	,,	Hodgkinson, S.	2768	,,	Stoneham, J.
2244	,,	Hodgkinson, J. A.	2748	,,	Stuebing, C.
2389	,,	Hyde, W. G.	2717	,,	Sullivan, V.
2497	,,	Hutchins, F.	2797	,,	Symons, R.
2734	,,	Johnstone, R. L.	2470	,,	Taylor, E. D.
2578	,,	Kershaw, S. F.	2573	,,	Taylor, M. J.
2580	,,	Kirby, A. A.	2637	,,	Toder, A. J.
2659	,,	Knight, H.	2638	,,	Trevor, V.
2828	,,	Lee, R. E.	2850	,,	Trinder, A. W.
2655	,,	Lingford, G. K.	2685	,,	Walker, W. J.
2654	,,	Louis, R. H.	2478	,,	Warburton, F. G.
2630	,,	Maytum, W. G.	2746	,,	Ward, D.
2718	,,	Maytum, A. W.	2691	,,	Webb, H. G.
2819	,,	Martin, H.	2549	,,	West, A.
2569	,,	Martin, F.	2595	,,	Webster, A. C.
2693	,,	Matthews, E. J.	2798	,,	White, P. T. A.
2669	Sh'sm'th	Matthews, F.	2574	,,	Wilson, P. S.
2694	Private	Masson, A. J.	2820	,,	Wright, W. F.
2482	,,	Maiden, W. A.	2686	,,	Wyatt, A. D.
2610	,,	McArthur, G. W.	2809	,,	Young, C.
2602	,,	McCurdy, D. J.			

Canadian Pacific—The Empire's Greatest Railway.

LORD STRATHCONA'S HORSE (R.C.)—*cont.* 257

Machine Gun Section.

Officer Commanding ... ... Lieut. O. A. Critchley

Regl. No.	Rank.	Name.	Regl. No.	Rank.	Name.
1673	Sergt.	Mitchell, L.	2719	Private	Francis, J.
2551	Corpl.	Drummond, L. D. B.	2696	,,	Huth, M.
2508	Private	Allen, W. P.	2881	,,	Lefroy, L. B.
2457	,,	Broadbridge, R.	2695	,,	Melhuish, J. L.
2751	,,	Brown, R. S.	2689	,,	Oland, C. F.
2525	,,	Carroll, R.	2633	,,	Robertson, H. M.
2512	,,	Campbell, H. G.	2840	,,	Robertson, A. P.
2848	,,	Campbell, J.	2833	,,	Steedman, C. D.
2849	,,	Carpenter, L.	2825	,,	Stewart, W. Y.
2523	,,	Cotterill, H. S.	2870	,,	St. Lo, M.
2546	,,	Crippen, N. B.	2642	,,	Vance, A. G.
2541	,,	Donald, J.	2683	,,	Vickers, H. H.
2826	,,	Duby, T.			

Base Details.

Officer Commanding ... ... Lieutenant C. K. L. Pyman

Regl. No.	Rank.	Name	Regl. No.	Rank.	Name.
2270	S.Q.M.S.	Rothery, J. H.	2793	Private	Madigan, F.
2800	Sergt.	George, E. W.	2441	,,	Matthey, G. A.
2662	,,	Macfarlane, C. A.	2422	,,	Miller, L. E.
2851	Corpl.	Blaylock, J.	2667	,,	Morrant, H. D.
2796	Private	Blaigners, A.	2761	,,	Munn, J.
2838	,,	Brown, J. H.	2879	,,	Marsham, J.
2791	,,	Bruce, W.	2412	,,	Poston, E.
2880	,,	Boyer, C. J.	2883	,,	Rhodes, C. R.
2781	,,	Cook, S.	2553	,,	Smith, J.
2861	,,	Cunningham, G.	2867	,,	Smythe, A.
2532	,,	FitzGerald, R. D.	2472	,,	Stallard, C.
2589	,,	Green, G.	2882	,,	Watt, J.
2775	,,	Holmes, J.	2886	,,	Wadsworth, E.
2856	,,	Lalonde, W.	2780	,,	Yorke, R. G.

Canadian Pacific—The Empire's Greatest Railway.

R

DIVISIONAL ARTILLERY HEADQUARTERS.

Officer Commanding	Lieut.-Colonel H. E. Burstall
Brigade Major	Captain C. F. Constantine
Staff Captain	Captain A. S. Wright
A.D.C.	Captain N. O. Reiffenstein
Extra A.D.C.	Lieutenant G. G. Blackstock
Chaplain	Hon. Capt. Rev. Father W.T. Workman
,,	,, ,, Rev. Canon J. M. Almond

Regl. No.	Rank.	Name	Regl. No.	Rank.	Name.
40001	Staff Sgt.	Hooper, R. E.P.	40011	Gunner	Tingman, William
40002	Corpl.	Traynor, Albert E.	40014	,,	Turner, Frederick C.
40003	Bombr.	Wallace, Charles R.	40015	,,	Shaughnessy, C.W.E.
40004	,,	Lowther, Osmond R.	40017	,,	McGrath, Earl
40005	,,	Quilter, George	40018	,,	Rose, Ernest
40006	Gunner	Cherry, Edward John	40019	,,	Harrison, Robert
40007	,,	Lewis, Stephen Thos.	40020	,,	Wright, Edward
40008	,,	Drake, George	40021	,,	Chamberlain, Wilfred
40009	,,	Swaddling, Charles	40022	,,	Smith, Herbert R.
40010	,,	Nicholls, Albert V.			

1st ARTILLERY BRIGADE AND AMMUNITION COLUMN.

Lieut.-Colonel	Morrison, E. W. B. (D.S.O.)
,,	Dodds, W. O. H.
,,	Maclaren, C. H.
Major	Britton, R. H. *DSO*
,,	McCrae, John
,,	Sharman, C. H. L.
Captain	Cosgrave, L. V. M.
Veterinary Officer	Captain Dixon, E. M.
Captain	Durkee, A. A.
,,	Goodere, L. C.
Paymaster	Hon. Captain Kelly, L. S.
Captain	Stewart, J. C.
,,	White, D. A.
Lieutenant	Alderson, F. H.
,,	Bick, A. H.
,,	Boville, K. H.
,,	Blue, W. E.
,,	Gillis, A. R.
,,	Godwin, C. R. M.
,,	Helmer, A. H.
,,	Macpherson, J. S.
,,	Matthews, H. S.
,,	Shaw, W. B.
,,	Taylor, H. W.
,,	Thackeray, R. G.
,,	Whitley, H.

Canadian Pacific—The Empire's Greatest Railway.

1st ARTILLERY BRIGADE & AMMUNITION COL.—cont. 259

Attached.

Major	Mills, J. E.	
Captain	Pickles, F. W.	
Lieutenant	Benson, V.	
,, ...	Young, R. T.	

Regl. No.	Rank.	Name.	Regl. No.	Rank.	Name.
40361	Driver	Abbey, W.	40368	Gunner	Bate, H. B.
40356	Gunner	Ackland, W.	40761	Driver	Bates, D. E.
40589	Driver	Ackley, W.	40098	Sergt.	Bates, W. M.
40590	Gunner	Acton, J.	40372	Driver	Bathgate, G.
40115	Bombr.	Adams, G. V.	40139	Gunner	Bauville, J.
40052	Gunner	Addison, W. G.	40775	,,	Beals, H.
40908	Corpl.	Aggett, S. E. G.	40777	,,	Beames, R.
40285	Gunner	Ainslie, —	40782	.,	Beames, S.
40524	Driver	Ainslie, J.	40597	,,	Beaubien, B.
40357	Gunner	Adkins, W.	40596	Driver	Beaumont, F.
40770	,,	Adkins, W. E.	40144	Gunner	Beeching, —
40333	Sad. Sgt.	Alcock, A.	40598	,,	Beckett, P.
40360	Gunner	Alexander, F. W. T.	40924	Shoe Sgt.	Beecham, J.
40359	,,	Allen, J. R.	40129	Gunner	Bell, J. M. G.
40051	Corpl.	Allinson, C. L. C.	40599	,,	Bell, K. W.
40050	Gunner	Allinson, J. D.	40564	,,	Bellmore, H.
40053	Bombr.	Allwood, F. H.	40553	Sergt.	Bellringer, W.
40123	Driver	Anderson, R. B.	40287	Gunner	Belton, A.
40591	Gunner	Amo, L.	40780	,,	Bennett, C. H.
40592	,,	Armstrong, J. B.	40926	Saddler	Bennett, J. W.
40593	,,	Armstrong, J. M.	40363	Driver	Benson, R. N.
40594	,,	Applin, J.	40600	,,	Bentham, J.
40771	,,	Arnold, E. G.	40521	,,	Berube, J. F. X.
40124	Driver	Arnold, F. S.	40056	Sergt.	Best, R. M.
40358	Bombr.	Arnoldi, J. R.	40776	Gunner	Bethune, L.
40285	Gunner	Ashmore, F.	40907	Shoe Sgt.	Biles, B. R.
40054	Trumpt'r	Ashton, V.	40094	Sergt.	Billman, R. S.
40523	Gunner	Ashworth, —	40380	Driver	Bird, G.
40772	,,	Ashworth, D.	40376	,,	Birnie, P.
40929	,,	Atkinson, W.	40585	Cook	Bishop, M.
40928	,,	Audette, J.	40765	Driver	Bishop, W.
40768	Driver	Audette, J.	40778	Gunner	Black, C. C.
40327	Gunner	Baber, W.	40601	,,	Black, J.
40378	,,	Badgley, F.	40602	,,	Black, M.
40381	Driver	Baillie, O. E.	40341	Corpl.	Black, W.
40740	Gunner	Baker, A.	40347	Act. Cpl.	Blackburn, W.
40137	Saddler	Baker, W.	40364	Gunner	Blaylock, E. G.
40369	Gunner	Balcombe, H. S. G.	40366	,,	Bleasdell, H. T.
40140	,,	Balderston, C. T.	40135	,,	Blyth, G. S.
40143	,,	Barbour, J. D.	40141	Driver	Boadley, J.
40595	Driver	Barrett, J.	40126	Gunner	Bochatey, A.
40128	Gunner	Bartlett, E.	40057	,,	Bonneville, S.
40350	Bombr.	Bartlette, E.	40107	,,	Boone, J. R.
40134	Driver	Barry, J.	40061	Driver	Boulger, G. J.
40382	Gunner	Batcheldor, D. A.	40055	Gunner	Bourbridge, H. W.

Canadian Pacific—The Empire's Greatest Railway.

R 2

260   1st ARTILLERY BRIGADE & AMMUNITION COL.—cont.

Regl. No.	Rank.	Name.
40603	Corpl.	Bovey, E. T.
40571	Driver	Bovey, R. J.
40587	Trumpt'r	Bovey, S.
40131	Gunner	Bowden, J. R.
40365	Driver	Bowen, C.
40773	Gunner	Bowen G.
40604	,,	Bowman, W.
40058	,,	Boyle, E. A.
40059	Driver	Bradley, —
40103	Corpl.	Brady, G.
40373	Gunner	Bray, A.
40781	,,	Braybrook, K. G.
40130	,,	Brehaut, R.
40060	,,	Breiter, J. P.
40606	Driver	Brennan, F.
40605	Gunner	Brennan, H.
40922	Shoe Sgt.	Brennan, S. L.
40133	Driver	Brew, S.
40138	Gunner	Brewer, W. D.
40370	,,	Bright, H. R.
40371	,,	Brisbois, R.
40779	,,	Briston, G.
40142	Driver	Broadwith, —
40379	Gunner	Bronskill, F. H.
40125	,,	Brown, C. G.
40132	Driver	Brown, E. A.
40607	Gunner	Brown, G.
40556	,,	Brown, G. H.
40774	,,	Brown, J. J.
40608	,,	Brown, M.
40127	,,	Bruce, W. G.
40367	,,	Bryan, D.
40609	Driver	Buchanan, J.
40923	Shoe Sgt.	Buck, E.
40348	Bombr.	Buck, R. G.
40913	,,	Buckell, E. R.
40610	Driver	Bullett, B.
40611	,,	Bullett, W.
40362	,,	Bunyan, B.
40286	Gunner	Burgess, W.
40374	Driver	Burns, E.
40375	Gunner	Burns, J. H.
40783	,,	Burns, M. L.
40567	Bombr.	Burns, P. J.
40526	Driver	Burns, R.
40612	,,	Burtch, A. A.
40565	Corpl.	Buss, T.
40136	Gunner	Butter, C.
40525	Driver	Butler, J. A.
40145	,,	Butt, G. A.
40377	Gunner	Byron, R. L.
40331	Q.M.S.	Cairns, S. J.

Regl. No.	Rank.	Name.
40387	Gunner	Campbell, N. G.
40613	,,	Campbell, R. H.
40788	,,	Campbell, W. G.
40152	Driver	Canning, E. G.
40386	,,	Carney, J.
40150	,,	Carr, C.
40390	Gunner	Carr, E. A. V.
40062	,,	Carrier, L.
40614	,,	Carter, E. D.
40615	Driver	Carter, S. H.
40616	,,	Carter, V. W.
40569	Bombr.	Case, J. W.
40557	Sergt.	Case, R.
40785	Gunner	Cayer, R.
40787	,,	Champagne, L.
40522	Driver	Charbonneau, —
40745	Gunner	Chatham, W.
40149	Driver	Chatwin, A. E.
40617	Gunner	Chester, W.
40441	Sergt.	Chevis, W.
40618	Driver	Chidley, W.
40349	Act. Cpl.	Chipman, C. C.
40899	Sgt.-Maj.	Chitty, L. M.
40619	Bombr.	Chisholm, J. A.
40155	Gunner	Christian, G. R.
40622	,,	Chouinard, —
40621	,,	Chubb, B.
40383	Driver	Church, J.
40147	Gunner	Claire, C. E.
40623	Driver	Clare, W. C.
40624	,,	Clark, H. J.
40063	Pay Sgt.	Clark, O. W.
40578	Gunner	Clark, R. A.
40391	,,	Clark, R. A. R.
40625	,,	Clark, R. K.
40288	,,	Clark, W. A.
40344	Corpl.	Clarke, S. S.
40901	Sergt.	Clarke, G.
40388	Driver	Clarke, G. E.
40746	Gunner	Clayburn, J.
40384	,,	Clayton, P.
40784	,,	Collins, E.
40151	Driver	Colville, G.
40154	Gunner	Compton, B. W.
40906	,,	Cooch, G. G.
40786	,,	Cook, V.
40385	Driver	Cooksey, F.
40156	Gunner	Cooney, R. P.
40626	,,	Corboy, J.
40627	,,	Cormack, W. J.
40628	Driver	Cornwell, A.
40064	Corpl.	Corry, J. H.

Canadian Pacific—The Empire's Greatest Railway.

1st ARTILLERY BRIGADE & AMMUNITION COL.—cont. 261

Regl. No.	Rank.	Name.
40389	Driver	Coulter, E. H.
16220	,,	Courtney, —
40290	Gunner	Cousins, C.
40292	Driver	Cousins, H.
40629	Gunner	Cowan, A.
40751	Driver	Cowan, J.
40630	Gunner	Cowlard, G.
40148	Driver	Crawford, J. H.
40789	Gunner	Crawford, R. H.
40153	Driver	Crilly, J. J.
40291	Gunner	Cronk, G.
40065	,,	Cruickshank, H.
40146	Driver	Cunningham, R.
40392	Gunner	Cunningham, R. J.
40631	Corpl.	Curson, H.
40632	Driver	Curson, J.
40328	Gunner	Dahl, J.
40796	,,	Dahlin, F.
40633	,,	Daish, B.
40560	Sergt.	Dale, J. A.
40159	Driver	Dalton, E.
40527	Gunner	Daly, G.
40161	,,	Daly, J. R.
40295	,,	Daly, M. G.
40395	Driver	Davidson, W. S.
40791	Gunner	Davis, A. E.
40157	Wheeler	Davis, A. E.
40634	Driver	Davis, E.
40399	Gunner	Day, F. B.
40635	Driver	Demar, R.
40636	,,	Dempster, H.
40158	,,	Depencier, C. E.
40160	,,	Derbyshire, —
40790	Gunner	Deslauriers, E.
40792	,,	Diamond, M.
40397	Wheeler	Dick, W. T,
40637	Bombr.	Diespecker, L.
40293	Gunner	Dillnut, H.
40638	,,	Dingle, E. E.
40577	,,	Dingle, E. W.
40639	Bombr.	Dowling, E.
40916	Gunner	Downe, W. L.
40393	Driver	Donald, W.
40330	Sgt.-Maj.	Donaldson, J. W. A.
40396	Driver	Donaldson, S.
40795	Gunner	Donohue, W. H.
40294	,,	Dopson, C.
40766	,,	Dorey, F.
40400	,,	Dorland, J. P.
40748	,,	Doughton, D.
40529	Driver	Doumouchel, E.
40793	Gunner	Downey, R.

Regl. No.	Rank.	Name.
40398	Gunner	Doxee, H. E.
40528	,,	Drouin, A.
40756	,,	Drummond, J.
40640	Driver	Dugan, T.
40794	Gunner	Dumbleton, J.
40328	,,	Duncan, M.
40905	Sergt.	Dunford, E.
40394	Driver	Dunn, A.
40559	Sergt.	Dunning, W.
40620	Gunner	Dyke, A. H.
40799	,,	Eagan, J.
40797	,,	Eakets, F.
40118	Bombr.	Eaton, J.
40165	Gunner	Eaton, W. H.
40112	Bombr.	Eden, W. G.
40163	Gunner	Edmunds, R.
40641	,,	Elliott, L.
40798	,,	Elliott, W.
40642	,,	Ellis, H.
40401	Driver	Eustace, W.
40164	Gunner	Evans, S. C.
40643	,,	Evans, T. G.
40166	,,	Evans, W. H.
33694	,,	Evans, S. H.
		(Water Details)
40644	,,	Ewart, H.
40801	,,	Ewing, B.
40800	,,	Eynonf, G.
40407	Driver	Falkner, A.
40403	,,	Farmer, G. E.
40168	Gunner	Farmer, J. E.
40402	Driver	Farmer, W.
40803	Gunner	Farrell, C.
40066	,,	Ferguson, R.
40902	Sergt.	Fernie, G.
40646	Gunner	Ferris, T.
40805	,,	Fielding, E. L.
40645	,,	Fieldson, F.G.
40167	,,	Finlayson, R. H.
40169	Driver	Finter, R.
40647	Gunner	Fitt, T.
40405	,,	Fitzpatrick, W. J.
40648	,,	Fleming, A.
40408	,,	Fleming, C. S.
40404	,,	Foley, E. E.
40410	Driver	Foreman, P.
40406	Gunner	Forrestal, M. J.
40649	,,	Foster, G.
40170	Driver	Foster, T. C.
40804	,,	Foster, W. H. W. A.
40409	Bombr.	Fownes, J.
40802	Gunner	Fraser, P.

Canadian Pacific—The Empire's Greatest Railway.

262 1st ARTILLERY BRIGADE & AMMUNITION COL.—cont.

Regl. No.	Rank.	Name.
40570	Bombr.	Fulcher, F. D.
40411	Driver	Furrier, E. F.
40808	,,	Gagnon, P.
40298	,,	Gallagher, E.
40176	Saddler	Gallagher, J. B.
40813	Gunner	Gardiner, H.
40173	Driver	Gardner, J. R.
40174	Gunner	Garrison, J.
40414	,,	Gatcum, C.
40342	Act. Sgt.	Gaunt, T. W.
33693	Corpl.	Gerrard, W. L.
40918	Signaller	Gerrard, C.
40580	Sh'sm'th	Gibb, W.
40178	Gunner	Gill, E. R.
40179	,,	Gill, V. K.
40561	,,	Gimlett, J.
40177	Driver	Godfrey, J. T.
40090	Gunner	Gogo, R. J.
40530	,,	Gomes, M. A.
40653	Driver	Goodridge, J.
40175	Gunner	Gordon, R.
40572	Corpl.	Gordon, W.
40068	Gunner	Gornal, W. G.
40181	,,	Graham, E. G.
40743	Driver	Grange, F.
40650	,,	Grant, C.
40297	Gunner	Grant, H.
40806	,,	Grant, R.
40296	Driver	Gravenall, C. E.
40807	Gunner	Graves, E.
40811	,,	Graves, J.
40413	,,	Green, A. H.
40652	Bombr.	Green, K. R.
40809	Gunner	Green, R. J.
40180	,,	Green, W. H.
40739	Driver	Gregory, A.
40651	Bombr.	Gregory, W.
40812	Gunner	Gregson, R.
40412	Driver	Greig, G. O.
40182	Gunner	Grice, A. S.
40172	Driver	Griffen, J.
40917	Corpl.	Grove, J.
40171	Gunner	Groves, E.
40810	Driver	Guernsey, H.
40568	,,	Gynane, J. E.
40816	Gunner	Haggart, J.
40343	Corpl.	Haig, H. G.
40299	Gunner	Hale, J.
40418	Driver	Halpenny, W. J.
40654	,,	Hamilton, C.
40419	,,	Hamilton, J. M.
40428	Gunner	Hanley, F. A.

Regl. No.	Rank.	Name.
40817	Gunner	Hanna, A.
40423	,,	Hannington, F. C.
40657	Wheeler	Hardy, A.
40658	Gunner	Harker, R.
40822	,,	Harper, P. L.
40426	,,	Harris, A. E.
40823	,,	Harris, G.
40422	,,	Harris, L. G.
40424	,,	Harrison, M. T.
40659	Driver	Harrison, R. C.
40302	,,	Hart, W. E.
40820	Gunner	Harte, A.
40576	,,	Harvey, R.
40188	Driver	Harwood, W. E.
40815	Gunner	Haworth, W.
40425	Trumpt'r	Hay, G. A.
40415	Driver	Hay, R.
40821	Gunner	Hayden, M. E.
40183	Bombr.	Haywood, M.
40662	Gunner	Hylton, C.
40191	,,	Hyslop, D. E.
40421	Driver	Healy, J.
40555	Sergt.	Heaton, J.
40184	Gunner	Henderson, —
40655	,,	Henderson, J.
40656	Driver	Henderson, W.
40353	Bombr.	Hendrie, J. M.
40900	Q.M.Sgt.	Herzog, G. L.
40192	Driver	Hicks, J.
40186	Gunner	Higgins, W. G.
40417	,,	Highley, C. A.
40352	Act. Cpl.	Highley, P. J.
40416	Gunner	Hill, C. B.
40193	Driver	Hill, W.
40189	,,	Hilton, A.
40531	,,	Hirst, T.
40190	Gunner	Hunter, G. R.
40427	,,	Hodson, St. J.
40744	Driver	Holland, F.
40532	Gunner	Holland, G. H.
40661	,,	Holland, S.
40300	,,	Honan, S.
40185	,,	Hope, G.
40187	,,	Horn, P. S.
40814	,,	Hornbey, J.
40819	,,	Howard, A. H.
40533	,,	Howard, J.
40818	Driver	Hudson, C.
40351	Bombr.	Hull, C. W.
40420	Trumpt'r	Hunt, C. T.
40190	Gunner	Hunter, G. R.
40301	,,	Hutchins, J.

Canadian Pacific—The Empire's Greatest Railway.

1ST ARTILLERY BRIGADE & AMMUNITION COL.—cont. 263

Regl. No.	Rank.	Name.
40429	Driver	Ingram, R.
40584	Gunner	Jackson, J.
40581	,,	Jackson, M.
40663	Driver	Jackson, W.
40198	,,	Jacob, E. H.
40195	,,	Jacob, M.
40664	,,	Jacques, F.
40665	Gunner	James, A.
40824	,,	Jameson, F. L.
40117	,,	Jamieson, J. G.
40666	Driver	Jeffries, D.
40573	Gunner	Jeffries, W.
40667	Driver	Jenkins, H.
40197	Gunner	Jessett, E. E.
40325	,,	Jewett, J. E.
40121	Bombr.	Jonas, C. H.
40194	Driver	Jones, R. G.
40826	Gunner	Judge, T.
40668	Driver	Kane, G.
40669	,,	Kane, P.
40200	Gunner	Keene, M.
40199	Driver	Kelly, A.
40436	,,	Kenna, T. H.
40201	Gunner	Kennedy, F. J.
40434	,,	Kennedy, G.
40437	,,	Kennedy, M.
40828	,,	Kennedy, R. J.
40431	,,	Kent, T. R.
40435	,,	Keogh, B.
40432	Sh'sm'th	Kimber, B.
40534	Gunner	King, H. L.
40827	,,	King, J.
40433	,,	Kiser, C. D.
40430	Driver	Knox, J.
40303	Gunner	Knox, W. J.
40536	,,	Lacey, J.
40670	,,	Lachapelle, J.
40212	,,	Lachapelle, B.
40209	,,	Lacroix, B.
40438	Driver	Lacroix, E.
40210	,,	Lacroix, H.
40305	Gunner	Lafferty, A.
40106	Corpl.	Lamplough, L. A.
40443	Driver	Lancaster, W.
40336	Sergt.	Langford, J. R.
40832	Gunner	Larocque, J.
40671	Driver	Lasha, K.
40833	Gunner	Latour, A.
40442	,,	Laundy, H. C.
40206	Driver	Lavoie, W.
40835	Corpl.	Leacock, H. W.
40763	Gunner	Lee, F.

Regl. No.	Rank.	Name.
40440	Gunner	Lee, F.
40304	,,	Lee, J.
40439	,,	Leggett, J. F. C.
40829	,,	Legros, C.
40207	,,	Lemire, L.
40441	Driver	Leonard, N.
40091	Sgt.-Maj.	Lewis, A. G. B.
40204	Gunner	Lewis, G.
40203	,,	Lewis, J. J.
40108	Corpl.	Lewis, P. A.
40089	Act. Sgt.	Lewis, W. M.
40535	Gunner	L'Heureux, H. E.
40831	,,	Liesham, A.
40836	,,	Littlewood, W.
40672	,,	Lloyd, G.
40838	,,	Lloyd, J. E.
40208	Driver	Loader, T.
40830	Gunner	Lock, A.
40750	,,	Lockwood, F.
40837	,,	Loney, L.
40211	,,	Long, W.
40673	Driver	Longworth, R.
40202	Gunner	Luch, J.
40755	,,	Lucy, R.
40754	,,	Lucy, T.
40205	Driver	Lund, J.
40834	Gunner	Lunn, D. M. A.
40552	Sergt.	Lunn, H.
40202	Gunner	Lush, J.
40462	,,	McCallum, K. C.
40113	Bombr.	McCarthy, J. P.
40074	Gunner	McCauley, D.
40839	,,	McCormack, M.
40674	Driver	McDonald, F.
40461	,,	McDonald, J.
40463	Gunner	McElary, V.
40075	Bombr.	McElroy, H. H.
40105	Corpl.	McFeat, J.
40760	Gunner	McGregor, A. P.
40334	Far. Sgt.	McHugo, G.
40222	Gunner	McInnes, —
40217	,,	MacInnes, W. F.
40842	,,	McKay, W.
40459	Driver	McKenna, W.
40446	,,	McKenzie, A.
40226	Gunner	McKinnon, S.
40218	,,	McLaughlin, W.
40676	,,	McLaughlin, W.
40851	Driver	McLeod, A.
40925	Wheeler	McLinton, R.
40675	Gunner	McMahon, F.
40225	,,	McMillan, D. M.

Canadian Pacific—The Empire's Greatest Railway.

264   1st ARTILLERY BRIGADE & AMMUNITION COL.—cont.

Regl. No.	Rank.	Name.	Regl. No.	Rank.	Name.
40677	Driver	McMillan, E.	40550	Q.M.S.	Mooney, F.
40583	Gunner	McMillan, M.	40453	Gunner	Moore, G.
40850	,,	MacMillan, M.	40685	,,	Moore, R.
40849	,,	MacMillan, R. J.	40221	,,	Moore, T. A.
40843	,,	McNee, P.	40749	,,	Moore, W. C.
40447	Driver	McPhail, N. R.	40538	,,	Morel, A. L.
40219	Gunner	McVittie, J. E.	40072	Driver	Morel, C.
40847	,,	Mackay, M.	40537	Gunner	Morel, R. S.
40678	,,	Mackney, H.	40753	,,	Morgan, W.
40071	,,	Maguire, —	40224	Bombr.	Morris, C.
40449	,,	Maguire, L. E.	40840	Gunner	Morton, R.
40450	Driver	Mahoney, J.	40215	,,	Moses, A. C.
40563	,,	Mann, R.	40460	Driver	Mossman, J.
40306	,,	Maples, J. T.	40686	Gunner	Muchmore, J.
33695	Gunner	Marble, R. W.	40220	Clerk	Muirhead, L.
40230	Driver	Marissette, C.	40911	Bombr.	Muggleton, G.
40214	,,	Maroney, J.	40102	Corpl.	Mulock, R. H.
40582	Saddler	Marriott, J.	40687	Gunner	Munden, J.
40458	Gunner	Marsden, H. C.	40759	,,	Munroe, R.
40679	,,	Marsden, R.	40688	Driver	Murray, F.
40910	Corpl.	Marsh, B. C.	40689	,,	Murray, H. W.
40451	Driver	Martelle, A.	40229	Gunner	Murray, W. M. H.
40454	Gunner	Martin, H.	40122	,,	Musgrave, T. H.
40227	Driver	Martin, H.	40234	Sh'sm'th	Naish, W. E.
40228	Gunner	Matthews, T.	40690	Gunner	Nalon, M.
40452	,,	Meade, T. H.	40921	Signaller	Napolis, B. A.
40680	,,	Meagher, J. J.	40853	Gunner	Neff, E.
40326	Clerk	Mee, C. T.	40232	,,	Neil, V.
40575	Bombr.	Meggs, F.	40691	,,	Nelson, T. H.
40841	Gunner	Meldrum, W.	40854	,,	Nesbitt, C.
40448	Sh'smth.	Melvin, T. P.	40099	Sergt.	Neville, E. W.
40455	Gunner	Merrifield, J. R.	40465	Driver	Newton, H. G.
40846	,,	Messinger, A. W.	40233	Gunner	Newton, J.
40845	,,	Messinger, L.	40692	,,	Newton, J.
40681	,,	Metcalf, G. F.	40231	Driver	Nichol, W. D.
40445	Driver	Metge, D.	40076	Gunner	Nicholson, A.
40444	,,	Metge, S. C.	40308	,,	Noel, H.
40097	Sergt.	Michel, S.	40852	,,	Nolan, H.
40457	Driver	Miller, G.	40464	,,	North, S.
40579	Gunner	Miller, G.	40239	Driver	O'Brady, W. K.
40682	Corpl.	Miller, H.	40856	Cook	O'Brien, J.
40456	Driver	Miller, T.	40693	Gunner	O'Connor, R.
40844	Cook	Miller, W.	40742	Sergt.	O'Halon, B.
40213	Trumpt'r	Miller, W. J.	40236	Gunner	O'Malley, C. R.
40683	Gunner	Milne, J.	40466	,,	O'Rourke, D.
40848	,,	Mills, W. C. A.	40237	,,	O'Shaughnessy, R.
40104	Corpl.	Mindenhall,	40694	Driver	Offord, F.
40307	Gunner	Mitchell, D.	40855	Gunner	Oliver, W. S.
40111	Bombr.	Mitchell, R. L.	40467	,,	Orde, R. J.
40684	Driver	Moffat, D.	40695	,,	Orr, J. C.
40073	,,	Moffatt, L. W.	40238	,,	Orvis, L. W.
40566	Corpl.	Monteith, W. B.	40696	Bombr.	Osborne, W. G.

Canadian Pacific—The Empire's Greatest Railway.

1st ARTILLERY BRIGADE & AMMUNITION COL.—cont. 265

Regl. No.	Rank.	Name.
40235	Driver	Owen, A. E.
40920	Signaller	Owen, T.
40309	Gunner	Page, A.
40354	,,	Paradise, G.
40077	,,	Parker, E. W.
40558	Sergt.	Parry, G.
40471	Driver	Parsley, J.
40698	Gunner	Parson, L.
40697	Driver	Parsons, E. J.
40699	Gunner	Parsons, S.
40857	,,	Passmore, F.
40469	,,	Paterson, W.
40475	,,	Patteson, E.
40476	,,	Payne, J.
40477	,,	Paynter, C. S.
40332	Sergt.	Paynter, J. J.
40245	Gunner	Paynter, W.
40472	,,	Pearson, J. O.
40861	,,	Pelletier, T.
40860	,,	Perranet, E.
40859	,,	Perrier, D.
40700	Driver	Perry, J.
40858	Gunner	Pharo, A. J.
40474	Driver	Phelp, R. J.
40701	,,	Phillips, A.
40243	,,	Phillips, A. W.
40470	Gunner	Phillips, E. T.
40767	Driver	Phillips, R.
40702	Gunner	Pippard, F.
40244	Driver	Pointer, S.
40703	Gunner	Pope, F.
40478	,,	Potts, J. W.
40310	,,	Powell, J. G.
40473	,,	Powell, C. H.
40241	,,	Pratt, A. M.
40242	,,	Pratt, H. R.
40345	Corpl.	Price, C. H.
40704	Gunner	Price, R. L.
40468	Bombr.	Price, W.
40479	,,	Prior, E. W.
40240	Driver	Pruner, J.
40862	Gunner	Quinn, J. A.
40246	Driver	Quintal, N.
40078	,,	Radcliffe, J.
40114	Bombr.	Rainey, H.
40481	Gunner	Ramsay, G. M.
40250	Driver	Ramsay, H. J.
40706	Gunner	Randalls, G.
40712	Driver	Rattan, A.
40574	Corpl.	Rattray, N.
40707	Gunner	Raven, C.
40705	Driver	Rea, C.

Regl. No.	Rank.	Name.
40586	Cook	Rea, S. H.
40311	Gunner	Read, E. E.
40588	Trumpt'r	Reagon, T. F.
40284	Gunner	Relph, S. F.
40708	Driver	Reynolds, J.
40487	,,	Richards, R. G. T.
40709	Gunner	Richardson, E.
40871	,,	Richardson, W.
40249	,,	Richer, C. E. M.
40870	Bombr.	Ritchie, A. B.
40867	Gunner	Ritchie, R.
40486	,,	Rivers, P. F.
40314	,,	Robert, A.
40482	Driver	Robinson, F.
40355	Bombr.	Robinson, H. L.
40247	Driver	Robinson, G. H.
40483	Gunner	Robinson, H. A.
40484	Driver	Robinson, J.
40485	Gunner	Robley, E. V.
40865	,,	Roch, J.
40868	,,	Rockwell, G.
40312	,,	Rollins, R.
40554	Sergt.	Rolson W.
40313	Gunner	Roper, V.
40869	,,	Rose, A.
40488	,,	Ross, J.
40710	Driver	Rothwell, J. H.
40079	Gunner	Rowan, J. C.
40480	Driver	Rowecroft, M. G.
40863	Gunner	Roy, R.
40864	,,	Roy, R. J.
40711	Driver	Runnet, F.
40866	Gunner	Ryder, H.
40539	,,	Salaway, J.
40338	Sergt.	Sargent, R.
40101	Far. Sgt.	Sarson, W. E.
40500	Driver	Saunders, C.
40752	Gunner	Saunders, H.
40261	Driver	Savinion, H.
40883	Gunner	Scarr, C.
40092	Q.M.Sgt.	Schelleter, C.
40540	Gunner	Schofield, M. E.
40492	,,	Scobie, —
40258	,,	Scott, H.
40081	,,	Scott, Moncrief G.
40503	Driver	Scott, R.
40337	Sergt.	Scullard, H.
40262	Trumpt'r	Sealey, G. H.
40489	Driver	Seaman, H.
40110	Gunner	Searle, P.
40315	Driver	Serviss, W. R.
40879	Gunner	Shannon, W. J.

Canadian Pacific—The Empire's Greatest Railway.

1st ARTILLERY BRIGADE & AMMUNITION COL.—cont.

Regl. No.	Rank.	Name.
40713	Gunner	Sharp, J.
40502	Driver	Sharpe, C. F.
40499	,,	Sheldon, F.
40873	,,	Sheehan, A.
40316	Gunner	Shirran, F.
40255	,,	Short, W. A.
40320	,,	Sills, J. C.
40497	,,	Simmonds, A. C. J.
40881	,,	Simpson, J. F.
40082	,,	Simpson, R.
40872	,,	Sirois, R.
40256	Driver	Smaile, A.
40265	Gunner	Small, C. S.
40251	Wheeler	Small, F. H.
40319	Gunner	Small, R.
40714	Driver	Smith, A. H.
40877	Gunner	Smith, C.
40080	Staff Sgt.	Smith, C. K.
40762	Driver	Smith, E.
40876	Gunner	Smith, F.
40317	,,	Smith, F. A.
40715	Driver	Smith, H.
40549	Br. S.-M.	Smith, J.
40716	Gunner	Smith, J.
40878	,,	Smith, J. H.
40318	,,	Smith, J. M.
40259	Driver	Smith, N. R.
40095	Sergt.	Smith, R. T.
40875	Gunner	Smith, W. A.
40494	,,	Smyth, A. K.
40335	Wh. Sgt.	Somers, J.
40874	Gunner	Southworth, C.
40339	Sergt.	Spafford, G. N.
40257	Gunner	Sparham, H. A.
40096	Sergt.	Sparrow, F. B.
40493	Driver	Spence, J.
40264	Shoe Sgt.	Springett, C.
40496	Driver	Stacey, H.
40562	Gunner	Stafford, C. B.
40490	Driver	Standen, J.
40491	,,	Standing, A.
40708	Gunner	Stark, J.
40880	Driver	Steele, J. F.
40260	,,	Steele, H. G.
40263	Gunner	Steven, G. K.
40261	Driver	Stevenson, H.
40253	Gunner	Stewart, I.
40498	,,	Storey, W. H.
40882	Driver	Stotts, H.
40717	,,	Street, C.
40915	Corpl.	Suttie, J. H.
40254	Driver	Sweeney, H. B.

Regl. No.	Rank.	Name.
40109	Shoe Sgt.	Sweeney, W. R.
40495	Gunner	Sweet, W.
40501	,,	Sword, S. A.
40886	,,	Tetlock, J. B.
40340	Corpl.	Tett, G. A.
40887	Gunner	Tew, R.
40267	Driver	Thomas, F. A.
40504	,,	Thomas, H.
40719	Gunner	Thompson, J.
40268	,,	Thompson, P. C.
40919	Signaller	Thornton, G.
40505	Driver	Thunder, P. A.
40885	Gunner	Timpson, H. W.
40720	Driver	Travers, W.
40888	Gunner	Traynor, O.
40884	,,	Tucker, B. J.
40266	Driver	Turner, A.
40721	,,	Turner, A. M.
40506	Storem'n	Twyman, T. G.
40070	Gunner	Tyndale-Lea, G.
40722	,,	Tyo, S.
40507	Driver	Tyron, H.
40889	Gunner	Usher, H. E.
40116	Bombr.	Vereker, S. R.
40890	Gunner	Vians, A.
40723	Driver	Vivian, B.
40903	Sergt.	Vogg, F. M.
40508	Driver	Vosdingh, H.
40119	Sh'sm'th	Waite, H.
40542	Gunner	Waite, H. E.
40724	Driver	Waker, E. J.
40725	Gunner	Walker, V. A.
40514	,,	Wallace, A.
40093	As.Q.M.S.	Waller, E.
40909	Corpl.	Wallis, E. E.
40509	Driver	Walshe, F. P.
40927	Gunner	Walters, W.
40726	,,	Walton, T.
40515	Driver	Ward, F. B.
40274	,,	Ward, J.
40322	,,	Ward, S.
40517	Gunner	Warren, H. G.
40280	,,	Warren, R.
40727	,,	Watson, C.
40728	Driver	Watson, J. A.
40273	Gunner	Watson, W. M.
40269	Driver	Watt, J.
40518	,,	Weaver, C. L.
40270	,,	Webb, F. G.
40100	Wheeler	Weeks, A.
40891	Bombr.	Weir, A. W.
40729	Driver	West, G.

Canadian Pacific—The Empire's Greatest Railway.

1st ARTILLERY BRIGADE & AMMUNITION COL.—cont.

Regl. No.	Rank	Name
40277	Gunner	West, J.
40895	,,	Westerdale, L.
40730	Driver	Westwood, H.
40757	Cook	Wheeler, G.
40896	Gunner	Wheeler, H.
40731	Driver	Wheston, M. F.
40741	,,	White, J.
40084	,,	White, L. W.
40272	,,	Whitestein, J.
40512	,,	Wickham, R.
40513	Gunner	Wilke, F. E.
40085	Driver	Wilkinson, H. E.
40733	Corpl.	Williams, R. H.
40516	Gunner	Williams, W.
40747	,,	Willis, F.
40275	Driver	Wills, W. J.
40083	Bombr.	Wilson, —
40734	Driver	Wilson, C.
40894	Gunner	Wilson, J.
40519	Driver	Wilson, W. A.
40279	Gunner	Wiseman, C. H.
40541	,,	Woods, M. W.
40893	,,	Woods, T.
40737	Gunner	Woolley, J. A.
40510	Driver	Wotton, R.
40764	,,	Wraight, J.
40511	Gunner	Wright, E. A.
40892	,,	Wright, F. B.
40278	,,	Wright, K. P.
40735	,,	Wright, L. B.
40271	Driver	Wright, R.
40736	,,	Wye, A.
40276	Gunner	Wylde, M.
40914	Sergt.	Wylie, R.
40897	Gunner	Yale, E.
40281	,,	Yateman, N.
40520	,,	Yatman, T. A.
40282	,,	Yeoman, F. L.
40283	,,	Yeomans, H. E.
40898	,,	Young, C.
40346	Sergt.	Young, F.
40086	Gunner	Young, J. A.
40912	Corpl.	Young, W. J.
40087	Gunner	Yuill, A.
40088	Act. Sgt.	Zala, V.
40738	Gunner	Zivian, J.

2nd CANADIAN FIELD ARTILLERY BRIGADE.

BRIGADE STAFF.

Lieut.-Colonel	Creelman, John J.
Captain	Hanson, Charles S.
Lieutenant	Duguid, Archer F.
,,	Burnham, Howard H.
,,	Coulombe, Aime E.
Paymaster	Hon. Major J. A. C. Mowbray

Regl. No.	Rank	Name
41668	Sgt.-Maj.	Flinter, Mervyn
41665	S. Sgt.	Dundas, Lawrence E.
41667	Sergt.	Foote, Frank A. J.
41666	S. Sgt.	Farlie, George H.
41664	B.S.M.	Slade, J. R.
41632	S. Sgt.	Rose, Michal
41634	Bombr.	Hyman, Thomas M.
41635	Act. Br.	Murray, David
41633	Bombr.	Warene, Harry
41636	Gunner	Ashe, Edward H.
41639	,,	Barker, Ronald
41638	Gunner	Brown, John A. M.
4399	,,	Bruin, Leonard
41640	,,	Clarke, Robert
41642	,,	Coderre, Eugene
41641	Driver	Cowan, Harry J.
41634	Gunner	Dallow, John
33698	,,	Dalzell, Bert
41645	,,	Davidson, Gerald H.
41644	,,	Davies, Peter
41646	,,	Duncan, Eldred C.
41647	,,	Dyer, James

Canadian Pacific—The Empire's Greatest Railway.

2ND CANADIAN FIELD ARTILLERY BRIGADE—cont.

Regl. No.	Rank.	Name.	Regl. No.	Rank.	Name.
41650	Gunner	Fairclough, Richard	41654	Gunner	Murray, David
41649	Trump'r	Farrell, Hubert	33699	,,	Rawson, Frederick
41648	Gunner	Faught, Thomas	41656	,,	Roberts, Willard R.
41652	,,	Hearn, J. Wilfred	41658	,,	Samuel, Robert A.
4501	,,	Hinton, Arthur	41657	,,	Schofield, Frank
41651	,,	Howarth, Walter F.	41659	,,	Taylor, Frank
33697	Corpl.	Jenkins, Claude	41660	,,	Torp, William
33700	Gunner	Kemp, George	41661	,,	Wright, Harry T.
41631	,,	Kirkman, John A.	41662	A.Bombr.	Waite, George C.
41653	,,	Kimber, Percy	41665	Gunner	Hedgecock, H.
41655	,,	McDonald, Roderick			

4th BATTERY, 2nd BRIGADE.

Major	...	...	...	McNaughton, Andrew
Captain	...	...	...	Hale, Edward Chalenor
Lieutenant	...	...	...	Fyshe, Francis
,,	...	...	...	Green, Frederick D. L.
,,	...	...	...	Hague, Owen, C. F.

Regl. No.	Rank.	Name.	Regl. No.	Rank.	Name.
41211	By. S.-M.	Price, John H.	41337	Cook	Bargman, Albert
41404	Q.M.Sgt.	Race, James	41288	Gunner	Barnes, William
41311	Sergt.	Carpenter, S. W.	41287	,,	Barrette, Alexander
41213	,,	Fraser, Gordon M.	41325	,,	Beaudoin, Horace
41247	,,	Grey, Walter B. J.	41330	,,	Beaudoin, Paul
41406	,,	Johnson, E. D.	41341	,,	Beaulieu, Wilfred
41288	,,	McLeod, Norwood	41278	Cook	Bell, John Neil
41212	,,	Rydberg, Leon A.	41347	Gunner	Blair, Floyd E.
48708	Far. Sgt.	Beardshall, H.	41362	,,	Blair, Silas A.
41284	Corpl.	Duncan, David L. C.	41361	,,	Bolton, Ernest
41215	,,	Keane, Thomas B.	41346	,,	Boucher, Arthur W.
41255	,,	Smith, William	41277	,,	Boucher, Thomas
41285	Bombr.	Arthur, Arnold E.	41377	Driver	Bourgeois, Joseph A.
41253	,,	Bonnell, G. H.	41328	,,	Bourne, Bertram K.
41217	,,	Brown, James J.	41370	,,	Bowker, Leighton S.
41375	,,	Butler, Thomas F.	41394	,,	Brewer, Chauncey H.
41216	,,	Cooper-Smith, E. J.	41329	,,	Brodie, Alexander
41345	,,	Cousins, Morton	41293	,,	Brown, Alexander
41315	,,	Flemming, Alex.	41312	Sh'sm'th	Bryson, Alexander
41218	,,	Hoar, A. E.	41396	Driver	Bushnell, James
41376	,,	McKenzie, Donald	41320	,,	Byrne, Francis
41314	,,	Shirley, Joseph	41317	Gunner	Campbell, Peter
41252	,,	Thomlinson, W. L.	41386	Driver	Candlish, James
41214	Trooper	Anderson, James C.	41384	,,	Candlish, Malcolm
41397	,,	Ford, Robert H.	41238	,,	Cockburn, Harold J.
41259	Gunner	Allen, Charles V.	41299	,,	Coleman, James
41273	Driver	Ashton, Frederick	41389	Gunner	Crisp, Charles

Canadian Pacific—The Empire's Greatest Railway.

4TH BATTERY, 2ND BRIGADE, C.F.A.—cont.

Regl. No.	Rank	Name	Regl. No.	Rank	Name
41297	Driver	Curwood, James	41258	Gunner	Mace, William A.
41363	,,	Dalton, Thomas E.	41260	,,	MacPherson, Stanley
41298	,,	Davidson, L. C.	41222	,,	Malpas, George
41286	Gunner	Dawe, Edwin	41307	,,	Morrison, Robert
41336	Driver	De La Durantaye, W.	41274	Driver	Maskell, George
41365	,,	Desilet, Zepher	41256	Gunner	Masterson, Herbert J.
41399	,,	Desrossiers, Donat	41233	Driver	Mawhinney, John
41308	,,	Dibble, James L.	41232	,,	Mawhinney, Radcliff
41241	,,	Donovan, Harry	41237	Gunner	McConnell, Murdoch
41266	,,	Dorion, Edgar J.	41373	,,	McCormack, Harold
41306	Gunner	Ducie, Peter	41268	Driver	McDougall, Edwd. J.
41318	,,	Dugas, Arthur	41290	Gunner	McDowell, Leo
41323	Driver	Durward, Peter	41352	,,	McGuiness, William
41360	,,	Edwards, Harry J.	41231	Driver	McGurk, Douglas
41393	,,	Edwards, Robert	41309	,,	McRae, George
41391	,,	Edwards, William G.	41369	Gunner	Minall, William
41245	,,	Elliott, Joseph	41388	,,	Monk, Montague
41269	,,	Erde, Herbert J.	41319	,,	Montague, Thomas
41348	,,	Everette, Albert C.	41212	Cook	Moran, Joseph
41236	,,	Ferguson, Percy A.	41226	Driver	Nash, Thomas
41366	,,	Florry, Frederick	41355	Gunner	Navin, John F.
41354	,,	Fox, William H.	41278	Driver	Nichols, Charles T.
41316	Gunner	Gale, Sidney	41263	Gunner	Nickle, Charles R.
41310	Driver	Gillespie, Peter	41254	,,	Nolan, Howard S.
41381	,,	Girdleston, Thomas	41380	,,	Nugent, John H.
41243	,,	Gittins, Thomas W.	41289	,,	Osmun, William E.
41276	,,	Graham, Arthur	41322	Driver	Padner, Frederick
41398	,,	Grantham, Alex.	41296	Gunner	Pearce, Edgar John
48831	,,	Graves, L.	41401	,,	Penticost, Albert G.
41291	Gunner	Haggerty, Michael	41364	Driver	Penticost, Joseph C.
41234	,,	Hall, William A.	41305	Cook	Perrin, John
41390	,,	Hansford, Stanley	41358	Gunner	Pierce, Claude
41228	,,	Harland, Hugh B.	41350	,,	Price, Charles L.
41339	Driver	Harrison, George	41383	,,	Randall, Frederick
41270	,,	Hartley, Joseph G.	41313	Wheeler	Ratcliffe, Joseph F.
41334	,,	Hogan, Hugh	41371	Sh'sm'th	Rhind, Gilbert
41229	Gunner	Holback, Eric O.	41356	Gunner	Richardson, Fredk.
41349	,,	Hurn, Horace S.	41271	Driver	Robertson, James A.
41321	,,	Hylands, James	41353	Gunner	Rodgers, Arthur A.
41359	,,	Jardine, James	41382	,,	Rowley, Samuel R.
41205	,,	Kennedy, Thomas	41327	Driver	Roy, Arthur
41301	Driver	Kerr, William C.	41239	,,	Roy, Joseph
41385	Gunner	Kiloh, Andrew	41324	,,	Sadler, Louis
41264	,,	Kittson, Arthur G.	41368	,,	Samson, Frederick
41240	Driver	Lake, Thomas	41281	,,	Seath, Robert W.
41351	Gunner	Lanoue, Arthur	41221	Gunner	Shand, Charles
41255	,,	Lewis, Frederick	41379	,,	Shea, Arthur D.
41257	,,	Lindsay, Patrick	41395	,,	Stanford, Edgar H.
41224	Driver	Lloyd, Alfred	41340	Driver	Starkey, Joseph S.
41342	Gunner	Long, Thomas	41338	,,	Starkey, Stephen
41272	Driver	Lowe, Harold	41357	,,	Stewart, James
41331	Gunner	Lucas, Walter	41265	Gunner	Stickland, Stanley

Canadian Pacific—The Empire's Greatest Railway.

4TH BATTERY, 2ND BRIGADE, C.F.A.—cont.

Regl. No.	Rank.	Name.	Regl. No.	Rank.	Name.
41400	Driver	Sutton, Ernest	41261	Gunner	Watt, Roderick M.
41392	,,	Swain, Wesley C.	41220	,,	Webster, James
41300	,,	Taylor, William	41378	,,	Wells, Mortley H.
41225	,,	Taylor, William J.	41244	Groom	Wenham, Charles E.
41227	Gunner	Thompson, Eric H.	41219	Driver	Whalen, Daniel
41304	Driver	Turner, James R.	41403	Groom	Widdicombe, Charles
41295	Gunner	Unwin, Charles	41262	Gunner	Williams, Claude
41235	Driver	Vawer, Frederick A.	41323	,,	Wilson, Charles
41326	,,	Vezina, Joseph	41322	,,	Winton, Frederick
41267	,,	Vincent, Leonard G.	41387	,,	Woods, Joseph
48821	,,	Wallace, D.	41303	Driver	Wright, William
41335	,,	Warne, S. D.			

Artificers.

41250	Wheeler	Daly, Joseph L.	41344	Cpl. S. S.	Marshall, Arthur B.
41248	Far. Sgt.	Forsythe, Thomas J.	41372	Saddler	Swartz, Harry
41283	Saddler	Gray, James			

5th BATTERY, 2nd BRIGADE.

Major	...	...	...	...	Hanson, Edward Gerald
Captain	...	...	...	...	Macdonald, John Angus
Lieutenant	...	...	...	...	Armour, I. D.
,,		...	...	...	Paterson, Alexander Thomas
,,		...	...	...	Green, John Kay MacDonald
,,		...	...	...	McNaughton, M. W. A.

Regl. No.	Rank.	Name.	Regl. No.	Rank.	Name.
4755	B.S.-M.	Carruthers, Kenneth	41031	Corpl.	Bennett, Harold O.
41028	Q.M.S.	Wallace, Thomas	41102	,,	Rice, Gitz Ingraham
41050	Sergt.	Christie, Douglas G.	41177	,,	Braye, Basil Hubert
41030	,,	Taylor, Walter M.	41002	,,	Eastlake, James E.
41016	,,	Young, George H.	41095	,,	McClintock, L. D.
41176	,,	Macdonald, A. K.	41055	Bombr.	Olsen, Olaf K.
41147	,,	Campbell, M. A.	41014	,,	Berkeley, M. K. F.
41033	,,	Weldon, Charles L.	41069	,,	Ball, Bernard B.
41017	,,	Holmes, Richard T.	41054	,,	Murray, George W.
41020	Far. Sgt.	Murray, John T.	41103	,,	McLennan, Hugh
41143	Cpl. S. S.	Brown, James	41023	,,	Greig, Donald G.
41140	Sh'sm'th	Fothergill, Wm.	41013	,,	Tomkinson, Thomas
41121	,,	McKenna, James J.	41073	,,	McClintock, G. A.
41134	,,	Saunders, Robert	41104	,,	Peck, Brian Alison
41052	Saddler	Connor, John	41151	,,	Congdon, David R.
41056	,,	Duncan, Gideon	41025	,,	Kieran, James R.
41035	Wheeler	Hughes, Thomas J.	41119	Gunner	Abbott, William H.
41051	,,	Murdock, Samuel	41088	,,	Anderson, Sedley C.
41041	Corpl.	Bennett, R. E.	41131	Driver	Arpin, Anthime L.

Canadian Pacific—The Empire's Greatest Railway

5TH BATTERY, 2ND BRIGADE, C.F.A.—cont.

Regl. No.	Rank	Name	Regl. No.	Rank	Name
41011	Driver	Askham, Horace	41169	Driver	Hill, Stanley
41022	Gunner	Barnaby, Hazen O.	41065	,,	Holmes, Albert John
41145	,,	Barden, Isaac	41009	Gunner	Hughes, Thos. James
41062	Driver	Black, Charles Eldon	41142	,,	Hurst, Wm. Edward
41125	Gunner	Black, Hugh L.	41128	,,	Hull, Harold L.
41010	Driver	Blank, Joseph	41005	Driver	Isaacs, Lionel Shirley
41114	Trumpt'r	Baugh, Charles W.	41172	,,	James, Thomas
41149	Gunner	Boyd, Alexander	41156	Gunner	Johnson, Malcolm
41186	Driver	Butler, James Lucas	41115	,,	Jones, George
41046	Gunner	Brooks, Ernest	41092	Driver	Joyce, Alfred Leslie
41180	,,	Bertrand, Edgar A.	41057	,,	Jackson, William
41098	,,	Cairns, George A.	41024	Gunner	Kearon, George T.
41029	,,	Carr, Lincoln F.	41001	,,	Kennedy, John F.
41021	,,	Carruthers, George A	41199	,,	Kernick, Wm. Henry
41012	Driver	Champ, George	41063	,,	Knight, William
41074	,,	Cohen, Robin	41174	,,	Landry, Herbert
41058	,,	Cooper, Harold E.	41132	,,	Langstone, Fredk. H.
41034	Gunner	Cotton, Charles P.	41105	,,	Larsen, John Fredk.
41194	Driver	Comer, John	41100	Driver	Laurie, Chas. Mason
41148	Gunner	Curry, Lauchlis, M.	41044	,,	Laurence, James J.
41008	,,	Davis, Stanley	41043	Gunner	Lavigne, Anthony A.
41007	,,	Davis, Frank Leslie	41150	Driver	Leah, John
41197	,,	Di Sanctis, Tesil C.	41040	Gunner	Lee, Errington B.
41101	,,	Di Gaspero, B.	41038	Driver	Leonard, Walter E.
41126	,,	Dougall, Allan Weir	41157	,,	Leonard, William
41045	,,	Edwards, Wm. G.	41161	,,	Levanger, Benjamin
41139	Driver	Elphick, Frederick	41004	Gunner	Lomer, John Muse
41191	Gunner	Ferguson, Wm. L.	41042	Driver	McIntosh, William
41123	Driver	Forman, John F.	41039	Gunner	Maddocks, Thos. H
41195	Gunner	Frost, Arthur G.	41066	,,	Mathewson, James L
41064	Driver	Fraser, David	41188	Driver	Masson, Alex. Stewart
41059	,,	Faulkner, F. W.	41124	Gunner	Macaulay, Robert V.
41093	Gunner	Galbraith, Henry H.	41168	,,	Mahoney, Wm. S.
41003	,,	Gordon, Cecil Alex.	41159	Driver	Mackay, Alexander
41076	,,	Gordon, Robert B.	41155	Gunner	McCormick, John
41026	Driver	Gouick, John Alex.	41113	Driver	McDonald, Chas. E.
41015	Gunner	Greig, James Alex.	41117	Gunner	McLeman, Wm. D.
41200	,,	Graham, Fredk. A.	41081	,,	McNaughton, Arch.
41080	,,	Gibson, Eric J. L.	41111	,,	Mitchell, Wilfred
41078	,,	Grant, George Edwd.	41082	,,	Morell, Douglas
41160	,,	Grant, James	41138	,,	Murray, John Stuart
41079	,,	Gallert, Samuel	41094	Driver	Marks, Arthur
41032	,,	Hamilton, Hugh P.	41099	Gunner	Motyer, Arthur John
41027	,,	Harrison, Joseph A.	41152	Driver	Macdonald, Alex. P.
41097	,,	Harkom, John F.	41153	Gunner	McDonald, Fredk. W.
41096	,,	Haskell, Ludlow St. J.	41162	Driver	McDonald, A. D.
41130	Driver	Hesketh, Thomas	41170	,,	McDonald, Dan H.
41167	,,	Hersey, Leman	41181	,,	McIsaac, John R.
41127	Trumpt'r	Hetherington, C. R.	41165	Gunner	McIsaac, Neil
41018	Driver	Hickley, Patrick J.	41166	,,	McKinlay, Wm. O.
41109	Gunner	Higgins, Joseph	41179	Driver	McLaughlin, Horace
41154	Driver	Higgins, James J.	41192	,,	McLean, John

Canadian Pacific—The Empire's Greatest Railway.

5TH BATTERY, 2ND BRIGADE, C.F.A.—cont.

Regl. No.	Rank.	Name.	Regl. No.	Rank.	Name.
41118	Driver	McLean, Harold E.	41077	Gunner	Schalman, Joseph
41182	,,	McLean, Fredk. J.	41106	Driver	Shaw, John Edward
41183	Gunner	McPhee, Hugh	41137	,,	Shaw, David
41135	Driver	Monahan, Richard	41047	,,	Smart, Joseph
41185	,,	Moulesong, Wltr. J.	41037	Gunner	Stephens, James
41193	Gunner	McDonald, D. N.	41072	,,	Stewart, Charles W.
41178	,,	McDonald, Dan A.	41173	,,	Stewart, Alfred
41158	Driver	McDonald, Alex. J.	41068	,,	Sproston, Joseph
41163	Gunner	McCormack, D. L.	41086	,,	Steele, David
41175	,,	McMillan, Robt. D.	41060	,,	Takin, Roland James
41190	,,	McAulay, John Jas.	41075	Driver	Taylor, Thomas H.
41198	,,	Musgrave, W. P.	41136	Gunner	Taylor, Heber Edw.
41070	,,	McMaster, Joseph	41189	,,	Tomlinson, Lancelot
41071	,,	Odell, Stanley R.	41164	Driver	Tucker, Edward T.
41122	Driver	Outhet, Edward	41036	Gunner	Turnbull, Harry
41116	Gunner	Paddon, Herbert A.	41049	,,	Turenne, Aimar A.
41087	,,	Patterson, Arthur L.	41171	,,	Taylor, Arthur
41019	,,	Patterson, Thomas I.	41133	,,	Taylor, James
41067	,,	Payne, James	41098	Driver	Thomas, Thomas S.
41108	Driver	Phillips, Percy E.	41184	,,	Vey, Thomas James
41084	Gunner	Powter, Arthur L.	41120	,,	Walker, Harry
41141	,,	Price, Willard J.	41053	,,	Warner, William
41144	Driver	Procter, Thomas	41091	Gunner	Warren, Leslie S.
41006	Gunner	Quick, Stuart Henry	41061	Driver	Webb, William C. H.
41048	,,	Richardson, Allan I.	41196	Gunner	Wiles, James
41187	,,	Roper, Harry David	41112	Driver	Williamson, Geo. M.
41146	,,	Richardson, W. F.	41107	,,	Wiseman, Edmund J.
41090	Driver	Richardson, Percy T.	41110	Gunner	Walbank, Fredk. K.
41083	Gunner	Rowat, William E. A.			

6th BATTERY, 2nd BRIGADE.

Major	Harvey G. McLeod.
Captain	Wm. A. McKee
,, ...	John G. Piercey DSO
,, ...	Arthur E. Barton
Lieutenant	John H. Evans
,, ...	H. F. Geary (R.C.A.)

Regl. No.	Rank.	Name.	Regl. No.	Rank.	Name.
41421	B.S.-M.	McLean, James D.	41430	Far. Sgt.	Beal, William
41422	B.Q.M.S.	Dobson, Frank E.	41431	Corpl.	Blake, Ernest O.
41423	Sergt.	Cook, Stanley	41432	,,	Grant, Percy
41424	,,	Ingraham, Robert J.	41433	,,	Kitchen, Thomas H.
41425	,,	Le Blanc, Ernest C. J.	41434	,,	Milburn, Arnold R.
41426	,,	Main, Lewis C.	41435	,,	Currie, John A.
41427	Corpl.	Randall, Robert P.	41436	,,	Robinson, George R.
41428	Sergt.	Steeves, Noah E.	41437	Gunner	Taylor, Edward B.
41429	,,	Wilson, Timothy	41438	B'dsm'n	Armstrong, Wm. F.

Canadian Pacific—The Empire's Greatest Railway.

6TH BATTERY, 2ND BRIGADE, C.F.A.—cont.

Regl. No.	Rank.	Name.	Regl. No.	Rank.	Name.
41439	B'dsm'n	Bagnall, Wynn	41490	Driver	Crossman, James E.
41440	,,	Blackwood, William	41491	Gunner	Curry, Wm. J.
41441	,,	Campbell, Clarence G.	41492	Driver	Curtis, Arthur B.
41442	,,	Garland, Alfred A.	41493	Gunner	Day, Jas. D.
41443	,,	Gunn, Fred C.	41494	,,	De Grace, Camille
41444	Driver	Harriman, Stafford	41495	,,	De Witt, Roy L.
41445	B'dsm'n	Hicks, Ainsley	41496	Driver	Devine, Albert
41446	,,	McMullen, Lawrence	41497	Gunner	Donovan, Michael
41447	,,	McKinnon, Neil E.	41498	,,	Dow, Millard F.
41448	,,	Turner, Gordon E.	41499	Driver	Duncan, David C.
41449	Trumpt'r	Micheau, Charles	41500	Gunner	Emin, Charles
41450	,,	Bowser, Ernest	41501	,,	Elsdon, Charles W.
41451	Driver	Adams, Carty	41502	Driver	Ferguson, Bryon W.
41452	,,	Adams, Francis J.	41503	Gunner	Fitzgerald, Thos.
41453	Wheeler	Adams, Roy	41504	Driver	Fitzpatrick, John P.
41454	Driver	Anderson, Ben	41505	,,	Fitzpatrick, Roy J.
41455	,,	Andrews, Irving W.	41506	,,	Frost, William R.
41456	,,	Appleby, Royal W.	41507	Gunner	Fry, Richard E.
41457	,,	Arnold, Gordon W.	41508	,,	Gammon, Herbert G.
41458	,,	Atherton, George	41509	Driver	Gifford, William
41459	Gunner	Atherton, George F.	41510	Gunner	Gillis, John A.
41460	,,	Atkinson, Thomas H.	41511	,,	Gillis, Michael
41461	,,	Ayer, John E.	41512	,,	Guthro, Martin L.
41462	,,	Bagnall, Webster	41513	,,	Green, Arthur E.
41463	,,	Bannister, Wm. H.	41514	,,	Hart, William J.
41464	,,	Bate, George J.	41515	,,	Havens, Clarence E.
41465	Driver	Bell, George A.	41516	Driver	Haywood, Eric
41466	,,	Bennett, Blanchard	41517	,,	Heifler, Harry E.
41467	,,	Biggar, Herbert	41518	,,	Hennessy, Chas. A.
41468	Gunner	Black, Reginald J.	41519	,,	Henry, Charles W.
41469	,,	Blake, Charles S.	41520	Gunner	Hooser, George A.
41470	Driver	Bleakney, R. C.	41521	,,	Horsman, Calvin E.
41471	Gunner	Bleakney, Uz. J.	41522	Driver	Horsman, John G.
41615	Driver	Bleakney, Von A.	41523	,,	Ingram, John A.
41472	Gunner	Bovard, Thos. J.	41524	Gunner	Jackson, Almanda G.
41473	Driver	Brown, John A.	41525	,,	Jacques, Howard J.
41474	,,	Bryan, Herbert J.	41526	Driver	Jamieson, Wylie F.
41475	,,	Bull, Norman, K.	41527	,,	Johnson, George F.
41476	,,	Butler, John F.	41528	Gunner	Judkins, John W.
41477	Gunner	Campbell, Alex. H.	41529	Driver	Kearns, Frank J.
41478	Driver	Campbell, Fred W.	41530	Gunner	Kelly, Arthur D.
41479	,,	Cantwell, Jas. W.	41531	Driver	Kelly, Ben F.
41480	Gunner	Carter, Jas. L.	41532	Gunner	Kelly, John J.
41481	,,	Cathcart, Leonard	41533	Driver	Keoughan, Pat J.
41482	Driver	Chambers, Leo. J.	41534	Sh'sm'th	King, Waldo A.
41483	Gunner	Chisholm, Wm.	41535	Driver	Kinnie, Judson L.
41484	Driver	Cobb, Harold L.	41536	Gunner	Knapp, Edward W.
41485	Gunner	Cochrane, Harold E.	41537	,,	Kyle, John J.
41486	,,	Coll, Arthur	41538	Driver	Lawlor, Michael
41487	Driver	Corneau, Joseph A.	41539	,,	Lawlor, Victor
41488	Gunner	Crocker, Clarence C.	41540	,,	Leaman, George H.
41489	Driver	Crossman, George O.	41541	,,	Lingley, John

Canadian Pacific—The Empire's Greatest Railway.

s

6TH BATTERY, 2ND BRIGADE, C.F.A.—cont.

Regl. No.	Rank.	Name.
41542	Driver	Maher, James
41543	,,	Masson, George M.
41544	Sh'sm'th	Marley, Charles A.
41545	Driver	Matheson, Alex.
41546	,,	McCullum, Wilfred L.
41547	,,	McDonald, Herbt. A.
41548	,,	McDonald, Hugh A.
41549	Gunner	McDonald, Malcolm
41550	Driver	McDonald, Robt. B.
41551	,,	McDougall, Fred J.
41552	,,	McIntyre, David W.
41553	Gunner	McIverney, Geo. V.
41554	C.S.Sm.	McKenzie, Alex.
41555	Wheeler	McKenzie, Sam. A.
41556	Gunner	McLeod, David D.
41557	Saddler	McMullin, John
41558	Gunner	McNeil, Oliver B.
41559	Driver	McQueen, Forbes F.
41560	Gunner	Miller, Leslie J.
41561	Sh'sm'th	Mills, Ira J.
41562	Driver	Mitton, Freeman J.
41563	Gunner	Moores, James H.
41564	Driver	Morrison, Hugh
41565	Gunner	Mowbray, Wm. J.
41566	Driver	Muggoh, Fred G.
41567	Gunner	Muree, Edward E.
41568	Driver	Myers, Fred
41569	Gunner	McKinnon, John A.
41570	Driver	Neilson, Arne E.
41571	Gunner	Niles, George M.
41572	,,	O'Brien, James F.
41573	,,	O'Brien, John A.
41574	,,	Owen, Frank
41575	,,	Patterson, George A.
41576	,,	Polleys, Edward H.
41577	Driver	Powell, Ralph D.
41578	,,	Poyser, George
41579	Gunner	Price, Ernest G.
41580	,,	Price, John S.
41581	,,	Nickerson, Jas. W.
41582	,,	Reid, Howard
41583	Driver	Reilly, Amos J.
41584	Gunner	Rhodes, Harry
41585	Driver	Robertson, Thos.
41586	,,	Rome, Joseph
41587	Gunner	Ross, Norman A.
41588	Driver	Ryder, Frank A.
41589	Gunner	Saunders, R. A.
41590	,,	Scott, George T.
41591	,,	Sewell, John C.
41592	,,	Smallwood, Clark W.
41593	Driver	Smith, Robert A.
41594	Gunner	Starratt Albert W.
41595	,,	Steeves, Henry W. B.
41596	,,	Steeves, Stanley A.
41597	,,	Stiles, Alvin E.
41598	Sergt.	Spence, Ralph E.
41599	Gunner	Stokes, Leslie T.
41600	,,	Stone, George F.
41601	Driver	Surette, Daniel
41602	Gunner	Swinimer, Alex. B.
41603	,,	Talbot, George
41604	,,	Thornton, Harry M.
41605	Driver	Tobin, Edward
41606	,,	Thompson, R. J.
41607	Gunner	Walker, George F.
41608	Driver	Wall, Arthur M.
41609	Gunner	Way, John R.
41610	,,	Welling, Albert M.
41611	,,	Wellington, F. D.
41612	,,	Wilson, Gordon A.
41613	Saddler	Wilson, John C.
41614	Gunner	Young, Ray D.

AMMUNITION COLUMN, 2nd BRIGADE.

Captain	Eakins, James Macdonald
Lieutenant	Hanson, W. Gordon
,, ...	Tingley, Frank Harvey *mc*
,, ...	Savage, Harold M.
,, ...	McMurtry, A. O.

Regl. No.	Rank.	Name.
41701	Br. S.-M.	Porteous, Wm. J.
41706	Q.M.Sgt.	Burnett, John T.
4121	Sergt.	Curtis, Francis Bert
41709	,,	McMullen, James

Canadian Pacific—The Empire's Greatest Railway

AMMUNITION COLUMN, 2ND BRIGADE, C.F.A.—cont. 275

Regl. No.	Rank	Name	Regl. No.	Rank	Name
41663	Sergt.	Laurence, Jas.	41762	Driver	Coyne, W. A.
41711	,,	Whitebone, Ernest A.	41764	Gunner	Cunningham, H.
41712	Far. Sgt.	Boyd, William	41765	,,	Cunningham, L.
41713	Crpl.	S.S. MacAulay, D. S.	41766	Driver	Currie, Richard
41714	Corpl.	Duncan, W. C.	41767	,,	Daley, Desmond D.
41715	,,	Dunsmore, George	41769	Cook	Dalziel, Alexander
41716	,,	Marshall, F. R. H.	41770	Driver	Dargovel, Lyle
41717	,,	Grubb, Harry	41910	,,	Danforth, R. K.
41718	Bombr.	Carroll, Jack	41771	,,	Davis, Edward W. M.
41719	,,	Mason, Alfred W.	41772	,,	Delorme, Joseph
41720	,,	McIsaac, John Alex.	41773	Gunner	Deslile, Alexander
41721	,,	Harris, Lionel	41774	Driver	Dryden, Edgar B.
41722	,,	Ward, James	41775	,,	Duncan, Alfred
41723	,,	Withey, William	41776	,,	Dunn, Joseph
41724	Trumpt'r	Morgan, Sidney W.	41777	,,	Dupree, Amede
41725	Gr. or Dr.	Albert, Joseph	41778	,,	Evans, Robt. A.
41727	,,	Allen, Carl	41779	,,	Ferguson, Frank G.
41728	,,	Allen, Joseph	41780	,,	Ferguson, Lorenzo
41729	,,	Allinson, Alfred	41781	,,	Forest, Henry
41730	,,	Archambault, J. E. A.	41782	,,	Foster, William
41731	,,	Arsenault, Joseph	41783	,,	Foster, Robert
41732	,,	Arsenault, John P.	41784	,,	Foyle, William
41733	,,	Atthill, Eric	41785	,,	Fraser, Lester
41734	Saddler	Absolom, Albert	41786	,,	Fraser, Peter
41735	Gr. or Dr.	Baron, Joseph	41704	,,	Gavin, Jno.
41736	,,	Barton, William	41703	,,	Graham, D.
41737	,,	Bartlett, Frederick	41788	,,	Giguere, Alphonse
41738	,,	Bennet, William	41789	,,	Gillin, James D.
41739	,,	Bentcliff, Jos.	41790	Gunner	Gilvear, George W.
41740	,,	Bertrand, Louis J.	41791	Driver	Gillett, Fred. W.
41741	,,	Berube, Joseph	41792	Gunner	Glancy, James
41742	,,	Berry, Robert	41794	Driver	Greenless, William
41743	Cook	Boucher, Adolph	41795	,,	Gouin, Henry
41744	Gunner	Boucher, Alex. P.	41796	,,	Gulliver, Rufus
41745	Driver	Bonaport, Lewis	41797	Gunner	Gunn, Walter
41746	,,	Brennan, Robt.	41798	,,	Hamill, David
41747	,,	Brodeur, Joseph	41799	,,	Harnish, Chas.
41343	,,	Buchanan, G. E.	41800	Driver	Harrigan, James B.
41748	,,	Baron, G. A.	41801	Gunner	Hardy, Joseph
41749	,,	Burke, John	41802	,,	Harvey, Robert
41750	,,	Casey, Gilbert	41803	,,	Harris, Thomas
41751	,,	Chappell, Ernest	41804	Driver	Hartley, Herbert
41752	,,	Charon, Albert	41805	Gunner	Hennegan, Sydney
41753	,,	Chelloner, Albert	41806	Driver	Hickson, Robert
41754	,,	Chelmondly, Robt.	41807	,,	Hill, Gerald M.
41755	,,	Clifford, Thos. F.	41808	Cook	Houle, Alfred
41913	,,	Coffee, T.	41809	Driver	Hughes, Owen
41756	,,	Coatsworth, Peter	41902	,,	Halstead, Ed.
41757	,,	Coderre, Napolean	41705	,,	Haynes, W.
41758	Gunner	Connor, Robt. H.	41810	Gunner	Hibbert, Jeffrey J.
41759	Driver	Copeland, William S.	41811	Driver	Hurtubise, Rene T.
41761	,,	Cox, Pearley R.	41812	,,	Keith, Douglas G.

Canadian Pacific—The Empire's Greatest Railway.

276 AMMUNITION COLUMN, 2ND BRIGADE, C.F.A.—cont.

Regl. No.	Rank	Name
41813	Driver	Kelly, James M.
41814	,,	Labelle, Joseph A.
41793	,,	Laurance, W. A.
41815	,,	Lafrance, Joseph
41816	,,	Lagneux, Oscar
41707	,,	Landry, T. E.
41817	,,	Lauzon, Henry
41818	,,	Lauzon, Francis
41819	,,	Lajoie, Arthur
41820	,,	Le Blance, Arthur
41821	,,	Letters, Hugh
41822	,,	Libersant, Arthur
41823	Gunner	Limmall, William
41824	,,	Livock, George
41825	Driver	Loundes, Amos
41826	Saddler	Marcovitz, Isador
41827	Driver	Martell, Edward
41787	,,	Marcotte, J. E.
41828	,,	Mathews, Frank
41829	Gunner	Mellish, John
41830	,,	Meurant, Chas.
41831	Driver	Malfoy, Frank
41832	,,	Miller, Joseph
41833	,,	Miller, Walter L.
41834	,,	Mitchell, Gordon
41835	,,	Mitchel, Charles
41836	,,	Mullen, Clyde E.
41837	,,	Mulhern, Milton
41838	,,	Murphy, Richard T.
41839	,,	McConnell, Leo A.
41840	,,	McCready, John
41842	Saddler	McDonald, John J.
41843	Driver	McDonald, Angus
41844	Gunner	McDonald, Chas. R.
41845	,,	McDonough, Alfred
41846	Driver	McElhetton, John
41847	,,	McKinney, John E.
41849	Gunner	McKennan, Daniel
41848	Driver	McLennan, Dan. A.
41850	,,	McNeil, George
41851	,,	Neary, Herbert J.
41852	Gunner	O'Keefe, James
41853	,,	Osborne, Alfred J.
41854	,,	Pelletier, Alzeal
41855	Driver	Perrault, Emile
41768	,,	Perrault, R.
41856	Gunner	Perrault, Verris
41857	Driver	Pheeney, Chas.
41710	,,	Porter, Chas.
41858	Driver	Picard, Joseph P.
41859	,,	Popow, Fred
41861	Gunner	Rae, George
41862	Driver	Randall, Albert
41863	,,	Rankeller, Alex.
41864	,,	Rawcliffe, Alfred
41865	,,	Redpath, Robert
41866	,,	Reed, William
41868	Gunner	Rimes, Harold
41869	,,	Sawyer, Albert
41870	Driver	Sayer, Harold N.
41871	,,	Scullion, Ernest
41872	Gunner	Scott, Cecil O.
41873	Driver	Sears, Stanley
41874	,,	Sears, Leonard A.
41875	,,	Shaw, William
41876	,,	Slonwhite, Stanley
41877	,,	Sloan, Herbert J.
41878	Gunner	Smith, Thos. J.
41879	Driver	Smith, Reginald
41880	Gunner	Smith, Bristol
41763	Driver	Smith, John
41881	Cook	Simard, Joseph
41882	Driver	Starr, Ernent
41883	,,	Stomps, Chas.
41884	Gunner	Stevenson, Chas.
41885	Driver	Stevenson, James
41886	,,	Strickland, Simeon
41887	,,	Sullivan, Anthony
41888	Gunner	Sutherland, Wm.
41889	,,	Swinden, Fred
41891	Driver	Thomas, Harry
41892	Gunner	Thurley, Edgar C.
41893	Driver	Tinker, Chas.
41894	Gunner	Tomkins, Edward G.
41895	,,	Vanbuskirk, Dan. A.
41896	,,	Wale, Gerald H.
41897	Driver	Wane, James E.
41898	,,	Webb, Ernest
41899	,,	Wetmore, William J.
41900	,,	Whitehead, William
41901	Gunner	Whiting, Geo. E.
41902	Driver	Whitehouse, Charles
41903	,,	Whitehouse, William
41904	Wheeler	Wilson, George
41905	Driver	Wilson, James
41906	,,	Withnell, Joseph E.
41907	,,	Woodcock, William
41908	,,	Youthed, Fred

Canadian Pacific—The Empire's Greatest Railway.

3rd BRIGADE, C.F.A.

BRIGADE STAFF.

Officer Commanding	Lieut.-Col. James H. Mitchell
Adjutant	Major George H. Ralston
Orderly Officer	Lieutenant Cecil V. Stockwell
Paymaster	Hon. Captain William R. Thomson
Veterinary Officer	Captain Charles G. Saunders
Medical Officer	Major David A. Clark
Chaplain	Hon. Captain Joseph B. Grimshaw
Supernumerary	Lieut. E. B. P. Armour

Regl. No.	Rank.	Name.	Regl. No.	Rank.	Name.
42001	Br.S.-M.	Kerry, Herbert G.	42864	Gunner	Fraser, Alex.
42023	Sergt.	Ellender, William A.	42865	,,	Boyes, John
42035	,,	Smith, Sydney G.	42866	,,	Feneton, Ernest
42002	,,	Egerton, Frank H.	42005	,,	Kuhry, Alban J.
42003	Corpl.	MacDonald, John Y.	42010	,,	Lander, William B.
42007	,,	Brown, Stanley	42020	,,	McKenzie, William
42024	Act.Bbr.	Douse, Henry	42017	,,	McPherson, Fredk. S
42008	Bombr.	Peach, Howard L.	42028	,,	Munn, Robert M.
42013	Gunner	Ashforth, Harold E.	42029	,,	Markle, Austin
42004	,,	Benson, George	42019	,,	Neill, Charles
42018	,,	Barton, William E.	42015	,,	Richardson, Wm. A,
42021	,,	Burke, Thomas	42027	,,	Rooney, Patrick
42022	,,	Brennan, R. M.	42006	,,	Smith, John W.
42031	,,	Boyle, Walter S.	42009	,,	Steven, Ian H.
42032	,,	Charles, Harry S.	42025	,,	Turner, Thomas H.
42033	,,	Cameron, Ian	42030	,,	Welch, Thomas
42016	,,	Gates, Chester R.	42026	,,	Williams, David A.
42012	,,	Hobbs, Thomas	42034	Q.M.Sgt.	Grute, Herbert
42011	,,	Jossa, Charles	42036	Corpl.	Wright, Donald
42014	,,	Joyce, William F.	42039	Private	Beardmore, H. E.
42853	,,	Minto, Harvey S.	42038	,,	Fraser, Fugl. D.
42852	,,	Mackenzie, Roderick	42037	,,	Pitt, William H.

7th BATTERY, 3rd BRIGADE.

Major	King, William B.
Captain	Bell, Charles J.
Lieutenant	Lancaster, Edward H.
,,	Ball, John C.
,,	Morgan, Ralph C.

Regl. No.	Rank.	Name.	Regl. No.	Rank.	Name.
42040	Br.S.-M.	Hampshere, John	42043	Far. Sgt.	Montgomery, John
42041	Q.M.Sgt.	Dunklee, John B.	42044	,,	Dicks, Sydney
42042	Sergt.	Holt, Eustace Otto	42045	,,	Wickham, Albert M.

Canadian Pacific—The Empire's Greatest Railway.

7TH BATTERY, 3RD BRIGADE, C.F.A.—cont.

Regl. No.	Rank.	Name.	Regl. No.	Rank.	Name.
42046	Far. Sgt.	Miller, James H.	42097	Gr.or.Dr.	Clay, Edward
42047	,,	Roberts, John	42098	,,	Collins, John
42048	,,	Guyalt, James	42099	,,	Cawley, Harry E.
42049	,,	Guerin, Tenniece	42100	,,	Cooney, Patrick
42050	Corpl.	Rudge, William	42101	,,	Clark, Edward
42051	,,	Hubbard, G. A. W.	42102	,,	Clark, Andrew
42052	,,	Allen, George Wm.	42103	,,	Day, William
42053	,,	MacDougall, C. G.	42104	,,	Daly, Richard
42054	,,	Cooper, Thomas R.	42105	,,	Daniels, George
42055	Bombr.	Young, Charles A.	42106	,,	Dixen, Henry
42057	,,	Branigan, Harry	42107	,,	Dorris, Ambrose
42058	,,	Archer, Arthur J.	42108	,,	Downey, Joseph Earl
42059	,,	Baker, Robert F.	42109	,,	Evans, David
42060	,,	Duke, Harry	42110	,,	Everett, James
42061	,,	McBride, Archer	42111	,,	Everett, Charles W.
42062	,,	Turnbull, Ernest	42112	,,	Everest, James
42063	,,	Rayner, Richard W.	42113	,,	Ellis, Frank
42064	,,	Fry, Oliver	42114	,,	Edmiston, G. H.
42065	,,	True, Thomas	42115	,,	Elliott, Robert
42066	Trumpt'r	Duff, Charles	42116	,,	Fairfield, Herbert
42067	Gunner	Adie, James A.	42117	,,	Fenton, Alexander
42068	,,	Ash, George	42118	,,	Finglah, Bert
42069	Gr. or Dr.	Aubron, Thomas	42119	,,	Forsyth, Fred
42070	,,	Aldred, Joseph	42120	,,	Fry, George H.
42071	,,	Ansell, Raymond	42121	,,	Findlay, George
42056	,,	Barton, Edgar	42122	,,	Fry, Francis
42072	,,	Bassford, John	42123	,,	Gibson, William
42073	,,	Baird, Ernest	42124	,,	Goodwin, Richard
42367	,,	Beddow, John Alfred	42125	,,	Graham, Fredk. C.
42074	,,	Beer, Lionel L.	42126	,,	Graham, Geoffrey
42075	,,	Bell, Andrew	42127	,,	Gunter, Arthur
42076	,,	Berkeley, William	42128	,,	Gray, Arthur E.
42077	,,	Biddecombe, Edwin	42129	,,	Golds, Percy
42078	,,	Billings, Edward J.	42130	Bombr.	Graham, William E.
42079	,,	Blott, Arthur E.	42131	Gr. or Dr.	Garrow, Henry J.
42080	,,	Bradley, John J.	42132	,,	Halpin, Michael
42081	,,	Brown, Duncan	42133	,,	Harris, Russell
42082	Bombr.	Boone, Gordon V.	42134	,,	Harcus, George R.
42083	Gr.or.Dr.	Brown, William	42135	,,	Hearn, Alfred E.
42084	,,	Baker, Herbert C.	42136	,,	Hawker, Reginald
48085	,,	Bamford, William	42137	Bombr.	Helliwell, Ivan H.
42086	,,	Chandler, James E.	42138	Gr. or Dr.	Higgins, James P.
42087	,,	Connelly, George H.	42139	,,	Hills, Bertram C.
42088	,,	Cadigan, Joseph	42140	,,	Hodgins, William J.
42089	,,	Clark, Williams J.	42141	,,	Holleran, James
42090	,,	Colquhoun, George P.	42142	,,	Haworth, Chris.
42091	,,	Clasby, Augustus	42143	,,	Hudson, Alfred J.
42092	,,	Campbell, Alexander	42144	,,	Hanton, John
42093	,,	Clarke, Horace	42145	,,	Hann, Arthur G.
42094	,,	Carpenter, Arthur	42146	,,	Ingham, Thomas
42095	,,	Coleman, Albert F.	42147	,,	Ireland, Wilfred
42096	,,	Chapman, Wm. H.	42148	,,	Johnston, Harold

Canadian Pacific—The Empire's Greatest Railway.

7TH BATTERY, 3RD BRIGADE, C.F.A.—cont.

Regl. No.	Rank	Name	Regl. No.	Rank	Name
42149	Gr.or Dr.	Joy, James R.	42192	Gr.or Dr.	Pratt, Charles N.
42150	,,	June, Arthur L.	42193	,,	Penman, Robert
42153	,,	Keating, Gus	42194	,,	Payne, William
42151	Trumpt'r	Jackson, George H.	42195	,,	Proudman, Walter
42152	Gr. or Dr.	Kadwill, George E.	42196	,,	Ross, William
42154	,,	Kett, Fred	42197	,,	Ripley, Douglas B
42155	,,	King, William	42198	,,	Rooney, Herbert
42156	,,	King, Mervyn F.	42199	,,	Roberts, James
42157	,,	Lavoie, Eugine	42200	,,	Riley, Henry
42158	,,	Luther, Sidney T.	42201	,,	Renoff, Edward
42159	,,	Lindsay, Daniel	42202	,,	Reynolds, Joseph
42160	,,	Levill, William	42203	,,	Rix, Walter
42161	,,	McPhearson, Neil H.	42204	,,	Saunders, Charles W.
42162	,,	McLean, Robert	42205	,,	Sullivan, Harry
42163	,,	McConnell, Samuel	42207	,,	Standen, Samuel
42164	,,	McIntyre, Peter	42208	,,	Simmons, George
42165	,,	McKenna, John J.	42209	,,	Stafford, Reginald G.
42166	,,	McNicholls, John F.	42210	,,	Smith, Joseph D.
42167	,,	McElwee, Wm. J.	42211	,,	Sandford, Arthur H.
42168	,,	McLean, John	42212	,,	Saxton, Ernest
42169	,,	McDonald, Thomas	42213	,,	Smith, Albert
42170	,,	McCormick, James	42214	,,	Stafford, Joseph
42171	,,	Martin, George J.	42215	,,	Saltrough, Nathan
42172	,,	Mackney, John	42216	,,	Stevens, Benjamin W.
42173	,,	Marriott, William	42217	,,	Steele, Harry
42174	,,	Mills, William N.	42218	,,	Steele, Frederick C.
42175	,,	Marshall, George S.	42219	,,	Smith, John C.
42176	,,	Mercer, Charles	42220	,,	Soady, Percy E.
42177	,,	Mesler, Benjamin	42221	,,	Stevens, Frederick
42178	,,	Messer, Adam	42222	,,	Spears, Samuel
42179	,,	Miller, David	42223	,,	Sloan, Bruce W.
42180	,,	Moore, George	42224	,,	Turner, Arthur W.
42181	,,	Mohun, George	42225	,,	Tranter, George W.
42182	,,	Morrow, George	42226	,,	Tugwood, Percy
42183	,,	Maess, Roy	42227	,,	Toohar, William P.
42184	,,	Newby, Mervyn L.	42228	,,	Wheeler, Alfred
42185	,,	Nicholls, Eli	42229	,,	Whitham, Walter
42186	,,	Nicholson, William	42230	,,	Whiffen, Peter
42187	,,	Nokes, Arthur	42231	,,	Woodward, Harry
42188	,,	O'Neill, Henry P.	42232	,,	Winterford, Arthur
42189	Bombr.	Parnell, Mathew	42233	,,	White, Charles
42190	Gr. or Dr.	Paskins, Cecil G.	42234	,,	Young, Arthur
42191	,,	Paxton, Norman J.			

Canadian Pacific—The Empire's Greatest Railway.

8th BATTERY, 3rd BRIGADE.

Major	... ...	Carscallen, Henry G.
Captain	... ...	Crerar, Henry D. G.
Lieutenant	... ...	Hendrie, William J. S.
,,	... ...	Scandrett, James H.
,,	... ...	Storms, Douglas H.
,,	... ...	Young, James V.

Regl. No.	Rank.	Name.	Regl. No.	Rank.	Name.
42235	Br. S.-M.	Griffiths, Joseph J.	42286	Gr.or Dr.	Cockrane, William J.
42236	Q.M.Sgt.	Brydges, James J.	42287	,,	Chambers, Wm. H.
42237	Sergt.	McLeod, Daniel E.	42288	,,	Canning, Russell J.
42238	,,	Doyle, James J.	42289	,,	Chadwick, Fred
42239	,,	Smithson, Ernest	42290	,,	Carr, John
42240	,,	Barnhill, John A.	42291	,,	Cox, Walter
42241	,,	Campbell, Roy O.	42251	,,	Connor, Thomas
42242	,,	Struad, John H.	42292	,,	Cavanagh, William J.
42243	Far. Sgt.	Adams, Henry	42247	,,	Cameron, Daniel
42244	,,	Barnacal, William	42293	,,	Chew, James W.
42255	Corpl.	Hulsman, Chester H.	42294	,,	Cotgreave, George
42256	,,	Oakley, Albert J.	42295	,,	Carson, William H.
42257	,,	Simmons, Robert S.	42296	,,	Clark, Charles O.
42258	,,	Fish, William C.	42297	,,	Comroe, Harry
42259	,,	Thorpe, Henry J.	42298	,,	Devall, William H.
42245	,,	Bosher, James T.	42249	,,	Dinham, Thomas
42260	,,	Kelly, John B.	42299	,,	Dunford, Thomas W.
42261	Bombr.	Aldridge, Fredk. G.	42300	,,	Duncan, Edward J.
42262	,,	Fletcher, John L.	42301	,,	Diggle, James
42263	,,	Buzza, John	42250	,,	Edgeler, Archibld.W.
42264	,,	Inch, George T.	42302	,,	England, George
42265	,,	Leaper, Claude A.	42253	Trumpt'r	Frame, Andrew
42266	,,	Archer, William	42303	Gr. or Dr.	Foley, Hugh
42267	,,	Marks, George J.	40067	Sergt.	Fish, Frederick M.
42269	,,	Ritchie, Thomas	42305	Gr. or Dr.	Fenton, Michael
42270	,,	Lawson, William S.	42306	,,	Frost, Dorman J.
42271	,,	Dodd, William D.	42307	,,	Fairbrother, Harold
42268	,,	Johnstone, Robert	42309	,,	Greenhough, Thomas
42272	Gr. or Dr.	Anderson, Johnston	42310	,,	Grigg, Thomas
42273	,,	Arnold, George	42311	,,	Gillespie, William C.
42274	,,	Andrews, William J.	42312	,,	Gee, Clarendon
42275	,,	Blackwell, Peter	42313	,,	Green, Charles
42276	,,	Boardman, George	42314	,,	Goatcher, Arthur
42277	,,	Britt, Robert	42315	,,	Gange, Harry
42278	,,	Boynton, Louis	42316	,,	Hampson, John S.
42279	,,	Burgess, Leonard	42317	,,	Hobson, James
42280	,,	Brady, John	42318	,,	Hills, Charles
42246	,,	Brown, Alfred T.	42319	,,	Hornung, John I.
42281	,,	Barker, Frederick H.	42320	,,	Harrison, Frank A.
42282	,,	Bowman, Frank H.	42321	,,	Howie, David C.
42283	,,	Benz, Sidney	42322	,,	Hayzelden, Chas. T.
42284	,,	Bowland, Ben J.	42323	,,	Hossock, James
42285	,,	Chase, Joseph T.	42325	,,	Husson, Frederick N.

Canadian Pacific—The Empire's Greatest Railway.

8TH BATTERY, 3RD BRIGADE, C.F.A.—cont.

Regl. No.	Rank.	Name.	Regl. No.	Rank.	Name.
42324	Gr.or Dr.	Husson, William E.	42375	Gr.or Dr.	Rasberry, Henry
42326	,,	Hunter, Ernest J.	42254	,,	Trumpt'r Rees, Joseph
42327	,,	Hore, Frederick J.	42376	Gr. or Dr.	Rattew, John
42328	,,	Hillman, Archibald R.	42377	,,	Rissidore, Fredk. D.
42329	,,	Hadley, Edward	42378	,,	Rodgers, Allan R.
42330	,,	Head, Sydney G.	42379	,,	Rissidore, Walter W.
42331	,,	Hayward, Edward M.	42380	,,	Randell, Peter
42332	,,	Heppell, Reginald M.	42383	,,	Ryan, John
42333	,,	Irwin, Arthur T. J.	42382	,,	Reynolds, Joseph
42334	,,	Inkson, Charles	42381	,,	Ryan, John James
42335	,,	Jeppesen, Andrew	42384	,,	Routh, Stanley C.
42336	,,	Jennings, Garfield	42385	,,	Snowdon, George T.
42337	,,	James, Thomas	42386	,,	Smith, William
42338	,,	Johnson, Frederick	42387	,,	Scholes, George
42339	,,	Knowles, Arthur J.	42388	,,	Smithers, Fred
42340	,,	Kincade, Garfield	42389	,,	Simpson, William
42341	,,	Kern, Charles E.	42390	,,	Stacey, John S.
42342	,,	Kane, Joseph	42391	,,	Stribbell, John L.
42248	,,	Knightley, Alfred J.	42392	,,	Silcock, Clarence C.
42343	,,	Kilhams, Sidney	42393	,,	Starling, James A.
42344	,,	Kelley, Harry	42394	,,	Salmon, Lord G.
42345	,,	Le Page, Edwin	42395	,,	Shea, Jeremiah
42346	,,	Leishman, James	42396	,,	Shea, Thomas
42347	,,	Laing, James	42397	,,	Shipton, William
42348	,,	Livesey, Peter	42398	,,	Smith, James
42349	,,	Murray, Richard	42399	,,	Smith, Stephen C.
42350	,,	Miller, George	42400	,,	Sutherland, Earl W.
42351	,,	Mercer, Robert H.	42401	,,	Steward, William J.
42352	,,	Mitton, William R.	42402	,,	Shelton, Charles W.
42353	,,	Mark, Henry R.	42403	,,	Taplay, Fred
42354	,,	Martin, Herbert	42404	,,	Tanner, Daryle C.
42355	,,	Marshall, John S.	42405	,,	Thompson, Ernest
42356	,,	Macdonald, John	42406	,,	Turner, Herbert A.
42357	,,	McWhinney, Hamltn.	42407	,,	Tye, Herbert
42358	,,	McConachie, James	42408	,,	Thomson, Roderick F.
42359	,,	Martin, Claud K.	42409	,,	Woodward, L. B.
42360	,,	Noble, Harold	42410	,,	Wheeler, William T.
42361	,,	Nevills, Andrew J.	42411	,,	Withers, Walter
42362	,,	Olliver, Reginald V.	42412	,,	Wesley, William C.
42363	,,	O'Regan, Patrick	42413	,,	Williams, William
42364	,,	Phinn, William	42414	,,	Williamson, A. W.
42365	,,	Pike, Fred J.	42415	,,	Wilson, Thomas H.
42366	,,	Perry, William	42416	,,	White, Algernon
42367	,,	Percival, Harry C.	42417	,,	Walker, William
42368	,,	Pratt, George	42418	,,	Westacott, Herbert
42369	,,	Pearson, Alexander	42419	,,	White, Harold V.
42370	,,	Powell, Frederick C.	42420	,,	Whiteside, Robert
42371	,,	Pyett, George	42421	,,	White, Fred W.
42372	,,	Pawson, Edward	42422	,,	Weatherill, Clair G.P.
42373	,,	Ryan, William	42252	,,	Yorkstone, Alexander
42374	,,	Rycroft, James	42308	,,	Young, Norman

Canadian Pacific—The Empire's Greatest Railway.

9th BATTERY, 3rd BRIGADE.

Major	... ...	MacDougall, Ewan A.
Captain	... ...	Wainwright, Arthur, C. S.
Lieutenant	... ...	Ross, James W.
„	... ...	Greene, Elliot A.
„	... ...	Craig, Charles S.
„	... ...	Ryerson, Arthur C.

Regl. No.	Rank.	Name.	Regl. No.	Rank.	Name.
42423	Br. S.-M.	Wildgoose, Richard	42431	Gr. or Dr.	Attwell, Robert
42424	B.Q.M.S.	Footitt, George E.	42432	„	Austin, George A.
42553	Sergt.	Muir, Thomas	42433	„	Austin, John F. L.
42538	„	Masters, Ernest J.	42436	„	Bailey, Percy H.
42489	„	Gamble, James	42437	Gunner	Ball, Wm. John
42535	„	MacNachtan, E. L.	42442	„	Biggs, John
42503	„	Hamilton, Harold H.	42440	Gr. or Dr.	Bentley, William
42614	„	Wright, Robert C.	42441	„	Berry, Ernest
42435	„	Badger, Wm. A. R.	42444	„	Boswell, Sidney R.
42574	Far. Sgt.	Richmond, A. R. B.	42445	„	Boyd, Thomas R.
42593	Shoe Cpl.	Stone, William G.	42446	„	Bregmann, Sidney
42478	Sh'sm'th	Down, Frederick W.	42447	„	Bristowe, Edward P
42481	„	Edwards, Albert G.	42449	„	Brown, John T.
42460	„	Clark, William J.	42450	„	Brown, Nathaniel C.
42448	Saddler	Bromhall, John C.	42451	„	Brownbill, Wm. G.
42439	„	Beardmore, Wm. B.	42452	„	Buhagiar, Felice
42579	Wheeler	Roper, John	42434	„	Badenoch, Alexander
42513	„	James, Joseph W.	42453	„	Carey, Martin J.
42501	Trumpt'r	Hall, Clarence A.	42455	„	Carrol, Patrick
42543	„	Mills, Alfred	42456	„	Carruthers, Thos.
42555	Corpl.	Mulholland, B. F. P.	42457	„	Carter, Edward J.
42611	„	Wilson, John W.	42458	„	Carter, Harry
42521	„	Lister, Richard C.	42459	„	Chalklin, Charles F.
42522	„	Love, Francis	42461	„	Collins, John N.
42559	„	Orton, Alfred	42463	„	Colyer, William J.
42606	„	Warrington, H. W.	42454	„	Carney, John
42466	„	Cruickshank, Arch.	42462	„	Colmer, Charles H.
42483	Bombr.	Evans, William	42464	Gunner	Cooper, John Robert
42572	„	Rhodes, Herbert A.	42465	„	Crosgrey, Roy
42438	„	Barker, William G.	42467	Gr. or Dr.	Currie, William P.
42541	„	Messenger, Arthur	42468	„	Dale, Raymond M.
42443	„	Blackburn, Joe	42469	„	Dalziel, William
42607	„	Webb, George	42470	„	Davidson, Edward
42427	„	Adams, Robert C.	42472	„	Davis, Alfred J. S.
42609	„	Welch, Leonard S.	42471	Gunner	Davies, David W.
42516	„	Ker, Alan W. W.	42475	„	Defrez Forbes, Elliot
42550	„	Moore, Philip J.	42473	Gr. or Dr.	Dawson, Joseph
42425	Gr. or Dr.	Adams, Charles	42474	„	Deacon, Thomas E.
42426	„	Adams, Gordon W.	42476	„	Dodd, William H.
42428	„	Aisthorpe, John W.	42477	„	Dow, James B.
42429	Gunner	Allcock, Frank D.	42479	„	Dunbar, Henry C.
42430	Gr. or Dr.	Amoore, Harry S.	42480	„	Dundas, Thomas H.

Canadian Pacific—The Empire's Greatest Railway.

9TH BATTERY, 3RD BRIGADE, C.F.A.—cont.

Regl. No.	Rank.	Name.	Regl. No.	Rank.	Name.
42482	Gr. or Dr.	Elliot, Ruben, J. F.	42546	Gr. or Dr.	Mintram, Andrew M.
42484	,,	Fairbrother, Geo. A.	42547	,,	Moles, George F.
42485	,,	Fallas, William	42548	,,	Monday, Bertram E.
42486	,,	Farnworth, Geo. H.	42549	,,	Moore, Charles D.
42487	,,	Fox, Arthur	42551	,,	Mouncey, George A.
42488	,,	Freeman, Robert	42552	,,	Mountain, Albert
42490	,,	Gemmell, John T.	42554	,,	Mulhall, Joseph W.
42491	,,	Gillmore, Charles J.	42556	,,	Neale, Alfred T.
42492	,,	Gillmore, George F.	42557	,,	Nicholson, Robert
42493	,,	Gilmour, James G.	42558	,,	Niven, William
42494	,,	Gilruth, Harold	42560	,,	Osler, Charles W.
42495	,,	Gosse, Walter H.	42561	,,	O'Toole, Joseph
42496	,,	Gough, Edward J.	42562	,,	Oxland, William C.
42497	,,	Grange, Frederick	42563	,,	Padmore, Arthur S.
42498	,,	Grant, Albert	42564	,,	Palmer, James F.
42499	,,	Gregson, Edward J.	42565	,,	Parker, Henry J.
42500	,,	Gustar, Alfred W.	42566	,,	Petrie, Herbert W.
42502	,,	Halliwell, John	42567	,,	Phillips, Joseph H.
42504	Gunner	Hanson, Samuel	42568	Gunner	Raymond, Edward J.
42507	,,	Holly, Thos. Walter	42580	,,	Russel, Joe
42505	Gr. or Dr.	Hedley, George E.	42569	Gr. or Dr.	Reid, Robert B.
42506	,,	Hetherington, S. G.	42570	,,	Relf, Edgar G. B.
42508	,,	Holt, Sydney	42571	,,	Reynolds, Arthur H.
42509	,,	Hopkins, Albert E.	42576	,,	Robson, William W.
42510	,,	Hopkins, F. W. A.	42577	,,	Roney, Foster J.
42511	,,	Hornbeck, Gerald R.	42578	,,	Roney, William J.
42512	,,	Hughes, Earl R.	42575	,,	Robert, Eugene J.
42514	,,	Jones, Harry G.	42573	,,	Riches, Finley
42515	,,	Jones, James A.	42581	,,	Sash, Ernest
42517	,,	King, Harry	42582	,,	Sidey, Leo
42518	,,	Lawrence, Thomas J.	42583	,,	Simmonds, Chas. E.
42519	,,	Lee, Joseph	42584	,,	Simmons, Edward L.
42520	,,	Le Gros, Henry A.	42585	,,	Sinclair, Archibald
42523	,,	Lovekyn, Vyvyan J.	42586	,,	Sleeman, George H.
42524	,,	Lye, John G.	42588	,,	Sparkes, Leonard
42527	,,	MacDonnell, Charles	42589	Gunner	Stewart Burton
42528	,,	Macdonnell, N. S.	42590	,,	Stinson, Chas. L.
42525	,,	MacBride, John	42594	,,	Strutt, Alexander
42526	,,	Macdonald, Colin R.	42596	,,	Summers, Jas. H.
42529	,,	McEwen, John D.	42591	Gr. or Dr.	Stobo, Isaac A.
42530	,,	McGee, Ernest B.	42592	,,	Stone, Alfred
42531	,,	McGill, Mordie	42595	,,	Sullivan, John L.
42532	,,	MacGregor, Lewis	42597	,,	Sutton, John E.
42533	,,	McIntosh, Norm. H.	42598	,,	Sykes, Henry
42534	,,	McKay, John N.	42587	,,	Smith, George
42536	,,	McVittie, George	42599	,,	Tachauer, David H.
42537	,,	Martin, Edgar A.	42600	,,	Thew, Christie
42540	,,	Medhurst, George H.	42601	Gunner	Turner, Percy David
42539	,,	Mearns, Archibald J.	42602	Gr. or Dr.	Uren, Frederick C.
42542	,,	Meiklejohn, Richard	42603	,,	Veitch, Mark B.
42544	,,	Mills, Andrew	42604	,,	Wade, Mathew
42545	,,	Millson, Samuel E.	42605	,,	Wakelin, William

Canadian Pacific—The Empire's Greatest Railway.

9TH BATTERY, 3RD BRIGADE, C.F.A.—cont.

Regl. No.	Rank.	Name.	Regl. No.	Rank.	Name.
42608	Gr. or Dr.	Welch, Harry C.	42615	Gr. or Dr.	Yates, Arthur J.
42610	,,	White, Asa	42616	Gunner	Yates, Jas. Ashley
42612	,,	Woodward, Hbt. J.	42617	Gr. or Dr.	Youden, Harry C.
42613	,,	Worthington, Geo.	42618	,,	Young, Charles A.

BASE.

Lieutenant ... ... Macdonnell, James M.

Regl No.	Rank.	Name.	Regl. No.	Rank.	Name.
42775	Q.M.Sgt.	Vance, Fred. W.	42813	Gunner	Harvey, Albert E.
42776	Sergt.	Lucas, John	42815	,,	Hazzard, Edward
42777	Bombr.	Walsh, George	42816	,,	Holloway, William
42778	,,	Hatt, Charles E.	42850	,,	Hoyden, George
42781	Gunner	Auger, Lewis G.	42817	,,	Hamilton, Thomas
42782	,,	Abery, Alfred	42820	,,	Hay, Robert A. W.
42783	,,	Allen, Arthur F.	42779	,,	Jackson, Albert M.
42784	,,	Armstrong, W. L.	42818	,,	Jones, Albert E.
42785	,,	Antill, William	42819	,,	Jamieson, Peter B.
42786	,,	Allen, James	42849	,,	Jordan, James
42787	,,	Beechey, George H.	42821	,,	Kemp, Sidney
42788	,,	Berryman, Rich. H.	42823	,,	Millwood, Ernest
42789	,,	Bird, George	42822	,,	McManus, John
42790	,,	Bolanger, Lewis	42824	,,	McMaster, Robert
42791	,,	Bradford, James	42825	,,	Mills, William J.
42792	,,	Burnett, Gordon H.	42826	,,	Park, James
42793	,,	Boulding, Walter	42827	,,	Pearson, Sidney
42794	,,	Biggar, Charles	42828	,,	Pidsley, John E.
42795	,,	Betts, Alfred	42829	,,	Saunders, Peter H.
42796	,,	Bonnyman, Alex.	42830	,,	Saunders, William A.
42797	,,	Bristow, George	42831	,,	Smith, Alexander W.
42798	,,	Bell, Albert E.	42832	,,	Smith, Arthur S. G.
42799	,,	Blackhall, Charles M	42833	,,	Stock, Fred. H.
42848	,,	Brett, Phillip	42834	,,	Sparrow, Arch. S.
42800	,,	Currie, James	42835	,,	Somerville, Frank L.
42801	,,	Clayton, Albert A.	42836	,,	Shoebottom, William
42803	,,	Caswell, Frank	42837	,,	Smith, William T.
42804	,,	Claridge, George	42847	,,	Sheridan, Joseph
42805	,,	Davison, Alex.	42838	,,	Taylor, William
42806	,,	Eames, Alfred	42839	,,	Thompson, Alex.
42807	,,	Eggiman, Felix	42840	,,	Van Sickle, Sheldon
42809	,,	Ellis, Fred	42841	,,	Vousden, Ernest
42808	,,	Foreman, Thomas	42842	,,	Westland, Wallace
42810	,,	Fenton, Ruben	42843	,,	White, Frederick W.
42811	,,	Gibson, Peter	42844	,,	Walker, Herbert
42812	,,	Green, Walter	42845	,,	Wilson, Edward
42780	,,	Grant, Duncan	42846	,,	Young, John

Canadian Pacific—The Empire's Greatest Railway.

AMMUNITION COLUMN, 3rd BRIGADE.

Captain ... ... McEwen, Alan B.
Lieutenant ... ... Burgoyne, Henry B.
    ,, ... Lovelace, Stanley E.

Regl. No.	Rank.	Name.	Regl. No.	Rank.	Name.
42619	Sgt.-Maj.	Connor, Wm. J. S.	42668	Gr. or Dr.	Clugston, James
42620	Q.M.Sgt.	Jones, Thomas E.	42666	,,	Clark, Roy
42623	Sergt.	Harris, Edward C.	42669	,,	Condie, Arthur G.
42622	,,	Harman, George	42656	,,	Claggett, John Wm.
42621	,,	Lewis, Frederick J.	42664	,,	Cross, Sydney
42624	,,	Cole, James A.	42674	,,	Craig, J.
42625	Far. Sgt.	Bletcher, Richard F.	42671	,,	Dean, Harry
42630	Corpl.	Stanning, Tom S.	42672	,,	Duncan, William P.
42626	,,	Grant, Malcolm R.	42670	,,	Dawe, Kenneth D.
42629	,,	Snell, William	42671	,,	Daniels, John
42628	,,	McCrudden, Charles	42673	,,	Ehmcke, William
42627	,,	Macdonald, Brodie	42674	,,	Fordyce, George
42632	Shoe Cpl.	Hollands, Henry J.	42676	,,	Falconer, Donald
42631	Whl. Cpl.	McKenzie, James M.	42677	,,	Finlayson, George
42633	Bombr.	Gustar, George	42678	,,	Forbes, Harry
42637	,,	Knight, William	42675	,,	Fox, William
42635	,,	Hayward, John	42679	,,	Gausden, William
42636	,,	Minott, Albert L.	42680	,,	Guilfoil, David
42634	,,	Simmonds, Frank J.	42681	,,	Gibbs, William
42645	,,	Archibald, Henry	42682	,,	Greaves, Percy S.
42644	Act.Bmr.	Machray, Robert S.	42684	,,	Grace, Walter
42638	Sh'sm'th	Jones, William J.	42685	,,	Gray, James
42639	,,	Hunter, John	42683	,,	Galbraith, Joseph
42640	,,	Smith, Harry	42686	,,	Haycock, Albert
42641	Saddler	Sinclair, Donald	42687	,,	Herod, William
42643	Wheeler	Durand, Daniel J.	42691	,,	Hainer, Charles
42646	Trumpt'r	Rogers, William P.	42692	,,	Hipper, Aubrey
42647	Gr. or Dr.	Allender, Samuel	42693	,,	Hurrell, Charles
42648	,,	Appleby, Ernest	42694	,,	Hurrell, Albert
42649	,,	Aitken, Archibald	42695	,,	Hubbard, Judson J.
42650	,,	Aitken, Jack	42689	,,	Hillson, George
42651	,,	Abbot, Arthur	42690	,,	Howse, Leonard
42652	,,	Armstrong, John	42700	,,	Jolliffe, Alfred
42654	,,	Bruce, James	42701	,,	Jones, Morris
42655	,,	Brakefield, Geo. W.	42696	,,	Jackson, Ernest F.
42658	,,	Barker, Herbert D.	42697	,,	Jones, Charles
42659	,,	Ball, Frank	42699	,,	Johnson, William
42657	,,	Burgess, Charles E.	42698	,,	Irving, Harry J.
42660	,,	Burkitt, Frederick	42703	,,	Kempster, Arthur
42653	,,	Bishop, Alfred	42706	,,	Kern, Harry
42656	,,	Buttery, Percy A.	42704	,,	Key, Herbert
42661	,,	Cockran, Sam	42702	,,	Knowsley, Thomas
42662	,,	Clarke, Eric Jones	42705	,,	Kerr, John
42663	,,	Craig, William R.	42707	,,	Livingstone, Joseph
42665	,,	Cutting, Charles	42708	,,	Large, Samuel
42667	,,	Currin, William J.	42709	,,	Lippiatt, Frank

Canadian Pacific—The Empire's Greatest Railway.

286 AMMUNITION COLUMN, 3RD BRIGADE, C.F.A.—cont.

Regl. No.	Rank.	Name.	Regl. No.	Rank.	Name.
42710	Gr. or Dr.	Ladley, John	42743	Gr. or Dr.	Smith, Henry G.
42714	"	McRae, John E.	42744	"	Sheerer, William
42715	"	McLean, Donald	42745	"	Smith, Harry W.
42724	"	McKay, John	42747	"	Smith, Richard
42711	"	Myron, Kenneth	42748	"	Smith, Charles W.
42712	"	Mitchell, Edward	42749	"	Saunders, Everton A.
42713	"	Methuen, Arthur	42750	"	Sprague, William
42716	"	Major, Horace H.	42751	"	Smith, John, Senr.
42717	"	McMillan, Nelson	42752	"	Shee, Albert
42718	"	Majory, Samuel	42855	"	Smith, John, Junr.
42725	"	Macdonald, John	42772	"	Simmonds, Geo. K.
42719	"	Murphy, William	42742	"	Stott, Arthur
42720	"	Miles, George	42746	"	Scott, Samuel
42722	"	Moyes, Alexander	42741	"	Slade, George
42723	"	Munroe, William	42753	"	Travis, Albert
42721	"	Martin, Edward	42754	"	Tuck, Harry
42773	"	Milburn, Daniel	42756	"	Tuff, Thomas
42854	"	Meehan, George	42759	"	Tasker, Benjamin
42726	"	Neale, John C.	42754	"	Taylor, Jabaz
42727	"	O'Neill, John	42757	"	Townley, David R.
42728	"	Petley, Walter J.	42758	"	Teale, Eli Leslie
42729	"	Phillips, Joseph B.	42770	"	Vincent, Stanley
42730	"	Page, George K.	42768	"	Vine, Herbert
42732	"	Peers, Harry L.	42769	"	Vines, George
42731	"	Papworth, Charles	42760	"	White, Matthew
42736	"	Robb, James	42761	"	Williams, Frederick
42733	"	Robb, Ernest G.	42762	"	Walker, William J.
42735	"	Ross, Ernest	42764	"	Warren, Walter
42737	"	Ramsay, William H.	42767	"	Walker, Richard
42734	"	Rennardson, Harold	42763	"	Wareham, Stanley
42738	"	Stevens, John Henry	42765	"	Walters, Alfred
42740	"	Simpson, David			

No. 1, HEAVY BATTERY.

Major ... ... Magee, Frank Cormack
Captain ... ... Hall, Geo. Ernest
Lieutenant (Brevet-Captain) Irving, William Alexander
" ... ... Ryan, John Alfred
" ... ... Leach, Richard James (R.C.A.)

Attached.

Veterinary Officer ... ... Caudry, M. T. A. (C.A.V.C.)
Paymaster ... ... Hon. Captain Lockhart Allen Chown

Regl. No.	Rank.	Name.	Regl. No.	Rank.	Name.
43222	B.S.M.	Ryan, Francis A.	43020	Act. Sgt.	Buckland, Thomas A.
43010	B.Q.M.S.	Cruchley, Alfred C.	43013	Sergt.	Fisher, A. Wellesley
43218	Pay Sgt.	Billings, Charles A.	43016	"	Hermitage, George A.

Canadian Pacific—The Empire's Greatest Railway.

No. 1, HEAVY BATTERY, C.F.A.—cont. 287

Regl. No.	Rank	Name.	Regl. No.	Rank	Name.
43009	Sergt.	Hopkins, Charles W.	43069	Gunner	Bouchard, Arthur
43012	,,	Glasgow, Samuel D.	43070	,,	Bousquet, Frederick
43019	,,	Litolff, Herbert	43071	,,	Bradford, Gilbert
43011	,,	Robblee, Charles C.	43072	,,	Brown, G.
43023	Corpl.	Brown, Sidney	43073	,,	Buchan, William
43024	,,	Davis, Albert	43074	,,	Bull, Charles
43025	,,	Dickson, Robert S.	43075	,,	Bullock, William
43022	,,	Harvey, Frank	43076	,,	Burns, A. G.
43014	,,	Jennings, George H.	43077	,,	Burrows, G.
43026	,,	Kirby, Sidney	43078	,,	Buttrey, Arthur
43017	,,	McHaffie, William	43079	,,	Callaghan, Thomas
43044	Act. Cpl.	Kerrick, James	43080	,,	Cameron, John
43030	,,	Angell, Joseph	43082	,,	Carroll, A.
43021	Bombr.	Bell, Ernest	43083	,,	Channon, Fredk. R.
43029	,,	Benton, Percy	43084	,,	Charboneau, Frank
43039	,,	Mather, Charles	43085	,,	Chevrier, William
43041	,,	Maybury, Henry D.	43086	,,	Clancy, William
43027	,,	Robertson, James	43087	,,	Clarioux, Ernest
43055	Act.Bmr.	Anderson, Bruce A.	43034	,,	Clarke, Robert C.
43137	,,	Gardner, Charles	43088	,,	Cobb, Percy
43035	,,	Hobson, William	43089	,,	Cochrane, Alex.
43133	,,	Inglis, James L.	43091	,,	Cooper, Alexander M.
43147	,,	Le-Brun, Mark	43090	,,	Cooper, Edward
43036	,,	Markell, Oliver	43092	,,	Cowell, W. R.
43037	,,	McMillen, Colin	43093	,,	Crawshaw, Harry
43033	,,	Miller, J. S.	43096	,,	Crisp, John
43031	,,	Noble, David	43094	,,	Crisp, William
43167	,,	Paul, John	43097	,,	Davies, Major
43032	,,	Sales, George E.	41771	,,	Davis, Edward
43038	,,	Stansfield, Joseph P.	43098	,,	Davy, T. H.
43046	,,	Tucker, E. R. H.	43099	,,	Day, Norman
43042	Far. Sgt.	Prinn, William C. V.	43100	,,	Delisle, Romeo
43043	Saddler	Valois, James	43102	,,	Denman, Reg. W.
43045	Wheeler	McLennon, Geo.M.M.	43101	,,	Desmarchais, W.
43046	,,	Warner, W. C.	43051	Trumpt'r	Doetzel, Frederick
43068	Sh'sm'th	Bonnette, Ernest	43103	Gunner	Dominique, Wilfred
43049	,,	Langford, Fredk. J.	43104	,,	Dewar, Robert
43047	,,	May, Victor W.	43082	,,	Docherty, Jos.
43052	Gunner	Abbott, Rowland	43106	,,	Doyle, Patrick J.
43053	,,	Ahearn, Robert	43107	,,	Drummond, Harold
43054	,,	Aird, Alfred	43108	,,	Duncan, James
43056	,,	Archer, Rupert	43109	,,	Dymock, John
43058	Pioneer	Barnett, John	43110	,,	Edwards, Stanley
43215	Gunner	Barrett, S	43112	,,	Essex, Llew.
43059	,,	Beaubien, Albert	43111	,,	Evans, Daniel
43060	,,	Beaver, Wilfred	43113	,,	Fletcher, Alfred W.
43062	,,	Bell, John	43114	,,	Foley, George
43063	,,	Bennett, Fred	43115	,,	Forgette, Jos.
43064	,,	Bissonette, A.	43116	,,	Foster, Frederick
43065	,,	Bodkin, Frederick J.	43117	,,	Garnish, P. E.
43066	,,	Boileau, Romeo	43118	,,	Glennie, George
43067	,,	Boisvert, Arthur	43119	,,	Groom, Frederick

Canadian Pacific—The Empire's Greatest Railway.

No. 1, HEAVY BATTERY, C.F.A.—cont.

Regl. No.	Rank	Name	Regl. No.	Rank	Name
43040	Gunner	Hadley, William	43169	Gunner	Payette, Rene
43121	,,	Haley, James	43170	,,	Pemberton, H. V.
43994	,,	Hall, F.	43172	,,	Penrod, C. E.
43122	,,	Handford, F. G.	43173	,,	Pepin, Gus.
43123	,,	Hannaford, Richard	43174	,,	Perkins, Ernest
43124	,,	Harris, George	43175	,,	Philp, Fred
43125	,,	Hart, W. J.	43176	,,	Polley, Frank
43050	Trumpt'r	Hayes, John	43177	,,	Porthin, Emile
43126	Gunner	Healey, Thomas	43178	,,	Quirk, Matthew
43127	,,	Heideman, James C.	43179	,,	Racicot, Lucius
43128	,,	Henley, Arthur	43180	,,	Ramage, John G.
43129	,,	Hill, Rowland	43181	,,	Reilly, John
43130	,,	Hiseman, Fredk. J.	43182	,,	Riddler, Harry
43131	,,	Holding, John	43183	,,	Robinson, John
43132	,,	Hope, Thomas	43184	,,	Rowley, Edgar
43028	,,	Houghton, J. R.	43185	,,	Saddler, Harry S.
43134	,,	Johnanassen, Bertel	43186	,,	Senior, Harry
43135	,,	Jowett, Ellis	43187	,,	Seymour, Emile
43136	,,	Kear, Allen	44039	,,	Stackhouse, J. C.
43138	,,	Kelly, F. C.	43188	,,	Stein, Edward
43139	,,	Kempton, Charles	43189	,,	Stanley, D. McN.
43140	,,	Kilfoyle, William	43190	,,	Stephenson, John
43048	,,	Kind, P.	44038	,,	Stop, W. C.
43141	,,	Kind, O.	43191	,,	Sunborg, Arthur
43142	,,	Kinnear, Alfred	43192	,,	Taylor Edwin D.
43143	,,	Knight, Launcelot	43193	,,	Thompson, W.
43144	,,	Labrache, John J.	43194	,,	Thompson, W.
43145	,,	Lamb, James	43195	,,	Thomson, Rbt. P.
43146	,,	Le-Brun, Ernest	43196	,,	Timms, Arthur C.
43149	,,	Linsell, Sydney N.	43197	,,	Thorogood, Francis
43150	,,	Lonsdale, W. P.	43198	,,	Treger, Auguste
43152	,,	Mahony, James	43199	,,	Twaits, John
43153	,,	Mansfield, Percy F.	43200	,,	Walker, Reginald W.
43154	,,	Marchant, Herbert	43201	,,	Wares, Percy A.
43155	,,	Marsden, Wm. J.	40202	,,	Whitefoot, E.
43156	,,	Martin, Roderick	40203	,,	White, James
43157	,,	Meldrum, James	43204	,,	Whiteman, Robert
43158	,,	Miller, Harry	43205	,,	Wilcox, John
43160	,,	Murphy, James	43206	,,	Wilkes, Charles
43163	,,	Macdonald, James	43207	,,	Wilkes, George
43164	,,	Neil, William J.	43208	,,	Wilson, Thomas
43165	,,	O'Connor, C.	43209	,,	Wolfenden, James
43166	,,	Partrick, William	43210	,,	Woods, Sydney L.
35514	,,	Patterson, W. F.	43211	,,	Wright, Guy W.
43168	,,	Paxton, Henry	43212	,,	Young, Douglas

Attached.

33714	Corpl.	Richardson, F. S. (C.A.M.C.) Water Detail	33715	Private	Latimer, William W. (C.A.M.C.) (Water Detail)

Canadian Pacific—The Empire's Greatest Railway

ROYAL CANADIAN HORSE ARTILLERY.

HEADQUARTERS.

Commanding Officer	Lieut.-Colonel Henri Alexandre Panet, D.S.O.
Adjutant	Captain Henry Eversley Boak
,, ...	,, George Sackville Browne
Paymaster	Hon. Captain William Gimblett
Chaplain	,, Rev. John A. Fortier

Regl. No.	Rank.	Name.	Regl. No.	Rank.	Name.
5053	Mtr.Gr.	Hird, Walter (W.O).	6260	Gunner	Clarke, F. E. J.
1531	R.S.M.	McIntyre, William (W.O.)	4607	Driver	Gigeurre, Ovilla
			5178	,,	Guy, George
6264	Q.M.Sgt.	Robert, Arthur A.	5031	,,	Huard, Henri
5341	,,	Marshall, Ernest F.	5867	Gunner	Jones, Albert E.
5694	Sergt.	Warburton, Egton	5844	,,	Kent, Frederick W.
5757	Corpl.	Kennard, Harry	5735	,,	Longshaw, Harry F.

Attached.

433   Arm. S. S.   Phillips, Harold (C.O.C.)

"A" BATTERY.

Major	Leslie, James Norman Stuart
Captain	Elkins, William Henry Pferinger
Lieutenant	Benson, Frederick Merrett
,, ...	MacPherson, Huntley Wilson
,, ...	Hughes, Laughlin Macleod
Medical Officer	Lieutenant Eric Charles Henry Winderler
Veterinary Officer	Major John Henry Wilson

Regl. No.	Rank.	Name.	Regl. No.	Rank.	Name.
4273	S.M.A.	Turner, Thomas J. (W.O.)	6257	Sergt.	Stacey, Gifford S.
			5691	,,	Setterington, G. W.
4694	B.S.M.I.	MacDonald, John H.	4801	Corpl.	Bilodean, Alfred
5097	B.Q.M.S.	Eggleston, T. W.	5635	,,	Clarke, Richard
5261	S.Sgt.F'r.	Blackely, Albert	5656	,,	McDermid, William
5987	Sgl. Sgt.	Atkinson, Albert	4495	,,	Dervent, Frederick C.
5772	Sergt.	Batten, Alexander	5826	,,	Hawker, Wm. A. G.
5690	,,	Botting, Cecil George	5834	,,	Hayes, John
5703	,,	Dalghleish, James	5847	,,	Knapton, William
6261	,,	Fencott, Thomas H.	5661	,,	Morris, George E.
3327	,,	Hubley, Edward C.	5734	Bombr.	Boutiller, Arthur
6260	,,	Inglis, Roger W.	5677	,,	Dennis, William
5963	,,	Lang, John	5110	,,	Newman, William
4863	,,	Lowrie, William	4774	,,	O'Leary, John
5609	,,	McKinley, Peter M.	5860	,,	Prince, Charles G.

Canadian Pacific—The Empire's Greatest Railway.

T

290 ROYAL CANADIAN HORSE ARTILLERY —cont.

Regl. No.	Rank.	Name.
5707	Bombr.	Simmonds, H. Wm.
5697	,,	Wolfe, Charles F.
6234	Saddler	Strain, William
5996	Wheeler	Conacher, John
6268	,,	Rider, James
6209	Trumpt'r	Hiscott, Bernard C.
5730	,,	Smith, Sidney
4464	Gr. or Dr.	Abba, Edmond
6251	,,	Adams, Walter
4860	,,	Aiken, Alex. I.
5933	,,	Aitken, Thomas
3522	,,	Akerley, Harvey H.
6214	,,	Ancrum, George H.
6206	,,	Anderson, Duncan A.
5496	Trumpt'r	Andrews, John H.
5911	Gr. or Dr.	Astley, Willoughby
5982	,,	Balmer, Thomas S.
5848	,,	Beckingham, F.
6231	,,	Bevis, John William
6208	,,	Biggar, Ernest B.
5944	,,	Bird, Joseph E.
5943	,,	Bird, William I.
5932	,,	Bissex, Davey Charles
5940	,,	Black, George
5127	,,	Blackman, Ernest
5993	,,	Blackman, Henry
6249	,,	Bond, Frederick H.
5927	,,	Boucher, Jack S.
5976	,,	Bradshaw, Leonard
6270	,,	Brander, Arthur P.
5949	,,	Brown, Percy
6245	,,	Burnside, William G.
5306	,,	Burrows, Charles
5171	,,	Cabrie, James
6240	,,	Carter, Charles E.
5928	,,	Cass, William E.
5953	,,	Chainery, Richard G.
5968	,,	Chainey, Charles E.
5951	,,	Chittick, John Irwin
6210	,,	Clark, William
5938	,,	Codd, Ronald C.
5952	,,	Coker, Frederick
5904	,,	Condor, Patrick
5920	,,	Countryman, G. A.
6263	,,	Cummings, G. G.
5925	,,	Curtis, George B.
6240	,,	Daniel, Godfrey D.
5983	,,	Davies, Frederick E.
5851	,,	Davis, Richard
5995	,,	De May, George
5670	,,	Dennis, Charles
5785	,,	Denton, William

Regl. No.	Rank.	Name.
5191	Gr. or Dr.	DeWilde, Alfonse
5709	,,	Dockerty, Charles
6241	,,	Dore, Gustave
5950	,,	Douglas, Robert
6269	,,	Elliott, Joseph L
5869	,,	Endersby, Frank
6224	,,	Evans, Frank
4549	,,	Ferrier, William
5964	,,	Fitzhenry, John
2601	,,	Fournier, George J.
5902	,,	Fox, Christopher
5984	,,	Freeman, Cedric
5958	,,	French, George
6218	,,	Fry, William James
5990	,,	Fuller, Vernon B.
6229	,,	Garnett, Lawrence H.
5890	,,	Gatland, Ernest J.
5170	,,	Gendron, Henry
6238	,,	Gettrall, William
4862	,,	Gingrass, Joseph T.
4128	,,	Glenn, Matthew
5930	,,	Green, Stanley Alfred
5917	,,	Greening, George
5818	,,	Groves, John
6252	,,	Hair, William L.
6244	,,	Harris, Ralph
4142	,,	Harrisson, William J.
6248	,,	Hay, William Hendrie
5716	,,	Herbert, William H.
5921	,,	Hobbs, George Stone
5971	,,	Hobson, George J.
6259	,,	Hogg, Albert M.
5948	,,	Honeysett, Hugh K.
4535	,,	Hopkins, Walter
6238	,,	Howard, George
5961	,,	Howe, Herbert L.
6262	,,	Howes, Thomas
6246	,,	Howlett, William
5946	,,	Hoyd, Percy Alfred
5913	,,	Husband, Alexander
5991	,,	Hyslop, Robert C.
6246	,,	Illingworth, George
5689	,,	Jamieson, Joseph F.
6201	,,	Jerram, William
5995	,,	Johning, William
4494	Bombr.	Johnson, Edward
6254	Gr.or Dr.	Johnson, Stewart
5945	,,	Jones, John
5121	,,	Kelly, Thomas
5759	,,	Kemp, Arthur
5704	,,	Kendall, William T.
6216	,,	Kent, William

Canadian Pacific—The Empire's Greatest Railway.

ROYAL CANADIAN HORSE ARTILLERY—cont. 291

Regl. No.	Rank.	Name.	Regl. No.	Rank.	Name.
5865	Gr. or Dr.	Kinghorn, Allen	4845	Gr. or Dr.	Richardson, James R.
4383	,,	Koehler, Charles H.	6200	,,	Robb, Gordon Bell
5688	,,	Lafferty, William	6271	,,	Rose, Bert
5947	,,	Landstrom, Erick	6207	,,	Ross, Andrew S.
5922	,,	Leach, John O.	5926	,,	Ross, Arthur Cecil
5959	,,	Le Barre, Gordon	1552	,,	Ryder, Edward
6221	,,	Lee, Harold Vernon	6220	,,	Salaman, Erick J. S.
5924	,,	Lewis, Harry Stewart	6230	,,	Salvage, George K.
5956	Bombr.	Lewis, Walter Aiken	6232	,,	Scholfield, Frank F.
5857	Gr.or Dr.	London, Edward	5736	,,	Scott, George
6227	,,	Maddox, Jerry	5765	,,	Seymour, Alfred J.
6226	Bombr.	Maich, Joseph	6253	,,	Sharpe, William Geo.
5997	Gr.or Dr.	Marke, Thomas	5713	,,	Shepherd, Davis
6205	,,	Marr, William	6243	,,	Shore, Richard
6212	,,	Martin, William	6211	,,	Siegrist, Earl Arthur
6203	,,	Mattinson, George F.	5868	,,	Simmons, Herbert
5954	,,	Miles, Roscoe Franklin	6228	,,	Simpson, Duncan P.
5673	,,	Mitchell, Arthur Wm.	6267	,,	Smedley, William A.
5908	,,	Mitchell, John	5141	,,	Smith, William
5985	,,	Moeller, August	6202	,,	Sparrow, Stanley
5916	,,	Moore, Allen C.	5992	,,	Staite, Harry J.
5960	,,	Moss, William	5957	,,	Stanley, Robert
5940	,,	MacAuley, F. R.	5771	,,	Steele, Walter James
6265	,,	MacKenzie, John K.	5913	,,	Stephens, John
5973	,,	McBeth, John	5980	,,	Stoddart, John
5919	,,	McCarthy, James	5915	,,	Struthers, Norman S.
5998	,,	McDonald, William	6225	,,	Stuart, Richard
5972	,,	McEwan, John Alex.	6235	,,	Talbott, Arthur
5934	,,	McIsaacs, John D.	6237	,,	Telfer, John Andrew
5910	,,	McMillan, Albert E.	5969	,,	Thompson, Wm. W.
5926	,,	McNair, James	6239	,,	Thorne, Frederick J.
5935	,,	McVeigh, Wilbert	5784	,,	Thurston, Lloyd Roy
5793	,,	Norwich, Alfred Chas.	5766	,,	Tibbetts, Alfred
5770	,,	Norwood, Percy Wm.	5986	,,	Tromba, Thomas
5967	,,	Nursey, George	5824	,,	Trusler, Thomas
5936	,,	O'Connell, George	5988	,,	Unwin, Shadforth H.
5975	,,	Palser, Sidney Charles	5763	,,	Wake, Joseph Albert
5914	,,	Parker, Robert Frank	5974	,,	Walker, John
5760	,,	Peacock, Andrew	5977	,,	Wallace, John Moffat
5000	,,	Pepin, Amedee	5987	,,	Ward, Alfred
5994	,,	Percival, Alfred	5901	Bombr.	Webster, Albert
6204	,,	Pinkerton, James S. R.	6252	Gr. orDr.	Welch, Alfred
5962	,,	Plaskett, Walter G.	5981	,,	Wheatley, Arthur
5810	,,	Potter, Albert E.	5842	,,	Whiting, John
5929	,,	Price, William Henry	6233	,,	Williams, Isaac Chas.
5900	,,	Pullin, Henry Reg.	5909	,,	Wilson, Alex. McC.
5746	,,	Purdy, Herbert	6256	,,	Wright, Fredk. H.
4941	,,	Purvis, Archibald	6258	,,	Yeates, William A.
5978	,,	Ramsbottom, Ernest	4905	,,	Young, Clarence A.

Attached—C.A.M.C. (*Water Detail*).

33710 Private Glanville, E. W. | 33711 Private Covington, C. J.

Canadian Pacific—The Empire's Greatest Railway.

T 2

ROYAL CANADIAN HORSE ARTILLERY—cont.

"B" BATTERY.

Major	Eaton, Vernon
Captain	Hagarty, William Grasett
Lieut. and Bvt. Capt.	Tremaine, Arthur Victor
Lieutenant	Lafferty, Heber Pembroke
"	Bishop, Clarence Vivian
Medical Officer	Lieut. Carr, O. E.
Veterinary Officer	" Souillard, P. P.

Regl. No.	Rank.	Name.	Regl. No.	Rank.	Name.
5248	Q.M.S.I.	Finney, Wilfred J.	6039	Gr. or Dr.	Arseneau, Charles
4129	B.Q.M.S.	Fowler, Herbert	6031	"	Askunas, Gilbert
5106	Sergt.	Adam, Charles	6052	"	Ashby, Percival
5243	"	Aldridge, Frank	6046	"	Atkinson, Arthur E.
5398	"	Gray, William	6047	"	Atkinson, John F.
5424	"	Hewitt, Thos.	6062	"	Austin, Adam
5667	"	McKinney, Jos. H.	5877	"	Ayers, Thomas Owen
5589	"	Salmon, Ed. W.	6145	"	Bailey, Wm.
5631	"	Stacey, Wm. John	6017	"	Barber, Robert H. W.
5884	Corpl.	Barter, Charles F.	6116	"	Barnbrook, F. J.
5363	"	Bland, John Henry	6013	"	Barrand, Albert E.
5592	"	Campbell, Michael W.	6037	"	Bartholomew, Edwin
5843	"	George, Edward T.	6091	"	Batstone, Frank O.
5543	"	Marshall, Charles A.	5718	"	Battle, Joseph
5845	"	Moore, Samuel	5849	"	Beckett, Walter G.
5798	"	Ridley, Archibald	6027	"	Benbow, George
4602	Wheeler	Smith, William	6141	"	Berry, Richard
6069	Bombr.	Champion, Ed.	6100	"	Biart, Eugene F.
5407	"	Clarke, George	6131	"	Bladen, Don Evelyn
5888	"	Considine, Michael F.	6148	Sh'sm'th	Blagg, James
5421	"	Crane, Wm A.	6057	Gr. or Dr.	Blythe, C. J.
6085	"	Davidson, Jas.	6148	"	Bracken, Kenneth, O.
5883	"	Dennes, Fredk.	5899	"	Brown, James W.
5897	"	Dodgson, Wm. C.	6089	"	Brown, Thomas E.
6054	"	Horswill, Hugh S.	6024	"	Cain, Richard C
5850	"	King, Ed. Arthur	6050	"	Campbell, Austin M.
6053	"	Lawrence, Benjamin	6106	"	Campbell, E. A. F.
5838	Act. Bmr.	McFarlane, Henry W.	5565	"	Campbell, Fredk. J.
5813	"	Reid, Samuel H.	6124	"	Carr, Frederick R.
1897	"	Vanalstine, Richard	5837	"	Carroll, Joseph
5520	Trumpt'r	Allcock, James	5539	"	Carter, Albert E.
5878	"	King, Frank	5905	"	Carter, Arthur Daly
6095	"	Lindsay, George W.	5906	"	Carter, Gerald
5808	Gr. or Dr.	Adair, Harry	5070	"	Chaplin, Wm.
4381	"	Aldcroft, George T.	5384	"	Clarabutt, Harold
6030	"	Allen, Herbert	6001	"	Clark, Chas.
5594	"	Allen, Edward J.	6094	"	Clark, James Dunbar
6015	"	Anderson, James L.	5862	Sh'sm'th	Cole, Edmond S.
6092	"	Anderson, William	6123	Gr. or Dr.	Coles, Herbert John
5593	"	Andrews, Ernest	6111	"	Cooke, Irving Deming
6063	"	Appleton, William	6121	"	Cox, Alfred Valentine
6061	"	Apps, F.	6043	"	Crossfield, Frank

Canadian Pacific—The Empire's Greatest Railway.

ROYAL CANADIAN HORSE ARTILLERY—cont. 293

Regl. No.	Rank.	Name.	Regl. No.	Rank.	Name.
5816	Gr. or Dr.	Cudbertson, Fred	5564	Gr. or Dr.	Le Blanc, Gerald
5272	,,	Cunningham, Jas.	5582	,,	Lockhart, Horace
6028	,,	D'Arcy, Joyce	6130	Sh'sm'th	Lord, Victor
5874	,,	Day, Roy	5539	Gr. or Dr.	Lowe, James
5467	,,	De Serres, Rene	6004	,,	Lynch, James
6059	,,	Dice, Thomas Henry	6073	,,	Malcolm, John Warn
6150	Sh'sm'th	Doughty, Albert E.	4004	,,	Manning, George
5144	Gr. or Dr.	Done, Frank	5835	,,	Mansfield, Frederick
5777	,,	Edwards, William C.	6118	,,	Marshall, Walter
6032	,,	Ellis, Alexander H.	5896	,,	Martin, John
6051	,,	Ellison, Le Roy	6019	,,	Meadus, Reginald H.
6146	,,	Ellwood, George	6060	,,	Mercier, Philip
6101	,,	Elwood, Clarence Ira	6099	,,	Miles, Ch. Russell
6147	,,	Evans, Robert	5823	,,	Moore, Ed.
5414	,,	Farmer, Neil	6110	,,	McCallum, Alasdair S.
6098	,,	Forbes, Robert James	6135	,,	McCue, Alva R.
3346	,,	Fradette, John George	5422	,,	McDonald, Charles
6021	,,	Franks, John Joseph	6071	,,	McGrath, Charles
5881	Sh'sm'th	Gash, George	5563	,,	McKay, Lemuel C.
6001	Gr. or Dr.	George, Alex. H.	6134	,,	McKay, Leonard Earl
6132	,,	Gill, Ernest E.	6083	,,	McKinley, Roy
6125	,,	Gimblett, Thomas	6067	,,	McLeod, David H.
6045	,,	Goerke, George	6108	,,	McMillan, William
5573	,,	Goldfinch, Alfred	4967	,,	Nelson, Arthur
6035	,,	Greaves, James N.	6105	,,	Nelson, Berkeley
6104	,,	Hammond, George	6143	,,	Nodder, Frederick
6068	,,	Hammond, Weston	6064	,,	O'Brien, Martin P.
6080	,,	Hancock, Walter	5786	,,	O'Connell, Charles
6081	,,	Hanson, Benjamin	5225	,,	O'Donoughue, John
6002	,,	Harper, Roy	5598	,,	O'Hara, Terence
6133	,,	Havens, Wilfred	6126	,,	Ostlund, Gillis
5595	,,	Hayes, Ed.	6018	,,	Paverley, Fred
6010	,,	Heffernan, Robert M.	6144	,,	Pearson, Fredk.
5599	,,	Hermann, Harry	6097	,,	Pelkey, Ernest
5819	,,	Hoelke, William	6119	,,	Pentz, David Winfred
6012	,,	Holland, Gerald A.	5529	,,	Phillips, Ernest
6022	,,	Howard, Everett, H.	6088	,,	Place, George
6055	,,	Howell, Walter	5827	,,	Plumpton, Floyd L.
6112	,,	Howden, Wm. Y.	6024	,,	Potts, John Charles
6113	,,	Humphries, W. G.	6056	,,	Powell, William
6086	,,	Hunter, Jn. E.	6065	,,	Pridgent, Montague J.
5448	,,	Hunter, Wm.	6136	,,	Reid, Addison
6036	,,	Ingram, Courtenay A.	6007	,,	Riddle, Thomas
5891	,,	Izzett, John	6107	,,	Robinson, Geo. H.
5553	,,	Jenkins, Thomas H.	6034	,,	Robinson, Wm. Henry
6033	,,	Jones, Herbert T.	6049	,,	Robinson, William F.
5392	,,	Kelly, William	6042	,,	Rogers, Clifford
6103	,,	Kennedy, James	6008	,,	Rooney, John
6078	,,	King, Cyril	6084	,,	Rycroft, Arthur
6096	,,	King, Edward Mark	6140	,,	Ryan, John D.
6120	,,	Kitchen, Charles H.	5433	,,	Scott, Francis Dow
5801	,,	Lace, Otho	6093	,,	Scott, George McKean

Canadian Pacific—The Empire's Greatest Railway.

ROYAL CANADIAN HORSE ARTILLERY—cont.

Regl. No.	Rank.	Name.	Regl. No.	Rank.	Name.
5253	Gr. or Dr.	Self, George	6025	Gr. or Dr.	Sutherland, R. D.
6016	,,	Sheppard, Harold S.	6114	,,	Taylor, Alfred Richd.
6072	,,	Shepherd, Henry T.	6003	,,	Terry, Saml. Jordan
6076	,,	Sherlock, David	6138	,,	Thurston, Roy H.
6029	,,	Simms, Sherman H.	6109	,,	Tullis, William M.
6006	,,	Simpson, James	6137	,,	Twelves, Claude F. H.
5898	,,	Skates, William John	6127	,,	Urquhart, Grant Wm.
6038	,,	Skinner, James	5894	,,	Valiquette, Alfred
6115	,,	Sky, George Edward	6122	,,	Waters, Stanley
6087	,,	Smith, Blanchard E.	4709	,,	Wathen, Henry
6102	,,	Smith, Alfred Francis	5893	,,	Warner, Edward
6058	,,	Stapley, Allan A.	6079	,,	Weiss, Cecil G.
5458	,,	Statham, William	5552	,,	Welch, Frank
5548	,,	Stead, Wilfred	6139	,,	Wheeler, Ronald W.
6048	,,	Streight, Samuel	5889	,,	Wiggins, Norman
5903	,,	Stewart, Alexander L.	5578	,,	Wilson, Wm. H.
6149	Cpl. S. S.	Ste. Croix, Philip T.D.	6066	,,	Wilson, Robert
6025	Gr.or Dr.	Sutherland, Robert D.	6006	,,	Winning, Robert
6129	,,	Steere, Edward	6023	,,	Wiskar, Stanley
6117	,,	Stevens, Jack Stanley	6020	,,	Woods, Alfred
6090	,,	Summer, Reg. G.	6128	,,	Woods, Robert

Attached—C.A.M.C. (Water Detail).

33712 Private Cassidy, P. J. | 33713 Private Fortier, C.

DIVISIONAL ENGINEERS.

HEADQUARTERS.

Lieut.-Colonel ... ... Lieut.-Colonel C. J. Armstrong
Major ... ... Major T. V. Anderson
Lieutenant ... ... Lieutenant J. B. P. Dunbar
Paymaster ... ... Hon. Captain A. J. G. Davidson
Medical Officer ... ... Captain P. Poisson, C.A.M.C. (attached)
Veterinary Officer ... ... Lieutenant A. B. Outcliffe, C.A.V.C. (attached)
Chaplain ... ... Hon. Captain Rev. A. H. McGreer

Regl. No.	Rank.	Name.	Regl. No.	Rank.	Name.
5581	Q.M.Sgt.	Parker, C. W.	5590	Sapper	High, W.
5552	Lce.-Sgt.	Scott, F. E. B.	5582	,,	Laidley, P. W.
5586	Sapper	Bates, W. O.	5584	,,	McGregor, T. N.
5588	,,	Bolton, —	5589	,,	Pearson, S. L.
5587	,,	Burns, J.	5583	,,	Wright, R. H.

Attached, C.A.M.C., 33681 Private Porter, H.

Canadian Pacific—The Empire's Greatest Railway.

DIVISIONAL ENGINEERS.

1st FIELD COMPANY.

Major	... ...	Melville, W. W.
Captain	... ...	Macphail, A.
Lieutenant	... ...	Vince, E. R.
,,	... ...	Hay, B. M.
,,	... ...	Cosgrove, J. P.
,,	... ...	Gendron, F. S.

Attached.

Captain	... ...	Hodgins, F. O.
,,	... ...	Fell, J. P.
Lieutenant	... ...	Rankin, F. S. /*Fé 2b*

Regl. No.	Rank.	Name.	Regl. No.	Rank.	Name.
5001	C.S.M.	Hudson, S.	5159	Lce.-Cpl.	McJannett, D.
5002	C.Q.M.S.	Turner, R. E. D.	5414	,,	Macphail, J. B.
5003	Sergt.	Botting, W.	5027	,,	Smith, H.
5005	,,	Beasley, F.	5022	,,	Smith, W. M.
5006	,,	English, J. H.	5032	,,	Wood, J. A.
5012	,,	Graham, A. E.	5037	Sapper	Acott, W.
5008	,,	Roberts, C.	5039	,,	Austin, H. L.
5209	,,	Smith-Rewse, M. B.W.	5034	,,	Aedy, A. G.
5010	,,	Serpell, W. D.	5035	,,	Allan, J.
5009	Far. Sgt.	Pringle, T.	5036	,,	Amer, H.
5079	Sgt. Cook	Chappell, A.	5040	,,	Andison, T. W.
5240	Corpl.	Bliss, L.	5041	,,	Brooker, C.
5013	,,	Booth, L. C.	5556	,,	Baker, H. S.
5319	,,	Free, H. B.	5042	,,	Bragdon, J. O.
5014	,,	Gradisky, C. G. E.	5043	,,	Bowser, H. S.
5010	,,	Mooers, R. C.	5044	,,	Branch, A. J.
5011	,,	Paul, D.	5047	,,	Balch, W. C.
5016	2nd-Cpl.	Allen, L. E.	5048	,,	Blackwell, R. E.
5017	,,	Anthony, H. J.	5049	,,	Blowers, A. E.
5021	,,	Holland, H.	5050	,,	Bennett, W. C.
5324	,,	Jammett, J. M.	5237	,,	Beynon, I.
5015	,,	Melville, A.	5051	,,	Blacklock, T. B.
5019	,,	Ross, A.	5052	,,	Blue, F. N.
5325	,,	Sersons, J. H.	5239	,,	Bridgewater, E. J.
5020	,,	Stedham, E. G.	5053	,,	Bright, C. J.
5338	Lce.-Cpl.	Bate, C. B.	5054	,,	Bird, A. S.
5340	,,	Birkett, E. H.	5055	,,	Bryan, J. F.
5341	,,	Bolton, R. A.	5056	,,	Brooks, F. G.
5023	,,	Brown, W. H.	5060	,,	Brown, J. O.
5025	,,	Dickinson, R.	5061	,,	Brown, T.
5028	,,	Field, G. B.	5059	,,	Brydon, K.
5029	,,	Fitzgerald, H.	5057	,,	Bogle, G. S.
5030	,,	Gordon, K.	5058	,,	Bowden, H. W.
5031	,,	Greaves, F. G. H.	5344	,,	Boyle, P.

Canadian Pacific—The Empire's Greatest Railway.

DIVISIONAL ENGINEERS—*cont.*

Regl. No.	Rank.	Name.	Regl. No.	Rank.	Name.
5560	Sapper	Buchanan, W. C.	5112	Sapper	Harmon, B. W.
5062	,,	Craik, C. V.	5113	,,	Hird, J.
5063	,,	Connolly, A. R.	5114	,,	Higson, G.
5064	,,	Carnahan, A.	5117	,,	Hamilton, G.
5065	,,	Code, A. G.	5118	,,	Hardy, E. T.
5067	,,	Charlton, E.	5119	,,	Hill, D. A.
5068	,,	Clark, R.	5120	,,	Hall, B. C.
5069	,,	Cornish, H. E.	5126	,,	Hugh, E. A.
5071	,,	Clark, R. A.	5121	,,	Harper, H.
5073	,,	Carlisle, F.	5123	,,	Herbert, B.
5074	,,	Connell, G. W.	5125	,,	Hodges, E.
5075	,,	Carey, J.	5122	,,	Howarth, H. F.
5076	,,	Campbell, J.	5124	,,	Humphries, R. H. W.
5077	,,	Casement, R. J.	5127	,,	Hunter, J. P.
5072	,,	Chillingworth, G.	5128	,,	Johnson, B.
5078	,,	Coate, K.	5129	,,	Jenkins, T.
5081	,,	Deeves, W. J.	5130	,,	Kemp, A. E.
5082	,,	Dixon, B.	5406	,,	Kerr, A. O.
5083	,,	Davis, A. W.	5131	,,	Kershaw, J. B.
5361	,,	Dougherty, J. W.	5132	,,	Knights, K. M. W.
5084	,,	Davis, C. A.	5034	,,	Longley, A.
5085	,,	Dymond, M. S.	5135	,,	Loxley, F.
5364	,,	Eaton, H. T.	5136	,,	Laidlaw, A.
5086	,,	Edwards, M.	5139	,,	Logue, R.
5087	,,	Evans, A. J. L.	5140	,,	McCulloch, W.
5004	,,	Evans, W. A.	5238	,,	McDougall, E.
5088	,,	Fisher, J. C.	5141	,,	Morrison, T.
5089	,,	Freer, L. H.	5142	,,	McGlashen, W.
5090	,,	Fielding, H.	5143	,,	McMillan, E. S.
5091	,,	Fawcett, C. J.	5144	,,	Milford, F.
5092	,,	Fullerton, G.	5145	,,	McIsaacs, D. H.
5499	,,	Garner, H.	5146	,,	McLeod, W. R.
5101	,,	Guige, J.	5147	,,	Mason, R. T.
5107	,,	Gaitskell, H. G.	5150	,,	Mitchell, J. R.
5094	,,	Gifford, V.	5154	,,	McIntyre, H. P.
5095	,,	Greer, P.	5153	,,	Mabbutt, C. S.
5096	,,	Greenwood, L. V.	5155	,,	McIntosh, J. T.
5097	,,	Green, W. A.	5156	,,	McKenzie, A.
5098	,,	Goad, A.	5157	,,	McPherson, J.
5102	,,	Gilchrist, E.	5158	,,	McIlroy, J.
5103	,,	Golding, K.	5420	,,	May, J. L.
5532	,,	Gordon, E.	5542	,,	Mellor, W. E.
5104	,,	Gray, G. W.	5439	,,	Millymaki, A.
5105	,,	Gillespie, H. S. P.	5160	,,	North, C. B.
5093	,,	Galbraith, A.	5161	,,	Neilson, A.
5106	,,	Gray, L. S.	5162	,,	O'Grady, B. T.
5108	,,	Howie, G.	5163	,,	Otto, H. W.
5109	,,	Hedger, E.	5164	,,	Owens, C.
5383	,,	Harris, H.	5165	,,	O'Connor, A.
5110	,,	Hartley, A.	5443	,,	O'Connor, C. D.
5384	,,	Haryett, H. C.	5166	,,	Oxley, R. E.
5111	,,	Hanna, J. J.	5167	,,	Prince, A. E.

Canadian Pacific—The Empire's Greatest Railway.

DIVISIONAL ENGINEERS—cont. 297

Regl. No.	Rank.	Name.	Regl. No.	Rank.	Name.
5168	Sapper	Pearson, J. M.	5461	Sapper	Shea, A.
5169	,,	Pryke, J. W.	5205	,,	Shrubsall, H.
5170	,,	Pow, J.	5463	,,	Sissons, G. E.
5171	,,	Phillips, A.	5206	,,	Samuels, S. A.
5172	,,	Palmer, W.	5207	,,	Steel, J. D.
5174	,,	Poulson, C.	5208	,,	Sommerville, C.
5177	,,	Phillip, J. R. D.	5197	,,	Sanderson, W. J.
5176	,,	Phillips, R. F.	5547	,,	Smith, L. G.
5178	,,	Philps, E. T. H.	5210	,,	Smithson, E. B.
5175	,,	Poitras, A.	5211	,,	Sutherland, G.
5179	,,	Proulx, E.	5212	,,	Selkirk, W. A.
5180	,,	Qua, A. H.	5464	,,	Spears, D. C.
5182	,,	Ross, C. F. D.	5128	,,	Turner, C. H.
5181	,,	Ridge, H.	5471	,,	Tett, H. B.
5183	,,	Ritchie, G.	5214	,,	Tobin, L. M.
5184	,,	Ransley, A. B.	5215	,,	Taylor, F. N.
5185	,,	Ryan, B. W.	5216	,,	Tompkins, J.
5186	,,	Russell, G.	5217	,,	Terriss, T. G.
5188	,,	Roberts, R. M.	5220	,,	Tuite, R. J.
5189	,,	Robinson, S. F.	5221	,,	Vickers, C.
5190	,,	Revell, G. E.	5226	,,	Whitehouse, W. P.
5191	,,	Reynolds, L. B.	5018	,,	Williams, J.
5193	,,	Reeves, B. S.	5229	,,	Warnock, J.
5187	,,	Revie, C. D.	5230	,,	Wilson, J.
5459	,,	Servage, E. G.	5231	,,	White, C. E.
5194	,,	Smiles, C. B.	5232	,,	Webster, G. B.
5195	,,	Spicer, J.	5233	,,	Warton, R. J. B.
5196	,,	Souter, E.	5234	,,	Woolley, A.
5198	,,	Shaw, A. B.	5222	Bugler	Walkem, W. R.
5200	Driver	Simmonds, W.	5224	Sapper	Walker, E.
5202	Sapper	Sawers, B. L.	5225	,,	Walker, R.
5203	,,	Scott, F. W.	5033	,,	York, A.
5204	,,	Stephenson, G.	5236	,,	Young, H.

2nd FIELD COMPANY.

Major ... ... Lindsay, W. Bethune
Captain ... ... Irving, T. C.
Lieutenant ... ... Robertson, N .R.
,, ... Milne, C. N. G.
,, ... Hertzberg, H. F. H.
,, ... Mathieson, D. M.

Attached.

Lieutenant ... ... Lynn, E. F.
,, ... Bell-Irving, D. P.

Regl. No.	Rank.	Name.	Regl. No.	Rank.	Name.
5301	C.-S.-M.	Chetwynd, G. R.	5303	Sergt.	Craig, J. S.
5302	C.Q.M.S.	McCuaig, O. B.	5307	,,	Robins, D. W.
5412	,,	Lawrence, A. S.	5308	,,	Bell, C. A.

Canadian Pacific—The Empire's Greatest Railway.

DIVISIONAL ENGINEERS—cont.

Regl. No.	Rank.	Name.	Regl. No.	Rank.	Name.
5309	Sergt.	Taylor, J. E.	5355	Sapper	Darley, A.
5310	,,	Ferris, C. B.	5357	,,	Dennehy, J. P.
5321	,,	Tanqueray, J. F. D.	5494	,,	Denton, G. R.
5338	,,	Fiset, J.	5358	,,	Dick, W.
5306	,,	Stern, E. L.	5359	,,	Dickie, J.
5304	Far.-Sgt.	Ellison, H.	5360	,,	Dinnen, R. J.
5313	Corpl.	Brown, W. H.	5080	,,	Dover, G. W. D.
5314	,,	Smith, W. H.	5348	,,	Down, J. H.
5316	,,	McDonald, J. A.	5362	,,	Dyer, W.
5317	,,	Ollivier, R. H.	5365	,,	Elliott, W. J.
5318	,,	Bevan, W. H. B.	5367	,,	Embleton, H. J. V.
5315	Sec.-Cpl.	McCutcheon, H. E.	5363	,,	Ewing, E. G.
5323	,,	Waugh, W. E.	5496	,,	Fisher, T.
5322	,,	Fenwick, E. S. R.	5369	,,	Fowlds, E. S.
5326	,,	Downie, R. W.	5370	,,	Fowler, J.
5327	Lce.-Cpl.	Smith, W. M.	5024	,,	Francis, S.
5385	,,	Henderson, G. V.	5371	,,	Gallagher, J. J.
5026	,,	Lyle, J.	5100	,,	Gibson, G. G.
5421	,,	McAndrew, P.	5372	,,	Gilbert, J.
5448	,,	Parker, F.	5531	,,	Gilhuly, H. R.
5401	,,	Johnson, W., Jr.	5378	,,	Gill, A. J.
5435	,,	Mountain, W. J.	5373	,,	Glidden, J. H.
5452	,,	Rankin, R.	5375	,,	Greenhill, W. G.
5192	,,	Rhodes, C.	5377	,,	Griffen, J.
5500	,,	Grimsdick, O. V.	5099	,,	Griffith, E. P.
5514	,,	Peareth, A. R. T.	5501	,,	Haldane, T.
5311	Trumpt'r	Follon, J.	5380	,,	Hanington, W. H.
5305	Sh'sm'th	Jelliff, C. A.	5381	,,	Hardman, J.
5312	Bugler	Rowlands, F. W.	5382	,,	Harris, Henry
5328	Sapper	Ainsworth, H.	5391	,,	Hirst, Henry
5330	,,	Anderson, E. S.	5116	,,	Hodgson, W. F.
5332	,,	Atkinson, J. F.	5386	,,	Holliday, F. P.
5333	,,	Atkinson, W. G.	5387	,,	Holt, F. T.
5334	,,	Atterbury, L. J. R.	5388	,,	Howard, C.
5038	,,	Avery, A.	5389	,,	Howard, F.
5335	,,	Balfour, J. W. A.	5392	,,	Hurst, John
5336	,,	Bargate, G.	5393	,,	Hurst, J. L.
5337	,,	Barker, S.	5394	,,	Hurst, W.
5339	,,	Bennett, H. S.	5395	,,	Husband, J.
5342	,,	Boomhower, E. M.	5115	,,	Husband, T. G.
5343	,,	Boyce, A. C.	5396	,,	Hyslop, D. W.
5345	,,	Brewis, H. W.	5397	,,	Illidge, W.
5045	,,	Browning, C. F.	5398	,,	Jenkins, A.
5046	,,	Bullock, J. P.	5399	,,	Jervis, M. H.
5066	,,	Calderwood, W. M.	5400	,,	Johnson, J. W.
5070	,,	Carling, T.	5402	,,	Jones, J.
5559	,,	Carr, O. D.	5403	,,	Kelly, W.
5350	,,	Cave, E.	5404	,,	Kempthorne, H. T.
5351	,,	Chester, G. W.	5405	,,	Kerr, D.
5550	,,	Clark, R.	5407	,,	Keys, H. J. F.
5352	,,	Cretney, J.	5408	,,	Kinloch, R.
5353	,,	Crompton, H.	5507	,,	Lashley, R. R.

Canadian Pacific—The Empire's Greatest Railway.

DIVISIONAL ENGINEERS—cont. 299

Regl. No.	Rank.	Name.	Regl. No.	Rank.	Name.
5138	Sapper	Lammie, W. L.	5366	Driver	Ellis, P. H.
5410	,,	Law, G.	5374	,,	Goring, A. F.
5137	,,	Leger, O. E.	5502	,,	Hunnisett, F.
5541	,,	Lyall, G. N.	5506	,,	Johnson, D.
5419	,,	Matthias, H. C.	5505	,,	Jenkins, T.
5430	,,	Mellan, J. P.	5504	,,	Jeanes, C.
5417	,,	Marr, G. W.	5503	,,	Jackson, J. R.
5418	,,	Matheson, P. J.	5509	,,	Lockhart, R. R.
5415	,,	Marryat, G.	5508	,,	Lock, A.
5431	,,	Miller, J. K.	5411	,,	Lawless, N.
5432	,,	Moore, A.	5512	,,	McArthur, A.
5433	,,	Moore, G.	5510	,,	McLeish, W. C.
5434	,,	Moore, G. M.	5511	,,	Martin, G. E.
5437	,,	Murray, H. S.	5513	,,	Murray, J.
5438	,,	Murton, H. S.	5515	,,	Pearson, J. H.
5422	,,	McBeath, A. G.	5516	,,	Reeves, G.
5423	,,	McBeath, D. A.	5517	,,	Russell, S. H.
5151	,,	McCovey, R.	5454	Sapper	Richardson, T.
5425	,,	McCullough, J. S.	5455	,,	Robertson, G. S.
5426	,,	McDonald, C. H.	5551	,,	Ross, A.
5428	,,	McGee, A.	5457	,,	Rowlands, E.
5427	,,	McGregor, R. S.	5458	,,	Rutherford, F. S.
5429	,,	McGuire, P.	5213	,,	Scoggins, J. B.
5148	,,	McIntyre, G.	5460	,,	Shaw, H. P.
5553	,,	McJannett, W. L.	5533	,,	Shead, G. H.
5548	,,	McKay, S. F.	5462	,,	Sheldon, B.
5416	,,	MacKenzie, W.	5201	,,	Sims, M. M.
5152	,,	McKinnon, P.	5558	,,	Skinner, C.
5546	,,	MacLachlan, R.	5555	,,	Soplett, F.
5413	,,	McNair, J.	5465	,,	Spencer, F. C.
5440	,,	Neate, F. G.	5466	,,	Stark, D.
5441	,,	Nicholls, E.	5467	,,	Steele, G.
5549	,,	North, W. H.	5468	,,	Stevens, E. G.
5442	,,	Nutt, F.	5469	,,	Stevenson, R. L.
5444	,,	Olive, S. A.	5199	,,	Strange, G. W.
5445	,,	O'Neill, W.	5518	Driver	Stanley, G. G.
5446	,,	Osborn, G.	5495	,,	Stoutenberg, E. M.
5447	,,	Oxley, A. C.	5520	,,	Thorpe, E. H.
5450	,,	Philp, W. M.	5521	,,	Trenham, E.
5170	,,	Pollock, W. C.	5522	,,	Turner, J.
5451	,,	Quinn, P.	5470	Sapper	Tait, V. H.
5453	,,	Redden, J.	5472	,,	Thomas, W.
5485	Driver	Anderson, E. E.	5473	,,	Timmins, N.
5488	,,	Browning, F. W.	5474	,,	Tinson, A. E.
5487	,,	Brooks, G. T.	5475	,,	Tocher, A. D.
5486	,,	Banfield, W.	5219	,,	Turnbull, W. J.
5490	,,	Clark, T.	5539	,,	Turriff, A. N.
5491	,,	Cook, T. P. B.	5476	,,	Vanbergen, L. C.
5489	,,	Clark, J. T.	5478	,,	Venables, A. G.
5492	,,	Daniel, L.	5540	,,	Vitty, C. E.
5493	,,	Davidson, J. A.	5477	,,	Vokes, N. J.
5498	,,	Franklin, W. J.	5523	Driver	Veitch, W. M.

Canadian Pacific—The Empire's Greatest Railway.

DIVISIONAL ENGINEERS—cont.

Regl. No.	Rank.	Name.	Regl. No.	Rank.	Name.
5528	Driver	Wyatt, C. A.	5543	Sapper	White, R. G.
5524	,,	Waugh, R.	5525	,,	White, W. F.
5526	,,	Wilson, G.	5484	,,	Wiles, F. B.
5527	,,	Whitelow, H.	5482	,,	Williams, J. G.
5480	Sapper	Walton, W. G.	5227	,,	Williams, W.
5235	,,	Welcher, R.	5483	,,	Wilson, D. M.
5228	,,	White, A. E.	5223	,,	Wiman, L.
5481	,,	White, G. M.	5554	,,	Young, T. W.
5557	,,	White, H. C.	5529	Driver	Younger, J. R.

Attached from C.A.M.C.

| 33720 | Private | Connors, J. | 33721 | Private | Croft, J. |

3rd FIELD COMPANY.

Major	...	...	...	Wright, G. B.
Captain	...	...	...	Connell, E. K.
Lieutenant	...	...	...	Nowlan, A.
,,	...	...	...	Pepler, E.
,,	...	...	...	Harrison, E. W.
,,	...	...	...	Thexton, R. D.

Attached.

Captain	...	...	...	Donnelly, C. O'C.
,,	...	...	...	Stubbs, J. H.
Lieutenant	...	...	...	Macdonald, J. C.
,,	...	...	...	Ridout, G. L.
,,	...	...	...	Daw, H.
,,	...	...	...	Parker, S. D.
,,	...	...	...	Drummond, L. Nieuport 17.
,,	...	...	...	Merkill, R. F.
,,	...	...	...	Sutherland, R. B.

Regl. No.	Rank.	Name.	Regl. No.	Rank.	Name.
45001	C.S.M.	Whyte, A. K.	45017	Corpl.	Kane, R. A.
45002	C.Q.M.S.	Smith, C.	45018	Sergt.	Harvey, J. P.
45004	Sergt.	Hicks, O. A.	45019	Sec. Cpl.	Morrison, D.
45008	,,	Campbell, G. F.	45020	Sapper	Baillie, W.
45005	,,	Cain, H.	45021	,,	Williams, F.
45006	,,	Turner, G. R.	45022	,,	Coulson, C. E.
45007	Sapper	Lake, F. A.	45023	,,	Collins, W. S.
45009	Far.Sgt.	White, C.	45024	,,	Ward, C.
45003	Sergt.	Manby, C. S.	45025	Lce.-Cpl.	Marlatt, H. S.
45011	Bugler	Arnold, L.	45026	,,	Haines, A. J. L.
45012	Corpl.	Probin, H. A.	45027	,,	Pugh, W. J.
45013	,,	Bowles, F.	45010	Car. Sm.	Brind, F. C.
45014	,,	Stein, C. D. P.	45028	Lce.-Cpl.	Ellery, W. H.
45015	,,	Allison, R. A.	45029	Sapper	Butland, E.
45230	,,	Ralph, R. C.	45030	Lce.-Cpl.	Probin, F. C.

Canadian Pacific—The Empire's Greatest Railway.

DIVISIONAL ENGINEERS—cont. 301

Regl. No.	Rank	Name	Regl. No.	Rank	Name
45031	Lce.-Cpl.	Rawson, C.	45082	Sapper	Clarke, C.
45032	,,	Hennesy, P. H.	45235	,,	Curtice, A.
45033	,,	McLean, K.	45079	,,	Cruikshank, G.
45034	,,	Platts, C.	45083	,,	Dowdeswell, A.
45035	Sapper	Leslie, F.	45084	,,	Douglas, R.
45210	Cpl.S.Br.	Smylie, W.	45085	,,	Dickie, A. H.
45036	Sapper	Adams, J.	45086	,,	Dyke, W. S.
45037	,,	Allen, G.	45087	Lce.-Cpl.	Dey, H.
45038	,,	Anderson, H. J.	45088	Sapper	Darwell, E. J.
45039	,,	Anderson, R.	45089	,,	Despatie, A.
45040	,,	Alford, R. C.	45090	,,	Drury, J.
45041	,,	Adams, A. W. H.	45091	,,	Douglas, E.
45042	,,	Anderson, J.	45092	,,	Dunning, R. J.
45234	,,	Anderson, John	45093	,,	Eadie, A. R.
45043	,,	Amess, R.	45094	,,	Evans, G. W.
45044	,,	Asbury, G.	45095	,,	Estey, F. B.
45045	,,	Ashby, H.	45096	Driver	Ferguson, R. W.
45047	,,	Ardern, W. C.	45097	,,	Fairchild, F.
45048	,,	Baverstock, H.	45098	,,	Fry, L. J.
45049	,,	Borrie, W. J.	45100	Sapper	Fotherby, G.
45050	,,	Brooks, C. R.	45101	,,	Finnie, A. C.
45051	,,	Bayne, J.	45102	Driver	Fraser, J. A.
45052	,,	Bristlon, F. T.	45103	Sapper	Fogg, E.
45053	,,	Bould, P. T.	45104	Driver	Gregory, A.
45054	Driver	Ballintine, J. E.	45105	Sapper	Goulding, J. J.
45055	Sapper	Bates, W.	45106	,,	Green, W.
45056	,,	Burden, J.	45158	,,	Guinness, F.
45057	,,	Bird, A.	45107	Driver	Giles, F. C.
45058	,,	Baker, A.	45108	Sapper	Greenhough, J. W.
45059	,,	Burnett, G.	45109	,,	Gleig, S. H.
45060	,,	Barry, J.	45110	,,	Griffith, F.
45061	,,	Brett, J.	45111	Driver	Grant, A.
45062	,,	Bullock, F.	45112	,,	Hall, A.
45063	,,	Bowen, F. N.	45113	Sapper	Hook, G. H.
45064	,,	Bousfield, A. P. H.	45114	,,	Henning, A. E.
45065	,,	Cripp, S.	45115	,,	Hornett, J. F.
45046	,,	Crowe, A.	45116	,,	Hepburn, A.
45066	,,	Cuzner, L.	45117	,,	Hague, R. D.
45067	,,	Campbell, T.	45118	,,	Hunt, L. J.
45068	,,	Campbell, D. M.	45119	,,	Hutcheson, A.
45069	,,	Cossie, W. H.	45120	Driver	Hussey, H.
45070	,,	Coad, J. A.	45121	Sapper	Hifle, G.
45071	,,	Chamberlain, A.	45122	,,	Holland, B.
45072	Driver	Carlo, J.	45123	,,	Hall, Alex.
45073	,,	Carman, W.	45124	,,	Histed, P. E.
45074	Sapper	Cherry, F. J.	45125	Driver	Heys, F.
45075	,,	Coutts, J.	45126	,,	Hamilton, R. G.
45076	,,	Crawford, D.	45127	,,	Hirons, W. J. K.
45077	,,	Clark, J. S.	45128	,,	Herd, R.
45078	,,	Campbell, W. J.	45129	Sapper	Henwood, A.
45080	,,	Cook, W. C.	45131	,,	Inglis, D.
45081	,,	Creed, A.	45132	Driver	Jones, F. H.

Canadian Pacific—The Empire's Greatest Railway.

DIVISIONAL ENGINEERS—cont.

Regl. No.	Rank.	Name.	Regl. No.	Rank.	Name.
45133	Driver	Jones, R.	45183	Sapper	Porter, C. W.
45134	Sapper	Johnson, H. L.	45184	,,	Pogson, J. W.
45135	,,	Johnston, W.	45185	,,	Player, F. E.
45136	Driver	Kilbey, C.	45186	,,	Pearston, G. M.
45137	Sapper	Kenning, J. W.	45187	,,	Parsons, T. W.
45138	,,	Kingsley, M.	45233	,,	Middleton, J.
45139	,,	Kennedy, A.	45232	,,	Payne, B.
45140	,,	Kendall, C. R.	45188	Driver	Ronayne, H. F.
45141	Driver	Lockhart, G. F.	45189	,,	Roy, A.
45142	Sapper	Lewis, G.	45190	,,	Richards, D. O.
45143	,,	Luck, A. F.	45191	Sapper	Ross, A.
45144	,,	Larkin, H. F.	45192	,,	Reid, S.
45231	,,	Lazenby, C.	45193	,,	Reid, G. A.
45145	,,	Martin, F. L.	45194	Driver	Stout, S. T.
45146	,,	Mountseer, C.	45195	,,	Scane, D. G.
45147	Driver	Moody, C.	45196	,,	Sexton, T.
45148	Sapper	Muirhead, J.	45197	Sapper	Scott, J.
45149	,,	Matthews, G. W.	45198	,,	Stuart, W. J.
45150	,,	Murray, T.	45199	,,	Sanders, T. D.
45151	,,	Moser, J.	45200	,,	Sinclair, W.
45152	,,	Morley, A.	45201	,,	Simpson, W.
45153	,,	Milburn, W. H.	45202	,,	Stevens, A. W.
45154	,,	Miller, R. E.	45203	,,	Simson, J.
45155	,,	Murphy, G. F.	45204	,,	Shaw, W.
45156	,,	Miller, A. L.	45205	,,	Skippon, E.
45157	,,	Maconochie, J.	45206	,,	Smyth, J. W.
45159	,,	MacKenzie, W. J.	45207	,,	Smallwood, A. B.
45160	,,	McDougall, A. M.	45208	,,	Steele, A.
45161	,,	McGowan, A	45209	,,	Steuart, A. J.
45162	,,	McCarthy, C.	45211	,,	Smith, R. R.
45163	,,	McGinley, J.	45236	,,	Stubbins, A. G.
45164	,,	McDonald, R. M.	45212	Driver	Thomas, W. H.
45165	Driver	McKay, H. M.	45213	,,	Turville, R.
45166	,,	McLean, E.	45214	,,	Tyrell, S.
45167	Sapper	McKee, A. C.	45215	Sapper	Taylor, E.
45168	,,	McNeil, J.	45216	,,	Taylor, W.
45169	,,	McCosker, E.	45217	,,	Taylor, W. M.
45170	,,	McCloskey, W. J.	45016	Corpl.	Urie, H. R.
45171	Driver	McGrenery, D.	45218	Sapper	Veary, G. T.
45172	,,	Neame, T. W.	45219	Driver	West, J. E.
45173	Sapper	Nolan, M.	45220	,,	Whitely, T. R.
45175	,,	Nixon, W. P.	45221	,,	Witcomb, W.
45176	,,	Nunn, W.	45222	Sapper	Walker, C. S.
45174	,,	Neales, W. S.	45223	,,	Webster, J.
45177	,,	O'Reilly, S.	45224	,,	Watson, J.
45178	Driver	Patrick, G.	45225	,,	Weston, H. C.
45179	,,	Pyle, W.	45226	,,	Wooley, T. W.
45180	Sapper	Pearson, E. W.	45227	,,	Whalley, A.
45181	,,	Porter, E.	45228	,,	Williams, W. J. H.
45182	,,	Pryor, G.	45229	,,	Woodcock, S. G.

Canadian Pacific—The Empire's Greatest Railway.

DIVISIONAL TRAIN.

HEADQUARTERS STAFF.

Lieutenant-Colonel	Simson, W. A.
Major	Spittal, C. D.
Captain	Greer, H. C.
Veterinary Officer	Captain Woods, T. Z.
Medical Officer	,, Rogers, K. F.
Paymaster	Hon. Captain Elliott, F. D.
Postal Corps	Hon. Lieut. Caldwell, B. McG.

Regl. No.	Rank.	Name.	Regl. No.	Rank.	Name.
33687	Corpl.	Wright	33688	Private	Woods, Wm.
33689	Private	Horspool	33690	,,	Halksworth, A. E.

HEADQUARTERS COMPANY.

Major	Coles, W. G.
Captain	Williams, E. E.
,,	Baxter, L. D. M.
,,	Trenaman, H. C.
Lieutenant	Connors, A. De V. *MC*
,,	Inkster, F. B.

Regl. No.	Rank.	Name.	Regl. No.	Rank.	Name.
30014	R.S.M.	Hennessy, P.	33025	Sdlr.Cpl.	Smith, F.
30001	C.S.M.	Waddell, A. G.	30019	Wlr.Cpl.	Webb, F. G.
30002	C.Q.M.S.	McCullough, J. L.	30018	,,	Matthias, F.
30146	S. Sgt.	Giles, V. A.	30070	Corpl.	Givens, R.
30149	,,	Courtney, S. H.	30067	Driver	Foster, T. J.
30017	W.S.Sgt.	Hendricks, F. J.	30035	,,	Abbott, A. J.
30023	Dvr. Sdlr.	Nunnerley, J.	30037	,,	Atkinson, W.
30028	Fars. Sgt.	Morrison, D.	30036	,,	Atkins, T. J.
30003	Sergt.	Black, H.	30008	Trumpt'r	Allen, H. S.
30004	,,	MacDonald, J.	30038	Driver	Auld, E.
30005	,,	Rust, J. C.	30045	,,	Burke, H. J.
30006	,,	Purton, M. S.	30165	,,	Bullen, G.
30007	,,	Davies, H. R.	30041	,,	Blanchard, J. J.
30150	,,	Humphrys, F. A.	30040	Private	Burden, E.
30009	Corpl.	Stewart, P.	30158	Driver	Bailey, T. J.
30010	,,	Theobald, H. A.	30042	,,	Bouchard, L.
30011	,,	Curry, C. L.	30043	,,	Brasse, L.
30012	,,	Taylor, H.	30044	,,	Brown, R. C.
30151	,,	Wade, J. C.	30154	Private	Bond, E.
30152	,,	Woodville, C.	30132	,,	Blair, J.
30016	Driver	Sharkey, G.	30147	,,	Bushell, R. W.
30125	Corpl.	Shaw, J. F.	30052	Driver	Connor, T. H. J
30060	,,	Davidson, A. D.	30049	,,	Christopher, A.
30137	,,	Bryan, T.	30050	,,	Church, S.
30030	Far. Cpl.	McLellan, M.	30048	,,	Carroll, W. J.
30029	,,	Fradgley, A. R.	30153	,,	Carley, W. B.
30024	Sdlr.Cpl.	Pawley, D. B.	30163	,,	Cuff, S. T.

Canadian Pacific—The Empire's Greatest Railway.

DIVISIONAL TRAIN—cont.

Regl. No.	Rank.	Name.	Regl. No.	Rank.	Name.
30046	Driver	Caldwell, S.	30101	Driver	Marshall, E. J.
30047	,,	Cameron, C. H.	30100	,,	Marsland, J. W.
30053	,,	Chivas, W. C.	30107	,,	Milks, E. K.
30051	,,	Condron, C.	30123	,,	MacDonald, F. P.
30055	,,	Cooper, G.	30108	,,	Morgan, W. J.
30148	Private	Campbell, P.	30105	,,	McDonald, D. H.
30063	Driver	Dutton, A.	30096	,,	McDonald, A.
30059	,,	Dinelle, A.	30097	,,	McFarlane, J. D.
30061	,,	Dormer, L.	30104	,,	McCartey, P.
30033	Dvr.Far.	Dillon, C.	30162	,,	Nolan, T.
30057	Driver	Dennett, J.	30109	,,	Napier, K. R.
30056	,,	Dabson, B. E.	30110	,,	O'Brien, T. J.
30156	,,	Dugal, R. E.	30113	,,	Pope, H. W.
30058	,,	Dinelle, W.	30116	,,	Porteous, J. H.
30069	,,	Freeman H.	30114	,,	Powell, G.
30065	,,	Foley, T.	30112	,,	Pearson, F. G.
30066	,,	Forrest, H. E.	30111	,,	Pearn, J.
30068	,,	Fraser, W. B.	30115	,,	Pate, S. A.
30031	Dvr.Far.	Grist, F.	30117	,,	Quesnel, E.
30071	Driver	Green, W.	30118	,,	Rankin, J. R.
30072	,,	Gunn, D.	30120	,,	Roberts, A.
30161	,,	Guy, G. H.	30119	,,	Riddell, T.
30078	,,	Hughes, J.	30022	Dvr.Wlr.	Riseley, P. H. W.
30074	,,	Harrison, E.	30032	Driver	Richmond, S. J.
30075	,,	Hawkshaw, S.	30122	,,	Saville, J. A.
30077	,,	Haltham, A. H.	30127	,,	Smethurst, J.
30076	,,	Hind, S.	30129	,,	Southwick, E.
30073	,,	Howes, W. R.	30131	,,	Stroh, W.
30079	,,	Huntley, T.	30126	,,	Smart, T. W.
30081	,,	Hutchins, H. F.	30026	Dvr.Sdlr.	Shergold, J. W.
30080	,,	Hutchings, F. A.	30128	Lce.-Cpl.	Smith, J.
30083	,,	Ingram, L. J.	30121	,,	Scaife, W.
30087	,,	Joy, W.	30124	,,	Sharpe, W.
30084	,,	Jasper, J.	30130	,,	Spears, W.
30088	,,	Joy, C.	30015	,,	Salusbury, N. H. P.
30085	,,	Jones, T. B.	30021	Dvr.Wlr.	St. Denis, C. Z.
30086	,,	Jones, F. G.	30164	Driver	Shepcott, T. R.
30089	,,	Jarvis, A. G.	30134	,,	Treadway, G. S.
30157	,,	Joyce, M. J.	30027	Dvr.Sdlr.	Tomlinson, A. E.
30090	,,	Kerr, A.	30133	Driver	Toothill, H.
30092	,,	Keys, W.	30135	,,	Trollope, G. B.
30091	,,	Kerr, G.	30013	,,	Timmis, G. C.
30155	,,	Kerse, C.	30136	Dvr.Wlr.	Vaughan, W. H.
30034	,,	Latimer, C. H.	30155	Driver	Vickery, E. J.
30093	,,	Laird, J.	30139	,,	Williamson, R.
30095	,,	Leamy, F. A.	30138	,,	Weskett, F.
30094	,,	Lister, S.	30143	,,	Wright, W. J.
33098	,,	Madeley, J. G.	30142	,,	Woodhead, H.
30099	,,	Maloney, T. P.	30141	,,	Wishart, T.
30102	,,	Martin, G.	30145	,,	Wilkes, H.
30106	,,	Merriman, W. L.	30140	,,	Wilson, A. S. W.
30103	,,	Martin, W. R.	30144	,,	Wyllie, D. C.

Canadian Pacific—The Empire's Greatest Railway.

DIVISIONAL TRAIN—cont. 305

No. 2 COMPANY.

Captain ... ... Greer, W. D.
Lieutenant ... ... Webb, R. H.
,, ... Hooper, G. B.
,, ... Hollister, S. J. F.
,, ... McDougall, K. W. A.

Regl. No.	Rank.	Name.
30252	S.S.M. (W.O.)	Sainty, Henry St. J.
30167	C.S.M.	Ploss, Herman Wm.
30168	C.Q.M.S.	Maloney, Palmer
30208	S. Sgt.	Hamilton, Chas.
30213	,,	Anderson, R. G.
30169	,,	Marshall, Frank
30170	,,	Eden, William
30171	,,	Nicholson, W. M.
30172	Sergt.	Tait, John
30173	,,	Dunham, W. B.
30211	Corpl.	Routledge, W. T.
30174	,,	Hawley, F. B.
30276	,,	Collins, Henry
30215	,,	Denson, Reg.
30177	,,	Hayward, E.
30178	Private	Kirkwood, G.
30206	Corpl.	Girvan, James
30232	,,	Petrie, Harry Leslie
30216	Trumpt'r	D'Arcy, Norman F.
30179	Private	Allan, Alexander E.
30180	Lce.-Cpl.	Allan, Fred G.
30181	Corpl.	Baird, W. J.
30175	Driver	Baker, H. W.
30182	,,	Barclay, Edward
30183	,,	Barton, G.
30184	,,	Blackledge, F.
30185	,,	Blake, J.
30186	,,	Bragg, S.
30187	,,	Brown, J.
30189	,,	Burbridge, J.
30188	,,	Burt, J.
30196	,,	Campbell, A.
30190	,,	Carroll, Chas.
30192	,,	Clark, W. H.
30193	,,	Clifford, Thos.
30194	,,	Cole, W.
30195	,,	Cooke, A.
30250	,,	Counter, F. C.
30197	,,	Cowper, Thos.
30198	,,	Dell, John
30199	,,	Dove, H. C.
30200	,,	Durie, W.

Regl. No.	Rank.	Name.
30203	Driver	Edmunds, G.
30201	,,	Entwhistle, R.
30202	,,	Evans, E. P.
30204	Private	Ferguson, H. M.
30205	Driver	Foley, J. M.
30207	,,	Gordon, Geo.
30209	Lce.-Cpl.	Graham, Geo.
30248	Driver	Gray, E. A.
30212	,,	Hagen, R. E.
30217	,,	Haines, O.
30214	,,	Harris, W. G.
30218	,,	Hill, A. W.
30219	,,	Johnston, R.
30220	,,	Land, W.
30221	,,	Lawrence, Thos.
30222	Private	Lee, H.
30223	Driver	Lowbridge, Thos.
30224	,,	Lovett, F.
30253	,,	Mackay-Kean, J.
30225	,,	Marks, C. E.
30226	,,	Mainwaring, Geo.
30227	Private	McCracken, G. C.
30228	Driver	McCubbin, Thos.
30229	,,	Noël, Chas. J.
30230	,,	Olliver, J. A. B.
30231	,,	Olson, C. J.
30233	,,	Powell, A. E.
30234	,,	Preston, A.
30235	,,	Puncheon, Ralph
30237	,,	Robin, O.
30249	,,	Ross, M. E.
30238	,,	Shenton, J.
30239	,,	Smith, H. O.
30191	,,	Strickland, C.
30240	,,	Sutcliffe, F.
30241	,,	Thompson, F.
30242	,,	Tindall, J.
30243	,,	Turner, F. J.
30244	,,	Whitehurst, F.
30245	,,	Willis, Thos.
30246	,,	Wilson, W. J.
30247	Corpl.	Wright, G. E.
30176	Driver	Wright, J.

Canadian Pacific—The Empire's Greatest Railway.

U

DIVISIONAL TRAIN—cont.

No. 3 COMPANY.

Captain ... ... Corrigan, C. A.
„ ... ... Findlay, W. H.
Lieutenant ... ... Morison, J. B.
„ ... ... Oliphant, J.
„ ... ... Watson, C. S. S.

Regl. No.	Rank.	Name.	Regl. No.	Rank.	Name.
30256	Sgt.-Maj. (W.O)	Sutton, J. H.	30322	Driver	Grimshaw, R.
			30309	„	Greig, G. A.
30257	C.S.M.	George, A. F.	30335	Private	Griswood, G. A.
30258	C.Q.M.S.	Crow, G.	30324	Driver	Haggar, A.
30266	S. Sgt.	Warburton, T. E.	30338	„	Heath, G. H. D.
30263	„	Cottrell, C.	30262	„	Hicks, B. S.
30260	„	Roberts, S. J.	30279	„	Jaggard, G. R.
30325	„	MacDonald, E. E.	30328	Private	Jacobs, A. C.
30334	„	Browne, W. R.	30310	Driver	Kibble, C.
30301	Sergt.	Last, A. C.	30305	„	Lampriere, J. G.
30333	„	Bowden, G.	30280	„	Little, A.
30313	„	Williams, J.	30282	„	MacDowall, H.
30267	Corpl.	Billington, H.	30284	„	Mead, Wm.
30264	„	Thompson, E. A.	30283	„	Malone, W.
30261	„	Ball, J. M.	30285	„	McLaughlin, W.
30326	„	Dawson, E. C.	30323	„	Mackenzie, H.
30336	„	Prosser, J. W.	30286	„	Morton, E. R.
30300	„	Dawes, W.	30287	„	Melvin, D.
30314	„	Forrest, J.	30269	„	Mason, G.
30259	„	Waggitt, J. C.	30311	„	Neill, J.
30340	„	Parnell, J.	30315	„	Nelson, J. G.
30276	„	Etty, W.	30472	„	Neville, A.
30298	Trumpt'r	Goacher, G.	30289	„	Openshaw, W.
30271	Driver	Anderson, R. Y.	30288	„	Oddie, W.
30270	„	Archer, J.	30316	„	Ormerod, J.
30272	„	Bird, P.	30317	„	Plinston, D.
30273	„	Brice, H.	30291	„	Rigby, T.
30302	„	Bowie, A. D.	30268	„	Rigby, J.
30265	„	Beckett, J. T.	30339	„	Roberts, W. E.
30303	„	Cullen, M. J.	30292	„	Rainford, G.
30304	„	Craig, J.	30299	„	Ring, E. E.
30294	„	Cremer, L.	30293	„	Ryall, E. N.
30327	Private	Cremer, G. E.	30290	„	Rosart, T.
30274	Driver	Des Bois, W. E.	30318	„	Stradwick, C. J.
30275	„	Duncan, R.	30295	„	Tonner, A.
30330	Private	Duke, H. H.	30319	„	Thurgood, F.
30306	Driver	Edwards, C.	30296	„	Thompson, D.
30307	„	Francey, T.	30329	Private	Thompson, G. G.
30308	„	Fleming, W. D.	30320	Driver	Wilson, J. W.
30331	„	Freeman, G. W.	30321	„	Walton, W. J.
30277	„	German, R.	30297	„	Woolnough, J.
30278	„	Grant, J. M.	30337	Private	Warwick, H. S. R.

Canadian Pacific—The Empire's Greatest Railway.

DIVISIONAL TRAIN—cont. 307

No. 4 COMPANY.

Headquarters of Company.

Captain	... ...	Lawson, H. O.
„	... ...	Ruttan, C. M.
Lieutenant	... ...	McLeod, W.
„	... ...	Franklyn, G. E.
„	... ...	Fortin, A. R.

Regl. No.	Rank.	Name.	Regl. No.	Rank.	Name.
30346	R.S.M. (W.O.)	Leach, S. H.	30369	Wheeler	Bryant, H.
			30376	Private	Berkeley, M. A.
30347	C.S.M.	Fletcher, W. C.	30375	„	Brand, J. R.
30348	C.Q.M.S.	Cuthbertson, J.	30445	Driver	Blake, H. L.
30485	S.S.M.	Halton (W.O.)	30443	„	Brown, A.
30486	C.Sgt.M.	Jordan, J. B.	30911	Private	Biggs, K.
30436	Staff Sgt.	De Graves, W. A.	30440	Driver	Bowie, F.
30349	„	O'Connor, W. H.	30479	Private	Bradley, A. S.
30350	„	Ewing, D.	30370	Driver	Burden, A.
30437	„	Rose, A. G.	30378	„	Chapman, E.
30491	„	Wylie, John	30379	„	Chapman, S.
30354	Far. S. S.	Knowles, W.	30383	„	Cheeseman, W.
30356	Wlr. S. S.	Coull, J.	30425	Private	Collinson, J.
30477	Far. Crpl.	Riddell, A. G.	30381	„	Cooper, G.
30364	Sad. Crpl.	Johnston, J.	30380	Driver	Coppock, J.
30365	Wlr.Crpl.	Mitchell, T. F.	30384	Private	Crowe, G. E.
30352	Sergt.	Campbell, D.	30377	Saddler	Curtis, S. E.
30489	„	Chubbuck, R. D.	30382	Driver	Clews, W. E.
30488	„	Dalton, G.	30385	Private	Cameron, D. I.
30351	„	Hatton, T.	30446	Driver	Crawford, J. M.
30430	„	Jones, W. H.	30447	„	Carter, J.
30487	„	Radcliffe, G.	30929	„	Clegg, E.
30359	Lce.-Sgt.	Canham, A. W.	30484	Private	Collins
30441	Corpl.	Breakey, N. J.	30387	Driver	Dack, F.
30363	„	Ellard, T.	30388	„	Davis, G. S.
30361	„	Frank, R.	30449	„	Davidson, G.
30460	„	Jeffery, W. E.	30389	„	Day, S.
30357	„	Martin, H. J.	30386	„	Duggan, G. H.
30362	„	McLaren, W. J.	30450	„	Ellison, H.
30360	„	Nicholls, W.	30391	Private	Ferguson, J. H.
30353	„	Thompson, J.	30368	„	Fleming, D. W.
30358	„	Wood, J. H.	30915	„	Fish, H.
30442	2nd Cpl.	Black, D. C.	30916	„	Fairfax, R.
30448	„	Dundas, F.	30451	Driver	Fullerton, J.
30390	„	Edwards, R. W.	30392	Private	Garratt, J.
30438	Driver	Aitken, G. E.	30453	Driver	Gissing, C.
30439	„	Atkinson, J.	30454	Private	Goodridge, G. A.
30444	„	Belsey, F. L.	30452	Driver	Gray, E.
30371	„	Bald, J.	30395	Driver	Hayward, W.
30373	„	Barrett, J.	30394	„	Hatton, R. H.
30372	Private	Beard, S.	30396	„	Horse, A. M.
30429	„	Bennet, W. C.	30393	„	Hughes, T. A.
30374	„	Blair, J.	30455	„	Hogg, R. D.

Canadian Pacific—The Empire's Greatest Railway.

u 2

DIVISIONAL TRAIN—cont.

Regl. No.	Rank.	Name.	Regl. No.	Rank.	Name.
30458	Driver	Hogarth, W. M.	30355	Saddler	Pickering, H.
40459	,,	Harrow, G.	30409	Driver	Prestwood, W.
30457	,,	Harper, J.	30475	,,	Pegg, K. H.
30456	,,	Hitchens, C.	30474	,,	Pilkington, W.
30398	,,	Johnston, M. W.	30476	,,	Quinlan, M. J.
30397	,,	Johnston, Jas.	30482	,,	Robbins, H. J.
30399	Private	Keyte, W.	30410	,,	Rockhill, C.
30461	Driver	King, H.	30414	,,	Scott, J. C.
30400	,,	Kinsey, F.	30417	,,	Sturgess, W.
30918	Private	Laponte, A.	30412	,,	Stokes, G. H.
30919	,,	Laroche, R.	30413	,,	Sturt, T.
30460	Driver	Le Rasle, A.	30411	,,	Sheppard, F.
30464	Private	Leacroft, R. F.	30416	,,	Simms, J. J.
30462	Driver	Lee, V.	30478	,,	Sherlock, B.
30401	,,	Lingwood, J.	30924	Private	Sutton, W.
30281	,,	Lofthouse, H.	30987	,,	Smith, C.
30407	,,	Manning, B.	30896	,,	Smith, A.
30404	,,	Mobbs, Chas.	30930	,,	Smith, W.
30405	,,	Moore, J.	30895	,,	Smith, Walter
30884	,,	Morris, S. W.	30922	,,	Smollet, C.
30403	,,	Morrison, W.	30899	,,	Shephard, J.
30402	,,	Marcham, W.	30415	,,	Sage, R.
30465	,,	Mulvaney, G.	30931	,,	Thompson, A. R.
30468	,,	MacDonald, D. F.	30481	Driver	Tierney, W.
30469	,,	MacDonald, D. W.	30910	Private	Toombs, J. B.
30470	,,	McDonald, J.	30418	,,	Toms, A. B.
30467	,,	McLean, M.	30419	,,	Turland, E. B.
30366	Private	McArthur, J. C.	30420	Wheeler	Wilson, H.
30406	,,	McMullan, A. R.	30426	Driver	Woodman, A. C.
30887	,,	McCausland, P. A.	30423	,,	Whyte, W.
30920	,,	McIlvenny, J.	30421	,,	Wilson, C.
30932	,,	McNereon, J.	30424	,,	Webb, J.
30466	Driver	Morris, J.	30422	,,	Wallace, G.
30881	Private	Mullett, H.	30427	Private	Weightman, R.
30933	,,	Murray, A.	30428	,,	West, A.
30367	Trumpt'r	Neilson, W.	30479	Driver	Wade, J.
30408	Private	Neale, R.	30480	,,	Warren, J.
30471	Driver	Nisbet, W.	30928	Private	Walker, R.
30473	,,	Neal, C. J.	30925	,,	Wellings, C. F.
30883	,,	Parrish, J. W.			

DIVISIONAL SUPPLY COLUMN, M.T.

Major	Moore, Montague
Captain	Spencer, J. V. N.
Lieutenant	Winch, C. V.
,, ...	Turpin, T. J.
,, ...	Gordon, George H.
Paymaster	Hon. Captain Binks, B. C.
Medical Officer	Captain Davis

Canadian Pacific—The Empire's Greatest Railway.

DIVISIONAL SUPPLY COLUMN, M.T.—*cont.* 309

Regl. No.	Rank.	Name.	Regl. No.	Rank.	Name.
36001	R.S.M.	Daniels, Harold C.	36242	Private	Baty, Arthur G.
36002	C.S.M.	Stenson, Frederick	36044	,,	Bennington, Harld. A.
36013	C.Q.M.S.	Milne, John	36043	,,	Barker, Almond
36009	Sgt.-Maj.	Martin, Harold P.	36041	,,	Bartlett, Walter G.
36008	Sergt.	Manley, Davison B.	36049	,,	Bland, Alfred J.
36004	,,	de la Mare, Ernest	36253	,,	Browne, William A.
36006	,,	Fenton, Ray Wm.	36048	,,	Bawden, Harry
36012	,,	Ray, Thomas	36052	,,	Burgoyne, Richard J.
36018	,,	Stark, Thomas B.	36047	,,	Berryman, Talbot A.
36010	,,	Packer, John P.	36051	,,	Boultbee, Ernest L.
36011	,,	Pennie, Thomas C.	36045	,,	Bostock, James A.
36003	,,	Abell, Roy Benjamin	36054	,,	Courtney, Herbert
36249	,,	Weghorn, George	36055	,,	Cosford, Edward J.
36007	,,	Gray, James Speers	36056	,,	Cole, Frederick C.
36087	,,	Francis, Frederick	36057	,,	Cole, Walter
36017	,,	Porter, William	36058	,,	Cochrane, James L.
36232	,,	Williams, E. W. R.	36059	,,	Clarke, George
36014	,,	Crisford, George T.	36060	,,	Chapman, Albert D.
36015	,,	Hollingshead, Jos. T.	36061	,,	Clark, William A.
36022	Corpl.	Francis, Norman B.	36062	,,	Chamberlain, Fredk.
36019	,,	Bell, Dean W.	36063	,,	Counsel, Ernest
36020	,,	Cooper, J. H.	36064	,,	Craig, Percival H.
36029	,,	Draper, Charles N.	36065	,,	Collins, William G.
36072	,,	Dunning, F. G.	36066	,,	Culling, William C.
36082	,,	Evans, R. A.	36067	,,	Cumming, Lewis
36024	,,	Hanson, James	36083	,,	Clemens, Stephen D.
36122	,,	Huston, Victor Henry	36068	,,	De Marrais, Leroy A.
36021	,,	Exworthy, Albert E.	36069	,,	Dawson, Frederick J.
36028	,,	Tordiffe, Francis M.	36070	,,	Dickson, John
36023	,,	Gittins, John R.	36071	,,	Davidson, Alexander
36210	,,	Sharman, John D.	36073	,,	Dight, Walter J.
36026	,,	Mainprize, Thomas	36154	,,	Douglas, William D.
36027	,,	Pugh, Richard W.	36075	,,	Dunn, John J.
36167	,,	Perks, Cecil Thomas	36076	,,	Davies, Arthur
36206	,,	Sewards, Thos.	36077	,,	Davis, Peter A.
36269	,,	Tracey, Thomas E.	36079	,,	Douglas, Thomas
36031	Lce.-Cpl.	Brown, Travers S.	36078	,,	Davis, Sydney B.
36030	,,	Whittome, Robt. W.	36080	,,	Edwick, Charles G.
36270	Private	Alderson, H.	36081	,,	Ellam, Leopold G. B.
36035	,,	Amey, Purcell	36085	,,	Ensor, Claude
36040	,,	Anderson, Arthur W.	36255	,,	Evans, George D.
36037	,,	Appleton, Geo. W.	36086	,,	Fox, A. E.
36036	,,	Aspen, William	36088	,,	Fraser, Ronald
36032	,,	Adams, George A.	36089	,,	Fraser, Henry Q. W.
36039	,,	Alcock, Gordon	36090	,,	Farquharson, James
36038	,,	Arnold, Edward J.	36091	,,	Findlay, George M.
36033	,,	Ainsbury, Charles	36092	,,	Flood, Timothy
36034	,,	Arnold, Lorne A.	36093	,,	Fox, Frederick W. S.
36053	,,	Bartoli, Peter	36094	,,	Finnigann, Thomas
36046	,,	Blackie, William M.	36095	,,	French, Arthur
36042	,,	Barnes, Alfred A.	36096	,,	Frewin, Walter
36050	,,	Bradley, Percival	36097	,,	George, Thomas W.

Canadian Pacific—The Empire's Greatest Railway.

310 DIVISIONAL SUPPLY COLUMN, M.T.—cont.

Regl. No.	Rank.	Name.	Regl. No.	Rank.	Name.
36098	Private	Giles, Francis	36145	Private	Mayfield, Alfred
36099	,,	Gillespie, Sam C.	36146	,,	Medhurst, George E.
36100	,,	Grant, Duncan	36147	,,	May, Samuel T.
36101	,,	Gabel, Lewis	36148	,,	Mair, Harry G.
36102	,,	Gibson, Reginald S.	36150	,,	Marshall, Charles H.
36103	,,	Gadd, William J.	36244	,,	Morrison, Maxwell
36104	,,	Goddard, James	36245	,,	Mudge, William
36105	,,	Greenslade, William	36246	,,	Muir, Matthew
36106	,,	Grierson, Malcolm	36258	,,	Martin, Reginald E.
36107	,,	Grisewood, Louis H.	36016	,,	Mitchell, James A.
36108	,,	Galbraith, William	36266	,,	Mitchell, James
36264	,,	Graham, George	36267	,,	Mussens, C. M.
36109	,,	Hunt, Dennis J.	36269	,,	McKeedie, Archibald
36110	,,	Hoskin, George H.	36151	,,	McCaffery, J. T.
36111	,,	Howaith, John R.	36152	,,	McAvenue, John
36112	,,	Henderson, Henry	36153	,,	McDermott, Edwd. C.
36113	,,	Hobbs, Sidney J.	36154	,,	McDermott, S. E.
36114	,,	Hunt, Frederick	36155	,,	McDonald, M. D.
36115	,,	Holdgate, Nathl. J.	36156	,,	McLennan, Alex. K.
36116	,,	Hannigan, Frederick	36157	,,	McCrea, Charles
36117	,,	Harford, Robert	36159	,,	McCreery, Robert
36118	,,	Herbert, Arthur J.	36279	,,	McDermott, J. F.
36119	,,	Hodgkinson, George	36160	,,	McLaren, Frederick
36120	,,	Holland, Clare A.	36161	,,	MacMillan, Colin
36121	,,	Hubbard, Chas.	36162	,,	McClintock, Henry G
36123	,,	Hutson, Reginald H.	36163	,,	Newby, Wallace R.
36124	,,	Hitchens, Harry	36164	,,	Nixon, John Dale
36125	,,	Hutcheon, George L.	36165	,,	Palmer, Ernest T.
36126	,,	Haydon, Ashley A.	36166	,,	Patterson, Hugh J.
36127	,,	Hurt, Charles Julien	36168	,,	Perry, Thomas N.
36243	,,	Hughes, William	36169	,,	Plumbtree, Ambrose
36251	,,	Harton, Norman Lee	36170	,,	Pease, George Wm.
36128	,,	Image, Herbert Geo.	36172	,,	Pinder, Sidney R.
86129	,,	Jackson, George	36173	,,	Pettigrew, Archibald
36130	,,	Jeffares, Rupert J.	36256	,,	Parsons, Herbert E.
36131	,,	Jobling, Ralph H.	36257	,,	Purvis, Andrew
86132	,,	Johnson, Edgar Allan	36174	,,	Richardson, Reginald
36133	,,	Judge, John	36271	,,	Robertson, G.
36262	,,	Jervis, Thomas	36175	,,	Read, John
36084	,,	Jeanes, Ernest O.	36176	,,	Robbins, Arthur
36250	,,	Jefferies, William H.	36177	,,	Robinson, John A.
36134	,,	King, Frank	36274	,,	Rush, Herbert John
36139	,,	Knowles, Charles E.	36178	,,	Ryan, Malcolm G.
36136	,,	Keene, George E.	36265	,,	Risley, George
36137	,,	Keene, Fred	36180	,,	Scott, James
36138	,,	Kelynack, Nicholas	36181	,,	Scott, Robert J.
36135	,,	Kappert, Garret Jan	36183	,,	Stevens, Frank
36025	,,	Kennedy, Alfred	36185	,,	Stevens, Fred Roy
36140	,,	Kennedy, William C.	36186	,,	Stevens, Henry
36273	,,	Lake, H.	36187	,,	Stokes, Douglas H.
36141	,,	Lord, Horace	36188	,,	Scarlet, Edward
36142	,,	Lintern, Henry	36189	,,	Sharratt, Bernard

Canadian Pacific—The Empire's Greatest Railway.

DIVISIONAL SUPPLY COLUMN, M.T —cont.

Regl. No.	Rank.	Name.	Regl. No.	Rank.	Name.
36190	Private	Stuart, William F.	36216	Private	Tenant, Wm. E. S.
36191	,,	Scatchard, William K.	36217	,,	Thompson, William J.
36193	,,	Spong, Charles G.	36218	,,	Tanner, Henry Percy
36194	,,	Salt, Charles M.	36220	,,	Underwood, John R.
36195	,,	Seear, James	36221	,,	Unwin, Patrick
36196	,,	Shultz, Frank	36252	,,	Vaughan, William
36197	,,	Sinclair, John Ernest	36222	,,	Warren, Arthur G.
36198	,,	Slater, John C.	36224	,,	Wilson, William
36199	,,	Sprayson, Henry	36225	,,	Wilson, William
36200	,,	Smith, Hugh	36226	,,	Woolford, Fred
36201	,,	Smith, Sidney	36227	,,	Wright, Horace W.
36202	,,	Speight, Norman H.	36228	,,	Watt, Thomas
36203	,,	Sabelle, Frank	36229	,,	Watson, Thomas
36204	,,	Slater, Joseph M.	36230	,,	Waldon, James
36205	,,	Simpson, James P.	36231	,,	Webster, Lorne E.
36207	,,	Singleton, James H.	26275	,,	Westall, J.
36208	,,	Smyth, Alfred W.	36233	,,	Williams, William A.
36209	,,	Sampson, Herbert	36234	,,	Woodhouse, Harold
36211	,,	Score, Hendall R.	36235	,,	Woodward, Donald A.
36248	,,	Stevens, Arthur Tyre	36236	,,	Waddington, Percy
36192	,,	Shadwell, M. L.	36237	,,	Ward, Sidney
36248	,,	Stacy, J.	36238	,,	Willis, George Edw.
36212	,,	Todd, William Henry	36247	,,	Wilson, Garnet E.
36213	,,	Taylor, George H.	36223	,,	Wilson, Frank
36219	,,	Towers, John	36239	,,	York, John Arthur
36214	,,	Tyler, Alfred E.	36240	,,	York, Frederick N.
36215	,,	Turner, Alfred	36241	,,	Young, David

DIVISIONAL AMMUNITION COLUMN.

HEADQUARTERS.

Commanding Officer	Lt.-Colonel John Jenkin Penhale.
Adjutant	Major Charles Edward Long
Supernumerary	Lientenant Frederick H. Crathern
Medical Officer	Major David Donald
Paymaster	Hon. Captain Robert Broadwell Thompson
Warrant Officer	Lieutenant Charles Edgar Edgett
Chaplain	Hon. Captain Alexander Dow Cornett
Y.M.C.A.	Lieutenant Christopher Graham

Regl. No.	Rank.	Name.	Regl. No.	Rank.	Name.
43501	Reg. S.-M.	Slade, James	43504	Sergt.	Warden, R. H.
43502	Bty. S.-M.	Kear, William G.	43507	Trumpt'r	Ball, Albert E.
43503	Bty. Q.M.S.	Cunard, Charles K.	43564	,,	Cooper, Harold
22000	Sergt.	Cottam, P. A. S.	43509	Gunner	Aitchison, A. W.
43506	,,	Long, Robert A.	43515	Driver	Andrews, G. W.
43505	,,	Sadlier, K. D.	43562	Gunner	Austin, Wm. John

Canadian Pacific—The Empire's Greatest Railway.

312 DIVISIONAL AMMUNITION COLUMN—cont.

Regl. No.	Rank.	Name.	Regl. No.	Rank.	Name.
43522	Gunner	Boxall, Henry W.	43513	Gunner	Lockett, R. J.
43510	,,	Clowery, F. G.	43630	,,	Lovell, Henry P.
43511	,,	Cassidy, John J.	43632	,,	Markwell, James
44064	,,	Elmslie, Charles	44022	,,	McPartland, J. H.
43512	,,	Howell, Albert	30101	,,	Marshall, Ernest
43678	,,	Holloway, James	43514	,,	Owen, Richard
43996	,,	Hayes, William H.	43747	Corpl.	Robertson, A. F.
43995	,,	Hanson, Cyril	44054	Gunner	Wilson, Thomas

No. 1 SECTION.

Major	...	...	...	...	Ralston, George Harrah
Captain	...	...	...	...	Greenlees, Frederick Henry
Lieutenant	...	...	...	...	Magann, George Lorenzo
Lieutenant	...	...	...	...	McTaggart, William Broder

Regl. No.	Rank.	Name.	Regl. No.	Rank.	Name.
43550	Sergt.	Blandford, George	43622	Gunner	Brooks, Joseph
43549	,,	Grant, Donald W.	43560	,,	Cromwell, John W.
43548	,,	Latham, E. D.	43625	,,	Clarke, William J.
43551	Far. Sgt,	Bowes, Matthew	43583	,,	Charles, Gerald
43517	Corpl.	McKenzie, T. J. B.	43584	,,	Charette, G. J.
43552	,,	Matthews, R. H.	43585	,,	Cheetham, G. E.
43554	Bombr.	Angles, Harry G.	43587	,,	Cameron, Azel B.
43556	,,	Archer, Robert C.	43588	,,	Cameron, W. H.
43555	,,	Goddard, Edward	43624	,,	Cameron, B. S.
43553	,,	Lagimodiere, A.	43591	,,	Cuthbert, C. E.
43557	,,	Monahan, Oscar	43593	,,	Campbell, W. F.
43594	Shoe Sgt.	Carroll, John J.	43081	,,	Campbell, Patrick
43740	,,	Jackson, Wilbert	43595	,,	Chessman, Thomas
43586	,,	Schock, Oscar	43597	,,	Collins, John
43653	,,	St. Germain, N.	43788	,,	Chandler, Walter
43558	Wheeler	Benford, Charles	43623	,,	Chevais, Norman
43518	,,	Ogilvie, George	43600	,,	Deary, James
43627	Saddler	Ling, Joseph	43301	,,	Dixon, William E.
43681	Gunner	Anderson, John	43602	,,	DeWolfe, Jacob G.
43682	,,	Andrews, Frank	43561	,,	Elliott, Richard D.
43519	,,	Avery, Arthur E.	43563	,,	Ewen, Alexander
43567	,,	Ayling, Herbert	43603	,,	Edmunds, M. B.
43520	,,	Bills, Edward M.	43523	,,	Finnegan, Joseph
43521	,,	Burton, V. F. B.	43559	,,	Fisher, W. H.
43568	,,	Blackwell, G. E.	43604	,,	Ferris, Andrew O.
43571	,,	Blair, Joseph M.	43719	,,	Flewelling, G. H.
43572	,,	Brooksmith, J. D.	43950	,,	Fidler, William
43573	,,	Boardman, Arthur	43524	,,	Gauvin, George
43574	,,	Ball, Walter	43525	,,	Gray, Herbert B.
43577	,,	Bird, Stanley	43526	,,	Godfrey, William
43578	,,	Button, Arthur F.	43605	,,	Graham, N. S.
43579	,,	Bates, Alfred	43606	,,	Gaffray, Etienne
43581	,,	Berry, Andrew	43607	,,	Grundy, Gordon
43621	,,	Baker, James	43608	,,	Goldsmith, A. H.

Canadian Pacific—The Empire's Greatest Railway.

DIVISIONAL AMMUNITION COLUMN—cont.

Regl. No.	Rank.	Name.	Regl. No.	Rank.	Name.
43546	Gunner	Gross, James	43637	Gunner	McAleese, W. J.
43989	,,	Gallagher, John	43159	,,	Morley, Patrick
43609	,,	Gardner, Henry S.	43638	,,	Oliver, Derrick E.
43723	,,	Gray, Orlo	43539	,,	O'Farrell, Arthur
43527	,,	Hamont, Louis	43589	,,	Owad, Vladimer
43529	,,	Howitt, Harold	43639	,,	Parberry, John H.
43610	,,	Horner, Archibald	43640	,,	Perrion, Arthur H.
43611	,,	Hartman, Howard	43540	,,	Payne, Harrold R.
43612	,,	Horan, Harold	43541	,,	Palmer, Martin
43613	,,	Hollands, John	44030	,,	Power, Adam
43789	,,	Horning, A. G.	43542	,,	Ridgway, Alfred
43614	,,	Illingsworth, H.	43641	,,	Randall, M. H.
43530	,,	Jackman, Narcisse	43642	,,	Russell, Edw. G.
43615	,,	James, Ivor	43769	,,	Rutherford, G.
43616	,,	James, Percy E.	43768	,,	Russell, Harold A.
43508	,,	Jones, Samuel	44031	,,	Russell, W. T.
43531	,,	Kirk, Samuel	43543	,,	St. Pierre, Wilfred
43617	,,	Kelly, Roy	43643	,,	Savoie, Joseph
43618	,,	Keenan, Stephen	43644	,,	Stone, Joseph
43619	,,	Kanneen, John R.	43646	,,	Saunders, E. D. L.
43620	,,	Livingstone, W. G.	43647	,,	Saunderson, E. D.
43626	,,	Levack, Alexander	43648	,,	Sinclair, Hugh L.
43628	,,	Luck, Allan John	43649	,,	Shaw, Frank
43629	,,	Long, Thomas W.	43650	,,	Smith, John R.
43631	,,	Lloyd, Thomas H.	43652	,,	Smeltzer, J. Albert
44009	,,	Limond, John L.	43547	,,	Simonds, SydneyC.
43151	,,	Lunn, Edgar	43654	,,	Simonds, Joseph
44008	,,	Lemon, Ezra L.	43651	,,	Spicer, John H.
43162	,,	McCleverty, A. M.	44033	,,	Smith, Edward
43532	,,	McDermott, W. P.	43779	,,	Stump, Wellington
43533	,,	McKerrill, G. S.	43544	,,	Thornton, John H.
43534	,,	McDonald, D. J.	43655	,,	Thomas, Harmon
43535	,,	McConnell, W.	43656	,,	Turner, Ronald
43566	,,	McKay, Mark H.	43781	,,	Thomas, Ernest A.
43536	,,	Milligan, A. McK.	43545	,,	Vaughan, G. F.
43537	,,	Martineau, Leo	43657	,,	Wildes, Harold
43757	,,	McPhee, William	43658	,,	Wilson, Joseph V.
43633	,,	Michael, Donald	43659	,,	Williams, F. C.
43634	,,	Miller, G. W. H.	44047	,,	Wylds, H. H.
43635	,,	Murray, G. F. T.	43660	,,	Yelverton,C.J.H.P.
43636	,,	MacDonald, A. D.	43661	,,	Youell, Edward A.

No. 2 SECTION.

Major	...	...	...	McGowan, John Thomas
Captain	...	...	...	Kennedy, Kenneth Edgar
Lieutenant	...	...	...	Churchill, Clifford Earl
,,	...	...	...	Harcourt, Robert Hamilton
,,	...	...	...	Moir, Robert H.
,,	...	...	...	Dowsley, Colin Gray
,,	...	...	...	Smith, William Fielding

Canadian Pacific—The Empire's Greatest Railway.

DIVISIONAL AMMUNITION COLUMN—cont.

Regl. No.	Rank.	Name.	Regl. No.	Rank.	Name.
43662	Sergt.	Denmark, John C.	43713	Gunner	Dorval, Guy
43665	,,	Setchell, Herbert	43714	,,	Dumais, Lorenzo
43949	,,	Terry, William P.	43599	,,	Dumont, Leopold
43666	Corpl.	Castera, Leon	43715	,,	Elston, Eugene E.
43064	,,	Henderson, E. W.	43716	,,	Farmer, John
43731	Bombr.	Hart, Stephen	43717	,,	Fell, Reginald H.
43667	,,	Ilott, Charles	43718	,,	Flemming, Richard
43668	,,	Stratton, James L.	43720	,,	Ford, Victor M.
43670	,,	Whitehead, A. E.	43721	,,	Fowke, Earle P.
43669	,,	Wilkinson, William	43952	,,	Fidler, Carrel Watt
43672	Sh'sm'th	Wells, Harold John	43722	,,	Goodwin, Albert
43673	Wheeler	Sherlock, Wm. O.	43724	,,	Greenhalf, Edward J.
43674	,,	Zeigler, Milton F.	43725	,,	Greenaway, Wm. L.
43676	Saddler	Anctil, Joseph A.	43726	,,	Grimshaw, C. D.
43675	,,	Mahoney, John	43727	,,	Gauthier, Joseph
43680	Gunner	Allan, Charles T.	43728	,,	Goulin, Joseph
43683	,,	Ansgood, Walter E.	43953	,,	Grass, George F,
43684	,,	Barber, Willard L.	43729	,,	Hack, Robert James
43685	,,	Barney, George H.	43730	,,	Hack, Charles A.
43686	,,	Beckman, Charles A.	43732	,,	Heskins, George
43687	,,	Beckman, Lloyd J.	43733	,,	Hill, John
43688	,,	Behan, Jean	43528	,,	Hewitt, George H.
43061	,,	Beck, Harry	43736	,,	Hodgins, William
43689	,,	Bewey, Samuel	43737	,,	Hogg, William
43690	,,	Boucher, Frank	43738	,,	Hillier, Edgar
43691	,,	Bradley, Clifford H.	43596	Wheeler	Holowatuk, Billy
43692	,,	Bramble, John R.	43739	Gunner	Hotson, John
43693	,,	Brentnell, Wm. H.	43741	,,	Jamieson, Charles R.
43694	,,	Buisson, Cyriague	43742	,,	Jolicoeur, Joseph L.
43695	,,	Burcombe, R. S. D.	44067	,,	Jackson, William H.
43696	,,	Bursey, William F.	43671	,,	King, Charles
44063	,,	Burnett, W. A.	43743	,,	L'Heureux, François
43697	,,	Cardinal, Emile	43744	,,	Longwell, Robert
43699	,,	Campbell, Charles E.	43745	,,	Lynes, William B.
43700	,,	Clark, William	43746	,,	Low, Arthur G.
43701	,,	Clayton, F. J., Jr.	43747	,,	La Rue, Joseph A.
43702	,,	Clegg, Albert C.	43807	,,	Lebreque, Arthur
43703	,,	Conley, Thomas	43748	,,	Masson, William E.
43704	,,	Costello, John	43749	,,	Miller, Lawrence F.
43705	,,	Crane, James	43750	,,	Morgan, Joseph
43706	,,	Crozier, Harold J.	43751	,,	Mowat, Mark
43707	,,	Cruse, John	43752	,,	McConaghy, S. C.
43708	,,	Cutting, George	43753	,,	McGrail, Thomas
43804	,,	Consigny, Charles	43754	,,	McKen, George
43805	,,	Carnell, James D.	43755	,,	McKen, Robert T.
43951	,,	Clayton, F. J., Sr.	43756	Shsm'th	McLennan, Alex.
43698	,,	Carrier, Leo W.	43758	Gunner	McVey, Patrick J.
43677	,,	Dayer, William H.	43663	,,	Martin, Edward
43709	,,	D'Amour, Jules	43810	,,	Marquis, Joseph
43710	,,	De Chateauvert, C.	43679	,,	Malcolm, Michael
43711	,,	De Chateauvert, H.	43759	,,	Norrish, William G.
43712	,,	Docksey, Parcy G.	43760	,,	Patman, F. Wm.

Canadian Pacific—The Empire's Greatest Railway.

DIVISIONAL AMMUNITION COLUMN—cont. 315

Regl. No.	Rank.	Name.	Regl. No.	Rank.	Name.
43761	Gunner	Peacock, Albert E.	43784	Gunner	Tovell, Robert James
43762	,,	Pearson, William	43785	,,	Tryan, Benjamin S.
43570	,,	Pegus, Ruthven	43786	,,	Turland, Horace G.
43590	,,	Pfeifer, John	43955	,,	Tomney, C. Ford
43763	,,	Pitcher, Clarence R	43808	,,	Thibault, Joseph
43764	,,	Pitcher, Leonard E.	43787	,,	Vachon, Alfred
43765	,,	Rex, Sidney A.	43790	,,	Virtue, Wesley
43766	,,	Robertson, C. R.	43791	,,	Walsh, Gilbert
44062	,,	Robinson, A. E.	43792	,,	Weist, Arthur
43770	,,	Sager, Oscar E.	43793	,,	Webb, Albert
43771	,,	Scott, Morris	43794	,,	Welch, Michael J.
43772	,,	Searle, William	43795	Sh'sm'th	Wilkinson, John Wm.
43773	,,	Short, George S.	43796	Gunner	Williams, George S.
43774	,,	Smith, James	43797	,,	Williams, Thilbert D.
43775	,,	Smith, Simon	43798	,,	Wills, Sydney G.
43776	,,	Smith, Ernest	43799	,,	Winegard, Arthur R.
43777	,,	Soper, John F.	43800	,,	Winegard, Claude D.
43778	,,	Stableford, Roy N.	43801	,,	Winn, Charles R.
43780	,,	Steeves, Albert F.	43802	,,	Wooley, Thomas S.
43592	,,	Shytka, Wasyl	43803	,,	Worswick, Edgar T.
43782	,,	Thomson, Thomas	44066	,,	Wood, Walter H.
43783	,,	Tidswell, Frederick	44068	,,	Wilson, Thomas

No. 3 SECTION.

Major ... ... Anderson, Samuel Boyd
Lieutenant ... ... Hayes, Ralph St. Clair
,, ... Parker, Harry Scott
,, ... Lefroy, Robert Perceval Philip
,, ... Garland, Charles Hieland Barnet

Regl. No.	Rank.	Name.	Regl. No.	Rank.	Name.
43897	Sergt.	Lockett, Albert Edw.	43821	Gunner	Andrews, James
43811	,,	Martin, Henry E.	43815	,,	Bland, Arthur A.
43813	,,	Pellowe, William J.	43823	,,	Beal, Roland S.
43812	,,	Weatherhead, A.	43824	,,	Belyea, Abner B.
43944	Far. Sgt.	Fisher, Wallace G.	43825	,,	Bird, Harold W.
43814	Corpl.	Tremain, Edward C.	43826	,,	Bamber, John
43945	Bombr.	Bradshaw, Robert E.	43827	,,	Beamish, George
43864	,,	Estey, Arthur T.	43828	,,	Bailey, Norman J.
43817	,,	Shear, Frederick H.	43829	,,	Barnard, Frank
43818	,,	Spencer, James	43830	,,	Baulch, Sidney B.
43822	Saddler	Althorp, George	43831	,,	Bell, James
43849	Sh'sm'th	Crowe, Levi	43832	,,	Blasby, Benjamin E.
43892	,,	Keith, Douglas F.	43833	,,	Biddiscombe, Chas. E.
43902	Wheeler	McLean, John W.	43834	,,	Boutilier, Ernest C.
43936	,,	Whitnect, Thomas C.	43835	,,	Brentnell, Arthur
43819	Gunner	Anderson, Edward R.	43836	,,	Burk, William S.
43820	,,	Anderson, Dixon	43837	,,	Bytrave, John

Canadian Pacific—The Empire's Greatest Railway.

DIVISIONAL AMMUNITION COLUMN—cont.

Regl. No.	Rank.	Name.	Regl. No.	Rank.	Name.
43943	Gunner	Brown, Arthur G.	43889	Gunner	Hemming, George
43816	,,	Clark, Edward Clay	43890	,,	Jenkins, George S.
43838	,,	Cole, Samuel S.	43891	,,	King, John H.
43839	,,	Crawford, John A.	43893	,,	Livingstone, W. R.
43840	,,	Cunningham, V. J.	43894	,,	Leary, Patrick
43842	,,	Coyle, Ernest A.	43895	,,	Lingley, Otto D.
43843	,,	Cowan, Robert M.	43896	,,	Lattimer, William R.
43844	,,	Cummings, Wm. D.	43898	,,	LeClair, George
43845	,,	Cameron, Leonard P.	43899	,,	London, Joseph
43846	,,	Campbell, S. W.	43900	,,	Luttman, Sidney W.
43847	,,	Campbell, C. McG.	43901	,,	McDougall, George A.
43848	,,	Collins, Stanley	43903	,,	McIlwrith, William
43850	,,	Connolly, Daniel	43904	,,	McLeod, Murray A.
43851	,,	Capson, Roy W.	43905	,,	McHugh, John
43852	,,	Chase, Charles W.	43906	,,	McAllister, Edwin A.
43853	,,	Clary, Alfred Edw.	43907	,,	Mathias, Alexander
43854	,,	Connolly, Arthur	43908	,,	Morrow, James H.
43855	,,	Dunn, Benjamin R.	43909	,,	Moore, Frederick
43856	,,	Dunn, John A.	43910	,,	Munro, Frederick H.
43582	,,	Duhaut, Gus.	43911	,,	Martin, Bernard
43857	,,	Downing, Norman	43912	,,	Mullin, George DeW.
43858	,,	Doyle, Alex. A.	43913	,,	Miller, James
43859	,,	Davis, Oscar G.	43914	,,	McDonald, James
43860	,,	DeRoche, Frederick	43915	,,	McGregor, Alex. E.
43861	,,	Durant, James T.	43916	,,	Mooney, John Harold
43862	,,	Damery, Fredk. K.	43917	,,	Nice, Frederick
43863	,,	Downes, Frank E.	43918	,,	Nordstrum, Nels
43865	,,	Elliott, John	43919	,,	Oppoli, Frederick
43866	Act. Cpl.	Farmer, Geoffrey	43947	,,	O'Keefe, John Chas.
43867	Gunner	Frizell, Patrick	43948	,,	Pincomb, Jacob Wm.
43868	,,	Friars, Louis S.	43920	,,	Pierce, George A.
43869	,,	Fowlie, Walter E.	43921	,,	Purcell, James R.
43870	,,	Favro, Louis	43922	,,	Roberts, William
43871	,,	Fraser, Nicholas W.	43923	,,	Ramsden, James E.
43872	,,	Forbes, Alexander J.	43924	,,	Sullivan, William
43946	,,	Frisk, Jacob	43925	,,	Smith, Joseph Henry
43873	,,	Garnett, George K.	43926	,,	Spragg, Arthur S.
43874	,,	Graham, Percy L.	43928	,,	Shepherd, Alfred
43875	,,	Gibson, Andrew	43929	,,	Stafford, George W.
43876	,,	Hickey, William L.	43930	,,	Skuse, William
43877	,,	Hilvorsan, Martin	43931	,,	Savage, Daniel
43878	,,	Hicks, Rufus	43932	,,	Todd, George H.
43879	,,	Hatt, Arthur E.	43933	,,	Verrall, Ernest
43880	,,	Hammond, Joseph A.	43934	,,	Wright, Harry Chas.
43881	,,	Howell, Cyril	43935	,,	Williamson, Geo. G.
43882	,,	Higgs, Antoine	43937	,,	Wiley, George A.
43883	,,	Hayes, Richard	43939	,,	Wasson, Hedley S.
43884	,,	Henderson, Alex. T.	43940	,,	Whelly, Richard G.
43885	,,	Haley, George	43941	,,	Walker, Charles E.
43886	,,	Hudson, Joseph E.	43942	,,	Wright, John H.
43887	,,	Hackett, Wilfrid	43938	,,	Walsh, John Francis
43888	,,	Humphrey, James A.			

Canadian Pacific—The Empire's Greatest Railway.

DIVISIONAL AMMUNITION COLUMN—cont. 317

No. 4 SECTION.

Captain ... ... Stern, Percival Theodore
Lieutenant... ... ... Dunlop, Hugh McDonald
     ,, ... Hoodless, Joseph Brenard

Regl. No.	Rank.	Name.	Regl. No.	Rank.	Name.
43959	Sergt.	Puddy, Edward J.	43569	Gunner	Ittis, George
43956	,,	Slader, Edward M.	43575	,,	Ittis, Albert
44057	Far. Sgt.	McIntyre, Hugh	44001	,,	Jackson, H. E. R.
43957	Corpl.	Evans, William J. W.	44002	,,	Johnson, John E.
44013	,,	Lugar, William R. B.	44003	,,	Journeay, Benj. L.
44059	Bombr.	Collins, Ambrose	44004	,,	King, John S.
43990	,,	Gaudet, Laurence S.	44005	,,	Kirkland, Harry
43958	Wheeler	Cook, James	43576	,,	Koynoff, Koynes
44012	Sh'sm'th	Long, Beverly	44006	,,	Knowles, Elmer M.
43962	Gunner	Avery, Frederick	44007	,,	Laskey, Frederick C.
43963	,,	Andrews, Harry	44010	,,	Lock, Alfred
44058	,,	Armstrong, Hen. T.	44011	,,	Loftus, John
43516	,,	Barber, James Jos.	44014	,,	Lloyd, David H.
43964	,,	Babbitt, William P.	43148	,,	Lepine, Alcide
43965	,,	Beale, William T.	44015	,,	Males, Charles
43966	,,	Bellefontaine, Alph.	44016	,,	Manley, Stephen
43967	,,	Beckingham, F. C.	44017	,,	Martin, James
43968	,,	Bryan, William	44018	,,	Meates, Barth. John
43969	,,	Burrell, Robert J.	44019	,,	Muir, James W.
43970	,,	Brown, John W.	44020	,,	Murphy, Henry J.
43971	,,	Capson, Guy Charles	44021	,,	McInnis, Charles A.
43972	,,	Carter, Albert E.	44023	,,	McNulty, Joseph W.
43973	,,	Clark, Lewis H.	44024	,,	McTigh, Thos. M. F.
43974	,,	Clattenbury, Lester	43961	,,	McDonald, Daniel A.
43975	,,	Cobham, Arthur G.	44025	,,	Noftel, Joseph
43976	,,	Coffey, Robert J.	44026	,,	Palmer, Frederick T.
43977	,,	Comeau, Henry T.	44028	,,	Penney, Stanley H.
43978	,,	Chandler, Lambert A.	44029	,,	Poulson, Alex. T.
43979	,,	Creaser, William	43960	,,	Pike, Harry W.
43980	,,	Davey, Ernest E.	43580	,,	Rudick, Christopher
43981	,,	Davis, John J.	44060	,,	Rogers, Henry
43983	,,	Dobbin, Norman A.	43565	,,	Schwartz, Charles F.
43984	,,	Dorion, Stephen L.	44032	,,	Shillington, Leslie F.
43985	,,	Derrick, Edward	44034	,,	Soper, Vernon B.
43105	,,	Dibble, John	44036	,,	Stark, John
43986	,,	Evans, John W.	44037	,,	Stone, Thomas J.
43987	,,	Force, Gordon	44039	,,	Tapley, George P.
43991	,,	Gorman, William	44040	,,	Thayer, Thomas C.
43992	,,	Gillett, Frank J.	44041	,,	Thompson, Frederick
43993	,,	Greentree, Geo. Hen.	44042	,,	Thompson, Wm. Hen.
43120	,,	Haire, Thomas	44043	,,	Thompson, Wm. Jas.
44061	,,	Hollingsworth, Jas.	44044	,,	Tolley, George F.
43997	,,	Horsman, Arthur S.	44045	,,	Townsend, Frederick
43998	,,	Hunter, William L.	44048	,,	Walker, Harry W.
43999	,,	Harley, Frank	44049	,,	Walker, David N.
44000	,,	Ingraham, Charles P.	44050	,,	Ward, Harold J.

Canadian Pacific—The Empire's Greatest Railway.

DIVISIONAL AMMUNITION COLUMN—cont.

Regl. No.	Rank.	Name.	Regl. No.	Rank.	Name.
44051	Gunner	Webb, William	44055	Gunner	Wade, Louis J.
44052	,,	Webb, Cyril	44056	,,	Ward, William B.
44053	,,	Williams, W. McL.			

DIVISIONAL AMMUNITION PARK, with C.F.A. (attached)

Major	Bell, Archibald de Mowbray
Captain	Goldie (Adjt), Edward Crosby
,, ...	Chaplin, Garnet Wolseley (attached)
Lieutenant	Lindsay, Norman James
,, ...	Mills, John Ross
,, ...	Steele, Samuel Coucher
Paymaster	Hon. Captain Cawdron, Ernest V.
Lieutenant	Schreiber, Eric B. (attached)
,, ...	Warren, James Delemere
Medical Officer	Captain Boyd, Harold Bently
Captain	Turnbull, Alan (unattached)
Lieutenant	Nicholls, Walter N. (attached)

Regl. No.	Rank.	Name.	Regl. No.	Rank.	Name.
37006	(W.O.)	Johnson, F. E. H.	37324	Corpl.	Smith, William C.
37008	Sgt.-Maj.	Bayliffe, Henry John	37115	,,	Kidby, Arthur J.
37010	Q.M.Sgt.	Harrison, Walter L.	37322	,,	Jones, Arthur W.
37009	Staff Sgt.	Murry, John S.	37106	,,	Jones, Arthur C. F.
37081	,,	Fawcett, Norman W.	37136	,,	Jones, Henry Charles
37313	,,	Shaw, Robert Albert	37239	,,	Robinson, Arthur E.
37340	,,	Woods, F. O. G.	37059	,,	Conduit, Alfred H.
37001	Sergt.	Allen, Arthur Nelson	37199	,,	Naylor, Cyril F.
37359	,,	Warburton, E. R.	37064	,,	Dunfield, Eber Atkin
37336	,,	Hay, Lionel	37326	,,	Shilling, Lewis James
37007	Staff Sgt.	Norris, Charles E.	37184	,,	Prince, Harold W.
37360	Sergt.	Smith, James W.	37016	,,	Barton, Arthur
37339	,,	Lyon, John Sydney	37063	,,	Dixon, William J.
37049	Staff Sgt.	Bright, David M.	37351	,,	O'Brien, Charles E.
37368	,,	Casson, George Dent	37095	,,	Gallwey, Lionel Guy
37076	Sergt.	Elliott, Henry S.	37022	,,	Ballantyne, Ralph M.
37142	,,	Webb, Frederick A.	37332	,,	Castree, George
37308	,,	Nicol, Arthur P.	37337	,,	Moser, Harry Tyler
37323	,,	Steele, Henry Wm.	37311	,,	Walker, David
37104	,,	Gilchrist, John	37183	,,	Powell, Wilfred B.
37253	Staff Sgt.	White, Ottie Earle	37317	,,	Temple, Thomas H.
37148	Sergt.	Hill, William	37252	,,	Wrigglesworth, V. G.
37194	Corpl.	Martin, Robert A.	37110	,,	King, William H.
37266	,,	Sparrow, A. K.	37111	,,	Kinghorn, Thomas
37122	,,	Lewis, Frederick Wm.	37204	,,	Rea, William John
37129	,,	Hunt, Godfrey B.	37246	,,	Wyncot, Jack
37288	,,	Scott, William C.	37373	,,	Manson, Alexander
37093	,,	Hoover, William E.	37089	,,	Garrett, George Chas.

Canadian Pacific—The Empire's Greatest Railway.

DIV. AMMUNITION PARK, with C.F.A. (ATTACHED)—cont. 319

Regl. No.	Rank.	Name.	Regl. No.	Rank.	Name.
37061	Corpl.	Cave, Reginald H.	37058	Private	Churcher, Edwd. W.
37116	,,	Kinnell, James S.	37057	,,	Crewson, John
37126	,,	Legassick, Arthur H.	37055	,,	Clarkson, Elmer
37114	,,	Kirkaldy, John G.	37056	,,	Clark, Charles
37375	,,	Cockell, William H.	37048	,,	Campbell, William
37388	,,	Corner, Wilfred R.	37051	,,	Cullen, Harold C.
37264	,,	Smiley, James	37097	,,	Carmack, Harry S.
37096	,,	Hartnell, John	37052	,,	Carter, Frederick W.
37011	Private	Ackroyd, Abraham	37067	,,	Dickie, Alexander K.
37017	,,	Bergenhagen, Alex.	37075	,,	Dekker, Henry C. C.
37036	,,	Bremner, Thomas	37068	,,	DeWinter, John W.
37026	,,	Bailey, Charles H.	37374	,,	Damour, Ludger
37021	,,	Black, Sydney A.	37083	,,	Dixon, William H.
37030	,,	Brown, Russell G.	37062	,,	Darlow, John H.
37012	,,	Booast, Herbert P.	37084	,,	Deegan, Lawrence
37032	,,	Bunyon, Sidney	37066	,,	Davie, Horace
37019	,,	Bryant, William	37069	,,	Eason, Samuel
37038	,,	Bremner, Robert D.	37074	,,	English, Frank
37046	,,	Bell, Thomas R.	37377	,,	Evans, John
37023	,,	Booth, Leslie	37071	,,	Easy, Harry
37035	,,	Bourne, Alfred	37072	,,	Earle, George
37033	,,	Bone, David	37073	,,	Edwards, William J.
37013	,,	Baxter, John R.	37070	,,	Ellison, James
37027	,,	Bricknell, Horace	37469	,,	Edwards, L. St. John
37014	,,	Barber, George	37079	,,	Flint, James
37090	,,	Baker, Joseph	37078	,,	Flurett, John James
37379	,,	Bowen, John	37112	,,	Finkle, Charles P.
37031	,,	Black, William A.	37144	,,	Fry, David
37005	,,	Burdge, Charles H.	37080	,,	Fraser, Jack M.
37041	,,	Bartholomew, Cyril	37077	,,	Fairbanks, E. V.
37018	,,	Bowman, Victor	37187	,,	Falconer, Edwd. A.
37043	,,	Butler, John	37082	,,	Fogden, Thomas
37039	,,	Brookes, Reginald A.	37085	,,	Gilboe, Arthur
37040	,,	Besse, Harry	37087	,,	Grimes, George E.
37270	,,	Baker, R. J.	37100	,,	Gardner, Roy
37024	,,	Barker, Thomas N.	37328	,,	Griffin, Walter E.
37028	,,	Bell, Elvis Albert	37195	,,	Gardiner, William
37025	,,	Brown, John	37130	,,	Gerry, John S.
37029	,,	Bentley, Cuthbert	37271	,,	Gofton, Alfred S.
37037	,,	Byrne, Thomas	37175	,,	Gregson, James H.
37366	,,	Barnett, Stanley	37090	,,	Garvie, Harold Ellis
37042	,,	Belben, Leslie	37196	,,	Gates, Fredrich A.
37020	,,	Boyle, Joseph Alex.	37394	,,	Gray, James
37382	,,	Chiolno, James	37101	,,	Gallwey, John N.
37044	,,	Clinger, Royden C.	37086	,,	Grant, James Stuart
37045	,,	Childs, Harold	37128	,,	Gunn, Claude Alfred
37060	,,	Cooper, James	37088	,,	Godsmark, A. E.
37047	,,	Cheeseman, Albert E.	37120	,,	Greenwell, W. E.
37053	,,	Cartledge, Norman	37387	,,	Gabbutt, Earle
37055	,,	Cox, James	37350	,,	Harkness, Thomas
37050	,,	Calvert, James E.	37132	,,	Howery, Clay G.
37099	,,	Chapman, Herbert E.	37272	,,	Harwood, James

Canadian Pacific—The Empire's Greatest Railway.

320   DIV. AMMUNITION PARK, with C.F.A. (attached)—con,

Regl. No.	Rank	Name	Regl. No.	Rank	Name
37134	Private	Huggins, Walter	37170	Private	Moore, Hugh
37135	,,	Hall, Newman A.	37137	,,	Masson, Gilbert A.
37376	,,	Hall, Arthur Leonard	37161	,,	Milne, Richard
37131	,,	Hopley, William J.	37295	,,	Muirhead, George
37353	,,	Hancock, Walter	37164	,,	Macklem, Norman
37133	,,	Hofley, Joseph T.	37273	,,	Mather, Lewis
37094	,,	Howson, Jack	37139	,,	Mott, George Hebert
37146	,,	Higginbotham, R. E.	37362	,,	Mathieson, James
37147	,,	Holley, Thomas G.	37333	,,	Miller, William
37145	,,	Hooper, Percy	37352	,,	Murphy, Owen
37291	,,	Hagman, William A.	37154	,,	Morton, William
37098	,,	Hunt, William Hy.	37173	,,	Mechan, Robert M.
37092	,,	Hannawin, Patrick	37171	,,	Montieth, Cyril I.
37149	,,	Hollingdale, John A.	37159	,,	Middleton, Alfred S.
37091	,,	Hutchison, Harry	37156	,,	Middleton, Owen W.
37003	,,	Hall, Thomas Sydney	37343	,,	Millier, Herbert J.
37143	,,	Howe, Andrew F.	37138	,,	Mansell, Harry
37102	,,	Irving, Andrew	37174	,,	Masterton, James
37152	,,	Johnstone, Thos. R.	37325	,,	Myers, George
37383	,,	Jarvis, James	37197	,,	Matthews, F. G.
37108	,,	Joyce, Morris Russel	37140	,,	Mulligan, Edgar
37107	,,	James, Samuel	37364	,,	McCollum, Winfield S
37319	,,	Johnston, Fredrick A.	37153	,,	McKee, John Samuel
37367	,,	Johnston, David A.	37361	,,	McNeill, Lewis
37103	,,	Jackson, George G.	37338	,,	McLean, Daniel L.
37150	,,	Jackson, Samuel	37167	,,	McIvor, Wilfred J.
37354	,,	Jones, Richard D.	37178	,,	McLaren, John S.
37117	,,	Kelton, Thomas	37172	,,	McDonald, Cornelius
37113	,,	Knapp, Fredrick E.	37163	,,	McNicol, Gordon R.
37151	,,	Kynnersley, Chas. H.	37193	,,	McDonald, Donald
37347	,,	Kennedy, William H.	37160	,,	McLaren, William L.
37329	,,	Klapproth, Herbt. C.	37168	,,	McKay, John Alex.
37188	,,	Kirkland, Harry	37236	,,	McKeigan, William
37372	,,	Leveque, Nathan E.	37169	,,	McDonald, Peter J.
37118	,,	Lessard, Achille	37162	,,	McDonald, Malcolm
37121	,,	Lawson, John	37305	,,	McGinty, William
37378	,,	Lemmon, Charles R.	37331	,,	McKenzie, Thomas
37385	,,	Larson, Max	37166	,,	MacKenzie, John
37119	,,	Lockard, A. L.	37165	,,	MacKenzie, Colin G.
37124	,,	Lewis, Arthur Walter	37330	,,	McInnes, R. C.
37125	,,	Law, Walter	37314	,,	Macrorie, James
37105	,,	Ludlow, John H.	37344	,,	McCuaig, Roy John
37127	,,	Leonard, Peter	37237	,,	McCartney, J. M.
37109	,,	Legallais, John E.	37015	,,	McInerney, Michael
37349	,,	Murphy, Patrick	37386	,,	Numbers, Ralph
37307	,,	Morrison, Samuel N.	37238	,,	Nicholson, Edward S.
37158	,,	Millar, James	37198	,,	Napier, Andrew D.
37157	,,	Magill, Samuel	37257	,,	Noble, Peter F.
37240	Lce.-Cpl.	Munford, Thos. A. S.	37296	,,	Netter, George J.
37310	Private	Montgommery, A. R.	37177	,,	Nelson, James
37318	,,	Mendes, Harvey	37274	,,	Nisbet, John
37155	,,	Moffatt, Archibald	37200	,,	Nixon, Fredrick C.

Canadian Pacific—The Empire's Greatest Railway.

DIV. AMMUNITION PARK, with C.F.A. (attached)—cont. 321

Regl. No.	Rank	Name	Regl. No.	Rank	Name
37241	Private	Neal, Eric Donald	37320	Private	Sparrow, Albert H.
37380	,,	O'Gara, James	37289	,,	Sutton, Thomas A.
37180	,,	Patterson, C. M.	37265	,,	Simmonds, Walter E.
37176	,,	Parker, William H.	37222	,,	Strachan, David L.
37179	,,	Powell, Fred.	37225	,,	Saxby, Ernest
37185	,,	Palfrey, John	37220	,,	Shiels, Peter
37218	,,	Pearce, Arthur	37340	,,	Slavin, Daniel
37215	,,	Pierce, Thomas	37268	,,	Skelcher, William
37393	,,	Prinn, Allan	37290	,,	Stewart, Howard W.
37189	,,	Purcell, Clarence G.	37223	,,	Smith, Alexander
37181	,,	Pimlott, George	37229	,,	Sutherland, Charles
37190	,,	Purcell, Robert S.	37226	,,	Sharp, Charles
37186	,,	Phillips, George H.	37227	,,	Stuart, Donald
37191	,,	Proctor, Walter J.	37224	,,	Solman, Gerald S.
37217	,,	Postlethwaite, Wm.	37302	,,	Sutherland, John C.
37216	,,	Phillips, Thomas G.	37267	,,	Strubb, Irving H.
37219	,,	Pinkham, William	37141	,,	Simpson, Herbert A.
37192	,,	Probert, John	37259	,,	Taylor, John
37275	,,	Plumbtree, W. G.	37261	,,	Taylor, Leonard C.
37182	,,	Parker, Alfred E.	37316	,,	Tonelli, Andrea
37292	,,	Patterson, Wm. R.	37262	,,	Tanner, Eric C.
37207	,,	Rayner, George W.	37293	,,	Thomson, T. H.
37201	,,	Redman, Jack	37357	,,	Tapp, John T.
37211	,,	Russell, Robert	37294	,,	Terry, Donald
37297	,,	Robinson, E. C.	37263	,,	Trudeau, Oliver
37206	,,	Royce, Ernest F.	37233	,,	Tollman, Robert
37321	,,	Reid, James, Jr.	37234	,,	Tilley, Henry Lewis
37278	,,	Rand, Walter	37232	,,	Travers, Charles W.
37203	,,	Rose, William John	37279	,,	Trotter, Harold C.
37208	,,	Rowe, Frank Ralph	37363	Lce.-Cpl.	Tytherliegh, Hugh
37277	,,	Reynolds, F. G.	37301	Private	Thompson, John
37210	,,	Rasmussen, Christie	37389	,,	Turner, Thomas
37205	,,	Robertson, Douglas	37356	,,	Thomas, Fredrick
37212	,,	Reid, James, Sr.	37231	,,	Thompson, Victor
37214	,,	Renaud, Constant J.	37260	,,	Taylor, George H. K.
37209	,,	Robinson, D. N.	37304	,,	Undsworth, Charles
37213	,,	Rooke, Berty	37345	,,	Urquhart, Thomas
37258	,,	Richardson, Thomas	37346	,,	Vine, William
37312	,,	Rawlings, Harry M.	37315	,,	Van Buskirk, M. B.
37276	,,	Rance, Walter	37002	,,	Wink, Thomas
37300	,,	Rees, Claud	37256	,,	Watson, William
37202	,,	Reed, George	37280	,,	Waite, Bert
37230	,,	Sparling, Howard C.	37248	,,	Wareham, Thomas
37221	,,	Stevens, Wm. H.	37327	,,	Weatherall, Fred R.
37269	,,	Smiley, Samuel	37285	,,	Wright, Charles
37034	,,	Spence, Claud	37306	,,	Watson, Gerald C.
37371	,,	Sutherland, Harry	37335	,,	Wilson, Dawson
33339	,,	Scott, Alex.	37341	,,	Williams, Ernest J.
37365	,,	Scott, George	37244	,,	Whyte, Hugh K.
37369	,,	Smith, John	37283	,,	Williamson, James
37342	,,	Shoemaker, E. H.	37384	,,	Wilson, Edward
37287	,,	Schrier, Ernest G.	37284	,,	Wallis, Rupert

Canadian Pacific—The Empire's Greatest Railway.

x

322 DIV. AMMUNITION PARK, WITH C.F.A. (ATTACHED)—cont.

Regl. No.	Rank.	Name.	Regl. No.	Rank.	Name.
37358	Private	Whatson, Albert E.	37255	Private	Walker, St. Clair
37334	,,	Warner, Vern	37245	,,	Walker, Wesley
37243	,,	Walker, Wilfred	37247	,,	Wilson, William
37355	,,	Watson, Robert	37298	,,	Webb, Alfred B.
37282	,,	Walsh, Harry	37251	,,	Wilson, Harry
37286	,,	Williams, William	37303	,,	Younger, George
37299	,,	Waterfall, John F.	37381	,,	Goldie, Thomas
37250	,,	Waugh, William	37392	Corpl.	Ward, Luke (Water
37254	,,	Webb, Basil			detail).
37242	,,	Wheeler, Walter	37391	Private	Trerise, Edward T.
37235	,,	Williams, John L.			(Water detail).
37281	,,	Woods, Edmund			

ARTILLERY DETAILS.

Major ... ... Gillmore, Edward Theodore Barclay
Captain ... ... Roy, Joseph George Emile

Regl. No.	Rank.	Name	Regl. No.	Rank.	Name.
37475	Sgt.-Maj.	Houghton, Charles J.	37471	Gunner	Fowler, Percy E.
37455	Sergt.	Carter, Edward J.	37480	,,	Grauer, Samuel
37473	,,	Davies, Harry L.	37419	,,	Gorst, Peter
37456	,,	Hoey, William	37452	,,	Graham, Thomas C.
37401	Act.-Sgt.	Morris, Henry W.	37477	,,	Griffiths, William
37403	,,	McNown, Ernest A.	37465	,,	Glass, William
37402	Corpl.	Barber, George	37435	,,	Hadlington, Solomon
37458	,,	Barrett, Vernon W.	37432	,,	Hutchison, S. McG.
37423	,,	McCabe, Henry P.	37406	,,	Henderson, John
37418	Gunner	Alley, Augustus C.	37412	,,	Hoskins, George
37472	,,	Angers, Frank Real	37405	,,	Higham, George
37427	,,	Budd, Alfred	37476	,,	Harper, Hanley
37481	,,	Budd, James	37450	,,	Hackett, Michael
37425	,,	Baughn, Frederick	37474	,,	Ingar, Joseph
37462	,,	Baker, William	37433	,,	Kenneally, H. M.
37428	,,	Brown, Playfair	37434	,,	Kerry, George
37411	,,	Brown, William A.	37407	,,	Knox, William
37479	Bombr.	Bray, George	37410	,,	Kennedy, James
37424	Gunner	Brabant, Joseph A.	37437	,,	Leonard, R. A.
37426	,,	Burton, William H.	37466	Bombr.	Logan, John
37417	,,	Butler, John	37436	Gunner	Learn, Clinton T.
37457	,,	Baldwin, F. A.	37451	,,	McDonald, William
37464	,,	Bolwell, William S.	37467	,,	McDonald, David
37429	,,	Cowman, John J.	37421	,,	McEwan, William N.
37430	,,	Campbell, Arthur J.	37478	,,	Moran, Henry
37415	,,	Connolley, Wm. J.	37453	,,	Moody, William L.
37459	,,	Curry, Robert	37439	,,	Nicholson, Charles
37422	,,	Dolga, Dominic	37440	,,	Noyes, Harry Wm.
37431	,,	Davies, Frederick	37408	,,	Penn, Edward H. M.
37468	,,	Dorman, Frederick	37441	,,	Penley, Henry
37463	,,	Fournier, Pierre	37460	,,	Reith, Walter
37470	Bombr.	Fisher, James	37469	,,	Sibberin, Harold

Canadian Pacific—The Empire's Greatest Railway.

DIV. AMMUNITION PARK, WITH C.F.A. (ATTACHED)—cont. 323

Regl. No.	Rank.	Name.	Regl. No.	Rank.	Name.
37409	Gunner	Shaw, Thomas	37404	Bombr.	Wills, Samuel
37454	,,	Street, Joseph	37414	Gunner	Wingate, Herbert
37442	,,	Shaw, Arthur Henry	37420	,,	Wilson, James
37443	,,	Smith, Henry B.	37446	,,	Wright, Christopher
37444	,,	Thomas, Owen A.	37449	,,	Walker, Edward W.
37413	,,	Thomson, Robert	37445	,,	Wilson, Gordon C.
37461	,,	Thomson, Gordon			

No. 1 RESERVE PARK.

Major	... ...	Adams, Charles
Captain	... ...	Heasley, Hugh J.
Lieutenant	... ...	Storer, John Cameron Hume
,,	... ...	Church, Eric James
,,	... ...	Gerrard, William James
Veterinary Officer	... ...	Lieutenant Douglas, Kenneth Leon
Medical Officer	... ...	Captain McDermot, Hugh Ernest
Paymaster	... ...	Hon. Captain Lacroix, L.

Regl. No.	Rank.	Name.	Regl. No.	Rank.	Name.
35326	Driver	Abbott, W. H.	35353	Driver	Buckley, Joseph
35327	,,	Adams, J. H.	35354	,,	Buckley, D. C.
35328	,,	Allan, T.	35355	,,	Burgess, F.
35329	,,	Allcock, F.	35356	,,	Burnett, G.
35330	,,	Allen, W.	35357	,,	Byers, C. J.
35331	,,	Anderson, J. G.	35358	,,	Bourque, J.
35332	,,	Armstrong, S.	35359	,,	Canavan, J.
35333	,,	Augustyn, L.	35360	,,	Chambers, L.
35334	,,	Bailey, W.	35361	,,	Clay, J.
35336	,,	Bairstow, W.	35362	,,	Clermont, J. B.
35335	,,	Baker, H. N.	35363	,,	Clitheroe, R.
35337	,,	Bate, E. C.	35364	,,	Cochran, D. A.
35338	,,	Bates, J.	35365	,,	Cole, D. H.
35339	,,	Bennett, W. R.	35366	,,	Cole, C.
35340	,,	Biggs, H.	35367	,,	Coneybeare, A. J.
35341	,,	Bissonnette, E.	35368	,,	Cook, F.
35342	,,	Blackledge, R.	35369	,,	Cook, W. H.
35343	,,	Blackman, H.	35370	,,	Coombes, F.
35344	,,	Bowie, F. E.	35371	,,	Cooper, D.
35345	,,	Bricklebank, E.	35372	,,	Corbett, J. J.
35346	,,	Briggs, P.	35373	,,	Cordes, E.
35437	,,	Brown, A.	35374	,,	Copley, C.
35348	,,	Brown, James	35375	,,	Cox, A. E.
35349	,,	Brown, R.	35305	Far. Sgt.	Crawford, J. H.
35324	Trumpt'r	Brown, W. J.	35376	Driver	Crawley, A.
35350	Driver	Brown, W. W.	35377	,,	Craig, A. M.
35351	,,	Brown, John	35378	,,	Crockett, W. A.
35352	Sh'sm'th	Buckenham, A. S.	35379	,,	Chapman, F.

Canadian Pacific—The Empire's Greatest Railway.

x 2

No. 1 RESERVE PARK—cont.

Regl. No.	Rank.	Name.
35380	Driver	Cross, D.
35381	,,	Cunningham, G.
35382	,,	Corkill, F.
38383	,,	Daley, H. C.
35384	,,	Davis, A. W.
35385	,,	Day, M. C.
35390	Sh'sm'th	Dearden, H.
35386	Driver	Decker, H. A.
35387	,,	Dixie, H. H.
35388	,,	Dodds, W. S.
35389	,,	Deacon, G. C.
35391	Far. Cpl.	Donaldson, W. A.
35392	Driver	Duncan, D.
35393	,,	Downes, W. H.
35394	,,	Davis, A.
35395	,,	Davis, James
35396	,,	De Vriendt, R.
35397	,,	Edgar, G.
35398	,,	Empson, L. W.
35321	Corpl.	Enticknap, A.
35399	Wheeler	Fage, E. L.
35400	Driver	Fairthorne, M.
35401	,,	Farr, A.
35402	,,	Farrance, P. H.
35320	Corpl.	Farrar, T. G.
35403	Driver	Faulkner, R.
35404	,,	Ferguson, T.
35405	,,	Fielder, H. A.
35406	,,	Fielding, H. C.
35407	,,	Findlay, F.
35408	,,	Fisher, J. A.
35307	Whr. Sgt.	Flower, C. P.
35409	Driver	Forster, F.
35410	,,	Fotherby, E. E.
35411	,,	Fowler, F.
35412	,,	Fox, M. W.
35310	Sergt.	Francis, R.
35413	Driver	Freestone, J. C.
35414	,,	Francis, J. W.
35415	,,	Gamble, J.
35416	,,	Gates, H. C.
35417	,,	Gear, E. F.
35418	,,	Gerrish, J.
35419	,,	Gotts, S.
35420	,,	Graham, W.
35421	,,	Grandison, D.
35422	,,	Grant, H. J.
35489	,,	Green, H.
35311	Sergt.	Green, H. P.
35423	Driver	Greenhalgh, D.
35424	,,	Greenwell, J.
35425	,,	Grice, W.
35426	Driver	Griffiths, G. A.
35427	,,	Gunn, D. S.
35428	,,	Hackett, T.
35429	,,	Haddrell, F.
35430	,,	Haggas, W. C.
35431	,,	Hall, E.
35432	,,	Hall, T. A. D.
35301	Sgt.-Maj.	Hamilton,F.S.(W.O.)
35433	Driver	Hankinson, E. G.
35434	,,	Harding, W. G.
35435	,,	Harley, A.
35436	,,	Harris, A.
35306	Wlr. Sgt.	Harris, G. A.
35437	Driver	Hawker, F. A.
35438	,,	Henault, L.
35439	,,	Henderson, H.
35440	,,	Hewitt, R.
35441	,,	Hill, J. W.
35442	,,	Holdsworth, F. C.
35443	,,	Horner, V.
35444	,,	Hough, R.
35445	,,	Houle, J. H.
35446	,,	Huggins, W. H.
35447	,,	Hutchings, H.
35448	,,	Hedges, J. A.
35449	,,	Jackling, J. H.
35450	,,	Jackson, P.
35303	Co.Q.M.S.	Jaffray, J.
35451	Driver	Jeffrey, C. W.
35452	,,	Jones, D. W.
35453	,,	Jones, H.
35454	,,	Jones, P.
35455	,,	Jagger, A. M.
35456	,,	Johnson, W.
35322	Corpl.	Johnson, G. H.
35457	Driver	Keenan, J. J.
35458	,,	King, A.
35459	,,	Lavallee, A.
35460	,,	Leavitt, A. E.
35461	,,	Lee, E. A.
35462	,,	Lees, C.
35463	,,	Lemay, J. A.
35464	,,	Leslie, W.
35465	,,	Lesperance, E.
35323	Lce.-Cpl.	Lewis, F. C.
35466	Driver	Little, H. S.
35467	,,	Liscoumb, C.
35468	,,	Livie, D.
35469	,,	Lofthouse, F.
35470	,,	Lord, J. H.
35471	,,	MacDonald, J. A.
35325	Pay Sgt.	MacLachlan, A. J.

Canadian Pacific—The Empire's Greatest Railway.

No. 1 RESERVE PARK—cont.

Regl. No.	Rank.	Name.	Regl. No.	Rank.	Name.
35472	Driver	McAnulty, C.	35522	Driver	Reddy, F.
35473	,,	McCarthy, B. A.	35523	Sh'sm'th	Reed, F. A.
35474	,,	McCarthy, L.	35524	Driver	Reid, H. A.
35475	,,	McBride, T.	35525	,,	Redfern, Joseph
35476	,,	McIntyre, C. E.	35526	,,	Regan, C.
35477	,,	McKenzie, A.	35527	,,	Rheaume, D.
35478	,,	McKeown, B.	35528	,,	Riley, H. A.
35479	,,	McLeod, T.	35529	,,	Rose, W.
35480	,,	McLearon, A.	35530	,,	Roux, F.
35481	,,	McMurray, W.	35315	,,	Russell, H.
35482	,,	McRae, P.	35531	,,	Saunders, J.
35483	,,	Mallette, E.	35532	,,	Scott, H.
35484	,,	Marcotte, E.	35309	Sad. Sgt.	Schwartz, J.
35308	Sad. Sgt.	Marshall, L. L.	35304	Far. S. S.	Scott, J.
35485	Driver	Martin, J. T.	35533	Driver	Sellen, L. E.
35486	,,	Marlatt, D. G. L.	35534	,,	Sharkey, G. F.
35487	,,	Marrison, F. D.	35535	,,	Sharples, J.
35488	,,	Maxwell, C. H.	35536	,,	Slack, W. S.
35317	Sad. Cpl.	Mayer, J. A.	35537	,,	Slavin, F. A.
35490	Driver	Meech, F.	35538	,,	Sims, E.
35491	,,	Melvin, J.	35539	,,	Smith, A.
35492	,,	Minifie, J. H.	35540	,,	Smith, G.
35493	,,	Minifie, J. T.	35541	,,	Smith, Joseph H.
35494	,,	Mitchell, V. W.	35542	,,	Smith, James
35495	,,	Mitchell, W. A.	35543	,,	Smith, W.
35496	,,	Morgan, A.	35544	,,	Smith, S.
35497	,,	Moxham, M. V.	35545	,,	Snelling, F.
35498	,,	Mayne, G. R. T.	35546	,,	Snoddy, W.
35499	,,	Nash, T.	35547	,,	Spencer, A.
35500	,,	Neame, W. F.	35548	,,	Spruce, R.
35501	,,	Nickson, R.	35549	,,	Stanley, C. F.
35502	,,	Noel, R.	35550	,,	Stead, G.
35503	,,	Nutt, W.	35551	,,	Stevenson, W. F.
35504	,,	Oakes, E.	35552	,,	Sticht, J. H.
35505	,,	Palmer, G. H.	35553	,,	Swatman, B.
35506	,,	Pankhurst, A. W.	35554	,,	Sproule, S. M.
35507	,,	Patterson, J.	35555	,,	Sullivan, O.
35508	,,	Peat, A.	35556	,,	Sullivan, F.
35509	,,	Perrott, O. C.	35557	,,	Tavner, J.
35510	,,	Phillips, R.	35558	,,	Taylor, J.
35511	,,	Pickering, W.	35302	Co. S.-M.	Tessier, R.
35512	,,	Pike, H. W.	35559	Driver	Teskey, T. S.
35513	,,	Porter, R.	35560	,,	Tomlinson, T.
35514	,,	Prendergast, D.	35561	,,	Thornton, G.
35515	,,	Preston, S.	35562	,,	Totten, P.
35516	,,	Price, A.	35563	,,	Tranter, C. T.
35517	,,	Proctor, J. F.	35564	,,	Turrell, E.
35518	,,	Pyke, P.	35565	,,	Upton, P. H.
35316	Far. Cpl.	Ramsay, W. H.	35566	,,	Vigor, A.
35519	Driver	Randall, A. E.	35567	,,	Wade, W.
35520	,,	Ranger, E.	35568	,,	Wakelyn, E. D.
35521	,,	Read, E. E.	35569	,,	Walker, D. K.

Canadian Pacific—The Empire's Greatest Railway.

No. 1 RESERVE PARK—cont.

Regl. No.	Rank.	Name.	Regl. No.	Rank.	Name.
35570	Driver	Walker, C. W.	35314	Wlr. Cpl.	Whimp, G. J.
35571	,,	Walter, F.	35585	Driver	Whimp, W.
35572	,,	Waller, H.	35579	,,	Whitcombe, A. C.
35312	Sergt.	Waters, P.	35318	Sad. Cpl.	White, H.
35573	Driver	Watts, S. J.	35319	Corpl.	White, S.
35574	,,	Waterton, J. H.	35580	Driver	White, T.
35575	,,	Way, C.	35581	,,	Williams, J.
35576	,,	Wearne, H. F.	35582	,,	Williams, H. R.
35577	,,	Wehrle, C.	35583	,,	Wilson, J. S.
35313	Sergt.	West, G. V. M.	35584	,,	Wilson, S. W.
35578	Driver	Wheeler, J. H.	35586	,,	Yates, W.

DEPOT UNITS OF SUPPLY, C.A.S.C.

No. 1.

Captain ... ... Cleary, Edward John

Regl. No.	Rank.	Name.	Regl. No.	Rank.	Name.
30600	Act.S.S.M.	McCallum, C. P.	30603	Act.S.Bkr.	Gibson, Frank
30601	Act.Staff S.	Simmonds, R. H.	30609	Act.Cpl.Bkr.	Farnsworth, D.
30605	Act. Sgt.	Robertson, L. R.	30610	Private	Barclay, William
30604	,,	Dicks, George	30611	,,	Carter, Frank G.
30607	Act. Cpl.	Sarles, Alfred J.	30616	,,	Gordon, John
30613	Private	Dicks, Isaac	30617	,,	Gollan, William
30614	,,	Dicks, John	30608	Act.Cpl.Bkr.	Holland, Cornelius
30626	,,	Williams, Albert	30619	Private	McAllister, Robert
30615	,,	Giffen, Ernest M.	30620	,,	McAllister, Samuel
30611	,,	Cole, Harry	30621	,,	Newton, Jim
30627	,,	Wilson, John B.	30622	,,	Page, James
30624	,,	Skelton, Richard	30623	,,	Sephton, Harry
30602	Act.S.S.Bkr.	Worton, Wm. S.	30625	,,	Durocher, Leon L.
30628	Act.Cpl.	Graham, John			

No. 2.

Lieutenant ... ... Bishop, Bradford Burton

Regl. No.	Rank.	Name.	Regl. No.	Rank.	Name.
30650	Act.S.S.M.	Turner, C. T. McL.	30655	Private	Gemmel, Geo. H.
30651	Act.Staff S.	Gemmel, T. M.	30659	,,	Hayman, P. W.
30652	Act. Sgt.	Gemmel, A. A.	30657	,,	Jakes, Frank
30653	Act. Cpl.	Sclater, Charles H.	30660	,,	Jackson, Charles
30654	,,	Parker, Herbert E.	30658	,,	Neville, Tom
30662	Private	Bryant, Sidney	30656	,,	Strong, G. N. E.

Canadian Pacific—The Empire's Greatest Railway.

DEPOT UNITS OF SUPPLY, C.A.S.C.—cont. 327

No. 3.

Captain ... ... McLennan, J. A.

Regl. No.	Rank.	Name.
30700	Sgt.-Maj.	Howe, P.
30701	Staff Sgt.	Carter, G.
30702	,,	Hosking, F.
30718	Sergt.	McMillan, J.
30709	,,	Goode, W.
30703	,,	Routledge, J.
30722	Corpl.	Turner, A.
30704	,.	Allen, A.
30708	,,	Curry, H.
30713	2nd Cpl.	Holley, H.
30726	,,	Westbrook, F.
30705	Private	Austen, H.
30707	,,	Beck, W.
30728	,,	Betty, R. J.

Regl. No.	Rank.	Name.
30710	Private	Gillespie, W.
30711	,,	Herzog, J.
30712	,,	Hayes, W. C.
30714	,,	Lyall, A.
30715	,,	Mitchell, W.
30716	,,	Matier, W. J.
30717	,,	Newell, A.
30719	,,	Nash, A.
30720	,,	Norman, J.
30721	,,	O'Donnell, J.
30723	,,	Taylor, W.
30724	,,	Withers, A.
30725	,,	Williams, D. J.
30727	,,	Wilson, G.

No. 4.

Captain ... ... Eaton, F. B.

Regl. No.	Rank.	Name.
30750	Sgt.-Maj.	Prikler, L.
30751	Staff Sgt.	Dunlevy, B. J.
30752	Sergt.	Ruddick, W. M.
30754	Lce.-Cpl.	Dowle, W. O.
30760	Corpl.	Parish, J. W.
30753	Private	Cook, C. W.
30755	,,	Hall, T.
30756	,,	Jorden, F.
30757	,,	McIntosh, N.
30758	,,	McLeod, T. R.
30759	,,	Olney, H. J.
30761	,,	Weston, J.
30762	,,	Wright, A.
30663	Staff Sgt.	White, H. E.

Regl. No.	Rank.	Name.
30664	Sergt.	Millar, George
30665	Corpl.	McCarthy, Chas.
30666	,,	Elliott, R. H. W.
30667	Private	Dival, Lewis
30668	,,	Fitzgerald, E. J.
30669	,,	Garey, David
30670	,,	Gibson, D. W.
30671	,,	Meek, Charles
30672	,,	McGill, Ignatius
30673	,,	Peters, Alfred
30674	,,	Rogers, William
30675	,,	Sampson, Peter
30676	,,	Stares, William
30677	,,	Wilson, S. A.

RAILWAY SUPPLY DETACHMENT.

Captain ... ... Baker, L. S.

Regl. No.	Rank.	Name.
30850	Staff Sgt.	Macnamara, W. B.
30851	,,	Harrison, E. D.
30852	,,	Cunliffe, J. A.
30853	Sergt.	Milner, R. W.

Regl. No.	Rank.	Name.
30854	Sergt.	Cunliffe, J.
30855	Private	Adcock, T. F.
30857	,,	Bowden, J.
30858	,,	Brown, C.

Canadian Pacific—The Empire's Greatest Railway.

328 RAILWAY SUPPLY DETACHMENT—cont.

Regl. No.	Rank.	Name.	Regl. No.	Rank.	Name.
30856	Private	Burton, F. A.	30883	Private	Menzies, A. E.
30867	,,	Campbell, J. J.	30885	,,	Miller, A. W.
30861	,,	Carr, W. S.	30882	,,	Mould, S.
30863	,,	Clement, T. H.	30889	,,	Newman, W. S.
30865	,,	Clements, S.	30890	,,	Poore, K. H.
30864	,,	Collins, A. E.	30891	,,	Postlethwaite, A.
30860	,,	Cooper, G. N.	30894	,,	Ranford, W.
30859	,,	Crew, C. L.	30936	,,	Rees, W.
30866	,,	Cumberbatch, J.	30892	,,	Robertson, R. E.
30862	,,	Cunliffe, F.	30893	,,	Rutledge, R.
30869	,,	Davey, R. J.	30934	,,	Scott, R. G.
30868	,,	Dewar, J. P.	30921	,,	Scanlon, E. L.
30913	,,	Dudley, L. W.	30897	,,	Smith, Albert
30870	Corpl.	Evans, C. R.	30923	,,	Stevens, H.
30914	Private	Ford, M.	30898	,,	Stewart, C. S.
30871	,,	Gotham, A. T.	30901	,,	Thomson, A.
30874	,,	Hanley, D. McN.	30904	,,	Thornton, J. L.
30873	,,	Haywood, F.	30902	,,	Tracey, W.
30872	,,	Higgins, A.	30903	,,	Trodden, P.
30876	,,	Kelly, C. H.	30900	,,	Turner, G. M.
30877	,,	Kelly, C. M.	30907	,,	Welch, D. H.
30875	,,	Kerr, T.	30926	,,	Whorton, J. F.
30878	,,	Little, R.	30909	,,	Williams, R.
30880	,,	Luxford, E. C.	30905	,,	Williamson, D.
30879	,,	Luxford, J. E.	30908	,,	Wilson, B. C.
30888	,,	McEwan, W.	30906	,,	Wyman, A.
30886	,,	McFarlane, R.			

No. 1 FIELD AMBULANCE.

"A" SECTION.

Lieut.-Colonel	Ross, Arthur Edward, A.M.C.
Captain	Duval, Josias Louis, A.M.C.
,, ...	Gorssline, R. M., P.A.M.C.
,, ...	McConnell, Arnold Davis, I.A.M.C.
,, ...	Boyce, George Joseph, A.M.C.
Paymaster	Hon. Captain H. Beaudry

Regl. No.	Rank.	Name.	Regl. No.	Rank.	Name.
32701	Sgt.-Maj.	Buswell, William,	32837	Corpl.	Rolland, Rudolph
33927	Staff Sgt.	Griggs, Thomas	32850	,,	McManus, Frank
32928	,,	Smith, Frank	32835	Lce.-Cpl.	Garnett, Welland
32820	Sergt.	Boone, Bert	32842	Private	Asbell, Ira
32819	,,	Blair, Kenneth	32840	,,	Andrews, Harold
32845	,,	Ross, Robert	32938	,,	Adams, James
32930	Lce.-Sgt.	Cameron, William	32823	,,	Bagley, William
32807	Corpl.	Barry, Arthur	32822	,,	Bardon, Walter
32826	Sergt.	Crozier, Leonard	32854	,,	Betts, Geo.

Canadian Pacific—The Empire's Greatest Railway.

No. 1 FIELD AMBULANCE—cont.

Regl. No.	Rank.	Name.	Regl. No.	Rank.	Name.
32799	Private	Britney, John	32832	Private	Merrick, John
32939	,,	Cairns, Robert	32943	,,	McAulay, Thomas
32948	,,	Carter, Gerald	32849	,,	McBriarty, Simon
32791	,,	Daly, Louis	32937	,,	McDonald, Angus
32818	,,	Day, Guy	32848	,,	McDonald, Roderick
32827	,,	Decormier, John	32855	,,	McNutt, Walter
32817	,,	Dupuis, Albert	32806	,,	Maggs, George
32857	,,	Desharnais, Rosier	32813	,,	Monteith, William
32936	,,	Davis, Arthur	32808	,,	Norman, John
32849	,,	Evans, Alfred	32980	,,	Nobles, Millard
32814	,,	Earl, Ernest	32841	,,	Orr, Earle
32924	,,	Edgecombe, Fred	32869	,,	Perrault, John
34116	,,	Fenwick, Alister	32846	,,	Pare, Gustave
32821	,,	Fletcher, Edward	32828	,,	Perrault, Wilfred
32940	,,	Forbes, Hedley	32834	,,	Phillips, Arthur
32838	,,	Gagnon, William	32833	,,	Price, Joseph
32839	,,	Gaynes, Frank	32843	,,	Robinson, Joshua
32942	,,	Glover, William	32858	,,	Roy, Charles
32852	,,	Gillis, Alfred	32944	,,	Scott, Geo.
32851	,,	Gordon, John	32811	,,	Shannon, Urban
32856	,,	Henry, Percy	32815	,,	Stuart, Donald
32831	,,	Harton, Thomas	32816	,,	Stuart, William
32954	,,	Hunt, Albert	32945	,,	Sullivan, John
32929	,,	Kelly, Thomas	32946	,,	Sultana, Frank
32848	,,	Kelly, Frank	32853	,,	Tebo, John
32844	,,	Lacey, John	32825	,,	Thomas, John
32846	,,	Logan, Walter	32797	,,	Walker, Frank
32977	,,	Lecain, John	32934	,,	Wood, Albert
32926	,,	Lutes, Guy	32947	,,	Wood, William
32935	,,	Mean, Henry			

"B" SECTION.

Major	... ...	Wright, Robert Percy, A.M.C.
Captain	... ...	Graham, Chas. Robert, A.M.C.
,,	... ...	Geggie, Robert Conrad, A.M.C.

Regl. No.	Rank.	Name.	Regl. No.	Rank.	Name.
32782	Q.M.Sgt.	Owens, John B.	32955	Private	Allan, Walter
32783	Staff Sgt.	Brown, John S.	32859	,,	Blouin, Adelard
32781	,,	Reade, Joseph	32860	,,	Bolideau, Francois
32785	Sergt.	Stensrud, Oscar P.	32861	,,	Badeau, Edward
32784	,,	Gibson, Archibald	32862	,,	Baker, William
32866	Corpl.	Cerusi, Adolph	32863	,,	Bolseret, Maurice
32786	,,	Hoad, Frederick	32864	,,	Bognes, Wm.
32787	,,	Quigley, Joseph	32865	,,	Cahill, Felix
32788	,,	Hurteau, Oscar	32867	,,	Cosgrove, John
32892	Lcc.-Cpl.	O'Connor, Maurice	32868	,,	Caronn, Albert
32789	Private	Aubin, Louis	32777	,,	Champagne, Wilfrid

Canadian Pacific—The Empire's Greatest Railway.

No. 1 FIELD AMBULANCE—cont.

Regl. No.	Rank.	Name.	Regl. No.	Rank.	Name.
32772	Private	Charron, Ulric	32779	Private	Moss, Walter
32870	,,	Crossman, Maurice	32891	,,	Neish, John
32871	,,	Dawson, John	32893	,,	Parent, Elphange
32872	,,	Dextras, John	32894	,,	Paulding, John
32873	,,	Doyle, William	32895	,,	Pearson, Frank
32874	,,	Edmunds, Anthony	32896	,,	Paradis, Joseph
32875	,,	Fortnum, Joseph	32897	,,	Perkins, Wm.
32876	,,	Fregault, Ferdinand	32898	,,	Pelletier, Joseph
32877	,,	Goudreau, John	32933	,,	Reveille, Albert
32879	,,	Gray, James	32899	,,	Robatille, Albert
32880	,,	Gillies, Charles	32900	,,	Spencer, Ben
32774	,,	Hainse, Adilion	32901	,,	Smith, Wm.
32881	,,	Hawkshaw, William	32902	,,	Silcott, Clarence
32882	,,	Hillier, Charles	32903	,,	Sylvain, Alphonse
32883	,,	Hagans, Robert	32904	,,	Sein, Milton
32884	,,	Hope, Clarence	32905	,,	Twohey, Leonard
32780	,,	Kendall, Phillip	32778	,,	Thomas, Geo.
32885	,,	Knight, Albert	32906	,,	White, Albert
32886	,,	Long, Wm.	32907	,,	Wass, John
32887	,,	Mayer, Alfred	32908	,,	Waring, Wm.
32888	,,	Mitchell, John	32909	,,	Wilkinson, Jas.
32889	,,	Marshall, Norman	32910	,,	Westby, Edward
32890	,,	McAllister, Stephen	32923	,,	Wingrove, Wm. A.

"C" SECTION.

Captain ... ... Howlett, George Patrick, A.M.C.
    ,, ... Stone, Ervin

Regl. No.	Rank.	Name.	Regl. No.	Rank.	Name.
32753	Staff Sgt.	Flint, Thos.	32731	Private	Childs, Gabriel
32728	,,	Mundell, Kenneth	32946	,,	Conway, Frank
32713	,,	Brown, Tyler	32737	,,	Cottee, Fred
32723	Sergt.	Bothwell, John	32736	,,	Cantrill, Thomas
32717	Corpl.	Hooper, Jas.	32733	,,	Chare, Francis
32729	,,	Armstrong, Nobel	32714	,,	Craig, Wm.
32753	,,	Spreckley, Robert	32961	,,	Denny, Alfred
32727	Private	Ahearn, Christopher	32962	,,	Dicken, John
32989	,,	Anderson, Isaac	32754	,,	Foran, Wm. Dennis
32756	,,	Anderson, Thomas	32722	,,	Forsyth, Robert
32755	,,	Brown, Henry	32746	,,	Fraser, Fred
32768	,,	Bezbie, Alex.	32763	,,	Gibson, Geo.
32712	,,	Bates, Harold	32734	,,	Granby, Thos.
32732	,,	Butler, Geo.	32719	,,	Haggarty, John
32720	,,	Babb, James	32724	,,	Hainsworth, Gilbert
32925	,,	Button, Wm.	32718	,,	Hewetson, John
32738	,,	Cockerman, Albert	32715	,,	Hill, Reginald
32735	,,	Cannon, Bruce	32716	,,	Holmes, Chas.
32730	,,	Carless, Joseph	32767	,,	Hutchins, Thos.

Canadian Pacific—The Empire's Greatest Railway.

No. 1 FIELD AMBULANCE—cont.

Regl. No.	Rank.	Name.	Regl. No.	Rank.	Name.
32726	Private	Livings, Jas.	32741	Private	Perrault, Wm. J.
32757	,,	Layzell, Donald	32742	,,	Roach, Bernard
32759	,,	Lees, John	32743	,,	Richardson, Albert
32960	,,	Maxwell, Clinton	32744	,,	Rose, Geo. W.
32760	,,	Medcalfe, A.	32956	,,	Smith, Chas.
32725	,,	Mills, Leslie	32745	,,	Smith, Thos.
32761	,,	Mullen, Thos.	32748	,,	Sugden, Ernest
32769	,,	McLeod, Wm.	32750	,,	Stewart, Arthur
32733	,,	Normoyle, Patrick	32762	,,	Shehyn, Roderick
32982	,,	Oakes, Edward	32758	,,	Smith, Wm. B.
32735	,,	Owen, William	32964	,,	Sauvage, Clifford
32749	,,	O'Connor, Austin	32751	,,	Tilling, Ernest
32739	,,	Patton, David	32721	,,	Woods, Fred
32764	,,	Peebles, Robert	32731	,,	Wilson, Richard
32740	,,	Peebles, Peter	32770	,,	Wilson, Thos.

Captain ... ... McGibbon, R. H.
,, ... Smith, A. (No. 3 F.A.)

Regl. No.	Rank.	Name.	Regl. No.	Rank.	Name.
32911	Sergt.	Moissant, Joseph A.	32974	Private	Labelle, Napoleon
32810	Corpl.	McKay, H.	32970	,,	Labelle, Eugene
32802	Private	Beaurram, Thos.	32951	,,	Leseaux, Ernest
32966	,,	Bearance, Russell E.	32798	,,	McCarthy, John
32913	,,	Berger, Emile	32801	,,	Martin, Emile
32912	,,	Brisbois, Adrienne	32805	,,	Martin, Hector
32914	,,	Chevalier, Alphonse	32952	,,	McCormack, James
32915	,,	Chasse, Joseph	32957	,,	Mills, Chas. H.
32704	,,	Crate, John	32918	,,	Monette, Arthur
32792	,,	Demeule, Edgar	32976	,,	Mortimer, John
32949	,,	Deseuve, Henry	32709	,,	Murphy, Chas.
32710	,,	Dougherty, Patrick	32975	,,	Murphy, Fred
32916	,,	Drolet, Ephraim	32804	,,	O'Brien, M.
32707	,,	Edwards, John	32919	,,	Perry, Alfred
32702	,,	Fannon, John	32711	,,	Pearn, Wm.
32765	,,	Ford, James	32920	,,	Rose, Sidney
32703	,,	Grant, H.	32790	,,	Soncartier, Ernest
32950	,,	Halligan, Thos.	32972	,,	Tremblay, Victor
32867	,,	Lavis, John	32922	,,	Trottier, Eugene
32917	,,	Lacourse, Louis	32971	,,	Treadway, Edward
32809	,,	Lewis, John	32921	,,	Trudel, Louis
32706	,,	Liberty, Albert			

Canadian Pacific—The Empire's Greatest Railway.

No. 2 FIELD AMBULANCE.

Major	... ...	Bentley, David Benjamin
Captain	... ...	Musson, George
,,	... ...	Brown, Percy Gordann
,,	... ...	Jeffs, Howard Brown
Paymaster	... ...	Hon. Captain R. Giroux

Regl. No.	Rank.	Name.	Regl. No.	Rank.	Name.
32969	Staff Sgt.	McIntosh, James	33114	Private	Moore, Alexander
32972	,,	Patterson, Edwin B.	33140	,,	Newton, John Ray
32977	Sergt.	Thom, C. A. S.	33143	,,	Naptheon, R. G.
32980	,,	Bach, Richard E.	33146	,,	Orgill, Joseph
32992	Corpl.	Hurst, George, E.	33150	,,	Perry, Arthur H.
32990	,,	Rowe, Arthur	33155	,,	Perry, Edmund T.
32988	,,	Holland, Thomas	33153	,,	Pompey, Samuel
33147	Lce.-Cpl.	Parmenter, William	33152	,,	Pitts, Charles Lewis
32998	Private	Archibald, C. H.	33154	,,	Pirrie, Thomas W.
33020	,,	Bryant, Walter	33164	,,	Rennie, John
33013	,,	Barker, Robert A.	33165	,,	Robertson, John
33002	,,	Brooks, Herbert	33166	,,	Roberts, William A.
33019	,,	Bowler, John	33159	,,	Rutherford, Frank
33001	,,	Bell, Adam	33162	,,	Rogers, John
33016	,,	Boswell, James Wm.	33163	,,	Rogers, Ernest
33014	,,	Buckle, John	33172	,,	Smith, James
33024	,,	Coyne, John E.	33180	,,	Symonds, Ernest
33038	,,	Coutts, Albert E.	33169	,,	Symonds, Walter
33037	,,	Cook, Richard	33184	,,	Seale, Thomas
33033	,,	Coutts, Alexander	33175	,,	Stewart, James
33032	,,	Crossman, T. C.	33183	,,	Sherrat, Harvey
33040	,,	Clay, Frederick	33191	,,	Turner, Frank
33045	,,	Devine, Frank	33187	,,	Turner, Guy
33074	,,	Gale, Alfred Ernest	33190	,,	Tarver, Ernest C. C.
33084	,,	Hammond, T. C.	33193	,,	Tyler, William
33087	,,	Inksater, George	33188	,,	Taylor, Robert
33089	,,	Jennings, Louis	33185	,,	Telford, George
33091	,,	Johnson, Thomas	33197	,,	Warren, Edward
33092	,,	James, Fred L.	33207	,,	Wheeler, Sydney
33103	,,	Latham, Ernest J.	33196	,,	Wilkinson, Frederick
33102	,,	Lovell, David T.	33208	,,	Warnes, Henry G.
33104	,,	Laird, Ernest W.	33202	,,	West, Edward
33105	,,	Lowe, Thomas	33201	,,	Warner, Arthur
33126	,,	Meads, George	33212	,,	Wilson, Robert
33128	,,	Murray, Wm. B.	33198	Bugler	Wray, Sydney A.
32981	Sergt.	Kells, Joseph	33017	Private	Bird, John
32978	,,	Perley, James	33004	,,	Bailey, Harry
33021	,,	Baskett, William Hy.	33010	,,	Breach, Jas. Harold
33168	,,	Shortill, Rbt. Lloyd	33000	,,	Bothwell, Harry
33216	,,	Venn, Charles James	33023	,,	Calder, Roderick Geo.
33173	Corpl.	Smith, Walter Francis	33022	,,	Cartwright, James
32983	,,	Rawlings, Harry, A.	33043	,,	Crooks, Albert

Canadian Pacific—The Empire's Greatest Railway.

No. 2 FIELD AMBULANCE—cont.

Regl. No.	Rank.	Name.	Regl. No.	Rank.	Name.
33039	Private	Carrick, Hugh	33123	Private	Mercer, George C.
33028	,,	Corner, William McL.	33129	,,	Manning, George M.
33044	,,	Cook, John	33142	,,	Nevan, Thomas
33048	,,	Duncan, Archie	33144	,,	Nunn, John
33058	,,	Elliot, John	33148	,,	Pilcher, Sydney Clark
33059	,,	Evans, Albert	33219	,,	Price, John
33062	,,	Finnie, David	33151	,,	Poultney, Herbert A.
33067	,,	Garrison, Russell	33218	,,	Parkinson, Henry
33071	,,	Greenwood, Robert	33157	,,	Quinton, Robert
33072	,,	Giles, Albert	33167	,,	Reid, Frederick
33082	,,	Hackett, Fred Thos.	33174	,,	Skinner, Frank
33081	,,	Hackson, William	33170	,,	Sunderland, Chas. O.
33086	,,	Hughes, Bernard	33177	,,	Serbert, William J.
33085	,,	Henratty, Walter	33210	,,	Wilson, William
33088	,,	Irwin, William	33204	,,	Wilson, George
33093	,,	Knapman, Frdk. S.	33206	,,	Woodman, Stanley S.
33106	,,	McGernon, John Geo.	33205	,,	White, Charles
33107	,,	McKendry Nelson C.	33199	,,	Walker, James
33109	,,	McIntyre, Niven	33209	,,	Walker, Louis
33133	,,	McGuire, Thomas. A.	33213	,,	Willis, Robert
33127	,,	Montroue, Arthur L.	33200	,,	Williamson, Hazen
33130	,,	Marshall, John			

NO. 3 FIELD AMBULANCE.

Lieut.-Colonel	Watt, Walter L.
Major	Gunn, John A.
,, ...	Templeton, Charles P.
Captain	Vesey, Eustace M.
,, ...	Panton, Kenneth D.
,, ...	Bell, Fred C.
,, ...	Smith, Stanley Alwyn
,, ...	Bell, Percy G.
,, ...	Donaldson, Anson Scott
,, ...	Woodiwiss, Edwin Sydney
Paymaster	Hon. Captain MacDougall, Donald H.
Captain	McQueen, John D.

Regl. No.	Rank.	Name.	Regl. No.	Rank.	Name.
33500	Sgt.-Maj. (W.O.)	Amps, Herbert F.	33427	Staff Sgt.	Owen, Harold H.
			33302	Sergt.	Bye, S. H.
33244	Q.M. Sgt.	Case, William E.	33254	,,	Francis, R. B.
33250	Staff Sgt.	Barlow, William	33403	,,	Mansfield, Russell C.
33243	,,	Bowen, George J.	33260	,,	Nelson, Frederick
33245	,,	Crowe, Charles W.	33261	,,	Northmore, Wm. H.
33235	,,	Francis, Charles	33445	,,	Roberts, Lewis
33246	,,	McArthur, Charles E.	33442	,,	Rotsey, Albert E.
33259	,,	Milborne, A. J. B.	33248	,,	Sherlock, F. R.

Canadian Pacific—The Empire's Greatest Railway.

No. 3 FIELD AMBULANCE—cont.

Regl. No.	Rank.	Name.	Regl. No.	Rank.	Name.
33253	Lce.-Sgt.	Ferguson, John	33301	Private	Burke, George W.
33247	,,	Morrison, Thomas J.	33252	,,	Burns, William C.
33249	Corpl	Ball, Frederick J. E.	33303	,,	Cameron, Herbert T.
33251	,,	Bennett, Charles	33304	,,	Cameron, John
33255	,,	Franklin, Wm. H.	33305	,,	Catlett, James A.
33256	,,	Frost, Oliver C.	33306	,,	Campbell, Thomas G.
33394	,,	McDonald, William	33307	,,	Campbell, William J.
33263	,,	Riley, William	33308	,,	Capstick, William E.
33268	,,	Stall, Montagu	33309	,,	Carr, George R.
33264	,,	Stuart, John	33310	,,	Cairns, Victor G.
33488	,,	Wilson, Harry B.	33311	,,	Clark, Raymond J.
33320	Lce.-Cpl.	Disley, Albert Price	33312	,,	Coleman, Frank G.
33335	,,	Fielding, Cecil C.	33313	,,	Cooling, Samuel
33351	,,	Hayes, William J.	33314	,,	Crapper, Arthur, J.
33364	,,	Hooley, Samuel	33315	,,	Croft, Thomas A.
33262	,,	Rogers, Alfred Wm.	33316	,,	Cunningham, C. W.
33457	,,	Smith, Robert W.	33317	,,	Currie, Henry E.
33267	,,	Southorn, Charles	33501	,,	Craddock, Gordon C.
33498	,,	Turner, Arthur	33318	,,	Daley, Barry
33492	,,	Woods, Andrew J.	33319	,,	Davidson, John G.
33270	Private	Anstey, John	33321	,,	Donald, Alec.
33271	,,	Agnew, William	33322	,,	Dyer, John Henry
33272	,,	Allen, Benjamin W.	33328	,,	Dickson, A. E.
33273	,,	Anderson, Alexander	33323	,,	Eckhoff, Philip
33274	,,	Ash, Cecil	33324	,,	Edwards, David C.
33275	,,	Ashcroft, Henry	33325	,,	Edwards, Richard G.
33276	,,	Arnold, Thomas	33326	,,	Ellis, Judson H.
33277	,,	Bailey, Bertram	33327	,,	Elkington, Wm. C.
33278	,,	Baird, William C.	33329	,,	Ennis, Albert L.
33279	,,	Barker, Ernest	33330	,,	Evans, David Owen
33280	,,	Bartley, Albert	33331	,,	Everitt, Frank H.
33281	,,	Barker, Frank	33332	,,	Fetherstone, John
33282	,,	Barrows, Edwin W.	33333	,,	Field, Frederick J.
33283	,,	Bateman, William	33334	,,	Finn, George A.
33284	,,	Bateson, George M.	33336	,,	Forbes, James
33285	,,	Bealey, Edgar	33337	,,	Frankenstein, M. L.
33286	,,	Beesley, Harold	33338	,,	Francis, Arthur
33287	Lce.-Cpl.	Bennett, F. E.	33341	,,	Fryer, Charles
33288	Private	Binfield, John C.	33340	,,	Freeman, Frederick
33289	,,	Binfield, Arthur	33339	,,	Fraser, David C.
33290	,,	Beach, Benjamin G.	33342	,,	Fullerton, Adam
33291	,,	Bent, Frederick W.	33343	,,	Fulthorp, Thomas
33292	,,	Billingsley, Lorne	33344	,,	Gall, William Duff
33293	,,	Blaney, Edgar T.	33345	,,	Galloway, Wm. A.
33294	,,	Blondal, Thor.	33346	,,	Gaylard, George S.
33295	,,	Black, William	33347	,,	Geddes, John
33296	,,	Boardman, John H.	33348	,,	Goose, Bertie
33297	,,	Bond, Jesse	33349	,,	Goode, James Allen
33298	,,	Boothe, Albert A.	33350	,,	Goodwin, Ralph D.
33265	,,	Bone, Charles F.	33257	,,	Gower, John William
33299	,,	Broadhurst, D. S.	33352	,,	Haire, James
33300	,,	Brown, William J.	33353	,,	Hallett, Clarence B.

Canadian Pacific—The Empire's Greatest Railway.

No. 3 FIELD AMBULANCE—cont.

Regl. No.	Rank.	Name.	Regl. No.	Rank.	Name.
33354	Private	Harlock, Mathew H.	33406	Private	Maloney, Corneils
33355	,,	Hammersley, R. D.	33407	,,	Mills, Clifford W.
33356	,,	Hammond, Wm. G.	33408	,,	Millen, Arthur
33357	,,	Hamilton, Wm. G.	33409	,,	Miller, Fernly
33358	,,	Head, Richard L.	33410	,,	Morrison, Charles
33359	,,	Hitch, George S.	33411	,,	Moore, Thomas
33360	,,	Higham, John F.	33412	,,	Morrison, Roy
33361	,,	Higgins, Gerald	33413	,,	Mowbray, Harry D.
33362	,,	Higgins, Frank T.	33414	,,	Morgan, George H.
33363	,,	Hodge, Alfred B.	33415	,,	Morrisey, James A.
33365	,,	Holloway, William J.	33416	,,	Morris, Stephen C.
33502	,,	Honneyman, E. H.	33417	,,	Muhich, Joseph
33366	,,	Hood, Alexande W.	33266	,,	Mayson, Richmond
33367	,,	Hughes, Leslie D.	33418	,,	Nelson, Axel
33368	,,	Hughes, Reginald A.	33419	,,	Neilson, Richard
33369	,,	Hughes, Charles	33420	,,	Newton, A. E.
33370	,,	Hutton, David A.	33421	,,	Nicol, David W. S.
33371	,,	Hussell, Le Roy E.	33422	,,	Nickerson, Allie L.
33372	,,	Huntley, Joseph H.	33423	,,	Nicholson, John
33258	,,	Hunt, Robert W.	33424	,,	North, Clifford D.
33373	,,	Iliffe, Henry George	33425	,,	Norman, Cyril
33374	,,	Jackson, Lawrence H.	33426	,,	Nuttall, Alfred
33375	,,	Jensen, Einar Bjorn	33428	,,	Partridge, William
33376	,,	Johnston, Harry C.	33429	,,	Parker, George C.
33377	,,	Johnston, Robert H.	33430	,,	Parker, Thomas J.
33378	,,	Jones, Hugh Price	33431	,,	Park, Hugh A.
33379	,,	Jones, Lea	33432	,,	Phillips, Harry G.
33380	,,	Kirkbride, John	33433	,,	Pickles, Tom
33381	,,	Kyle, Hugh F.	33434	,,	Porteous, James
33474	,,	Kerrison, Henry G	33435	,,	Pottinger, James
33382	,,	Lamond, Gordon M.	33436	,,	Pratt, Hugh B.
33383	,,	Landstrom, G. A.	33437	,,	Pulcine, Michael
33384	,,	Levere, Cameron A.	33438	,,	Quandt, Carle C.
33385	,,	Leckie, James C.	33439	,,	Randall, Frank
33386	,,	Livingstone, J. R.	33440	,,	Reid, Henry Muir
33387	,,	Lisney, Frederick J.	33441	,,	Ritchie, William J.
33388	,,	Longthorne, James	33443	,,	Roe, Luke
33389	,,	Lockery, John D.	33444	,,	Robinson, David
33390	,,	Lyttle, Charles W.	33446	,,	Sarson, Henry S.
33391	,,	Lymburn, James F.	33447	,,	Scholefield, Herbert
33392	,,	McArthur, John M.	33448	,,	Secord, George
33393	,,	MacDonald, A.	33449	,,	Sherk, Joseph N.
33395	,,	McIntosh, A. B.	33450	,,	Shearing, John A.
33396	,,	McKay, Archibald M.	33451	,,	Simmons, Arthur
33397	,,	McKellar, Thomas	33452	,,	Skinner, Roderick
33398	,,	McKenzie, John L.	33453	,,	Smith, John
33399	,,	McMaster, George E.	33454	,,	Smythe, William F.
33402	,,	MacMillan, F. A.	33455	,,	Smart, Walter T.
33400	,,	MacMillan, Alex.	33456	,,	Smith, Frederick G.
33401	,,	McKeon, William P.	33458	,,	Spencer, Harold
33404	,,	Marshall, Ernest	33459	,,	Spooner, F. H. P.
33405	,,	Main, Thomas	33460	,,	Spiers, James

Canadian Pacific—The Empire's Greatest Railway.

No. 3 FIELD AMBULANCE—cont.

Regl. No.	Rank	Name.	Regl. No.	Rank.	Name.
33461	Private	Stewart, Hugh G.	33480	Private	Walsh, Alexander W.
33462	,,	Stinson, Clifford J.	33481	,,	West, H.
33463	,,	Street, George R.	33482	,,	Wemyss, R. P.
38464	,,	Sutherland, G. J.	33483	,,	Weeks, Henry G.
33465	,,	Teal, Ernest O.	33483	,,	Westmoreland, J. W.
33466	,,	Thompson, Wm. M.	33485	,,	White, Norman H.
33467	,,	Thompson, Wm. R.	33486	,,	Whitehead, M. B.
33468	,,	Tongs, Edward	33487	,,	Whitefoot, T. W.
33469	,,	Towle, Sidney	33489	,,	Wilkinson, W. L.
33470	,,	Tomkins, Charles B.	33490	,,	Williams, Jack
33471	,,	Turnbull, Wm. A.	33491	,,	Wilde, Reginald B.
33472	,,	Urquhart, William	33493	,,	Wright, Meiklejohn
33473	,,	Varty, Charles F.	33469	,,	Wood, Arthur
33475	,,	Vince, Horace A.	33494	,,	Wright, Frank
33476	,,	Watts, William J.	33495	,,	Yates, Thomas
33477	,,	Watson, Oscar Guy	33496	,,	Yeates, C.
33478	,,	Watson, John	33497	,,	Young, Robert B.
33479	,,	Way, Cecil Frank			

CLEARING HOSPITAL.

Lieut.-Colonel	Ford, Frederick Samuel Lampson
Major	Chisholm, Hugh Alexander
,, ...	Mackinnon, Wm. Thomas Morris
Captain	Peat, Gilbert Bamfylde
,, ...	Dickson, Charles Harold
,, ...	Dowsley, George William Ogilvie
,, ...	Macdonald, Ronald Hugh
,, ...	Pickup, Wm. Alfred
,, ...	Stewart, John Murdoch
Paymaster	Hon. Captain A. Chute
Hon. Captain and Chaplain ...	Frost, Harry Arthur

Regl. No.	Rank.	Name.	Regl. No.	Rank.	Name.
33801	Sgt.-Maj.	Robart, Reigh C.	33809	Corpl.	Ware, James
33802	Staff Sgt.	Dexter, Ernest	33813	,,	Hunt, Edward
33803	,,	Burnett, Frederick	33814	,,	Spencer, Ernest
33805	Sergt.	Brown, Reginald	33819	,,	Lantz, Harold
33806	,,	McGill, Chester	33875	Lce.-Cpl.	Watney, Robert
33812	,,	Morris, Andrew	33834	,,	Downer, John
33807	,,	Dumbrell, David	33856	,,	McLeod, Clark
33808	,,	Feindel, John	33821	Private	Baird, Andrew
33810	,,	McGillicuddy, Donald	33822	,,	Barnes, Clifford
33820	Pay Sgt.	Smith, Brenton	33823	,,	Bell, Montgomerie
33859	Bugler	Metcalf, Ernest	33824	,,	Bell, Raymond
33816	Lce.-Sgt.	Holden, Charles	33825	,,	Bernardine, Wm.
33879	,,	Walton, Arthur	33826	,,	Binns, Thalberg
33851	,,	Trefry, Alfred	33817	,,	Bird, Francis

Canadian Pacific—The Empire's Greatest Railway.

CLEARING HOSPITAL—cont.

Regl. No.	Rank.	Name.	Regl. No.	Rank.	Name.
33827	Private	Brooks, William L.	33853	Private	McGowan, Edward
33828	,,	Campbell, William	33854	,,	McKeegan, Frank
33829	,,	Clark, Kenneth	33855	,,	McLeod, James
33830	,,	Conrad, Edward	33857	,,	McIntyre, Alexander
33831	,,	Conrad, George	33858	,,	Malcomson, David
33832	,,	Crane, Albert	33804	,,	Mason, Vere
33833	,,	Crouse, Allen	33860	,,	Metcalf, Harry
33835	,,	Evans, Albert	33861	,,	Neily, Melbourne
33836	,,	Farr, Gordon	33811	,,	O'Reilly, Wm.
33837	,,	Fell, Harold	33862	,,	Papkee, John
33838	,,	Flint, Edgar	33863	,,	Parkinson, James
33839	,,	Fraser, Cleveland	33864	,,	Patton, John
33818	,,	Frost, Lawrence	33865	,,	Proctor, James
33840	,,	Glaab, Peter	33866	,,	Rafuse, George H.
33841	,,	Hallett, John	33867	,,	Reed, Kenneth M.
33842	,,	Heron, Albert	33868	,,	Reynolds, Leonard
33843	,,	Holman, Lawrence	33869	,,	Robart, Arthur C.
33844	,,	Horne, Robert	33870	,,	Robart, Carman
33845	,,	Howard, Wm.	33871	,,	Rowell, James
38846	,,	Joudrey, Grover	33872	,,	Rumney, Norman
33847	,,	Joudrey, Archibald	33873	,,	Timmins, Arthur
33848	,,	Joudrey, William	33874	,,	Turner, Arthur
33849	,,	Keddy, Donald	33876	,,	Waterworth, John
33850	,,	Keeping, Lance	33877	,,	Wood, Vernon
33851	,,	Kennedy, Francis	33878	,,	Yates, Samuel
33852	,,	Leiper, Andrew			

No. 1 GENERAL HOSPITAL.

Officer Commanding	Lt.-Colonel Murray MacLaren
Lieut.-Colonel	Cameron, Kenneth
,, ...	Finley, Frederick Gault
Major	Wylde, Charles Fenwick
,, ...	Vaux, Francis Leonard
,, ...	Le Bel, Edouard Albert
,, ...	Campbell, Roland Playfair
,, ...	Doherty, Charles E.
Captain	Rankin, Allan Coats
,, ...	Forbes, Alexander Mackenzie
,, ...	Hill, John Travers
,, ...	Shanks, George
,, ...	Corbet, George Graham
,, ...	Fyshe, James Carlyle
,, ...	Hunt, John Garnet
,, ...	Ramsey, George Stuart

Canadian Pacific—The Empire's Greatest Railway.

No. 1 GENERAL HOSPITAL—cont.

Captain	Wilson, Robert
,, ...	Robson, Charles Harold
,, ...	Lomer, Theodore Adolphe
,, ...	Ellis, Arthur William Mickle
,, ...	Johnson, Arthur L. (Supernumerary)
,, ...	Bennett, Allan Edward Hingston
Hon. Captain and Quartermaster	Kirkpatrick, Robert
Hon. Captain and Dental Surgeon	Hassard, Oscar Garnet

Attached.

Captain	MacNutt, Lewis W.
Hon. Major and Chaplain (R.C.) ...	O'Leary, Peter M.
Hon. Captain and Chaplain (C. of E.)	Ingles, George L.
Paymaster	Hon. Captain McCullough, Hugh

Regl. No.	Rank.	Name.	Regl. No.	Rank.	Name.
34401	W.O.	Murphy, Donald M.	34435	Private	Bradford, E.
34402	,,	Galbraith, Archie C.	34436	,,	Brocklebank, H.
34403	S. Sgt.	Scott, William	34437	,,	Brophy, J.
34404	,,	Scott, Henry Robert	34438	,,	Brown, H. E.
34405	,,	Doran, Albert James	34439	,,	Brunet, O.
34406	,,	Bell, George Alex.	34440	,,	Buchanan, J. A.
34407	,,	Borden, Henry Edgar	34441	,,	Burgess, A.
34408	,,	Evans, Herbert Parry	34443	,,	Case, E.
34418	Sergt.	Saunders, Fredk. W.	34445	,,	Cameron, G. C.
34410	,,	Aitken, Hugh	34446	,,	Couborough, C.
34409	,,	Repen, James Henry	34447	,,	Cowling, H.
34411	,,	Slater, Frederick	34448	,,	Currie, W.
34412	,,	Millard, Mordecai F.	34449	,,	Curtiss, G.
34413	,,	McGregor, C. S.	34450	,,	Davidson, R.
34414	,,	Scott, Russel Alvyn	34451	,,	Davies, G.
34417	Corpl.	Henshaw, F. W.	34452	,,	Davis, J.
34420	,,	Fraser, S.	34453	,,	Degasse, A.
34421	,,	Ilott, W. G.	34454	,,	Deighton, E.
34422	,,	McDonald, S. K.	34455	,,	Desjardins, J. N.
34442	,,	Burridge, J.	34456	,,	Dennis, J.
34510	,,	O'Shea, G. A.	34457	,,	Eavers, L. B.
34533	,,	Sisterson, R. J.	34458	,,	Eekman, —
34423	Bugler	Gillespie, N.	34459	,,	Falzon, G.
34424	,,	Hobson, E.	34460	,,	Flay, F.
34425	Private	Albert, D.	34461	,,	Fenn, P.
34426	,,	Aubin, L.	34462	,,	Flannigan, T.
34427	,,	Beetson, W.	34463	,,	Forbes, A.
34428	,,	Bilodeau, P.	34464	,,	Ford, A.
34429	,,	Black, Thos. Geo.	34465	,,	Fry, W. J. F.
34431	,,	Boulay, J.	34466	,,	Garfoot, G. H.
34432	,,	Bowden, J.	34467	,,	Gittleson, H.
34433	,,	Bridgeman, A.	34468	,,	Glad, H. A.
34434	,,	Brier, G. A.	34469	,,	Godard, W.

Canadian Pacific—The Empire's Greatest Railway.

No. 1 GENERAL HOSPITAL—cont.

Regl. No.	Rank	Name	Regl. No.	Rank	Name
34470	Private	Graney, P.	34514	Private	Patterson, W. F.
34415	,,	Hague, J.	34515	,,	Pattinson, G. E.
34471	,,	Harris, P. V.	34516	,,	Peerless, F.
34472	,,	Hawkins, E.	34517	,,	Pelletier, A. H.
34473	,,	Hatton, A. H.	34518	,,	Pirie, D.
34474	,,	Hermitage, A.	34519	,,	Pouliot, William
34475	,,	Hewett, H.	34520	,,	Pratt, J. W.
34476	,,	Hicks, C.	34521	,,	Purdy, W.
34477	,,	Hill, W.	34522	,,	Robinson, H.
34478	,,	Hill, A.	34523	,,	Rooney, J. A.
34479	,,	Hillman, N.	34524	,,	Rosser, H.
34480	,,	Holzberg, S.	34525	,,	Ryan, P.
34481	,,	Hyde, A.	34526	,,	Sanson, T.
34419	,,	Jardine, G.	34527	,,	Saxby, S.
34482	,,	Jennings, C.	34528	,,	Scully, T. T.
34483	,,	Lafrance, V.	34529	,,	Setterstrom, E.
34484	,,	Lalonde, J. N.	34531	,,	Shaughnessy, J.
34485	,,	Lalonde, E.	34532	,,	Sipling, George
34486	,,	Lalonde, A.	34534	,,	Skinner, A.
34487	,,	Lapointe, S.	34535	,,	Soden, R.
34488	,,	Lawson, A.	34536	,,	Spellman, F.
34489	,,	Lewis, F. C.	34537	,,	Stokel, T.
34490	,,	Lortie, Napoleon	34538	,,	Southwick, W.
34491	,,	Mackay, A.	34539	,,	Strachan, W.
34492	,,	Mackenzie, J.	34540	,,	Stuttaford, H.
34493	,,	Mackenzie, R.	34541	,,	Tabb, F.
34494	,,	McKeown, J.	34542	,,	Thistle, W.
34495	,,	McGregor, D.	34543	,,	Thompson, R.
34496	,,	Maher, A.	34544	,,	Teuma, A.
34497	,,	Malcolm, W.	34545	,,	Turner, E.
34498	,,	Marlow, H.	34547	,,	Vaillancourt, Arthur
34499	,,	Marr, S.	34177	,,	Vernon, Wm.
34500	,,	May, F.	34546	,,	Verschoyle, A.
34501	,,	Melbourne, T.	34548	,,	Vien, A.
34502	,,	Mooney, C.	34549	,,	Walsh, R.
34503	,,	Moore, E.	34550	,,	Ware, T.
34504	,,	Morgan, T.	50001	,,	Warwick, J. C.
34505	,,	Miller, E.	50002	,,	Watson, D. M.
34506	,,	Miller, G. G.	50003	,,	Wentzell, F.
34507	,,	O'Brien, W.	50004	,,	Wilson, R.
34508	,,	O'Rourke, P.	50005	,,	Wilson, S.
34509	,,	O'Shea, G.	50006	,,	Wilson, J.
34511	,,	Overton, L.	50007	,,	Wilkins, G. S.
20915	,,	Parker, Harry	50008	,,	Wood, A.
34512	,,	Parsons, A.	50009	,,	Whiteside, A.
34513	,,	Pashby, C.			

Canadian Pacific—The Empire's Greatest Railway.

No. 2 GENERAL HOSPITAL.

Lieut.-Colonel	Bridges, James Whiteside
,, ,, ...	Scott, Wallace Arthur
,, ,, ...	Rudolph, Robert Dawson
Major	Clarke, John Thomas
,, ...	Dillon, William Pearson
,, ...	Gardner, Robert Lorne
,, ...	Goldsmith, Perry Gladstone
,, ...	Gorrel, Charles Willson Farren
Captain	Abbot, Rev. Brinley
,, ...	Bethune, William
,, ...	Burke, Frederick Sypher
,, ...	Calhoun, John Campbell
,, ...	Cole, C. E. Cooper
,, ...	Ellis, Stayner
,, ...	Leslie, Norman Victor
,, ...	MacBeth, William Lewis Colquhoun
,, ...	MacKay, Fred. Holland
,, ...	McLeod, Neil
,, ...	Menzies, Percival Keith
,, ...	Morgan, James Douglas
,, ...	Nichols, Ronald Herbert
,, ...	Tytler, William Howard
Lieutenant	Kelly, Frederick William Bruce
Hon. Captain and Paymaster ...	Lemieux, Victor

Regl. No.	Rank.	Name.	Regl. No.	Rank.	Name.
34551	Sgt.-Maj.	Wallace, James M.	34573	Corpl.	Reid, Clarence D.
34552	,,	Wiltshire, A. L. G.	34571	,,	Smith, Samuel
34561	Staff Sgt.	Adair, Edward	34567	,,	Sinclair, Daniel
34556	,,	Foxcroft, Thomas P.	34576	,,	Sutherland, William
34610	,,	Gray, John Calvery	34569	,,	Wood, William
34555	,,	Jackson, Leonard R.	34613	Lce.-Cpl.	Hardacre, Walter
34553	,,	Robinson, Wallace	34582	Bugler	Rankin, Thomas M.
34559	,,	Rutledge, David S.	34581	,,	Smith, William E.
34557	,,	Spracklin, John C.	34583	Private	Bartlett, Samuel H.
34554	Sergt.	Down, Richard E.	34584	,,	Binner, Percy
34562	,,	Downard, Edward	34585	,,	Beswick, George T.
34558	,,	Duncan, John A.	34586	,,	Bryant, Ernest John
34565	,,	Gwilliam, Thos. B.	34587	,,	Bullocke, Gordon W.
34564	,,	MacFarland, Roy H.	34588	,,	Burbridge, Arthur
34566	,,	Wood, Hubert T.	34589	,,	Clarke, Harry W.
34563	Lce.-Sgt.	Smith, James Roy	34590	,,	Clark, William
34580	Corpl.	Althorpe, Wm. H.	33036	,,	Cliff, Mathew
34579	,,	Arnott, John Orr	34591	,,	Collins, Victor W.
34578	,,	Chalkley, William A.	42699	,,	Condie, Arthur J.
34572	,,	Dalton, Robert E.	34592	,,	Crick, Jack N.
34575	,,	Griffith, Robert	34593	,,	Curtin, Edward
34577	,,	Harris, George	34594	,,	Dale, Francis G.
34618	,,	Hogg, William	34595	,,	Dalton, Sydney D.
34568	,,	Irwin, Thomas B.	34596	,,	Dickson, Robert

Canadian Pacific—The Empire's Greatest Railway.

No. 2 GENERAL HOSPITAL—cont.

Regl. No.	Rank.	Name.	Regl. No.	Rank.	Name.
34597	Private	Dooley, Francis	34643	Private	Nightingale, Wm. N.
34598	,,	Epps, Cecil Hubert	34644	,,	Ogden, James L. M.
34599	,,	Etchells, Thomas	34645	,,	Over, Sidney R.
34600	,,	Farrell, Joseph	34646	,,	Page, Vernon C.
34687	,,	Fleming, E. A. W.	34647	,,	Parker, George
34603	,,	Fletcher, Duncan A.	34648	,,	Paton, Harold McL.
34602	,,	Foley, Frederick J.	34649	,,	Paton, Robert S.
34604	,,	Frost, Harold	34652	,,	Payne, Percy John
34601	,,	Fryer, William	34650	,,	Pickard, William K.
34605	,,	Fuller, John Richard	34651	,,	Pick, William H.
34606	,,	Gilmour, Albert E.	34653	,,	Pidgeon, William C.
34607	,,	Glover, Raymond R.	34654	,,	Pike, Joseph James
34608	,,	Goodman, Albert V.	34656	,,	Poole, Charles
34609	,,	Gray, Albert	34657	,,	Preston, F. M.
34611	,,	Graham, John	34655	,,	Priest, John T.
34612	,,	Green, Edward	34659	,,	Rochford, Charles
34614	,,	Hawkins, William	34660	,,	Rogers, Kenneth D.
34615	,,	Hayward, Hubert O.	34661	,,	Rowand, George H.
34617	,,	Hogan, Julian A,	34570	,,	Scadding, Charles A.
34616	,,	Hone, James	34665	,,	Scarborough, E. T.
34619	,,	Houghton, W. A. E.	34663	,,	Scott, Alexander
34620	,,	Hughes, Ernest G.	34662	,,	Searle, William J.
34621	,,	Ingram, Jack McA.	34666	,,	Shahan, Daniel
34622	,,	Isherwood, Geo. W.	34664	,,	Sheard, Herbert
34623	,,	Jackson, Frank	34667	,,	Sheppard, Matt. J.
34625	,,	Jennings, D. F.	34668	,,	Simons, Frank H.
34624	,,	Jewell, George H.	34669	,,	Sinclair, Alex. T.
34626	,,	Johnson, Juno C.	34670	,,	Sinclair, Colin
34628	,,	Kelly, Norman	34671	,,	Sinclair, Donald J.
34629	,,	Knowlton, S. C.	34672	,,	Skeffington, A. G.
34630	,,	Lafontaine, J. F.	34674	,,	Small, James Elias
34631	,,	Lock, Stanley E.	34673	,,	Smith, Thomas
34640	,,	McBride, Claude A.	34675	,,	Strange, Percy
34574	,,	MacDonald, E. L.	34676	,,	Sykes, Joseph W.
34641	,,	McLean, John	34677	,,	Thomas, Percy R.
34642	,,	McQuey, Peter	34678	,,	Thomson, Robert C.
34632	,,	Mannock, Harry	34679	,,	Treleaven, George B.
34633	,,	Marshall, William A.	34680	,,	Turpin, Christopher
34636	,,	Meilak, Dominic	34681	,,	Varley, John
34638	,,	Mould, William T.	34686	,,	Watts, James
34639	,,	Moule, Robert B.	34684	,,	Webb, Geoffrey F.
34635	,,	Mulvey, Reginald	34682	,,	Welsby, Tom
34637	,,	Munro, Archibald	34685	,,	Wyatt, Frank
34560	,,	Nicholls, Norman E.			

Canadian Pacific—The Empire's Greatest Railway.

No. 1 STATIONARY HOSPITAL, A.M.C.

Officer Commanding	Lieut.-Colonel Drum, Lorne
Major	McKee, Samuel Hanford
,, ...	Williams, Edward Johnston
Captain	Morris, Clarence Hamilton
,, ...	Munroe, Hugh Edwin
,, ...	Mayrand, Robert
,, ...	Bauld, Wm. A. G.
,, ...	Johnson, John Guy Watts
Quartermaster	Hon. Capt. Currey, Frederick Esliada
Surgeon Dentist	Captain Neilly, Bayard Lamont

Regl. No.	Rank.	Name.	Regl. No.	Rank.	Name.
34110	W.O.	Vokey, Walter	34181	Private	Girard, Joseph
34102	Staff Sgt.	O'Brien, F. Chas.	34141	,,	Goddard, Frank
34104	,,	McInnes, John Lewis	34142	,,	Harris, William
34106	,,	Paton, Robert Knox	34143	,,	Hargraves, George
34107	,,	Melia, Patrick	34145	,,	Hodgkinson, Stanley
34108	Sergt.	Roberts, Harold	34146	,,	Hughes, Harold
34167	,,	Quigley, David	34148	,,	Isnor, George
34111	,,	Ansty, Archibald	34149	,,	Jackson, L.
34119	Corpl.	Gale, L. H.	34150	,,	Jewell, Andrew
34103	,,	Gough, A. M.	34151	,,	Kelly, William
34112	,,	La Rochelle, Emile	34152	,,	Kline, Gerald
34113	,,	Manning, George	34184	,,	Lalonde, Henri
34133	Lce.-Cpl.	Cottrell, Thomas	34153	,,	Le Brock, Clifford
34144	,,	Hoare, Ernest	34183	,,	Luissier, Aime
34164	,,	Nelson, Stanley S.	34154	,,	Mansfield, James
34157	,,	Marr, J. L.	34155	,,	Manahan, Leo.
34118	,,	Mitchell, Alexander	34156	,,	Marshall, George
34101	Bugler	Clarke, Harry	34159	,,	McDonald, Chester
34120	Private	Appleby, Andrew	34160	,,	McGrath, Robert
34121	,,	Appleby, Percy	34161	,,	McPhedran, Norman
34122	,,	Andrews, Arthur E.	34105	,,	McMenamon, T. A.
34123	,,	Ardron, Arthur	34162	,,	Melvine, William
34124	,,	Bassett, Percival	34114	,,	Myatt, Joseph
34125	,,	Bendell, Thomas	34163	,,	Naylor, Bernard
34126	,,	Berkley, John	34165	,,	O'Shaughnessy, Geo.
34127	,,	Bruce, Thomas	34166	,,	Potter, Raymond G.
34128	,,	Brewer, Percival	34168	,,	Reynolds, Norman
34129	,,	Brimelow, Thomas	34169	,,	Rooke, Harold
34115	,,	Brown, James	34170	,,	Ryan, James
34130	,,	Bonnell, John	34188	,,	Schofield, J. F.
34131	,,	Cameron, Don. Oxley	34171	,,	Shaw, Albert
34180	,,	Coté, Ludger	34185	,,	Simard, William
34135	,,	Crawford, Lionel	34173	,,	Sotirianakis, Nicholas
34137	,,	Dougan, Robert McA.	34174	,,	Stamatakis, Stanley
34455	,,	Desjardins, J. N.	34175	,,	Stewart, Alfred
34138	,,	Edwards, Charles	34176	,,	St. Aubin, Amede
34139	,,	Eynon, Percival	34178	,,	Ward, Charles T.
34182	,,	Francour, Irene	34179	,,	Waxman, Michael
34140	,,	Furlong, Redmond	34186	,,	Willsher, Stephen J.

Canadian Pacific—The Empire's Greatest Railway.

No. 2 STATIONARY HOSPITAL.

Lieut.-Colonel	Shillington, Adam T.
Major	Elliott, Henry Charles Schomberg
,,	Bell, Frederick McKelvey
Captain	Pentecost, Reginald Sterling
,,	Young, Charles A.
,,	Wood, James H.
,,	Fisher, Stuart MacVicar
,,	Bentley, William Joseph
Quartermaster	Walker, James Stewart (Hon. Capt.)
Paymaster and Hon. Captain	Costigan, C. T.

Regl. No.	Rank.	Name.	Regl. No.	Rank.	Name.
34251	Sgt.-Maj.	Law, Harry E. (W.O.)	34279	Private	Dickenson, Arthur T.
34255	Staff Sgt.	Cadman, Vivian E.	34278	,,	Duncan, Robert A.
34252	,,	Fox, Harold, V.	34280	,,	Eatell, Alfred
34253	,,	MacDonald, John A.	34281	,,	Fletcher, Joseph B.
34254	,,	Jones, Allen Ernest	34282	,,	Fawcett, Harry E.
34302	Sergt.	McGibbon, Hugh	34283	,,	Fraser, Roderick
34338	,,	Westwater, Robert	34284	,,	Fowler, Thomas E.
34294	,,	Hughes, W. S.	34285	,,	Fitzgerald, William
34275	,,	Young, William A.	34286	,,	Gregg, Thomas A.
34323	Lce.-Sgt.	Smuck, John Wesley	34287	,,	Gerard, Charles
34334	Act. Sgt.	Warren, Joseph A.	34288	,,	Gerard, Frank
34343	,,	Lancefield, George R.	34290	,,	Goddard, Alfred
34262	Corpl.	Bartlett, Frank A.	34291	,,	Hayes, Herbert
34256	,,	Ackerman, Arthur	34292	,,	Hood, Charles Wm.
34267	,,	Battley, Sinclair	34293	,,	Hewson, Alfred Lee
34342	,,	Webb, Herbert McN.	34295	,,	Jordan, Ernest
34319	,,	Rees, John Andrew	34296	,,	Joseph, Fredrick E.
34300	,,	Luscombe, John C.	34299	,,	Kirby, Cecil Howard
34289	Lce.-Cpl.	Gardiner, Alexander	34297	,,	Knight, Fredrick J.
34309	,,	Newton, Herbert J.	34298	,,	Knight, Earl R.
34337	,,	Ward, Jack	34301	,,	Livingstone, F. E.
34257	Private	Andrews, William H.	34304	,,	McLean, John
34258	,,	Aubin, Joseph	34303	,,	McLean, Frank
34259	,,	Bailey, John A.	34305	,,	McIntyre, James
34260	,,	Bailey, Charles Roy	34306	,,	Maycock, Joseph
34261	,,	Bartlett, Sidney A.	34307	,,	McWhinnie, Hamiltn.
34263	,,	Brown, William	34308	,,	Moody, John
34264	,,	Barclay, Thomas W.	34310	,,	Niles, John
34265	,,	Boyce, Herbert A.	34311	,,	Ouelette, Raymond
34266	,,	Burnie, William Rae	34312	,,	Owen, Christopher N.
34268	,,	Brennan, Francis D.	34313	,,	Orton, William A.
34269	,,	Cliffe, Jabez Andrew	34314	,,	Oxford, John
34270	,,	Chappelle, Charles J.	34315	,,	Powell, Percy Van V.
34271	,,	Cox, Samuel	34316	,,	Penhallerick, William
34272	,,	Cox, Enoch Ernest	34317	,,	Pepper, Edward L.
34273	,,	Cowan, Frank Harold	34318	,,	Pearson, James
34274	,,	Chambers, John A.	34320	,,	Rycroft, Edwin
34276	,,	Crossman, Francis	34321	,,	Russell, Orval Elmer
34277	,,	Carleton, Frank D.	34322	,,	Roy, Donat

Canadian Pacific—The Empire's Greatest Railway.

No. 2 STATIONARY HOSPITAL—cont.

Regl. No.	Rank.	Name.	Regl. No.	Rank.	Name.
34324	Private	Stephen, Thomas	34332	Private	Tribe, William John
34325	,,	Steen, John Clifford	34333	,,	Viancour, Thomas P.
34326	,,	Sage, Roy Grant	34335	,,	Weston, Arthur
34327	,,	Starratt, Gladstone I.	34336	,,	Wilson, James Frank
34328	,,	Taylor, Albert	34339	,,	Watson, William
34329	,,	Teahan, Edgar Alex.	34340	,,	Wendover, Ellery L.
34330	,,	Thompson, Wm. W.	34341	,,	Winson, Ernest A.
34331	,,	Taylor, Harold F.			

ADVANCED DEPÔT MEDICAL STORES.

Officer Commanding	Captain Nyblett, H. G.
Captain	Cockburn, G. L.
,, ...	MacNutt, L. W.
,, ...	MacKeen, G. W.
,, ...	Smith, A. H. C.
,, ...	Jardine, G. H.
,, ...	Ruttan, F. S.
,, ...	Boyd, H. B.
,, ...	Bennett, A. E. H.
Quartermaster	Thurgar, E. J. (Hon. Captain)

Regl. No.	Rank.	Name.	Regl. No.	Rank.	Name.
33301	Sgt.-Maj.	Muir, D. P.	33321	Private	Frampton, A. B.
33302	Q.M.S.	Brown, B.	33324	,,	Galarneau, A.
33303	O.R.Sgt.	Arthur, J.	32941	,,	Gauthier, A. M.
33304	Cook Sgt.	Gotzger, H.	33323	,,	Geffrion, A.
34634	Sergt.	Mitchell, T. F.	33322	,,	Giroux, H.
34683	,,	Weaver, A. E.	33343	,,	Hanlon, J.
33309	Corpl.	Berry, A.	33325	,,	Heron, L.
33307	,,	Couder, V. F.	33328	,,	Holmes, W.
33306	,,	Orron, C.	33326	,,	Huband, T.
33308	,,	Wagner, H. W. C.	34109	,,	Mason, H.
33310	Cook Cpl.	Giguere, A.	33330	,,	Masters, G. A.
33313	Private	Addler, M. J. U.	33329	,,	Mather, W.
33314	,,	Anouf, M. L.	43161	,,	Murray, J.
33312	,,	Auclair, A.	33333	,,	Payne, H.
33315	,,	Beecroft, E.	34658	,,	Prosser, H. H.
33305	,,	Blincoe, H.	33334	,,	Proulx, J.
33316	,,	Cavanough, G.	33335	,,	Rivet, A.
34132	,,	Conrad, W.	33336	,,	Robillard, J.
33342	,,	Cote, M.	33331	,,	St. Martin, A.
33317	,,	Coulter, W. H.	33332	,,	St. Martin, P.
34134	,,	Courtney, T.	33337	,,	Sekonuk, J.
34136	,,	Day, A.	33338	,,	Simard, G.
33318	,,	Duff, R.	33340	,,	Wilson, C.
33319	,,	Fincham, H.			

Canadian Pacific—The Empire's Greatest Railway.

CANADIAN ARMY VETERINARY CORPS.

No. 1 SECTION.

Captain ... ... Evans, T. Charles
Lieutenant ... ... McCarrey, John J.

Regl. No.	Rank.	Name.	Regl. No.	Rank.	Name.
48501	S.-Sgt.	Shirt, Arthur John	48546	Trooper	Fredette, George
48504	Sergt.	Buttling, William J.	48547	,,	Fitzsimmons, M.
48503	,,	Kenner, Harry B.	48548	,,	Gales, Frederick S.
48502	,,	Moores, William	48549	,,	George, Norman
48505	,,	Smith, Willie	48550	,,	George, William
48506	,,	White, Oliver C.	48551	,,	Graham, John A.
48507	Corpl.	Cave, Clem. A. C. B.	48552	,,	Grahame, Harry
48545	,,	Feeley, John	48553	,,	Green, George
48508	,,	Hurst, Andrew G.	48554	,,	Hamilton, Richard I.
49509	,,	Pynn, Joe	48555	,,	Hancock, Robert
48510	,,	Sullivan, John	48556	,,	Henningsen, Clifford
48511	,,	Vosburgh, Gordon	48557	,,	Hill, Arthur
48512	,,	Wenham, William	48558	,,	Huestis, Ralph
48513	Trooper	Anderson, Thomas	48559	,,	Insall Bert Augustus
48514	,,	Ashton, Fredk. G.	48560	,,	Jupp, George
48515	,,	Atkinson, George	48561	,,	Kendall, Henry G.
48516	,,	Bates, Ben	48562	,,	Kernan, Albert
48517	,,	Beer, Thomas	48563	,,	Kilpin, Waldemar E.
48518	,,	Bilst, Arthur	48564	,,	Larkin, George
48519	,,	Biscoe, Charles H.	48565	,,	Leeds, Charles
48520	,,	Bottomley, Thos. H.	48566	,,	McBeth, Norman
48521	,,	Brownrigg, W. A.	48567	,,	McClintock, Frank
48522	,,	Burden, Gladstone	48568	,,	McDonagh, Edward
48523	,,	Burn, John	48569	,,	McIlroy, John
48524	,,	Casey, Joseph A.	48570	,,	McLaurin, Neil
48525	,,	Champion, Joseph	48571	,,	McPherson, George
42526	,,	Cheval, Matthew	48572	,,	Merritt, Arthur John
48527	,,	Clark, Frank	48573	,,	Miller, John W.
48528	,,	Clark, Thomas O.	48574	,,	Millicent, Thos. J.
48529	,,	Clark, William H.	48575	,,	Millington, Edward
48530	,,	Clisdell, John	48576	,,	Mole, Wm.
48531	,,	Cocks, Harry	48577	,,	Moore, Jack
48532	,,	Collin, Thomas	48578	,,	Murray, Frank T.
48533	,,	Coveyduck, Albert	48579	,,	Nickle, James
48534	,,	Creasey, Albert J.	48580	,,	Norton, William
48535	,,	Croft, Edward F.	48581	,,	O'Keefe, James
48536	,,	Cross, James	48582	,,	O'Malley, Charles
48537	,,	Crossley, Hugh	48583	,,	Papinie, Peter
48538	,,	Cutts, Arthur G.	48584	,,	Perkins, William E.
48539	,,	David, George A.	48585	,,	Pilot, John
48540	,,	Dodds, Walter	48586	,,	Poole, Frank
48541	,,	Doughty, Frederick	48587	,,	Price, Frederick
48542	,,	Elder, Thomas G.	48588	,,	Prichard, Thomas
48543	,,	Escott, Edward	48589	,,	Reddy, William
48544	,,	Fall, Fred	48590	,,	Richardson, John

Canadian Pacific—The Empire's Greatest Railway.

CANADIAN ARMY VETERINARY CORPS—cont.

Regl. No.	Rank.	Name.	Regl. No.	Rank.	Name.
48591	Trooper	Ricketts, Alfred	48603	Trooper	Tuggey, Henry A.
48592	,,	Russell, George R.	48604	,,	Upwood, Stephen
48593	,,	Scott, Walter	48605	,,	Vance, James
48594	,,	Sheiding, Rudolph	48606	,,	Wallace, Robt. A. B.
48595	,,	Shaw, Alec Weadon	48607	,,	Wallace, Robert
48596	,,	Sheridan, Walter R.	48608	,,	Webster, John
48597	,,	Stark, Sidney C.	48609	,,	Wilson, Joseph
48598	,,	Starnes, James A.	48610	,,	Whatley, Edwin
48599	,,	Stewart, James	48611	,,	Wooster, William J.
48600	,,	Sweet, John	48612	,,	Young, Richard
48601	,,	Taylor, John F. A.	48613	,,	Young, Thomas
48602	,,	Trapnell, Donald			

No. 2 SECTION.

Captain ... ... Daigneault, Frederick Alphonse
Lieutenant ... ... Grignon, Louis Maurice

Regl. No.	Rank.	Name.	Regl. No.	Rank.	Name.
48701	Staff Sgt.	Foster, Harry	48732	Trooper	Dunkley, William
48702	Sergt.	Akerman, Alfred C.	48738	,,	Dupperault, Victor
48703	,,	Cotton, John	48731	,,	Durand, Joseph
48704	,,	Gosselin, Joseph E.	48730	,,	Durand, Stanilas
48705	,,	Hay, John	48733	,,	Drysdale, George
48706	,,	Turner, Seth. R. J.	48740	,,	Edridge, Godfrey C.
48708	Corpl.	Bennett, George	48739	,,	Ellis, Alfred
48709	,,	Hyatt, Melvin	48741	,,	Erskine, John
48710	,,	Kendall, Frank	48742	,,	Flynn, Daniel
48711	,,	Stevens, Gilbert R.	48144	,,	Fournier, Adolf
48707	,,	Stratton, William F.	48743	,,	Fowler, Thomas
48712	,,	Threlfall, Merton S.	48745	,,	Gatenby, William
48715	Trooper	Attewell, Albert J.	48750	,,	Ganthier, Frank
48716	,,	Attewell, George	48751	,,	Ganthier, Ulderic
48714	,,	Austin, Joseph	48744	,,	Geary, Edgar
48718	,,	Baker, William	48754	,,	Gibbs, Edward
48717	,,	Barton, William	48752	,,	Gill, Edward
48723	,,	Baynham, Edward	48746	,,	Goldsmith, James B.
48722	,,	Belcher, George	48753	,,	Gore, Albert Jas.
48719	,,	Blencowe, Bert	48747	,,	Greenough, James
48726	,,	Biggs, John	48748	,,	Guinan, James
48724	,,	Bradburn, R. M.	48749	,,	Glendennen, James
48720	,,	Brown, William M.	48758	,,	Hackett, John
48725	,,	Budd, Albert	48811	,,	Harbury, Chas.
48721	,,	Buller, William	48757	,,	Harbert, George
48727	,,	Chauvin, Felix	48759	,,	Harrison, Harry
48729	,,	Cordoniere, James	48761	,,	Hatfield, Edward J.
48728	,,	Couture, Ernest	48756	,,	Hayes, Chas. Jas.
48737	,,	Dennis, Adolf	48755	,,	Hull, Reg. Armitage
48736	,,	Donaldson, Charles	48760	,,	Humble, Ernest
48735	,,	Doust, Thos.	48762	,,	Jones, Arthur R.
48734	,,	Dugmore, W. S.	48763	,,	Jutrand, Emil

Canadian Pacific—The Empire's Greatest Railway.

CANADIAN ARMY VETERINARY CORPS—cont.

Regl. No.	Rank	Name	Regl. No.	Rank	Name
48764	Trooper	Keir, Archie	48788	Trooper	O'Rourke, Patrick
48768	,,	Lasierre, Aime	48789	,,	Pallett, Arthur
48767	,,	Laviolette, Oscar	48793	,,	Pavey, Horace
48769	,,	Leahy, Patrick	48791	,,	Pearce, William
48766	,,	Lessard, Wilfred	48796	,,	Pepper, Edward
48765	,,	Lovell, Frank	48792	,,	Perkins, Edgar F.
48770	,,	Murphy, Thomas	48795	,,	Phillips, Jack
48771	,,	Murphy, Frank	48790	,,	Poulton, Arthur
48772	,,	Machan, George W.	49794	,,	Plunkett, Arthur
48773	,,	Myers, Edward	48797	,,	Richardson, James
48774	,,	Madden, John James	48798	,,	Rioux, Edgar
48775	,,	Mills, James	48799	,,	Scrivener, George
48776	,,	Marlow, Charles	48800	,,	Shaw, Gervese
48777	,,	Menard, Cyril	48801	,,	Stewart, Alexander
48778	,,	Martin, Edwin	48802	,,	Tournour, Robert
48779	,,	Mead, David	48805	,,	Val de Verr, A.
48780	,,	Morton, Ernest	48803	,,	Valiquette, George
48781	,,	Meloche, Patrick J.	48804	,,	Veir, Robert
48782	,,	Montgomery, George	48807	,,	Wales, Oscar
48783	,,	McCall, George	48806	,,	Walker, George P.
48784	,,	McDonald, Arthur	48810	,,	Weller, Norman F.
48785	,,	MacDonald, E. G.	48809	,,	Williams, Harold H.
48786	,,	McDonald, Herbert	48808	,,	Winwood, Arthur
48787	,,	Nickle, James J.			

CANADIAN MOBILE VETERINARY SECTION.

No. 1.

Lieutenant ... ... O'Gogarty, M. G.

Regl. No.	Rank	Name	Regl. No.	Rank	Name
34706	Sgt.-Maj.	Southern, T.	34726	Private	Ballinger, Fred.
34709	Sergt.	Court, E.	34721	,,	Buckboro, N. B.
34711	,,	Farr, J.	34720	,,	Mullen, J. A.
34706	,,	Watterson, J.	34724	,,	Richards, Stanley
34713	Corpl.	Brodie, G. L.	34725	,,	Smith, James
34714	,,	Oliver, Herbert	34729	,,	Southern, Robert

No. 2.

Lieutenant ... ... Edwards, C. L.

Regl. No.	Rank	Name	Regl. No.	Rank	Name
34702	Sgt.-Maj.	Johnson, F.	34722	Private	Chase, George
34707	Sergt.	Burton, J.	34731	,,	Collinson, Fred.
34705	,,	Cameron, J. F.	34723	,,	Evans, Arthur G.
34712	,,	Doak, H.	34717	,,	McCay, John
34716	Corpl.	Henderson, Gordon	34730	,,	Salmon, James
34715	,,	Miller, W.			

Canadian Pacific—The Empire's Greatest Railway.

CANADIAN VETERINARY BASE SUPPLY DEPÔT.

Lieutenant and Quartermaster ... Frape, A. E.

Regl. No.	Rank.	Name.	Regl. No.	Rank.	Name.
34704	Sergt.	Denton, W.	34728	Private	Frape, James F.
24710	Corpl.	Johnson, G.	34732	,,	Groome, S. B.
34733	Private	Conroy, A. J.			

Supernumerary.

34727	Private	Collett, Howard B.	34719	Private	Walmsley, C.
34718	,,	Skinner, Geo.			

REMOUNT DEPÔT.

Lieut.-Colonel	... ...	Hendrie, W.
,,	... ...	Morden, W. Grant
Major	... ...	Thurston, E. C.
Captain and Adjutant	... ...	Van Allen, W.
,,	... ...	Smith, R. B.
Lieutenant	... ...	Dyer, E. A.
,,	... ...	Shanly, C. N.
,,	... ...	Laver, E.
Lieutenant and Quartermaster		Cowan, C. G.
Lieutenant and Veterinary Officer		Du Chene, H. D. J.

Regl. No.	Rank.	Name.	Regl. No.	Rank.	Name.
49047	S.M.	MacDonald, W. J.	49035	Private	Beard, F.
49046	Q.M.S.	Niemeyer, C. W.	49007	,,	Bergstrom, R.
49082	Fr. Q.M.S.	Dunbar, C.	49087	,,	Bignell, H.
49049	Fr. Sergt.	O'Connor, J. C.	49005	,,	Blacklaw, D.
49056	Sergt.	Bethell, A.	49006	,,	Blake, J.
49037	,,	Prince, C. J.	49026	,,	Bowerman, R.
49041	,,	Rendall, W.	49045	,,	Brown, J.
49032	,,	Salter, C. J.	49027	,,	Bubar, G.
49102	Lce.-Sgt.	Giles, J.	49063	,,	Buchanan, R.
49029	Corpl.	Hanson, F.	49058	,,	Cinq-Mars, O.
49075	,,	Haverson, A. E.	49042	,,	Clowes, B.
49030	,,	Hoggarth, Geo.	49008	,,	Collins, H. E.
49003	,,	MacDonald, L.	49009	,,	Conrad, H.
49078	,,	Paulin, D. G.	49010	,,	Corley, C.
49002	,,	Walmsley, F. M.	49050	,,	Crawford, A.
49001	Lce-Cpl.	Brand, J.	49011	,,	Crawford, R.
49081	,,	Collett, E.	49074	,,	Crook, B.
49054	,,	Leduk, A.	49051	,,	Desharnais, H.
49090	,,	Sutton, W. J.	49093	,,	Dieroff, F. W.
49034	Private	Anderson, G.	49012	,,	Doll, E.
49095	,,	Angus, A. R.	49013	,,	Downes, R.
49004	,,	Banwell, E.	49014	,,	Dubé, M.

Canadian Pacific—The Empire's Greatest Railway.

REMOUNT DEPÔT—cont. 349

Regl. No.	Rank.	Name.	Regl. No.	Rank.	Name.
49096	Private	Dufour, H.	49097	Private	McKay, H.
49028	Trumpt'r	Douglas, M.	49069	,,	Milverton, H.
49119	Private	Earthy, C.	49084	,,	Moisan, R.
49052	,,	Fillion, J.	49065	,,	Moon, H.
49015	,,	Fisk, H. J.	49089	,,	Morris, F.
49016	,,	Giffin, A.	49059	,,	Mullin, F.
49017	,,	Gillespie, W.	49040	,,	Norman, W.
49098	,,	Gillott, J. G.	49092	,,	Phillips, B.
49036	,,	Harwood, G.	49033	,,	Robins, C. E.
49018	,,	Hadwin, T.	49079	,,	Robitaille, A.
49088	,,	Hardcastle, H.	49055	,,	Ross, A.
49101	,,	Harding, W.	49043	,,	Sale, E. M.
49099	,,	Hemstock, P.	49062	,,	Simes, E.
49038	,,	Hickey, D.	49068	,,	Smith, T.
49019	,,	Hilchey, W. E.	49061	,,	Sowden, T. N.
49020	,,	Homenuk, J.	49025	,,	Taylor, T.
49118	,,	Horan, J.	49024	,,	Venus, R. W.
49103	,,	Hunter, G.	49072	,,	Walker, R.
49057	,,	Jackson, M.	49080	,,	Williamson, G.
49031	,,	Johnson, H.	49100	,,	Wilmot, T.
49076	,,	McBride, J.	49086	,,	Wiseman, N.
49066	,,	McDonald, M.	49022	,,	Woods, J. H.
49060	,,	McGreary, T.	49023	,,	Young, D.

AUTO MACHINE GUN BRIGADE, No. 1.

Major ... ... Brutinel, Raymond
Captain ... ... Browne, James Edwards
,, ... Hawkins, Charles Francis
,, ... Donnelly, Harold Higman
Lieutenant ... ... Wilkin, Francis Alfred
,, ... Bradbrooke, Charles Alfred
,, ... Scott, Morris Alexander
,, ... McCarthy, William Everett Carlton

Regl. No.	Rank.	Name.	Regl. No.	Rank.	Name.
45501	Private	Aldersley, John	45544	Private	Bolton Clifford
45548	,,	Alder, Frank	45574	,,	Brotherton, Tom
45601	,,	Anderson, Albert	45549	Corpl.	Brooks, Charles
45502	,,	Beeson, Harold	45550	Lce.-Cpl.	Brown, George T. S.
45503	,,	Beeson, Augustus	45507	Private	Bellas, Robert
45585	,,	Banks, Archibald	45620	,,	Baker, Alfred Edw.
45558	,,	Brassart, George	45624	,,	Baker, Edward
45593	Lce.-Cpl.	Blair, Donald	45625	,,	Boyd, Alexander
45504	Private	Black, David	45626	,,	Brown, Robert J.
45542	,,	Bundy, James	45592	,,	Code, Edmund
45615	,,	Bowden, G. Sinton	45551	,,	Carr, David
45505	,,	Beecroft, Arthur	45508	,,	Coles, George
45543	Lce.-Cpl.	Bach, Bert	45509	,,	Connell, Robert
45506	,,	Budd, James	45540	,,	Clark, Roy

Canadian Pacific—The Empire's Greatest Railway.

AUTO MACHINE GUN BRIGADE, No. 1—cont.

Regl. No.	Rank.	Name.	Regl. No.	Rank.	Name.
45590	Private	Campbell, Thomas	45525	Private	Mastin, Walter
45598	,,	Clark, John	45589	,,	McDowell, Herbert
45606	,,	Clark, John Dalton	45605	,,	Matthews, Percy
45587	,,	Chapman, George	45611	,,	Mitchell, James
45622	Corpl.	Colclough, Charles	45613	,,	McDonald, Albert
45627	Private	Crawford, H. McG.	45637	,,	Machanack, Kupun
45628	,,	Cruse, Reginald W.	45638	,,	Malcolm, Kenneth N.
45629	,,	Cornish, Thomas	45639	,,	Martin, James Harry
45630	,,	Cuddington, Frank	45640	,,	Miller, Alfred
45566	,,	Dann, Alfred	45641	,,	Murr, Christopher
45510	Corpl.	Durham, William	45642	,,	Myles, John
45559	Sergt.	Dowling, Allen	45643	,,	McDonald, T. Lattie
44511	Private	Diver, Victor	45644	,,	McKenzie, W. David
45560	,,	Fisher, Donald Alex.	45526	,,	Orrell, Walter
45512	,,	Friend, Edwin	45608	,,	O'Donnell, James
45513	,,	Fallows, Frank	45614	,,	Oxtoby, Boswell
45631	,,	Farrell, Joseph	45581	,,	Philp, Fred
45632	,,	Fee, Charles Herbert	45541	,,	Park, Frank
45633	,,	Finley, John	45527	,,	Pentleton, James
45634	,,	Fisher, Robert	45570	,,	Paterson, Allan
45635	,,	Francis, Lionel G.	45645	,,	Pearson, John
45595	,,	Gilmore, Allan	45646	,,	Ptolemy, John Alex.
45515	Lce.-Cpl.	Gould, Harry	45571	,,	Rouse, John
45596	Private	Girouard, Hector	45557	,,	Rawlings, Cecil
45636	,,	Gawthroup, Harry	45616	,,	Ritchie, Allan Bruce
45545	,,	Harvey, Sidney	45647	,,	Robinson, Harry
45576	,,	Hinds, Thomas	45773	,,	Smith, Allan
45516	,,	Hayden, Edgar	45528	,,	Singleton, George
45577	,,	Hetherington, John	45583	Corpl.	Stokey, Fred
45517	,,	Hicks, Edward	45530	Private	Sanders, James
45552	,,	Hargreaves, Sidney	45572	Sergt.	Sinclair, David
45519	,,	Hardie, Ventry	45617	Private	Smith, John
45520	,,	Hulbert, Dwight	45602	,,	Shore, George
45522	,,	Hazlitt, Lyle	45604	,,	Shine, Cornelius
45546	,,	Hotrum, Fred	45621	Corpl.	Sanderson, R. H.
45619	,,	Hubbell, Earl Darius	45623	Private	Savill, Ernest H.
45603	Sergt.	Howard, G. V. W.	45648	,,	Searle, Charles G.
45607	Private	Hallam, Douglas	45650	,,	Stoneman, W. J.
45518	,,	Hoyle, Joseph	45651	,,	Sutherland, J. R.
45654	,,	Hazlitt, Thomas A.	45653	,,	Skeet, John
45554	,,	Jensen, James	45652	,,	Thomas, William
45547	,,	Johnson, Ben	45531	Corpl.	Turner, Arthur
45591	Sergt.	Kerr, Nelson	45532	Sergt.	Thorne, Thomas
45555	Private	Keene, Louis	45584	,,	Uhthoff, Richard
45578	,,	Kirkham, George	45609	Private	Utman, Henry
45586	,,	Kevan, John	45533	,,	Vosburgh, Dumonte
45600	,,	Lewis, Harry	45536	,,	Waywell, Thomas
45563	,,	Lawlor, John	45538	,,	Winson, Walter
45523	,,	Lewis, Edwin	45588	,,	Wilding, George
45524	,,	Lang, George	45534	,,	Waghorn, Frank
45556	,,	Macoun, Stewart	45539	,,	Young, Sidney
45564	,,	Messenger, Harry			

Canadian Pacific—The Empire's Greatest Railway.

BASE PAY DEPÔT UNIT.

Paymaster ... ... Lieut.-Colonel C, N. Shanly
„ (Assistant) ... ... Captain C. M. Ingall

Regl. No.	Rank.	Name.	Regl. No.	Rank.	Name.
35002	Sgt.-Maj.	Horgan, D.	35015	Sergt.	Cragg, S. V.
35004	Staff-Sgt.	Kelly, P.	16492	„	Cox, R. G.
35006	Sergt.	Laurie-Dighton,T. E.	35016	Private	Warren, J.
35008	„	Picken, D. G.			

PAY AND RECORD OFFICE, LONDON.

Chief Paymaster and Officer i/c Records ... Colonel W. R. Ward
Paymaster ... ... Captain J. L. Regan
„ ... ... Captain C. Warne Ward
„ ... ... Captain J. W. Dowding
Lieutenant ... ... J. S. Redmayne

Regl. No.	Rank.	Name.	Regl. No.	Rank.	Name.
35001	Sgt.-Maj.	Baxandall, S.	35010	Private	Green, J.
35003	Q.M.Sgt.	Spink, B. J. W.	35011	„	Bishop. F. W.
35007	Sergt.	Boocock, B.	35013	„	Chapman, J. E.
35009	„	Grimmer, D. S.			

Major F. Logie Armstrong, D.A.A.G. } For Record Duties
1802 Sergt.-Major A. W. Kelly, C.M.S.C.

CANADIAN ORDNANCE CORPS.

Regl. No.	Rank.	Name.	Regl. No.	Rank.	Name.
234	Sb.-Cndr.	Pitman, J. D.	386	Lce.-Cpl.	Bennett, H.
87	S.Q.M.S.	Spicer, R. H.	503	Private	Rudland, G. R.
228	Staff-Sgt.	Bentley, A.	385	„	Taylor, G. A.

Artificers.

| 161 | Sergt. | Root, E. W. | 465 Private Shaw, W. |
| 480 | Private | Delafosse, C. R. | |

Armourers.

1193 Sgt.-Maj. Davis, E. | 34801 Sergt. Laman, T.

Canadian Pacific—The Empire's Greatest Railway.

POSTAL DETACHMENT.

Lieutenant ... ... Murray, Kenneth A.
" ... ... Caldwell, Bruce M.

Regl. No.	Rank.	Name.	Regl. No.	Rank.	Name.
35204	Sergt.	Ross, George Wm.	35203	Private	Boyd, W. A.
35211	Corpl.	Gow, W. J.	35215	"	Chagnon, Fredk. H.
35208	"	McPherson, Daniel V.	35210	"	Edwards, Ledman
35214	"	Taggie, Frederick A.	35213	"	Livingstone, Hugh W.
35202	"	Wallis, George T.	35209	"	Murray, Thomas H.
35206	Private	Baldock, George H.	35207	"	Smith, Clarence G.
35216	"	Belanger, Joseph H.	35205	"	Terry, Benjamin J.

NURSING MATRONS AND NURSING SISTERS.
CANADIAN ARMY MEDICAL CORPS.

Matron-in-Chief... ... ... Macdonald, Margaret Clotilde
Nursing Matron... ... ... Ridley, Ethel
" (acting) ... Charleson, Eleanor Margaret
" (acting) ... Goodeve, Myra

Nursing Sisters.

Allen, Anne Doctor
Attrill, Alfreda Jean
Bell, Jean Isabell
Bigue, Marie
Binning, Daisy Medd
Black, Emma Gertrude
Blewitt, Beatrice Jean
Bowden, Clare
Bruce, Constance Elspeth
Burns, Louise Wills
Burpee, Eleanor Bell
Cameron, Nancy Tupper
Campbell, Edith
Clint, Mabel
Cromwell, Bertha May
Davis, Agnes Balfour
DeBellefeuille, Katie
Denmark, Ida Georgina
Dixon, Effie Mae
Domville, Mary Lucretia
Doucette, Yvonne
Dover, Annie
Dussault, Alexina

Follette, Minnie Asenath
Fraser, Margaret Margery
French, Gertrude
Frew, Frances Maitland
Galt, Cecily
Geen, Celestine
Graham, Harriet
Grattan, Rose Myrtle
Greenwood, Ethel
Halpenny, Gertrude Eleanor
Hambley, Eva May
Hammell, Ada Winifred
Hare, Catherine Margaret
Hervey, Rebecca
Hinchey, Annie Ruby
Holmes, Ethel Marie
Howard, Amy
Hudson, Edith
Hunter, Florence Alexandra
Ivey, Pauline
Jamieson, Mabelle Clara
Johnston, Jean
Kennedy, Margaret Cecile

Canadian Pacific—The Empire's Greatest Railway.

NURSING MATRONS AND NURSING SISTERS—cont.

Nursing Sisters—cont.

Lambkin, Kathleen Marian
Leslie, Elsie Hogg
Little, Kathleen
Mabe, Lily Maud
Macallister, Charlotte Forbes
Macdonald, Jeanette MacGregor
Massy, Georgina Annie Graham
Mattice, Brenda Florence
McCallum, Florence E. M.
McCullough, Georgie Beach
McCurdy, Nellie Clare
McKiel, Theodora
McLean, Rena
McLeod, Margaret Christina
Meikeljohn, Naomi Frances
Mellen, Penelope
Mercer, Eleanor Cowan
Mills, Margaret Mostyn
Muir, Mary McBride
Nesbitt, Violet Claire
Nichols, Florence Maud
O'Loane, Nano
Parkins, Mildred Florence
Parks, Margaret
Pelletier, Juliet Marie
Ponting, Elizabeth Anne
Prinsep, Pearl

Pugh, Murnay May
Pense, Emma Florence
Richardson, Marcella Percy
Riverin, Ursule
Robertson, Jessie Helen
Robertson, Mildred
St. Arnaud, Rose
Sampson, Mae Belle
Scatcherd, Rhoda
Scoble, Catherine Isabelle
Scott, Amy Winifred
Smith, Ida
Smith, Lydia Vernon
Smith, Margaret
Strathy, Isabella Dora
Stronach, Jean
Strong, Annie Cornelia
Sword, Jean Elizabeth
Tremaine, Vivian Adelard
Tupper, Addie
Watson, Bessie Irving
Webb, Margarie Mabel
West, Florence Caroline
Willoughby, Bertha Jane
Winter, Dorothy Elizabeth
Wylie, Florence
Younghusband, Charlotte

Canadian Pacific—The Empire's Greatest Railway.

www.ingramcontent.com/pod-product-compliance
Lightning Source LLC
Chambersburg PA
CBHW031132160426
43193CB00008B/114